Rapid Application Development with Mozilla™

BRUCE PERENS' OPEN SOURCE SERIES

- *Managing Linux Systems with Webmin: System Administration and Module Development*
  Jamie Cameron
- *Implementing CIFS: The Common Internet File System*
  Christopher R. Hertel
- *Embedded Software Development with eCos*
  Anthony J. Massa
- *Rapid Application Development with Mozilla*
  Nigel McFarlane
- *The Linux Development Platform: Configuring, Using, and Maintaining a Complete Programming Environment*
  Rafeeq Ur Rehman, Christopher Paul
- *Intrusion Detection Systems with Snort: Advanced IDS Techniques with Snort, Apache, MySQL, PHP, and ACID*
  Rafeeq Ur Rehman

Rapid Application Development with Mozilla

Nigel McFarlane

PRENTICE HALL
Professional Technical Reference
Upper Saddle River, NJ 07458
www.phptr.com

Library of Congress Cataloging-in-Publication Data

McFarlane, Nigel
Rapid application development with Mozilla / Nigel McFarlane.
p. cm. — (Bruce Parens' Open source series)
Includes index.
ISBN 0-13-142343-6 (paper)
1. Internet programming. 2. Computer software—Development. 3. Netscape Mozilla. I. Title. II. Series.
QA76.625.M38 2003
006.7'6—dc22
2003065645

Editorial/production supervision: BooksCraft, Inc., Indianapolis, IN
Cover design director: *Jerry Votta*
Cover design: *Nina Scuderi*
Art director: *Gail Cocker-Bogusz*
Manufacturing buyer: *Maura Zaldivar*
Publishing partner: *Mark L. Taub*
Editorial assistant: *Noreen Regina*
Marketing manager: *Dan DePasquale*
Full-service production manager: *Anne R. Garcia*

Publishing as Prentice Hall Professional Technical Reference
Upper Saddle River, New Jersey 07458

Prentice Hall books are widely used by corporations and government agencies for training, marketing, and resale.

For information regarding corporate and government bulk discounts please contact:

Corporate and Government Sales (800) 382-3419 or corpsales@pearsontechgroup.com

Printed in the United States of America
1st Printing

ISBN 0-13-142343-6

Pearson Education LTD.
Pearson Education Australia PTY, Limited
Pearson Education Singapore, Pte. Ltd.
Pearson Education North Asia Ltd.
Pearson Education Canada, Ltd.
Pearson Educación de Mexico, S.A. de C.V.
Pearson Education—Japan
Pearson Education Malaysia, Pte. Ltd.

For Colleen, my magnificent sister, whose humor, intelligence, and adventurous nature are exceeded only by her grounded humanity. You are so appreciated.

About Prentice Hall Professional Technical Reference

With origins reaching back to the industry's first computer science publishing program in the 1960s, and formally launched as its own imprint in 1986, Prentice Hall Professional Technical Reference (PH PTR) has developed into the leading provider of technical books in the world today. Our editors now publish over 200 books annually, authored by leaders in the fields of computing, engineering, and business.

Our roots are firmly planted in the soil that gave rise to the technical revolution. Our bookshelf contains many of the industry's computing and engineering classics: Kernighan and Ritchie's *C Programming Language*, Nemeth's *UNIX System Administration Handbook*, Horstmann's *Core Java*, and Johnson's *High-Speed Digital Design*.

PH PTR acknowledges its auspicious beginnings while it looks to the future for inspiration. We continue to evolve and break new ground in publishing by providing today's professionals with tomorrow's solutions.

Contents

Acknowledgments

Thanks first and foremost to Megan Pearce, whose substance is of a quality and strength one rarely witnesses. Thank you very much for your understanding and patience and for the joy of your company.

This book would be a far lesser work were it not for the accuracy and insight of some very talented reviewers. Thanks very much to: Neil Rashbrook, Mozilla XPFE maven extraordinaire; Eve Maler, Sun Microsystem's XML Standards Architect and W3C member; and the incredibly busy yet helpful Dr. Alisdair Daws. Thanks also to Brendan Eich, Scott Collins, and Ben Goodger for support and specialist feedback.

Introduction

Welcome to Software Development the Mozilla Way

The Mozilla Platform is a large software development tool that is a modern blend of XML document processing, scripting languages, and software objects. It is used to create interactive, user-focused applications. This book is a conceptual overview, reference, and tutorial on the use of the platform for building such applications.

The Mozilla Platform encourages a particular style of software development: rapid application development (RAD). RAD occurs when programmers base their applications-to-be on a powerful development tool that contains much pre-existing functionality. With such a tool, a great deal can be done very quickly. The Mozilla Platform is such a tool.

One strategy for doing RAD is to make sophisticated HTML pages and display them in a Web browser. This book does not explain HTML, nor does it show how to create such pages. It has very little to do with HTML. Instead, it shows how to create applications that require no browser, and that might appear to be nothing like a Web browser. Such applications might be Web-enabled, benefiting from the advantages that Web browsers have, or they might have nothing to do with the Web at all.

Because Mozilla is closely linked to the Web in people's minds, this last point cannot be emphasized enough. The Mozilla Platform is far more than a browser. Here are some statistics:

- Mozilla contains well over 1,000 object types and well over 1,000 interfaces.
- It is highly standards compliant, supporting many standards from bodies such as the W3C, IETF, and ECMA. These bodies are, respectively, the World Wide Web Consortium, the Internet Engineering Task Force, and the European Computer Manufacturers' Association.
- Mozilla is built on a very big source code base and is far larger than most Open Source projects. It is 30 times larger than the Apache Web Server, 20 times larger than the Java 1.0 JDK/JRE sources, 5 times bigger than the standard Perl distribution, twice as big as the Linux kernel source, and nearly as large as the whole GNOME 2.0 desktop source—even when 150 standard GNOME applications are included.
- As a result of the browser wars in the late 1990s, the platform has been heavily tested and is highly optimized and very portable. Not only have hundreds of Netscape employees and thousands of volunteers worked on it, but millions of end users who have adopted Mozilla-based products have scrutinized it as well.

This extensive and tested set of features is a huge creative opportunity for any developer interested in building applications. These features also offer an opportunity for traditional Web developers to broaden their existing skills in a natural way.

This book covers the Mozilla Platform up to version 1.4. Changes between minor versions (e.g., 1.3 and 1.4) are small enough that most of this book will be correct for some time.

USEFUL KNOWLEDGE

Some experience is required when reading this book. Some familiarity with Web standards is assumed. This list of skills is more than enough preparation:

- A little HTML or XHTML
- A little XML
- A little JavaScript, or another scripting language, or one of the C languages (C, C++, C#, Java, IDL)
- A little CSS2
- A little Web page development
- A little SQL
- A little experience working with objects
- The pleasure of having read the W3C's DOM 2 Core standard at least once

All the standards for these technologies, except SQL and JavaScript, are available at *www.w3.org*.

To read this book with very little effort, add these skills: a little Dynamic HTML; a little Prolog; more experience with an object-brokering system like COM or CORBA; additional experience with another RAD tool like a 4GL or a GUI Designer; and more SQL experience.

It is common for advanced Mozilla programmers to have a full copy of the Mozilla Platform source code (40 MB, approximately). This book sticks strictly to the application services provided by the platform. There is no need to get involved in the source code, unless that is your particular interest.

The Structure of This Book

Chapter 1, Fundamental Concepts, is an overview of Mozilla. The remaining chapters mimic the structure of the Mozilla Platform. The early chapters are about the *front* part of Mozilla, comprising XML markup, which displays the elements of a graphical user interface. As the chapters proceed, the subject matter works its way to the *back* of Mozilla. The back consists of objects that silently connect to other computing infrastructure, like file systems, networks, and servers. To summarize:

- Chapter 1 is a concept overview.
- Chapters 2–4 describe basic XUL markup. XUL is a dialect of XML.
- Chapter 5 explains the JavaScript language.
- Chapters 6–10 describe interactions between the DOM, JavaScript, and XUL.
- Chapter 11 explains the RDF data format.
- Chapters 12–14 describe interactions between XUL and RDF.
- Chapter 15 explains how to enhance XUL using XBL.
- Chapter 16 describes many useful XPCOM objects. XPCOM is Mozilla's component technology.
- Chapter 17 describes how to deploy a finished application.

Within this flow from front to back, each chapter follows a set structure:

- Facing the start of each chapter is a special diagram called the NPA diagram.
- The first few paragraphs of a chapter introduce the chapter concepts, expanding on brief remarks in Chapter 1, Fundamental Concepts. Read these remarks to identify whether the chapter is relevant to your need.
- For more difficult material, these concepts are expanded into a concept tutorial. Read this tutorial material when looking through the book for the first time, or if a concept seems very foreign.
- Next, all the technical detail is laid out in a structured manner. Many examples are provided to support a first-time read, but this detail is designed to be flipped through and revisited later when you've forgotten something.

- In later chapters, this reference material is followed by a scripting section that explains what JavaScript interactions are possible. Read this when XUL and RDF alone are not enough for your purposes.
- "Style Options" describes the impact of the CSS standards on the chapter. Read this when a window doesn't look right.
- "Hands On" contains the NoteTaker tutorial that runs throughout the book. Read this when you need to get into the coding groove.
- "Debug Corner" contains problem-solving advice and collected wisdom on the chapter's technology. Read this before coding and when you're really stuck.
- Finally, the summary closes with a reflective overview and exits gracefully in the direction of the next chapter.

Some of these structural elements are discussed in the following topics.

The NPA Diagram

The core of the Mozilla Platform is implemented in the C and C++ programming languages, using many object classes. To understand how it all works, one could draw a huge diagram that shows all the object-oriented relationships explicit in those classes. Such a diagram would be quite detailed, and any high-level features of the platform might not be obvious. Although the diagram might be accurate, it would be a challenge to understand.

The NPA diagram is a simplified view of Mozilla's insides. NPA stands for *not perfectly accurate*. It is a learning aid. No one is arguing that Mozilla is built exactly as the diagram shows; the diagram is just a handy thinking tool. There is no attempt to illustrate everything that Mozilla does.

The NPA diagram appears prior to each chapter of this book. The subject matter of a given chapter is usually tied to a specific part or parts of the diagram.

Style Options

Mozilla makes extensive use of cascading stylesheet styles. In addition to features described in the CSS2 standard, Mozilla has many specialist style extensions. An example of a Mozilla-specific style is

```
vbox { -moz-box-orient: vertical; }
```

Most chapters contain a short section that describes Mozilla-style extensions relevant to that chapter.

The NoteTaker Tool

NoteTaker is a small programming project that is a running example throughout this book. There isn't room for developing a full application, so the compromise is a small tool that is an add-on. NoteTaker is a Web browser enhancement that provides a way to attach reminder notes (Web notes) to displayed Web pages. The browser user can attach notes to the pages of a Web site, and when that Web site is visited at a later date, the note reappears. This is done without modifying the remote Web site at all. Notes can be created, edited, updated, and deleted.

Figure 1 is a screenshot of NoteTaker at work.

The browser window shown has a new toolbar, which is the NoteTaker toolbar. That toolbar includes a drop-down menu, among other things. The displayed HTML page includes a small pale rectangle—that is the Web note for the page's URL. That rectangle does not appear anywhere in the displayed test.html file. Also shown is the Edit dialog window, which is used to specify the content and arrangement of the current note.

As an idea, it doesn't matter whether NoteTaker is pure genius or horribly clumsy. Its purpose is to be a working technology demonstrator. Each chapter enhances NoteTaker in a small way so that, by the end of this book, all Mozilla's technologies can be seen at work together.

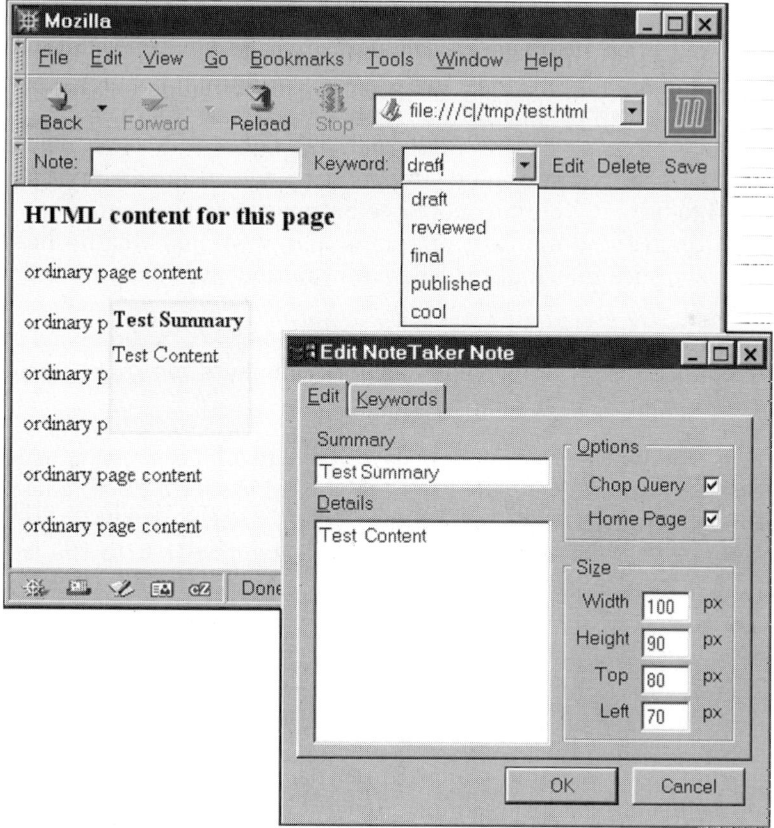

Fig. 1 Classic Mozilla browser window showing NoteTaker installed.

There is no generally agreed upon technical term for describing NoteTaker. The relationship between the tool and a browser is a little like the relationship between a Java applet and a Java application. It is an add-on that is more than a mere configuration option but less than a plugin.

This example project is attached to a Web browser. Generally speaking, Mozilla applications should run in their own windows with no Web browser in sight. There is no implication that all Mozilla applications should be designed like NoteTaker—it is just that NoteTaker is too small as described here to stand by itself.

Hands On: Tools Needed for Development

Even this short introduction attempts to follow the chapter structure described earlier. To begin development with Mozilla, you need a computer, software, and documentation.

Microsoft Windows, Macintosh, and UNIX/Linux are all acceptable development systems, although MacOS 9 support is slowly being dropped and perhaps should be avoided. The computer does not need to be Internet-enabled or even LAN-enabled after the platform is installed. The Mozilla Web site, *www.mozilla.org*, is the place to find software. Chapter 1, Fundamental Concepts, discusses software installation in "Hands On."

The sole warning in this introduction relates to documentation. This book alone is simply not enough information for all development needs. It would need to be a 10-volume encyclopedia to achieve that end. Just as UNIX has man(1) pages and applications have help systems, Mozilla has its own electronic reference information. That information complements the material in this book.

Unfortunately, that help information is widely scattered about and must be collected together by hand. Here are the documents you should collect while you are downloading a copy of the platform:

- From the W3C, *www.w3.org*, download all of these standards: CSS2, CSS2.1, XML 1.0, XHTML 1.0, DOM 1 all parts, DOM 2 all parts, DOM 3 all parts, and RDF. These standards are nearly all available in high-quality PDF files and can be viewed electronically with the free Adobe Acrobat Reader (at *www.adobe.com)*. The CSS2, DOM 2 Core, and DOM 2 Events standards are the most important ones; the others are rarely needed.
- From ECMA, *www.ecma.ch*, download the ECMA-262 ECMAScript standard. This is the JavaScript standard. You can do without it, but it is occasionally handy.
- From Prentice Hall's Web site, *http://authors.phptr.com/mcfarlane/*, or from the author's Web site, *www.nigelmcfarlane.com,* download sets of XPIDL interface files. These definition files describe all the object inter-

faces in Mozilla. These files are extracted from the source code and bundled up for your convenience.

- ☞ Also from *http://authors.phptr.com/mcfarlane* or from *www.nigelmcfarlane.com,* download class-interface reports. These specially prepared files are a nearly accurate list of the class-interface pairs supported by the platform. These lists help answer the question: What object might I use? They can be manipulated with a text editor or a spreadsheet.
- ☞ Finally, it would be helpful to possess a Web development book with a JavaScript focus.

If you are very detail oriented and have copious free time, then you might consider adding a full copy of the Mozilla Platform source code (40 MB approximately). That is not strictly required.

It is common for advanced application programmers to retain a full copy of the Mozilla Platform source code (40 MB, approximately). This book sticks strictly to the application services provided by the platform, so there is no need to get involved in the source code, unless that is your particular interest.

Debug Corner: Unreadable Documentation

Make sure that any documentation you download has the right format for your platform. The UNIX tools unix2dos and dos2unix can help; also UNIX files can be read on Microsoft Windows with any decent text editor (e.g., gvim at *www.vim.org*).

The font system on Linux is sometimes less than adequate and can make PDF text hard to read. To fix this, follow the suggestions in the Mozilla release notes. For other font problems, see the discussion on fonts in Chapter 3, Static Content.

Some standards are written in HTML. If you save these files to local disk and disconnect from the Internet, sometimes they display in a browser very slowly. This is because the browser is trying to retrieve stylesheets from a Web server. To fix this, choose “Work Offline” from the File menu, and reload the document.

Summary

Mozilla is a massively featured development environment with origins in XML, objects, and the Web, and application developers can easily exploit it. I hope you enjoy reading this book as much as I enjoyed writing it. I wish you many constructive and creative hours exploring the technology, should you choose to take it up. With that said, here we go…

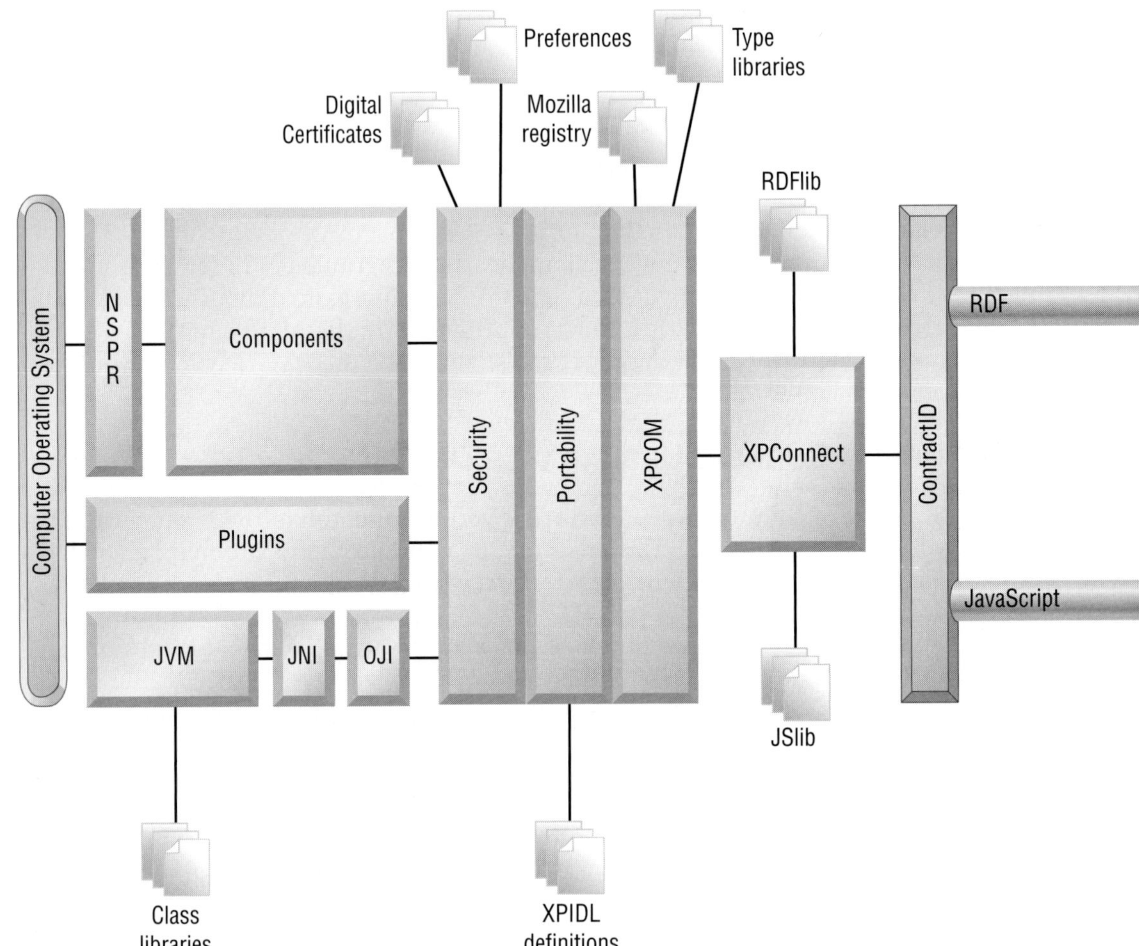

Preferences
Type libraries
Digital Certificates
Mozilla registry
RDFlib
Computer Operating System
NSPR
Components
Security
Portability
XPCOM
XPConnect
ContractID
RDF
JavaScript
Plugins
JVM
JNI
OJI
JSlib
Class libraries
XPIDL definitions

CHAPTER 1

Fundamental Concepts

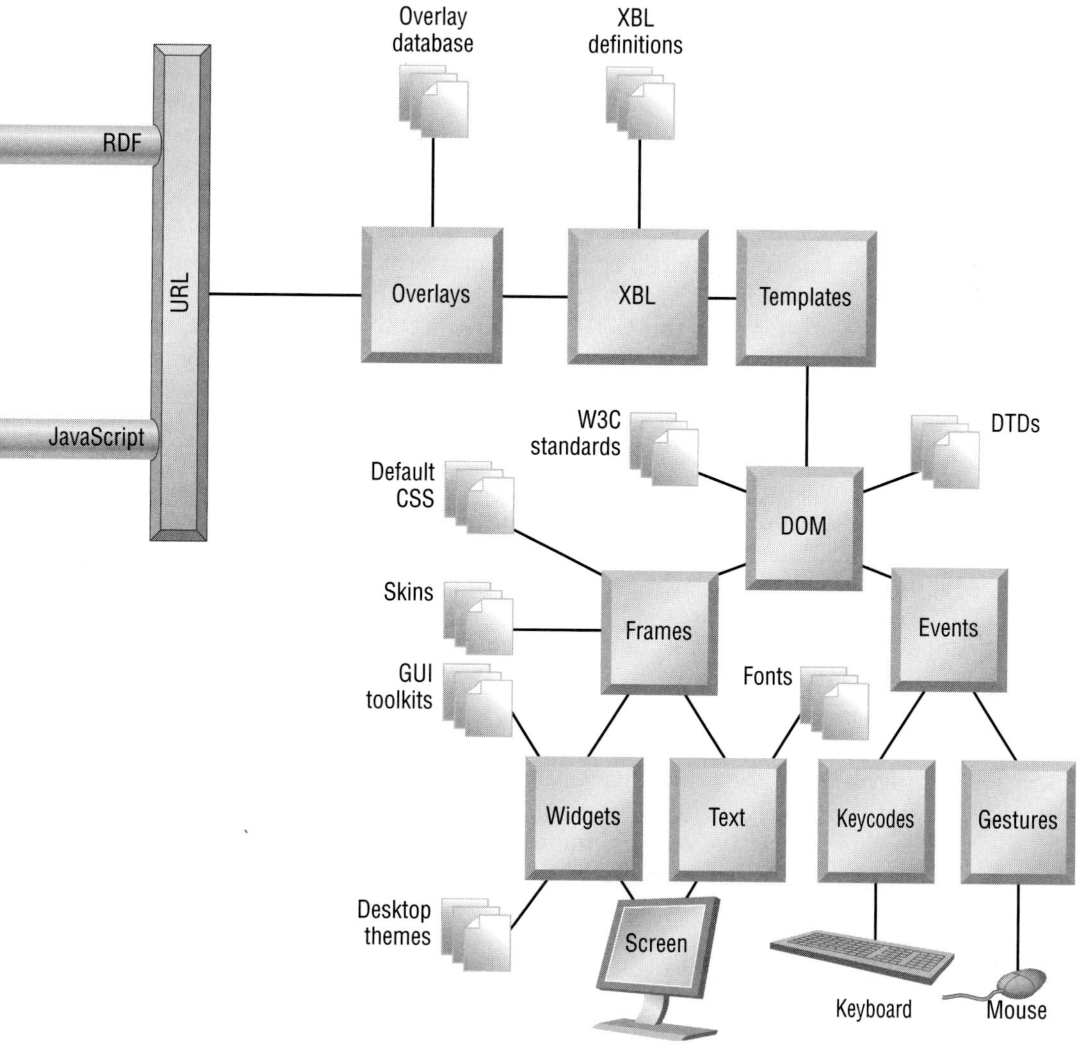

This chapter is an overview of Mozilla architecture and concepts, and it contains only a little code. If you are new to Mozilla, this chapter provides orientation and explains what you get for your time and effort. It explains what the platform is, how Mozilla fits in with XML technologies, and how it supports rapid application development. If you already appreciate some of the architecture, skip directly to Chapter 2, XUL Layout.

The "Hands On" session in this chapter contains some trivial programming examples. It pokes around inside an existing Mozilla-based application, writes a traditional "hello, world" program, and begins the NoteTaker project that runs throughout this book.

The NPA (Not Perfectly Accurate) diagram at the start of this chapter is a structural diagram of the Mozilla platform. Each rectangular box is a complex subsystem that represents a chunk of technology. Each chunk is about equal in size to one or more software standards. These rectangular boxes are embedded inside the program that makes up the Mozilla platform; they are not particularly separate. The small stacked rectangles represent files that sit in a computer's file system. The platform reads and writes to these files as necessary.

Without knowing anything much yet, it can be seen from the NPA diagram that there is a fundamental split in the platform. On the right (the *front*) are the more user-oriented, XML-like technologies like events, CSS (Cascading Style Sheet) styles, and the DOM (Document Object Model). URLs (Uniform Resource Locaters), the basis of the World Wide Web, are a key access point to these technologies. On the left (the *back*) are the more system-oriented, object-like technologies, such as components. Contract IDs (a Mozilla concept) are a key access point to these technologies. The two halves of the platform are united by a programming language, JavaScript, and a data format, RDF (the Resource Description Framework). JavaScript is very well suited to the technologies inside the Mozilla Platform.

It is easy to see these two parts of the platform. Open a window on any Mozilla-based product, for example the Netscape 7.0 Web browser or email client, and everything you see in that window will be made from XML. Writing a small piece of JavaScript code that submits an HTML form to a Web server is a trivial example of using objects associated with the back of the platform.

The view provided by the NPA diagram does not translate into a tricky or radical programming system. Programming with the Mozilla Platform is the same as with any programming environment—you type lines of code into a file. Unlike the restrictive environment of a Web page, you are free to work with a very broad range of services.

1.1 Understanding Mozilla Product Names

The word *Mozilla* was originally a project name. Proposed by Jamie Zawinski, an employee of Netscape Communications, in the 1990s, *Mozilla* was also the name of the green reptile mascot for that project. It is a contraction of "Mosaic

Killer," coined in the spirit of competitive software projects. The Mosaic browser was the predecessor of the Netscape 1.0 browser.

Since then, the term *Mozilla* has because increasingly overused. At one time it stood for a project, a product, and a platform; and *mozilla.org* came to stand for an organization. Now, Mozilla is a generic term for a cluster of technologies, just as Java and .NET are. Other terms are also used for products and technologies within that cluster. Mozilla's home on the Web, still referred to casually as mozilla.org, can be found at

```
www.mozilla.org
```

Mozilla first gained public visibility when the Netscape Communicator 5.0 Web application suite was announced as an Open Source project in 1998. The open source tradition allows for public scrutiny, public contributions, and free use. As time passed, Mozilla became a catch-all term for everything related to that 5.0 project. After more time, Mozilla 1.0 was declared ready in June 2002. That 1.0 release renamed the 5.0 project to *Mozilla 1.0*. The 5.0 status of that project can still be seen in the user-agent string of the browser (type `about:mozilla` into the Location bar to inspect this).

Now, versions 6.0, 6.5, 7.0, and onward refer to the still-proprietary Netscape-branded products, like Netscape Navigator. Versions 1.0, 1.1, 1.2, and onward refer to the Mozilla Platform version, as well as to the Web applications built by mozilla.org, that originate from the Netscape Communicator Web application suite.

In this book, the terms *Mozilla* and *Mozilla Platform* mean the same thing—the platform. Any Mozilla-based application (e.g., an email client) uses and depends upon a copy of the Mozilla Platform. The platform itself consists of an executable program, some libraries, and some support files. If the platform executable is run by itself, without starting any application, then nothing happens.

The separation between the Mozilla Platform and mozilla.org applications has become more obvious with time. What was once considered to be a very large application suite is now considered to be a large platform on which a set of smaller applications are built.

Until at least version 1.4, these smaller applications still carry their Netscape names—*Navigator*, *Composer*, and *Messenger*. They are also tightly integrated with each other. On one hand, this integration presents a unified face to the user, a face rich in functionality. On the other hand, this integration is inefficient to maintain because changes to one part can affect the other parts. For that reason, the browser and email applications have been reinvented as separate nonintegrated products at about version 1.5. These replacement applications have the names *Mozilla Browser* (project name: Firebird) and *Mozilla Mail* (project name: Thunderbird). The integrated suite continues to be available as well.

This split-up of the suite is not a fundamental change of any kind. Both integrated and de-integrated browsers share the same platform. Toolkits used by old and new browsers are also very similar. The application logic for old and new browsers does differ markedly, however.

Because the new nonintegrated applications are still in flux, and because they are narrow in focus, this book uses the older, integrated applications as a reference point and teaching tool. Those integrated applications are well tested, demonstrate nearly all of the platform technology, are better documented, and are still up-to-date. They are a useful training ground for grasping Mozilla technology.

In this book, *Classic Browser* means the established and integrated mozilla.org browser that is part of an application suite. *Classic Mozilla* means the whole application suite. *Navigator* means a Netscape-branded browser such as 7.0 or 4.79. The Classic Browser may display its content using the Classic theme (which looks like Netscape 4.x suite of products) or the Modern theme (which looks like the 5.0 suite of products). The Classic theme is therefore one step older than the Classic Browser.

A final product of the Mozilla project is *Gecko*, also called the *Gecko Runtime Engine*. This is a stripped-down version of the platform that contains only a core set of display technology. It has not yet emerged as a clearly separate product, but with increased use of this name, it is likely that Gecko will be recognized separately.

To summarise all that naming detail, this book is about the Mozilla Platform only. It uses the Classic Browser and other parts of Classic Mozilla to explain how the platform works, but it is about building applications separate from those applications. The NoteTaker running example adds a tool to the Classic Browser because it is too small to be an application of its own. If you download anything for this book, download the 1.4 release of Classic Mozilla, which contains the version 1.4 Mozilla Platform.

The remainder of this topic looks at some of the other names associated with Mozilla technology.

1.1.1 Platform Versions

Fundamental to Mozilla is the Classic Mozilla software release. Many versions of this combination of platform and Web application suite exist. Classic Mozilla contains a large subset of all features with which the platform is capable of dealing. The remaining features are unavailable. The main versions of Classic Mozilla follow:

Stable or major releases. These are versions x.0 or x.0.y; they provide a guarantee that critical features (interfaces) won't change until the next major release. Examples: 1.0, 1.01.

Feature or minor releases. These have versions a.b, where b is greater than 0. Feature releases provide enhancements and bug fixes to major releases. Example: 1.4.

Alpha, Beta, and Release Candidate releases. Before version 1.4 is finished, versions 1.4alpha and 1.4beta are versions of 1.3 that are more than 1.3, but neither finished nor approved for release as 1.4. The Release Candidate versions are near-complete beta versions that might become final releases if they pass last-minute testing.

Talkback releases. Alternate versions of any release might include Talkback technology, which captures the browser state when it crashes and emails the result back to mozilla.org. This is used for mean-time-between-failures engineering metrics and for debugging purposes.

Nightly and debug releases. Releases created nightly are compiled from the very latest changes and are the releases least likely to work. They are compiled with additional debugging features turned on, which very technical users can use as analysis tools. Both the platform and applications contain debugging features.

Custom versions. Because the source code is freely available, anyone with a suitable computer can compile the platform. Numerous compile time options change the set of features included in the final binary files. By modifying the default set of features, custom platforms run a risk. The risk is that the majority of forward progress assumes that the default features are always available. Special custom versions must live with the fact that they may not keep up with mainstream changes to the platform and may not run some Mozilla applications.

This book uses final, minor, or major releases of the standard platform.

1.1.2 Example Applications

Some of the better-known Web applications built on the Mozilla platform follow:

Netscape 7.0. This is the commercial edition of Mozilla and includes features to support AOL Time Warner's business goals in the Web and Internet space. The main technical differences are: support for the AOL concept of screen name; integration with AOL's server-side facilities; lack of popup window suppression; custom cookie handling; and a general cleanup of the user interface. Netscape 7.0 is based on Mozilla 1.01. Netscape 6.x is also based on Mozilla; however, it is based on version 0.94 and is highly buggy.

Compuserve 7.0. AOL also owns this older Web and Internet client-based service, which still has a large user base. Version 7.0 is a Mozilla 1.01–based tool.

AOL 8.0 for MacOS X. This is AOL's flagship Web and Internet client, with a very large user base and a highly custom interface. With version 8.0, the Macintosh version of AOL has been moved from Internet Explorer to Mozilla 1.01.

Mozilla Browser. This mozilla.org Web browser is to be more compact and streamlined than the Classic Browser.

Two very extensive examples of non-Web applications are given by OEone and ActiveState.

OEone (*www.oeone.com*) produces products intended to make personal computers easily useable by novices. Their OEone HomeBase product is a custom combination of Linux and an enhanced version of the Mozilla platform called Penzilla. It provides a complete system for interacting with a computer. Figure 1.1 shows an arrangement of this Mozilla-based desktop.

ActiveState (*www.activestate.com*) produces integrated development environment (IDE) tools for software developers. Their Komodo product is based on the Mozilla platform. Figure 1.2 is a screenshot of that product.

In addition to Web and non-Web applications, highly customized applications are possible. The standard Mozilla Platform provides the same interface on every desktop, which involves some compromise. There have been a number of attempts to create browser products that match the exact look and feel of one specific platform. These are deeply customized offshoots of Mozilla. Such offshoots use embedding technology not covered in this book:

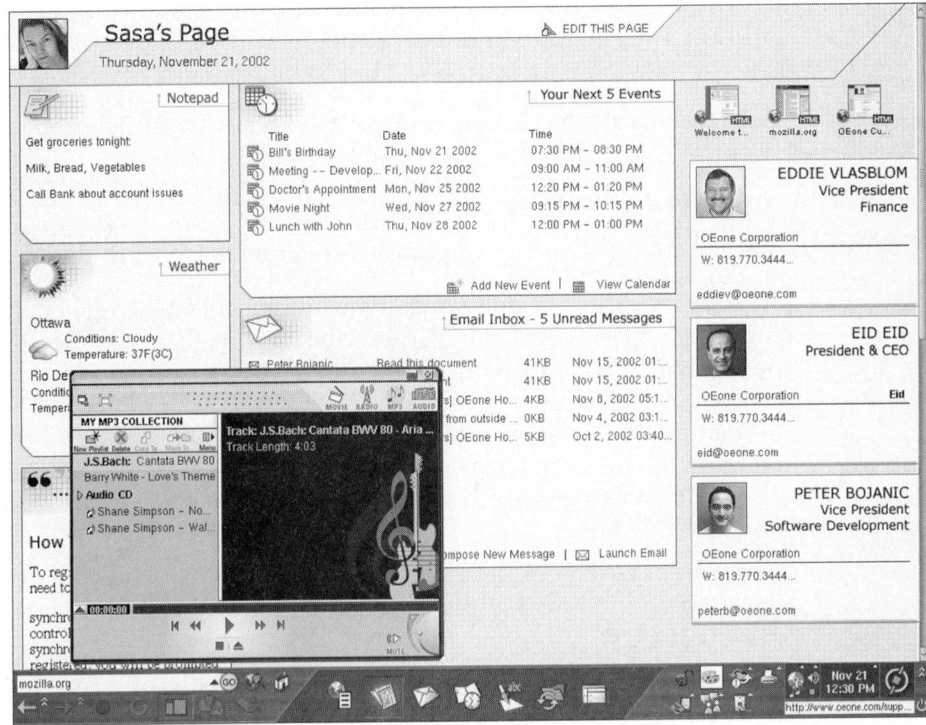

Fig. 1.1 OEone HomeBase desktop. Used by permission of OEone Corporation (*www.oeone.com*).

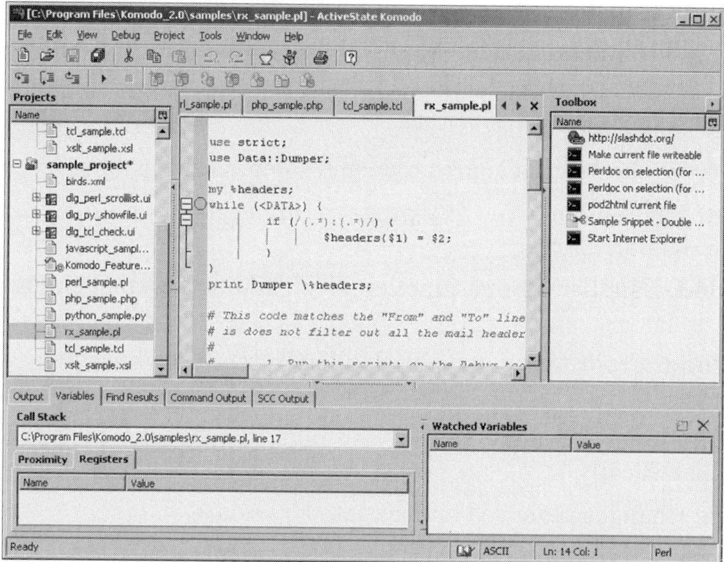

Fig. 1.2 ActiveState's Komode 2.0 IDE. Used by permission and courtesy of ActiveState (*www.activestate.com*).

Chimera. A Macintosh MacOS X browser based on the Cocoa interface, with traditional Macintosh menus.

Galeon, Nautilus. Browsing tools integrated closely with the GNU/Linux GNOME desktop interface. Some of this integration is addressed in the standard platform with forthcoming support for GTK 2.0.

K-Meleon. A Microsoft Windows browser that turns Mozilla into an ActiveX control. Toolbars are very similar to a simple Internet Explorer.

The number of applications based on the Mozilla platform is steadily growing, with announcements every month or so. The community newscenter *www.mozillazine.org* is a good place to pick up announcements of new Mozilla products.

1.1.3 Jargon Buster

Mozilla culture and mozilla.org documentation contains some convoluted slang. Covering it all is a hopeless task. Refer to *www.mozilla.org/docs/jargon.html* and to *http://devsupport.mozdev.org/QA/thesaurus/*. A few of the more visible terms follow:

XP. Cross platform, meaning portable, as in XPCOM, XPFE, XPInstall, XPIDL.

FE. Front end, the graphical display part of Mozilla.

BE. Back end, the networking part of Mozilla.

I18n. Internationalization = I + 18 characters + n. Multilocale support.

L10n. Localization = L + 10 characters + n. Customizations for a given locale.

The tree. The Mozilla source code and compilation system.

Bloat. The tendency for any program undergoing enhancement to get bigger.

Landed. Usually "landed functionality": adding finished changes to the tree.

Dogfood. From "eat your own dog food": testing where you trial your own fixes.

Porkjockeys. Derived from "flying pigs." Those who seek to redesign Mozilla radically.

r=ada. Changes reviewed and accepted by Ada.

sr=ada. Changes super-reviewed (architecturally reviewed) and accepted by Ada.

Zarro Boogs. Zero bugs; no current defect reports.

Finally, there is an endless list of overlapping technical terms for the core capabilities of Mozilla: Seamonkey, NGLayout, Necko, and more. Very few of these terms map cleanly to a single, obvious application technology, so they are generally avoided in this book.

1.2 The XML Environment

XML (the Extensible Markup Language) is a hugely successful standard from the World Wide Web Consortium (the W3C, at *www.w3.org*). Mozilla has extensive support for XML, so we briefly review what that standard is good for.

The primary goal of XML is to provide a notation for describing and structuring *content*. Content is just data or information of any kind. The central XML standards provide a toolkit of concepts and syntax. That toolkit can be used to create a set of descriptive terms that apply to one type of content, like vector graphics. Such a set of terms is called an *application* of XML. The most well-known XML application is XHTML, which is the XML version of plain HTML.

XHTML describes content that contains text, images, and references to other XHTML documents, commonly known as links. Any particular example of this content is called an *instance* or a *document*. Thus, XHTML defines *hypertext* documents, as opposed to any other kind of document. There are many other publicly defined XML applications, such as SVG (*vector graphics* content), MathML (*mathematical* content), and RDF (*resource description* content). Mozilla's own XUL specifies *graphical user interface* content. As an XML example, Listing 1.1 is a trivial SVG document.

Listing 1.1 A document that is an instance of SVG 1.0, an XML application.

```
<?xml version="1.0" encoding="iso-8859-1"?>
<!DOCTYPE svg PUBLIC
 "-//W3C//DTD SVG 1.0//EN"
 "http://www.w3.org/TR/2001/REC-SVG-20010904/DTD/svg10.dtd"
>
<svg width="500" height="400">
  <rect x="35" y="32" width="300" height="85"/>
  <text x="50" y="67">A Rectangle</text>
</svg>
```

The first five lines of this example specify the document type; the rest is the document content. Using an XML application definition, programmers create software that can process documents of that application type. Such processing can be either quite simple or complex. In the case of Figure 1.1, a program might take this document and display a rectangle with the words "A Rectangle" inside it. A Web browser is an example of such a program. Processing of such documents can be very sophisticated. XML documents can be transformed, transmitted, created, chopped up, and combined, as well as merely displayed.

The great success of XML rests on the following few simple principles.

1.2.1 Common Underlying Format

All XML documents, regardless of application, have the same underlying format. This common format makes analysis of all such documents similar. It saves a great deal of energy that would otherwise be wasted arguing about syntax. Such arguments typically have little bearing on the actual information that those formats contain. That saved energy can be put to more important tasks, and software no longer needs special adaptors to read the special formats of other systems.

A further consequence of this common format is that it promotes reuse and enhancement of software tools. Common operations on the XML format are now well known. Consequently, finding or making a tool that processes XML is easier. Programmers can rely on these features being present in most modern tools, including Mozilla.

1.2.2 The Open-Closed Principle

The open-closed principle originates from the world of object-oriented (OO) programming. It captures the idea that a piece of software can be both finished (closed) and yet still available for further change (open). This thinking also applies to XML. The core XML standards are finished and certain, as are various applications of XML; nevertheless, anyone can create a new XML application at any time. This is a highly flexible arrangement. Furthermore, the XML standards allow partial instances of XML applications (called *document fragments*) to be mixed together in one document. One document might contain both XHTML and SVG content. That is also highly flexible.

Such flexibility is a highly fluid situation and provides fertile ground for innovation. Document authors are free to make any instance of a particular XML application, which is just common sense. Software developers, however, are free to make any XML application definition. New application definitions can be the basis for a whole range of new document instances in a new content or application area.

Mozilla benefits from this flexibility. It implements several innovative XML applications, primarily XUL (XML User-interface Language) and XBL (XML Binding Language), upon which many special-purpose XML documents are based. It allows programmers to process generic XML content and many specific XML applications, like RDF and XHTML.

1.2.3 Beyond English

Another benefit of XML is its ability to be expressed universally.

The Unicode standard is a list of every character concept used in human writing. When a Unicode character reference and a font are combined, a visual character (also called a glyph) can be displayed. XML documents can refer to any entry in the Unicode standard, so XML is a useful way to express information in any language on Earth.

Early successes in the modern world of computing occurred in the English-speaking part of the West, some at the University of California, Berkeley Campus, and some at AT&T. It seemed at the time that eight bits (one byte) was sufficient to capture all the glyphs in common English text. This resulted in the ASCII character set, the C language's `char` type, and processing technology in the UNIX operating system all being fixed to one byte. This legacy has created a hurdle for the Unicode standard, which overall requires two bytes per character. XML is one way around this hurdle since it starts again from the beginning with a new format based on Unicode standards.

Mozilla is an example of a tool that handles internationalization issues by relying on XML and Unicode technology. Its main supported language, JavaScript, is also based on Unicode.

1.2.4 Hierarchical Thinking

The final strength of XML is in its internal structure. Documents created to XML standards consist of fragments of content nested inside each other, in a hierarchical way. Hierarchical organization is a concept that humans find easy to grasp. As the riddle goes, the man from St.Yves had seven wives, each wife

these layout and rendering objects and display automatically happens without any further programmer effort. This topmost, visual aspect of the platform can be seen in any Web browser window.

Finally, XML content and XPCOM objects can be tied together. This can be done with an XBL binding, an XUL template, or other less obvious approaches. These Mozilla-specific tactics extend the automatic processing done by sophisticated XPCOM objects so that even high-level tasks require only small amounts of scripting. The "tabbed navigation" feature of the Mozilla browser is an example of a tag/object combination created in XBL.

If that were all of the Mozilla Platform, then the platform would be no more than a JavaScript interpreter and a huge object library—not much different than Perl, Tcl, Visual Basic, or even Java. The platform, however, also includes at the topmost level an *application shell*. This shell is a mass of platform code that binds many of the XPCOM objects together into an executable program. This program is able to automate and coordinate many tasks, like connections to server software, basic document management, and installation processes. The application shell, plus many special-purpose XPCOM objects, represents a ready-made development framework. It is more immediately useful than a passive set of libraries that can't do anything until a programmer chooses to use them. The application shell provides the organization and integration features that allow applications to run on top of the platform. It is also the platform's application execution engine. The `mozilla` (or `mozilla.exe`) executable is a copy of the platform wrapped up in an extensive application shell.

A substantial portion of a programmer's work can be done merely by creating XML documents. These are then supplied to the application shell.

These layers of the platform do not hide each other from the programmer. An application programmer's script can perform operations at any level, in any order, subject to security constraints. Common tasks that are in keeping with the interactive, visual orientation of the platform can be achieved with very little code that exploits the highest layers of the platform. Highly application-specific tasks require a more traditional programming style in which lower-level objects are combined for an end result.

The remainder of this discussion of architecture considers some of these layers in more detail.

1.3.1.2 XPCOM Component Model A great strength of Mozilla is its internal structure.

At the lowest level, the platform itself is written in the C and C++ programming languages. In the case of a simple C/C++ program, adding functionality means compiling and linking in more objects or functions. For large projects, this is an impractical and naïve approach for many reasons.

One reason is that the resulting program will grow huge and inefficient to run. It is also impractical because keeping track of all the implemented objects is difficult. Finally, if several different projects are to use the software, each one might require only a portion of the platform. In other words, each project must heavily modify the platform for its own ends or live with a miscellany of objects that it has no use for. There needs to be a cleverer approach, and there is.

An object broker (also called an object directory, object name service, or object discovery service) is a piece of code that finds objects and makes them available. If all objects built provide a standard or common interface that the broker can use, then all members of a large set of objects can be handled the same way. That imposes some uniformity on objects.

Mozilla objects are organized into individual components. Components are built out of objects and interfaces. A component registry (a small database) maintains a list of all the available components. A component name service that turns a component name into an object (in object-oriented terms it is a factory) is also available, as are a thousand components and a thousand interfaces. Here is an example of a component name, written in *Contract ID* form. The trailing digit is a version number:

```
@mozilla.org/browser/httpindex-service;1
```

The infrastructure on which these components are standardized is XPCOM. XPCOM is a little like CORBA and a lot like COM, two other object broking systems.

CORBA (Common Object Request Broker Architecture) is a system for gluing together objects written in any of a number of programming languages. In order to do that it describes all object interfaces using a language-neutral syntax called IDL (Interface Definition Language). Mozilla includes a variant of the CORBA IDL specification technology. The Mozilla version is called XPIDL (Cross Platform IDL). It is a portable (hardware- and operating-system-independent) language that is used to generate portable code and type libraries.

COM (Common Object Management) is a system for gluing together different objects written under Microsoft Windows. Mozilla also includes a variant of COM, called XPCOM (Cross Platform COM). XPIDL and XPCOM work together in Mozilla as a hybrid system that acts on COM-like objects that are described by CORBA-like specifications. There is no attempt to make XPCOM a distributed system, like DCOM (Distributed COM). It is restricted to one computer alone, and currently to one executable. Although object specifications are CORBA-like, the XPCOM system duplicates the features of COM quite closely.

Nearly all of Mozilla is reduced to XPCOM components, and nearly all of these components are scriptable via JavaScript. Many components implement Web protocols or other networking standards. This component model plus available network components makes Mozilla look like a miniature version of Microsoft's .NET framework. If platform components are written in C/C++, as most are, then they must be written according to strict portability guidelines, just as XPCOM is.

1.3.1.3 Support for XML Software support for XML standards is a matter of degree. A program might merely be able to read an XML document, like a file filter, or it may have its entire purpose dedicated to XML analysis, like an XML database server. Mozilla lies somewhere between these two extremes.

Mozilla does a better job of supporting XML standards than just reading documents of that format. Mozilla has considerable infrastructure for management of retrieved XML documents; in particular, it has a simple but sophisticated processing model for RDF. The best way to view Mozilla's XML support is as a system that can get XML from *here* and put it *there*. To assist that process, a number of transformation techniques can be applied. Example techniques include merging and filtering documents, managing document fragments, and performing fine-grained insert, update, and delete operations on the document structure and its content.

A fairly complete list of Mozilla-supported XML applications is: XML, XML Namespaces, XLink, XHTML (and HTML), MathML, SVG, XSLT (Extensible Stylesheet Language Transformations), RDF, SOAP, WSDL (Web Services Description Language), and XML Schema.

Mozilla also supports two XML applications unique to the platform: XUL and XBL. XUL documents specify arrangements of graphical widgets. XBL documents represent bindings that blend together a JavaScript object and XML content into a new piece of content. XUL is a crucial technology for application developers. Look at any Classic Mozilla window or dialog box—everything you see (except for any displayed HTML) is XUL content.

Mozilla supports DTDs (document type definitions) for many of these standards. It supports XML Schema definitions for none of them. Of the supported standards, the only ones that are intended for visual display are XHTML/HTML, SVG, MathML, XUL, and XBL. The rest are used only for data processing purposes.

1.3.1.4 Gecko Content Display Model To show the user XML content, some kind of display system is required. That is the job of the rendering objects inside the platform that form part of the Gecko display subsystem.

The rules that determine the layout of XML documents (and particularly layout of HTML) have been shifting in the last few years. Where those rules used to appear in standards such as HTML, they now are collected into the styling standards, such as CSS, DSSSL (Document Style Semantics and Specification Language), and XSL-FO (XSL Formatting Objects). This trend is reflected in the Mozilla Platform, where all layout is controlled by a modern CSS2 implementation, which includes many Mozilla-specific enhancements. The powerful CSS2 engine inside Mozilla is also the heart of the Gecko layout system. Mozilla also uses CSS2 for printing.

XML documents are not immutable. If delivered from a remote location, they can arrive incrementally. If acted on by a programmer, they may grow or shrink. Modern display tools need a sophisticated content model to support all kinds of dynamic content changes during display. Mozilla has a third-generation content display system, also part of Gecko, whose architecture is contrasted against earlier approaches in this short list. Although the list refers to XML, the most obvious example of a display system is one that displays HTML.

Mark I strategy. Read an XML document's tags one at a time and display as you go. Pause the display process when not enough tags have arrived to figure out the next step, making the user wait. Very early browsers did this with HTML, like Netscape 1.0.

Mark Ib strategy. Read all of a document's XML tags into memory, putting the user on hold. Analyze the document. Display the entire document at once. No popular browsers ever did this, but XSLT performs batch processing in a similar way when used in specialist printing software.

Mark II strategy. Read XML tags one at a time and display the page using placeholders for content that is anticipated but not yet read. When that content arrives, dynamically replace the placeholders with the real content. Shuffle everything around to clean up changes each time placeholders are filled. Internet Explorer 4.0+ and Mozilla 1.0+ do this.

Mark III strategy. Read XML tags as for Mark II, but possibly read control information as well. When the user or the server manipulates the control information, fetch or remove matching content and update the display with it. Do this even after the document is fully loaded. Mozilla 1.0+, which uses RDF as the control information, does this.

It requires a complex design to implement a Mark III display model, and Mozilla's internals are quite sophisticated in this area.

1.3.1.5 Support for Web Standards For traditional Web page display, Mozilla's Web standards support is the best yet seen in a Web client. The closest current competitor is the Opera Web browser. Although this book is not about HTML, a brief review is not entirely irrelevant, since HTML can be combined with XUL in several ways.

In the world of HTML, Mozilla has a *legacy compatibility mode,* a *strictly standards-compliant mode,* and a *nearly standards-compliant mode*. The legacy compatibility mode does its best to support old HTML 4.01 and earlier documents. The strict mode supports the newer XHTML 1.0 only. The nearly strict mode is the same as the strict mode, except that it provides a migration path for older Web pages that look bad when displayed strictly according to standards. Directives at the start of a Web page determine which mode will process that document. In all modes, enhancements to the standards are allowed and some exist.

Mozilla supports complementary Web standards such as HTTP 1.1; CSS2; DOM 0, 1, and 2; and ECMAScript Edition 3 (JavaScript). Mozilla's Cascading Style Sheet (CSS2) support has received a great deal of standards attention, and a number of Mozilla extensions look forward to CSS3, or are merely innovative in their own right. Only some parts of DOM 3 are supported. Mozilla supports some of the accessibility statements made by the W3C.

The world of HTML is being reduced to a number of small, separate standards and standards modules that together make up the whole of HTML. Mozilla supports XLink but not XForms. Similarly, some of the DOM 3 modules are supported, while others aren't. Since Internet Explorer 6.0 supports only the DOM standards to DOM 1, Mozilla is well ahead in the standards adoption game. Chapter 5, Scripting, explores standards compliance for the DOM standards in more detail.

Mozilla support for MathML and SVG is not complete. The MathML support is close to being complete and is extensive enough to be fully functional, but the SVG support is only partially implemented and is not available by default.

1.3.1.6 Custom Tags and Objects Mozilla provides a specification mechanism for pairing textual XML tags and compiled objects. This specification language is called XBL, an XML application invented for Mozilla. XBL is assisted by JavaScript, CSS, and other XML standards.

With the help of XBL, a new XML tag that is not mandated anywhere else can be defined. This tag can be hooked up to processing logic. The W3C calls this logic an *action*, but it is better known by the Microsoft term *behavior*. In Mozilla, such logic is created in the form of a full object-oriented object definition. The connection between the new tag and the processing logic is called a *binding*. The object logic can be written to take advantage of any of the services available to the platform, including all the XPCOM objects and other custom tags that possess their own bindings.

Because XBL allows new tags to be specified, Mozilla must be particularly liberal when processing content. Any XML tag might have meaning defined somewhere. XBL contributes to the near-zero validation aspect of Mozilla, discussed under the heading "Consequences."

1.3.2 Innovations

The Mozilla Platform does not reduce to a set of objects and a set of XML standards ticks. It also includes infrastructure that holds together processing and applications designed to exploit those objects and standards.

Some of this infrastructure contains new and innovative ideas. Most of it is required if application programs are to be created, installed, and operated correctly.

1.3.2.1 Chrome and Toolkits The installation of a Mozilla application can be divided into three parts. One part is a set of files specific to the user of the application, such as email addresses and bookmarks. One part is a set of binary files containing the executable programs of the platform, plus a few configuration files. The final part is a set of application files stored under a directory with the name `chrome`. Chrome is a central concept for Mozilla-based applications. An exploration of the chrome directory is included in the "Hands On" session in this chapter.

Inside the chrome directory there are many subdirectories, data files, documents, scripts, images and other content. Together, the sum of the chrome content, merely called the chrome, represents a set of resources. This set of resources is responsible for all the user interface elements presented by the applications installed in the platform. An application may exist entirely as a set of files in the chrome.

Mozilla refers to files in the chrome with the special URL scheme `chrome:`. An example of a chrome URL is

```
chrome://notetaker/content/NoteTaker.xul
```

A `chrome:` URL is usually a special case of a `resource:` URL. The Mozilla-specific `resource:` URL scheme points to the top of the platform installation area, so this URL is usually equivalent to the preceding URL:

```
resource://chrome/notetaker/content/NoteTaker.xul
```

Both `resource:` and `chrome:` URLs represent a subset of all the resources that can be located using a `file:` URL. The `chrome:` and `resource:` URL schemes, however, are processed specially by the platform, and a `file:` URL cannot always be used as a substitute.

Generally speaking, everything in the chrome directory is portable. Although there are always exceptions, an application installed in the chrome of Mozilla on Microsoft Windows should have files nearly identical to the same application installed in chrome on UNIX or Macintosh. XUL documents are usually stored in the chrome.

Chrome is more than a desktop theme, since it can contain both GUI elements and general application logic. It is more like a sophisticated X11 window manager such as the GNOME desktop's Sawfish (used on Linux/UNIX), or an advanced theme engine on Microsoft Windows. Take the example of Sawfish. Sawfish can be configured using scripts written in a programming language. This typically results in the addition of buttons and decorations to a window's title bar. Sawfish cannot reach inside the windows it decorates; it can only place decorations on the outside of those windows. Mozilla's chrome, on the other hand, cannot reach outside the edges of a window, but it can modify all the elements inside it. If Microsoft Word were implemented using Mozilla and ran on UNIX, Sawfish could remove the stylized W from the top left corner of the title bar, but it couldn't change any of Word's toolbars. Mozilla's chrome, on the other hand, couldn't remove the stylized W, but it could change the toolbars. Figure 1.3 shows a combination of these GUI elements together in a single window. The window contains Sawfish window decorations, Mozilla chrome status bar and toolbars, and a simple HTML document.

Sawfish adds a fancy title bar with at least four buttons. Files in the chrome add at least two toolbars, a menu bar, a status bar, and a collapsed sidebar. The rest is HTML.

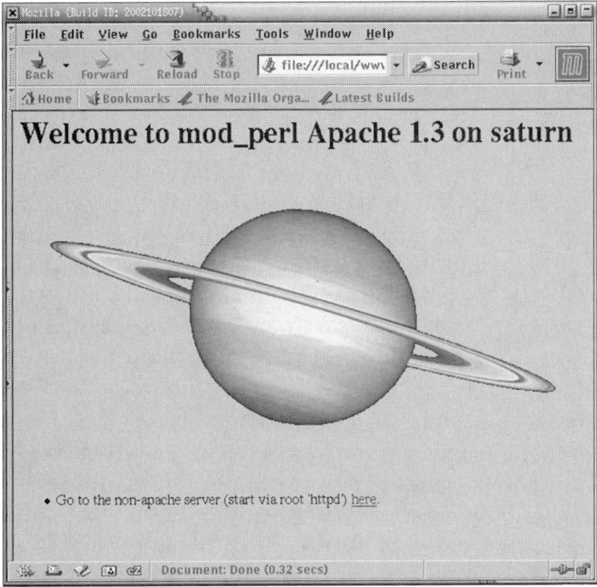

Fig. 1.3 GNU/Linux Mozilla with Sawfish Window Manager. Used by permission of Arlo Rose.

The chrome also contains a special file named `toolkit.jar`. This file is an archive that contains a collection of commonly used files. The most important thing in this archive is a set of definitions that state which XUL tags exist and what they do. Since Mozilla applications are built out of XUL, the presence and content of this file is of vital interest to application programmers, and little can be done without it. This toolkit is supplied with all complete releases of the platform. It is undergoing minor change during the development of the new Mozilla Browser.

1.3.2.2 Themes, Skins, and Locales The Mozilla Platform supports a *theme system* that allows the appearance of an application to be varied and a localization system that allows the language that an application is expressed in to be varied. Both systems work inside the chrome directory.

Individual themes in the theme system are built out of skins. A *skin* is a file specifying the nonstructural aspects of a Mozilla window, such as colors, fonts, and images. Skin files are a subset of the chrome that is automatically selected by the current browser theme. "Theme" in the language of Mozilla means "All skins stored under the name of this theme." Some Mozilla advocates are passionate about designing their skins. In the commercial world, skins are a way to package and brand applications with corporate colors and marks or to make them fit look-and-feel or desktop integration standards.

Chrome URLs are modified by the current browser language (the *locale*) as well as by the current theme. This means that supporting both an English and a Russian Back button is just a matter of having chrome files expressed in both languages.

1.3.2.3 Data Sources and Content Sinks An innovative system used extensively inside the platform is the Producer and Consumer design pattern. This pattern is normally seen inside object-oriented libraries and languages. The Mozilla Platform includes infrastructure support for a number of Producer/Consumer combinations, with special attention to handling of RDF-style data.

The Producer/Consumer approach dedicates pieces of code to supplying data (i.e., Producers, called *data sources* in Mozilla) and other pieces of code to absorbing it (i.e., Consumers, called *content sinks* in Mozilla). This separation of supply and demand allows information to be pumped around inside the platform in a flexible way.

RDF is one of the more obscure W3C technologies, and little more can be said in this chapter without starting a long discussion. Data sources and sinks inside the platform give the programmer an opportunity to drive information around an application using operations that are not so different from database operations. This in turn allows the platform to behave a little like a 4GL tool used to build database client software.

The most sophisticated use of data sources and sinks involves pooling up RDF data for special processing. Inside the Mozilla Browser, RDF sources and sinks can be connected by intermediary processing that acts like a sophisticated filter. This filter allows the content in RDF data flows to be combined and split. This is done after the data flow is sourced but before it is sunk. In computer science terms, this is a simple knowledge processing system that is unusual for browser-like software.

1.3.2.4 Competitive Features In addition to good design, the Mozilla Platform seeks to provide a competitive alternative to Microsoft's Internet Explorer. To that end, it needs features that give it an edge over that Microsoft browser.

Mozilla's main strength is compliance with W3C standards. The problem is that standards compliance is invisible to end users—when things go as expected, there is nothing to note. So Mozilla also has flashy features that can compete in the end-user market. Some examples of these features follow:

Auto-completion of forms. Mozilla can remember what you typed in last time.

Type-ahead find. You can reach a link or any content on a page by typing text.

Quick launch. Mozilla has caches and options that make it start up faster.

Image resizing. Mozilla proves size controls for images displayed by themselves.

Junk email filtering. Mozilla has a filtering system to combat spam.

The Mozilla engineering staff also maintains a set of performance objectives for the product based on competitive benchmarks with Internet Explorer and Opera. There are regular initiatives designed solely to trim inefficient processing from the platform, and from the browsers built upon it.

1.3.2.5 Remotely Sourced Applications The Mozilla Platform contains two methods of access to Mozilla-based applications located on a remote Web server.

The simpler of the two methods is the ability to download an application and run it immediately. Just as a remote HTML document can be displayed locally, giving the user the option of filling in and submitting a form, or clicking a link, so too can a remote XUL document be displayed locally, giving the user the option of working with a forms- and menu-driven window that acts like a locally installed program. This aspect of the platform is most similar to that of Microsoft's .NET initiatives.

The other method is to use the platform's XPInstall technology. This is a remote installation system that downloads an archive from a remote Web site and installs it in the local chrome directory permanently. A script guides the installation process, and the archive can contain XUL-based applications and other files of any kind.

In both cases, the remote source applications have some security restrictions, although those restrictions can be lifted if the correct approach is taken.

1.3.3 Consequences

Finally, some aspects of the Mozilla Platform emerge from the sum of many small changes.

1.3.3.1 GUI Integration Mozilla is a display-oriented tool, which is very different from other Open Source tools like Apache. Apache just sits on a simple network connection and waits. Mozilla is intimately connected to the user and the user's environment. It contains several strategies for working with GUIs and desktops.

At the lowest level, Mozilla relies on GUI widgets from a suitable native toolkit for the current platform. This means GTK on Linux, Win32 on Windows, and the Macintosh toolkit. A port of Mozilla that uses the Qt widget set exists, but it hasn't been maintained for a long time. There is no raw X11 implementation. The platform abstracts user input away from operating system formats using the DOM 2 Events standard.

At the desktop level, Mozilla responds normally to window operations such as focus, iconization, and exit operations. It is well behaved on UNIX under most X11 window managers. Recent versions of Mozilla support native desktop themes in Windows XP and in GNOME 2.0. Mozilla supports content selection and cut 'n' paste to a degree, but this must sometimes be hand-implemented, and only happens automatically in the most obvious cases. Mozilla also supports multiformat clipboard copying. This means that some of the formatting in a piece of selected content can be preserved when it is pasted to another application, such as Microsoft Word. Mozilla supports drag-and-drop mouse operations within the context of the application, but again, some hand-implementation is required. Simiarly, objects can be dragged from elsewhere on the desktop to a Mozilla window Without hand-implementation, nothing will happen, and no visual feedback will appear. Most Mozilla-based applications include logic that supports some drag 'n'drop operations.

Finally, at the application level, one of Mozilla's great strengths is its XUL widget description language, which allows GUI elements to be brought together in a very simple and efficient way.

1.3.3.2 Portability Mozilla runs on many different operating systems and desktops. At *www.mozilla.org*, the Mozilla Browser Platform is test-compiled every night, and the results are bundled into downloadable and installable files. At least the following operating systems are supported:

UNIX: Linux i386/PowerPC, FreeBSD, HP-UX, Solaris i386/SPARC, AIX, Irix

Mini computers: OpenVMS

Personal computers: Windows 95/98/Me/NT/XP, MacOS 9.x/X, OS/2, BeOS

There are also experimental ports to other platforms such as the Amiga. Mozilla has well-established support for the GNU/Linux operating system, and GNU/Linux is widely ported itself. It is probably feasible to port the Mozilla software to most GNU/Linux hardware.

Mozilla's portability extends beyond mere platform availability. Most features supported are intended to be identical across platforms. In particular, the file types required to build a Mozilla application (XUL, CSS, DTD, properties, JavaScript, RDF, etc.) are all entirely portable formats. In theory, a Mozilla application should run on all operating systems that the platform runs on, without a porting cost. In practice, minor differences mean that very few applications are 100% portable without some testing and occasional fixes.

1.3.3.3 Near Zero Validation In the world of communications programming, a fundamental design is this: Transmit strictly according to standards, but when receiving, accept anything that it is possible to comprehend. This strategy is designed to increase standards usage in new systems without isolating older systems.

The Mozilla Platform is a communication device, frequently receiving Web pages, email, and other messages. It follows a communication design and that design is visible to a programmer. Except in the case of strict mode for HTML, the platform interprets received XML and other documents very liberally, adapting to or ignoring many simple mistakes, omissions, and additions.

For an end user like a Web surfer, this liberal interpretation is a good idea because irritating error messages are kept to a minimum. For a programmer, this liberal interpretation is a bit of a nightmare. It is very easy to add information to a Mozilla application, only to have it silently ignored or silently recorded. This silence could result if supplied additions are not implemented, contain typos, or are simply incorrect. As a programmer, an extra degree of alertness is required when writing code for Mozilla.

Fortunately Mozilla does the most basic of checks correctly: XML content must be well formed, and JavaScript and CSS code must at least parse properly. That is a beginning, but it is cold comfort for more advanced areas where errors are more obscure.

1.3.3.4 Extensibility A strength of Mozilla is that it is a platform, not just a product. Alas, a weakness is that it is only version 1 so far, and the platform is not as flexible or as complete as one might hope.

Nevertheless, it is sufficiently flexible that it can be extended in many ways, from trivial to fundamental. New objects can be added, even XPCOM objects; new XML tags can be added; and new themes or locales or applications can be added. There is no need to register anything with some central body or to fit it in with someone else's logic.

Because the platform's source code is available, any enhancement at all is possible. Because Mozilla's chrome and XPCOM system are easy to use, many experiments can be performed with ease. Some experiments are done within the Mozilla organization itself, like attempts to produce a `<canvas>` tag for XUL. Many other people experimenting with Mozilla extensions can be found at *www.mozdev.org*.

1.3.3.5 Security Mozilla supports the security features of Netscape 4.x, including the powerful "Same Origin" policy. That policy insists that insecure operations, like writing a file, be heavily restricted. An insecure operation retrieved from a given internet location (a URL) can be attempted only on a resource that comes from the same location. This restriction allows Java applets to speak to their server of origin only. Similarly, it allows HTML or XUL applications to submit data to the Web server at which they originated.

The most noteworthy aspect of security in the platform is that applications installed in the chrome have no security restrictions at all. Security restrictions imposed by the operating system still apply.

The platform has several security models to pick from; they are described in Chapter 16, XPCOM Objects. The standard platform installation includes support for most digital encryption standards and certificate authority certificates.

1.4 The RAD Environment

Having covered the platform briefly, let's look at the rapid application development (RAD) style of software development and see what it consists of.

RAD projects have some unique characteristics. The primary characteristic is just what it says: rapid application development. RAD projects have fast delivery of finished work as a primary goal.

The Mozilla Platform itself is not a RAD project. It is an Open Source project, where peer review, innovation, and architectural strategy are at least as important as fast delivery. Furthermore, the platform can be used in embedded software projects, a topic not covered in this book. Embedded software has as its main constraints footprint size, robustness, and low maintenance. Fast delivery is not a critical priority for embedded software either.

Because there are alternatives, speedy development is not just a matter of adopting the platform. It is both a mindset and a process. Here are some of the essential characteristics of RAD projects.

1.4.1 Less Time, Same Effect

The quickest solution you can find that achieves a desired end is probably the best solution. This is an essential characteristic of RAD projects—there is no allegiance to any rigid rules. Whatever does the job fastest, wins. Even if the technique you chose isn't that beautiful, isn't that sophisticated, and maybe isn't even that flexible, the fact that it gets the job done is essential. If your labor can be polished up afterward, that is a plus.

Don't agonize for years over the perfect design. Make something work.

1.4.2 Visual Prototypes

Human users are the ultimate challenge in software development. They can't be programmed reliably, and their subjective processes go straight through the structured rules of software. It takes time and many experiments before a user and a user interface are happy with each other. In the acronym RAD, the A for *application* guarantees the need for flexible user-interface experiments. RAD projects need the ability to create visual prototypes efficiently.

RAD projects are not based on the concept "build it and they will come." Flexible, changeable user demos are critical.

1.4.3 Vertical Solutions

RAD projects are used to build products that have a narrow purpose, whether it be a museum catalog or a stock analysis package. Those products are so-called vertical solutions. There is usually no need to make the product so flexible it can be applied to other uses. That can be a later goal if the product works as is. So why insist on a low-level, generic tool, such as C++, Perl, or Tcl/Tk, as the basis for a product that is a point solution? Use instead a specialized tool that fits the problem space—one that is suited to the task will be more efficient. Mozilla is specifically aimed at several vertical problem spaces.

RAD projects can be built on a narrow technology base. Very generic tools aren't always better.

1.4.4 COTS Software Versus Home Grown

The "not invented here" argument of software development, in which programmers object to using other people's software, is becoming harder and harder to sustain. As the total amount of code in the world increases, the chance that your job has been done for you also increases. Using COTS (common-off-the-shelf) software is a good technique for saving time and effort. It greatly reduces the amount of pure programming labor and gets you a result. Using COTS software makes perfect sense for RAD projects.

RAD projects use other people's work first and build things by hand second.

1.4.5 Destructured Testing

The constraints of low-level programming languages like C are well known. Pointer problems and strong typing make the use of a good compiler essential. The argument goes that using the compilation phase will save time later because it is a rigorous process. Less human testing will be needed if a compiler with a `--pedantic` option is used.

If programmers have a fixed defect rate per hour, this argument is probably correct, even if the language is a scripting language. This argument, however, assumes that a nontrivial program is being developed. In the case of RAD, using a large existing tool (like Mozilla) means adding small program fragments rather than big standalone chunks of code. A small program fragment is easier to create correctly at the start because it contains few branch points (few `if` statements). When program fragments reside in a larger tool, the tool also acts as a permanent test harness. Highly formal testing in such a case can be overkill.

RAD destructures testing because many small code fragments are more likely to be correct than one big program.

1.5 Effective RAD Projects with Mozilla

Mozilla might be an efficient development tool, but it also comes with a catch: there is too much slow information. Mozilla's source code takes too much time to understand. Mozilla's bug database is a jungle to get lost in, and the mozilla.org Web site freely mixes new and old documentation without regard for accuracy or age. Attempting to absorb all this can undermine the reasons for choosing Mozilla in the first place. To keep the RAD benefits of Mozilla intact, so that you can get something done, here are some recommendations.

Most importantly, grab the documents listed in the "Hands On" section in the introduction of this book. Those documents, plus a decent book, are enough documentation to get going. For a RAD project, it's rare to need a copy of the Mozilla source code.

You will occasionally need to peek at application files in the chrome to see how other people solved a problem you've encountered. If you want to search chrome files effectively, get one snapshot of the Mozilla source and index it with a tool like UNIX's `glimpseindex(1)`; or just index a set of unarchived chrome files.

When building user interfaces with XUL, avoid perfection. If you find yourself setting out windows to exact pixel measurements, you are doing it incorrectly. Do everything very roughly, and only make fine adjustments at the very end. Don't fight the tool; use it the easy way. If, for example, you find that you don't like the `<grid>` tag, but there's nothing else appropriate, just make do with `<grid>` anyway. Always display the JavaScript console, but don't write a line of JavaScript code until your customer has seen the XUL screens you've created.

When prototyping or experimenting, don't be too clever with XPCOM. Most processing can be handled just by submitting an HTML form to a Web server. Keep it basic, and don't try to master all the XPCOM components. You'll never use them all. If you have no server, use the `execute()` method to run a separate program. Don't worry about it being ugly, you can neaten it up later.

When stuck on a technical problem, try not to become distracted by unhelpful detail. Most problems are little more than syntax errors or misunderstandings. Everything in the platform is interpreted from XML to CSS, and syntax errors creep in everywhere. The source code will not help you with these—it takes a month of study before the source makes any sense, anyway. The Bugzilla bug database (at `http://bugzilla.mozilla.org`) can also be very distracting and time consuming.

A better approach to problems is to make a copy of your code and chop bits off until the problem area is clear. Then look at a book, or post to a newsgroup. If the problem won't go away, at least you have an effective test case for the Bugzilla database, and someone might respond quickly if you lodge a bug. If you change your code slightly, it may well go away. Because of the platform's near-zero validation behavior and poorly documented Mozilla internals, you won't always have a deep reason *why* some trivial change made something work again. There's always a rational explanation, but it often takes a long time to find. Move on.

If, however, you are passionate about Open Source, then don't expect working on the Mozilla Platform itself to be a RAD project. Working on the platform is the same as working on any C or C++ project. You can make a difference month by month, not day by day. Unless you are lucky enough to get paid for it, it's a very long-term hobby. Applications can be rapidly developed with Mozilla, but the platform itself is not as easily developed.

1.6 Hands On: Cranking Up the Platform

This "Hands On" session provides a first exploration of the Mozilla Platform and more steps that set up the NoteTaker project.

1.6.1 Installation

This book recommends downloading the 1.4 release of the platform, which includes Classic Mozilla and the platform. Later releases are also probably fine. You might want to check *www.nigelmcfarlane.com* for recent updates if this book has been in print a while.

The installation notes on mozilla.org are quite complete and should be read for your platform. They can be reviewed from the official download pages. Some less obvious effects are briefly covered here.

On Windows 95/98/Me, your user profile will be installed in this obscure location:

```
C:\Windows\Application Data\Mozilla
```

Under Windows NT/2000/XP technology, look in the equivalent path for the current user. On UNIX, the profile can be found here:

```
~/.mozilla
```

It's recommended that you do two whole installations of Mozilla, each into a separate directory. One will be your reliable version; one will be for development. On Windows and UNIX, if you have only the default user profile, that profile will be shared by both installations. Alternatively, create a different profile name for each installation. If you do this, disable email on the profile for the development installation, or confusion will result. Two installations give you two sets of chrome, one of which you can experiment on, leaving the other intact and working.

If you install Mozilla twice, or if you install two versions, be very careful when running them together. You can tell the differences between them from the date in the title bar (on Windows), but starting one when the other is already running is confusing, especially during testing. This is because Mozilla uses a signaling mechanism. The version you started might signal a running copy of Mozilla and then die straight away. That running copy then opens a new window. It looks like you start a new window and a new instance of the platform, but you really just opened another window of the existing, running platform. If you are accustomed to viewing Web pages while you develop, then the cleanest way to do that on Windows is to install Internet Explorer as well. Use that for viewing documentation. On UNIX, it is easy to run separate instances of the platform—just use the command line.

This book assumes standard installation directories. On Microsoft Windows 95/98/Me, the install directory is here:

```
C:\Program Files\Mozilla
```

Under UNIX, installing applications into `/usr` is overrated and makes subsequent version control tasks harder. Ask any system administrator. The installation directory is assumed to be here:

```
/local/install/mozilla
```

In both cases, Mozilla's chrome is stored in a `chrome` subdirectory underneath these directories.

If you do two UNIX installations, you need to review the installation notes about setting the environment variable MOZILLA_FIVE_HOME. If you want to run the program from a GNOME icon, read the installation notes. The GNOME Panel is the bar across the bottom of the desktop. You can drag a newly made icon from the panel directly onto the desktop.

The following systems were used to test this book: Microsoft Windows 98SE with Internet Explorer 6.0 and patches; Red Hat GNU/Linux 7.2 with GNOME 2.02. We also briefly tested with Microsoft Windows XP and MacOS X.

1.6.2 Command Line Options

Command-line help for the Mozilla Browser is available on UNIX using `--help`. On Microsoft Windows, `-h` or `-help` will display a help message but only if Mozilla's output is sent to a file. Table 1.1 shows the available options, but not all are available on all platforms.

1.6.3 Chrome Directories and the Address Book

The quickest way to see what Mozilla application development is like is to see something working. The Address Book of Classic Mozilla is an easy starting point. Like many Personal Information Managers (PIMs), it's just a set of names and contact points, including email addresses. The address book is tied to the Classic Mail & Newsgroup client, from which it automatically collects new names. Its database of contacts also assists the user when the Mail & Newsgroup client tries to auto-complete a partially typed-in address.

Structurally, the address book is a piece of the Mail & News package. That package is written entirely as a RAD client, using Mozilla's chrome concept. That means it contains no C or C++, although it makes heavy use of C/C++ XPCOM components. It also means that you can customize and rewrite the interface of the Classic Mail & News client as you see fit. The interface is written in JavaScript and XUL, plus some complementary technologies. The Classic Mail & News Client is stored in the chrome.

The chrome directory contains plain textfiles and JAR files. JAR stands for Java Archive. It derives from Sun Microsystem's Java project. For Mozilla, such files are in plain ZIP format on Windows and UNIX. On Windows, it's convenient to associate these files with a tool like WinZip, or else the Java JVM will try to execute them when they are double-clicked. File associations with WinZip are a little tricky. If double-clicking a JAR file zips it up a second

Table 1.1 Command-line option for Mozilla

Option name	Mozilla starts with
-addressbook	the email address book
-chat	the IRC chat client, if installed
-compose field1=val1, field2=val2,etc	the email message composer
-chrome URL	a chrome window, contents at URL
-console	an additional command-line window that displays diagnostic messages and the output of dump()
-contentLocale L	a normal window but HTML content locale set to L
-CreateProfile PNAME	a normal window, under a new profile of PNAME
-edit URL	the Composer HTML editor, editing the file at URL
-h -help—help	nothing; display command-line help instead
-height N	a window N pixels high
-installer	the Netscape 4.x migration tool
-jsconsole	the JavaScript console
-mail	the email and news reader
-news	the email and news reader
-nosplash	without the splash screen
-P PNAME	the user who's profile is PNAME
-ProfileManager	the profile manager tool
-ProfileWizard	the profile creation tool
-SelectProfile	the profile selection tool
-quiet	without the splash screen
-UILocale L	a normal window but with the XUL locale set to L
-venkman	the JavaScript debugger, if installed
-width N	a window N pixels wide

time, then fix that with the WinZip Command Line Support Add-on from *www.winzip.com*. In the absence of the add-on, just use File | Open Archive... to inspect the JAR file. On UNIX, `zip/unzip` are the correct tools, not `gzip/gunzip`. On the Macintosh, StuffIt! or a similar tool is required.

Figure 1.4 shows a typical example of the chrome directory on Microsoft Windows.

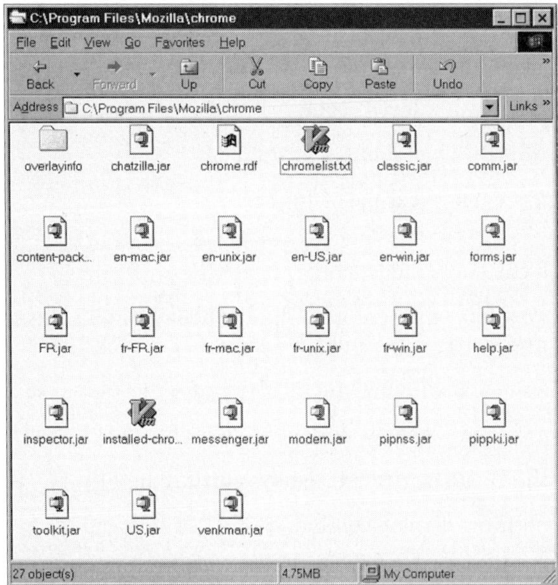

Fig. 1.4 Chrome directory on Microsoft Windows.

This screenshot shows a Mozilla installation with `en-US` (U.S. English, the default) and `fr-FR` (standard French) localizations. Mozilla auto-generated the `overlayinfo` directory and solitary text files; however, they can be edited by hand.

- `chrome.rdf` is a text-based database of all the JAR files.
- `toolkit.jar` contains general-purpose utilities that make up a "global" piece of chrome content.
- `classic.jar` contains the Classic skin.
- `messenger.jar` contains the Mail & News Client.
- `comm.jar` contains the chrome for a normal Web browser window and for the HTML editor.

It might seem that some pattern is implied by these file names, but that is not strictly true. There is merely a JAR naming convention that keeps language packs, themes, and components separate. It is not mandatory to use JAR files—files can be stored on their own, uncompressed and un-archived, anywhere inside the chrome directory. A second naming convention applies to the directory structure underneath the chrome directory. If it is not applied, some features of the platform won't work, so that convention is more important. An example of this second convention is shown in Figure 1.5.

This chrome directory contains two application packages, `packageA` and `packageB`. The most important directories are underlined: `content`, `locale`, and `skin`. Content contains the application. Locale contains language-specific

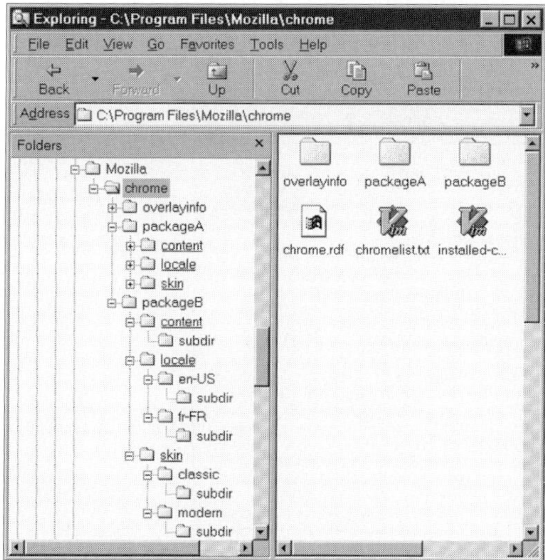

Fig. 1.5 Chrome subdirectories for all platforms.

elements of the application. Skin contains theme-specific elements of the application (decorative information). By splitting an application into these three components, an application can be reused across different languages and themes. Underneath these three directories, subdirectories can be nested as deep as you like, as the `subdir` examples show.

If you examine the files inside any JAR archive, you will see that they are distributed across this standard directory layout. Thus, `modern.jar`, a JAR file containing the modern skin, holds files for the skin subdirectory only, whereas `venkman.jar`, the JavaScript debugger, contributes files to all three top-level chrome directories. The directories inside a JAR file are slightly inverted so that they don't match the hierarchy of Figure 1.5. This is done to make searching the JAR file faster. Mozilla automatically converts these non-standard directories back to those of Figure 1.5 if necessary.

All these naming and structural conventions can be completely ignored at two costs. First, your application is likely to become a disorganized mess. Second, chrome URLs are magically modified to pick up the current theme and current locale. If your MyTheme skins and MyLocale text aren't in the right directories, they might display because they are hardcoded in, but they won't respond to the chrome system when the *current* theme or locale is switched to MyTheme or MyLocale.

For the address book, Figure 1.6 shows a slice of the applicaiton's insides.

From this screenshot, it's clear that chrome applications can be large—this JAR file expands to 1.5 MB (megabytes) of source code. Some JavaScript scripts in this JAR file are nearly 100 KB (kilobytes) alone. There is no compilation to do on any of these files; they all run in Mozilla exactly as they are.

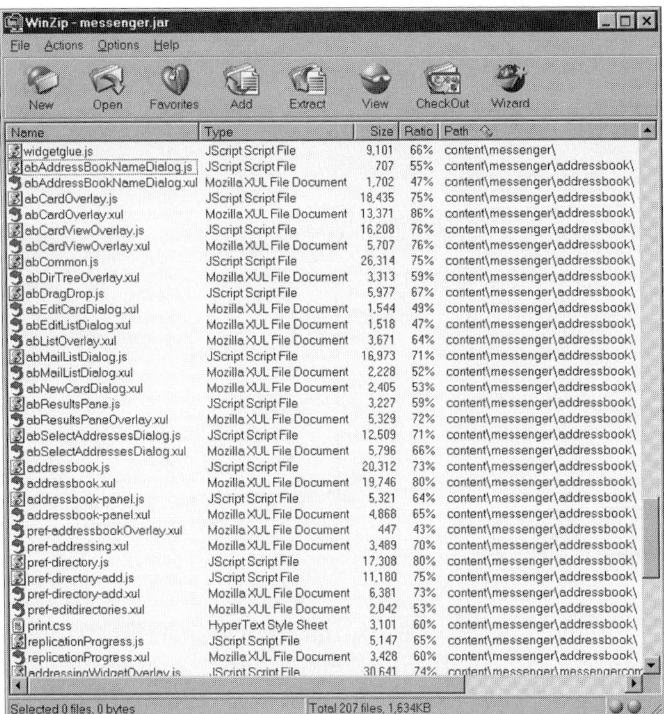

Fig. 1.6 Address book portion of messenger.jar chrome file. Used by permission of WinZip Computing, Inc.: Copyright 1991-2001 WinZip Computing, Inc.WinZip®is a registered trademark of WinZip Computing, Inc. WinZip is available from *www.winzip.com*. WinZip screen images reproduced with permission of WinZip Computing, Inc.

The nearest equivalent in the address book to a `main.c` is the `addressbook.xul` file. It is a good example of Mozilla's features at work. If you view this file, get out your XML experience, and spot the following general items: XML notation; use of `<?xul-overlay>`, `<?xml-stylesheet?>`, and `<script>` to include other files; extensive use of DTDs and entity references; XML namespace declarations; event handlers; and a big pile of tags that sound descriptive of GUIs.

This JAR file is not the only one that contains address book files. More can be found in other files, such as the JAR files holding Classic and Modern skins. If you delete all the chrome, or wreck it, you can't use the address book, and may not be able to start Mozilla at all. Chrome is vital to Mozilla.

It's also possible to modify Mozilla from outside the chrome directory. Chapter 17, Deployment, covers XPInstall, which allows most files in the Mozilla installation to be replaced. Some of these files, like preference files, make sense to modify, and this book points out when that is a good idea. Others, like some of the resource files under the `res` directory, are better left alone. Ignoring these files is a good idea because they have been thoroughly tested. Binary files can also be changed, but that is a C/C++ coding job for another day. Finally, there are configurable files under the individual Mozilla user profiles. The `.js` preference files in there are probably the only files that occasionally require hand-modification.

1.6.4 "hello, world"

No programming book is complete without a go at this simple program, made famous by Kernighan and Ritchie in *The C Programming Language*. The original "`hello, world`" was upgraded to "`Hello, World!`" after C gained an ANSI standard. Mozilla is in its formative days, so the early version is the appropriate one to follow here.

Mozilla supports all the simple versions of HTML-based "hello, world" you can think of. There are endless variations. Listing 1.2 shows trivial versions for legacy and standard HTML dialects, in case anyone has forgotten.

Listing 1.2 "hello, world" in legacy HTML and in XHTML 1.0.

```
<html><body>
  hello, world
</body></html>

<?xml version="1.0"?>
<!DOCTYPE html PUBLIC
"-//W3C//DTD XHTML 1.0 Strict//EN" "DTD/xhtml1-strict.dtd">
<html xmlns="http://www.w3.org/1999/xhtml" lang="en">
<body>
  hello, world
</body></html>
```

For rapid application developers, a more appropriate "hello, world" uses XUL, Mozilla's GUI markup language. Again, there are endless variations, but the simplest case, which reveals very little about XUL, looks like Listing 1.3.

Listing 1.3 "hello, world" in legacy Mozilla's XUL.

```
<?xml version="1.0"?>
<!DOCTYPE window>
<window xmlns= "http://www.mozilla.org/keymaster/gatekeeper/
          there.is.only.xul"
>
  <box>
    <description>hello, world</description>
  </box>
</window>
```

The main thing to note is that XUL requires a special tag (`<description>`) with an inconveniently long name for simple text. XUL files don't usually contain much plain text; they contain other things. The XML namespace identifier is an oblique reference to the movie *Ghostbusters*, based on the fact that some pronounce XUL like this: *zool*. This string appears nowhere but inside Mozilla. There is a placeholder XML page at the Web address give by this string, but it is not used for anything.

To get this going, save the content to a file called `hello.xul` in any directory. No use of chrome is necessary for simple cases. Load it into Mozilla using a `file:` URL, typed into the location bar as for any URL. The result might be as shown in Figure 1.7, if the file were located in `/tmp/hello.xul`.

Mozilla XUL content does not have to appear inside a browser window. Shut down Mozilla, and start it from the command line using the `-chrome` option. A typical one-line UNIX command is

```
/local/install/mozilla/mozilla -chrome file:///tmp/hello.xul
```

A typical one-line Microsoft Windows command is

```
"C:\Program Files\Mozilla\mozilla.exe" -chrome "file:C:/tmp/
     hello.xul"
```

In either of these cases, the result is likely to be as illustrated in Figure 1.8.

This last expression of "hello, world" is typical of applications developed with Mozilla. It's a beginning.

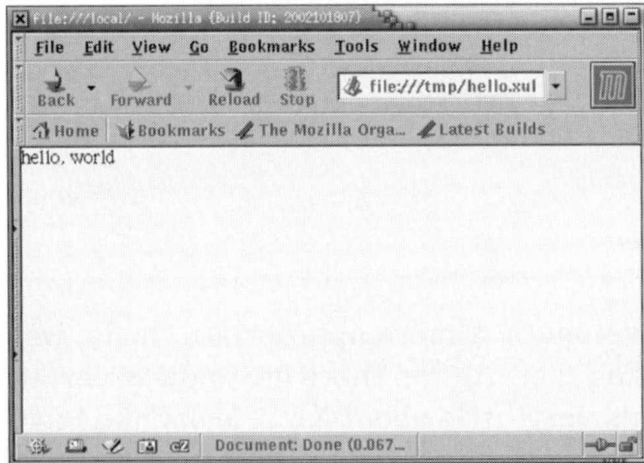

Fig. 1.7 XUL version of "hello, world" displayed as a document.

Fig. 1.8 XUL version of "hello, world" displayed as chrome.

1.6.5 NoteTaker Preparation

The NoteTaker application is a tiny example application running through this book. Rather than standing by itself, it works with the Mozilla Classic Browser. When end users install NoteTaker, all the setup is done for them automatically. As developers, we must make our own road, right from the beginning.

The only step required for NoteTaker setup is to create some directories and to register the name *notetaker* as an official Mozilla chrome package. As an official package, it will be accessible via the `chrome:` URL scheme. Here are instructions for creating the directories:

1. In the Mozilla install area, change the current working directory to the `chrome` directory.
2. Make a subdirectory `notetaker`, and change to that directory.
3. Make subdirectories named `chrome`, `locale`, and `skin`.
4. Inside `locale`, make an `en-US` subdirectory.
5. Inside `skin`, make a `classic` or `modern` subdirectory, or both.

Package registration is done in the `chrome/install-chrome.txt` file. To register NoteTaker as the chrome package "notetaker," just add this line to the end of that file, and restart the platform.

```
content,install,url,resource:/chrome/notetaker/content/
```

This syntax is very fragile and must be added exactly as shown. On the application side, nothing more is required at this point, although we'll revisit these directories frequently. It is recommended that you also follow the advice in the "Debug Corner" section that's next.

1.7 Debug Corner: Debugging from Outside

Mozilla is quite a complicated system. If you don't have it configured correctly, working applications are harder to achieve. The number of mysterious problems is reduced with every bug fix, but it's better to set yourself up for success from the beginning.

You can apply a number of overall settings to Mozilla to make life easier. The most obvious technology to learn is the JavaScript debugger, code-named Venkman. It's located under Tools | Web Development | JavaScript Debugger. If you like visual, integrated debuggers, then this is the way to go. This author prefers the UNIX philosophy of many small tools, so there's no Venkman tutorial here. To start the debugger, add this line to the scripts in your application:

```
debugger;
```

Netscape 7.0 doesn't come bundled with the debugger (version 7.1 does), but you can still download and auto-install it at any point. To find it, look on the DevEdge Web site, at `http://devedge.netscape.com`.

1.7.1 Important Preferences

The most important thing to get right is Mozilla's preferences. Mozilla has over a thousand preferences. Only a tiny subset are available from the Edit |

Preferences menu. The rest should be hand-coded using a text editor. Mozilla cannot be running while doing this because it rewrites the preference files every time it shuts down. This is the same as Netscape 4.x products.

You can also see and edit the majority of preferences by typing the URL `about:config`. Beware that the editing system does not modify the preference that you right-click on; it modifies any preference. There are hidden preferences as well as those shown.

To change a preference on disk, either modify the `prefs.js/preferences.js` file in the appropriate user profile, create a new preference file called `user.js` in the user profile, or modify the `all.js` file under the Mozilla install area. That last file is in `defaults/prefs`. Just duplicate an existing line and modify it. Preference order is not important.

Table 1.2 lists preferences that, for application developers, are best changed away from the default.

There are numerous other dumping and debugging options, but they are of limited assistance. Make sure that the normal browser cache is set to compare pages with the cache every time they are viewed.

You might want to test your Mozilla applications on Netscape 7.0 as well as on the mozilla.org platform. Netscape 7.0's Quick Launch feature is hard to turn off under Microsoft Windows. Even if you choose "no" during the installation, it may still be activated. If so, look in the Windows registry here for something to remove:

```
HKEY_CURRENT_USER\Software\Microsoft\Windows\CurrentVersion\Run
```

Table 1.2 Important nondefault developer preferences

Preference	Set to	Reason
browser.dom.window.dump.enabled	`true`	Enables diagnostic function dump().
nglayout.debug.disable_xul_cache	`true`	By default your XUL application is cached by Mozilla. During testing you want the real, genuine file loaded at all times.
javascript.options.strict	`true`	Adds more diagnostic reports to the JavaScript Console.
nglayout.debug.disable_xul_fastload	`true`	A second cache for XUL, loaded at startup time from an .MFL file. Possibly confusing when left on.
signed.applets.codebase_principal_support	`true`	Lifts all security restrictions on downloaded content except that the user must still grant access.
xul.debug.box	`false`	Can be turned on from inside an XUL file if required.

1.7.2 Multiwindow Development

When Mozilla is running, it generally manages more than one window at a time. It is easy to be confused by this arrangement, especially if you have multiple versions of Mozilla installed.

1.7.2.1 Microsoft Windows Behavior If a new Mozilla window is opened on Microsoft Windows, then it will be attached to any currently running Mozilla program. That means that there can be at most one version of Mozilla running at any given time, and at most one instance (running executable) of that version.

If a window is started from the command line or desktop icon, then the program executed does no more than look for an existing, running Mozilla. If one exists, that existing copy is sent an "open window" instruction, and the command line or icon-based program ends. Only if there is no other Mozilla program running will a command line or icon start a whole new platform instance.

This means that if you have two version of Mozilla, in the simple case, you can't run them both at the same time on Windows. In the complex case, it is possible to overcome this restriction. To do so, start by making a copy of the Mozilla executable. Modify the copy's resources with a resource editor tool (e.g., Microsoft Visual C++). Change resource strings 102 and 103 in the String Table section to something new. Save the copy. The copy can now be run as a separate instance to the original executable. It should also use a separate profile. If you do this, you also have to remember this modification is in place.

Second, it is possible (and sometime easy) to create poorly formed XUL-based applications. When windows holding these applications are displayed, everything seems normal, although they may not work as intended. In rare cases, when those windows are closed, the running platform can linger on. If this happens, the next window opened will use the existing platform, which may be in a buggy state as a result of the poorly formed application previously tested.

If you suspect that this is happening to you, use Control-Alt-Delete to check for any Mozilla processes still running, even though all windows are gone. Such a process is safe to kill.

1.7.2.2 UNIX X11/GTK Behavior On UNIX/Linux, a Mozilla command line or desktop icon will not interact with an existing, running instance of Mozilla. This is the opposite of Microsoft Windows and is true for versions at least as modern as 1.4.

This behavior is something of a nuisance because a XUL application does not usually have standard Mozilla menus. These menus are the access points for diagnostic tools like the DOM Inspector, Debugger, and JavaScript Console. Without these menus, there's no obvious way to start these tools. So it is difficult to apply them to the XUL application under development. On Windows, you can just start another Navigator window and open the standard menus from there. On UNIX, you cannot.

There is a very easy workaround for the JavaScript console; just add this option to the command line:

```
-jsconsole
```

A more general workaround is to include a piece of script in your XUL application, as shown in Listing 1.4. For this script to work, the XUL application must be installed in the chrome, since it requires that no security be in place.

Listing 1.4 Starting Mozilla tools with an application.

```
<script>
var options =
        "chrome,extrachrome,menubar,resizeable,scrollbars,status,toolbar
        ";
var domins = "chrome://inspector/content/inspector.xul";
var jscons = "chrome://global/content/console.xul";
if (window.name == "_blank") {
  setTimeout("window.open('"+location+"','test','chrome')",5000);
  setTimeout("window.close()",6000);
  window.open(domins,"_blank",options);
  window.open(jscons,"_blank",options);
}
</script>
```

This script opens the DOM Inspector and JavaScript Consoles when the current document loads and then replaces the current document with an identical copy in another window. This last step is done so that the application window loads last. This loading order allows the DOM Inspector to notice the application window, which can then be inspected.

There are many systems between Mozilla and the screen under UNIX. If you experiment aggressively with the application, it's possible to trip over bugs hiding elsewhere in the desktop. If something locks up or goes mad, the first thing that attracts blame is Mozilla, but the blame may well lie elsewhere. Use `top(1)`, `ps(1)`, and `kill(1)` to shut down and restart one system at a time until the problem is gone. A suitable testing order follows:

1. Kill and restart all Mozilla processes and clean up `XUL .mfasl` files, if any.
2. Kill and restart the window manager (sawfish, twm, enlightenment, etc.).
3. Kill and restart the whole desktop (GNOME, KDE, OpenStep, etc.).
4. Kill and restart the X-server (Xfree86, vncserver, etc.).
5. Logout and login.
6. Reboot the computer.

Such problems are rare, but a systematic approach to solving them will save a great deal of time. It will also save Mozilla from an undeserved bad name.

1.7.3 Compile-Time Options

If you are willing to wrestle with the compilation process for Mozilla, you can build a binary with additional programmer-level debugging support. Some of this support can be activated by setting various magic environment variables. Be warned that some of these options spew out vast amounts of information.

The gateway to a more debuggable version of Mozilla is the `--disable-debug` option. This is an option to the `configure` tool set right at the start of the compile process. When turned on, many sections of debug code throughout Mozilla are included in the compiled code. To turn this option on, or to turn other options on, you can generate a custom file that `configure` can take advantage of from a form on mozilla.org. That form is located at `http://webtools.mozilla.org/build/config.cgi`.

To understand what environment variables make sections of debug code do something, read the Mozilla source code. To find other debug assistance at the compile level, such as `#ifdef EXTRA_DEBUG` directives, read the source code.

1.8 Summary

Mozilla is a browser-like tool that can be used to create applications faster than traditional 3GLs (Third-Generation Languages). It brings some of the benefits of Web-based applications to traditional GUI-based applications. The highly interpreted nature of such environments creates an opportunity to do very rapid iterative development and efficient prototyping. This efficiency must be balanced against a desire to look more deeply into the tool, which is a time-consuming activity, and against syntax problems, which rest heavily on the shoulders of the developer.

Mozilla has its roots in the evolution of Web browser technology, and it has much to offer in that area. It has up-to-date standards support and is highly portable. For UNIX platforms, it is the obvious, if not the only, browser choice. The architectural extensions inside Mozilla, however, are of most interest to developers. The componentization of Mozilla's internals presents a developer with a ready-made set of services to work with, and innovative GUI markup languages like XUL are powerful and convenient. This piece-by-piece structure allows Mozilla to be considered a development platform, although it suffers a little from being version 1.0.

Mozilla is backed by an organization that is both commercially and community driven. It provides a plethora of resources for a technical person to take advantage of and asks nothing in return. The organization has many partners in commerce, academia, and standards communities and shows no sign of shutting up shop. It seems likely that the technology it develops has a fair chance of being useful, influential, and popular.

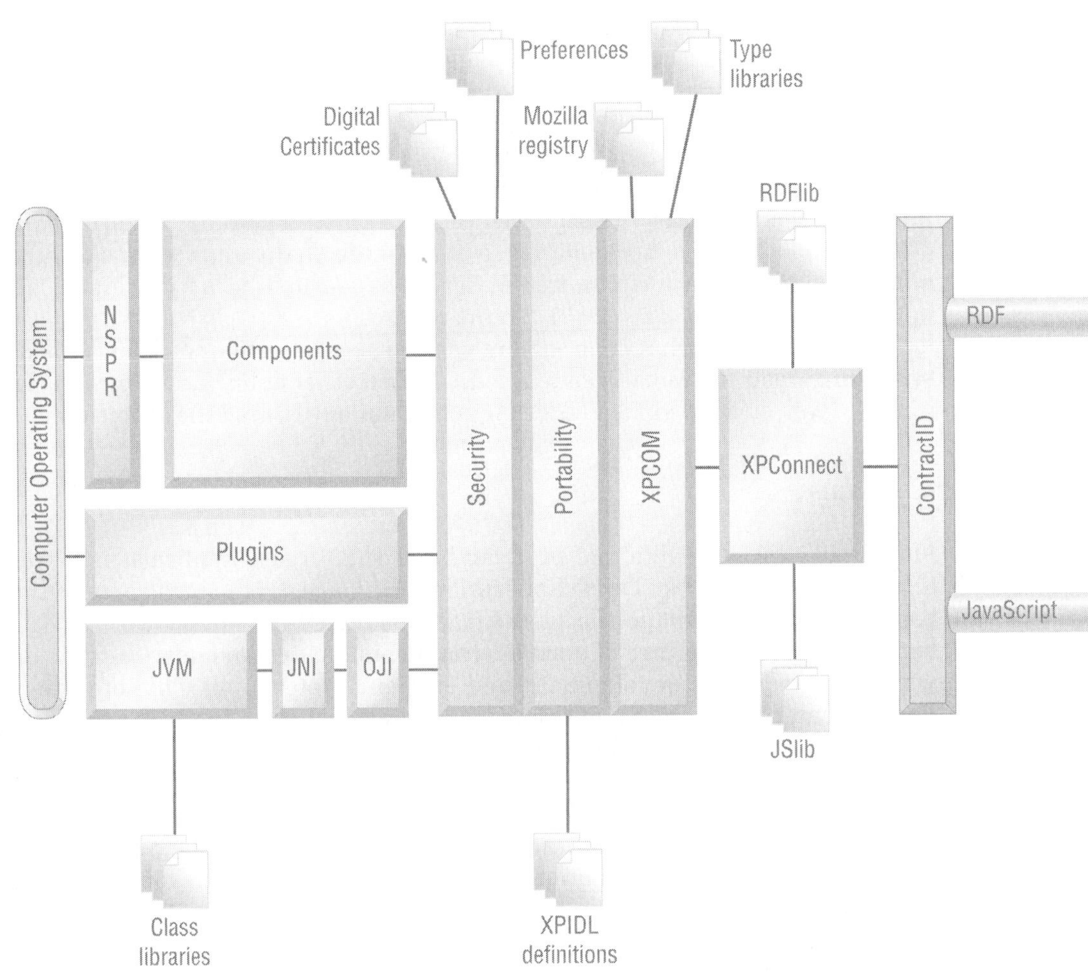

Preferences
Type libraries
Digital Certificates
Mozilla registry
RDFlib
Computer Operating System
NSPR
Components
Security
Portability
XPCOM
XPConnect
ContractID
RDF
JavaScript
Plugins
JVM
JNI
OJI
JSlib
Class libraries
XPIDL definitions

CHAPTER 2

XUL Layout

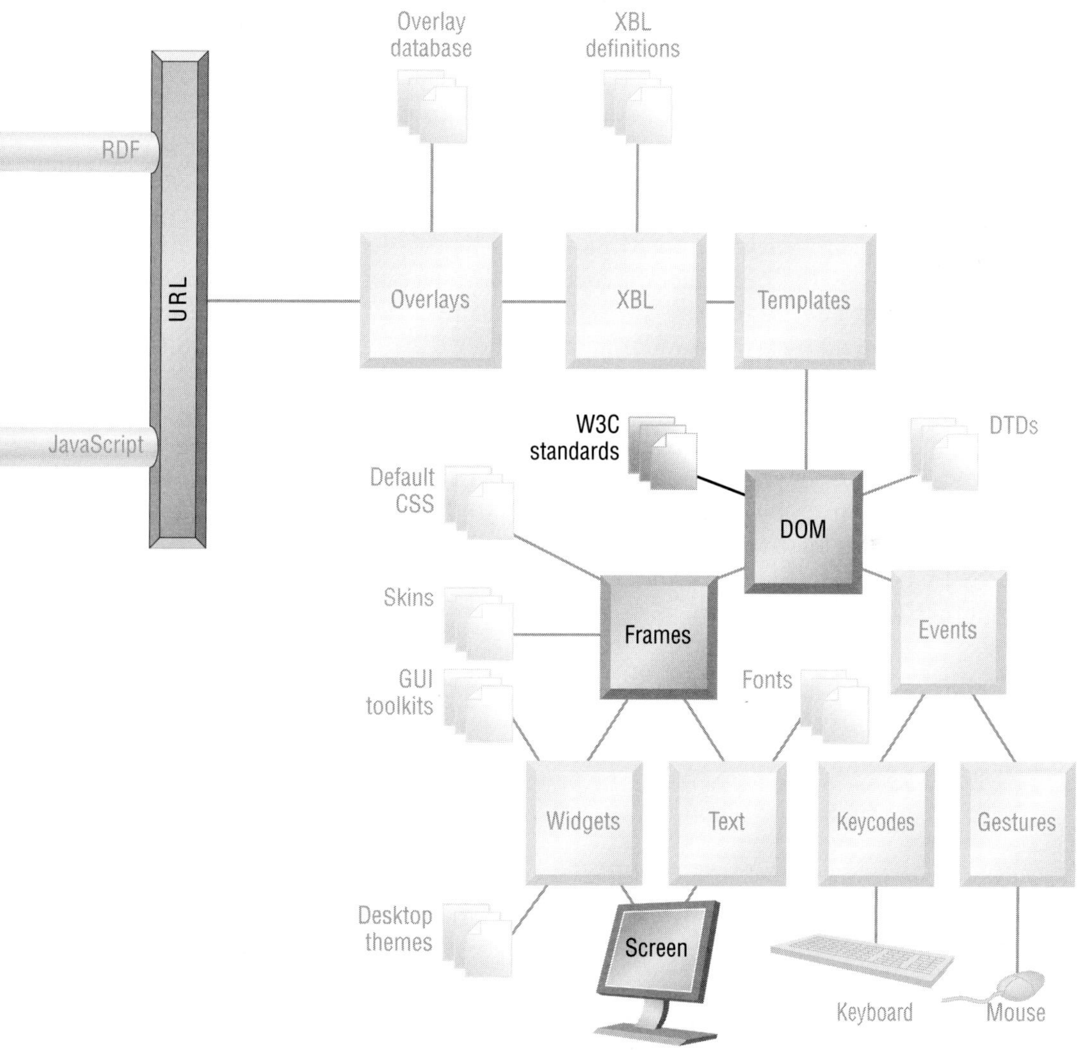

Most computer applications contain a visual interface, and—no wonder—humans process visual information easily. A Mozilla application uses XUL documents to specify its visual interface. XUL is one of the most efficient ways of creating a GUI in existence.

XUL stands for *XML User-interface Language*. This chapter describes the bones and whole skeleton of the language. That means the structural aspects that all the fancier features of the language depend upon. Without a proper understanding of that core structure, the flashier and somewhat more distracting features of the language can be frustrating to use. Therefore, we start at the beginning.

XUL's basic structure is a layout system that determines the geometric position of other XUL content. That positioning is dictated by the <box> tag and a few similar tags.

The NPA diagram at the start of this chapter illustrates the extent of these skeletal XUL features inside Mozilla. From the diagram, it's not surprising that those features sit on the display side of the platform, in the so-called front-end (the right-hand half of the diagram). The layout system maps out where other content will appear on the user's monitor, but it is mostly concerned with two big in-memory structures: frames and the DOM. These structures reflect the geometry and the data of a XUL document. Being so fundamental, many W3C standards affect their features. A few small files help along the way.

The DOM is not so interesting from a display point of view; we merely note that it exists. It is the frame system that programmers use on an everyday basis when they are creating a heap of XUL tags for a new user interface. Although the frame system is not manipulated explicitly, every XUL tag carries information used by that system.

Listing 2.1 repeats the "hello, world" example from Chapter 1, Fundamental Concepts.

Listing 2.1 "hello, world" revisited.

```
<?xml version="1.0"?>
<!DOCTYPE window>
<window xmlns= "http://www.mozilla.org/keymaster/gatekeeper/
          there.is.only.xul">
  <box>
    <description>hello, world</description>
  </box>
</window>
```

The outside <window> tag is a hint that says this document should appear in a separate window, but it is only a hint. Its main function is to act as the root tag of the document. XML requires that all documents have a root tag. It is the <box> tag that says how the document content should be displayed. Learning XUL means learning about boxes. In fact, the root tag (<window>)

also acts as a <box> tag to a degree, but it is a less powerful layout tool than <box>.

To benefit effectively from this chapter, a little XML and a little CSS is mandatory. Recall that for XML the <?xml?> and <!DOCTYPE> directives and the xmlns attribute act together to define what kind of document is present. So the first three lines in Listing 2.1 ensure that the content of the document will be laid out according to the XUL layout system rather than the HMTL Layout system. This system can be overridden or modified at any time by use of CSS2 style rules. Recall that for CSS2 such rules originate from this simple syntax:

```
selector { property : value-expression; }
```

selector is usually a tag, class, or id name. CSS2 style rules are not themselves XML and must be stored as the value of an XML attribute, or in separate .css files. An example of a rule that ensures the <window> tag is displayed using the XUL layout system is

```
window { display : -moz-box; }
```

The implications of that line of code are discussed extensively in this chapter. For more on CSS2's traditional use in HTML, consult the standard at *www.w3.org*, or explore any Web page or Mozilla window with the DOM Inspector tool.

2.1 XUL Means Boxes

When learning HTML, <P> tags and heading tags like <H1> are a common starting point. Only after some experience do you realize how invisibly powerful the <SPAN> tag is. An <H1> tag, for example, is just a <SPAN> tag with some CSS styles applied, like display:block and font-size:large. It's not the only such tag either—many are just <SPAN> plus some styling. HTML does not teach <SPAN> first because a plain <SPAN> tag doesn't appear to "do" anything; it's normally invisible.

XUL's <box> tag has the same role as HTML's <SPAN> tag, except that <box> is necessary right from the beginning. It's important that you master your XUL boxes straight away. Listing 2.2 is an XUL fragment showing typical use of boxes to structure content.

Listing 2.2 XUL fragment illustrating box-structured code.

```
<box orient="horizontal">
  <box orient="vertical">
    <description>Apples</description>
    <description>Oranges</description>
  </box>
  <box orient="vertical">
    <description>HTML</description>
    <box orient="horizontal">
     <description>XUL</description>
```

```
      <description>XBL</description>
    </box>
  </box>
</box>
```

This code contains as many <box> tags as "real" tags. This is normal for XUL. Expect to use <box> tags automatically. Figure 2.1 shows how this content might appear on Microsoft Windows, if it were the content of a complete XUL document:

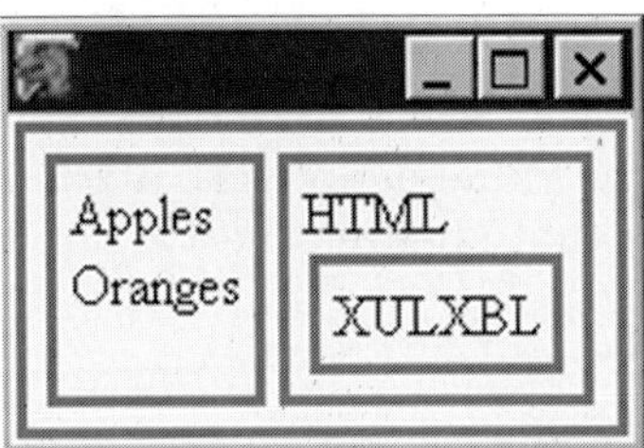

Fig. 2.1 Displayed results for box-structured code.

In this screenshot, the XUL content has had a simple CSS style applied so that you can see where the boxes are. Each box contains two tags, and those two tags are clustered either side by side or one on top of the other. That is the whole purpose of <box>. Normally, only one or two boxes would have borders. Listing 2.3 shows the style used.

Listing 2.3 Simple stylesheet that reveals borders of boxes.

```
box { border : solid;
      border-color: grey;
      padding: 4px;
      margins: 2px;
}
```

Obviously, styling and laying out XUL content is similar to styling and laying out HTML content—at least in terms of basic approach. But just how similar are they? Learning boxes right from the start means learning the layout rules. After we've covered the rules, you are encouraged to experiment with CSS styles—a great deal can be revealed about XUL layout that way.

2.2 Principles of XUL Layout

XUL layout is the process of turning tag information into content a human can appreciate. XUL layout is different from application layout. The browser automatically takes care of the former. The latter is a design task allocated to a programmer or graphic designer. Automatic layout is described here.

The layout rules for HTML include something called the *Box Model*, defined in the CSS2 standard, section 8 (see *http://www.w3.org/TR/REC-CSS2*). HTML and XUL share a number of CSS2 styles, including box decorations. It is easy to conclude that the Box Model applies to XUL as well. It does, but this is only about one-third of the truth. Boxes are so important that we need to clear up any confusion at the start.

One issue is that Box Model boxes and <box>es are not identical. Many XUL tags follow the Box Model, but <box> in particular is not fully described by that model.

A second issue is that although the grandly capitalized Box Model defines one layout concept, it is not a whole layout strategy. A layout strategy also needs an output device, and a system for mapping the layed-out content to that output device. If the layout device is a computer monitor, then a *visual formatting model* is the required plan (i.e., sections 9 and 10 of the CSS2 standard, separate from the Box Model). Critical to the CSS visual formatting model are the concepts of a *block* and a *line box*. A block is just a rectangular region on the screen. If the content of a block extends over more than one line, then each line within the block is a line box.

The visual formatting model documented in CSS2 applies only to HTML. XUL has its own visual formatting model, which is different and not well advertised. The XUL model somewhat resembles the way HTML table rows are layed out. The resemblance is not exact.

Mozilla's extended version of CSS2 is a notation that provides layout rules for both HTML and XUL tags. The platform supports HTML and XUL layout with a single, general-purpose layout implementation. In principle, the two types of layout are served by separate CSS2 layout rules. In practice, the two layout types share some rules and can be mixed together in one document. It is better to stick to pure XUL or pure HTML layout, however.

There is one other piece of jargon. Inside Mozilla the concept of a *frame* is very important. It is, in fact, important enough to appear on the NPA diagram. A frame is an object representing the visual rectangle that a tag takes up on the screen.

Between these many concepts, there's more than enough hair-splitting to keep standards people happy. The path to simple understanding is this: First consider a single XUL tag, and then consider a group of XUL tags. We will do this shortly. A summary of the correct relationships between all these concepts is

- ☞ HTML and XUL tags follow the rules of the Box Model.
- ☞ HTML and XUL have different visual formatting models. Line boxes stretch and shrink differently for HTML and XUL.
- ☞ Some HTML tags are like CSS2 line boxes and some XUL tags are like XUL line boxes. <box> is like an XUL line box but also follows Box Model rules.

- ☞ Most HTML and XUL tags have a CSS2 block, which is the "home rectangle" for the tag and its contents, but "block" is a confusing term. Inside Mozilla, "block" is used only for HTML, "box" is used for XUL. "Frame" is used for the underlying concept that applies to both HTML and XUL. Use "frame" and ignore "block."
- ☞ For both HTML and XUL, content can overflow a tag's CSS2 block. This makes everything more complex, and it's best to ignore overflow until the rest is clear or forever.

The simplest way to see the difference between XUL and HTML is to experiment. For practice, take the contents of Listing 2.2, and change every `<box>` to a `<DIV>`. Change the style to match. Put the new content inside an XHTML 1.0 document, and load that file into a chrome window. Play with window sizes and compare how HTML and XUL versions react. They are subtly different. Just how they differ is described next.

2.2.1 Displaying a Single Tag

Displaying a single XUL tag means using the CSS2 Box Model. Most XUL tags, including `<box>`, are styled this way. Figure 2.2 illustrates this model based on the diagram in section 8.1 of that standard.

Figure 2.2 shows text (the word "Anything") as the content of this box, but the content could be anything literally: text, an image, a button, a scrollbar, or a checkbox. Section 8, Box Model, and section 14, Colors and Backgrounds, are the only sections of the CSS2 standard that are completely correct for XUL.

Standard sizing styles may also be applied to a XUL tag. Supported properties are

```
minwidth width maxwidth minheight height maxheight
```

For a single tag, these tags work the same as they would for HTML, but a surrounding tag may narrow or widen the contained tag in a way that is subtly different from HTML. This means that the size calculations in the CSS2 standard are not reliable for XUL. The top and left properties work only in

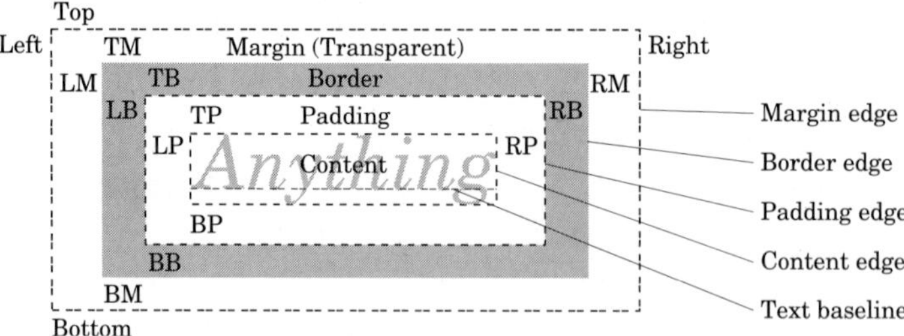

Fig. 2.2 CSS2 Box Model.

special cases; the bottom and right properties do not work at all. Understanding why this is so leads immediately to the subject of positioning. Top and left are also discussed in the "Stacks and Decks" section.

In CSS2, a tag that is a Box Model box can be positioned—placed somewhere. Positioning XUL tags is simpler than positioning HTML tags, but *the same style properties are used.* In CSS2, positioning is controlled by the four properties `display`, `position`, `float`, and `visibility`.

> **`display`**. In CSS2, `display` can take on many values. The only CSS2 values supported in XUL are `none` and `inline`. Although `none` works, the XUL `hidden` attribute is a better, albeit identical, solution. `none` applies to all XUL tags, whereas `inline` is used to tell a tag that it lives within another `<box>`. XUL has many, many custom values for the display property, nearly one per XUL tag, and nearly all are too obscure to be useful. The `-moz-box` option, for example, is described after this list.
>
> **`position`**. XUL does not support absolute or fixed positioning. These styles have been known to crash Mozilla and should be avoided. There is some support for relative positioning, but only if the XUL tag styled is an immediate child of a `<stack>` or `<bulletinboard>` tag.
>
> **`float`**. Float is not supported at all in XUL.
>
> **`visibility`**. Set to `hidden`, this property makes a styled element invisible. Although this approach works, the XUL attribute `hidden` works just as well. There are no tables in XUL, but setting this property to `collapse` does effectively the same thing to the styled element—margins are retained. The `collapsed` attribute is the preferred approach for collapsing, although it is identical to using `visibility`. Both apply to all XUL tags, except that the `<menuitem>` tag only supports `hidden`.

For XUL, the lowest common denominator style is `display: -moz-box`, a special Mozilla display type. This means that all existing XUL tags and all user-defined tags in an XUL document act like `<box>`, unless they have additional styles of their own. That is why boxes are so central in XUL. `-moz-box` makes XUL tags different from HTML tags.

Inside the chrome is a standard archive called `toolkit.jar`. That archive contains a file called `xul.css`. This file included the basic style definitions for all XUL tags. These styles are applied to an XUL document before anything else, including global styles or skins. This is where `-moz-box` is set.

2.2.2 Displaying Multiple Tags

To display multiple tags in XUL, put them inside a `<box>` tag. There are other options, but `<box>` is the simplest. The problem is that `<box>` doesn't act like a real-world box. Figure 2.3 illustrates how sticking things inside other things can be done in different ways.

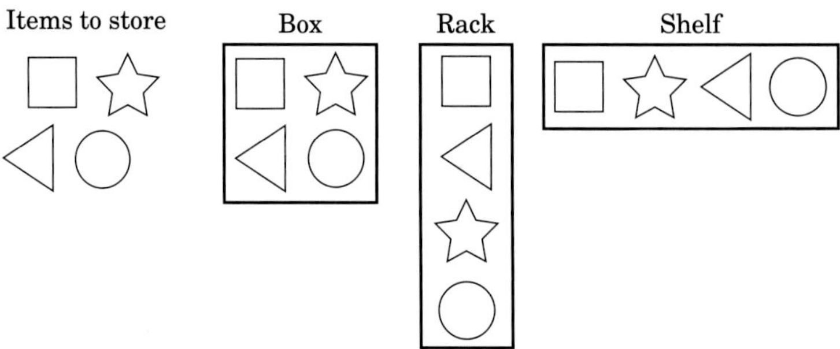

Fig. 2.3 Containment strategies for storing items.

Clearly a traditional box is a two-dimensional affair, whereas a real-world shelf is not. <box> is like a shelf. A shelf can handle only one row of content. If the `orient` attribute is set to "vertical," then <box> acts like a real-world rack, which holds several shelves. The rack for a <box> tag is only one item wide, like a free-standing CD tower.

Many HTML elements also look like shelves, but this appearance is deceiving. Most HTML elements support line-wrap, so an overly long line is folded into two or more lines. This does not usually happen with XUL. If there is a shortage of space, a line will be truncated. If you start a recent version of a Microsoft Windows tool like Microsoft Paint, you can narrow the window until the menu options wrap over to take up two lines. If you do this with Mozilla, the menus are truncated, not wrapped. This is because <box> does not line-wrap its contents, and tags that are <box>-like do not line-wrap their contents.

There are two exceptions to this rule: The `<description>` tag and the `<label>` tag will line-wrap their contents as needed. The XUL `<description>` tag displays content the way most HTML tags do.

A horizontal <box> and its contents act like a CSS2 line box. The main difference has to do with size calculations. In both HTML and XUL, a line box must be big enough to fit its contents, but some negotiation is possible. In HTML, this negotiation involves calculating the space required for content and laying it out until it is all done. If the window width reduces, line-wrap might split the content across two lines. In XUL the same negotiation involves calculating the space required for content and allocating exactly that amount of space. The content must then fit inside that space. In the XUL case, line-wrap is not an option, so if the window width is reduced, the <box> must try to squish its content into a smaller space. If the minimum size of each piece of content is reached, no more squishing can be done. The box then has no choice but to overflow and clip the content so that it appears truncated to the viewer. This behavior is dictated by the visual layout model.

A vertical <box> acts like a pile of CSS2 line boxes, one exactly on top of the other. The same rules apply to these line boxes as in the horizontal case, except that each line box contains only one piece of content (one child of the `<box>` tag).

2.2.3 Common Box Layout Attributes

Just as in HTML, layout can be left up to the browser, or you can take control. A standard set of tag attributes is used to distribute the content of a <box> tag. These attributes apply to any container tag, since most XUL tags act like box tags. Figure 2.4 shows the conceptual arrangement of these attributes.

Figure 2.4 illustrates the `orient="horizontal"` case, which is the default for <box>. To see the `orient="vertical"` case, turn this book 90 degrees clockwise. Each of the words in the diagram is a XUL attribute that affects where the <box> content is located. Every item inside a <box> must be a tag in its own right.

Historically, some of these attributes derive from attributes in the CSS2 standard. This soon became confusing, so it is less confusing to look at these attributes as being entirely separate. In particular, the `valign` CSS2 attribute should be avoided, even though it is still supported. The recognized layout attributes follow. See Table 2.5 for a matching illustration.

- **`orient = "horizontal" | "vertical"`**. The `orient` attribute states whether the content will be layed out across or down the page and determines the *primary direction*. The primary direction is rightward for `horizontal` and downward for `vertical`. `horizontal` is the default.
- **`dir = "ltr" | "rtl" | "normal" | "reverse"`**. The `dir` attribute is like the `dir` attribute in HTML. Content will be layed out left to right or right to left in the primary direction. `normal` is the same as `ltr`; `reverse` is the same as `rtl`. For vertical boxes, left to right means top to bottom, and right to left means bottom to top. `ltr` is the default.
- **`pack = "start" | "center" | "end"`**. The `pack` attribute justifies the contents of a box along the primary direction, like justification in a word processor. `start` means left- or top-justify, `center` means centered content, and `end` means right- or bottom-justified. Normally, a box expands lengthwise to fit the available space. In that case, `pack` is useful. If the box does not expand `pack` does nothing. Expansion depends on the `align="stretch"` attribute. `start` is the default for `pack`.

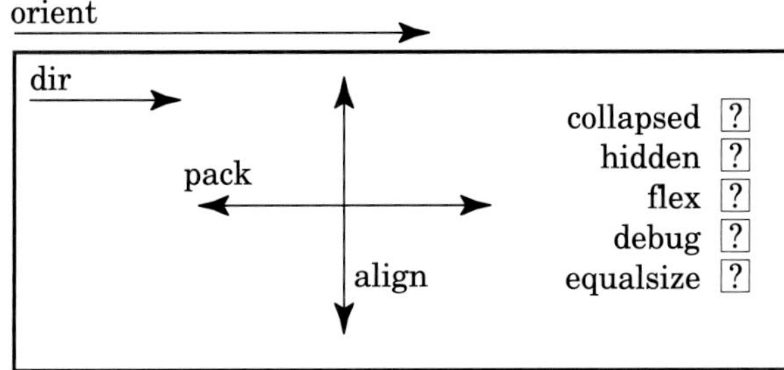

Fig. 2.4 Standard layout attributes for XUL container tags

- ☞ **align = "start" | "center" | "end" | "baseline"| "stretch"**. The `align` attribute justifies the content in the box's transverse (cross-ways) direction. At all points along the box, there is only one content item in this direction, so `align` shifts every item up/down or left/right. This is meaningful only if the box's transverse size is greater than some part of the content. For a horizontal box, `baseline` shifts content to the CSS2 text baseline, which aligns all text but puts other items to the bottom of the box. `stretch` means full justification, but since there is only one content item at every transverse point, that item is made bigger until it touches the start and end sides. This applies to nested boxes, images, and widgets but not to plain text. The default is `stretch`.
- ☞ **equalsize = "always"**. If this attribute is set to `always`, and if all child tags have a `flex` attribute, then all contents of the box will be given equal size in the primary direction. This is useful for a tabular or grid-like layout. Any other value turns `equalsize` off.

Mozilla also supports the **ordinal**attribute. This attribute is recorded automatically when Mozilla saves and recalls information about XUL documents via the `persist` attribute. The persistence system is discussed in Chapter 12, Overlays and Chrome. It is not particularly relevant to the application programmer. Nevertheless, here is its use.

`ordinal` applies the child tags of any given tag, and holds an integer whose lowest value is zero. It specifies the order of those child tags within their parent. Normally that order follows automatically from the order of the tags in the XUL document. `ordinal` is sometimes used to record the state of the columns of a `<tree>` tag.

For all these attributes, a value of `inherit` has the same meaning as in CSS2; in that case, the value will be taken from the parent tag's style information. An `inherit` value, however, can only be specified from the CSS styles equivalent to these tag attributes (see the "Style Options" section). Figure 2.5 illustrates the effect of these tags.

The screenshots in Figure 2.5 required a total of 82 `<box>` tags, although the layout in this case is somewhat artificial. The other commonly used layout attributes apply to all tags, not just to tags used as box containers. These layout attributes follow:

- ☞ **collapsed = "true" | "false"**. Set to `true`, the tag will be collapsed as though as though the CSS2 style `visibility: collapse` were used. It takes up no space on the screen, which affects how any containing box lays out its children. Set to `false`, or anything else, the tag reappears. Dynamically changing `collapsed` causes reflow, which is a heavy processing job for Mozilla. CSS2 `collapse` is present tense; XUL `collapsed` is past tense.
- ☞ **hidden = "true" | "false"**. Set to `true`, the tag will disappear from the screen as if CSS2 `display: none` were set. The tag still takes up space.

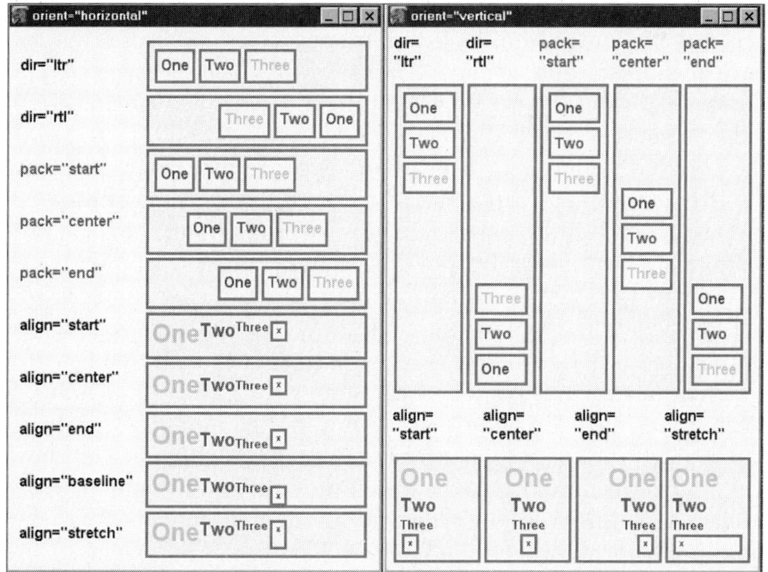

Fig. 2.5 Standard XUL box alignment options.

If it is set to `false` or anything else, the box is re-exposed. Dynamically changing the `hidden` attribute does not cause reflow.

☞ **flex = "*integer*"**. If `flex` is set to a whole number greater than 0 (zero), then the tag to which it belongs may stretch larger than its normal size. This simultaneously removes the effect of any pack attribute, unless the space the tag can stretch into is constrained in some way. Flex is discussed with an example in the section entitled "Box Layout Tags" in this chapter. The equivalent style is `-moz-box-flex`.

☞ **debug = "true"**. Setting the `debug` attribute reveals structural information about the current layout of the tag. This option is discussed in the "Debug Corner" in this chapter. Setting `debug` distorts the normal layout of the content.

Many other attributes also have an effect on layout, but these are the central ones. For further analysis of the layout system, we need to go back to Mozilla's use of styles.

2.2.4 Frame and Style Extension Concepts

The layout features described in the preceding section are all driven from XML content; they are tag attributes. There is, however, another side to the layout coin. Mozilla has very extensive enhancements to the CSS styling system. These style extensions are used at least as much as XUL attributes. Central to these styles is the important concept of a *frame*.

2.2.4.1 What a Frame Is A frame is an implementation concept inside the Mozilla Platform that manages the display state of a single tag. In complex cases, zero or many frames can match a tag, but the *one frame, one tag* rule is a good rule of thumb for thinking about frames. Frame information is a complementary concept to the "objects" described in the W3C DOM standards. DOM objects, really just interfaces on objects, are internal representations of an XML entity, usually a whole tag. They provide a data-oriented view of that tag. Frames are internal representations of the CSS style associated with a whole tag. Most tags have a frame. The frame provides a view of the tag that is spatial, visual, and geometric. Frames include both standard CSS styles and Mozilla CSS style extensions.

Frames are important to XUL because (eventually) you need to know whether a tag has a frame or not: `<box>` tags always have a frame.

When styles cascade, when windows resize, and when a tag is dynamically updated, frames are responsible for coordinating the display changes that result. This all happens automatically inside Mozilla, just as event processing does for the DOM standards.

To an application programmer, frames are a more abstract concept than DOM interfaces, and there's no need to interact with them directly. The Gecko rendering engine manages all the required frames for you. Frames are important only if you become deeply tangled up in layout issues. At that point, a useful guiding rule is *no frame, no proper layout*. Whether a visual element acquires a frame or not is a Mozilla source code question. A rough rule is *every viewable element that resides at* `z-index:0`*, and that occupies a distinct rectangular area, has a frame.* Many other visible elements, such as HTML absolutely positioned content, also have frames. Flyover help popups do not have frames. XUL tree tags have tricky frame support.

The main reason for discussing frames is to give Mozilla's CSS2 style extensions a home. Style extensions are used a great deal in Mozilla applications.

2.2.4.2 Styles and Style Extensions Affect Frame State and Content Mozilla adds to the CSS2 set of properties. All extensions start with a "`-moz`" or a "`:-moz`" prefix. These additions might be genuine extensions, obscure internal features, experiments under test, or debugging tools, or they may anticipate features of future standards. Some of these additions have obvious purposes within a stylesheet-rendering model, and some have purposes that are more programmatic.

Style properties and extensions are defined at the source code level in C/C++ header files. If you are curious, look for file names that end in `List.h`, like `nsCSSPropList.h`. You will find that the list of extensions is huge. Why are there so many?

The answer has to do with implementation. The set of standard CSS2 properties can be seen as a big state machine (a finite state automaton) because each displayed tag or frame has a set of states. A set of states matching CSS2 properties may be enough to describe what the display looks like, but it is not enough for a complete CSS2 display system. Such a display system must keep extra housekeeping information. For example, CSS2 properties might be sufficient to describe how a button looks, but the CSS2 engine inside Mozilla also needs to know if the XML button contains a button widget from some GUI toolkit. Such a widget would need to be managed. That extra piece of information (that a widget is present) might as well be stored as a Mozilla style extension, like `-moz-gc-wrapper-block`. This example is really of interest to the developers of Mozilla only.

It follows, therefore, that some style extensions are *intrinsic* while others are *extrinsic*. The intrinsic ones, created mostly for internal purposes, can be ignored. The extrinsic ones, created in order to add fancy features, are provided for the use of document authors and application programmers and should be considered. Of course, there is a gray area between, and you are free to apply intrinsic styles if you research them carefully. This book documents extensions that have an obvious extrinsic use.

A similar intrinsic versus extrinsic distinction applies to styled-up content. The content of a given tag, even one without child tags, may be broken into several different bits. These internal bits might have style information of their own, even though they are not accessible from outside. An example is a drop-cap character, typically used as the first character of a paragraph. Although the CSS3 standard now reveals that character via a pseudo-class `:initial-letter`, it is implemented as an intrinsic frame in Mozilla. These intrinsic bits are as obscure to application developers as intrinsic styles. They are the lowest level nuts and bolts of the display system, Mozilla-specific, and likely to change subtly over time. Stick to the extrinsic features where possible simply because they are plainer and more straightforward.

These last few paragraphs can be viewed as a warning. Unless you want to help maintain the Mozilla Platform, getting tangled up in low-level internals is a waste of time and energy.

An example of a useful extrinsic style extension is this (abbreviated) line from the `html.css` stylesheet that accompanies the Mozilla installation. It has a new style property and a new style value. Mozilla may not directly support CSS2 outline properties, but it has extensions that are close:

```
input:focus {-moz-outline: 1px dotted -moz-FieldText;}
```

`-moz-outline` means apply an outline. `-moz-FieldText` means apply the color used by the desktop for field text.

Earlier it was noted how layout can be done with XUL attributes. That system uses meaningful tag names, meaningful XML attributes, and meaningful values for attributes. An example is this bit of XUL:

```
<mybox align="start"> ... </mybox>
```

All the English words in this markup fragment (`mybox`, `align`, `start`) give hints about the layout of the content. The simplest thing to do with these keywords is to turn them into style properties. Many of Mozilla's style extensions are merely equivalent in meaning to an XUL keyword. Some XUL tags depend entirely upon these equivalent styles for their behavior so that the meaning of the tag actually originates in a style. The preceding bit of XUL can be stated as

```
mybox { -moz-box-align: start; }
```

There is no C/C++ code for <mybox>; the whole tag depends entirely upon styles.

In addition to Mozilla's new style properties, there are also new style rules.

2.2.4.3 Style Rule Extensions Access Additional State

The CSS concept of *pseudo-class* is a powerful one that Mozilla exploits both intrinsically and extrinsically. The intent of pseudo-classes is to provide a query-like mechanism for identifying styled elements in a specific state. A pseudo-class can thus be seen as a trivial way to query the set of styled elements for a feature or state not covered directly by CSS—an intrinsic state. Mozilla contains numerous pseudo-class selectors matching internal state information. Using these selectors is a matter of separating the very handy from the uselessly obscure.

The section entitled "Style Options" in this chapter (and in most other chapters) explores all the Mozilla extensions available for the subject matter at hand. For this chapter, that means extensions that are meaningful to basic layout. "Style Options" covers both style property extensions and style rule extensions.

2.3 Box Layout Tags

Structural tags are XUL tags that affect layout but that aren't necessarily visible themselves. In the simplest case, they have no content of their own.

2.3.1 Boxes

As stated earlier, all XUL tags, including unknown tags, have the style display `-moz-box` applied to them. Those tags with special purposes are then overridden, leaving the rest to act like <box>. That means <xyzzy> and <happy-sad> are XUL box tags, although not particularly obvious ones. There are three tags put forward as the standard way to express boxes:

1. **<box>**. This tag is a horizontal box with defaults as described under "Common Box Layout Attributes."
2. **<hbox>**. A horizontal box. This tag is exactly the same as <box>. The name merely helps to remind the reader of its use.
3. **<vbox>**. A vertical box. This tag is exactly the same as <box orient="vertical">, except that it is easier to type. The name is again suggestive.

A <vbox> is no more than a format-free, user-defined tag like <xyzzy> with the -moz-box-orient:vertical style extension applied to it. That extension is equivalent to orient="vertical" and is the very essence of a <vbox>. One can argue that <vbox> follows the style, not the other way around. A <vbox> isn't really a thing in its own right.

Another source of boxes is the root tags of XUL documents. <window>, <dialog>, <page>, and <wizard> are all box-like. These tags are discussed in Chapter 10, Windows and Panes, with the exception of <wizard>, which is covered in Chapter 17, Deployment. For the purposes of layout, these tags act just like <box>, with flex applied as described in the next section.

2.3.2 Flex and Spacers

When laying out a user interface, you need a quick way to stretch tags bigger, and a quick way to put space between tags. This section describes the tools available. These tools are mostly user-defined tags (tags without any special features) that have become popular as design tricks within Mozilla.

2.3.2.1 `flex=` and `align=` The only mechanisms for stretching out XUL tags are the flex and align attributes. flex and align apply to all XUL tags that are box-like; flex is also used in several special-purpose tags. align is described under "Common Box Layout Attributes." Typical flex syntax is

```
<hbox flex="1"> ... content ... </hbox>
```

This attribute is not inherited from parent to child tags.

A flexible tag can stretch in both *x*- and *y*-directions. Adding flex="1" or align="stretch" to a tag does not guarantee that it will get bigger. Whether a tag stretches or not also depends on the tag in which it is contained (i.e., on its parent tag). The rules for flexing are different for the *x*- and *y*-directions for a given tag. Recall that a box's parent dictates the primary direction for layout. The transverse direction is at right angles to the primary direction. The rules for the primary direction follow:

- ☞ Stretching in the primary direction is determined by the flex attribute.
- ☞ If the flexing tag has an attribute or style that sets a maximum width or height, then stretching will never exceed that width or height.
- ☞ If there is unused space inside the parent's box, then the flexing tag will stretch to gobble up some or all of it.
- ☞ If there is no unused space inside parent's box, the tag will stretch only if the parent is able to stretch so that it has more space inside. The parent follows the same set of rules with respect to its parent.

The transverse case follows:

- ☞ If the parent tag has align="stretch" (or if align is not set at all), then the tag will stretch in its transverse direction.

It follows from these rules that if a tag is to change size in both directions when the window is resized by the user, then the tag and all its ancestor tags must have the `flex` attribute set, and/or `align="stretch"`. That usually means that many tags must have `flex` added.

If the XUL document is very complex, flex can be set using a global style selector and overridden for those special cases where it is not required. "Style Options" in this chapter describes how to do this.

If a <box> contains several tags, then those tags can all flex different amounts in the primary direction. The spare space in the containing box will be allocated using a shares system. All the flex values are totaled, and the available space split into shares equal to the total. Each tag then gets extra space matching the number of shares it holds. Example code is shown in Listing 2.4.

Listing 2.4 Container box with weighted flexing of contents.

```
<box width="400px">
  <box id="one"   flex="1"/>
  <box id="two"   flex="2"/>
  <box id="three" flex="3"/>
</box>
```

In this example, assume that the parent box has no borders, padding, or margins, so that all `400px` is available to share out between the three child boxes. Further assume that the child boxes use up `100px` in the beginning. In that case:

Total unused space: `400px - 100px = 300px`.

Total shares called for by the child boxes: `1 + 2 + 3 = 6`.

Space for one share: `300px / 6 = 50px`.

Therefore, each child box changes as follows:

Box "one" stretches `1 share * 50px = 50px`

Box "two" stretches `2 shares * 50px = 100px`

Box "three" stretches `3 shares * 50px = 150px`

Alas, because of the mathematics inside Mozilla, this is a close estimate, not an exact prediction. Margins, padding, and borders also affect the final calculation. Use this as a rule of thumb only.

2.3.2.2 `<spacer>` and Other Spacing Tags The "Common Box Layout Attributes" section explains how to use XUL attributes to justify box contents. You can't separate just two boxes that way, unless you use many <box> tags. Spacing boxes apart can be done using the `<spacer>` tag and flex.

The <spacer> tag is just a user-defined tag. It has no special processing; it has no styles at all. Using it is just a convention adopted in XUL, so it is in the XUL tag dictionary by stealth. It is used like this:

```
<hbox flex="1"><box/><spacer flex="1"/><box/><box/></hbox>
```

This thing is a horizontal box with four pieces of content. You only need to follow the preceding flex rules to see what happens. Only <spacer> seeks shares of any leftover space, so it will gobble up all the spare space. There will be one box on the left, a blank area where the spacer is, and then two boxes on the right. The spacer has separated the boxes on either side of it.

<spacer> displays nothing at all if `flex="1"` is omitted and there is no `width` or `height` attribute. That might seem useless, but it allows the space to be dynamically collapsed if required. It could be argued that <spacer> should be automatically styled to include flex. That hasn't happened yet. Figure 2.6 shows the results of different flex settings for the preceding line of code. Style `border: solid thin` has been added to the <spacer> tag so it can be seen. Normally, <spacer> is invisible.

There are other XUL tags that do what <spacer> does. A semicomplete list is <separator>, <menuseparator>, <toolbarseparator>, <treeseparator>, and <spring>. In fact, any user-defined tag with `flex="1"` will act like a spacer. What are all these tags?

<separator> and <toolbarseparator> are user-defined tags that pick up specific styles. They are design concepts rather than raw functionality. They do no more than <spacer> does, but they have specific roles for which each Mozilla theme should provide styles. <toolbarseparator> provides a stylable object that appears between toolbar buttons, whereas <separator> provides a stylable object between toolbars and other generic content. The presence of these objects gives themes additional design options. These tags are something like HTML's <HR> or the dreaded one-pixel GIF. The only people interested in these tags are theme designers. These tags don't use flex.

<menuseparator> is a similar concept for drop-down menus. It provides an <HR> style mark across a menu, dividing it into two sections. Menus are discussed in Chapter 7, Forms and Menus, and Chapter 8, Navigation.

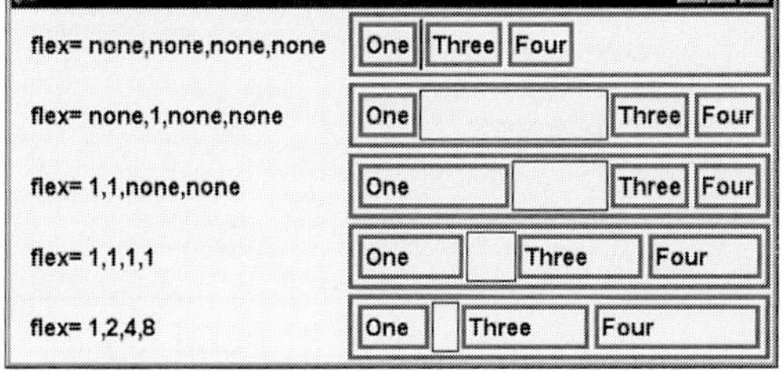

Fig. 2.6 Variations of <spacer> and flex values in a box.

<treeseparator> is special and is described in Chapter 13, Listboxes and Trees. As the name suggests, it applies to trees. Don't use <treeseparator> by itself.

Finally, <spring> is a design concept tag used in the Classic Composer. The flexing behavior of XUL boxes is supposed to overcome the need for spring-like objects, but there are occasionally special cases to cater for. The Composer is the last place in Mozilla yet to convert to <spacer>. <spring> should be avoided not just because it will complicate your flexing layout but also because it has fallen out of favor as an XUL concept. If you think you require a <spring> or <strut> tag, first read the discussion in the "Debug Corner" section in this chapter.

2.3.3 Stacks and Decks

XUL tags can be placed on top of each other, but XUL does not support CSS2 absolute or fixed positioning. It is done using a technique that goes back at least as far as Hypercard for the 1980s Macintosh. In this technique, a rectangle of the screen is treated as the top of a pack of ordinary playing cards, with all the cards facing up. XUL content is drawn onto the faces of the cards and is visible from "above" the pack.

Mozilla supports <stack> and <deck> card packs. A <stack> is like a pack of cards printed on transparent paper. A <deck> is like a pack of cards made of normal white paper, except that only one card is examined at a time. In both cases, the *x*- and *y*-dimensions of the pack are equal to the card with the largest size in that direction. Consequently, all cards are initially the same size, even if the content of some cards requires less space. This standard card size can be reduced for a given card if that card is relatively positioned. In that case, the card's top-left corner is indented from the other cards' top-left corner, and so its dimensions are reduced by the amount of the indentation.

Variations on <stack> and <deck> include <bulletinboard>, <tabbox>, and <wizard>.

2.3.3.1 <stack> Listing 2.5 shows a <stack> at work.

Listing 2.5 A <stack> example.

```
<stack>
  <image src="spade.gif"/>
  <box style="left:30px; top:30px;">
    <description>Another Card</description>
  </box>
  <description top="10" left="10">I am a Card</description>
</stack>
```

The XUL attributes left and top are the same as the CSS2 properties left and top. Inline styles are never recommended; use a separate style sheet. One is used here only to illustrate the technology. Each tag that is a child of the <stack> tag forms a single card, so there are three cards. Cards that appear "on top" cover cards "underneath" if they have opaque content, which is the normal case. The last tag is the topmost tag, so when creating a stack, create the content bottom-up. The widest part of the content is the text, but the tallest part is the image, so the final card size is a composite of those two largest dimensions. Figure 2.7 shows the result of this stack code. Some basic styles have been applied to make the layout clearer.

The <stack> tag is the most important XUL tag for animated effects, such as games or effects that would otherwise be attempted using Dynamic HTML. Because there is no absolute positioning in XUL, ordinary animation of content must occur entirely inside the box edges of a <stack>. The template system is an alternate dynamic arrangement, but has little to do with animation.

There is another restriction on animation—it is not easy to shuffle a <stack>. The order of cards in the stack is not tied to a `z-index` CSS2 property and so cannot be changed using Dynamic HTML techniques. This means that one card is permanently "in front" of all preceding cards. Two cards can't pass behind each other using CSS styles. The two cards can, however, pass behind each other by using JavaScript and the DOM standard to reorder the content tags inside the <stack> tag. This requires a remove and insert operation. Reordering tags causes a lot of expensive processing inside Mozilla, so this solution is not ideal. A better solution is to repeat content as shown in Listing 2.6.

Listing 2.6 Duplicating cards in a <stack>.

```
<stack>
  <description id="a2">Fish One</description>
  <description id="b1">Fish Two</description>
  <description id="a1" hidden="true">Fish One</description>
</stack>
```

In this stack, the topmost element is "Fish Two," with "Fish One" behind. If the visible "Fish One" tag is hidden and the previously hidden tag is made

Fig. 2.7 <stack> layout at work on three pieces of content.

visible, the stacking order of the *visible* cards is swapped. For N content tags, this technique requires $N^2 - 1$ tags total, which is a lot of tags if N is 10 or more. This overhead can be reduced by designing animation so that it has a number of planes (each a thick layer). A card belongs to a given plane. Typically you need a backdrop plane, a sprite plane (for aliens and spaceships), a transient plane (for bombs and pick-me-ups), and an effects plane (for kabooms). Using such a system, you might avoid all cases where multiple ordering is required, or at worse you may need to duplicate just part of the animation. Using this design you can control the animation with JavaScript, CSS styles, and a much reduced use of the DOM1.

If you want to animate a single element of your animation scene, you can either use a progressive GIF image or make that card of the `<stack>` a `<stack>` itself. Nested `<stacks>` are supported.

Mozilla's `-moz-opacity` custom style can be used to make the content of a `<stack>` card semitransparent. Normally only the noncontent area of a card is transparent.

The `selectedIndex` attribute of `<deck>`, discussed next, does not work with `<stack>`. If `flex="1"` is added to any tag that is a stack card, it will have no effect.

2.3.3.2 `<deck>` The `<deck>` tag is the same as the `<stack>` tag, except only one card is visible. The other cards are not "underneath" that card; they are removed entirely from the pack. They can be imagined as being present in the pack but invisible. Behind the single visible card is whatever content surrounds the `<deck>` tag. Listing 2.7 illustrates the same content for `<deck>` as was used earlier for `<stack>`.

Listing 2.7 A `<deck>` example.

```
<deck selectedIndex="1">
  <image src="spade.gif"/>
  <box style="left:30px; top:30px;">
    <description>Another Card</description>
  </box>
  <description top="10" left="10">I am a Card</description>
</deck>
```

A `<deck>` does not have the same ordering as a `<stack>`. The content tags of the `<deck>` are numbered from top to bottom starting with 0 (zero). By default, the first content tag is the one on top, so a `<deck>` pack of cards appears to be ordered the reverse way to a `<stack>` pack of cards. In reality, there is less card ordering in a `<deck>` than in a `<stack>`. For `<deck>`, there is only the card on top. The number indexes given to the individual cards work just like identifiers. If `selectedIndex` is set to an identifier that doesn't have a matching card, then the deck displays a blank card. In Listing 2.7, the `selectedIndex` attribute of `<deck>` is used to make the second content tag appear on top, rather than the first. Figure 2.8 shows the result of this code.

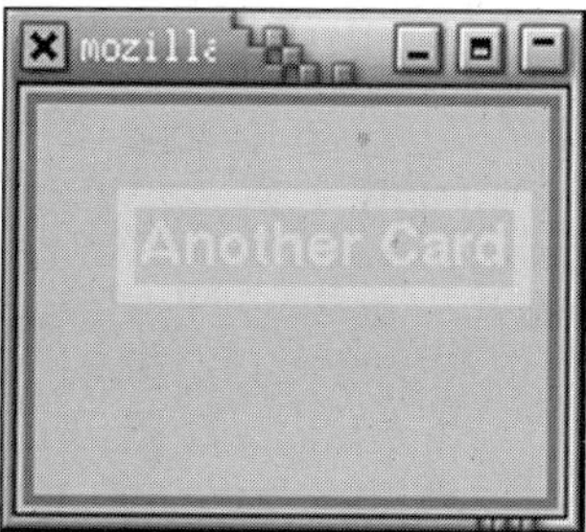

Fig. 2.8 <deck> layout at work on three pieces of content.

Animation and other fancy effects are fairly pointless with a deck. The most you might attempt is to flash through the set of cards by changing `selectedIndex`. For decks with a small surface area, this can display quite quickly without needing a top-end computer.

2.3.3.3 <bulletinboard>, <tabbox>, and <wizard> When <stack> was first added to Mozilla, relative positioning of card content was not supported. The <bulletinboard> tag was invented to support the use of left and top attributes and styles. Imagine a cork board with paper notes pinned all over it—that's a bulletin board. Eventually, this left and top functionality was added to <stack>, as described earlier, making <bulletinboard> redundant. It still lurks around in Mozilla's standard stylesheets, but it has no unique purpose of its own anymore. Use <stack> instead: The syntax is identical.

A more serious problem exists with <deck>. Having created one, how does the user pick between the various cards? The basic <deck> tag provides no solution; you need to add some buttons and scripts (or whatever).

<tabbox> and <wizard> are complex XUL tags that solve this problem. <tabbox> wraps up a <deck> inside a set of controls that provides one clickable icon per card. <wizard> wraps up a <deck> inside a set of buttons labeled "Previous" and "Next." Both of these tags automate the process of making the new card visible, putting it "on top".

<tabbox> is discussed in Chapter 8, Navigation. <wizard> is discussed in Chapter 17, Deployment. The <wizard> tag is commonly used to allow the end user to add new software components to his or her Mozilla Browser installation.

2.3.4 Grids

Plain <box> can't lay out visual elements so that they line up both horizontally and vertically, unless you use a lot of tags. So <box> by itself is not equivalent to HTML's table layout. The <grid> tag is XUL's answer to organized two-dimensional layout. It can be used to display tables, spreadsheets, matrices, and so on. There are other, less general solutions called <listbox> and <tree>.

XUL's grid system consists of five tags:

```
<grid> <columns> <column> <rows> <row>
```

XUL documents store hierarchically organized tags, and hierarchical systems are a clumsy way to represent two-dimensional structures. XUL's solution is typically ugly, but it does the job and is somewhat flexible. The grid system is just a collection of <vbox> and <hbox> boxes positioned on top of each other, with some special support to make them a bit more grid-like.

Making a grid works as follows: Specify all the columns and all the rows, and use a single content tag for each row-column intersection point. That content tag is effectively a cell. That content tag may contain any amount of XUL itself. This system has a problem: Where do you put the content tags—inside the row tags or inside the column tags? XUL's answer is that either works, but inside the rows tags is a much better solution. It doesn't matter whether you state the rows or columns first; it just matters which ones contain cell content. Listing 2.8 shows a 2×3 (two-row, three-column) grid of text specified rowwise and then columnwise:

Listing 2.8 Two identical <grid> examples.

```
<grid>
  <columns>
    <column/><column/><column/>
  </columns>
  <rows>
    <row>
      <description>One</description>
      <description>Two</description>
      <description>Three</description>
    </row>
    <row>
      <description>Four</description>
      <description>Five</description>
      <description>Six</description>
    </row>
  </rows>
</grid>

<grid>
  <rows>
    <row/><row/>
  </rows>
  <columns>
    <column>
      <description>One</description>
      <description>Four</description>
    </column>
    <column>
      <description>Two</description>
      <description>Five</description>
    </column>
```

```
      <column>
        <description>Three</description>
        <description>Six</description>
      </column>
    </columns>
  </grid>
```

Even though some tags are empty (<column> in the first example, <row> in the second), they should still all be stated. This is to give the XUL system advance warning of the final size of the grid—this problem is similar to that of the HTML table layout. XUL does not provide attributes that state the size of the <grid>. Grids do not have header rows, captions, or other fancy features. They are as plain as <stack>.

Turn border styles on, and a grid will appear as a spreadsheet. Leave border styles off, and the column and row edges will act as application layout lines for the enclosed content. Specifying layout lines for a new UI (user interface) is the first step of any UI design process. Figure 2.9 shows the example grid displayed four times, with a little bit of flex added to make the displays tidy. The first display has no borders. The second display has complete and neat borders. The other two displays illustrate styling differences between the two strategies used in Listing 2.8.

Gray borders are used for the empty columns or rows, and black borders are used for the populated columns or rows. As you can see from the diagram, when it comes to grid styles, order does matter. If there is to be any margin or padding, then only the columnwise case correctly lays out the cell contents. If you examine the top-left grid carefully, you can see a one-pixel gray line. Mozilla's grid code has some very subtle problems with grid borders. Perhaps they'll be gone by the time you read this.

In a grid, the total number of rows must match the number of content items in a given column. If they do not, Mozilla will cope, but layout might not be exactly as you expect. The reverse applies if you choose to populate rows with content instead of columns.

Finally, it is possible to add content to both columns and rows. If you do this, then it follows that one cell will receive one content tag from a <row> tag

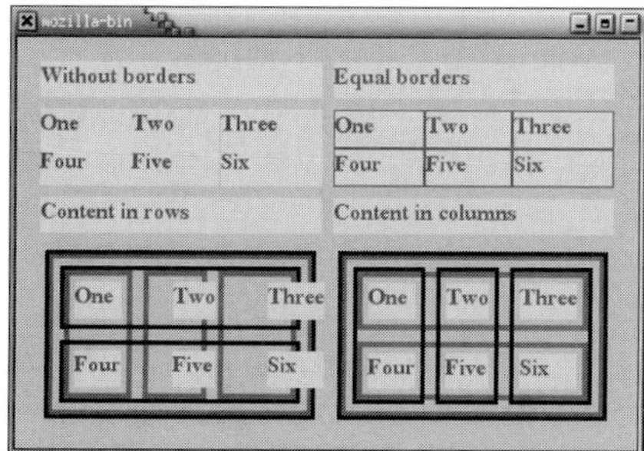

Fig. 2.9 <grid> layout showing border variations resulting from content ordering.

and one from a <column> tag. That cell will act like a two-item <stack>, with the first-appearing content tag underneath. This is a useless feature, except perhaps for some obscure purpose. If you need a <stack> in a cell, then just make the cell contents a <stack> in the first place.

The major use of <grid> is as an application layout assistant. If you use plenty of flex on the <column> and <row> tags of the grid, your content should line itself up neatly and fill the window as well. The Find dialog under the Edit menu of Mozilla contains an example of a <grid> tag at work.

If you don't like <grid>, then consider the <listbox> and <tree> functionality described in Chapter 13, Listboxes and Trees.

2.4 A Box Improvement: <groupbox> and <caption>

This chapter has covered all the basic structure and content tags that XUL has to offer. What on Earth can the rest of this book be about then? The answer is that the basic <box> technology is enhanced in an amazing variety of ways. The simplest example is a pair of tags: <groupbox> and <caption>. A related XUL tag is <radiogroup>, covered in Chapter 5, Scripting.

<groupbox> and <caption> are to XUL what <fieldset> and <legend> are to HTML. They allow a set of content items to be surrounded with a border. This is the same as a border CSS2 style, except that the border can have a title embedded in it. The purpose of the <groupbox> tag is purely visual. By collecting a number of related items together, they are "chunked" and easier for the human brain to process. They also serve to identify an area of the window that has a common purpose. That is an aid to interpretation. Listing 2.9 shows a typical group box.

Listing 2.9 Example of a <groupbox> tag.

```
<groupbox>
  <caption image="menu.png" label="Today's Menu"/>
  <description>To start with: Widget Soup</description>
  <description>Main course: Widget Steak</description>
  <description>Finishing up: Widget Ice-Cream</description>
</groupbox>
```

The three entries in this menu would be better aligned if more boxes were used, perhaps with a left column as the course name and a right column as the dish. All such content can be placed inside a <groupbox>. Figure 2.10 displays the result.

There are some basic rules for using the <caption> tag. If it is an empty tag, the content must be specified in a label and/or image attribute. Both of these attributes are optional. The label content cannot be generic XUL, just text. The image always appears before the label, unless dir="rtl" is added. If it is not an empty tag, any content can appear in the caption. The <caption> tag must be the first piece of content inside the <groupbox>.

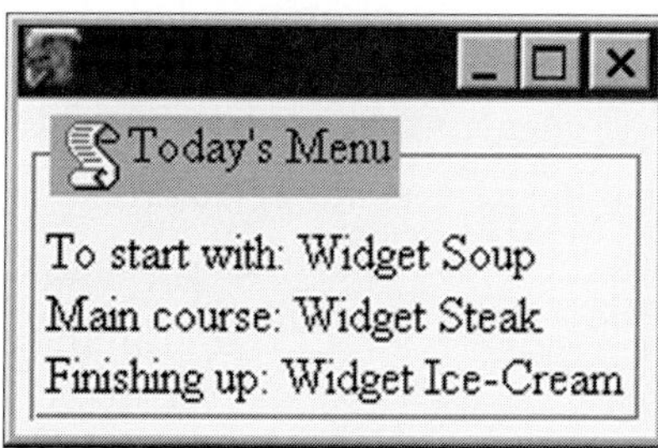

Fig. 2.10 Example of <groupbox> tag with no theme applied.

It's possible to use <caption> by itself, outside of a <groupbox>, although there are few reasons to do so. One reason might be a separate heading that is to be styled the same as the captions in a set of groupboxes. It's also possible to mess up the position of the caption by adding standard box attributes like `pack` and `align`.

Beyond its obvious utility, <groupbox> introduces a few new concepts to XUL.

First, it's clear that <groupbox> is somewhat novel. No obvious combination of the tags noted so far can mimic it. So <groupbox> must be implemented by some real C/C++ code. On the other hand, it seems easy to mess up—just try adding a box alignment attribute like `pack`. That kind of fragility sounds more like a stylesheet specification. The truth is somewhere in between. The essential part of a <groupbox> is implemented in C/C++, but special handling of attributes and content is implemented in XBL, which is a human-readable XML document. Many of XUL's tags are like this. XBL is discussed in Chapter 15, XBL Bindings.

Second, the requirement that enclosed content must have a certain order is new. The first tag inside the <groupbox> tag must be a <caption>. This kind of prescriptive rule is very common for the more complex tags in XUL, and that is also a feature of XBL.

Finally, the image in Figure 2.10 is skinless (themeless). It matches neither the Classic nor the Modern theme of Mozilla. It is entirely possible to avoid skins, but it is fairly pointless, since theme support provides a polished finish for near-zero effort. To avoid applying any theme, just forget an important stylesheet or two.

That ends the discussion of basic structure tags in XUL. All that remains before moving on to Chapter 3, Static Content, is to wrap up some loose ends and give XUL a spin.

2.5 General-Purpose XUL Attributes

XUL is an XML application that is similar to HTML. It's no surprise that familiar attributes from HTML also apply to XUL.

id. XML supports the concept of tag identity, simply called *id*. HTML's id attribute is named `id`. XUL's id attribute is also named `id`. That is straightforward.

style. Inline styles can be specified for XUL as for HTML.

class. As with HTML, CSS syntax makes it particularly easy to apply style rules to elements of a particular class, or to all elements of the same class.

onevent handlers. XUL tags support most DOM inline event handlers like `onclick`. They are numerous and covered in Chapter 6, Events.

XUL also has its own set of generally useful attributes, like `flex`, `debug`, `height`, and `width`, discussed earlier. One attribute not yet discussed is the `persist` attribute.

The `persist` attribute is used by the Mozilla Browser to save information about a given XUL document. The most obvious example of `persist` is to save the *x*- and *y*- positions of the window on the computer desktop: The next time that a window is opened, it is located in the same place on the screen as before. `persist` can be used to save the value of any XUL attribute, and that information survives the browser's shutting down. It is stored on disk in an RDF file and reloaded each time the browser starts up. The browser does all this automatically after the attribute is set.

In fact, there are many attributes with special behavior like `persist`. `observes`, `command`, `key`, `uri`, and `commandupdater` are all examples. Each one is discussed later in this book where the features of XUL are further explored.

2.6 Good Coding Practices for XUL

Developing XUL applications means creating XML documents. The best way to do this is by hand, as there are no good GUI builders for XUL yet. It is very important that sloppy habits left over from HTML are stopped before they start. Listing 2.10 shows a typical piece of legacy HTML code.

Listing 2.10 Unstructured HTML development.

```
<HTML><HEAD>
  <STYLE>
    P { font-size : 18pt; }
  </STYLE>
  <SCRIPT>
    function set_case(obj)
    {
      if (obj.value)
        obj.value = obj.value.toUpperCase();
      return true;
    }
```

```
  </SCRIPT>
</HEAD><BODY BGCOLOR="yellow">
  <P>Enter a name</P>
  <FORM>
    <INPUT TYPE="text" ONCHANGE="set_case(this)">
</FORM>
</BODY></HTML>
```

This code is not very modern, but it works. XUL will not stand for this lazy treatment. It requires more formality. It is also important that XUL documents be well organized. Although XUL is faster to use than coding against a GUI library, it is still structured programming. Good coding practices for XUL follow:

1. Always use XML syntax. XUL has no pre-XML syntax like HTML anyway.
2. Avoid using embedded JavaScript. Put all scripts in a `.js` file.
3. Avoid using embedded stylesheets. Put all style information in a `.css` file.
4. Keep inline event handlers to a minimum. One onLoad handler is enough. Install the rest from JavaScript using `addEventListener()` (see Chapter 6, Events, for how).
5. Avoid using inline styles. Do everything from a stylesheet.
6. Avoid putting plain text in a XUL document. Only use custom DTD entities.

This is a fairly harsh restriction. It can be dropped if the XUL application needs to work in only one language.

If these rules are applied to the example HTML, then the results might be similar to those in Listing 2.11.

Listing 2.11 Structured HTML development.

```
<!-- text.dtd -->
<!ENTITY text.label "Enter a name">

/* styles.css */
p    { font-size : 18pt; }
body { background-color : yellow; }

// scripts.js
function load_all()
{
  document.getElementbyId("txtdata").
    addEventListener("change",set_case,0);
}
function set_case(e)
{
  if (e.target.value)
```

```
    e.target.value = e.target.value.toUpperCase();
  return true;
}

<!-- content.html -->
<?xml version="1.0"?>
<?xml-stylesheet href="styles.css" type="text/css"?>
<!DOCTYPE html [
  <!ENTITY % textDTD SYSTEM "text.dtd">
  %textDTD;
  ] >
<html><head>
  <script src="scripts.js"/>
</head><body onload="load_all()">
  <p>&text.label;</p>
  <form>
    <input id="txtdata" type="text"/>
  </form>
</body></html>
```

This code has gone from 18 to 28 lines and from one to four files, but the actual HTML has dropped from 18 to 14 lines, of which now only 8 lines are content. This is an important point: The content has been stripped right back to the minimum. XUL development is very much like this.

This structured example is how you should approach XUL from the start. Your first step should be to create a `.xul`, `.css`, `.js`, and perhaps a `.dtd` file. The `<?xml-stylesheet?>` tag is a standard part of core XML and always available—it is vaguely similar to C's `#include`. Adding a DTD file is not common in HTML, but it is a regular event in XUL.

Prototype development is usually a hasty affair, and you might find a few emergency hacks creeping into your new, reformed practices. If so, beware of one or two scripting traps that can wreck your document.

A trap with XML syntax involves terminators. In both legacy HTML and Mozilla XML applications, the `<script>` tag contains code, usually JavaScript. In the legacy case, if that code for any reason contained the string "`</script>`," that string would be recognized as an end tag. The solution is to break up the string:

```
var x = "</scr" + "ipt>";
```

This still applies to Mozilla's legacy HTML support. The same problem exists in XML and XUL.

A more serious problem is the use of JavaScript's && and & operators. XML and XUL documents treat & as the start of an XML entity reference. This also can cause early termination. Similarly, the << and < operators are treated by XML and XUL as the start of a tag.

The solution to all these problems for inline code is to use CDATA literals as shown in Listing 2.12.

Listing 2.12 Use of XML CDATA literals to encapsulate scripts.

```
<script><![CDATA[
    if ( 1 < 2 )
    {
       var x = "harmless </script>";
    }
]]></script>
```

This solution has an early termination weakness of its own. This line of code causes early termination because it contains the string "]]>":

```
if ( a[b[c]]> 0 ) { return; }
```

When creating Mozilla applications, the real solution is to avoid inline code entirely.

There is a second trap with XML scripts. In legacy HTML, there was special coordination between HTML and JavaScript. If the first line of the code was the XML opening comment tag:

```
<!--
```

then special processing meant the code was still interpreted. Use of XML comments in XUL or XML code will hide the code from the JavaScript interpreter entirely.

In all these cases, the real solution is to avoid inline code. That goes for stylesheets as well.

2.7 Style Options

Recall from the discussion on frames and style extensions earlier that many aspects of the XUL tag set also exist in Mozilla's extended style system. This can makes the XUL language appear quite transparent. You can define a new XML element (perhaps using a DTD), add a style to it, and have the element act as though it were the official XUL element matching the style. Mozilla's most obvious CSS2 extensions exactly match an XUL tag, as Table 2.1 shows.

These styles define what kind of thing a particular XUL tag is. Unfortunately, these styles cannot always be assigned to a user-defined tag like `<mystack>`. Inside the Mozilla C/C++ code there are occasional assumptions that tie a tag name to a given display value. The Mozilla project has as a goal of elimination of these assumptions, and by version 1.4, most are gone. How do you find out if a tag called `<mystack>` will act like `<stack>` if the display style is set to `-moz-stack`? The answer is: Try it out.

There is another set of style extensions that apply to structural tags. These extensions match tag attributes rather than whole tags, and their values exactly match the values that those attributes can take on. Table 2.2 describes these attribute-like style properties.

The visual layout models that Mozilla uses can be extremely complex in parts. There is some common functionality between XUL, HTML, and MathML, and the situation is further complicated by compatibility modes for legacy HTML documents. The upshot of all this is that there are a few styles that act as layout hints to the styling system. For pure XUL, or even for mixed XUL and HTML, these styles are last-resort solutions to your visual layout problems. You're probably trying to do something the complicated way. These styles are noted in Table 2.3.

Table 2.1 "Display" style extensions for structural XUL tags

Value for CSS display: property	Equivalent XUL
-moz-box	<box>
-moz-stack	<stack>
-moz-deck	<deck>
-moz-grid	<grid>
-moz-grid-group	<columns> or <rows>
-moz-grid-line	<column> or <row>
-moz-groupbox	<groupbox>

Table 2.2 Style properties for XUL box layout attributes

New CSS property	Equivalent XUL attribute
-moz-box-align	align=
-moz-box-direction	dir=
-moz-box-orient	orient=
-moz-box-pack	pack=
-moz-box-flex	unique flex= value
-moz-box-flex-group	equalsize=

Table 2.3 Style extensions providing layout hints to Mozilla

Property	Values	Use
-moz-box-sizing	border-box, content-box, padding-box	Instructs the layout engine what part of the styled element to use when calculating its edges.
-moz-float-edge	border-box, margin-box, content-box, padding-box	Dictates which outer limit of a floating element should be used when content flows around it.

CSS3 is in development as this is written, and Mozilla has partial support for it. CSS3 will include support for Internet Explorer 6.0's "border box model," often called the broken box model by Microsoft cynics. Mozilla will likely support this model eventually.

2.8 Hands On: NoteTaker Boilerplate

It's time to apply XUL structure to a real example—the NoteTaker browser enhancement. In this and subsequent chapters, all we do is start work on a dialog box.

2.8.1 The Layout Design Process

The dialog box we want appears when the Edit button on the NoteTaker toolbar is pressed. Figure 2.11 shows this dialog box at the conceptual stage.

This diagram looks like it might be a tabbed box, each tab revealing different content. We don't know how to do tabs yet, so we'll ignore that part of the problem. We also don't know how to do textboxes, checkboxes, or buttons. We can, however, do some basic layout.

The layout process is stolen from the world of graphic design—we just want everything to align nicely. This means doing a bit of up-front planning. It might be more fun to charge in and create the UI in an ad hoc way, but in the end that will take more time. From an engineering point of view, doing layout design is a reliable starting point for the visual part of Mozilla application development.

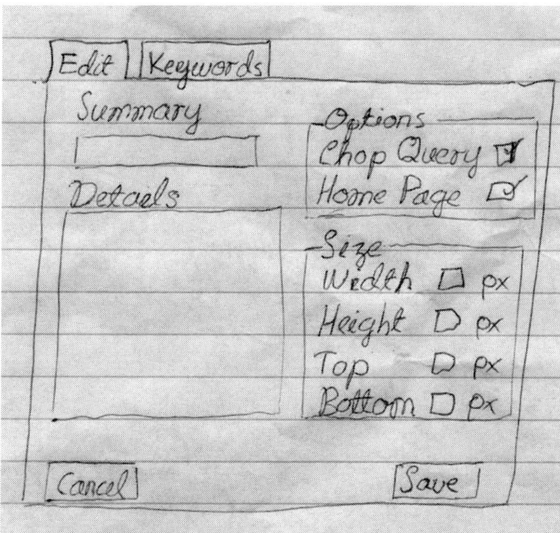

Fig. 2.11 Sketch diagram of a dialog box.

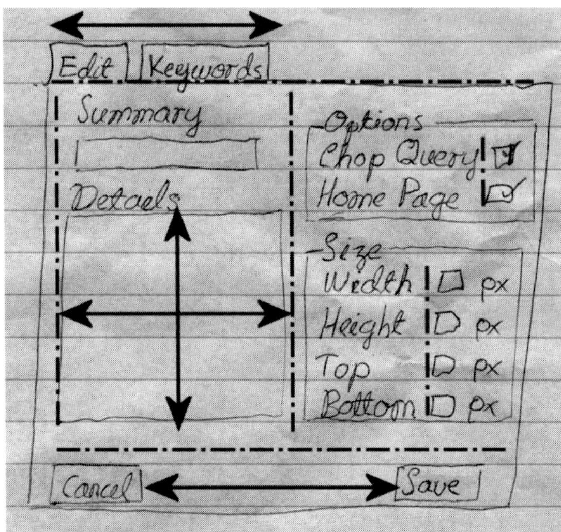

Fig. 2.12 Breaking down a sketch into alignment.

Layout design is really trivial. Seeing alignment inside the drawn dialog box is easy. Figure 2.12 shows the original diagram with some alignment marked in.

Dot-dashed lines are our guesses where content should line up. Double-headed arrows show where we suspect things should flex. This is not a formal notation, just useful scratching on a page. It's a kind of markup, but no formality is needed. It's just a thinking tool.

This kind of scratching is not locked in stone either. User interfaces are fragile and easily broken by the user's perspective on them. We'll need to revisit this design frequently. What we're attempting to do is plan a little, which will pay off especially if the application under development is very large.

From these scratched registration lines (as they're sometimes called), we can imagine the required boxes without much effort at all. The whole dialog box is a <vbox> containing three <hbox>es. The second <hbox> contains in turn two <vbox>es, and so on. Actually making the boxes is easy. Listing 2.13 shows a box breakdown for the dialog box.

Listing 2.13 Box breakdown for the NoteTaker dialog box.

```
<vbox>
  <hbox></hbox>
  <hbox>
    <vbox></vbox>
    <vbox>
      <groupbox>
        <caption/>
```

```
        <grid>
          <rows><row/><row/></rows>
          <columns>
            <column></column><column></column>
          </columns>
        </grid>
      </groupbox>
      <groupbox>
        <caption/>
        <grid>
          <rows><row/><row/><row/><row/></rows>
          <columns>
            <column></column>
            <column></column>
            <column></column>
          </columns>
        </grid>
      </groupbox>
    </vbox>
  </hbox>
  <hbox></hbox>
</vbox>
```

At the start of the chapter, we discussed how important boxes are to Mozilla applications. This fairly simple example makes that obvious. With a little extra styling—thick borders for boxes, thin borders for grids and groupboxes—Figure 2.13 shows the result of this code.

Until your eye gets a little XUL practice, this doesn't look too much like the needed layout. After we add some flex, however, matters improve. The only lines that need flex are near the top, as shown in Listing 2.14.

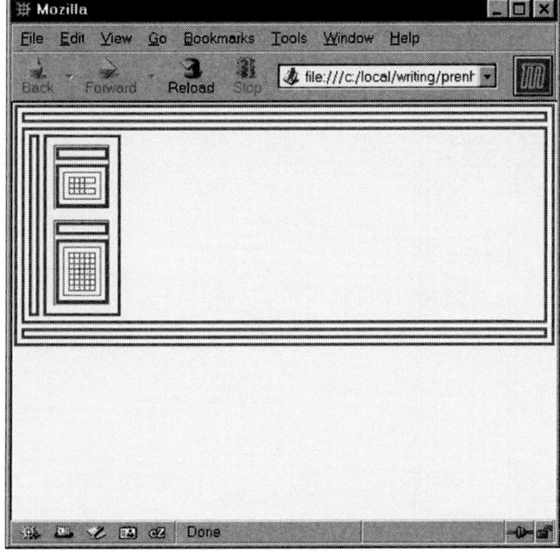

Fig. 2.13 Simple box breakdown for the NoteTaker Edit Dialog window.

Listing 2.14 Flex additions for the NoteTaker dialog box.

```
<vbox flex="1">
  <hbox>
  </hbox>
  <hbox flex="1">
    <vbox flex="1">
...
```

With this flex in place, Figure 2.14 shows the improved solution.

That concludes the layout process. It's not hard. If you need to provide many different but similar screens, a layout skeleton showing the common elements is a good investment.

This simple document can also be installed in the chrome and run from there. To do that, copy the XUL file to this Microsoft Windows location.

```
C:\Program Files\Mozilla\chrome\notetaker\content\editDialog.xul
```

or for UNIX, copy it to here:

```
/local/install/mozilla/chrome/notetaker/content/editDialog.xul
```

This file can now be viewed using the `chrome://notetaker/content/editDialog.xul` URL, provided the setup in the "Hands On" section in Chapter 1, Fundamental Concepts, has also been done. For now, we can use the `-chrome` command line option if a separate window is desired. We can also view this URL in an ordinary browser window.

2.8.2 Completing Registration

We registered NoteTaker as a package name in Chapter 1, Fundamental Concepts, but we didn't register the NoteTaker package with the Mozilla chrome

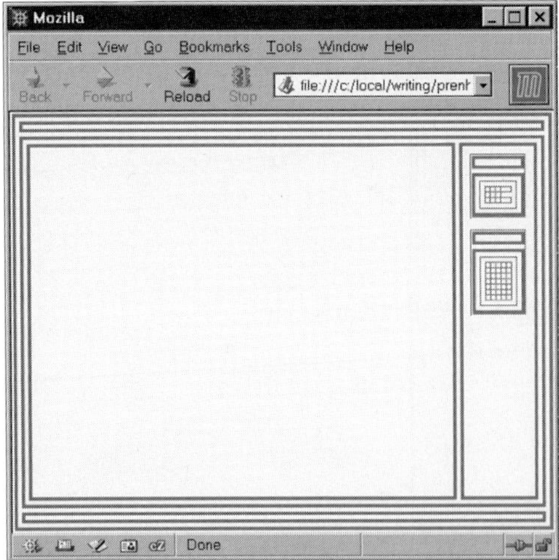

Fig. 2.14 Simple box breakdown for the NoteTaker Edit Dialog window.

registry. That registry (described in more detail in Chapter 12, Overlays and Chrome) allows our application to use features like skins, locales, and overlays. We don't need those things yet, but we might as well get ready for them. Now that we're editing XML-based XUL files, we might as well edit an XML-based RDF file at the same time.

An extra file called `contents.rdf` is required if the chrome registry is to be used. We need to put that file in this subpath of the install area:

```
chrome/notetaker/content/contents.rdf
```

Note that this file path partially matches the path added to `installed-chrome.txt` in Chapter 1. This file is an XML document consisting of RDF tags. RDF is discussed beginning in Chapter 11, RDF.

All this file needs to say in order to register NoteTaker with the chrome system is shown in Listing 2.15.

Listing 2.15 `contents.rdf` file required to register the NoteTaker package.

```
<?xml version="1.0"?>
<RDF:RDF
  xmlns:RDF="http://www.w3.org/1999/02/22-rdf-syntax-ns#"
  xmlns:chrome="http://www.mozilla.org/rdf/chrome#">

  <RDF:Seq about="urn:mozilla:package:root">
    <RDF:li resource="urn:mozilla:package:notetaker"/>
  </RDF:Seq>

  <RDF:Description about="urn:mozilla:package:notetaker"
    chrome:displayName="NoteTaker"
    chrome:author="Nigel McFarlane"
    chrome:name="notetaker">
  </RDF:Description>

</RDF:RDF>
```

The `<Seq>` tag adds NoteTaker to the list of packages; the `<Description>` tag adds one record of administrative information about the package. This very standard piece of RDF can be reused for other packages—just replace the string "`notetaker`" everywhere with some other package name.

To make this change stick, we just need to resave the `installed-chrome.txt` file so that its last-modified date is brought forward to now. The next time the platform starts up, the chrome registry will read our `contents.rdf` file, but that file does nothing significant in this chapter. It merely says that the NoteTaker package exists.

That ends the "Hands On" session for this chapter.

2.9 Debug Corner: Detecting Bad XUL

The Mozilla Platform provides some simple analysis tools for diagnosing your XUL. They are your friends, and engaging them in a little idle experimentation can expand your understanding of the technology enormously. This "Debug Corner" covers basic syntax errors and the `debug` attribute.

Most programmer support tools are located under Tools | Web Development.

The command line is a good place to start Mozilla under both Windows and UNIX. It is particularly handy for loading documents into undecorated `-chrome` windows because command line history allows you to reload a document into a new window with just two keystrokes. The test-debug-fix loop is particularly quick for XUL since everything is interpreted, and fast keystrokes save you from messing around.

On older Microsoft Windows versions you really need `doskey` if you plan to use a DOS box command line. `doskey` provides command-line history and is available on all older Windows versions; newer versions have that functionality built into the command processor. Edit `C:\autoexec.bat` and add a line `"doskey"`. If you want to do this the GUI way, then the following process might get you there, depending on your version and the tools installed from your Windows CD: Start | Programs | Accessories | System Tools | System Information. From the new window, choose Tools | System Configuration Utility. Finally, choose the autoexec.bat tab, click New, then type **doskey**, click OK, and finish by shaking your head in disbelief.

On UNIX, most shells, but particularly the bash shell, provide command-line history after you put the command `set -o vi` or `set -o emacs` in your `~/.bash_profile` file. Either the vi or emacs keys are then available (see the `readline(3)` or `bash(1)` manual page for details).

2.9.1 Warnings and Silence

Debugging comes down to what you're told and what you're not told. Older Web browsers are somewhat unreliable about reporting errors. In the past, it was common for the reported line number to be wrong or for the line of content causing the error to be wrong. Those days are over. Mozilla's error messages are pedantically correct, just as compiler error messages are pedantically correct.

Mozilla produces warnings for basic errors. The simplest error is to forget to close a tag. This, and basic syntax errors, result in a standard error window. Figure 2.15 shows this screen.

It's very important that this window be dismissed after it has appeared. You can't retest your document properly until it is gone. If you leave it, loading a fixed document will yield the same message. That is very frustrating if you accidentally hide it behind some other window.

One of Mozilla's design themes is near-zero validation. The amount you are not told is quite high, and you must be aware of that. You are not told any of the following items; consequently, you must check them all by eye if it's not working:

- The tag name, attribute name, or attribute value is unknown.
- The style selector, property, or property value is unknown.
- An id value was repeated across tags.

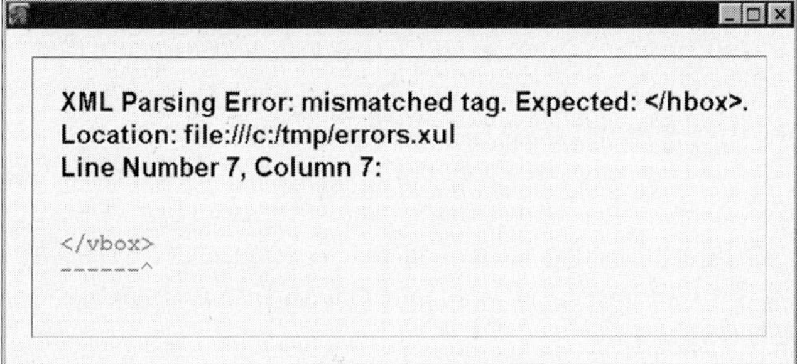

Fig. 2.15 Basic error message from Mozilla.

- ☞ A style property was repeated in a single style.
- ☞ That attribute value or attribute doesn't work on this tag.
- ☞ That content shouldn't be enclosed in this tag.

XUL's more advanced tags are seductively easy to use. However, if you haven't grasped the first principles of layout, you have no idea how to cope after your first mistake. Make an effort to understand what's going on.

2.9.2 Debug Springs and Struts

The `debug` attribute helps you diagnose layout problems. If your boxes aren't lining up the way you want, then turning debug on gives you some visual clues why that is so. Using a preference, debug can be turned on for individual tags or for the whole page. When used extensively, it adds much visual information to the screen, possibly too much. It's recommended to use debug sparingly. Listing 2.16 shows a simple piece of content with `debug` added in various spots.

Listing 2.16 XUL content instrumented with `debug="1"`.

```
<hbox flex="1" debug="true">
  <box flex="1"><text value="One"/></box>
  <box><text value="Two"/></box>
</hbox>
<vbox debug="true">
  <box flex="1" debug="true"><text value="One"/></box>
  <box><text value="One"/></box>
</vbox>
```

In this chapter, most XUL examples include border styles so that the layout of the content can be seen. In this case, there are no styles of any kind. Figure 2.16 illustrates.

This screenshot is double normal size so that the small debug markings are clearer. A box with a thick border across the top is a `<hbox debug="true">`. A box with a thick border along the left is a `<vbox`

debug="true">. From the preceding listing, it's clear that debug is inherited because the boxes inside the <hbox> tag all have a debug border but don't have the attribute. The content of the thick border provides the layout clues.

These border clues consist of a number of pieces. Each piece is either a straight line (a *strut*) or a wiggly line (a *spring*), terminated on both ends with a small lug. These names come from mechanical engineering. A strut is a stiff bar that holds its shape and keeps things apart. A spring is a stretchy coil that adapts in length when the things it is anchored to move together or apart. A lug is just a bit that sticks out.

In the thick debug border, the number of springs and struts present equals the number of box-like content items inside the current box. These pieces make statements about the content items. A strut means that the matching content item is of fixed size equal to the strut's length. A spring means the content item is flexible in size.

These debug borders can be used to answer the question: Which tag took all the extra space? To understand the answer, look at the supplied example. The <hbox> across the top half has one spring and one strut. Therefore, the first <box> inside it must be flexible and the second must not be flexible. Checking the code, this is true. By looking at the first <box>, it's clear that this box has flexed, since its content is a strut, but the length of the strut is shorter than the length of the parent spring. The space to the right of the <box>'s strut is the share of extra space that the box acquired from flex. This share expands and contracts as the window size changes.

Note that for the <hbox>, in the perpendicular direction (transverse to the primary direction), there are no layout hints. This is because, in the ordinary case, boxes can always expand in the transverse direction.

These debug borders can also be used to answer the question: Why didn't this box flex? In the example, the <vbox> across the bottom half of the diagram has one flexible piece of content and one not. This also matches the code. If the <vbox>'s content was other <vbox>es, then the situation would be anal-

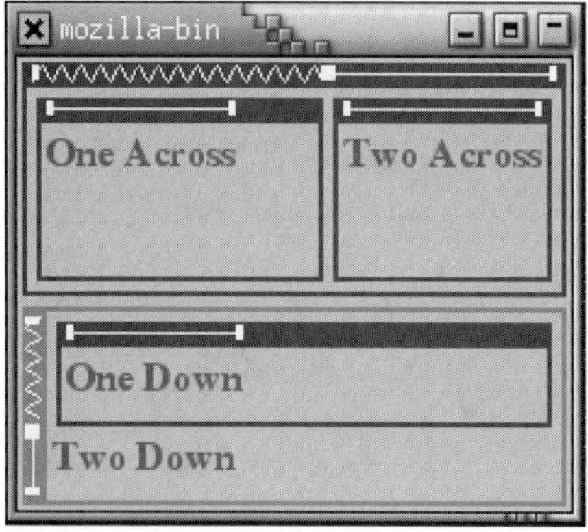

Fig. 2.16 XUL document showing debug springs and struts.

ogous to the <hbox> example. After examining the aligned borders, you could see that no extra space is allocated to the interior boxes, no matter what the window size. In other words, the parent box should have flex but doesn't. That conclusion matches the code, but it's easier to see using debug="true".

The <vbox> case is actually more complicated again because it doesn't have <vbox> content. Instead, it has <hbox> content (<box> acts like <hbox>). You don't have a matching set of debug borders to compare, but you do have a rule from earlier that you can apply: Boxes always flex in the transverse direction. Therefore, both content boxes must flex along the <vbox> direction, regardless of what the <vbox> springs and struts say. Since they haven't, if the window is large in size, you can again conclude that the outside <vbox> is missing flex.

Springs and struts are the nuts and bolts of resizable displays. Most GUI systems have something based on them. The automatic expansion of XUL and HTML tags is really a management system for springs and struts. You're not supposed to care about the lower level concepts because the intelligent layout design does the work for you. This is why it's a step backwards to invent or use <spring> and <strut> tags. Exploit the automatic layout instead.

Thinking a lot about spring and strut tags usually means that your XUL is getting too complex. It's only a window, not a work of art. Some basic structure should be all you need. If you need to lock down the layout of your tags very tightly, then you are probably trying too hard. The debug attribute is supposed to be a diagnostic aid, not a design tool.

2.10 Summary

XUL is like HTML, but it is more programmer-oriented in the services it provides. XUL documents have URLs and are loaded like any Web document, although use of the -chrome command-line option is common. XUL requires more structured thinking than HTML; consequently, better coding habits are essential. Inline code is generally bad practice in XUL documents. XUL requires a proper understanding of its main tag, <box>, right from the beginning.

Inside Mozilla is the central concept of a frame, which is complementary to the W3C's concept of a DOM. The concept of a frame supports a layout system. The layout system provides an orderly way to arrange the elements of a graphical user interface. Unlike most programming languages, that layout is done declaratively.

Debugging XUL can be challenging. You can peek inside Mozilla's layout system using the debug attribute. Although you get some help when typos happen, you must keep a sharp eye out for errors that are silently passed over. It's very important to adopt a structured approach right from the start.

XUL without any content is a bit like a bride without a bridegroom. In the next chapter, you'll see how to add basic, static text to a document. That kind of content is one of few features shared with HTML.

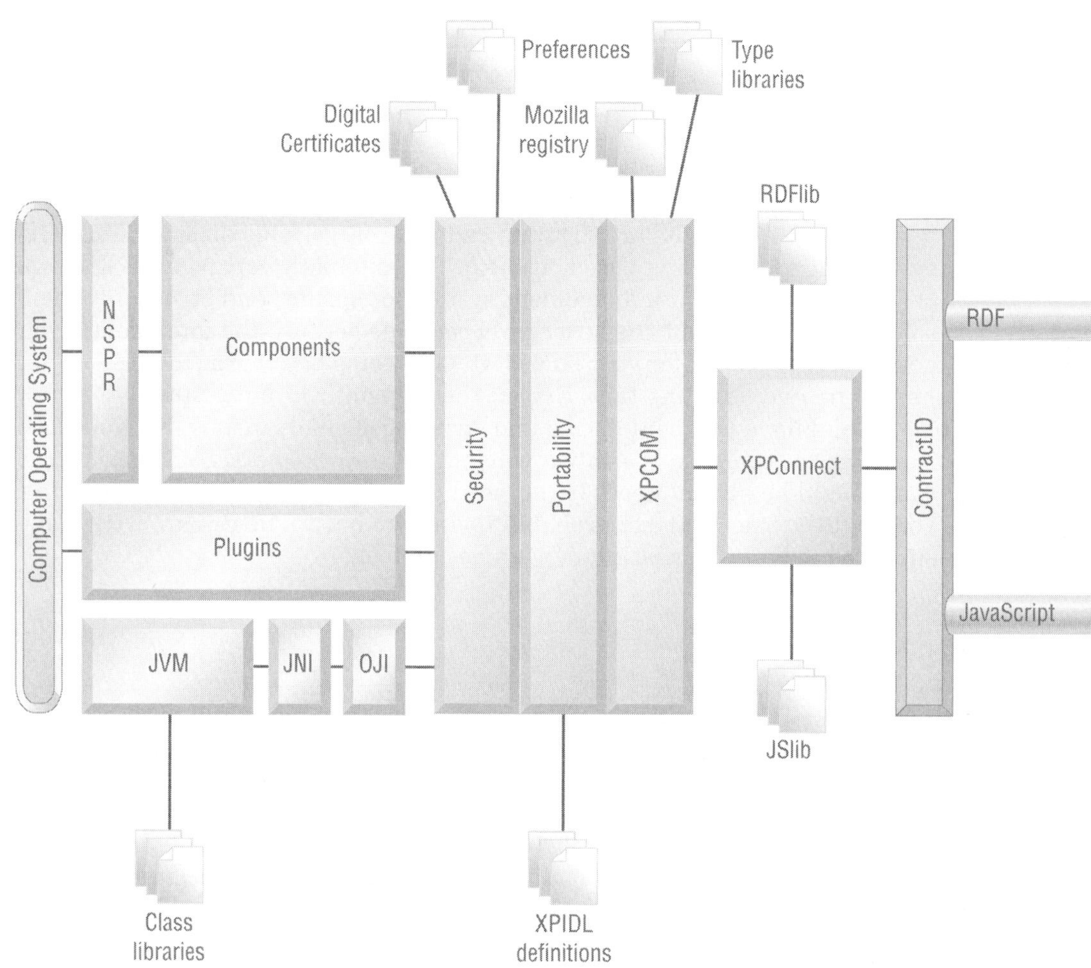

Preferences
Type libraries
Digital Certificates
Mozilla registry
RDFlib
Computer Operating System
N S P R
Components
Security
Portability
XPCOM
XPConnect
ContractID
RDF
JavaScript
Plugins
JVM
JNI
OJI
JSlib
Class libraries
XPIDL definitions

CHAPTER 3

Static Content

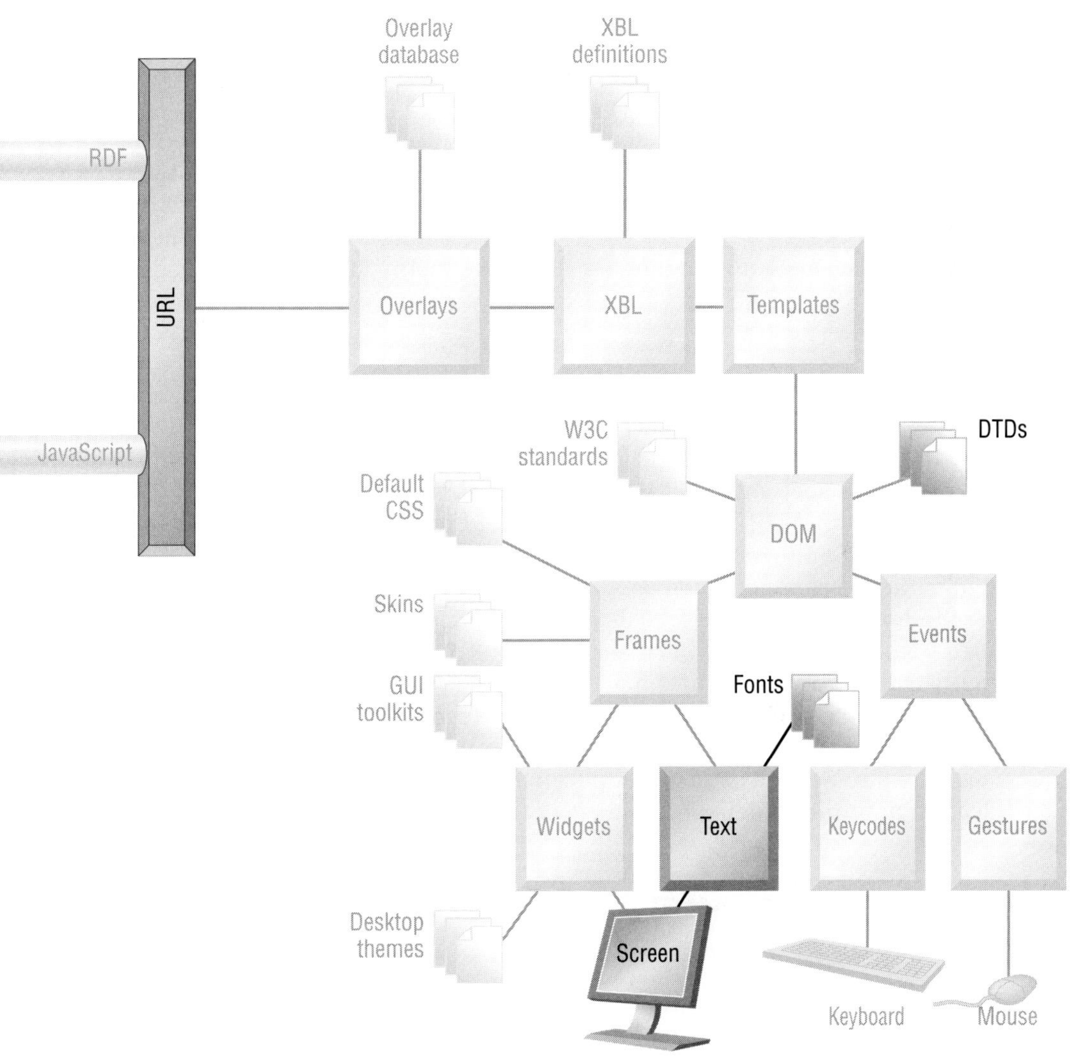

This chapter explains how to add noninteractive text, images, and borders to a XUL application.

This kind of simple, noninteractive content is very easy to work with. It's no accident that this part of XUL is similar to HTML, but similarities are mostly confined to this chapter and to Chapter 7, Forms and Menus. A significant difference between XUL and HTML is that HTML has a fixed set of tag names, but the set of XUL tag names can be extended with trivial effort. For now, we consider just the standard XUL content tags.

The NPA diagram for this chapter illustrates the impact of static content on Mozilla. Textual information can be supplied directly inside a XUL file, or it can come from an external DTD file. Although DTDs aren't much used in HTML-based Web applications, their use is common in XUL. Later when we have some scripting technology, we will be free to get text from any information source. XUL also allows images to be loaded via a URL just as HTML does.

Font information is another aspect of static content display. The Mozilla Platform is a good tool for UNIX application development, but care needs to be taken that the finished application benefits from correctly organized fonts.

Given that XUL and HTML are somewhat similar in this area, XUL's existence as a separate language needs some justification. That discussion is up first.

3.1 XUL and HTML Compared

Why should anyone bother with XUL at all? Isn't HTML good enough? Doesn't layout succeed in HTML already? Surely HTML tables or CSS2 styles is all you need? Well, HTML is not enough. Figure 3.1 illustrates a message from a public and commercial HTML-based Web application, in this case a high-volume e-commerce travel site.

In terms of user-interface design, this is truly awful. First, it is about the third time the users have been asked to confirm their transaction. Second, it's highly fragile: Any accidental move by the user can obviously wreck the application. Finally, the implication is that no feedback will be given. When do users find out that the job is finished? Overall, it's weird, scary, and confusing. Such a popup window is just an apology for a bad user interface. HTML is not ideal for application delivery because of the pre-existing navigation controls at

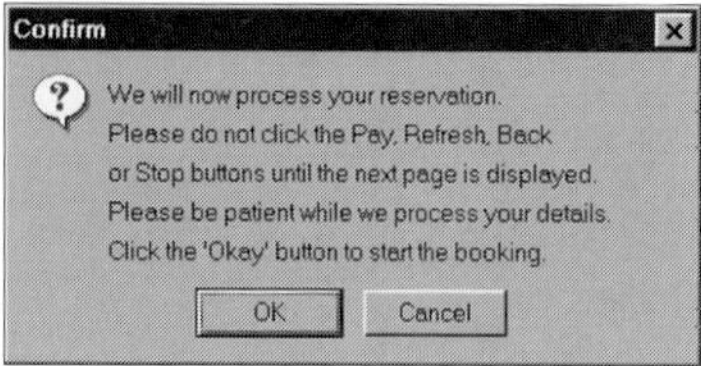

Fig. 3.1 HTML's user interface problems.

the top of every browser window—the user can press them at any time. HTML is also not ideal because of the difficulty of building reliable navigation systems out of HTML tags.

There is no need for this kind of bad design when using XUL. XUL allows the programmer to do away with the browser toolbars that allow the user to disrupt an HTML-based application. XUL also gives the application programmer more control over application processing, via sophisticated and feature-rich widgets.

It might seem that XUL is a minor technology compared with HTML. Nothing could be farther from the truth. Every window of the Classic Browser (and all other Mozilla-based Web browsers) is a XUL application, even `alert()` popups. Some browser windows, like the Navigator window, may have large sections dedicated to other kinds of content (like HTML pages), but every window is a XUL application first and foremost. These windows interoperate by sharing definition files and by scripting mutually accessible components. Everything you see when looking at a Mozilla Browser is wrapped up in XUL. Even though HTML is well known, under the Mozilla Platform it is a second-class citizen when compared to XUL.

To understand how XUL works in a finished application, consider typical uses of HTML first. HTML Web pages use form submission, links, and Dynamic HTML to get their jobs done. The actual form submission, link navigation, and DHTML objects are services provided by the browser. They don't exist in the HTML document, although some HTML tags are closely tied to them. The HTML documents *assume* that the browser provides those needed services. For HTML, those services are defined mostly in the DOM standards.

In the case of XUL, a XUL document describes all the GUI elements. The assumption is that there is something for these GUI elements to do. Mozilla's XPCOM provides the components with which these GUI elements can work. As for HTML, the document content and the services of the browser go together. XPCOM components are generally more powerful than DOM interfaces. If necessary, XUL can also use DOM objects.

Although both XML and HTML can be identified by namespace strings, there is also a crucial difference. There is no DTD for XUL. The tags that make up the language come from a variety of sources inside the Mozilla Platform. There is no authoritative specification.

In fact, there is no exact or binding agreement on just what XUL tags exist. The language is like a bit of clay. This is because each of several technologies contributes XUL tags, and more tags can be added at any time. Thus, there is also no such thing as a "correct" XUL document. The question is rather: Do all the tags in this document do something useful?

Matters are not quite as extreme as they might seem; there is a well-defined set of basic XUL tags. These make a good starting point, but, overall, XUL is not as fixed as HTML is. Learning XUL tags is about building up a dictionary: Put a tag in the dictionary if it is in common use, regardless of where it comes from.

3.2 XUL CONTENT TAGS

This chapter considers only static content, which means text, images, and style effects. If you're looking for buttons, see Chapter 4, First Widgets and Themes.

3.2.1 Text and Strings

The <description> tag is the simplest, if somewhat verbose, way to put textual characters on the screen. There are other ways as well. The full list of useful textual tags includes

```
<description> <text> <label> <stringbundle> <stringbundleset>
    <caption>
```

Because XUL is XML, there is always the option of working with generic XML features. For text, that means entities and entity references. Some of these options allow strings to be stored in separate files, so those mechanisms are also examined.

Note that the XUL <description> tag and the RDF <Description> tag are entirely separate and different in meaning.

3.2.1.1 <description>, <text>, and <label> The <description> tag is the workhorse of XUL plain text. The <label> tag is exactly the same as <description>, except that it supports the control attribute. The control attribute associates the text of a label with a form element. To understand how that works, see Chapter 6, Events. <label> is basically a smarter version of <description>. The <text> tag provides a simpler display mechanism than the other two tags.

<description> and <label> tags are the only tags in XUL that will line-wrap their content if it is long. Line-wrapping involves using more than one line to display the text. When text is wrapped, it is done so on a breaking-whitespace character (like space or tab). XUL does not support the   non-breaking-space character entity reference: If it's needed, use the equivalent . If the text cannot be wrapped before the maximum line width is reached (because no breaking character is encountered), then the line will overflow. It will be clipped at the edge of the next fixed width box (usually the window's edge). It will also do this if the window size changes.

<description> and <label> can contain any type of content, not just text. That includes <box> or other XUL tags. The content inside these tags will be wrapped across lines as well. Line-wrap can also occur where an end tag and start tag meet inside a string of <description> or <label> content. In short, <description> and <label> are like HTML's <P> tag. <description> supports one special attribute:

```
value
```

<label> supports two special attributes:

```
value crop
```

Both can have their content stated between start and end tags, or in the XML string assigned to the `value` attribute.

The `crop` attribute can be set to `start`, `center`, or `end`. By default none of these values applies. If the `crop` attribute is set, a <label> tag will no longer line-wrap. If the content would overflow the width of the enclosing box, then it will be clipped and truncated. This truncation is severe enough that there is room left over for ellipses (three dots, "...") to be added. In the case of `crop="start"`, the ellipses appear at the beginning of the label content. In the case of `crop="end"`, they appear at the end of the content. For `crop="center"`, they may appear at both ends. The ellipses indicate to the user that more text is available to read.

A few restrictions apply to these tags. First, XUL documents consist of 8-bit character encodings, usually UTF-8, so non-ASCII and multibyte Unicode characters must be specially referenced. That is the case for all XML. Second, if the `value` attribute is used, then not all of the CSS2 styling that applies to text can be applied to the content, so beware. The `value` attribute also does not allow generic XML (or XUL) content to be specified, only plain text. Enclose the content between begin and end tags for maximum flexibility.

The <text> tag is the same as the other two tags, except that its content does not wrap to a second line. If the content would overflow the width of the enclosing box, then it may be clipped and truncated by adding a flex attribute. In that case, it acts like a <label crop="end"> tag. The <text> tag is therefore most useful in menus and toolbars where temporarily shrinking a window might hide part of a short text string.

<description>, <label>, and <text> are real XUL tags in the sense that they are backed by a C/C++ implementation. They do not originate from a design practice based on a user-defined tag, as <spacer> does.

3.2.1.2 DTD Text Document type definitions are used in Mozilla XUL applications to replace language-specific text with more generic terms.

The XML 1.0 standard defines syntax for DTDs. In general, DTDs are used to specify what terms are available to an XML document. In the most complex case, a DTD defines the whole of an XML application's tagset, like all the XUL tags. In the more common simple case, a small DTD fragment adds new terms that document authors find convenient.

As an example, a DTD fragment can make a memorable name like ` ` (an HTML no-break-space character) available to the document author. XUL does not define ` ` so, without such assistance, an author must remember the raw and obscure ` `.

Memorable entities can stand for whole strings (entity references) as well as single characters (character entity references). If this seems unfamiliar, then review section 4.2.2 "External Entities" of the XML 1.0 standard. In summary, a DOCTYPE declaration like

```
<!DOCTYPE html [ ... ]>
```

makes extra ENTITY declarations (or other DTD content) available. A piece of code in a XUL file, like that in Listing 3.1, is the same (roughly) as a `#include` in C/C++ or `require` in Perl:

Listing 3.1 Use of a DOCTYPE declaration to include XML entities from a file.

```
<!DOCTYPE html [
  <!ENTITY % textDTD SYSTEM "text.dtd">
  %textDTD;
  ] >
```

The `text.dtd` file is human-readable and contains one or more lines like this:

```
<!ENTITY text.welcome "Welcome to my Application">
```

To use such an entity, the equivalent XUL or XML looks like this:

```
<description>&text.welcome;</description>
```

or like this:

```
<description value="&text.welcome;"/>
```

Therefore, using entities, an application can be completely translated to Esperanto, Klingon, or whatever. Only the DTD file needs to be modified. The XUL document doesn't need to be touched. Many examples of these `.dtd` files can be seen in the chrome of Mozilla.

Because these entities can appear in XML attribute values, they can also store style information. This is for the rare case where one localized version needs to be styled differently from another. Perhaps a Cantonese menu should be red or a Western bridal invitation should be white.

The most significant thing about DTDs is that they are read-only. This is sufficient for 90% of an application's text needs, but not all.

3.2.1.3 `<stringbundle>`, `<string>`, and Property Files DTDs are of no use if a displayed string of text needs to change while the application is running. Mozilla provides a separate mechanism for storing strings that can be read and manipulated. Such strings are often required for error messages, user feedback, and all occasions where a string needs to contain some computed value. In Mozilla, a collection of such strings is called a string bundle.

Mozilla stores string bundles in a property file, which is similar to a Java property file. The nearest Microsoft Windows technology is an `.ini` file. The nearest UNIX technology is perhaps `strfile(1)`. A Mozilla property file has the extension `.properties`, and the content of the file consists of single lines of human-readable text. An example is

```
instruct-last=To continue, click Next.
```

"instruct-last" is a string name, "To continue, click Next." is the string value. A set of these lines makes a string bundle—a tiny database of strings—for a Mozilla application to work with.

Such property files must be stored in the locale subdirectory of a chrome package. A full URL for a string bundle is, therefore,

```
chrome://packagename/local/filename.properties
```

From the point of view of pure XUL, string bundles are boring. Listing 3.2 shows everything you can do with them.

Listing 3.2 String bundles declared from XUL.

```
<stringbundleset>
  <stringbundle id="menus" src="menus.properties"/>
  <stringbundle id="tips" src="tips.properties"/>
  <stringbundle id="status" src="status.properties"/>
</stringbundleset>
```

None of these tags produce any visible content. All they do is make string bundles available to JavaScript scripts. The `<stringbundleset>` tag isn't even a real tag—it's just a user-defined container that holds the `<stringbundle>` tags. Both tags have enough default styling to make them completely invisible.

This kind of XUL demonstrates an important feature of the language. The use of a container tag, usually with a name ending in `-set`, is a common idiom. Even though tags such as `<stringbundleset>` do nothing, using them to collect together a group of like statements (the `<stringbundle>` tags) is good coding practice. It is tidy and highly readable. It's recommended that you always collect your invisible sets of tags together like this and put them at the start of your XUL document.

JavaScript does all the work when it comes to string bundles. Chapter 5, Scripting, explains and has an example. It's also possible to access a string bundle directly from code without using any XUL content at all.

In addition to all these text mechanisms, JavaScript scripts and RDF documents can supply textual content to a XUL application. That kind of content is even less static than string bundles.

3.2.2 Images and `<image>`

HTML has the `<IMG>` tag; XUL has the `<image>` tag. They are the same. An example piece of code is

```
<image src="myimage.jpg"/>
```

Images have a minimum width and height matching the image to be displayed. If flex is applied to an <image> tag, the image loses those minimums and can be squeezed quite small. To preserve those minimums, reapply width and height styles or attributes.

There are two very useful image techniques. Both relate to the decorative information stored in Mozilla skins and themes. Even though XUL has an <image> tag, images used in skins or themes should not be stated that way; they should be specified in the stylesheet. A style containing an image URL can be attached to a content-less tag like this:

```
<description class="placeholder"/>
```

An example of a matching style is

```
.placeholder { list-style-image: url("face.gif"); }
```

Second, a large number of images can be reduced to a single file. The clipping features of CSS can be used to display from the large file the subimage required as follows:

```
#foo {-moz-image-region: rect(48px 16px 64px 0px); }
```

and similarly

```
#foo:hover {-moz-image-region: rect(48px 32px 64px 16px); }
```

Using this technique, image rollovers caused by mouse movements and other CSS pseudo-class effects are implemented. Such rollovers, where one image is replaced with another, had in the past required separate JavaScript code, but CSS2 advances have made that unnecessary. This technique is used routinely in Mozilla's own skins and themes. Figure 3.2 shows the Classic

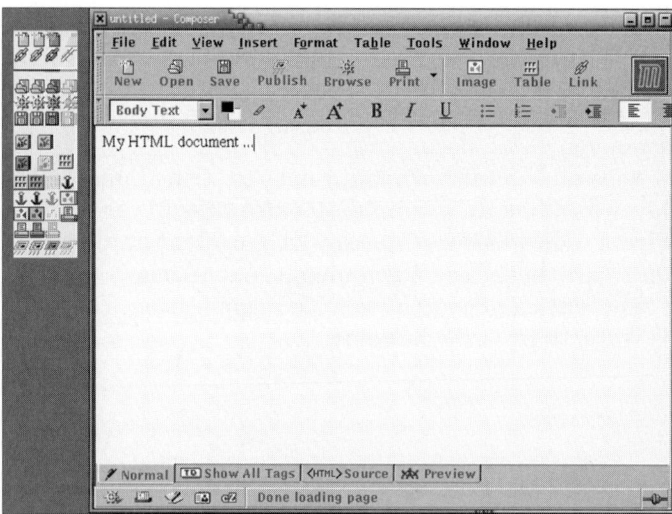

Fig. 3.2 Composer window with clipped images and original image.

Composer with classic skin, and a chrome file from `classic.jar` that is responsible for many of the visible icons.

Mozilla also has new support for the Microsoft Windows `.bmp` image format.

3.2.3 Border Decorations

Mozilla supports an extensive set of border decorations based on CSS2, plus some extensions. These are covered in the "Style Options" section of this chapter. One entirely standard CSS2 style that deserves special mention is `overflow:scroll`.

A typical use of this style is to provide a scrollable region of static text, such as a license disclaimer. All that is required is two user-defined tags, one inside the other, with the desired content inside both. For HTML, such a tag is `<SPAN>`; for XUL, use `<box>`.

Note that these scrollbars are not themselves scriptable objects, which is something of a weakness. This styling technique is recommended only where the state of the scrollbars is not important. In the default XUL case, CSS2 scrollbars are always visible.

XUL has a number of better methods for managing scrollbars, including a quite general `<scrollbox>` tag. Scrollbars are discussed more generally in Chapter 8, Navigation.

3.3 Understanding Font Systems

Displaying text is not a simple process at all. To display text on a bitmapped interface (a non-character-based terminal), every character in the text must be rendered into a set of pixels. Mozilla is sensitive to the way this is done, and applications or HTML pages can look good or bad as a result. Problems exist mostly on UNIX platforms. Figure 3.3 shows the letter A as rendered on the screen by Mozilla under four different circumstances.

Each of these characters (a glyph) is taken from one Mozilla window. In each case, the style

```
{ font-family : Times; font-size : 72pt; }
```

has been applied, although a little cheating with `font-size` is done to make the letters appear about the same across different desktops. The blob under

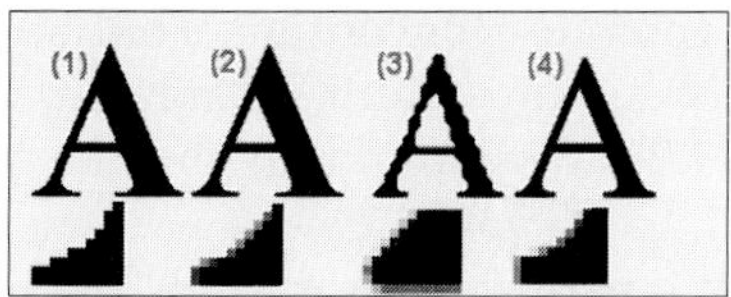

Fig. 3.3 Four Mozilla glyphs for the letter A across Windows and UNIX.

each letter is the bottom tip of the left stroke of the letter, magnified five times. Obviously, things need to be set up correctly if character glyphs are to look their best on the screen.

Images (1) and (2) of Figure 3.3 are taken from Microsoft Windows; images (3) and (4) are taken under UNIX, using the X-Windows system, which is the fundamental display technology for UNIX/Linux. Clearly the letters are different shapes across the two operating systems. That is because there were at least three versions of the Times font at work; a TrueType version on Windows; a "scalable" bitmapped font on UNIX, and a Type1 font on UNIX. If your XUL application is to be perfectly portable, then the same implementation of a given font, stored in the same font format, must be available on all platforms. That is the best step toward sanity. Another step is to arrange matters so that the font looks good.

The two Windows version of "A" differ only by the rendering process. In the Microsoft Windows Control Panel, in the Display Control, under the Effects tab, the option "Smooth edges of screen fonts" is ticked in one case but not in the other. This option turns on an *anti-aliased* rendering of glyphs. In Microsoft-speak, this is also called sub-pixel accuracy.

What is anti-aliasing? First, aliasing is the process of taking a font description of a single glyph and converting it to a rectangle of dots or pixels for display. Because many points in the initial description end up in the same pixel, those points are said to have the same alias. This system relies on the final glyph being one solid color. This is the first-generation way to bit-render fonts. Anti-aliasing takes advantage of the increased color depth of modern monitors. It partially shades extra pixels to improve the appearance of the glyph. This is called anti-aliasing because fewer points on the original glyph match a given pixel. Even so, there is still quite a bit of aliasing going on. Anti-aliasing is the second-generation way to render fonts. Anti-aliasing makes characters look smoother, but fuzzier. It is only recommended on fonts where the font size *measured in pixels* is not too small. It also requires a monitor that supports many shades of gray—more than 256 colors per pixel, ideally. Anti-aliasing is at work in three of the four magnified images in Figure 3.3.

In the UNIX versions of "A", both glyphs are anti-aliased, but one looks awful. Clearly, a smart rendering algorithm is not enough; Mozilla must be able to find a decent font as well. This is an issue for both the platform and the operating system. The better image (4) comes from Mozilla 1.0, the worse image (3) comes from Mozilla 1.21. That is not what you might expect. The reason is that the better image comes from a special custom version of Mozilla 1.0. That version was compiled with extra pieces of X-Windows support bundled together using the `--enable-xft` compile-time option. That support is not available by default in Mozilla for UNIX. The default Mozilla 1.0 displays "A" no better than the default of Mozilla 1.21. Why would an obvious improvement not be in the standard distribution?

This extra X support is turned off for a performance reason. The reason is complex and has to do with the architecture of X-Window. X-Window works as follows: Programs send instructions to a dedicated X-server (like Xfree86, VNC, X-Terminal firmware, or Reflection), which then draws things on the screen. All X-based applications are no more than pictures drawn by an X-server as directed by the application. There is a standard set of instructions that the server can accept. This set is the X11 Protocol, and it doesn't include sophisticated font display. The X11 Protocol supports extensions, which are optional features of the server. The RENDER extension supports sophisticated font display—exactly what you need. Most servers do not (yet) implement that extension. So Mozilla cannot rely on it being present in the server. Consequently, there is first a functionality problem, not a performance problem. To see if your server does support RENDER, run `xdpyinfo` at the command line.

The performance problem is introduced because the `--enable-xft` version of Mozilla uses RENDER anyway. Instead of telling the server to do it, the Mozilla client has RENDER built in. It uses this extension to turn every glyph from a character code plus font information plus a RENDER X11 instruction into a rendered pixmap (an image) and a standard X11 instruction. This means all characters are sent to the X-server as images. Instead of requiring a few bytes per character, RENDER uses over 100 bytes per character—and as much as 1,000 bytes for a large character. That is the performance issue.

This change from characters to images is not always a killer. The X-Window system already has a performance issue of its own that dwarfs anything that Mozilla might add. An understanding of X11's issue will help you decide whether the RENDER support in Mozilla is worth having.

Modern X-based applications, like Mozilla, the GIMP, and OpenOffice, contain many images used for icons, buttons, and other user-interface cues. The X11 system was originally designed for monochrome monitors (one bit per pixel), but now monitors are 8-, 24-, or 32-bits per pixel. Therefore, images have become both more common and a lot bigger. The communication traffic between X-servers and X-clients is now dominated by those images, in the same way that most internet bandwidth is spent on Web-based images. If this is the environment that Mozilla works in, then adding more images is not going to make much difference. In that case, use the RENDER support if you like. A typical example that applies in this case is when all of your computing technology is running on a single UNIX or Linux computer, and you use KDE or GNOME.

When the X11 system uses few images, or it operates over a slow connection, then Mozilla with RENDER support can become a real issue and should be avoided at that point. The most common scenario is when the X-server is remote. This is how Reflection works. It is also the case if you run an X-server at home (on a PC or an X-terminal) and dial up to a host running X-applications at work. This is *not* the case for VNC. The VNC server is remote to the VNC client, and the server contains an X-server. Mozilla won't affect VNC performance.

For desktop integration, Mozilla 1.0–1.4 is based on the GTK 1.x widget library that sits on top of X-Windows. The existing X enhancements will work under GNOME 2.0 or KDE or later because the older GTK libraries exist on those newer versions as well. Thus, choosing to use a RENDER-enabled version of Mozilla does not create an upgrade problem for your current desktop.

If these UNIX font issues grab your attention, there is much to learn. You can begin your search in several different places. The file fonts HOWTO is a standard FAQ delivered with most Linux systems; the subject of *twips* is a deep architectural matter that applies to Mozilla font display, Microsoft Windows, and graphical displays in general; the matters at `www.fontconfig.org` will explain the basics of the Xft font-serving system; and the X-Window organization can be found at `www.x.org`.

Finally, Figure 3.3 is unnecessarily harsh on the default version of Mozilla. A simple solution is just to get more fonts. The Linux fonts HOWTO document contains pointers to many fonts. Mozilla can even look beautiful with just plain bitmapped fonts (the most primitive and brain-dead of fonts). All that is required is an X-installed bitmap font for every font at every point size used in your Web documents. Such fonts take a long time to make, unless you're a font specialist. Mozilla does not support embeddable fonts (fonts downloaded "live" from the Web).

If you don't want to compile Mozilla yourself, an `--enable-xft` version for GTK1.x can be had from `ftp://ftp.mozilla.org` in RPM format. This version will install only on top of the standard Mozilla installation that exists in `/usr/bin/mozilla` and `/usr/lib/mozilla`.

3.4 Style Options

Mozilla's most decorative extensions relate to the Box Model of CSS2. That model describes how a box of content can have a rectangular border. That border can have a simple line style applied to it. Mozilla supports CSS2 borders; however, some line styles do not work.

Mozilla's extensions allow for even more decorative borders. Borders can have fancy corners and may be multicolored. Borders can have transparent lines along their length. Table 3.1 lists these extensions.

These extensions bear some explaining. Mozilla has two separate border enhancements, and they don't work together. Listing 3.3 illustrates both.

Listing 3.3 Mozilla border style examples.

```
#box1 {
    border:solid thick;
    border-width:20px; margin:20px; padding:20px;
    border-color:gray;

    -moz-border-radius-topright: 20px;
    -moz-border-radius-bottomright: 40px;
    }
```

```
#box2 {
    border:solid thick;
    border-width:20px; margin:20px; padding:20px;
    border-top-color : gray;

    -moz-border-right-colors :
    #000000 #101010 #202020 #303030
   #404040 #505050 #606060 #707070
   #808080 #909090 #A0A0A0 #B0B0B0
   #C0C0C0 #D0D0D0 transparent #000000;

    -moz-border-bottom-colors :
    #000000 #101010 #202020 #303030
   #404040 #505050 #606060 #707070
   #808080 #909090 #A0A0A0 #B0B0B0
   #C0C0C0 #D0D0D0 transparent #000000;
}
```

The first enhancement provides corner rounding, but the border must be one solid color. A few border-style values (like double) are supported, but not all are maintained. The second enhancement allows a border to be shaded different colors. In this case, the border is drawn as a series of concentric lines one pixel wide. Each line is drawn in a different color from a supplied color list, starting from the outside edge of the border. If colors run out, the last color is used until the border is finished. If rounding is attempted for a shaded

Table 3.1 Style extensions for Box Model borders

Property or Selector	Values	Use
-moz-border-radius	As for margin, use px units only	Dictates the roundness of the corners of a border or outline.
-moz-border-radius-topleft	-moz-border-radius-topright	-moz-border-radius-bottom-left
-moz-border-radius-bottomright	Px	Roundness or flatness of a single border corner. 0 for square. Curved for single-color borders; slanted for multicolor borders.
-moz-border-bottom-colors	-moz-border-top-colors	-moz-border-left-colors
-moz-border-right-colors	Color list plus "transparent" and CSS2 special values	Colors for a single border. Any number of colors may be specified, with each color painted one pixel wide. The last color fills the remainder.

border, then the corners are drawn cut instead of rounded. Figure 3.4 shows the result.

It is possible using these extensions to create jagged, nonmatching border corners, but that is a consequence of poor XUL use rather than any fundamental flaw in Mozilla.

Some of these border styles also apply to CSS2 outlines. Mozilla's outline support is described in the "Style Options" section of Chapter 7, Forms and Menus.

Mozilla also supports style extensions for images. The `list-style-image` property discussed earlier is a standard CSS2 property, not an extension. Table 3.2 illustrates.

Separate to both layout and content issues are a few miscellaneous and generally applicable style extensions. They are noted in Table 3.3.

Note that XUL does not support the CSS2 text-decoration style. That style provides underline and strikethrough decorations.

CSS3 is in development as this is written, and Mozilla has partial support for it. CSS3 will include support for Internet Explorer 6.0's "border box model." Mozilla will likely support this eventually, but that has not happened yet.

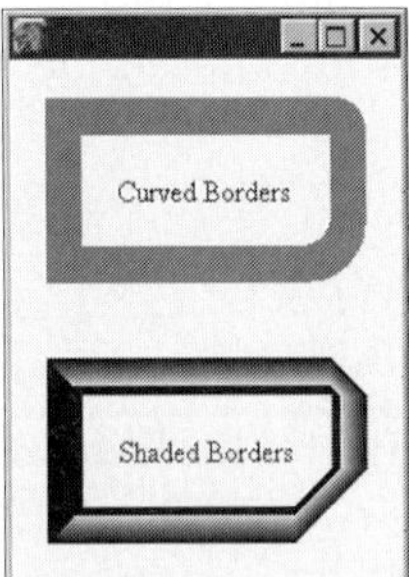

Fig. 3.4 Mozilla custom border styles.

Table 3.2 Style extensions for HTML—new features

Property	Values	Use
-moz-background-clip	Border, padding	Near-complete CSS3 background-border support. Mozilla 1.2+.
-moz-background-origin	Border, padding, content	Near-complete CSS3 background-origin support. Mozilla 1.2+.
-moz-force-broken-image-icon	1=true, 0=false	Display the "image failed to load" image instead of a real image.
-moz-image-region	As for clip	Display only a portion of an image.

Table 3.3 Style extensions applicable to most XULtags

Property	Value	Use
Any property	-moz-initial	Set this property to the value it would have if there were no style cascading or inheritance.
Most properties	inherit	As for HTML/XHTML.
Any font property	Desktop fonts	See "Style Options," Chapter 10, Windows and Panes
Any color property	Desktop colors	See "Style Options," Chapter 10, Windows and Panes
-moz-binding	None or url()	Attaches a nominated XBL binding to the tag. See XBL.
-moz-opacity	0.0 to 1.0	Make content semitransparent—equivalent to an alpha channel

3.5 Hands On: NoteTaker Boilerplate

In this "Hands On" session, we will fill with text the skeletal structure of the dialog box started in the last chapter. We also will explain how to set up locales, although they're not used in the NoteTaker running example.

Layout is a kind of content, but to the user it's invisible. Real user content is visible. Boilerplate text is text in the panel of a window that never changes. The term *boilerplate* comes from the early days of printing and is also used in form design. Our content strategy is to include enough boilerplate text that a useful screenshot can be taken. Our overall goal is to produce something ultra-quickly that we can throw to the wolves: that is, to the users, analysts, and usability people. They will almost certainly tear it apart, and large pieces will be thrown out. By providing a very early draft, hours rather than weeks of work are thrown out. Ideally, this will all happen long before the specification stage—by then the details of the screens will be rigidly locked down.

3.5.1 Adding Text

Because we haven't covered any widgets yet, the content part of this dialog box will be fairly simple. Anywhere a widget should be, we'll just put an empty box as a placeholder, with its border turned on. Listing 3.4 shows the fragments of content added to the layout.

Listing 3.4 XUL content for the NoteTaker dialog box.

```
<text value="Edit"/>
<text value="Keywords"/>
```

```
<description>Summary</description>
<box/>
<description>Details</description>
<box flex="1"/>

<caption label="Options"/>
<description>Chop Query</description>
<description>Home Page</description>

<caption label="Size"/>
<description>Width</description>
<description>Height</description>
<description>Top</description>
<description>Left</description>

<box/>
<box/>
<box/>
<box/>

<description>px</description>
<description>px</description>
<description>px</description>
<description>px</description>

<text value="Cancel"/>
<spacer flex="1"/>
<text value="Save"/>
```

As you can see, this is all fairly trivial. Note how `<text>` is used where the content has a command-like purpose and `<description>` is used where the content has an instructional purpose. By systematically listing the content, we have already picked up and corrected one error: *Bottom* should read *Left*, since content elements are positioned with the top and left pair of style properties.

The result of adding this content is shown in Figure 3.5.

All that remains is to clean up the styles so that unwanted box borders disappear. Proud as we are of this achievement, the resultant window is still pretty ugly and primitive. It needs real widgets, and it needs a beautifully designed stylesheet. In the next chapter, we'll add button widgets and a skin to NoteTaker.

We can stop there, and we will, but we also have the option of internationalizing NoteTaker so that it can be presented in different languages. To do this, we use a DTD file (with `.dtd` extension) and set up Mozilla's locale system. Doing that reduces the readability of the examples in this book, so we don't apply it here.

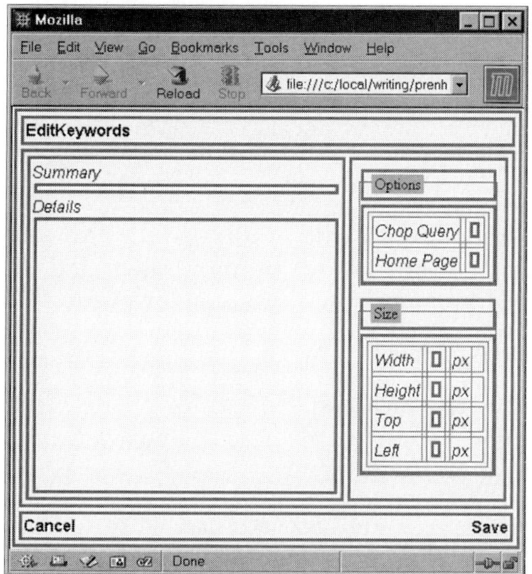

Fig. 3.5 First draft of the NoteTaker dialog box.

3.5.2 Configuring and Using Locales

For your own projects, here is how to get localization working. First, all static text in the original XUL must be replaced with XML entity references. That means that a tag like

```
<text value="Cancel"/>
```

gains a suggestively named entity reference like

```
<text value="&editDialog.cancel"/>
```

In this chapter, we identified all the static text, so the set of changes is totally obvious. The entity `editDialog.cancel` needs to be declared and defined in a DTD. We merely create a file with one or more lines like this in it:

```
<!ENTITY editDialog.cancel       "Cancel">
```

It really is that simple. Since "Cancel" is English, this file must contain an English language locale, such as `en-US`, or `en-UK`. For U.S. English, we put this file at this path:

```
chrome/notetaker/locale/en-US/edit.dtd
```

The name `edit.dtd` just reminds us this file is for the edit dialog we're making. It could be used for the whole NoteTaker application, or any part of it. This DTD fragment must be included in the application, so we expand the `<!DOCTYPE>` declaration in `editDialog.xul` to do that, using standard XML syntax. It goes from

```
<!DOCTYPE window>
```

to

```
<!DOCTYPE window [
<!ENTITY % editDTD SYSTEM "chrome://notetaker/locale/edit.dtd">
%editDTD;
]>
```

Note that this `chrome:` URL doesn't have any locale name. It will be mangled by Mozilla at run time so that the locale name is added. If the current locale is `en-US`, the URL will be mangled to read:

```
chrome://notetaker/locale/en-US/edit.dtd
```

This matches where we put the locale-specific information. In fact, that new URL is incompletely changed. It illustrates how the current locale is substituted in, but the fully modified URL will be:

```
resource://chrome/notetaker/locale/en-US/edit.dtd
```

Finally, we want the platform to understand that this locale-specific information is available for use, and that NoteTaker should benefit from it. Otherwise, Mozilla won't bother to look for package-specific locale files. To do that, we need to give the locale a `contents.rdf` file and to update the `installed-chrome.txt` file again. The `contents.rdf` file looks like Listing 3.5.

Listing 3.5 `contents.rdf` for a chrome locale.

```
<?xml version="1.0"?>
<RDF
  xmlns="http://www.w3.org/1999/02/22-rdf-syntax-ns#"
  xmlns:chrome="http://www.mozilla.org/rdf/chrome#">

  <Seq about="urn:mozilla:locale:root">
    <li resource="urn:mozilla:locale:en-US"/>
  </Seq>

  <Description about="urn:mozilla:locale:en-US">
    <chrome:packages>
      <Seq about="urn:mozilla:locale:en-US:packages">
        <li resource="urn:mozilla:locale:en-US:notetaker"/>
      </Seq>
    </chrome:packages>
  </Description>

</RDF>
```

This file can be used for any locale, just by changing the strings "en-US" and "notetaker." Just treat this file as an anonymous block of text for the minute. RDF is described in detail from Chapter 11, RDF, onward. The three `chrome:` attributes of the `<Description>` tag can be dropped if the locale exists anywhere in the chrome already. In this case, they could be dropped because the Classic Browser already uses U.S. English. This file just says that the locale `en-US` exists (the three early lines), and that the notetaker package has `en-US` locale information (the seven later lines).

After creating this file, bring the `installed-chrome.txt` file up to date. It needs this one additional line:

```
locale,install,url,resource:/chrome/notetaker/locale/en-US/
```

That tells the platform that the locale exits, and the saved file tells the platform to reinspect the chrome the next time it starts. If the user swaps locales in the platform preferences, then `notetaker` will now automatically use `different.dtd` files for its referenced entities.

The chrome locale system also supports versioning. Version information can be supplied in the `contents.rdf` files in the chrome. See Chapter 15, XBL Bindings, for more information on versions.

3.6 Debug Corner: The DOM Inspector

The DOM Inspector is a tool supplied with the Classic Browser. It is a great toy to play with and has two immediate uses: It is a diagnostic aid, and it is a learning aid. Here we point to those immediate uses. You can explore its functionality for yourself.

To get the DOM inspector working, start it from the Tasks | Web Development menu in a Navigator window. From the DOM Inspector window, choose File | Inspect a window ... and then choose any window except the one labeled "DOM Inspector." Avoid selecting DOM Inspector because it's confusing to look at a window that's analyzing itself. That inspect action should put content in the left and right panels of the DOM Inspector window. In the DOM Inspector window, under Edit | Preferences, make sure Blink Selected Element is ticked, and that Blink Duration is set to at least 2,500 milliseconds (for beginners).

It turns out that most of the DOM Inspector main menu items are of trivial use. The two most useful things to press are the small icons at the top left of the two content panels. They look like tiny Windows Explorer windows in "small icons" mode. These icons are buttons and drop-down menus. From the left menu, choose DOM Nodes; from the right menu choose Computed Style. You are now ready to explore the content of any Mozilla window. This setup is shown in Figure 3.6. Interesting items to press are circled.

The left panel is a tree-oriented view of the full XML hierarchy that makes up a Mozilla window. Since all Mozilla windows start with XUL, this is a hierarchy of XUL tags. Some Windows, like Navigator windows, also include HTML tags. You can drill down the hierarchy just by clicking on the branches of the tree, or you can click-select a single tag. When you click on a tag, that tag flashes a red border in the real window it comes from. If the tag is invisible, then a zero height or width border (a line) flashes. This left panel usually

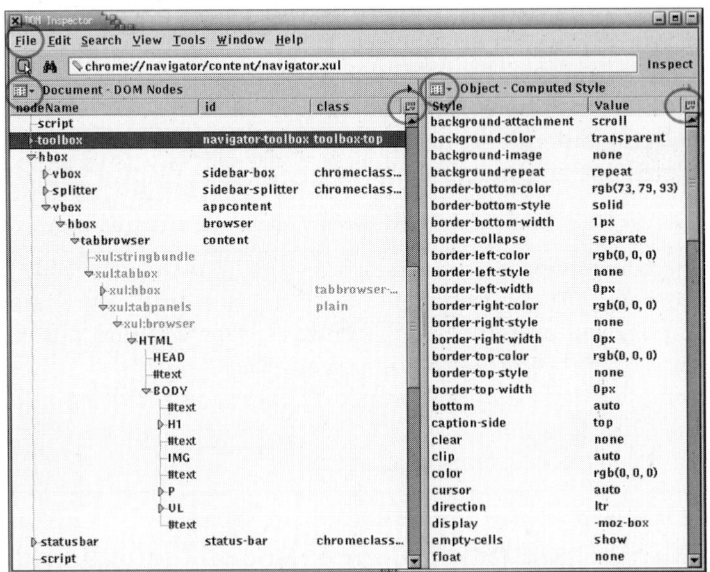

Fig. 3.6 DOM inspector breakdown of a Navigator window showing HTML.

shows three columns: NodeName, id, and class. More columns can be added with the column picker icon at the top right of the panel.

The right panel shows one of a number of specialist panels, which also have column pickers. These panels reveal content for the currently selected tag. As an example, the Computed Style panel shows the style of the currently selected tag after all the CSS2 cascading has taken place. This is the "real" style of the tag, as it appears on the screen.

The circles on the screenshot show the bits of the DOM Inspector that are interesting to press. If, on Microsoft Windows, you happen to find a button in the DOM Inspector labeled "Capture", then pressing it is a great way to crash the platform before it has a chance to work.

The simplest use of the DOM Inspector is diagnosis. It can help you make sense of complex XUL documents by showing you the live state of the document. The tree-structured view of your document and the flashing red borders makes it easy to see what tag in the tree is responsible for what visual element. It may give you ideas for a better breakdown of your XUL. The id and class columns let you see immediately if the styles you expected are attached to the right tags.

The other obvious use of the DOM Inspector is spying, also called learning. It allows you to deconstruct all the XUL supplied with the Classic Browser—or in fact, any Mozilla-based product. This is a fascinating activity that can teach you a great deal about how the Mozilla programmers created the standard chrome content. It also completely smashes the myth that the Classic Browser is built mysteriously and cryptically by hard-core programmers. Much of Mozilla is just XUL documents and friends. Try the DOM Inspector on everything including alert boxes and the preferences window. Figure 3.6 shows a DOM Inspector breakdown of a Classic Browser window. Both the browser's XUL and the contained HTML document are shown in the screenshot.

3.7 Summary

The simplest thing you can do with XUL is display static text and images. Such content is very easy to add. The `<description>` tag has powerful line-wrap features but usually only supplies small amounts of text at a time. Images and styles in XUL are very much like HTML. Fancy borders are a Mozilla feature of both, and Mozilla has numerous style extensions, some of which are content- or layout-specific.

XUL without GUI widgets is hardly more than HTML. In the next chapter, you'll see how to add that most famous of widgets, the button. Improving the overall appearance of XUL is also a theme for Chapter 4, First Widgets and Themes.

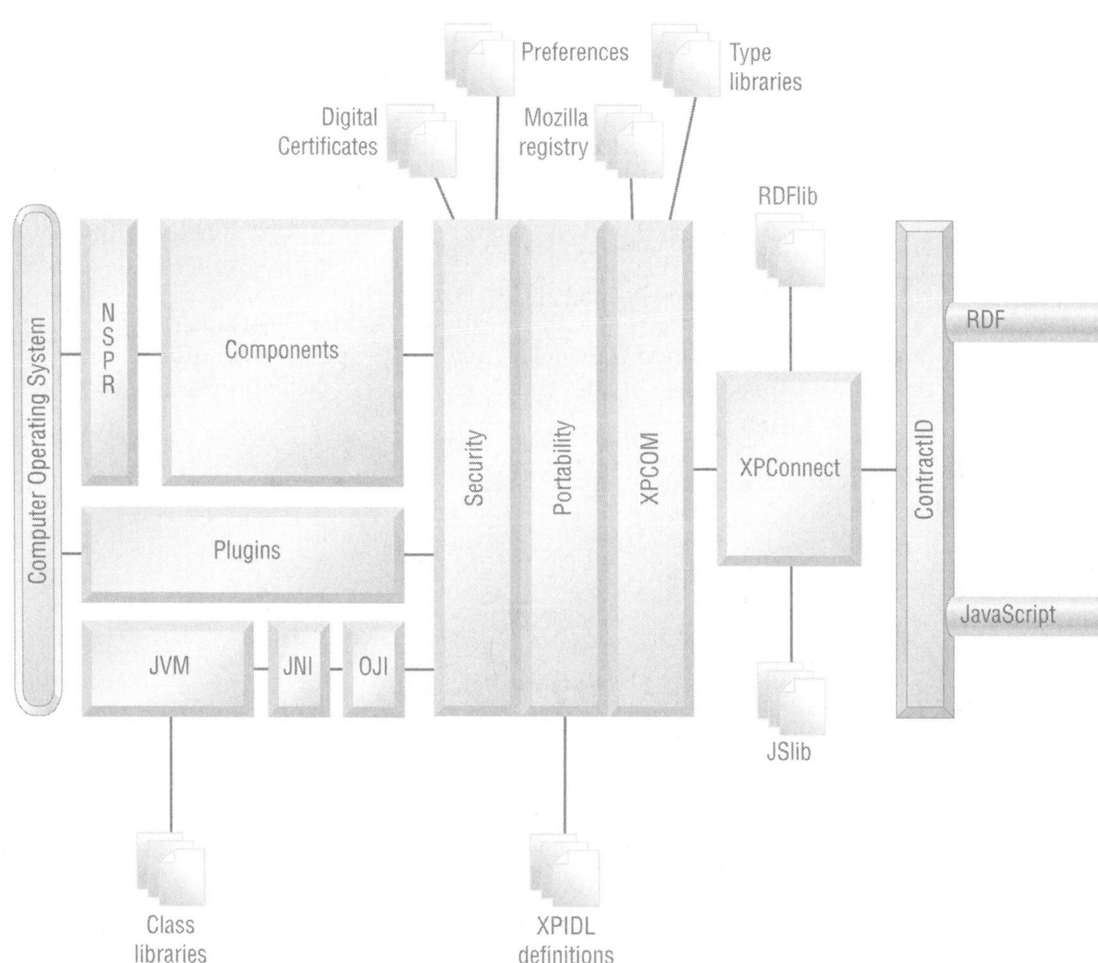
Preferences
Type libraries
Digital Certificates
Mozilla registry
RDFlib
Computer Operating System
NSPR
Components
Security
Portability
XPCOM
XPConnect
ContractID
RDF
JavaScript
Plugins
JVM
JNI
OJI
JSlib
Class libraries
XPIDL definitions

CHAPTER 4

First Widgets and Themes

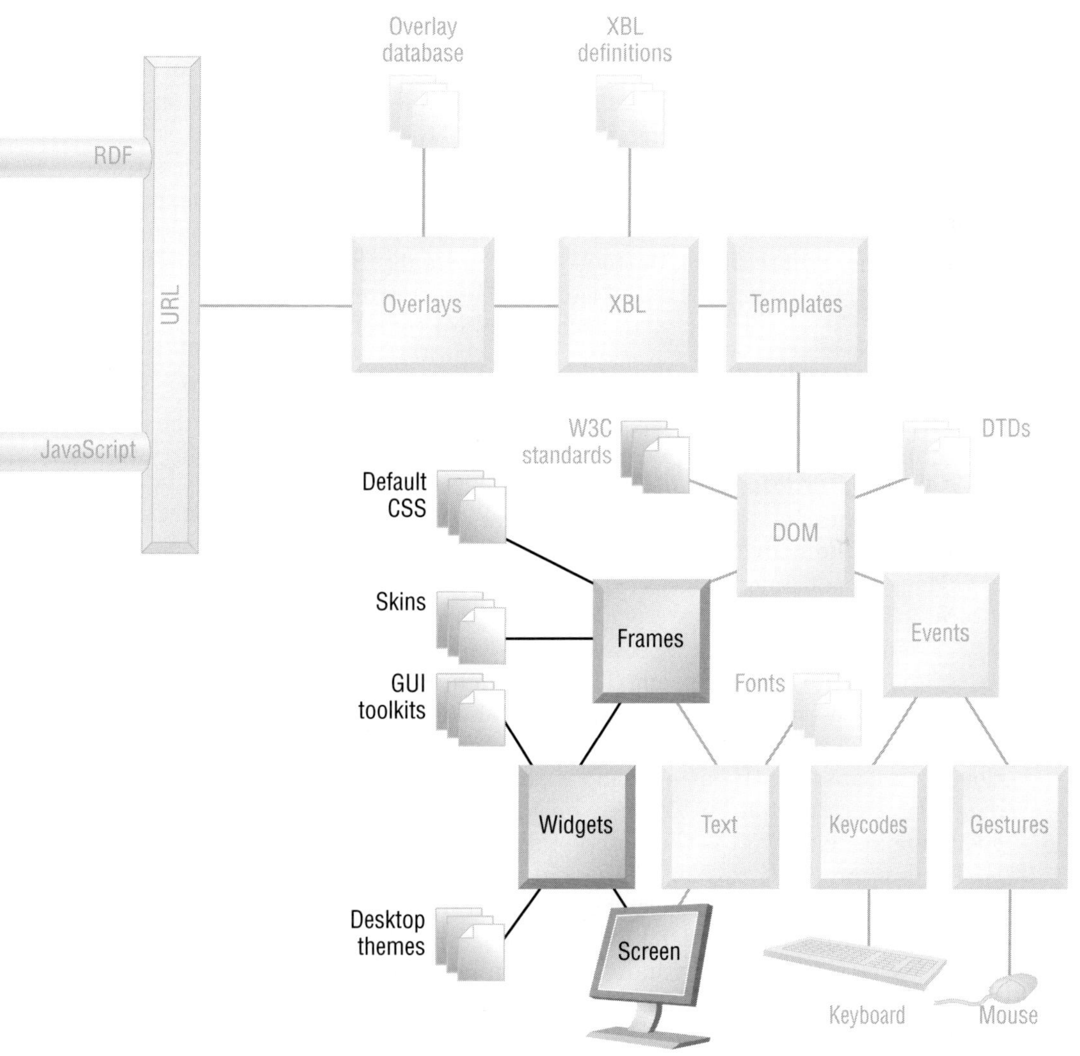

This chapter explains how to use XUL buttons and how to change their appearance with the Mozilla theme system. The Mozilla theme system can be used to change the appearance of all XUL tags.

Mozilla applications are interactive, which means that there are screen controls that users can manipulate. The simplest control available is the humble "Press Me" button. Buttons are so useful that Mozilla has a wide variety, although all are expressed in XUL markup. The simplest example of a button is the `<button>` tag, expressed as easily as this:

```
<button label="Press Me"/>
```

This is a very quick way to create a useable button and therein lies the value of XUL. A button also needs some kind of script, or else pressing it may have no ultimate effect. Effect-less buttons are hardly useful for practical applications. This chapter is more concerned with learning about buttons than about implementing their actions.

Buttons are easy in concept. Just look around you; they cover the surface of most technological devices: the phone, the CD player, the dashboard, and even the rice cooker. It seems like a significant part of life's purpose is to press them. For the lighter side of buttons, try "The Really Big Button That Doesn't Do Anything" Web page; it's also a cautionary tale for UI designers. In Mozilla, buttons are the simplest way to decorate plain text and image content with widgets.

A *widget*, of course, is a small graphical building block for GUI-based applications. The most common widgets are those that make up menus, forms, and scrollbars. Some widgets can move, transform, change, or animate; others can't. Widgets are the concern of programmers, since they typically come in 3GL or OO libraries, like GTK, Qt, Swing, and Win32. When a user and a widget interact, the widget changes appearance so that the user knows that they have done something. Widgets are all about helping the user's brain complete interactive tasks. Buttons are perhaps the simplest widget.

From a technology perspective, some widgets (including buttons) are not as simple as they might seem. There's much going on in button-land. This complexity is a great excuse to learn more about the Mozilla Platform.

The NPA diagram at the start of this chapter shows the bits of Mozilla closely associated with buttons, and with the content of this chapter. From the diagram, it's clear that buttons rely heavily on a widget toolkit provided by the operating system. That is the functional side of a button. What is less obvious is that buttons also rely on the world of styles, themes, and skins. This is because a button's appearance is as fundamental as its function. If it doesn't look like a button, then it isn't one. So far, this book has managed to sidestep any discussion of themes by hand-waving a lot about styles. Before complicating Mozilla too much, the theme system needs to be explained. It is explained in this chapter.

A subtle aspect of buttons is the way in which they interact with other XUL tags. So far, the only interaction between tags has involved one tag being the content of another. Buttons, however, interact with tags in a number of novel ways. This chapter describes those interactions; it could even be subtitled: "Secret Relationships Between Tags." A full-blown description of XUL's complex tag systems is left to later in the book. The goal here is just to expose some of the simpler interactions as a taste of what's ahead.

The broader issues of building forms and of handling user input via keystrokes and clicks are covered in Chapter 6, Events. There's more than enough in simple buttons to fill this chapter.

4.1 What Makes a Button a Button?

Markup languages like HTML and XUL provide many options for visual display. Sometimes it's hard to tell what is "real" and what is just clever animation and a bit of scripting. The discussion on buttons and widgets starts by looking at what a Mozilla widget really is. Thinking about XML-based widgets can be a bit messy, as the following example shows.

Figure 4.1 is a simple XUL application containing one "real" button and two fakes. Which is the real one? Although the third candidate is in the middle of a mouse-click operation, any of the three could be clicked.

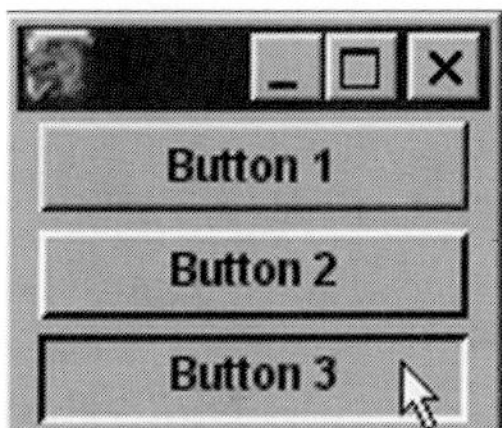

Fig. 4.1 Fake and real buttons in Mozilla.

In this figure, button 1 is the "real" button. The other two buttons are just `<vbox>` tags with a sole `<description>` tag as content. The `<vbox>` tags are styled as shown in Listing 4.1.

Listing 4.1 Button-like styles for <box> tags.

```
vbox
{
    border : solid;
    border-width : 2px;
    margin : 2px 6px;
    -moz-box-align : center;
    border-left-color : ButtonHighlight;
    border-top-color : ButtonHighlight;
    border-right-color : ThreeDDarkShadow;
    border-bottom-color : ThreeDDarkShadow;
}
```

```
vbox:active
{
    border-left-color : ThreeDDarkShadow;
    border-top-color : ThreeDDarkShadow;
    border-right-color : ButtonHighlight;
    border-bottom-color : ButtonHighlight;
}
```

The two styles make a <vbox> act a bit like a familiar button when clicked on. These border styles are not identical to the border of the real Button 1, but they could be. Such a styled-up box is not a real Mozilla widget.

On the other hand, even though widget style information doesn't make a widget, style remains important from a user's perspective. Figure 4.2 shows the JavaScript console (under Tools | Web Development), which includes some slightly controversial buttons.

A user could argue that the words "All," "Warnings," and the like aren't much like buttons. If you hover the mouse over these items, then button-like outlines appear, but there is no clue that you should do this. For a new user, these items aren't "normal" buttons, even though functionally they work just fine. The only thing that helps the user out is the fact that such buttons are a common feature of software, but even so, they should contain images rather than text.

Clearly there is a tension between things that look like buttons but don't act like them, and things that act like buttons but don't look like them. Saying "this is a button" can be a hasty statement.

There is a famous GUI design pattern called Model-View-Controller (MVC), which is the key to understanding Mozilla widgets. This piece of design is widely used for GUI systems. It separates a widget into three parts: M, V, and C. The widget's visual appearance is the job of the View. Holding the widget's data is the job of the Model. The Controller is a piece of software that ties the visual appearance of the widget to the data the widget works on.

Each aspect of the MVC pattern holds a different kind of content. The Viewer holds the appearance of the widget. A button must look like a button. The Model holds the application use of the widget, which might either be browser information or form data. A button must also act on the application.

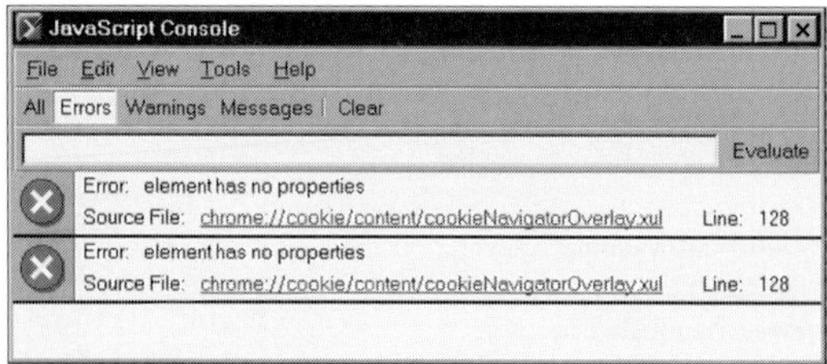

Fig. 4.2 Hidden buttons on the JavaScript console.

The Controller holds the capabilities or the behavior of the widget—what actions the widget can take.

Mozilla widgets are defined by their capabilities. In Mozilla, you can take away a button's appearance (the Viewer) by ignoring style and trivial content. You can take away a button's effect in an application by removing the data (the Model) that it works on. What remains is what a button's *might* do. Anything it might do is a capability (and part of the Controller). Such capabilities make the button what it essentially is. Capabilities are what this chapter tries to focus on.

As an example, the XUL `<button>` tag has some simple and some complex capabilities. The simpler capabilities are button state, event handlers, and button-specific XML attributes. The more complex capabilities include accessibility features for the disabled, navigation list membership, the ability to handle buttons from a GUI toolkit, and the ability to handle native themes.

4.2 The Origins of XUL Widgets

The NPA diagram gives an overview of the technologies used inside Mozilla as a whole. The boxes in that diagram can be rearranged to show the anatomy of a single XUL widget. XUL contains a wide variety of tags, and not all of them are constructed along the same lines. Figure 4.3 is a useful guide that applies in most cases.

At the bottom of the stack are the resources provided by an operating system like Windows, MacOS, or UNIX. At the top of the stack is a user control in a finished application. In between, the low-level services of the operating system are gradually abstracted and simplified into a single XUL tag.

The most primitive widget is that provided by a GUI toolkit library, such as GTK or Win32. It is a native widget, meaning that it is not portable across operating systems. Mozilla supports several different graphic libraries. Sophisticated graphic libraries support desktop themes, so a theme definition may be applied to a native widget.

Fig. 4.3 Widget construction stack.

A Mozilla widget hides the details of the native widget and provides an interface inside Mozilla that is the same for all platforms and all GUI. It is an implementation detail that is not accessible to the application programmer. Several native widgets might be required to make one Mozilla widget.

When a widget is displayed because a document is being loaded into a window, a frame is created to position the widget on the screen. The frame and all the items below it on the stack are written in C/C++. All the items above it in the stack are interpreted, being either XML or CSS documents. As discussed in Chapter 2, XUL Layout, the frame manages any stylesheet information relevant to the item it displays.

Mozilla supports a theme system separate from any desktop system. Each Mozilla theme consists of a set of stylesheets. Each theme stylesheet is known as a skin, and at least one skin provides a set of styles for widgets. This information is applied to any frames holding widgets.

It is very common for a widget to have an XBL definition. An XBL definition is an XML document that defines the XUL tag name, tag attributes, object properties, and object methods for the widget. It does this by attaching a binding to the XUL tag. Finally, an example widget will appear as content in an application document as a single XUL tag. That tag may have other tags (possibly also widgets) as content.

Although Figure 4.3 seems fairly clean and orderly, that is not necessarily the case inside Mozilla. The tag name, for example, can appear in any layer down to "Mozilla Widget," as well as elsewhere inside the platform. The layers are linked together; they are not perfectly separated.

It is not clear from the preceding description why there should be multiple places inside Mozilla where a widget is defined. It's understandable that Mozilla provides a platform-independent widget because that aids portability, but why have an XBL definition as well? Can't it all be done in the one place? The next topic explains Mozilla's strategy.

4.2.1 Split Widget Design

The implementation of most XUL widgets is split in half. The `<button>` tag is a typical example.

The `<button>` tag has both simple, specific capabilities and complex, general capabilities. Some capabilities, like the `type` attribute, are specific to the button. The `type` attribute has a special meaning for the button tag alone. Other capabilities, like navigation list membership, are closely linked to general processing in the Mozilla Platform. Navigation list membership puts a widget in a list that the user can cycle through with the Tab key. When the user presses the Tab key, input focus moves from one widget to the next automatically. These two types of capabilities are handled separately.

The specific parts of the `<button>` tag, including tag attributes, state information, and methods, are all defined in an XBL file. This information is easy to change as the XUL language grows and is fairly independent of other changes to the Mozilla Platform. Chapter 15, XBL Bindings, describes how to make such files. Application programmers that deeply customize Mozilla might choose to modify or copy these files. Modifying an XBL file changes the surface personality of a given widget.

The more integrated part of the <button> tag requires complex logic that reaches across the Mozilla Platform. This is implemented in efficient C/C++ code, using shared aspects of the platform. Such features can only be added by developers of the Mozilla Platform, and so this lower-level set of features appears fixed to application programmers. Making changes at this level modifies the very essence of a given widget.

There is a very rough analogy between this split and the way relational databases store data. In a relational database, each table is assigned a storage type. That type might put data into a B-tree, a hash table, or a heap. Only a few storage types are available, as they come from deep inside the database server. A table using such a storage type is far more flexible than a table whose structure is fixed. This is because the flexible version may be created to have any columns or indexes that seem like a good idea. Like a table, a XUL tag that is a widget is restricted to the features implemented in C/C++, but the XBL definition for the tag can be flexibly created so that the final widget has various characteristics.

4.3 XUL Buttons

XUL provides a number of button-like tags. Two tags fit most common requirements: <button> and <toolbarbutton>. It's rare that you'll need anything more than these. Nevertheless, there are three other button tags worth examining: <autorepeatbutton>, <thumb>, and <scrollbarbutton>. These five tags are the most button-like of the XUL tags. Some of these tags are several button types in one.

Separate from these five tags are a number of other button-like tags. Grippy tags are button-like tags that are attached to other widgets. <label> has some button-like features as well. <statusbarpanel> is discussed in Chapter 8, Navigation, rather than here. Finally, a few tags are worth avoiding because of their incompleteness or their age.

4.3.1 Five Fundamental Buttons

XUL button tags are defined like any other tag and can enclose any content:

```
<button><description label="Tools"/><button>
```

Although any content can be put between the open- and close-tags, Mozilla does not correctly display all combinations of button and content. The goal of XUL 1.0 has been to produce a functional XML language for GUIs. That means that all the straightforward button-content combinations work but that support for more esoteric combinations is patchy. The easiest way to find out if particular content works inside a button is to try it.

Figure 4.4 shows these five buttons in three states each: a normal state; a state with the mouse hovering over; and a state when it has been clicked on but the mouse has not yet been released. A blank entry means that there is no change in appearance for that mouse action.

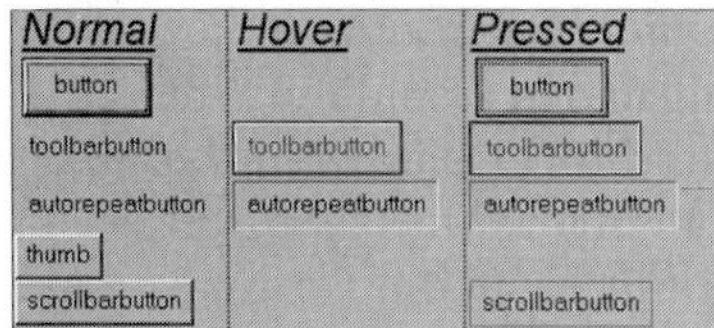

Fig. 4.4 Visual cues given by XUL buttons under the Classic theme.

In Figure 4.4, the content of each button is just a description tag, as shown earlier in the one-line example. Each of the buttons appears and behaves differently from the others. Less obvious is the fact that the internal processing of each button is different. Looking forward briefly to Chapter 6, Events, each of these buttons also supports a subset of the DOM2 events, and therefore a set of JavaScript event handlers.

It is nontrivial to display Figure 4.4 if your version of Mozilla is 1.21 or greater. From that version onward, the Classic theme (only) has special widget support. That support means that widgets such as buttons will look like operating system widgets rather than a Mozilla theme. You can see Mozilla-themed widgets by using an earlier version of Mozilla, by changing the Mozilla theme away from Classic, or by modifying the Classic theme. The section entitled "Themes and Skins" in this chapter explains how all that works.

4.3.1.1 `<button>` The `<button>` tag is the workhorse of Mozilla buttons and is equivalent to the `<button>` tag in HTML. As the most sophisticated of XUL's buttons, it contains many features not found in other buttons:

- It can receive input focus. Input focus can be seen in Figure 4.4 as a dotted border just inside the button border.
- It can be a member of the document navigation list, which means that it has a numbered place in the navigation order in the page.
- It automatically wraps all its content up into an invisible `<hbox>`. This extra box can be affected by global styles.
- It supports Mozilla's accessibility services, which ensures that it can be reached using only the Tab key, or an equivalent to the Tab key.
- It provides "standard" button feedback to the user: It looks like a button before, during, and after user interaction.

The following XML attributes have a special meaning for the <button> tag:

```
disabled checked group command tabindex image label accesskey crop
```

<button>'s disabled and checked attributes can be set to true. disabled removes the button from the navigation list and de-emphasizes its appearance. The checked attribute allows a <button> to be pushed in permanently. checked has no effect if disabled is true. Figure 4.5 shows <button> with these attributes set. Note that the checked appearance is different from the pressed appearance shown in Figure 4.5.

The image, label, accesskey, and crop attributes relate to <button> content. <button> always adds an <hbox>, but if <button/> is specified without any content, it will add default content. This default content, excluding styles, is equivalent to Listing 4.2:

Listing 4.2 Default contents for <button>.

```
<hbox align="center" pack="center" flex="1">
  <image/>
  <label/>
</hbox>
```

The <image> and <label> tag display nothing because they are missing src and value attributes. The <button> attributes image and label supply this information. accesskey and crop also affect the label part of the <button>'s default content. An example is

```
<button image="green.png" label="Go" dir="rtl"/>
```

A <button> created with this tag might appear as shown in Figure 4.6.

The two content items appear reversed in order because the dir attribute has also been specified.

<button> will also show its default content if content tags do exist but consist of only a few special tags. Those special tags are <observes>, <tem-

Fig. 4.5 <button> alternate appearances under the Classic theme.

Fig. 4.6 Example of <button> with parameter attributes for default content.

plate>, <menupopup>, and <tooltip>. Such exceptions may sound a bit arbitrary, but these four tags are just commonly used content tags for a button. Chapter 15, XBL Bindings, explains how to read an XBL file, which is where such exceptions are specified.

Standard layout attributes, like align, if applied to the <button> tag, will propagate to the inside <hbox> tag. The other <button>-specific attributes noted previously apply to several XUL tags, not just button, and are discussed in Chapter 7, Forms and Menus.

As we will see later, the <button> tag supports most events in the DOM2 Events standard, such as onfocus, onclick, and onmouseover, as well as CSS2 pseudo-selectors such as :active, :hover, and :focus.

What makes <button> different from a user-defined XUL tag like <foo> is its internal processing. When you click on a button, that click event stops at the <button> tag. This is not the standard processing model for events in an XML document. The standard processing model requires that events pass from the <button> tag down into the content that the button tag holds, like a <description> or <image> tag. In the standard model, such an event will ultimately reach the most specific content tag under the mouse pointer, where it might be processed, and then returns back up to the <button>. This does not happen for a XUL <button>. Inside Mozilla, in the C/C++ code for a button, this event processing is changed as though the stopPropagation() DOM2 Event method were called on the <button> tag for all events. The content of a <button> acts as though it were sealed in amber—it receives no events at all. This behavior is the essence of the <button> tag.

To see this fundamental feature of <button> at work, try this piece of code, which appears to be two nested buttons:

```
<button><button onclick="alert('Hi')" label="B2"/></button>
```

The inner <button> does not provide visual feedback to the user, nor does it ever receive user input. It is frozen in place by the surrounding outer <button>.

4.3.1.2 <toolbarbutton> <toobarbutton> is the alternative to <button>. The following attributes have special meaning to <toolbarbutton>:

```
disabled checked group command tabindex image label accesskey crop
     toolbarmode buttonstyle
```

These attributes are almost the same as those for <button>, so why does <toolbarbutton> exist? The origin of this tag is a story about GUI systems. The most common way to attach commands to a graphical window is to add a menu system. Menus tend to be large and slow, so the concept of a toolbar arose. A toolbar presents frequently used commands in an easy-to-apply way. An easy way to provide a command on a toolbar is to use a button. Stacking buttons next to each other is confusing to the user's eye, so buttons on toolbars have no border unless the mouse is over them. This reduces the visual clutter. XUL has a

<toolbar> tag, and in it you can put a <toolbarbutton> for each such command. Just look at the window of the Classic Browser for many examples.

The <toolbarbutton> tag can be used outside a <toolbar>. There is no cast-iron link between a <toolbarbutton> tag and a <toolbar>. The two are entirely separate.

The <toolbarbutton> tag is a modification of the <button> tag. It has the same default content as <button>, but that default content always follows any content supplied by the user of the tag. Unlike <button>, the default content always appears.

Figure 4.7 shows the `checked` and `disabled` attributes at work on <toolbarbutton>.

The `toolbarmode` and `buttonstyle` XML attributes are special support for the Classic Browser application only. They are used inside Classic Browser skins (stylesheets) only and are not globally available. `toolbarmode` set to "`small`" will make the Classic Browser's navigation buttons small. `buttonstyle` set to "`pictures`" will hide the <label> part of the default content. Set to "`text`," it will hide the <image> part of the default content.

In the Classic Browser, <toolbarbutton> is used for the items in all the various toolbars. This includes the bookmarks on the Personal Toolbar. Such bookmarks are a first example of the complexity introduced by heavy stylesheet use—a single bookmark put on this toolbar looks nothing like a button. It looks like an HTML hyperlink instead. A further example of stylesheet creativity is the Modern theme. This theme removes the button-like borders from <toolbarbutton> entirely. If <toolbarbutton> is to have any identity at all, then appearance clearly has nothing to do with it.

The essence of a <toolbarbutton> is this: It is the same as a <button>, except that it visually suits a toolbar, it doesn't wrap its contents in an <hbox>, and it has special support for context menus. Context menus generally appear when you right-click a GUI element. <toolbarbuttons> can contain menus of their own. For the Back and Forward browser buttons *only*, special code inside Mozilla makes sure that both left- and right-clicking such a button always yields the contained menu. This feature is designed to reduce confusion for the user.

4.3.1.3 <autorepeatbutton> The <autorepeatbutton> is a button whose action occurs more than once. <autorepeatbutton> has very little use by itself, but it is an essential tool for constructing other, more complex user-interface elements. It is based on the <button> tag, but it has no default content and no special XML attributes.

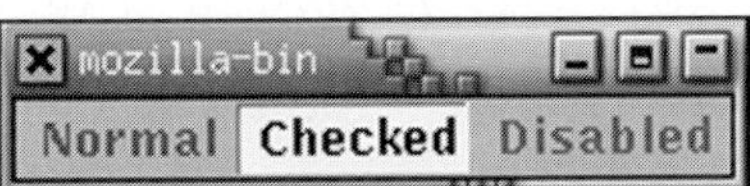

Fig. 4.7 <toolbarbutton> alternate appearances under the Classic theme.

If the user hovers the mouse over such a button, an oncommand event fires 20 times per second. These events can be captured by an oncommand event handler. All other events occur as for a user-defined tag.

<autorepeatbutton> is used in the construction of the <arrowscrollbox> tag, where it is used to implement continuous scrolling. It also appears in drop-down menus when the menu has so many items that they can't all be displayed at once. When a button at the end of the <arrowscrollbox> is held down, the box scrolls. <arrowscrollbox> is discussed in Chapter 8, Navigation.

If <autorepeatbutton> appears as a component of this larger tag, then its content is a single image that is supplied by stylesheet information. The image matches the direction of scroll. Each time an <autorepeatbutton> event fires, it searches for a parent tag that can be scrolled, and operates on it to perform the scroll action.

<autorepeatbutton> is interesting because it is not yet an independent button. If it appears outside the context of <arrowscrollbox>, it will not work properly. If the parent tag is not of the right kind, then <autorepeatbutton> will do what you want, but it will also spew error messages to the JavaScript console, which is ugly. The only way to stop these messages and make <autorepeatbutton> more generally useful is to modify its XBL definition in the chrome. Such a modification can be supplied with any Mozilla application.

4.3.1.4 <thumb> The <thumb> tag is a <button> tag that has a single <gripper> tag as content. The <gripper> tag is a user-defined tag. The <thumb> tag is used to implement the sliding box that appears in the center part of a scrollbar.

<thumb> is interesting because it exposes a native widget for display. The combination of <thumb>, <gripper>, and Mozilla-style extensions (see the "Style Options" section in this chapter) makes <thumb> transparently display the desktop version of a scrollbar thumb, not Mozilla's idea of scrollbar thumb.

<thumb> can work partially outside of a scrollbar, but it was not intended to be a general-purpose desktop-specific button. It does not display text or other content, just the outline and texture of a native button. It shows in a simple way how to create natively themed buttons. The <thumb> styles that do this can be seen in the chrome file xul.css in toolkit.jar.

4.3.1.5 <scrollbarbutton> <scrollbarbutton> is the tag that provides the button at each end of a scrollbar. In XUL, scrollbars are implemented with the <scrollbar> tag. If <nativescrollbar> is used instead, then no <scrollbarbutton> tags are involved. The arrow on a <scrollbarbutton> is supplied by style information.

<scrollbarbutton> is a modified <button> tag, and the XML attributes of <button> apply to it. This tag also supports the type attribute.

This attribute can be set to "`increment`" or "`decrement`" and has two purposes. It is used to determine stylesheet icons for the button, and it is used by the scrollbar to identify which way the scrolling action should occur. *Increment* means scroll in the forward direction; *decrement* means scroll backward.

`<scrollbarbutton>` is similar to `<autorepeatbutton>` in that it only works properly within the context of a larger tag. Unlike that other button, it is implemented without XBL code, so there is nothing an application programmer can modify that will make the tag easier to use. At least, this tag produces no error messages.

The pieces that make up a XUL `<scrollbar>` tag are, in general, tightly coordinated in Mozilla. `<thumb>`, `<scrollbarbutton>`, and `<slider>` all perform poorly on their own. Leave them inside `<scrollbar>`.

4.3.2 Button Variations

The `<button>` and `<toolbarbutton>` tags can display buttons with three different content arrangements. Which arrangement is shown depends on the type attribute. This attribute can be left off (the default case) or set to any of the following values:

```
menu menu-button radio checkbox
```

These alternatives are displayed in Figure 4.8.

The first two options, `menu` and `menubutton`, change the appearance of the button so that it supports content that is a menu. Such content consists of a single `<menupopup>` tag and its children. Menus are covered in Chapter 7, Forms and Menus. The small triangles in the figure are `<dropmarker>` tags. They are no more than an `<image>` tag with specific styles. Recall that the `<button>` tag surrounds its content with an `<hbox>`. If type is set to `menu`, then the `<dropmarker>` is inside that `<hbox>`, and the `<dropmarker>` is part of the clickable button. If type is set to `menu-button`, the `<dropmarker>` is outside the `<hbox>`. In that case, the button's face and the `<dropmarker>` are separately clickable. In either case, clicking the `<dropmarker>` reveals the contained `<menupopup>`. A separate style ensures that the button and dropmarker remain horizontally aligned, even when the `<dropmarker>` is

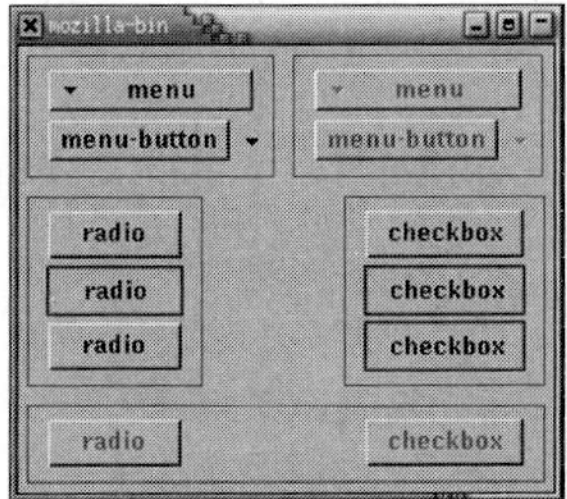

Fig. 4.8 `<button>` with type attribute set to various values.

outside the button's <hbox>. If used outside the context of a drop-down menu, <dropmarker> displays nothing.

The other two type options, radio and checkbox, change the response of the <button> tag when it is clicked. They cause it to mimic the <radio> and <checkbox> tags, also described in Chapter 7, Forms and Menus.

In the radio case, clicking the button will change its style so that it appears indented. Further clicks will have no effect. If the button has a group attribute, then clicking the button affects other buttons with the same group attribute. When the button is clicked, all other buttons with a matching group will no longer appear indented. If another button in the group is clicked, the original button changes to normal again.

In the checkbox case, clicking the button toggles its appearance between indented and normal. Such changes do not affect other checkboxes.

The <button> tag and its variations can be examined from JavaScript, like any XML tag. All these variations have type, group, open, and checked object properties that can be examined from JavaScript. These properties mirror the <button> attributes of the same name. The open property states whether the <menupopup> menu is currently showing.

4.3.3 Grippys

Grippys are small, secondary widgets that appear on or next to other, larger, primary widgets. Their purpose is to give the user some control over the appearance of the larger widget, a bit like changing a watch face by turning the small knob on top. The best-known examples of grippys are the corners and edges of a window, although the grippys themselves are not always obvious. When the mouse moves over the corner and edge grippys, the cursor icon changes, and the grippy can be dragged with the mouse, altering the window size.

Although grippys are often button-like in appearance, their ability to move or transform other graphical items makes them different from normal buttons. A scrollbar thumb is somewhat like a grippy, except that it operates on itself instead of on the scrollbar. A XUL <dropmarker> is also somewhat like a grippy, although it doesn't affect the tag it is attached to either.

In Mozilla and XUL, there are several grippys. A complete list is <grippy>, <toolbargrippy>, <resizer>, and <gripper>.

4.3.3.1 <grippy> To see a grippy in action, turn on the Mozilla sidebar using View | Show/Hide.. | Sidebar on the Navigator window. The <grippy> is the small vertical mark on the narrow border at the right edge of the sidebar.

The <grippy> tag is used inside the <splitter> tag. The <splitter> tag is a thin divider that looks like a visible spacer between two pieces of flexing content. By dragging the <splitter>, the content on one side shrinks while the content on the other side expands. <splitter> gives the user control over how much of a window is occupied by what content. It is discussed in Chapter 8, Navigation.

The <grippy> tag is very simple. It has no special-purpose attributes or content. Its appearance is entirely the result of styles. It is put at the center of the <splitter> to remind the user that there is something to drag. Any part of the <splitter> can be used as an initial drag point, not just the <grippy>. Use of the <grippy> tag is really trivial:

```
<splitter><grippy/><splitter>
```

The sole special use of the <grippy> is that it can hold event handlers by itself. This allows click-actions to be collected for the <splitter>, which normally only recognizes drag-actions. These click-actions might hide the splitter, move it to some predesignated position such as the extreme left or the middle, or clone it so that an additional splitter appears.

The <grippy> tag has almost no special logic. The sole unusual feature is that the <splitter> tag expects to have a <grippy> tag as content and sometimes modifies the grippy's layout attributes if the <splitter> itself changes. <grippy> is not a user-defined tag because its name is known and used inside the implementation of the platform.

4.3.3.2 <toolbargrippy> The <toolbargrippy> tag is used to collapse a toolbar down to a small icon so that it takes up less space. To do this, the toolbar must be a XUL <toolbar> tag inside a <toolbox> tag. Such a toolbar has a small button at the left-hand side that is the <toolbargrippy>. Figure 4.9 shows these grippys at work.

The <toolbargrippy> tag is subject to much argument. Even though it exists in Mozilla 1.02, it was withdrawn for version 1.21. In 1.3 it returned, and current policy is that it is here to stay. The argument in favor of <toolbargrippy> goes something like this: It is familiar to existing Netscape users; it is innovative design; and Internet Explorer can't emulate it easily. The argument against <toolbargrippy> goes like this: It is unusual and confuses users; it prevents toolbars from being locked; it derives from a specific desktop environment (Sun's OpenLook) and should only appear there.

The following remarks apply to Mozilla versions that support <toolbargrippy>.

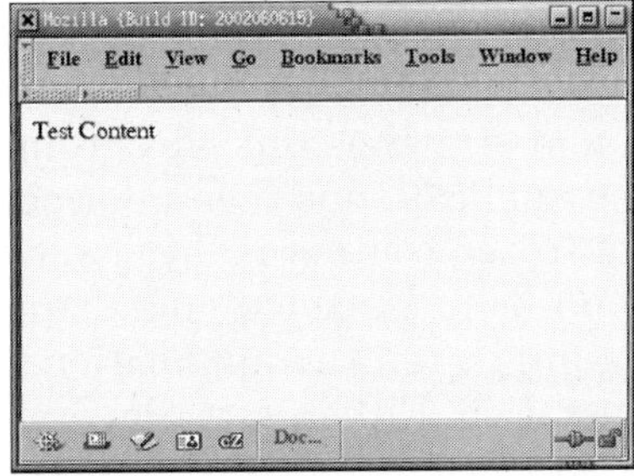

Fig. 4.9 <toolbargrippy> tags for uncollapsed and collapsed toolbars.

Like <grippy>, there is little point in using <toolbargrippy> by itself. It is little more than an <image> tag. A <toolbargrippy> tag is created automatically by a <toolbar> tag and is never specified by hand. The marks on the grippy's face do not come from any widget in the native desktop; they are just images that happen to look like widgets from the Open-Look desktop.

<toolbargrippy> has no special attributes or content of its own. The <toolbar> it resides in has one special attribute. The grippytooltiptext provides a tooltip (also called flyover help) for the grippy when the toolbar is collapsed. This tooltip identifies which toolbar the sideways grippy belongs to.

<toolbargrippy> behavior is implemented completely using JavaScript and the XBL definition of <toolbar>. When the grippy is clicked, it and the toolbar are hidden. A new, sideways-oriented grippy with different styles and content is then created from nothing and added to the XUL document. This is done using scripts that can create new content using the DOM1 interfaces described in the next chapter. The sideways grippy, when it appears, is therefore new content. If this sideways grippy is clicked, the process is reversed. The sideways grippy is stored in a special <hbox> of the <toolbox> tag. This <hbox> is empty and invisible unless sideways grippys are added to it.

4.3.3.3 `<resizer>` The <resizer> tag is used to resize the current window. The user can click on the content of a <resizer> and drag the window smaller or larger. The whole window is resized, regardless of where in the content the <resizer> tag is placed. The placement of <resizer> in the content has no special effect on layout.

There are two ways to resize an application window, and only one of those two uses the <resizer> tag.

One way to resize is to send a window hints from the desktop's window manager. This is done by grabbing the decorations on the outside of the window with the mouse. This is an instruction to the window manager, not to the application. The desktop window manager might change the window's border on its own initiative, without telling the application. A famous example of this is the twm window manager under X11, which has a "wire frame" option. When the user chooses to resize a window using the twm window decorations, the application content freezes, and a wire frame (a set of box-like lines) appears on the screen. The user moves and stretches this wire frame to suit and then releases the mouse button. The application is then informed that it must resize to fit that frame; the now-unfrozen content is layed out over the frame. In this way, the application only needs to do layout once. Fancier window managers, like GNOME's Sawfish, might tell the application to resize multiple times during the user's drag operation. Either way, this first method is the "outside in" method where the application receives instructions from outside.

The second method applies to the `<resizer>` tag. In this method, the application receives raw mouse events from the desktop, but no specific instructions to resize the window. The application itself (Mozilla) works out that the mouse actions imply resizing the window. The application directly or indirectly tells the window manager that the window is resizing. The application still has the choice of laying out the content repeatedly as the window grows or shrinks, or only laying out once when the resizing action is complete. In this second method, resizing is driven by the application, not the window manager. If there is no window manager, as might be the case in a small embedded system like a set-top box or a hand-held computer, then this is the only way to resize.

The `<resizer>` tag causes layout to happen continuously, not just once. Layout of displayed content updates as fast as possible when the window stretches and shrinks.

How `<resizer>` affects the window borders depends on the value of its special `dir` attribute. Use of `dir` for `<resizer>` is different than use of `dir` as a generic box layout attribute. For `<resizer>`, `dir` means the direction in which the window will expand or contract. It can take on any of the following values:

```
top left right bottom topleft topright bottomleft bottomright
```

The default value for `dir` is `topleft`. The first four values allow the window to change size in one direction only, with the opposite side of the window fixed in position. The other four values allow a corner of the window to move diagonally toward or away from the fixed opposite corner. A quick review of Mozilla's source code reveals the `direction` and `resizerdirection` attributes. These do not work like `dir`, nor do they do anything fundamental; they are simply used to hold data.

The `<resizer>` tag has no default content and no default appearance. It must be styled and provided with content if it is to be visible at all. In Mozilla, up to version 1.21, the default styles and content for `<resizer>` are missing, so it cannot be used without some trivial preparation. On more recent versions, it appears as expected in the bottom-right corner of a given window.

4.3.3.4 `<gripper>` The `<gripper>` tag is the single piece of content that goes inside a `<thumb>`, which in turn goes inside a `<scrollbar>`. It is a user-defined tag with no content, attributes, or special meaning, and it never needs to be used by itself. Ignore it. The name "gripper" is just an alternate piece of jargon for "grippy."

4.3.4 Labels and `<label>`

The `<label>` tag provides plain textual content, as described in Chapter 3, Static Content, but it does more than that. `<label>` also supplies content to other tags, assists with user input, and provides information needed for disabled access. The navigational and accessibility aspects are covered in Chapter 7, Forms and Menus. Here is a look at <label> helping out an ordinary button.

<label> has two button-friendly features. It can supply content to a button, and it can act as a button itself. Suppling content is the same as for any content tag. A trivial example is

```
<button><label>Press Me</label></button>
```

There is, however, an alternate syntax. Many XUL tags support the `label` attribute. In the case of <button>, this attribute sets the content of the visible button. The same example using this attribute is

```
<button label="Press Me"/>
```

The difference between `label` and `value` attributes is not obvious. At this point, it is sufficient to say that the two are the same visually, but that `label` has special uses. One such use is its capability to act as a button.

If a label is applied to the <checkbox> or <radio> tags (discussed in Chapter 6, Events), then the label text appears next to the tag's widget and can be clicked as if it were a button. A visual hint is supplied on some desktops if the mouse hovers over the text, or if the button has the focus, but the text is otherwise unadorned. This just makes it easy for users to strike the widget; they can strike the text as well as the rest of the widget.

The `label` attribute is difficult to master because it has multiple uses and doesn't apply to all tags. It can be used to supply ordinary content to most tags, but <checkbox> and <radio> are the only practical examples of <label> text acting like a button.

4.3.5 Bits and Pieces

The XUL part of Mozilla is fairly new and has taken time to reach version 1.0. It still has gaps and uncertainties in it. There are a number of other button tags lingering around in the discussion of XUL. These tags can cause endless confusion if you don't know what they are, not to mention the endless paperchase required to work out what their current status is. A few of the most obvious errant tags are noted here.

- ☞ <menubutton>, not the same as <button type="menu-button">, is an abandoned experiment in combining buttons and menus. Ignore it, and use the `type` attribute instead.
- ☞ <titledbutton> was an early attempt at combining images and text in a button, before plain <button> reached its current form. Ignore it, and use <button>.
- ☞ <spinner> is an attempt to create a widget that is sometimes called a spinbox. Such a widget consists of a box containing text with two small buttons to one side. These buttons are on top of each other, one being the

"up" button, one being the "down" button. These buttons allow the user to "spin" through a series of values that are displayed one at a time in the textbox. The user can either type in the wanted value or use the buttons to step to the wanted value. `<spinner>` is not finished and is not useable yet.

- ☞ `<spinbuttons>` is a further attempt at spinbox support but consists of the button pair only, without the textbox. It has a complete XBL definition, except that style information, including images, is missing. This is the same issue that `<resizer>` has. It is at best a starting point for a fully functional spinbox tag.
- ☞ `<slider>` is the final tag that contributes to a `<scrollbar>`. It is the clickable tray in which the `<thumb>` tag moves inside a scrollbar. `<slider>` is deeply connected to the `<scrollbar>` tag and can crash the Classic Browser if used alone. Avoid at all costs.

This list brings to an end the possibilities for independent buttons in Mozilla's XUL.

Many of XUL's more complex tags also contain button-like elements. In such cases, it is meaningless to try to separate the buttons. Tags like `<tabbox>`, `<listbox>`, and `<tree>` are discussed as complete topics in their own right.

Buttons also serve as thinking points for desktop integration issues. Will your Mozilla application blend in with the other applications that the user runs on their computer? If your buttons match theirs, that is a first step. The mechanics of making that happen are discussed next.

4.4 Themes and Skins

Themes and skins change the appearance of a piece of software. Whether called a theme, skin, profile, or mask, a theme usually consists of configuration information rather than whole programs. Apply a theme to a button, and the button's appearance changes.

Early theme systems were little more than a few user-driven color preferences. Examples of early theme systems are the Appearance options provided by Windows 9x/Me under the Display item in the Control Panel, and X11 resource files.

Beyond early theme systems are theme engines. A theme engine is a specialist part of a GUI library. When the library needs to draw a button, it consults the theme engine, which supplies graphical information matching the current theme. The engine understands the current theme from configuration information. These themes are typically crafted by an enthusiast and made available to the public for downloading. Windows XP, MacOS 10, and GNOME 2.0 are all examples of desktop systems that support a theme engine, and each supplies two or more themes to choose between in the default installation.

Themes based on theme engines make little difference to the features that the software provides because appearance and functionality are generally separate. From a programmer's perspective, such themes are about ornamentation rather than use. This is just one view. A graphic design perspective says that the icon-rich world we live in is full of practical instructions and directions. Stop signs are an example. From that perspective, a good theme is critical to making an application easy to use.

Very modern theme systems provide more options than just ornamentation. Such systems, like the Sawfish window manager's lisp engine or the SkinScript skin system used in Banshee Screamer (this author's favorite alarm clock software), can reorganize the user interface of an application entirely, as well as change the colors and textures of its visual elements.

Many software products use themes, with WinAmp and Mozilla further examples. Even mobile phones support themes in the form of ringtones. The `themes.freshmeat.net` Web site lists themes for a wide range of theme-enabled software, including Mozilla.

Parallel to the issue of themes is the issue of localization, in which content is adapted to a given language or platform. In Mozilla, localization works in a way that is very similar to themes. It is discussed in Chapter 3, Static Content.

4.4.1 Mozilla Themes

Mozilla themes and skins are two completely different things. A Mozilla theme is a design concept, with a little bit of software support. Themes can be used to brand the Mozilla platform, to project a certain image, or just to minimize performance issues. The obvious examples in Mozilla are the Classic and the Modern themes.

The theme system inside Mozilla is roughly equivalent to a theme engine. It is intended to modify content appearance only, not content itself. In extreme cases, it can be bent to modify content as well. Mozilla's theme system relies heavily on the CSS2 stylesheet support inside Mozilla. The theme system operates on some simple principles:

- Mozilla themes apply only to XUL. Except for scrollbars, they do not apply to HTML. Native themes, however, apply to both. They are discussed separately.
- There is a current theme, with a unique name. Mozilla remembers this name at all times, even when shut down.
- The current theme's name in lowercase is also a directory name in the chrome. Mozilla themes are stored in the chrome.
- For a theme to work fully, it must be implemented for each participating package in the chrome, and for a special package named global. `messenger` is an example of a package name. That name is used for the Classic Mail & News client.

- ☞ The theme information in the global package is used for all packages. This is a convention, not a requirement.
- ☞ All theme information must be specifically included in application documents. No theme information is included automatically.
- ☞ Mozilla automatically modifies theme-related URLs to include the current theme name. This allows documents to include the current theme without knowing its name.

This last point is discussed in the next section. It is the only thing in Mozilla that provides special support for themes. Everything else about Mozilla themes is just routine use of other technologies and a few naming conventions.

The current theme can be changed. In the Classic Browser, View | Apply Theme can be used to download new themes and to change the current theme. The browser must be restarted for the new theme to apply. Themes can also be installed from a normal Web link using the XPInstall system explained in Chapter 17, Deployment. Because themes are stored in the chrome as ordinary files, and because XPInstall is a general and flexible process, there is little stopping you from breaking many of the theme rules. For fastest results and pain-free maintenance afterward, it makes sense to create themes in the standard way.

Themes built for the Classic Browser will not necessarily work for the Netscape 7.x browser or the Mozilla Browser. Simple themes will work everywhere, but well-polished themes are likely to have flaws when moved to one of the other browsers. Many theme creators are now putting support for the Mozilla Browser before the Classic Browser. Therefore, themes are not always portable.

You can design a theme on paper or in a graphic design tool, but to put it into action, you must also implement it. Implementing a theme means creating skins.

4.4.2 Mozilla Skins

A Mozilla skin is a set of files that implement a theme for one application package installed on the platform, or for the global package that is used for all parts of the platform.

A skin can contain any type of file, but the types that make the most sense are stylesheets and images. Each skin is centered around a stylesheet that changes the appearance of a XUL document. If you use various CSS2 syntax tricks like `@import` and `url()`, those stylesheets might drag in other stylesheets or images. Together these items build up the whole styled appearance of the application. This is the primary reason why XUL documents should not contain inline styles. Good XUL design uses and reuses skins for appearance rather than re-inventing the wheel every time.

Chapter 1, Fundamental Concepts, briefly outlined the structure of the Mozilla chrome directory. It is the skin top-level subdirectory that contains all the theme information in Mozilla, for all packages. To create a skin, install constructed files underneath this directory. To use a skin, specify a URL that points to this directory. This use of a URL is where Mozilla's special processing comes in. An example illustrates.

Suppose a Mozilla chrome package called `tool` has a skin file called `dialogs/warnings.css`. This skin file is all the styles for the matching content file `dialogs/warnings.xul`. A programmer would include this skin in the `dialogs/warnings.xul` content file as follows:

```
<?xml-stylesheet href="chrome://tool/skin/dialogs/warnings.css"
     type="text/css"?>
```

Here, `tool` is a package name. There is nothing magical about skins—this is just a hard-coded inclusion. From this line, the URL for the skin file must be

```
chrome://tool/skin/dialogs/warnings.css
```

Suppose that the current platform theme is the Modern theme, with matching directory name `modern`. Mozilla will internally translate the preceding URL into the following directory path, relative to the install directory:

```
chrome/tool/skin/modern/dialogs/warnings.css
```

This translation has added the theme name (`modern`), and moved the package name (`tool`) further down the path. This directory also has a URL:

```
resource:/chrome/tool/skin/modern/dialogs/warnings.css
```

The `resource:` scheme just points to the top of the platform install area.

If the current theme were Classic instead, the translated directory path would be

```
chrome/tool/skin/classic/dialogs/warnings.css
```

This means that the application programmer must supply a skin file for every theme that might be installed in the platform. That is a lot of work, and sometimes it is impossible to forecast what themes the user might have. The easiest way to get around this requirement is to use the global skin for the current theme. This global skin can be included with a second `<?xml-stylesheet?>` tag using this URL:

```
chrome://global/skin/
```

This URL lacks a trailing `.css` file name. In this case, Mozilla will retrieve the file with the default name of `global.css`. This is the same as when `index.html` is retrieved by default for a Web site. The translated directory name in this example will then be one of

```
chrome/global/skin/modern/global.css
chrome/global/skin/classic/global.css
```

Since all responsible theme designers include a `global.css` in their themes, the problem of supporting unknown themes disappears by using this skin. The application programmer need only add specialist skins for unusual features of their application.

Creating a set of skins for a theme is a nontrivial task. The human factors problems are difficult enough, but the process of creating functional styles and images is also challenging. There are two reasons for this. First, your global skin must be sufficiently flexible to be reliable for "all" applications that might want to use your skin. That is a portability challenge. Second, for your new theme to be useful, you must also create skins for the well-known applications inside Mozilla: Navigator, Composer, Messenger, Address Book, Preferences, and so on. That is a challenge because there are many applications, and because it requires intimate knowledge of the classes, ids, and structure of the content in those applications. To get that intimate knowledge, you must either intensively study the application with the DOM Inspector or study the Modern or Classic theme skins. Creating skins for a new theme is a labor of love, or possibly some marketing person's clever idea.

Good coding practices when using or creating skins follow:

1. The global skin should be included before other, more specific skins.
2. The global skin is enough for most purposes.
3. If you create a special skin, have it `@import` the global skin so that only one skin needs to be referred to in the XUL file.
4. Don't modify the global skin unless you are responsible for the whole theme.

The skin directories can contain any type of file. JavaScript, XUL, HTML, or DTD files can all be put into a skin. There are always unique circumstances when this might make sense, and it is occasionally done in the Classic Browser, but in general you should avoid it. After you start doing this, you are effectively moving theme-independent content into theme-dependent skins, which multiplies the implementation and maintenance workload by the number of themes you intend to support. This practice is not recommended.

Skins will not work if they are merely copied into the chrome directory. The "Hands On" section in this chapter describes how to get a skin (or any other chrome file) in place the quick-and-dirty way.

4.4.3 The Stylesheet Hierarchy

Skins must be added by hand to a XUL application, but that is not the whole Mozilla story. Mozilla automatically includes a number of CSS2 stylesheets. A discussion of Mozilla themes and skins is not complete without considering these special sheets.

The CSS2 standard provides three structural features that can be used to organize a stylesheet hierarchy. Mozilla uses all three methods. These structural features are separate from the structure of the styled document.

The most obvious structural feature in CSS2 is support for cascaded and inherited styles. See section 6 of the CSS2 standard for details. Briefly, styles can be applied both generally and specifically as Listing 4.3 shows.

Listing 4.3 Selector hierarchy for progressively darker color.

```
* { color: lightgreen; }
text { color: green; }
text.keyword { color: darkgreen; }
#byline { color: black; }
```

In this example, all tags are light green; those tags that are `<text>` tags are green, tags that are `<text class="keyword">` are dark green, and one tag with `id="byline"` is black. If the earlier styles are put into highly general `.css` files, and the latter styles are put into more specific `.css` files, then regardless of the order of inclusion, all styles will apply. As examples, Mozilla provides highly general stylesheets called `xul.css` and `html.css`. `xul.css` includes the style rule:

```
* { -moz-user-focus: ignore; display: -moz-box; }
```

This style rule makes all XUL tags, whether user-defined or otherwise, act like boxes.

The second way that CSS provides structure is through ordering. If two styles exist for the same selector and property, then only the latter one applies. In that case, the order of stylesheet application is important. Although this can be relied upon in Mozilla, it is bad practice because style definitions are supposed to be *rules*. The point of a rule system is that all rules apply simultaneously, which is not the case if one rule overwrites an earlier one.

Finally, the `!important` CSS2 modifier can be use to break ties between identical style rules. Mozilla supports the CSS2 concept of *weight*, which is implemented with a two-byte value (0-65535). If a rule is `!important`, the weight is increased by 32768. In Mozilla's DOM Inspector, when the left-hand Document panel has a styled node selected, and the right-hand Object panel is set to CSS Style Rules, the Weight column shows the weights of the different style rules that apply to the selected node.

Table 4.1 shows all the sources of style rules that can be applied to XUL and HMTL documents. The most general sources are at the top. The special files `xul.css` and `html.css` have the lowest weight, which is 0.

4.4.4 Native Themes

Mozilla's own theme system doesn't apply to other non-Mozilla applications. If all applications on a given desktop are to have the same look and feel, then some common theme system must be used. The theme system of the desktop itself, called the native theme system in Mozilla-speak, is that common solution.

Table 4.1 Sources of style rules for XUL and HTML

Purpose of style rules	Supplied per theme?	XUL source	HTML source
Implement style properties	No	Built into Mozilla C/C++ code	Built into Mozilla C/C++ code
Fundamental styles that are always applied	No	xul.css with URL chrome://global/content/xul.css	html.css, forms.css, and quirks.css with URLs like resource:///res/html.css
Theme support for standard XUL widgets	Yes	Skins under the global package for XBL widgets (e.g., chrome://global/skin/button.css)	None
Global theme support used by all chrome packages	Yes	global.css with URL chrome://global/skin/	None
Specialist theme support for one or more chrome packages	Yes	Skins scattered throughout the chrome that are not under the global package	None
Inline styles	No	Should be avoided; otherwise, inside .xul content	Inside .html files
User options	No	None	Per-user preferences under Edit | Preferences, Appearance
Per-user custom styles	No	chrome/UserChrome.css for each user profile	chrome/UserContent.css for each user profile

Some parts of the content that Mozilla displays can be made to match the native theme. The restrictions follow:

- The Mozilla version must be 1.21 or higher.
- The desktop system must be Windows XP or MacOS 10.2 or have GTK 1.2 support.
- The native theme information applies to HTML form elements.
- The native theme information applies to XUL tags that are like widgets.
- Native themes work for XUL only if the current theme is Classic.
- The native theme can work with other Mozilla themes, but only if they are built using the technique that the Classic theme uses.

Native themes are implemented in a very simple way. The Mozilla CSS2 extension `-moz-appearance` turns native theme support on and off for a single tag. If it is set to `none`, then native theme support is off. If it is set to a key value, then that key value determines what native widget the native theme system will use. The native theme system will then try and render (display) that widget in place of the usual Mozilla content.

There are more than 60 different key values for this extension. Most of the common ones have the same name as the XUL tag they support, so for `<button>`, use

```
-moz-appearance: button
```

It's entirely possible, but not recommended or even sensible, to render a menu as a button using `-moz-appearance`. The best way to proceed is to use the Classic theme's skins as a guide. For a complete list of the keywords, see the array `kAppearanceKTable` in the Mozilla source file `content/shared/src/nsCSSProps.cpp`.

The Classic theme includes styles that match Netscape Navigator 4 widgets, but they are ignored because `-moz-appearance` is set. If `-moz-appearance` is set back to none, then the old, familiar styles will again be used. To turn off native theme support without damaging the existing themes, add this line to a suitable global `.css` file like `xul.css` or `userChrome.css`:

```
* { -moz-appearance : none ! important; }
```

The next topic shows native themes at work.

4.4.5 Theme Sampler

Figure 4.10 shows a simple Mozilla window under a variety of theme combinations. Three different XML pages are displayed. The first two are XUL; the last is HTML. The two XUL documents differ only in their stylesheet support.

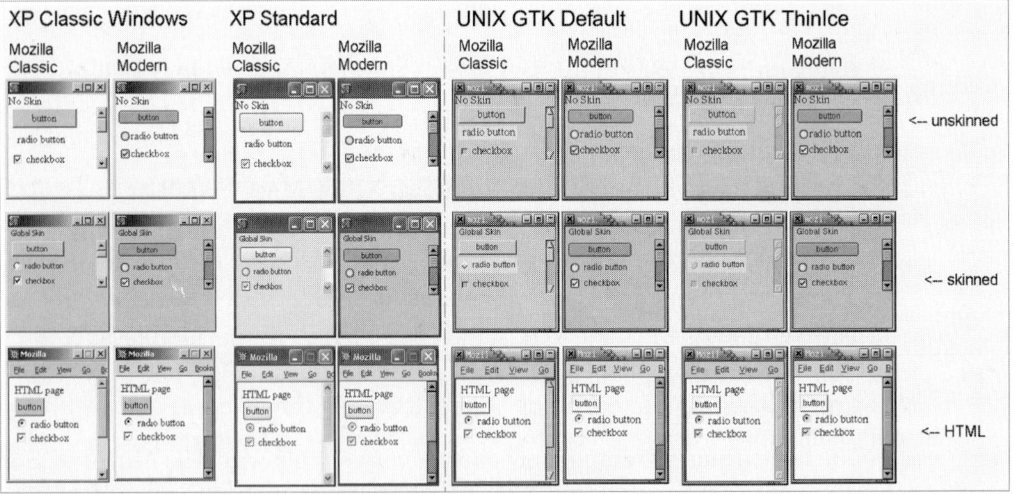

Fig. 4.10 Sampler of Mozilla and Desktop theme combinations.

The "No Skin" version includes no stylesheets at all, and so doesn't benefit from the current Mozilla theme. The "Global Skin" version includes the global skin for the current theme, which is sufficient for full theme support. The "HTML page" shows that its use of theme information differs from XUL's use.

In all the displayed screenshots, Classic Mozilla's Modern theme is the most resistant to change because it includes few uses of the `-moz-appearance` style. Similarly, HTML pages are presupplied with standardized style settings when `-moz-appearance` is used heavily, as it is in the Classic theme, or when no theme is present to mask out default behavior.

4.4.6 GTK and X-Windows Resources

The UNIX versions of Mozilla rest on the GTK graphics library, which in turn rests on the X-Windows system. It is common for X-Windows applications to be styled using so-called Xresources, whose master copies are typically found in `/usr/lib/X11/app-defaults` on UNIX. This invites the question: Can Mozilla be styled as other X11 clients are? The answer is no, because the GTK library does not support use of X11 resources.

GTK has its own styling system that revolves around the `gtkrc` file. The documentation for GTK explains how to modify this file so that per-widget custom styles are created. These styles will show through on Mozilla if widgets are drawn with the native theme.

A window manager under UNIX may or may not use the GTK toolkit. If it does not, then Xresources may be available to style that window manager. Examples of managers that do have Xresources are `twm` and `fvwm2`. But window managers don't affect application content.

4.5 Style Options

All the CSS2 styling information is available for use on buttons and in skins.

The proposed CSS3 style `font-family: button`, which sets the font to match the font used for `<button>`, can be applied with this Mozilla extension:

```
font-family: -moz-button;
```

The `-moz-appearance` property, which turns on native theme support, accepts the following values for the button tags described in this chapter:

```
button
resizer
scrollbarbutton_down
scrollbarbutton_left
scrollbarbutton_right
scrollbarbutton_up
scrollbargripper_horizontal
scrollbargripper_vertical
scrollbarthumb_horizontal
```

```
scrollbarthumb_vertical
toolbarbutton
toolbargripper
```

Finally, both here and in all subsequent chapters, style selectors and class attributes defined for the standard Mozilla applications (Navigator, Messenger, etc.) may be reused for other applications if it makes sense to do so. These selectors and attributes make up a layer of complexity on top of the style system. They represent a set of application targets against which styles can be applied. You are free to reuse these targets in the design of your own application. It makes sense to do that if your application overlaps with standard parts of the Classic Browser, or if it shares design features with any of those parts.

4.6 Hands On: NoteTaker Buttons and Themes

In the last two chapters, we added layout structure and basic textual content to the NoteTaker application. In this chapter we'll add buttons. The job is to

- ☞ Turn the Save and Cancel operations into buttons.
- ☞ Temporarily turn the Edit and Keywords operations into buttons. In a later chapter we'll get a proper tab control, supplying tab-like buttons, for this control.
- ☞ Put theme support in.

The XUL file that contains the application window we're developing is the only file that needs substantial changing. The required changes for the buttons are very simple, as Listing 4.4 shows.

Listing 4.4 NoteTaker changes required to turn text into buttons.

```
<!-- change this: -->
<text value="Cancel"/>
<spacer flex="1"/>
<text value="Save"/>

<!-- to this: -->
<button label="Cancel"/>
<spacer flex="1"/>
<button label="Save"/>

<!-- and change this: -->
<text value="Edit"/>
<text value="Keywords"/>

<!-- to this: -->
<toolbarbutton label="Edit"/>
<toolbarbutton label="Keywords">
```

When these changes are done, the dialog box looks a bit like Figure 4.11. The Keywords button is highlighted because the mouse was over it when the screenshot was taken.

Note that the appearance of the buttons isn't very striking yet. Also, they're a little confused by the diagnostic boxes we included in Chapter 2, XUL Layout. To add theme support, we need to get rid of the styles we threw in temporarily in past chapters and to include the global skin for the current style.

Looking at Figure 4.11, we want to get rid of all custom styles for text, and maybe some of the box borders. We'll leave a few box borders in just to remind us that there's more work to do. The main outstanding job is to find and add appropriate widgets, but we only have buttons so far. So that we can delay replacing all the boxes with widgets, we'll just make sure that the boxes with borders have `class="temporary"` and change the border-drawing style rule appropriately. The stylesheet inclusions in the `.xul` file will change from

```
<?xml-stylesheet href="boxes.css" type="text/css"?>
```

to

```
<?xml-stylesheet href="chrome://global/skin/" type="text/css"?>
<?xml-stylesheet href="boxes.css" type="text/css"?>
```

Figure 4.12 shows the results of this work when displayed first in the Classic theme and then in the Modern theme.

From Figure 4.12, it's clear that the `<button>`, `<toolbarbutton>`, and `<groupbox>` tags have adopted standard appearances based on the given themes. Fonts for the text have also changed.

If this XUL file is installed in the chrome, then the `boxes.css` stylesheet must be located in the same directory. That is good enough for testing, but is not ideal if themes are to be supported.

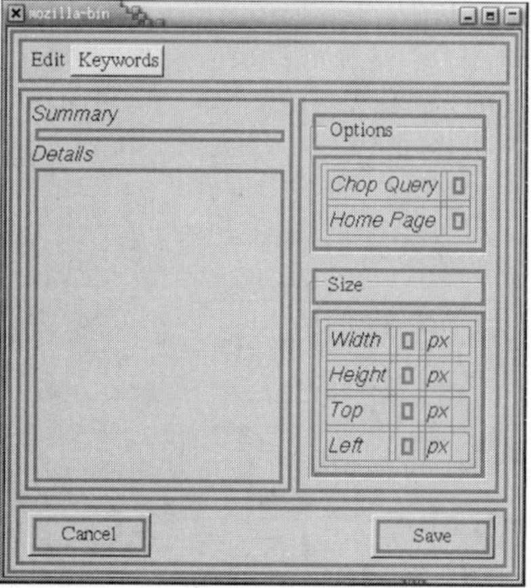

Fig. 4.11 NoteTaker with buttons included.

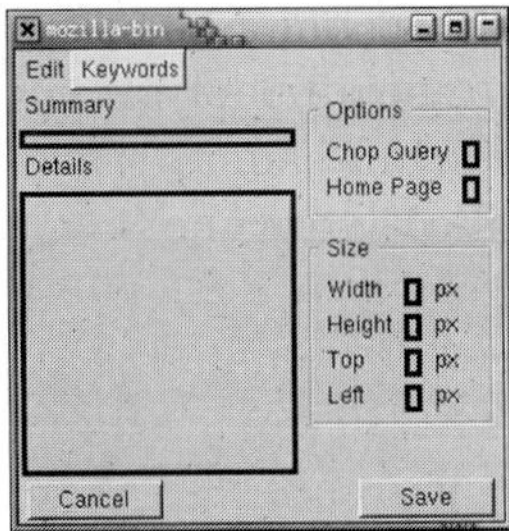

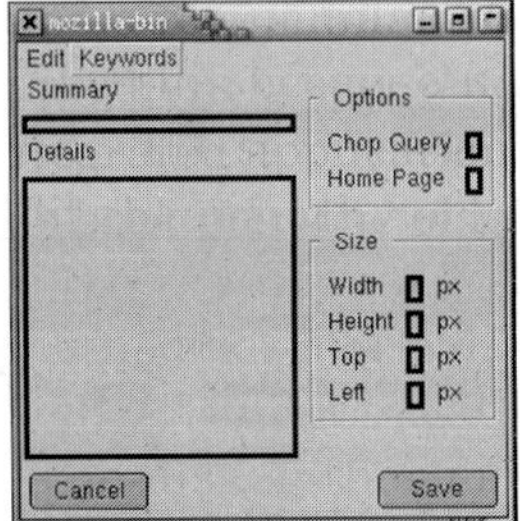

Fig. 4.12 NoteTaker with theme support showing Classic and Modern appearance.

To support themes, we need to change this line in the XUL content:

```
<?xml-stylesheet href="boxes.css" type="text/css"?>
```

to read

```
<?xml-stylesheet href="chrome://notetaker/skin/boxes.css" type="text/
    css"?>
```

Afterwards, we move the `boxes.css` file to this location in the chrome:

```
chrome/notetaker/skin/modern/boxes.css
```

Finally, we have to register the skin in the chrome registry, just as we had to register the package name in Chapter 1, Fundamental Concepts, and (optionally) the locale in Chapter 2, XUL Layout. Again this means creating a very standard `contents.rdf` file, this time in the skin directory. Listing 4.5 shows the required RDF.

Listing 4.5 `contents.rdf` required to register a chrome skin.

```
<?xml version="1.0"?>
<RDF
  xmlns="http://www.w3.org/1999/02/22-rdf-syntax-ns#"
  xmlns:chrome="http://www.mozilla.org/rdf/chrome#">

  <Seq about="urn:mozilla:skin:root">
    <li resource="urn:mozilla:skin:modern/1.0" />
  </Seq>

  <Description about="urn:mozilla:skin:modern/1.0">
    <chrome:packages>
      <Seq about="urn:mozilla:skin:modern/1.0:packages">
        <li resource="urn:mozilla:skin:modern/1.0:notetaker"/>
      </Seq>
    </chrome:packages>
  </Description>
</RDF>
```

Again, you need to look at Chapters 11–17 to decipher what all this RDF means. If we're confident that the skin already exists (which we are for Modern and Classic), then attributes of the <Description> tag that are prefixed with chrome: can be dropped. So those attributes are dropped here. The first part of the file states that the modern theme exists; the second, larger part says that the NoteTaker package has theme-specific skin information for that theme.

For the purposes of getting going, we need to make an exact copy of this file and to replace skin names ("modern/1.0" here) and package names ("notetaker" here) with whatever we're working on. The package name "modern/1.0" includes a version number, which is stated in the style of application registry names, discussed in Chapter 17, Deployment. Here, it's just a string that we must spell correctly. To see the correct spelling for existing themes, just look at other contents.rdf files in other packages that use that theme.

Finally, we need to update the installed-chrome.txt file so that the platform knows that there's a new skin implementation. So we add this line, save, and restart the platform:

```
skin,install,url,resource:/chrome/notetaker/skin/modern/
```

If we don't put a copy of boxes.css and contents.rdf in the equivalent place in the Classic skin, then our application won't have the styles we've carefully left behind under that skin.

For testing purposes, unless you are specifically building a skin, it's easiest to keep all your css files in the contents directory and to worry about putting stylesheets into skins when the application has been shown to work.

The NoteTaker window is now starting to look like a piece of software rather than just a sketch of some kind. We can't yet add widgets for two reasons: First, we have only a limited knowledge of the XUL widgets available, and second, we haven't considered the data that those widgets must handle.

If this were a book on database design, we'd next have a long discussion about schemas and types. The schema information would be discussed with the users, debated, and finalized, and the correct types would be chosen for each of the placeholders in our application. This is not a book on database design, so we'll avoid that step and just use some common sense as we go. Because plain buttons carry no data (they are generally functional rather than stateful), we don't need to do any data analysis here anyway. If we had a checkbox-style button, that would be a different matter.

4.7 Debug Corner: Diagnosing Buttons and Skins

If you are creating a theme, you may need to understand more deeply the way buttons (or any widget) are styled. Table 4.1 helps to understand the structure of the style system, but that is not a specific example. It is possible to trace the most important style information for an XUL widget directly. Here is how to do it for the <button> tag. This process can be applied to many tags.

The first step is to look at the file xul.css. Its URL is chrome://global/content.css, but the best way to find it is to look in the toolkit.jar file stored in the chrome and extract it. Inside this extracted file are one or more style rules for each XUL tag. It is the -moz-binding style property that is of interest. For the <button> tag, this reads:

```
-moz-binding: url("chrome://global/content/bindings/button.xml#button");}
```

This URL refers to an XBL file that's also inside toolkit.jar. You don't need to know XBL to understand the style information. The trailing #button text in this URL is the name of an XBL binding. It is coincidental that this name matches the <button> tag's name, but it is obviously a handy convention.

If you extract the named button.xml file, you can then search for a <binding> tag with id="button". In this tag will be a <resources> tag, and in that resource tag will be a <stylesheet> tag. That <stylesheet> tag names the stylesheet for the <button> widget, and it is a skin. You can examine it by opening any JAR file with a theme name, like classic.jar or modern.jar, since all good themes provides these standard skins.

A second difficult question is this: Is the button (or widget) being displayed a native button (or widget)? The short answer is that it doesn't matter too much except for scrollbars. For scrollbars, there is a separate <nativescrollbar> tag that is used when the whole scrollbar is to be a native widget. If you really want to know if a given tag has a native appearance, you can check the -moz-appearance property's value from a stylesheet, or from JavaScript. For example, this style rule makes all native buttons appear red:

```
button[-moz-appearance="button"] { background-color:red; }
```

For publicly available applications this is not recommended, since the user controls the themes at work in a browser, and relying on subtle details of layout is a guaranteed way to create a fragile application. If you really must have complete control over the appearance of your widgets, then avoid supporting themes entirely and supply a full set of application stylesheets. As the theme sampler in Figure 4.11 shows, this can carry risks of its own.

To diagnose problems with skins, you must find a content problem.

First, try the application with explicit stylesheets rather than a skin. That tests if the stylesheet content and XUL content agree. If the two work together, then the application content is probably fine. Check the original order in which skins are included in the XUL files; the global skin should be first; any application-specific skins go next; and the specific nonskin stylesheets are last. If the two don't work together, go back to the DOM Inspector and make sure that you know what you are doing with styles, ids, and classes.

If all that seems in order, then the problem is probably in the content of a contents.rdf file. It is very easy to make syntax mistakes in there. The simple way to be sure that your `contents.rdf` file is being read is to check the contents of the file named `chrome.rdf` at the top of the chrome hierarchy.

The platform generates this `chrome.rdf` file each time it reexamines the chrome. If your skin-package combination (or locale-package combination) doesn't appear in the lists embedded in this file, then your `contents.rdf` files are either not being read, not syntactically correct, or structured incorrectly. Reexamine them.

The other part of this content problem is the `installed-chrome.txt` file, which is fussy about syntax. All directories must have a trailing slash, all entries about a locale must include a locale name, all entries about a skin must include a skin name, and paths in the chrome must begin with `resource:` or `jar:`.

4.8 Summary

Mozilla's XUL language is full of widgets, and the `<button>` tag is the simplest of them. Because buttons are such a common concept, there are a number of variations to consider. `<button>` and `<toolbarbutton>` cover most requirements. Although the capabilities of a button make it unique, users are very sensitive to appearances as well. A button must look and act like a button.

The business of appearances is linked directly to themes. Mozilla uses CSS2 stylesheet technology as the basis for its themes, plus some simple URL modification trickery. Themes apply to every window of a XUL application, and each window adopts one or more skins from a given theme. A skin is just a document-set of styles that follow the guidelines of a theme's design, plus any associated files.

Just as applications might support themes via stylesheet inclusion, so too do themes support applications, by implementing skins for standard widgets, packages, and style targets. These standard skins are the source of work for theme designers.

One aspect of the stylesheet system that brings the discussion full-circle back to buttons and widgets is the `-moz-appearance` extension. This extension allows a XUL tag to be displayed according to the rules of the native theme, that is, the current theme of the desktop. Using this `-moz-appearance` attribute, the Mozilla styling system becomes transparent in places to the native theme. This system works only for XUL tags that match native desktop widgets. This support is implemented in the Classic theme, but it can be put into any theme.

Buttons are just the first of many widget-like tags in Mozilla's XUL. Before exploring the others, you need to understand how to get the `<button>` tag to do something. The way to do this is to use a script. Scripting and the JavaScript language are described in the next chapter.

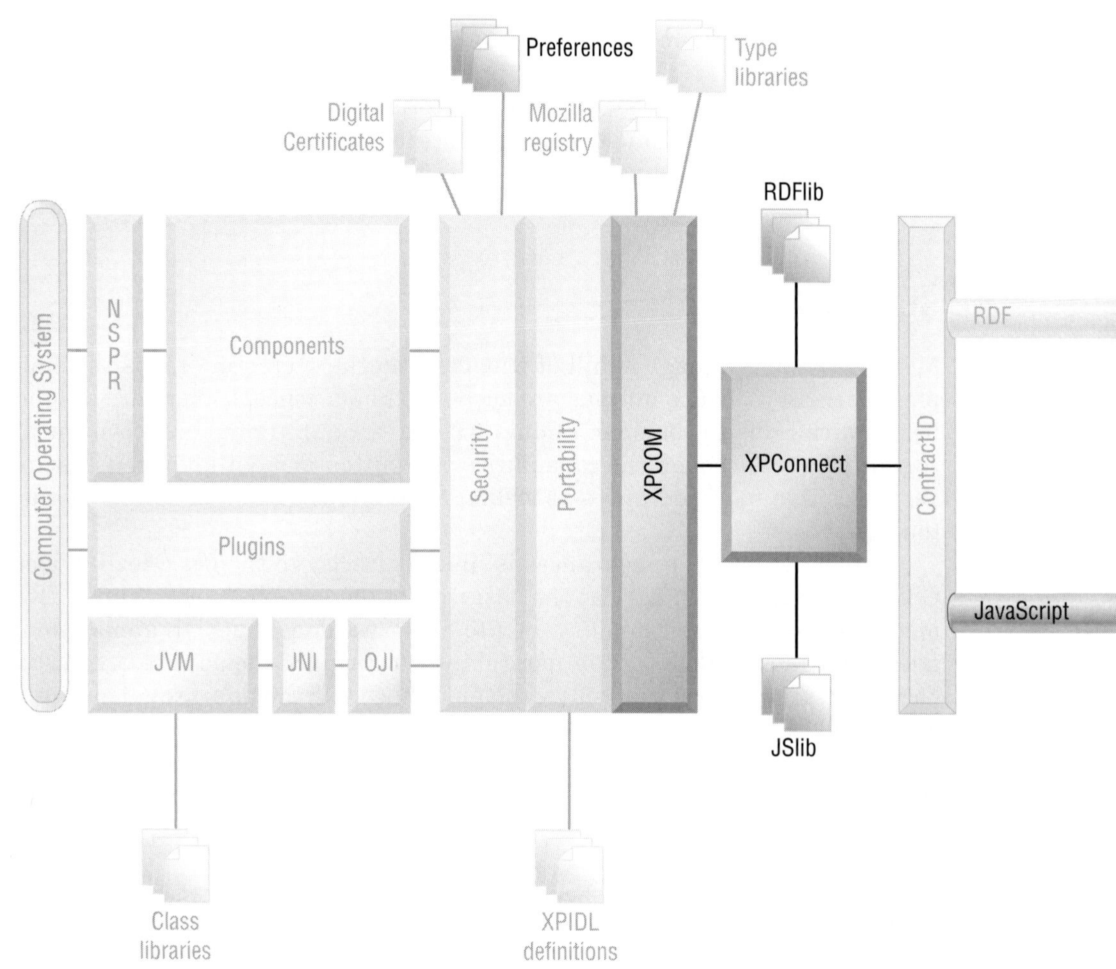

Preferences
Type libraries
Digital Certificates
Mozilla registry
RDFlib
Computer Operating System
NSPR
Components
Security
Portability
XPCOM
XPConnect
ContractID
RDF
Plugins
JavaScript
JVM
JNI
OJI
JSlib
Class libraries
XPIDL definitions

CHAPTER 5

Scripting

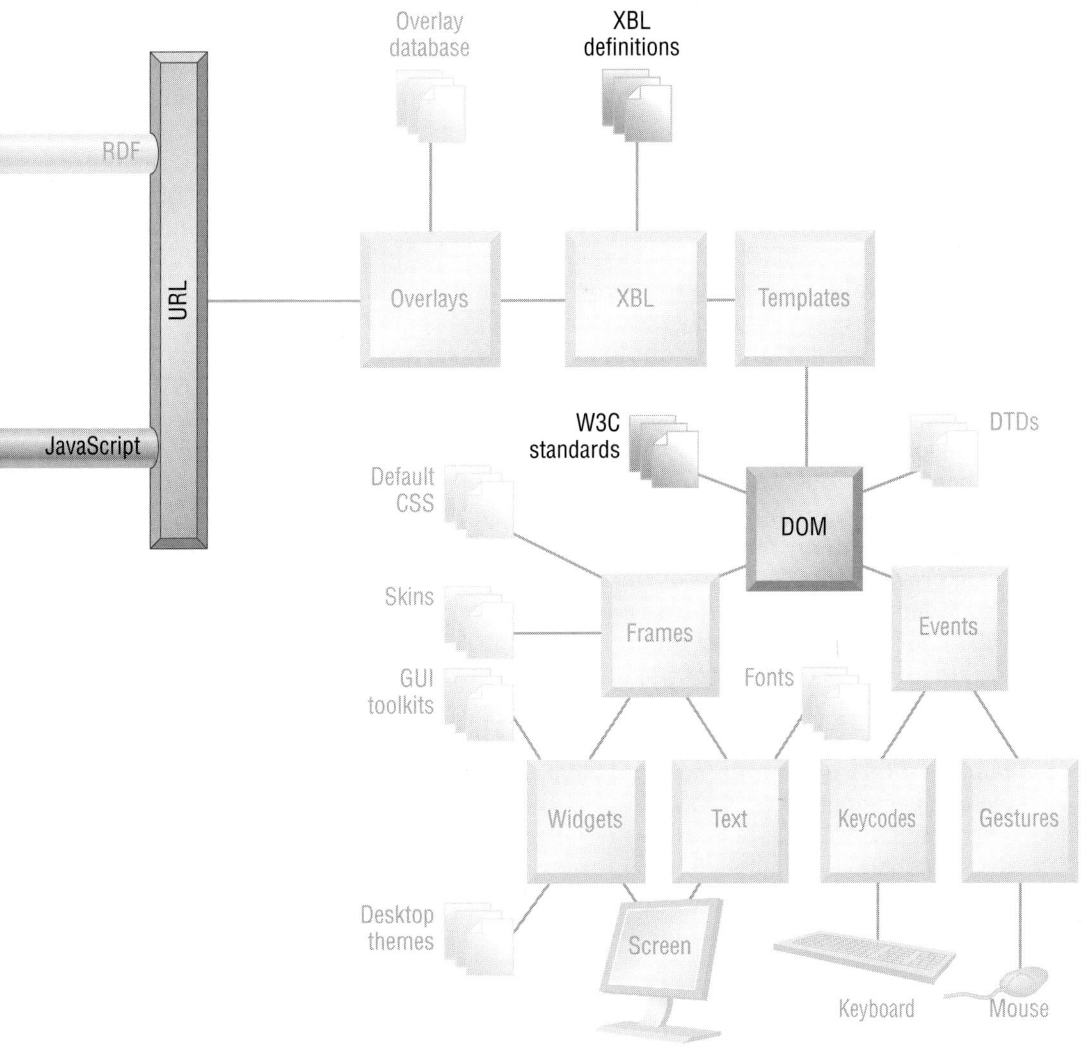

JavaScript is a lightweight programming language with C-like syntax that is an essential part of the Mozilla Platform. JavaScript programs, or program fragments, are called scripts. By adding scripts to XUL, read-only documents become dynamic interfaces that can do something in response to the user's commands. Writing scripts is a task for a programmer, not for a Web page author or a content provider. Mozilla applications can be developed only by a programmer.

This chapter describes the JavaScript language itself. It also provides an overview of the many services of the Mozilla Platform that are exposed to JavaScript scripts. These features and services are examined in more detail throughout the rest of this book. Whole books have been written on JavaScript. This chapter is a complete description, but it is also brief.

JavaScript scripts that are part of a Mozilla application might follow one or more traditional programming styles, depending on how ambitious the application is.

Lightweight Mozilla applications contain scripts similar to the scripts used in Web pages. In Web pages, these scripts are often added to HTML content as an afterthought. When such scripts become larger, they are sometimes called Dynamic HTML. Even so, such scripts do little more than rearrange HTML content in a pleasing way. Simple macros used in products like Microsoft Word are similarly lightweight.

Middleweight Mozilla applications use scripting more systematically than lightweight applications. Other environments like this are 4GL tools such as Sybase's PowerBuilder or Oracle's SQL*Forms. In such cases, scripts are responsible for much of the basic activity put into the software. Use of Python in the Zope application server is an Open Source example.

Heavyweight Mozilla applications, like ActiveState's Komodo development environment, have so much scripting that the scripts overwhelm the basic browser-like features of the platform. In such cases, JavaScript can act like other standalone scripting environments such as Visual Basic, Perl, and Tcl/Tk, or perhaps emacs' elisp. In such heavily engineered programming, scripts drive the behavior of the Mozilla Platform from beginning to end.

It is the middleweight approach, however, that application programmers use the most. XUL, JavaScript, XPCOM, and default platform processing are combined into a final application. JavaScript is the glue that holds the other technologies together.

The NPA diagram at the start of this chapter shows the bits of Mozilla that are most responsible for scripting support. From the diagram, JavaScript is both away from the user and away from the computer's operating system. This is because JavaScript and its scripts are embedded technologies that hide within other software. Scripts rarely drive Mozilla from the outside. The two most important boxes, XPConnect and the DOM, are deep inside the Mozilla Platform. They have a large number of APIs (Application Programming Interfaces), which are all available to JavaScript scripts. The scripted use of these interfaces is the main construction task when developing a Mozilla-based application. Being able to manipulate these interface script saves the programmer from having to use more laborious languages like C and C++.

The simplest use of JavaScript involves XML and the `<script>` tag. For both XUL and HTML documents, the following content will change the words in the title bar of a document's window:

```
<script> window.title = "Scripted Title"; </script>
```

Scripts like this can change any part of a displayed Mozilla window, including any part of the content. Such scripts can also interact indirectly with the wider world, including the Internet. The content of the `<script>` tag itself is highly meaningful and needs to be specially processed, just as the CSS2 content of the `<style>` tag is specially processed.

The Mozilla Platform itself is partly made out of JavaScript scripts. Such scripts are mostly found in the chrome, although a few outside exceptions, like preference files, also exist. Since the chrome is designed to contain Mozilla applications, it is no surprise that many scripts are stored there.

Before plunging into the language syntax, it's worth asking: Why pick JavaScript? That question is answered next.

5.1 JavaScript's Role as a Language

JavaScript is a member of the C family of programming languages. The most visible members of this family are C and ANSI C, Objective-C, C++, Java, JavaScript, PHP, C#, and awk.

The members of this family share syntax and some structure. These languages are all third-generation procedural languages, meaning that programs are specified as a series of ordered steps. They all contain the `if` keyword. Some of these languages are advanced enough to include support for objects. Objects provide structure on top of procedural steps.

JavaScript's essential qualities make it a (nearly) unique member of this group. It is designed to be the most accessible and easiest to use language in the family. It is also designed to be a take-anywhere language. It is highly portable, has tiny resource requirements, and doesn't need the support of a traditional compiler. This ease of use gives it wide appeal.

JavaScript code runs inside an interpreter, a virtual machine like Java's JVM, but one that is very small by comparison with that technology. It can be used in embedded devices, although the device must support 32-bit shifts and floating-point operations. Because JavaScript code is interpreted, variables are late-bound and weakly typed. This makes for an environment where it is very easy to get small programs working quickly, but very hard to get the last bugs out of big programs.

Because it is so small, JavaScript is heavily dependent on other software (called host software) before it can do anything meaningful. This is very similar to C, which can't do much without access to its companion `stdio` libraries, or a `stdio` equivalent. The Mozilla Platform, in the form of a set of libraries and an executable, provides a host for the JavaScript interpreter.

Because the host is typically large, most of the time spent scripting in JavaScript is spent exploring what the host has to offer. Inside Mozilla, JavaScript has a role similar to Visual Basic for Applications (VBA) as used inside Microsoft Word and Microsoft Excel. This is also the kind of use with which Web developers are familiar.

5.2 STANDARDS, BROWSERS, AND <SCRIPT>

Mozilla supports the ECMA-262 standard, specifically ECMAScript version 1, edition 3. This standard is also named ISO-16262. ISO is the international standards organization (but ISO is not an acronym). ECMA is the European Computer Manufacturers' Association. Web addresses are `www.iso.org` and `www.ecma.ch`. ECMAScript standards in PDF form can be downloaded for free. With a little effort, the standard is useable as an everyday language reference. There are two other ECMAScript standards. Mozilla does not support either of them.

ECMA-327 "ECMAScript Compact Profile" is a near-identical version of ECMAScript intended for embedding in tiny devices. It removes a few features considered too complex for tiny implementations. It can be viewed as an attempt to compete against the WAPScript language, and other languages designed for embedded use.

ECMA-290 "ECMAScript Components" specifies how to create modular JavaScript programs using XML-based module files. It is the basis of Microsoft's Windows Scripting Components technology. Mozilla uses XBL instead.

ECMAScript is the official name for JavaScript, because Sun Microsystems owns the Java trademark. Trademark protection includes words that extend an existing mark or derive from one. Long ago, JavaScript's pre-release name was LiveScript. Mozilla's implementation of ECMA-262 edition 3 is called JS 1.5 and is nicknamed SpiderMonkey. It is an interpreter implemented as a C library.

SpiderMonkey also supports old versions of JavaScript, including the somewhat unusual version 1.2. That version contained a variety of new features, some of which failed to become popular. Support for early versions can be turned on if required, following the approach of older Netscape browsers. In a XUL application, the latest version should always be used. In other markups, such as HTML, any version may be chosen. The `<script>` tag, supported in both HTML and XUL, is the way to make this choice.

The correct way to include JavaScript code in an XML document is like this:

```
<script type="application/x-javascript" src="code.js/>
```

This next method is deprecated, so avoid it, even though it will still work:

```
<script type="text/javascript" src="code.js/>
```

Another method can be used to choose specific versions of JavaScript:

```
<script type="JavaScript1.2" src="code.js/>
```

This final method assumes the language is JavaScript and defaults to the latest version:

```
<script src="code.js/>
```

For a new Mozilla application, the first syntax is ideal. The final syntax is a useful alternative, but to be correct and precise, the `type` attribute should always be added. All these examples have the default encoding of `encoding="UTF-8"`.

Chapter 2, XUL Layout, under "Good Coding Practices," explains why JavaScript code should always be stored outside an XML document in a separate file. The section "Using XPCOM Components" later in this chapter shows how to include a JavaScript file from another JavaScript file.

The Mozilla organization has a second JavaScript interpreter, one written in Java rather than in C. This version, called Rhino, is not used or packaged with the Mozilla Platform; however, it is available to download. It is also ECMA-262 version 1 edition 3 compliant.

5.3 ECMAScript Edition 3

This section describes the features of the JavaScript language that come from the ECMAScript standard. Enhancements are discussed in the next section. Objects provided by the host software rather than by the standards are discussed after that.

5.3.1 Syntax

Here we look at the text of the JavaScript language. Because the ECMAScript standard is nearly readable by itself, this chapter goes over that syntax only briefly. Where it is possible, an attempt is made to explore consequences of the syntax.

Mozilla JavaScript scripts are stored in plain text files. The content of those files must be encoded in UTF-8 format. This means that characters from the ASCII character set are stored as a single byte. This is normal for English-speaking places, and no special preparation is required. Just use a plain text editor for scripts.

Some computers use the unused ASCII values from 128 to 255, perhaps for European characters such as the *é* in *résumé*. In the past, this tradition has been a handy way to create text in other languages. Such practices do not follow the UTF-8 encoding rules, which demand two or more bytes for all non-ASCII characters. Embedding such 8-bit European characters won't work in scripts. "Ã©" is the correct UTF-8 encoding for *é*, or at least that is what the correct encoding looks like when viewed with a simple-minded text editor.

Even correctly specified, multibyte UTF-8-encoded characters have restricted use. They can only appear inside JavaScript string literals, inside comments, and sometimes in variable names. In general, stick to ASCII characters for your code; don't use other characters except as data. If you are European and want to use Latin1 characters for variable names, then in general they are safe if correctly expressed in UTF-8. For the fine points of Unicode support, see section 7.6 of ECMA-262 edition 3 and section 5.16 of the Unicode 3.0 standard.

Working with arbitrary Unicode characters is still possible in strings. See the section entitled "Data Types" for details.

5.3.1.1 Text Layout JavaScript is a free-format language like XML and C. Statements aren't restricted to a single line. Recognized whitespace characters include space and tab; recognized end-of-line characters include linefeed (hex 0A) and carriage-return (hex 0D). Beware that Windows, Macintosh MacOS 9, and UNIX all have a different concept of end-of-line. This doesn't affect the interpretation of scripts, but it can make editing them on the wrong computer harder.

Comments in JavaScript are written C-style. Single line comments are supported:

```
// Single line comment
```

as are parenthetic comments:

```
/* comment that can span
   multiple lines */
```

All combinations are possible except that multiline comments cannot appear inside other multiline comments. JavaScript does not have a special comment used for documentation. Scripts are not preprocessed before they are interpreted. There is no preprocessor like C's `cpp`.

5.3.1.2 Statements The basic unit of work in JavaScript is the statement. A statement is terminated by a semicolon, but that semicolon is optional. The one place that it is not optional is between the three expressions in a `for(;;)` statement. In all other cases, the JavaScript interpreter will automatically assume that a semicolon is present if it is left off. Three equivalent statements are

```
x = 5;
x = 5
x = 5   // same as previous line, even with this comment
```

This semicolon feature is designed to allow Visual-Basic style developers to feel comfortable with JavaScript. It is recommended that semicolons always be used. Not only is it clearer, but future versions of JavaScript will insist that one be present.

Scripts do not require a `main()` or any other kind of structure. Like Perl, statements can appear outside functions and outside objects from line 1 onward. JavaScript also supports the do-nothing statement:

```
;
```

JavaScript supports compound statements using the brace characters `{` and `}`, but they are different from compound statements in C (see the section entitled "Scope Rules." Bare compound statements aren't that useful in JavaScript, even though they are supported:

```
{ x = 5; y= 5; }
```

In this chapter, *statement* means either a single statement with trailing semicolon or a compound statement without a trailing semicolon.

5.3.1.3 Data Types

JavaScript has the following native data types:

```
Undefined Null Boolean Number String Object
```

There is also a hidden data type with no name that is a 32-bit signed integer.

In JavaScript, types are associated with data items, not with structures that hold data, like variables. There is an ancient analogy between programming variables and shoeboxes. In this analogy, a piece of data is a shoe, and a structure for holding it (a variable) is a shoebox. In JavaScript the type of information is attached to the shoe; it cannot be found in the shoebox. Variables holding types `Boolean`, `Number`, or `String` imply a shoebox with a single shoe of one kind in it. Type `Object` refers to a shoebox containing many shoes tied together into a single bundle. Type `Null` refers to a shoebox with nothing in it, and type `Undefined` refers to a shoebox whose contents aren't yet specified.

The `typeof` operator can be used to identify types. It will return one of the following strings for normal JavaScript data, or a custom string if the data tested come from the host software:

```
"undefined" "boolean" "number" "string" "object" "function"
```

"`object`" is returned if the data is of the `Null` type. Let's consider each type in turn.

The `Undefined` type has just one value (undefined) and no literal values. The global object (see later) has a single property named `undefined` that has this value. If necessary, the undefined value can be generated with the `void` operator, or with `undefined`:

```
x = void 0;
X = undefined;
```

The Null type has just one value: null. null is also a literal and can be used to empty a variable or in a comparison.

```
x = null;
```

The Boolean type has two values, true and false. true and false are literals for these values. False does not equal 0 (zero) as it does in C, but the conversion process between false and 0 is so seamless that any subtle difference can usually be ignored.

```
x = true;
```

The Number value stores a 64-bit double-precision floating-point number, as described in the IEEE 754 standard. That standard is not free, but a near identical draft can be had from http://www.validlab.com/754R/.

Floating point is an inexact attempt at representing a real number and is accurate to at least 15 digits, unless mathematical operations introduce further error. The IEEE 754 standard allows for Not-a-Number values (possibly resulting from dividing zero by zero, or taking the inverse sine of 2), and for Infinite values (possibly caused by overflow). The isNaN() and isFinite() methods can be used to test for these conditions. JavaScript has no literals for these values, but the global object has an NaN and an Infinity property, and the Math object has several handy properties:

```
POSITIVE_INFINITY NEGATIVE_INFINITY NaN MAX_VALUE MIN_VALUE
```

These properties can be used for comparisons. Floating-point literals support exponential notation up to about +/- 10^{300}:

```
x = -3.141592654;   y = 1.0e+23;    z = 234.555555E-100;
```

Number literals can also be specified in hexadecimal by using a 0x or 0X prefix, followed by the digits 0–9 and A–F in upper- or lowercase.

```
x = 0xFEFF;
```

JavaScript's method of comparing NaN values matches the recommendations in IEEE 754, but the unique identity of different IEEE 754 NaN values is not preserved by the ECMAScript language.

Because floating-point numbers are inexact and subject to error, they are poor choices for programming counters and indices. Integers are a better solution for such common tasks. Inside Mozilla's JavaScript interpreter, Number data are actually stored as 31-bit signed integers until there is a clear need for floating-point accuracy. The end result is that by avoiding division and by keeping numbers below about 46,000 (the square root of 2^{31}), most simple calculations in JavaScript are exact integer arithmetic without any floating-point error. These whole integers are also big enough to store any Unicode value or any CSS2 RGB (Red-Green-Blue) color value.

Several situations can cause a value to be stored as a true floating-point number. Some examples are: if a number literal has a decimal point; if division occurs where a remainder would result; if a function that has a real result (like `sin()`) is applied; or if mathematics results in a number bigger than 2^{31}. At all other times, `Numbers` are stored as integers.

If a number is converted from integer to floating-point representation, floating-point errors do not automatically occur. The IEEE 754 floating-point representation has 54 bits of precision, which is enough accuracy for all but the most intensive and repetitive calculations.

The `String` type represents a Unicode sequence of characters stored in a UTF-16 encoding (i.e., two bytes per character). Each string appears immutable as in Java; strings cannot be worked on "in place" as they can in C. String literals are delimited by a pair of single or double quotes. Special notation can be used for common nonprintable characters. This notation is inspired by special characters used in C strings. The JavaScript versions are

```
\b \t \n \v \f \r \" \' \\ and \x and \u
```

These characters are backspace, tab, newline, vertical tab, formfeed, carriage return, double quote, single quote, backslash, and the byte and Unicode leader characters. The byte leader character must be followed by two hexadecimal digits and specify a Unicode character whose code-point (character index) is between 0 and 255. This includes the ASCII characters and the non-breaking whitespace character (0xA0). It also includes ISO 8859 (Latin 1 - European) characters. The Unicode leader character must be followed by four hexadecimal digits and specifies any Unicode character you can think of. A trivial example is

```
str = "hello, world\n";
```

The `Object` type will be discussed in its own section shortly.

JavaScript provides automatic type conversion between most types. This means that a piece of data used in a context where a certain type is expected will be converted to that type before use. Such conversion is also discussed later. JavaScript does not have a casting system, but methods that can convert between types explicitly are available.

5.3.1.4 Variables JavaScript is a 3GL and therefore has user-defined variables. Variable names must start with an alphabetic letter or underscore or with $. $ should be avoided because it is rarely used in handwritten code. There is no limit on the length of a variable name. Alphanumeric characters, the dollar sign, and the underscore are the allowed characters. Variable names are case-sensitive.

```
my_variable x counter5 interCapName not$common _secret
```

Naming conventions recommend that all capitals be used for constants, with underscore as word delimiter (like Java); an initial capital be used for object constructors; and an initial underscore be used to indicate a variable is not intended for informal use.

Variables are undefined unless declared with the var keyword. If they are used without being declared, then that is a syntax error. If they are declared but nothing is assigned to them, then they are undefined. Variables are therefore defined when declared or on first use, whichever comes first. Initial assignment of variables in JavaScript is not restricted to constant expressions as is the case in C. Any expression may be used for initial assignment, and a variable can be declared anywhere in a script.

```
var x;
var y = 2, z = 3.45;
var product = x * y * z;
```

JavaScript variables store one item of data each. That item of data is either a simple value or a reference to an object. In the section entitled "Objects," it is explained that variables are also properties. JavaScript does not have pointers, and there is no syntax supporting references explicitly. Variables names may not be reserved words like `if`. The thing named `this` is a special variable that always refers to the current object.

5.3.1.5 Arrays JavaScript supports single-dimensioned arrays, like C, but their size can be specified by a nonconstant expression. Arrays are created using the new keyword, which is used to create objects of many kinds. There are several syntactic options for array creation:

```
var arr1 = new Array();              // zero-length array
var arr2 = new Array(5);             // array of 5 items
var arr3 = new Array(11,12,13);      // array of 3 items
var arr4 = new Array(2,"red",true); // array of 3 items
```

All array elements will be undefined unless content for the elements is specified at creation time. Each element of an array may contain data of any type. An array may also be created from a literal array, using the `[` and `]` bracket characters. These examples match the last ones, and are often preferred because the `Array()` method is a little ugly and confusing:

```
var arr1 = [];                // zero length array
var arr2 = [, , , , ,];       // array of 5 items
var arr3 = [11,12,13];        // array of 3 items
var arr4 = [2,"red",true];    // array of 3 items
```

Array literals can be nested so that array elements can themselves be arrays:

```
var arr5 = [ 6, ["red","blue"], 8, [], 10];
```

Array elements are referred to by their indices, which start at 0. The `length` property of an array is an integer one larger than the highest array index in the array. It is not equal to the number of elements in the array. It is kept up to date automatically:

```
a[0];           // first element of array a
b[2];           // third element of array b
c.length;       // one greater than highest index in c
c[c.length-1]; // last element of array c
d[1][4];        // see below
```

The last line in the preceding example is an array `d` whose second element `d[1]` is an array. Therefore, `d[1][4]` is the fifth element of the `d[1]` array.

Arrays are not fixed in size. The length property can be changed, either by assigning to it or by setting an element with a higher index.

```
arr1 = new Array(3);    // length is 3
arr1.length = 5;        // length is now 5;
arr1[8] = 42;           // length is now 9;
```

Arrays are sparse. In the preceding example, when the element with index 8 is set, the elements between index 5 and 8 are not created unless they are used in later statements. Because indices have the range of 32-bit unsigned integers, gaps between elements can be very large.

Looking ahead a little, arrays are also objects (of type `Array`). All objects support a little syntax that allows them to act like an array. When this is done, the object treated like an array does not gain a `length` property; it is merely allowed to use the square-bracket array notation. This array syntax can be used to find properties on all object-like data, but this flexibility doesn't benefit arrays, only other objects, as this example shows:

```
obj.prop_name == obj["prop_name"] // legal and always true
obj[1] != obj.1                   // illegal syntax
```

The syntax in the second half of the first line is useful when an object property needs to be created whose name is not a legal variable name. For example,

```
obj["A % overhead"] = 20;
```

A subtle trap with this array syntax support is caused by type conversion. Array element indices that are not integers are *not* rounded to the nearest integer. They are converted to strings instead:

```
obj[12.35] == obj["12.35"];
```

This example results in an object property being set rather than an array element because there are no floating-point indices. Array indices are typically stored in variables. If an index has been converted from an integer to a floating point as a result of some calculation, then this subtle type conversion can happen invisibly. It is difficult to spot because the property that is set will be used somewhat reliably, until the floating-point value is rounded or accumulates a fractional part due to calculation error. At that point, it will convert to a subtly different string that points to a different property. The value set also can't be recovered via a normal object property because the property name

12.35 is an illegal variable name. The moral is: Don't do complex mathematics on indices.

5.3.1.6 Expressions JavaScript expressions follow C, C++, and Java's expressions very closely and provide a means to do mathematics, bit operations, Boolean logic, and a few operations on objects. Expressions consist of variables, literals, and the operators noted in Table 5.1.

Table 5.1 JavaScript operators

Name	Binary?	Precedence	Symbol
Force highest precedence	Unary	0	( )
Array literal	Unary	0	[ ]
Object literal	Unary	0	{ }
Function call	Unary	0	( )
Property of		1	.
Element of	Binary	1	[ ]
Object literal	Unary	1	{ }
Create object	Unary	2	new
De-reference property	Unary	3	delete
Convert to undefined	Unary	3	void
Reveal type as a string	Unary	3	typeof
Pre- and postincrement	Unary	3	++
Pre- and postdecrement	Unary	3	--
Same sign	Unary	3	+
Opposite sign	Unary	3	-
32-bit bitwise NOT	Unary	3	~
Logical NOT	Unary	3	!
Multiplication		4	*
Division		4	/
Modulo		4	%
Addition, concatenation		5	+
Subtraction		5	-
32-bit left shift		6	<<
32-bit signed right shift		6	>>

Table 5.1 JavaScript operators (Continued)

Name	Binary?	Precedence	Symbol
32-bit unsigned right shift		6	>>>
Matches given type		7	instanceof
Matches object property		7	in
Ordinal comparisons		7	< > <= >=
Equality		7	== !=
Strict equality		7	=== !==
32-bit bitwise AND		8	&
32-bit bitwise XOR		9	^
32-bit bitwise OR		10	|
Logical AND		11	&&
Logical OR		12	||
Conditional	Ternary	13	?:
Simple assignment		14	=
Compound assignment		14	*= /= %= += -= <<= >>= >>>= &= ^= |=
List element delimiter		15	,

Precedence of 0 is the highest precedence. JavaScript roughly follows the left-to-right and right-to-left conventions of C for equal-precedence operators. It also supports short-circuit Boolean expressions, which means that an expression consisting of many `&&` and `||` operations is processed from left to right only until the final result is sure, not until the final term is evaluated.

One area where JavaScript Boolean logic is closer to Perl than C is in *multiplexed value sematics*. In this arrangement, `&&` and `||` used in expressions are evaluated as control-flow conditions similar to `?:` rather than as simple Boolean expressions. Thus in

```
var x = flag && y;
```

variable `x` evaluates to `y` if flag is `true`, and `false` otherwise, rather than evaluating to the Boolean result of "flag and y."

For mathematical expressions, a mixture of `Numbers` stored as integers and floating points results in all `Numbers` being promoted to floating points. If bitwise operations are attempted on `Numbers` stored as floating points, the floating-point numbers are first chopped down to 32 bits in a manner that is generally useless and unhelpful. Make sure that bit-operations only occur on `Numbers` stored as integer values.

5.3.1.7 Flow Control JavaScript supports C-style flow control. The standard forms are as follows, with the placeholder *statement* being either a single statement or a list of statements surrounded by { and }.

```
if (expression) statement
if (expression) statement else statement
while (expression) statement
do statement while (expression)
for (expression; expression; expression) statement
switch (expression) {
  case expression: statement; break;
  case expression: statement; break;     // as many as needed
  default: statement; break;
}
```

The argument to `switch()` can be anything, not just a variable. The `case` selectors are not restricted to literals either. The following two `if`s are the same:

```
if (a) statement else if (b) statement else statement
if (a) statement else {if (b) statement else statement}
```

As for many C-like languages, beware of the dangling `if` trap in which an `else` clause is attached to the last `if`, regardless of indentation; that trap is avoided by using the second, explicit syntax in this last example.

The `for` statement has a variant for stepping through the properties of a JavaScript object. Only the properties that are *not* `DontEnum` (see section 8.6.1 of ECMA-262) participate:

```
for ( variable-name in object ) statement
```

JavaScript has no `goto` statement. It does have labels, which are named as for variables but they are in a separate namespace. `continue` ends the current iteration of a loop; `break` leaves a loop or a switch statement permanently. A label can be used to break up more than one level when loops are nested several levels deep:

```
mylabel: statement;
break;
break label;
continue;
continue label;
```

JavaScript also has an exception system. It is not an optional add-on. It is part of the core language. It catches run-time errors and exceptions.

```
try { statement; }
catch (variable) { statement; }
finally { statement; }
```

There can be more than one `catch` block. The `finally` block is optional. Inside a `try` block, or anywhere, `throw` can be used to generate an exception:

```
throw expression;
```

The expression thrown can equate to any type of information from a simple number to a complex purpose-built object. To mimic the exceptions thrown by the XPConnect part of the platform, always throw a 32-bit integer, preferably including one of the values of the `Components.results` object.

Scripts are often written hastily with a quick purpose in mind, and exception handling is a less well-understood feature of 3GL languages. In reality, for a robust script, most processing should be contained in `try` blocks, as exceptions should never, ever reach the user. The simplest and most efficient way to ensure this is to wrap everything in a single, top-level `try` block

The `with` statement is discussed under "Scope."

5.3.1.8 Functions JavaScript supports functions. Functions are untyped and support a variable number of arguments, like C's `printf()`. Functions can also have no name, in which case they are anonymous. Listing 5.1 shows a typical function:

Listing 5.1 Ordinary JavaScript function syntax.

```
function sum(x, y)
{
  if (arguments.length != 2)
  {
    return void 0;
  }
  return x + y;
}

var a = sum(2,3);            // a = 5
var b = sum(1,2,3);          // b = undefined
var c = sum("red","blue");   // c = "redblue"
var d = sum(5, d);           // d = 5 + undefined = NaN
var e = sum;                 // e is now a function
var f = e(3,4);              // f = 7
```

The `arguments` object acts like an Array object, except that it is static—if more elements are added to the array, its `length` property will not be updated. It contains all the arguments passed in to the function. Functions can be anonymous as well:

```
var plus = function (x,y) { return x + y; }
var a = plus(2,3);
```

The benefit of anonymous functions is that they don't automatically create an extra variable with the name of the function. Consequently, it is possible to set methods on objects without globally defined function variables hanging around. Globally defined function names can also be avoided by placing a named function's definition inside an expression:

```
var five = (function sum(a,b){return a+b;})(2,3);
```

If a function is called by itself, not as an object method, then any use of the keyword `this` is resolved by scoping rules.

5.3.1.9 Regular Expressions JavaScript supports Perl5 regular expressions, with some obscure and rarely seen differences. Obscure differences exist because regular expression syntax is subtle in detail and always evolving and being fixed. UNIX systems have *file*, *normal*, and *extended* variants of regular expressions. Perl and JavaScript support extended regular expressions that very, very roughly match `egrep(1)`, or the "Wildcards" feature of Microsoft Word's Find dialog box. The Perl `man(1)` manual page `perlre` is easier to understand than the ECMAScript definition, but not much. Look for an online tutorial.

All regular expression operations in JavaScript are methods of the String object or the `RegExp` object; they do not have standalone existence like Perl's `m//` operator:

```
match(re)               // "red".match(/e/) == ["e"];
replace(re,string)      // "red".replace(/e/,"o") == "rod";
replace(re,function)    // "red".replace(/e/,myfn);
search(re)              // "red".search(/e/) == 1;
split(re)               // "red".split(/e/) == ["r","d"];
```

`replace()` returns a string; `search()`, an integer; and `match()` and `split()` return an array of strings each.

Regular expressions have a literal syntax that can be typed into source code anywhere that a string literal might occur. It is converted immediately to a `RegExp` object. The syntax is

```
/pattern/flags
```

`pattern` is any of the convoluted syntax of regular expressions; flags is zero or more of `g` (replace everywhere), `i` (ignore case), and `m` (match lines of multiline targets separately).

5.3.2 Objects

JavaScript has objects, but at version 1.5, it is not fully object oriented. JavaScript's report card for the many descriptive terms that apply to object-like systems is shown in Table 5.2.

All Objects and their attributes are late-bound in JavaScript. Attempting to write fully object-oriented code is a technical feat that should generally be avoided. JavaScript is designed for simple manipulation of objects, not for creating complex (or any) class hierarchies. Most of the objects used in a JavaScript script come from the host software and are implemented in another language.

There are no class definitions in JavaScript 1.5; there are only run-time types. A normal object class system allows objects to be created using an abstract specification—a class. This is like using a sketch plan to carve a

Table 5.2 JavaScript object support

Object system concept	Syntax support	Ease of use
Aggregation	High	Easy
Containment	High	Easy
Delegation	High	Medium
Encapsulation	Low	Medium
Inheritance	Medium	Difficult
Information hiding	Low	Medium
Interfaces	None	Difficult
Late-binding	High	Easy
Object-based	High	Easy
Object-oriented	None	Difficult
Multiple inheritance	None	Difficult
Run-time type reflection	High	Easy
Templates	None	Difficult

statue. JavaScript uses a prototype system to create objects instead. This is like carving a statue by starting with another statue. All JavaScript objects, except Host objects, are created using another object as the initial ingredient. This is more flexible than a class-based system, but to do anything sophisticated with it in JavaScript results in somewhat messy syntax.

5.3.2.1 Plain Objects A piece of data of type `Object` in JavaScript has a set of properties that are the contents of the object. Some properties contain Function objects and therefore are also called object methods. The special global object's properties are also called variables and functions. Just about everything in JavaScript is a property of some other object. There is no information hiding: In C++ or Java terms, all properties are public.

All properties have attributes, but these attributes are a subtle feature of the language and have no syntax of their own. You can read about attributes in the ECMAScript standard, but you should really just forget them. They are different from XML attributes.

To create an object of your own, use either `new` or an object literal as in Listing 5.2.

Listing 5.2 Examples of object creation in JavaScript.

```
// explicit approach
var obj = new Object;
```

```
obj.foreground = "red";
obj.background = "blue";

// literal approach
var obj = { foreground:"red", background:"blue" }
```

To add a method to an object, just use a function or an anonymous function as a property's value. Anonymous functions can also appear in object literals as shown in Listing 5.3.

Listing 5.3 Examples of method creation in JavaScript.

```
function start_it() { this.run = true; }

// explicit approach
var obj = new Object;
obj.start = start_it;
obj.stop = function (){ this.run = false; }

// literal approach
var obj = { start: function (){ this.run = true; },
            stop: function (){ this.run = false; }
          }

// execute the methods
obj.start();
obj.stop();
```

The `this` operator refers to the object that the function using `this` is a property of.

Objects may contain other objects:

```
var obj = {
  mother:{name:"Jane", age:34},
  father:{name:"John", age:35}
};
var my_ma_name = obj.mother.name;
```

Containment and association are the same thing in JavaScript because there is no information hiding. It is possible to do some information hiding by messing around with the properties of `Function` objects in the prototype chain. This can create permanent properties that are in scope only when a function runs—effectively a private variable. That obscure technical trick is generally unnecessary. Only do it if you are supplying a library of precreated objects for someone else's consumption, and you want the library to be absolutely rock-solid. See also the section entitled "Language Enhancements" for information on property getters and setters.

If many objects with similar properties are to be created, then fully specifying each one by hand is a tedious solution. An object constructor is a better solution. This is a function called as an argument to new. Inside the function, whatever standard properties the object needs are set. The constructor function can then be reused for each new object, as Listing 5.4 shows.

Listing 5.4 Examples of object construction using a constructor function().

```
function Parents(ma, pa)
{
  this.mother = { mother:ma; };
  this.father = { father:pa; };
  this.dog = "Spot";
}
var family1 = new Parents("Jane","John");
var family2 = new Parents("Joanne","Joe");
```

This system can be further improved. As soon as the constructor function exists, its prototype object can be modified. The prototype object for a constructor is an object that contributes default properties to the constructed object. The following lines could be added to Listing 5.4, immediately after the function definition for `Parents`:

```
Parents.prototype.lastname = "Smith";
Parents.prototype.ring = function (){ dial(123456789); };
```

When `family1` and `family2` get new parents, they will also have properties matching those in the prototype, for a total of five properties. Not only will they both have a dog named Spot, but they will both be Smith and both be able to ring on the same number. In fact, the `lastname` and `ring` properties are shared between the two objects. If one object updates its `lastname` property, that value will override the prototype's `lastname` property, and the object will cease to share the `lastname` property of the prototype. If the prototype object's `lastname` property is updated, then any objects sharing that property will see the change. This is not the case for the `dog` property, which is unique to each object created.

The purpose of this system is to allow an object to be extensively modeled once (by the prototype object) and then to permit that model to be reused by the constructor when a copy is created. The constructor can be restricted to dealing with construction parameters and running any initialization methods that might be required. Unfortunately, the prototypes system is somewhat unencapsulated because the prototype properties must be set outside the constructor.

See also the section entitled "Prototype Chains" in this chapter.

5.3.2.2 Host Objects Host objects exist outside JavaScript in the host software in which the interpreter is embedded. In Mozilla, such objects are typically written in C++. A piece of C code attached to the JavaScript interpreter finds them when they are asked for, constructs a simple internal interface that looks like a JavaScript object, hooks this up to the Host object, and thus exposes the Host object to scripting. The tricky part is finding the object in the first place, and JavaScript needs assistance from the host software (the Mozilla Platform) for that. The `document` object is an example of a host object.

Host objects appear the same as plain JavaScript objects to programmers, unless you try to turn them back into code using `toString()`. Because functions and methods are also objects in JavaScript, this difference applies to single functions or methods as well. For example, this piece of code attempts to discover the function body of the `alert()` function (which in XUL is a method of a host object of type `ChromeWindow`):

```
var str = "" + alert;
```

The resulting string, however, shows that `alert()` has no JavaScript source:

```
"\nfunction alert() {\n    [native code]\n}"
```

5.3.2.3 Native Objects A JavaScript interpreter has its own range of objects. Their names and types are

```
Object Array Boolean Number String Math Date RegExp Function Error
```

Objects can be created automatically and on the fly by the JavaScript interpreter, or they can be created by hand, which requires a constructor. These object names are also the names of the matching object constructor objects. Therefore, construct an object of type `Boolean` with the `Boolean` object constructor object. That constructor object is named `Boolean`:

```
var flag = new Boolean();
```

Technically it makes a difference whether an object prototype object or an object constructor object is used with `new`, but in practical terms they are the same. The latter case requires function parenthesis, whereas the earlier case doesn't.

The `Object` and `Array` types have already been discussed. `Array` objects maintain a length property, whereas `Object` objects don't.

The `Boolean`, `Number`, and `String` objects match the basic data types of the same name. JavaScript freely and automatically converts between simple data and objects of the same kind, even for literals. This example shows automatic conversion of literals to objects, which then execute a single method.

```
"Test remark".charAt(3);     // result: "t"
1.2345.toFixed(2);           // result: 1.23
true.toString();             // result: "true"
```

The `Math` object provides numerous basic mathematical operations, such as `Math.sin()`.

The `Date` object stores dates and has many accessor methods. `Date` objects only support a version of the Western Gregorian calendar extended forwards and backwards in time. They support dates before the UNIX Epoch (1 January 1970) and are not 32-bit `time_t` values. They are IEEE double precision and reach backward and forward 280,000 years. Dates are accurate to one millisecond, provided that the computer has an accurate clock. The zero value for dates matches the UNIX Epoch, so all `time_t`'s are valid `Date` values. Do not use the `getYear()` method, which is old; use the `getFullYear()` method instead.

The `RegExp` object holds a regular expression pattern and flags. Some methods related to regular expressions also exist on the `String` object.

The `Function` object is the object that represents functions and methods. It has clumsy constructor syntax. Anonymous functions or the `function` keyword syntax are almost always preferred to using "`new Function`".

The `Error` object reports run-time errors and exceptions that aren't caught by `catch` or `finally`. It is little use to application programmers, who can just look at Mozilla's JavaScript Console for the same information.

When studying one of these objects, use the ECMA-262 standard as a reference. The properties and methods for object of type X are described in section 15 under "Properties of the X Prototype Object" and "Properties of X Instances." This rule applies for all cases except the `Math` object (see the next section).

5.3.2.4 Built-in Objects and Similar Effects When the JavaScript interpreter starts, some objects are made available without any user scripting. These are called *built-in* objects if they are native objects. It's also possible for host objects to appear before any scripting occurs. Such automated setup is always done for convenience reasons. The best examples are the `Global` object, the `Math` object, and the `document` object.

The global object sits at the top of an object containment hierarchy. It is the root object in JavaScript. It is not the property of any other object, and a global object cannot be created without creating a separate and independent run-time environment. In Mozilla, the Window object (for HTML) and ChromeWindow objects (for XUL) are global objects. Therefore, each Mozilla window is a separate run-time environment. These global objects are implemented so that they have a `window` property. That window property refers back at the global object (a loop). Programmers use this window object as the "top-level object" in scripts.

A `Math` object is also created every time a JavaScript instance starts. This is referenced by a property of the global object called `Math`. It allows the following shorthand syntax for mathematical operations:

```
var one = Math.sin(Math.PI/2);
```

If a document is loaded into a Mozilla window, then that loading process can automatically populate JavaScript with many additional objects. These objects are familiar to Web programmers as the Document Object Model, level 0. In HTML, these objects form a large containment hierarchy commonly used like this:

```
window.document.form3.username.value = "John";
```

The explicit use of a `window.` prefix is optional. Equivalent prefixes are `this` and `self`.

By comparison with HTML, XUL has a very limited set of precreated objects. It uses an XPCOM name service to find host objects that are not precreated.

5.3.3 Processing Concepts

Separate to visible syntax is the way the JavaScript interpreter crunches through your script. There are a number of novel concepts to the language.

5.3.3.1 Operator Precedence Precedence of operators is noted in Table 5.1. The left-to-right and right-to-left ordering that JavaScript uses is similar to that of C, C++, and Java.

5.3.3.2 Argument Passing All function and method arguments are passed by reference, except for Booleans, numbers, null, and undefined. Those few cases are passed by value (copied).

5.3.3.3 Type Conversion JavaScript automatically converts data between all simple types and the `Number`, `String`, and `Boolean` types. It forces type conversion so that expressions can be evaluated in all cases. Every object in JavaScript has a `toNumber()` method and a `toString()` method that are used to assist in this process. Casts are not required; it is done according to an extensive set of rules in the ECMA-262 standard. These rules can be boiled down to just two rules:

> Rule 1: Never assume that conversion will work when trying to change a string into a number.
>
> Rule 2: Don't use binary operators on objects whose types you aren't sure of.

Rule 1 exists because the contents of a string might be an invalid number literal. This code will cause the JavaScript interpreter to return `NaN` and, in worse cases, the interpreter may halt:

```
var str = "123stop45";
var x = str * 3;          // str isn't a number.
```

Halting can only occur if syntax errors or run-time errors occur. To guard against such things, use the `parseInt()` and `parseFloat()` functions explicitly instead:

```
var x = parseInt("123stop45") * 3;
```

Rule 2 exists because the comparison operators (<, ==, etc.) and + are overloaded for Strings and Numbers. The rules that decide whether to ultimately treat both operands as strings or numbers are not immediately obvious, and they have different senses for comparison and concatenation operators. If in doubt, see Rule 1.

5.3.3.4 Scope Scope is the process of deciding what variables, objects, and properties are available to use at what point in the code. Scope in JavaScript has two sides.

The first side is traditional variable scoping. This is the same as C and C++ where variables may be local to a function or global. In JavaScript, functions can have a local variable with the same name as a variable outside the function. When the function is interpreted, the local variable is used. When statements outside the function are interpreted, the global variable is used.

In C and C++, in addition to function and global scopes, every statement block has its own block scope. This means that the scope of a variable declared inside a set of statements surrounded by { and } is different from that of variables declared outside. In JavaScript, such a statement block does *not* create a new scope. It has no such effect.

In C and C++, variables declared partway through a scope are valid from that point onward in the scope. In JavaScript, variables declared partway through a function (or through a global section of code) are valid for the entire scope. This code, illegal in the equivalent C/C++, is valid JavaScript.

```
function f() {
  alert(x);      // reports "undefined"
  var x = 42;
  alert(x);      // reports "42";
}
f();
```

The second side to scope is JavaScript's unusual concept of scope chains. A scope chain is an ordered list of objects that has at one end the global object. When a function call occurs, the interpreter must first find the function matching the function call. It does so by looking at the objects in the scope chain. The first object found that has a method with the same name as the function will be executed as that function. This is the mechanism that allows event handlers in Web pages to call functions based on the window object, even though the current object is something else. A scope chain makes services from several objects available at the same time.

The `with` statement in JavaScript adds objects temporarily to the scope chain. In Listing 5.5, you can see that the `toString()` function is used repeatedly, and each time it is found in a different object. At the same time, the `myflag` variable is always found in the `window` object because none of the other objects has a `myflag` property.

Listing 5.5 Example of JavaScript scope chains at work.

```
// scope chain = window
var myflag = "Test String";
```

```
var x = toString();      // "[object ChromeWindow]"
with (document)
{
  // scope chain = document, window
  x = toString();        // "[object HTMLDocument]"
  x = new Object;
  with (x)
  {
    // scope chain = x, document, window
    var y = toString(); // "[object Object]"
    var x = myflag;      // window.myflag
  }
}
```

Scope chains are a distant cousin to the vtables inside C++ that implement inheritance, except that scope chains are not fixed sizes and do not implement classical object inheritence. For application programmers, scope chains are handy but usually require no thought.

5.3.3.5 Stacks and Garbage Collection C, C++, and Java use two kinds of memory for data: a stack and a pool (also called a heap). The stack is used automatically as required, and the pool is used whenever `new` or `malloc()` is called. JavaScript has no stack, or at least no stack with which the programmer can work. Everything goes into the memory pool. Neither array elements nor function arguments are guaranteed to be contiguous. Stacks are used to implement passing of function arguments in the Mozilla SpiderMonkey implementation, but that stack mechanism is not visible to JavaScript programmers.

Java is a pointer-free garbage-collected language, as is JavaScript. JavaScript has one garbage collector per run-time instance. It is possible for objects in one window to contain references to objects in other windows. When a window is destroyed, any user-defined JavaScript objects are marked for collection. JavaScript's garbage collector does not run in a separate thread as Java's does.

5.3.3.6 Run-time Evaluation JavaScript has the capability to interpret new code at run time. The most powerful and general way to do this is by using the global object's `eval()` method. `eval()` can be used to execute any legal JavaScript:

```
var x = 5;
var code = "x = x + 1;";
eval(code);               // x = 6
x = x + 1;                // x = 7
```

Other methods for evaluating code at run time are not specific to the interpreter itself. In Mozilla, they include the `setTimeout()` and `setInterval()` methods, the very limited `parseInt()` and `parseFloat()`, and the javascript: URL. See the section entitled "Using XPCOM Components" for a further script-evaluation mechanism.

5.3.3.7 Closures JavaScript supports closures. This example illustrates:

```
function accumulate(x) {
  return function (y) { return x + y };
}
var subtotal = accumulate(2);
var total    = subtotal(3);   // total == 5
```

When the anonymous function is called, what will the return value be? If the x argument's state is cleaned up when the accumulate() function's scope ends, then it won't be available to contribute to the return value of the subtotal() call.

Closures are a solution to this problem. A closure is a collection of data that needs to live beyond the end of a function. It is basically a copy of scoped variables that refer to other objects. The copies are returned; therefore, the referred-to data doesn't lose its last reference when the originals are cleaned up. This prevents garbage collection of created objects when the scope ends. Closures are invisible to the programmer. Closure behavior makes sense for any language that supports run-time code evaluation.

5.3.3.8 Prototype Chains Perhaps the most complex feature of JavaScript is the prototype system. It is specified in a rather dense fashion in section 4.2.1 of the ECMAScript, 3rd Edition standard. Earlier we noted that every constructor has a prototype object, and that such a prototype object can be used to model the common parts of the objects that a constructor constructs.

In fact, every object in JavaScript has a prototype object, which is named __proto__, including objects used as prototype objects. This makes the following code perfectly valid:

```
MyConstructor.prototype.__proto__.value = 5;
```

Such a set of prototypes, whether explicitly stated or not, is called a prototype chain. The chain comes to an end with the Object.prototype object, which has no prototype of its own. All elements of the chain contribute properties to a final constructed object. The chain is an ordered list of its elements, so properties are contributed in that order. One effect of this order is *shadowing*, in which properties contributed later can override the values of properties with the same names contributed earlier.

Prototypes can be used to implement object-oriented inheritance. The simplest way to do this is to change a prototype to a new "base class," that is, to a new prototypical object. From Listing 5.4, this could be done as follows:

```
function Family() { };              // Some constructor.
Family.prototype = new Parents;     // New base "class".
```

The prototype property can also be set from within the constructor, providing that enough variations on shared, unshared, and cloned parts of the chain allow many tricks. Even multiple inheritances can be implemented, but they are applied rather awkwardly. Before attempting to work with multiple inheritance, read carefully section 4.2.1 of the standard. For most purposes, this complexity should be avoided. One base class as shown here is usually enough. Give it methods but no other properties.

Mozilla applications occasionally use the prototyping system to create custom objects. This is mostly done when more than one object of a given type is required. It is verbose to create explicitly several objects using object literals, so an object constructor is created once and used for each object needed instead.

5.4 Language Enhancements

Mozilla's JavaScript language has a few features beyond ECMA-262 Edition 3.

5.4.1 Mozilla SpiderMonkey Enhancements

Mozilla's interpreter, SpiderMonkey, is relaxed about what constitutes a valid statement:

```
x++ % y++;
```

This is standards-compliant behavior but other JavaScript implementations do not support it.

Perhaps the most useful standards extension is a feature that allows JavaScript `get` and `set` methods to be attached to an object property. In other words, when the property is read or written to, a whole function runs as a side-effect. The function must implement the normal action that occurs when a property is read or written as well. Listing 5.6 illustrates these extensions at work.

Listing 5.6 Creating an active property on a JavaScript object.

```
var obj = {
  get foo ()    { effect1(); return this._real_foo; },
  set foo (val) { effect2(); return this._real_foo = val;},
  _real_foo: "bar"
  }

var x = obj.foo;  // effect1() runs, and x = "bar"
obj.foo = "zip";   // effect2() runs, and _real_foo = "zip"
```

In this example, the `_real_foo` property stores the true state of the `foo` property, which really only exists as an interface. In ECMAScript standards terminology, these special functions allow you to implement the [[Get]] and [[Put]] operations on a property with functions of your own design.

Mozilla also provides some management functions that can be used on the same getters and setters. These functions are

```
_defineGetter__("property-name", function-object);
_defineSetter__("property-name", function-object);
_lookupGetter__("property-name");
_lookupSetter__("property-name");
```

The first two functions have the same effect as the syntax noted in the previous example. The second two functions return the function installed as either the getter or setter.

Mozilla also supports a __parent__ property that reflects the [[Scope]] internal property of function objects. Mozilla's JavaScript also provides this property on all native and host objects.

Finally, Mozilla supplies a __proto__ property that can be used to set explicitly or read the internal [[Prototype]] property described in the standard.

5.4.2 ECMA-262 Edition 4 Enhancements

Edition 4 of ECMAScript, currently in draft, is an overhaul of the language with numerous goals. In general, it is an attempt to broaden the language to include full object-oriented support, packages, better interfaces to other languages, and numerous other small enhancements. It replaces the prototype system with classes and has a strict mode that requires all code to match Edition 4. It also has a nonstrict mode for backward compatibility.

Few of the proposed features of Edition 4 are present in SpiderMonkey 1.5, but the standard is close to being finished. A starting point for Edition 4 issues is http://www.mozilla.org/js/language/.

A simple Edition 4 extension is support for constants:

```
const varname = 5;
```

Mozilla has a javascript.options.strict preference, which can be set to true. This also appears in the Debug part of the preferences dialog box if a nightly build of the platform is used. This option is not the same as edition 4 strict mode; it is just additional checks against normal edition 3 code. For developers, it is a recommended preference.

SpiderMonkey 2.0 is planned to be equivalent to Edition 4 of the standard.

5.4.3 Security Enhancements

The Mozilla Platform runs interpreted scripts on the user's computer, which is a potential security problem. Features in the platform address security problems in a variety of ways, and a couple of these apply to JavaScript. For a more general discussion on security, see Chapter 16, XPCOM Objects.

A script will generate an error if processing exceeds a very large (4194304) number of backflow instructions. Roughly, one backflow instruction is any script processing that is a function return, a new loop iteration, or an aborted scope due to an exception. Such processing is seen as a denial-of-service attack that prevents user input from being processed. In a browser, such an error results in a popup warning to the user, who can then stop the script.

It is still possible to do lengthy, CPU-intensive processing in a script—just divide the work into chunks, and submit each chunk via the `setTimeout()` or `setInterval()` methods. This creates a scheduling opportunity between chunks that allows user input to be received and in turn prevents popup warnings.

Mozilla's general strategy on security is the "same origin" principle. A script loaded from one Web site (domain and path) may not interact with a document or resource from another Web site (less qualified path). This keeps Mozilla windows separate from each other. Attempts to set variables in windows where access is disallowed by security results in an exception (an error).

Scripts stored inside the chrome are released from security restrictions. The largest restriction is that the `Components` property of the `Window` or `ChromeWindow` object is fully accessible. This property is the entry point to all of Mozilla's XPCOM components. None of these components are directly accessible from outside the chrome. Some of these objects underlie other functionality that is independently made accessible. An example is the object that implements the `Form` object that is made available in HTML documents.

JavaScript scripts may be signed using digital certificate technology. In that case, the script may be granted capabilities equal to those of chrome scripts.

5.5 Mozilla's Scriptable Interfaces

Like a hand in a glove, a JavaScript interpreter and the host software in which it is embedded go together. This topic describes the host software's contribution to that partnership.

As for C, the JavaScript language has no input or output operations. All input and output must be done via host objects. At least a trivial piece of host software is required to provide those host objects.

If basic input/output (I/O) features are provided, then a script can draw in other scripts from elsewhere. In theory, such scripts can be used to create very large programs. This is similar to Perl's module environment, but it is not common practice in JavaScript. In JavaScript, the expectation is that most of a program's functionality will be implemented by host objects. Because of this expectation, learning the language syntax and semantics is trivial compared to learning typically extensive object libraries.

Host objects are a JavaScript concept. Although such things appear as objects inside a script, the host software services behind those objects needn't be objects in turn. In Mozilla's case, scriptable functionality provided by the platform consists of sets of interfaces. Many of these interfaces are indistinguishable from objects, and many of these interfaces are implemented as C++ objects. They may also be implemented in pure JavaScript. Such things are called interfaces just to make the point that they formally and precisely expose features of the platform. The concept of interface in Mozilla follows Java's and Microsoft COM's concepts of interface—a selection of features that an object might provide, a selection that is not necessarily all of the object's functionality.

5.5.1 Interface Origins

All host objects are the same from a script's point of view, but host objects come from different places. Technologies that contribute host objects include:

- **World Wide Web Consortium standards.** The W3C DOM standards describe extensive programming interfaces to XML documents. These interfaces give scripts almost total control over document content.
- **Application and Browser Object Models** (AOM and BOM). In addition to DOM objects, the Mozilla Platform provides further objects that are available when an HTML or XUL document is displayed in a window. Some of these objects are supported by other Web browsers; some are not.
- **XPConnect and XPCOM.** This system is unique to the Mozilla Platform and provides access to all the components that make up that platform. Those components do much of the processing that goes on inside an application. Components also represent a library or toolbox of tools useful for standard programming problems, like access to sockets.
- **XBL bindings.** The XBL markup language, described in Chapter 15, XBL Bindings, combines an XML document, JavaScript, and a style rule to add scriptable interfaces to an XML document. Although these interfaces are specified in files outside the Mozilla Platform, logic in the platform is responsible for parsing them and tying them to scriptable objects.

These interfaces are all combined in the Mozilla environment. In particular, they can all be used inside a single window, which represents the root global variable of JavaScript's object system. Together they make for a rich programming environment.

Mozilla also has smaller scale JavaScript support. Some aspects of the platform, such as the preference system and the install system, have their own, independent JavaScript environments. These environments include a very small number of host objects dedicated to a specific purpose. The interpreted scripts that use them are cut off from the rest of the platform and its services. This chapter calls these environments *island interfaces.*

5.5.2 W3C DOM Standards

The Document Object Model standards are numbered starting from 0 (zero) and are designed to be independent of any particular piece of software. Mozilla supports all of DOM 0, all of DOM 1, most of DOM 2, a little of DOM 3, and numerous nonstandard extensions. Non-Mozilla Web browsers, like Internet Explorer 6 and Opera, support at least DOM 0 and DOM 1. There are many programming libraries that can be used to add DOM 1 support to an application that must process XML content.

Where Mozilla implements a DOM feature, that feature is exactly the same in Mozilla as in the standard. It is very straightforward.

The downloadable PDF (Portable Document Format) versions of these standards are good enough that they can be used as electronic help while programming. All versions from 1 onward are available at `www.w3.org`. To save not-yet-final drafts, which are typically available only in XHTML, use a recent version of Mozilla and save the file as "Web page, complete." Displaying such XHTML files saved locally might be slow if you are offline. If that happens, choose File | Work Offline for an immediate solution.

The appendices in these standards include a JavaScript binding for each interface, but those bindings are quite wordy. The IDL syntax used throughout those documents is close in syntax to JavaScript. It can be read and trivially translated into JavaScript scripts. That is the recommended way to go.

If you can understand the IDL syntax in these standards documents, then you are perfectly placed to understand the XPIDL files that describe Mozilla's XPCOM components. We will discuss those components in more detail shortly.

5.5.2.1 DOM 0 Mozilla supports DOM 0 in HTML documents only. Many objects available in XUL are inspired by equivalent DOM 0 objects, so DOM 0 should be used as a guide that says what to expect in XUL.

DOM version 0 has no W3C standard and represents early JavaScript support for HTML only. The contents of DOM 0 are roughly equivalent to the scriptable features of version 3 Web browsers. The best documentation on those features is available on Netscape's DevEdge Web site—`http://devedge.netscape.com`—where historical documents are still retained. Look for guides to early versions of Navigator under "archived information."

DOM 0 applies to HTML, not XML or XUL. As noted earlier, it provides a standard set of precreated objects that are made available to the scripter when an HTML document is loaded. The most famous example is the `Image` object that has been used extensively to implement the DHTML image rollover technique. See any book on intermediate Web page design.

DOM 0 objects often exactly match one HTML tag; for example, the `<input>` tag has an `InputElement` or `FormElement` object. In XUL, use the HTML tag nearest the XUL tag as a guide to the DOM 0 object for that XUL tag.

5.5.2.2 DOM 1 Mozilla supports DOM 1 completely.

Of the many features that the DOM 1 standard provides, the interfaces named `Node`, `NodeList`, `Element`, and `Document` provide 90% of the needs of scripts. The important properties and methods of these interfaces are listed in Table 5.3.

Table 5.3 Most useful features in the DOM 1 standards

Property or method	DOM interface	Use
parentNode	Node	The parent tag of the current tag
childNodes	Node	All the child tags of the current tag, as a NodeList
firstChild	Node	First child tag of the current tag
nextSibling	Node	Next child tag of the current tag's parent tag
Node insertBefore(aNode, existingNode)	Node	Add a tag or text before the stated child tag or text
Node removeChild(existingNode)	Node	Remove a tag or text from the immediate children of this tag
Node appendChild(aNode)	Node	Add a tag or text to the end of the children of this tag
String getAttribute(attString)	Element	Return the value of an existing attribute on this tag, or ""
void setAttribute(attString, value)	Element	Set attribute="value" text for this tag
void removeAttribute(attString)	Element	Remove the given attribute, if any, from this tag
Boolean hasAttribute(attString)	Element	Report existence of the stated attribute
Element createElement(tagString)	Document	Create a tag; the tag exists separate from the current document
Node createTextNode(value)	Document	Create text; the text exists separate from the current document

Table 5.3 Most useful features in the DOM 1 standards (Continued)

Property or method	DOM interface	Use
Element getElementById(idString)	Document	Get the tag with the specified id
NodeList getElementsByTagName(tagString)	Element, Document	Get all the tags with the specified tag name
Node item(i)	NodeList	Get the ith node in the list
length	NodeList	Return the number of nodes in the list

Because `Element` and `Document` interfaces are also `Nodes`, all the properties and methods noted against `Node` apply to those other interfaces.

The DOM1 standard ignores the history of DOM 0 and starts out afresh. It consists of two parts.

The first part is very general and applies to all XML documents, including MathML, SVG, and XUL. It also applies to XHTML and HTML. It breaks a text document up into a treelike structure, much as you might see in the "auto-indented tag view" of an HTML editor. Mozilla will display such a structure if you load an XML document whose XML application type it doesn't understand. This structure is a containment hierarchy.

Everything in DOM 1 part 1 is a Node object. Documents, tags, tag attributes, and tag contents are all objects that are subtypes of Node. The document tree is a tree of Nodes, with the top node being the Document object. The DOM 1 part 1 tree knows nothing about specific tags (such as XUL tags). So there is no `<button>` object. There is only a generic Element object, used for all tags. Processing is the same for XML, HTML, or XUL.

There are two ways to navigate such a tree. The first way uses a query system. You can use the DOM 1 equivalent of Microsoft's `document.all()`, or a Mozilla enhancement:

```
document.getElementsByTagName("button"); // all XML
document.getElementsByAttribute("class", "*"); // only XUL
```

The `"*"` parameter indicates that all values for the attribute are allowed. The other navigation technique is to step through the tree explicitly, using data structures and algorithms. For example, this code reaches down two levels into a document:

```
document.firstChild().firstChild().getAttribute("type");
```

DOM 1 part 1 also provides a complete set of features for inserting, updating, and deleting XML content, but this must be done by constructing objects, not by submitting fragments of XML content. Constructing objects can be a lengthy and unwieldy process if the content changes are significant. Mozilla has a single enhancement to make these jobs easier: the `innerHTML` property. This improvement is inspired by Internet Explorer and allows XML content to be added directly to a tag's content. Despite the name, this works for XML and XUL as well as HTML:

```
tag_object.innerHTML = '<box><button value="On"/></box>';
old_content = tag_object.innerHTML;
```

Mozilla does not support the Internet Explorer extensions `innerText`, `outerHTML`, or `outerText`.

The second part of DOM 1 is intended to be HTML-specific. DOM 1 part 2 provides handy methods and attributes for a HTML document. If a tag is an HTML tag, then the matching node in the DOM tree will have properties matching the HTML attributes of that tag. So a `<FORM>` tag is a node in the tree with `action`, `enctype`, and `target` properties, among others.

DOM 1 part 2 provides two more ways to access tag collections:

```
document.getElementsByName('myform1');
document.getElementById('testid');
```

`getElementById()` is also supported for XUL and is used everywhere. `getElementsByName()` is not recommended, not even for HTML, because the name aspect of HTML is being dropped from the standards.

To summarize, DOM 1 breaks down a whole XML or HTML document into a big data structure that's fully modifiable. If the document is an HTML document, then attributes are reflected as object properties for known tags. In either case, collections of similar tags can be extracted from the data structure simply. You can call DOM 1 the "canonical" (authoritatively accepted) interface.

5.5.2.3 DOM 2 Mozilla almost fully supports DOM 2.

The DOM 2 standard fills in a number of gaps in the DOM 1 standard. It is a superset of DOM 1. DOM 1 is written in one document, but DOM 2 is written in six documents. They are:

1. DOM 2 Core
2. DOM 2 HTML
3. DOM 2 Events
4. DOM 2 Style
5. DOM 2 Traversal and Range
6. DOM 2 Views

The DOM 2 Core and HTML documents are the same as the DOM 1 document. Some small fixes are present, but recent editions of the DOM 1 standard also have these fixes. A minor enhancement remains. The DOM 2 Core/HTML standards call everything in DOM 1 the "fundamental interface." The "extended interface" in DOM 2 provides several nice-to-have features that are allowed only in XML, not HTML. These features are interfaces that give access to

- Entity references like `&`
- Processing instructions implemented by languages such as XSLT
- The `<!ENTITY>` declarations in the document's defining DTD

The DOM 2 Events standard also provides the well-known Web browser events. In addition to the mouse events (`'click'`) and HTML-specific events (`'submit'`), there are general XML events (`'DOMFocusIn'`). There are also events that fire when the document tree is changed or "mutated." No key press events (`'keydown'`) are documented in DOM 2 Events. The DOM 2 Events standard also says how events travel around the document tree. Events are discussed in detail in Chapter 6, Events.

The DOM 2 Style standard compliments the CSS2 standard, giving JavaScript access to styles. In DOM 1, the only thing you can do is update the style attribute of a tag (an inline style). The DOM 2 standard lets you work with style rules as though they are objects, not just text content. It also lets you examine and change the fully cascaded style of any given tag. The following code

```
document.getElementById("greeting").style.color ="red";
```

changes a piece of text to red, regardless of what mix of external or inline styles exist. This interface, however, *is not supported in XUL*. It is supported in HTML only.

The DOM 2 Traversal and Range standard caters to user cut 'n' paste actions. This feature requires careful examination of the DOM tree to see what tags the user has selected. For this examination, better ways of stepping through the tree are needed. That is the Traversal part, where new objects called `Iterators` and `TreeWalkers` are specified. The Range part creates a collection of tag objects matching the tags selected with the mouse. In Mozilla, cut 'n' paste, where it exists, is done using this standard. The Range standard also does a little sophisticated processing of tags. It can chop tags in two, insert content between tags, and perform a few other conveniences. The ability to insert content more easily into an XML document while being guaranteed that the document will remain well formed is a powerful feature.

The DOM 2 Traversal and Range standard is mostly intended for building new software. This is even more true for the DOM 2 Views standard. Its purpose is to provide interfaces that let the DOM tree display in several windows at once. The most obvious use of this is in a Web page editor like HomeSite, where there is a user view, a source code view, and a document structure view, all visible at once. Updating the underlying model via one view updates the others. DOM 2 Views explains the interfaces needed so that you can build such an editor.

Of the six DOM 2 documents, two are from DOM 1, two are very useful (events and styles), and two are more obscure. You might call the DOM 2 standards the "user interaction" standards in the sense that they provide features that accommodate user input and page display.

5.5.2.4 DOM 3 Mozilla supports only a little of the DOM 3 standards.

The DOM 3 standards are very new, but they are near completion as this book goes to print. Much of the standardized functionality is not available in browsers yet. There are five parts to DOM 3:

1. DOM 3 Core
2. DOM 3 Events
3. DOM 3 Load and Save
4. DOM 3 Validation
5. DOM 3 XPath

DOM 3 Core makes minor changes to the DOM 2 Core. Two things are significant. This DOM 3 example

```
document.getInterface("SVG");
```

allows other standards implemented in the browser to be revealed to script use. This is equivalent to `use` in Perl. If SVG support in the browser provides an SVG interface to JavaScript, and it's not visible to you by default, this is the way to make it visible.

The second significant change is this example:

```
document.setNormalizationFeature("format-pretty-print");
```

which gives you additional control over an XML processor. The processor engine makes many decisions when loading a XUL or an HTML file, like how whitespace is handled and when errors are reported. As soon as DOM 3 Core is implemented, you will be able to control these decisions.

DOM 3 Events supplies the keypress events (now called text events) missing from DOM 2 Events. Most of the PC keys like Alt, Caps Lock, and F12 are specified. Multiple event handler listeners are also new. This feature allows two event handlers on the same tag to fire when just one event occurs. This is the only part of DOM 3 that Mozilla comes close to supporting.

The DOM 3 Abstract Schemas and Load and Save standard, which bears quite a lengthy name, is another two-part standard. The Abstract Schemas part provides full read-write access to the DTD of an XML document. This is more likely to be useful in an XML database than in a browser. The Load and Save part describes how to go from XML text to a DOM tree and back again. It is a serialization or encoding standard. This is the standards-based solution to the problem that the `innerHTML` property solves.

DOM 3 Validation adds a constraint system to document manipulation operations. Using the other DOM standards, it is possible to change a document so that it no longer conforms to its document type. For example, it is possible using the DOM 1 interfaces to add a `<circle>` tag to the content of an

HTML document, even though `<circle>` is not an HTML tag. The DOM 3 Validation standard checks the type definition of a document (either a DTD or an XSchema definition) every time one of the other DOM interfaces is used to modify the document. If the modification would break the rules implicit in the document type, the change is not allowed. It acts as a type of police officer.

Finally, DOM 3 XPath brings yet another method of stepping through the DOM tree to JavaScript, based on the W3C XPath standard. DOM 3 XPath exposes the XPath system to JavaScript.

You might call the DOM 3 standards the "heavy engineering" DOM standards. It will probably be a long time before the DOM 3 standards are ever used for publicly accessible XML pages. On the other hand, they are of vital interest to application developers working on high-end tools like WYSIWYG (What You See Is What You Get) document processors. Perhaps one day Mozilla will have full support.

It is unlikely that a DOM 4 set of standards will appear any time soon, if ever.

5.5.2.5 DOM Compatibility Ticks The DOM standards supply a `DOMImplementation` interface, which contains a `hasFeature()` method. This method can be called from JavaScript to reveal the standards that Mozilla claims to support. A suitable line of script is

```
f = document.implementation.hasFeature("XML","1.0");
```

Some past debate on `hasFeature` is recorded in Mozilla's bug database. Table 5.4 shows the results for Mozilla 1.0 and 1.4. "FALSE" is capitalized in the table only for ease of reading.

The results are the same for both XUL and HTML scripts, which makes reporting of the "HTML" feature incorrect when in an XUL document. XUL also has support for its own so-called `KeyEvents`, but that is not yet reported by `hasFeature()`.

A result of `false` for a particular feature is not a disaster. If a standard is completely implemented except for a single item, then `false` is the correct value to report. Finished parts of the implementation may still be used if they are known to exist. Knowing that they exist is a matter of reading and research.

If a feature has DOM support, the relevant DOM interfaces are available to script. Interfaces are used by programming languages. There are, however, other ways to interact with the services of a browser. Stylesheets and XML are two examples. A feature may have stylesheet support but not DOM support, or vice versa. `hasFeature` reports only on DOM support.

Some browser features may eventually make their way into the DOM standards. The Mozilla 1.0 features most likely to receive standards attention are drag-and-drop support, keystroke events, scrolling events, and key shortcuts.

Separate from HTML DOM 0 support is XUL DOM 0 support. XUL DOM 0 has no standard or central design document yet. It is undocumented except for remarks about specific tags in this book.

Table 5.4 DOM standards support for Mozilla 1.0 and 1.4

Feature string	Version string	hasFeature reports
HTML	1.0	true
XML	1.0	true
Core	2.0	true
HTML	2.0	true
XML	2.0	true
Views	2.0	true
StyleSheets	2.0	true
CSS	2.0	true
CSS2	2.0	true
Events	2.0	true
UIEvents	2.0	FALSE
MouseEvents	2.0	true
MouseScrollEvents	Not a W3C feature	true
MutationEvents	2.0	FALSE
HTMLEvents	2.0	true
Range	2.0	true
Traversal	2.0	FALSE
Xpath	3.0	true
All other DOM 3 features	3.0	FALSE

Mozilla specifies object interfaces using its own XPIDL language. The XPIDL files that programmers need when working with XPCOM objects are also used for DOM objects. Because XPIDL and IDL syntax are so similar, it is trivial to translate from one to the other. Mozilla's XPIDL definitions, however, located in the source directory `dom/public/idl`, are the official word on DOM and DOM-like interface support. They include restatements of both the DOM IDL definitions and the available XUL DOM-like interfaces. They also state Mozilla-specific enhancements to those standards. Beware that some implemented event handlers do not appear in these files.

5.5.3 Mozilla AOMs and BOMs

DOM objects are about XML documents. Some of these objects are made available when an XML document loads because they're handy to have. The `Document` object, and the document variable that points to it, is an obvious example.

There are other objects you might want to script that have nothing to do with documents. The window the document resides in is an obvious example. You might want to change the text of its titlebar, make a modal dialog box appear, or change the document that the window displays.

These nondocument objects are part of the Browser Object Model that exists in most Web browsers. This object model is small when compared with the DOM. It consists of a few objects only in a small hierarchy. The top of the hierarchy is a so-called `Window` object that represents the desktop window that the document is displayed in. The window variable refers to this object. The small BOM hierarchy is very familiar to Web developers and contains objects such as

```
navigator screen history location frames
```

This book doesn't dwell on these objects much (any Web-oriented JavaScript book covers them extensively). There is some further discussion on the window object in Chapter 10, Windows and Panes.

The Mozilla Platform is not just a Web browser but also a basis for applications. When XUL documents are being displayed, it makes more sense to talk about an Application Object Model rather than a BOM. XUL windows also start with a window variable that is the top-most object in the application hierarchy, but the matching object type is a chrome window, not a window. Figure 5.1 shows the AOM hierarchy for a chrome window.

Each word in Figure 5.1 is an object property that holds an object, although occasionally one may hold `null` or an empty string instead. The hierarchy that starts at window is always present. The hierarchy that starts with Element exists for every DOM 1 Element object. Dark lines exist for both XUL and HTML; lighter lines exist only for XUL. A dashed line means that the object is available only when security barriers are lifted. Where these terms match names in the Web browser BOM, the meanings are the same. The other terms are discussed throughout this book.

A brief summary of the XUL-specific AOM objects goes like this: `arguments` is passed in when a window is open; `content` points to the document held in a `<browser>` tag in the XUL page; `controllers` is a set of command controllers, either for the window or for one tag; `commandDispatcher` is also part of the command system; `focus` controls the focus ring; `boxObject` contains all the details of a single tag's frame, for both ordinary XUL tags and special XUL tags like `<scrollbox>`; `builder` exposes a tree builder for the `<tree>` tag; and `database` and `datasource` are part of the XUL template system.

In addition to these objects, Chapter 10, Windows and Panes, explores some of the less obviously exposed objects. Many of these objects are associated with the overall mechanics of displaying a XUL or HTML document.

The XUL window object is very similar to the HTML window object. It has a history property, for example. This arrangement is quite misleading because it implies that these properties do something. They don't do anything.

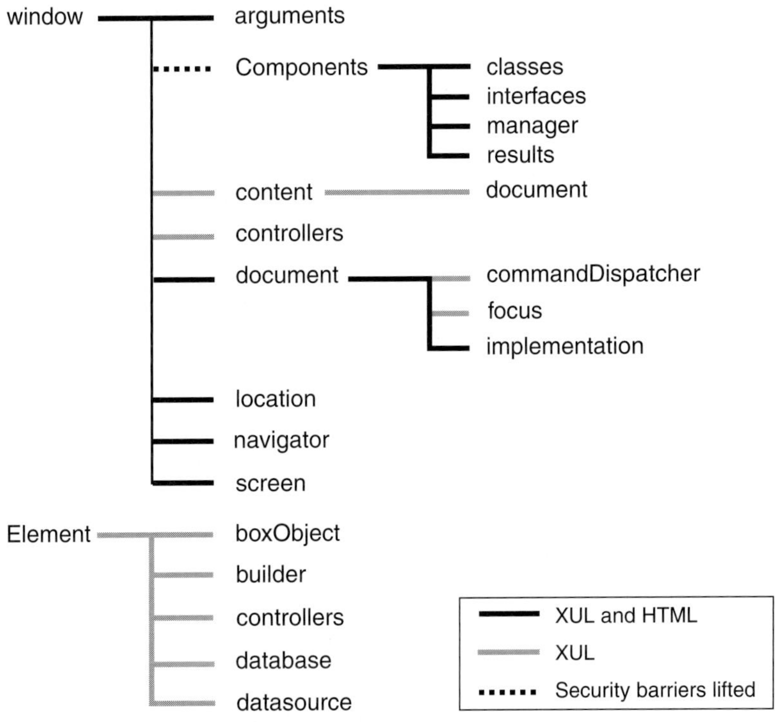

Fig. 5.1 Mozilla's XUL Application Object Model.

They exist because the many scripts and XUL documents that together make up a browser application expect them to be in place. Under normal conditions (a Classic Browser), these properties rely on extra scripting support to function. That scripting support isn't present in a plain XUL window, unless your XUL is designed to reimplement the features of a browser. Ignore these HTML-like properties.

As for HTML, all the implemented DOM interfaces are directly available to XUL. The properties and methods of the `window.document` object are the entry points to those interfaces.

Both HTML and XUL windows contain one special property: the `Components` property. That property is the starting point for the majority of Mozilla's unique interfaces. These interfaces are discussed next.

5.5.4 XPCOM and XPConnect

The DOM standards provide interfaces that make content accessible to scripts. By comparison, XPConnect and XPCOM provide interfaces that make the building blocks of the Mozilla Platform itself accessible to scripts.

XPCOM is entirely internal to the Mozilla Platform. XPConnect is the glue that turns XPCOM-compliant objects and their interfaces into JavaScript host objects. Chapter 16, XPCOM Objects, describes application-oriented use of this system extensively. This chapter just gives an overview of these two technologies.

From the application programmer's perspective, the XPCOM system appears mainly as the `window.Components` object (see Figure 5.1). The `classes` and `interfaces` properties of this object are lists of all the available XPCOM Contract IDs and interface names. The `manager` property is the XPCOM component manager. The `results` property is a list of all the possible exceptions that might be thrown and result values that might be returned. Results are 32-bit numbers.

These lists could in theory change dynamically, but that is not done in the standard platform. The standard platform registers all the known components at startup time, and a large part of that registration overhead is performed only once the first time the platform starts. The set of components registered can be recalculated by running the tool `regxpcom` (`regxpcom.exe` on Microsoft Windows). That tool is provided with any standard platform installation bundle. Using `regxpcom` is necessary only when new components (i.e., whole modules, not merely objects; see Chapter 16, XPCOM Objects) are created or installed.

From the application programmer's perspective, the XPConnect system is all but invisible, making the interfaces of C/C++-based components available to JavaScript. In order to do this, the XPConnect system relies on a set of type libraries (with `.xpt` extensions) that are stored in the `components` directory under the platform installation area. XPConnect also provides script access to browser plugins, to the DOM interfaces, and to Java and Java applets. Although these things may seem unrelated to XPCOM, in the end they are all XPCOM components.

All XPCOM components that provide more than one XPCOM interface should implement the `nsISupports` interface. This interface provides the `QueryInterface()` method, which can be used to find other interfaces supported by an object.

5.5.4.1 Finding XPCOM Components The Mozilla Platform is large, and many parts of it have been separated into building blocks: Each is an XPCOM component that has some identity of its own. Not all of Mozilla is so separated; there are still bits that sit anonymously inside the platform.

There are at least a thousand XPCOM components, each with one or more interfaces. That is an overwhelming number and is equivalent to a huge class library. This large number presents problems for the newcomer. At first glance, Mozilla functionality seems like a fragmented mess. It is not. There is simply too much to learn in one sitting, and structure is not obvious. Finding documentation on all the components of Mozilla is also problematic. At two pages per component, that's two thousand pages. Such huge books might exist one day, but they don't as this goes to print.

To find a suitable component, you need to look. The thing you ultimately want is an object that is used for a specific task. Not all objects need to be accessed directly via their XPCOM interfaces. Many objects exist in other forms. Before diving into XPCOM, ask yourself: Could the needed object appear in any of these other forms?

- As a standard JavaScript object (e.g., Date or Math). If so, look at the ECMAScript standard.
- As a piece of the DOM. If the object relates to any kind of XML document fragment, it will be covered in the W3C DOM standards.
- As a part of the BOM. A Web-based JavaScript book will tell you if the object is a standard feature of HTML scripts. The AOM in this chapter advises of standard XUL scriptable objects.
- As an XBL binding. Nearly all objects that have a matching XUL tag also have an XBL binding. The binding definition can be read from the file `toolkit.jar` in the chrome.
- As a floating object service. Some objects are separate from the DOM but still available for immediate use (e.g., Image and Option [HTML]; XMLHttpRequest and SOAPService [HTML and XUL]).

If there is no choice but to look for an XPCOM object, then here is how to proceed. An object is manufactured from an XPCOM interface and an XPCOM component that implements that interface. So you must locate these two things. Interfaces have names; components have Contract IDs (which are also names). To find these things, any of the following strategies will do:

- Look in the index of this book under a keyword that matches your problem area. Many component-interface pairs are recommended throughout this book.
- Download the summary reports from this book's Web site (at `www.nigelmcfarlane.com`), and look through those.
- Download the XPIDL bundles from this book's Web site (at `www.nigelmcfarlane.com`) or from the mozilla.org source, and look though those.
- Explore the chrome-based applications that come bundled with Classic Mozilla. That code contains many tested and proved examples.
- Search the mozilla.org organization's resources, like Web sites, newsgroups, and IRC. Well-stated questions posed in those fora often attract quality responses.

Of all these strategies, reading this book and acquiring a copy of the XPIDL files and other reports is the most immediate solution.

In the end, most, but not all, useful interfaces start with this prefix:

```
nsI
```

and all components' Contract IDs start with this prefix:

```
@mozilla.org/
```

As soon as you have a component-interface pair, the object can be created as follows.

5.5.4.2 Using XPCOM Components Here is a simple example of using a component. The Perl language has the `'require'` keyword, which allows one Perl script to load in the contents of another script. JavaScript has no such equivalent, but Mozilla has a component to do the job. Listing 5.7 illustrates.

Listing 5.7 Inclusion of JavaScript scripts using a Mozilla XPCOM component.

```
var comp_name = "@mozilla.org/moz/jssubscript-loader;1";
var comp_obj = Components.classes[comp_name];

var if_obj = Components.interfaces.mozIJSSubScriptLoader;

var final_obj = comp_obj.createInstance(if_obj);

final_obj.loadSubScript("file:///tmp/extras.js");
```

This script is equivalent to running `eval()` on the contents of the file `/tmp/extras.js`.

The two pieces of information needed to create an object are the component name (`comp_name`, a string) and the interface to use (`if_obj`, a property name). After the object is retrieved (`final_obj`), its methods can be put to use. In this case, the `loadSubScript()` method imports the contents of the file `extras.js` as though it were a string processed by `eval()`.

Typical of a Mozilla component, a line of documentation in the XPIDL definition for `mozIJSSubScriptLoader` states that the loaded JavaScript must be located on the local computer. Brief and sparse documentation is usual for Mozilla components.

5.5.4.3 Object Creation Alternatives In Listing 5.7, the `createInstance()` method was used to create the object. That is one of two main alternatives. The other main alternative is to use `getService()`. The `getService()` method is used when a given XPCOM component is designed to provide a single instance of an object only (the object is a singleton). Such objects may contain static or global information that cannot be coordinated across multiple object instances. In Listing 5.7, the equivalent line of code that uses `getService()` would be

```
var final_obj = comp_obj.getService(if_obj);
```

How do you tell which of `createInstance()` or `getService()` is required? If the Contract ID or the interface name contains the word *service* (any capitalization), then use `getService()`; otherwise, use `createInstance()`.

The `createInstance()` and `getService()` methods also have a zero argument form. If no argument is supplied, then the object created or returned has the `nsISupports` interface. That interface can then be used to acquire whatever other interface might be needed. We can modify Listing 5.6 to create an example of this use for `createInstance()`:

```
var anon_obj  = comp_obj.createInstance();
var final_obj = anon_obj.QueryInterface(if_obj);
```

If several objects of the same kind are to be created, then it is possible first to create a constructor, and then to use that constructor object to create the individual objects. This code replaces the first four lines of Listing 5.7:

```
var Includer = Components.Constructor(
                 "@mozilla.org/moz/jssubscript-loader;1",
                 "mozIJSSubScriptLoader",
                 null
               );
var final_obj = new Includer();
// var another_obj = new Includer()
```

Note that in this case the interface name is spelled out as a string. The third argument of the `Constructor()` method is an optional string. If stated, it is the name of a method to call as the initialization method when an object instance is created. Any arguments passed as arguments to the `Includer` object constructor will be passed to this initialization method.

Finally, it is possible to create objects with XPCOM interfaces directly in JavaScript. This can be done only for simple interfaces that have no special processing of their own. Continuing the variations on Listing 5.6, we can create an object using the code of Listing 5.8.

Listing 5.8 Creation of a JavaScript object with XPCOM interfaces.

```
var final_obj = {

  // interface nsISupports
  QueryInterface : function(iid) {
    var Ci = Components.interfaces;
    if ( !iid.equals(Ci.nsISupports) &&
         !iid.equals(Ci.mozIJsSubSCriptLoader )
      throw Components.results.NS_ERROR_NO_INTERFACE;
    return this;
  },

  // interface mozIJSSubScriptLoader
  loadSubScript : function (url) {
```

```
    // code to load a script goes here
    return;
  }
};
```

This object supports both the nsISupports and the mozIJsSubScriptLoader interfaces. If it were certain that no calls to QueryInterface() would ever be made on this object, then the nsISupports part of the object could be left off. Of course, this object has a major problem: How can it properly implement the second interface? It would need to contain a long piece of code that opens a file system file, reads the contents, and then calls eval() on that content. For that effort, you might as well use the existing implementation of the object. This by-hand construction of objects is sometimes highly useful. The most frequent use is in the creation of call-back objects used for observers and listeners—see Chapter 6, Events.

The createInstance() method is itself implemented by the nsIComponentManager interface; getService() is implemented by the nsIServiceManager interface.

5.5.4.4 Plugins and DOM Browser plugins have been scriptable since version 3.0 Web browsers. At that time, Netscape enhanced the version 1.1 NPAPI plugin standard to be scriptable, and hundreds of plugins were created to work with it. Mozilla still supports this standard, but very recent versions of both the platform and the plugins (especially Macromedia's Flash) are required if everything is to work without hiccups.

A series of scriptable XPIDL interfaces exists for plugins. Using these, individual plugins can be driven directly from JavaScript. The easiest way to handle plugins is still to use the HTML <embed> (deprecated) or <object> (recommended) tag and the DOM 0 plugins array. See Chapter 10, Windows and Panes, for a discussion on combining HTML and XUL.

A series of scriptable interfaces also exists for the DOM standards, so DOM interfaces can be retrieved using the Components object. There is little need for this, however, because those interfaces are automatically available on the window object, and on the DOM objects that are made and retrieved by the window object.

5.5.4.5 Java Web browsers have supported scripting Java applets since version 3.0; Mozilla also supports scripting Java. The architecture used in the Mozilla 1.x platform is different from that used in Netscape Communicator 4.x, but it is backwardly compatible for script writers.

In Netscape Communicator 4.x, the browser depended entirely on Java 1.1's security model. For that browser to make any security decisions, a request that Java examine a special class library provided by Netscape was required. Java and JavaScript were connected, and this was done by a technology called LiveConnect.

In Mozilla, this Java dependency is gone. Netscape manages its own security. No Java is required, and Java is no longer tightly integrated in the platform. There is no LiveConnect in the original sense; there is only XPConnect. Integration features provided by LiveConnect still exist, but they are buried in the code behind XPCOM. Mozilla's visible Java support now consists of a set of XPCOM interfaces like everything else, and Java support is considered to be similar in status to a plugin. The functionality of LiveConnect is still visible when Java and JavaScript objects are wrapped up for access in the language alternate to their origin.

Mozilla provides two pieces of technology that accommodate Java. The first is OJI (Open Java Interface). This is an API like the NPAPI (plugin) API that is supposed to work with any vendor's Java platform. XPCOM interfaces provide access to the OJI. The second piece of technology is a LiveConnect emulator for backward-compatibility. It also is an XPCOM interface, defined in the interface `nsIJRILLiveConnectPlugin`. This emulator handles Mozilla's C/C++ requests that were previously sent to Netscape 4.x's Java JVM.

As for plugins, the easiest way to use Java inside Mozilla is still to use an `<applet>` or `<object>` tag inside an HTML file. Again, see Chapter 10, Windows and Panes, for a discussion on combining HTML and XUL.

Some programmers come to the Web from a Java background. If you have a sophisticated Java environment and want to integrate it with Mozilla, tread cautiously. On the one hand, the most simple and obvious interactions between JavaScript and Java work fine. On the other hand, JavaScript, Java, and Mozilla are all quite complicated systems, and perfect interaction on every point is a large goal. Sophisticated interactions still have problems, and you're encouraged to study the remaining Java-related bugs in Mozilla's Bugzilla bug database carefully.

The best way forward is this: Stick to Sun Microsystem's Java implementation, and then use only version 1.4 or greater. A very recent version of Mozilla is recommended to keep the outstanding issues to a minimum.

Apart from some remarks in Chapter 10, Windows and Panes, that is all this book has to say on Java.

5.5.5 Scripting Libraries

Mozilla relies on the XPCOM system to draw in functionality from elsewhere, but a few small libraries written entirely in JavaScript exist. These libraries attempt to simplify particular aspects of the XPCOM system.

The most useful of these libraries are JSLib and RDFLib. RDFLib is really just a subset of JSLib. JSLib makes working with files and folders less painful. The RDFLib subpart makes working with RDF data sources less painful. This library creates JavaScript objects that simplify the XPCOM objects that they are based on.

This library can be downloaded from `http://jslib.mozdev.org`. Files in this library are written in ASCII, in UNIX format.

Beware that these libraries receive only occasional updates. Examine the headers when downloading them to see whether they have been recently maintained.

To use the library, include the top-level `jslib.js` file, which provides utility routines and constants. The most important of these routines is the `include()` function, which acts the same as Perl's `require` (or cpp's `#include`). Then include whatever other JSLib functionality is needed. The library contains nearly a dozen subdirectories, but the most significant ones are `io` (for file processing) and `rdf` (for RDF processing). Figure 5.2 shows the dependencies between these libraries.

Scripts with outgoing arrows require the targets of those arrows to be loaded first. Files with no dependencies are not shown. Clearly the library is divided into two main parts, which this book calls RDFLib and JSLib. There are two separate implementations of RDF file access: `rdf/rdfFile.js` and `io/RDF.js`. They present different interfaces for approximately the same task; `rdf/rdfFile.js` is the more extensive interface and uses subobjects.

The library uses the `window.Components.Constructor()` method to create object constructors for XPCOM components (see the section entitled "Object Creation Alternatives" for instructions describing how to do this). It also implements JavaScript object constructors using the JavaScript prototyping system. A prototype-based constructor is used to create a new JavaScript object. During the construction process, XPCOM object constructors are used to set properties on the new JavaScript object. Those properties hold one

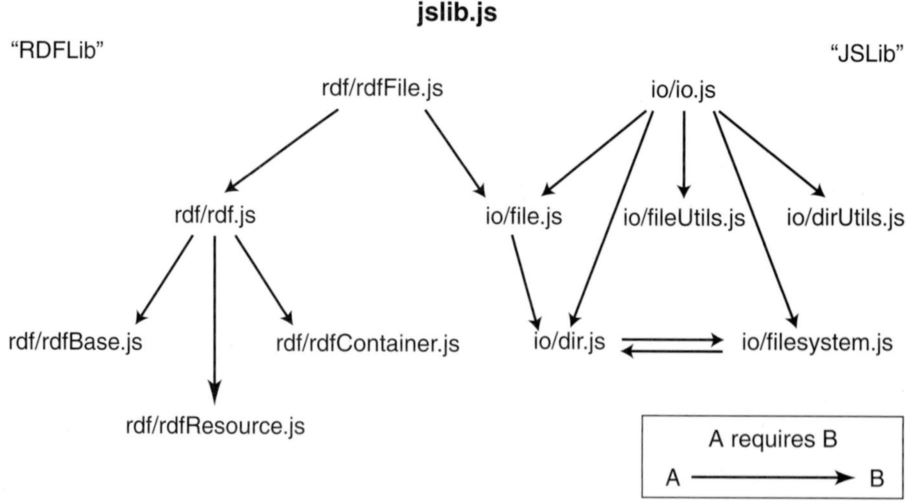

Fig. 5.2 JSLib and RDFlib file dependencies.

XPCOM object each. The final JavaScript object therefore contains (or uses) one or more XPCOM objects and is a wrapper or façade for those XPCOM objects. This is a simple and widely applicable technique.

Such new JavaScript objects contain error-checking, coordination, and translation code that makes the XPCOM components easier to use. They represent a simplification or specialist view of the XPCOM component system, intended for common tasks. Table 5.5 shows the objects created by this library.

In Table 5.5, a "data-source" argument is an `nsIRDFDataSource` object, not an `rdf:` URL. The JSLib library contains several other useful objects, but they are not as extensive or as complete as the objects in Table 5.5. The `Zip` object, for example, which is defined in the `zip/zip.js` file, performs only about half the work required to unzip a compressed file.

Most of the files in the JSLib have extensive documentation in the form of preamble comments. These preamble comments show how to use the objects supplied.

Table 5.5 Objects created by JSLIb and RDFLib

Constructor	Source file	Uses objects	Purpose
include() method	jslib.js		Include other .js files.
Dir(filePath)	io/dir.js	FileSystem()	Manage a folder on the local disk.
DirUtils()	io/dirUtils		Find install-specific directories.
File(filePath)	io/file.js	FileSystem()	Manage a file on the local disk.
FileSystem(filePath)	io/filesystem.js		Manage any file system entry on the local disk.
RDF(url, urn, xmlns, sync_flag)	io/rdf.js		Read and write a single special format RDF container in an existing RDF file.
RDFFile(file_url, urn, xmnls, sync_flag)	io/rdf.js	RDF()	Read and write a single special format RDF container in a local RDF file.
Socket()	network/socket.js		Set up and read/write a Domain socket.

Table 5.5 Objects created by JSLIb and RDFLib (Continued)

Constructor	Source file	Uses objects	Purpose
SocketListener()	network/socket.js		Handles asynchronous reads from a socket.
RDF(url, sync_flag)	rdf/rdf.js	RDFBase()	Read and write an RDF document fact-by-fact.
RDFBase(datasource)	rdf/rdfBase.js		Read and write an RDF document fact-by-fact, using an existing data source.
RDFContainer(type ownerURI, subjectURI, datasource)	rdf/rdfContainer.js	RDFResource()	Manage or create an RDF `<Seq>`, `<bag>`, or `<alt>` container using facts.
RDFResource(type, ownerURI, subjectURI, datasource)	rdf/rdfContainer.js	RDFBase()	Manage or create a URI that is useable as an RDF subject, predicate, or object.
Sound(url)	sound/sound.js		Play a sound from a URL.

5.5.6 XBL Bindings

JavaScript can also use interfaces supplied by XBL definitions. Those definitions are included in an XML file with the `-moz-binding` CSS2 style property. Such a binding attaches the definition to a tag or tags. Although XBL definitions can include content, it is also possible to create a definition that is just a set of functionality—an interface. Being able to add an arbitrary interface to an arbitrary tag is clearly a powerful feature.

If the DOM 1 standard is used to retrieve an `Element` object for a tag that is bound to an XBL definition, then the resulting JavaScript object will include the properties and methods implied by that definition. Those properties and methods can then be manipulated as for any host object. The platform automatically manages this task.

XBL definitions therefore make some DOM objects smarter by providing them with custom features. XBL definitions can also establish themselves as XPCOM components, so they are also accessible through XPConnect. The only good reason for doing this is if the XBL component needs to be accessed from C/C++ code.

Chapter 15, XBL Bindings, discusses XBL at length.

5.5.7 Island Interfaces

Mozilla has three scriptable island interfaces. These interfaces have their own JavaScript interpreter and their own global object. Because they are separate from the rest of Mozilla, they have their own AOM.

Mozilla's preferences system is the first of these islands. Its AOM consists of a single `PrefConfig` object that acts like a global object. It has only two properties, both of which are methods: `pref()` and `user_pref()`. The preference files, `prefs.js`, consist of repeated calls to these methods, but in actual fact, the full JavaScript language is available. Any use of this language availability is obscure at best. The preference system also presents two components to XPCOM. They are named

```
@mozilla.org/preferences-service;1
@mozilla.org/preferences;1
```

When these components are scripted from the normal Mozilla scripting environment, preferences can be changed, but the `prefs.js` files cannot be modified directly. Changes to these preferences do affect the regenerated `prefs.js` files that are written when the platform shuts down.

Mozilla's network-enabled component installation system is the second of these islands. Chapter 17, Deployment, discusses this environment and its AOM fully. This system also exposes XPCOM components to general scripting, but the interfaces provided are low-level and of little use to general tasks. They allow the XPInstall system to be notified when content is available from elsewhere (e.g., over the Internet) and accept that content for processing. These limited interfaces mean that XPInstall is good for installation tasks only.

`xpcshell` is Mozilla's third island interface. It is a program separate from the Mozilla Platform executable that isn't available in the downloadable releases. It is available in the nightly releases, or if you compile the software yourself (it requires the `--enable-debug` option). `xpcshell` is a standalone JavaScript interpreter that is used to test scripts, the SpiderMonkey interpreter, and the XPConnect/XPCOM system. Its AOM consists of a single global object and XPCOM-related objects. The most useful properties of the global object are listed in Table 5.6.

The `Components` array makes `xpcshell` a good place to test scripts that make heavy use of Mozilla components. Because `xpcshell` uses plain `stdin` and `stdout` file descriptors, it can easily be run in batch mode by automated testing systems. `xpcshell` is Mozilla's JavaScript equivalent of the Perl interpreter, except that it is little more than a test harness.

In theory, a script run through `xpcshell` could create and use enough components to build up a whole browser. In practice, the Mozilla executable sets up low-level initialization steps that the `xpcshell` doesn't use. Therefore, `xpcshell` is best left to simpler tasks.

Table 5.6 xpcshell global object properties

Property	Description
Components	The XPConnect/XPCOM components array, provides access to most components in the Mozilla Platform.
dump(arg)	Turns the sole argument into a Unicode string and sends it raw to stdout.
load(arg1,arg2,...)	Attempts to load and interpret the files (not URLs) specified.
print(arg1,args2,...)	Turn arguments to strings and sends them slightly formatted to stdout, using printf("%s ").
quit()	Stops xpcshell and exit.

5.6 Hands On: NoteTaker Dynamic Content

In this section, we'll add some scripts to the NoteTaker Edit dialog box. These scripts will modify the way the XUL document works after the platform displays it. In the process, we'll manipulate several types of objects discussed in this chapter.

5.6.1 Scripting `<deck>` via the DOM

The first NoteTaker change involves keyword content in the dialog box. This Edit dialog box actually supports two separate panes. Each panel is represented by one of the `<toolbarbutton>` tags, "Edit" and "Keywords." We'd like to display the dialog box with one or the other of the panes visible. Because the content of the keyword panel isn't yet decided, we'll just use a placeholder.

To support this two-panel system, we'll use a `<deck>` tag. The content for the Edit panel will appear as one card of the deck; the content for the Keyword panel will appear as the other card. Previously, the content underneath the two `<toolbarbutton>` tags was for the Edit button. Now, we'll make that content one card of a deck and make the other card like this:

```
<hbox flex="1">
  <description>Content to be added later.</description>
</hbox>
```

Figure 5.3 shows the structure of the XUL document before and after this change.

All we've done is add a `<deck>` tag and the new content at the right spots. This could have been done in Chapter 2, XUL Layout; however, it's not possible to swap between the cards of a plain `<deck>` without using a script. Now that we have JavaScript, we can do that swapping. Briefly sneaking ahead to Chapter 6, Events, we note that `<toolbarbutton>` tags support an

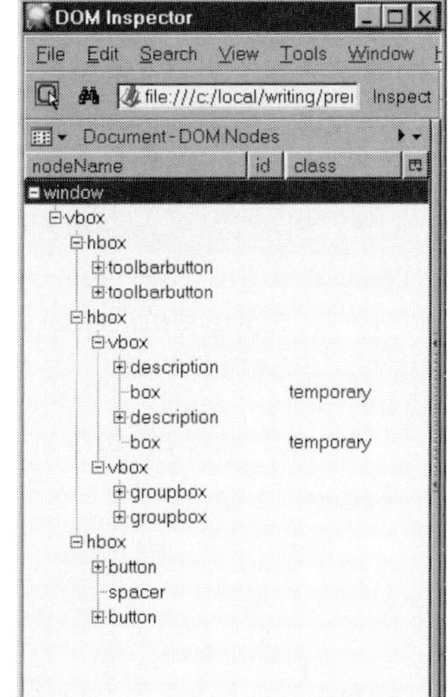

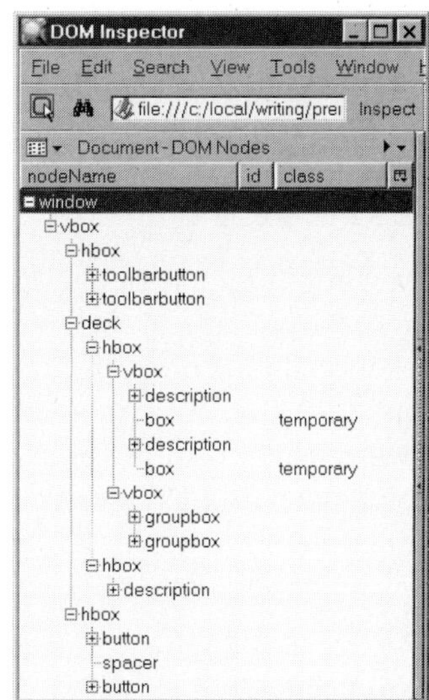

Fig. 5.3 Adding a <deck> to NoteTaker.

`onclick` event handler. We'll hook the script logic in there so that it's fun to play with.

There are numerous ways to make this work, but they all come down to adding some tag id attributes; writing a function, which we'll call `action()`; and adding an `onclick` handler. The `onclick` handlers look like this:

```
<toolbarbutton label="Edit" onclick="action('edit')"/>
<toolbarbutton label="Edit" onclick="action('keywords')"/>
```

The new ids look like this:

```
<deck flex="1" id="dialog.deck">
<hbox flex="1" id="dialog.edit">
<hbox flex="1" id="dialog.keywords">
```

The `action()` function looks like Listing 5.9.

Listing 5.9 Simple NoteTaker function that accepts commands as arguments.

```
function action(task)
{
  var card = document.getElementById("dialog." + task);

  if (!card || ( task != "edit" && task != "keywords") )
    throw("Unknown Edit Task");

  var deck  = card.parentNode;
  var index = 0;
```

```
  if ( task == "edit" ) index = 0;
  if ( task == "keywords") index = 1;

  deck.setAttribute("selectedIndex",index);
}
```

We want to get into the habit of passing command-like arguments to functions, since that's a very common practice for Mozilla applications. If we include this code in the .XUL file with a <script> tag, we'll have very obscure errors as described in the section entitled "Debug Corner" in this chapter, unless we're careful and use a <![CDATA[]]> section. It's better to put this script in a separate file right from the start and include that

```
<script src="editDialog.js"/>
```

The action() function calls the window.document.getElementById() method. This method is the most common starting point for script access to the DOM. It is passed the value of an XUL or HTML id attribute and returns an object for the tag with that id. You can then operate on that object via its properties and methods.

The remainder of the function navigates to the <deck> tag using the parentNode DOM property and sets the selectedIndex attribute there using the setAttribute() DOM property. Because this is a property meaningful to the <deck> tag, the XUL display system reacts to the change automatically, and the numbered card is displayed.

If command-like arguments are avoided, we can achieve the same effect with a quick-and-dirty solution. Equivalent onclick handlers that still use DOM interfaces look like these:

```
document.getElementById("dialog.deck").setAttribute("selectedIndex",0);
document.getElementById("dialog.deck").setAttribute("selectedIndex",1);
```

Whether structured or quick, just three interfaces of the DOM 1 Core standard are all we need to get most tasks done. These three are the Document, Element, and Node interfaces.

5.6.2 Alternative: Scripting Styles via the DOM

The use of <deck> is just one of many ways to script a XUL document. Another, equally valid alternative is just to modify CSS styles after the document has been loaded.

Starting from the <deck> example, remove the opening and closing <deck> tags. Now each set of content is enclosed in an <hbox> that can be treated like an HTML <div>. Listing 5.10 shows an alternate version of the action() method.

Listing 5.10 Simple NoteTaker function that accepts commands as arguments.

```
function action(task)
{
  var card = document.getElementById("dialog." + task);

  if (!card || ( task != "edit" && task != "keywords") )
    throw("Unknown Edit Task");

  var oldcard;  // the content to remove
  if (task == "edit")
    oldcard = document.getElementById("dialog.keywords");
  else
    oldcard = document.getElementById("dialog.edit");

  oldcard.setAttribute("style","visibility:collapse");
  card.removeAttribute("style");
}
```

This solution uses the same DOM interfaces as Listing 5.6 but modifies different attributes on the DOM hierarchy for the window. When the style rules for the content change, the rendering system inside the platform automatically updates the display. This use of the style attribute is a little clumsy. XUL provides a more useful collapsed attribute that can be set without affecting any other inline styles that scripts might add. The replacement lines follow:

```
oldcard.setAttribute("collapsed","true");
card.removeAttribute("collapsed");
```

The XUL `hidden` attribute shouldn't be dynamically updated because of the damage it does to XBL bindings (described in Chapter 15, XBL Bindings).

In addition to the `<deck>` and styled approaches, the DOM interfaces can be used to physically remove or add parts of the DOM hierarchy from a document. This approach is the third way to make content appear or disappear; however, it is an overly complex approach for simple tasks.

5.6.3 Alternative: Scripting `<deck>` via the AOM and XBL

When an XUL document is turned into a DOM hierarchy, more information is present than the W3C's standard DOM interfaces. There is also a set of interfaces resulting from Mozilla's XBL system. These extra interfaces add properties and methods to the DOM objects that are XUL-specific. Those properties and methods are extremely convenient and make the scripting job easier. Sometimes the pure DOM standards are a bit clumsy to use.

Let's see if the `<deck>` solution can be made easier using one of these interfaces. The tag we're most likely to script is the `<deck>` tag. We start by looking at the `xul.css` file. This file is stored in the `toolkit.jar` archive in the chrome. It's worthwhile keeping an unzipped copy of this JAR file somewhere handy. Viewing that file with a simple text editor, we look for "deck" and find:

```
deck {
  display: -moz-deck;
  -moz-binding: url("chrome://global/content/bindings/
     general.xml#deck");
}
```

The `-moz-binding` line tells us that `<deck>` does have a binding, so there are some goodies to look at. The binding is called deck, and it's in `general.xml`. So we view that file, and look for a line like

```
<binding id="deck">
```

Sure enough, it's there. Part of the binding reads

```
<binding id="deck">
  <implementation>
    <property name="selectedIndex" ...
```

That's all we need. Property names in XBL and attribute names in XUL generally match each other, and those names also generally match the names used for HTML objects. The `selectedIndex` property matches the `selectedIndex` attribute of the `<deck>` tag. We'll use that. In the `action()` method, replace this

```
deck.setAttribute("selectedIndex",index);
```

with this

```
deck.selectedIndex = index;
```

That's a trivial change, but it shortens the code enough that we can throw away the index variable and save a few lines. If the deck binding had a `setCard()` method, for example, then we could use that instead of writing `action()`. Perhaps it will arrive one day. The last few lines of the `action()` method can be collapsed to

```
var deck  = card.parentNode;

if ( task == "edit" )     deck.selectedIndex = 0;
if ( task == "keywords") deck.selectedIndex = 1;
```

5.6.4 Reading String Bundles via XPCOM

The second change we'll make to NoteTaker is to put external data into the displayed window from outside the XUL document. In short, we'll load content that appears inside the boxed areas. Over the course of this book, we'll change the way this information is loaded, saved, and displayed several times.

To get access to the outside, we don't need to use XPCOM components. We could submit a URL, which is explained in Chapter 7, Forms and Menus. Here we'll use a string bundle.

We can use string bundles, a.k.a. properties files from XUL or from JavaScript. If we do it the XUL way, it's the same as scripting `<deck>`—we add some tags, and look for an XBL definition that supplies useful interfaces. Here, we'll work with a string bundle in raw JavaScript. Because it uses XPCOM, we must store our files inside the chrome.

We need an object that acts on properties files. In other words, we need a useful XPCOM interface and a component that implements that interface. If we choose to look through the XPIDL files (or this book's index), then it's easy to spot the interfaces in the `nsIStringBundle.idl` file. There are two interfaces, `nsIStringBundleService` and `nsIStringBundle`. Because "Service" is in the name of the first interface, it must be an XPCOM Service; that's a starting point for us. Recall that services produce an object using `getService();` nonservices produce an object using `createObject()`.

We also note that the `createBundle()` method of that interface looks like this:

```
nsIStringBundle createBundle(in string aURLSpec);
```

OK, so this method creates an object with `nsIStringBundle` interface from a URL. That's easy enough to understand. The `nsIStringBundle` interface has a `getStringFromName()` method, which will extract a string from the string bundle (properties) file. We're not too concerned that the XPIDL files use their own `wstring` and `string` types; we know that XPConnect will convert those types to something that JavaScript can discern—a string primitive value that will appear as a `String` object.

This interface file also states at the top the associated XPCOM Contract ID, so we have found our XPCOM pair:

```
@mozilla.org/intl/stringbundle;1 nsIStringBundleService
```

We don't need a Contract ID for the `nsIStringBundle` interface because the service will create objects with that interface for us when we call `createBundle()`. We do need to get the service object in the first place. It is easy to ask for it using our discovered XPCOM pair:

```
var Cc = Components.classes;
var Ci = Components.interfaces;
var cls = Cc["@mozilla.org/intl/stringbundle;1"];
var svc = cls.getService(Ci.nsIStringBundleService);
```

If no errors appear in the JavaScript Console (and none should), then `svc` now holds the service object we've grabbed. We're ready to code. Listing 5.11 shows the results.

Listing 5.11 NoteTaker code to read in strings from a string bundle.

```
var Cc = Components.classes;
var Ci = Components.interfaces;
var cls = Cc["@mozilla.org/intl/stringbundle;1"];
var svc = cls.getService(Ci.nsIStringBundleService);
var URL = "chrome://notetaker/locale/dialog.properties";
var sbundle = svc.createBundle(URL);
```

```
function load_data()
{
  var names = ["summary", "details", "chop-query", "home-page", "width",
          "height", "top", "left"];
  var box, desc, value;

  for (var i = names.length; i>0; i--)
  {
    value = sbundle.getStringFromName("dialog."+ names[i]);
    desc  = document.createElement("description");
    desc.setAttribute("value",value);
    box   = document.getElementById("dialog." + names[i]);
    box.appendChild(desc);
  }
}
```

The `sbundle` variable contains a URL-specific XPCOM object. The URL we've chosen must follow the rules for property files. The function `load_data()` reads properties from that file and manipulates the DOM so that a `<description value="string">` tag is added to each placeholder <box> tag as content. Note how the object for `<description>` is built up and then added to the box tag at the end. That is more efficient than adding things piece by piece to the existing DOM.

This code also relies on the XUL document having some ids in place. We must add these ids by hand to the XUL. To do that, change every example of

```
<box class="temporary"/>
```

to something like

```
<box class="temporary" id="dialog.summary"/>
```

Finally, we'll run this `load_data()` function from another event target stolen from Chapter 6, Events: the `<window>` tag's `onload` attribute. Doing it this way ensures that the whole document exists before we start operating on it:

```
<window xmlns= "http://www.mozilla.org/keymaster/gatekeeper/
     there.is.only.xul" onload="load_data()>
```

Because the properties file is stored in the locale part of the chrome, the locale needs to be set up as described in the "Hands On" section of Chapter 3, Static Content. In other words, a `contents.rdf` file must be in place, and the `installed-chrome.txt` file must be up to date. The properties file itself might look like Listing 5.12.

Listing 5.12 dialog.properties property file for NoteTaker.

```
dialog.summary=My Summary
dialog.details=My Details
dialog.chop-query=true
dialog.home-page=false
dialog.width=100
```

```
dialog.height=90
dialog.top=80
dialog.left=70
```

The path of this file relative to the top of the chrome should be

```
notetaker/locale/en-US/dialog.properties
```

After all that work, the NoteTaker dialog box now looks like Figure 5.4.

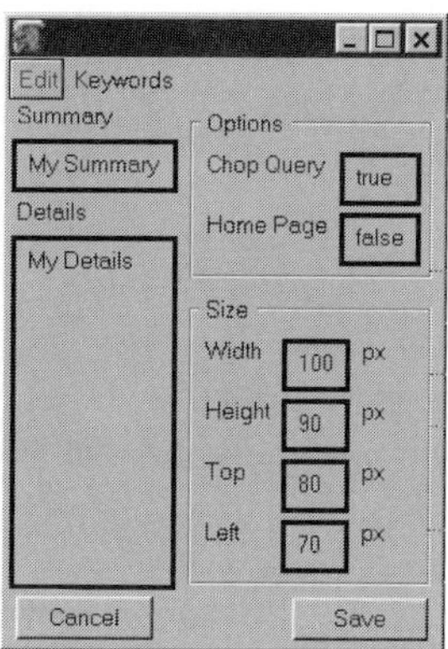

Fig. 5.4 NoteTaker dialog box with scripted property strings.

We've now successfully used XPCOM to interact with resources outside the loaded document. That's a big step, even if all we did was read a file. We'll leave writing this information out to a file to another day. Writing files (and reading them) is a long story. That story is told in Chapter 16, XPCOM Objects.

To summarize this activity, we've worked with DOM, AOM, XBL, and XPCOM objects. JavaScript has full access to the loaded content and, when installed in the chrome, can do anything it wants to do to that content. Most of the functionality we've added in this chapter has just been fancy little tricks. In future chapters, we'll replace those procedures with more professional work.

5.7 Debug Corner: Script Diagnosis

JavaScript is not a fully compiled language; consequently, it leaves the programmer with quite a bit of work in the area of detecting bugs. Because variables, properties, and methods are all resolved at run time, many bugs can lie hidden until very late in the development cycle. It's essential that the test-and-debug process have some structure and not be reduced to guesswork. This section describes the tools that can be applied to that process.

Good coding practices are probably the best defense against bugs. Keep your JavaScript code separate from XML. Always use terminating semicolons, meaningful variable names, and indentations. Always check arguments that are supplied to your functions, and return meaningful values at all times. Always use try blocks if the Mozilla interfaces you are using are capable of exceptions. Heed the advice on preferences in Chapter 1, Fundamental Concepts.

The `dump()` method of the window object is a very useful tool. When it is enabled, you can start Mozilla with the `-console` option and have diagnostic text spew out to a window without affecting the platform's own windows. That output can also be captured to a log file. On UNIX, `-console` can be used only from the command line. If your scripts include timed events, either generated by you or received by you, logged output is sometimes the only way to know what the order of events was in the processing.

Mozilla also supports a `javascript:` URL. This URL is useful for ad hoc tests of a document's state. If the document is loaded into a Navigator window (XUL documents can be loaded into Navigator as for any Web document), then `javascript:` URLs can be used to test the document's content. This is most useful when the document receives extensive input from the user. That input is usually stored as state information, which can be probed with statements like

```
javascript:var x=window.state.formProgress; alert(x);
```

`alert()`, of course, is a small dialog box that displays one or more lines of text. It can be placed anywhere in a script that is attached to a Mozilla window and can provide simple feedback on the state of the scripting environment and its content. `alert()` also pauses the JavaScript interpreter, which is a good thing for basic processing but a bad thing where information is supposed to be consumed in a time-critical way by the script (like streaming media). `alert()` is a trivial debugger.

Watchpoints are another trivial but extremely useful debugging tool. Every JavaScript object created has a `watch()` method. This method is used to attach a hidden function to a property of the object. This hidden function acts a little like Mozilla's "`set function ()`" syntax. Listing 5.13 illustrates.

Listing 5.13 Logging of object property changes using watchpoints.

```
function report(prop,oldval,newval)
{
   dump(prop + "old: " + oldval + "; new: " + newval);
   return newval;  // ensures watched code still works
};

var obj = { test:"before" };

obj.watch("test",report);
obj.test = "after";           // report() called
obj.unwatch("test");
```

The function `report()` has arguments imposed on it by `watch`. When the test property is watched, every change results in the `report()` function being called as a side effect. When the property is unwatched, the side effect ceases. This is also a tactic for logging changes as they occur.

Finally, the `debugger` keyword can be inserted in scripts anywhere. It starts the JavaScript Debugger, whose commands can be learned about by typing **/help** in the command line at the bottom of its window. This debugger is based on the XPCOM pair:

```
@mozilla.org/js/jsd/debugger-service;1 jsdIDebuggerService
```

If you don't like the JavaScript Debugger, you can implement something on top of this component and its `jsdIDebuggerService` interface yourself.

When obscure problems occur, shut down Mozilla completely, restart it, and retest. Always show the JavaScript Console (under Tools | Web Development), and always clear the console log before loading test documents so that new errors are obvious. On Microsoft Windows, occasionally check if zombie Mozilla processes are hanging around without any windows to identify them.

5.8 Summary

The JavaScript language is small and easy to master. It is much like many other languages in the C family of languages, except for its unique treatment of objects. The scope and prototype chain features of the language are curious and subtle, and many hours can be spent crafting clever uses. JavaScript 2.0 will de-emphasize prototype chains in favor of classes.

Compared with the core language, the interfaces that JavaScript uses are very extensive. They range from simple and convenient to remarkably obscure and encompass Java, plugins, and legacy browser support.

Well-trained Web developers will find Mozilla's support for DOM interfaces easy to use, familiar, and powerful. It is immediately applicable to XUL-based applications. The extensive standards support is something of a relief after years of cross-browser compatibility checks. Beginner XML programmers are advised to study the XML half of DOM 1 closely until the concepts of Node, Element, Document, and factory method sink in.

XPConnect and XPCOM infrastructure is the brave new world of Mozilla. With over a thousand components (and a thousand interfaces), there's only one way to eat this elephant: one bite at a time. You will probably never use some interfaces; your use of other interfaces will depend on how deeply you attempt to customize the platform and how aggressive your application is.

XPCOM provides a world of objects with the potential to make JavaScript programming as complex as the programming worlds of Java, C, or C++. XPCOM interfaces each have an XPIDL definition that is easy to read after it is located. Browsing through these interfaces can give you an early hint of Mozilla's full capabilities.

Rather than delve into XPCOM and never return, we next go back to the world of user interfaces and consider user input.

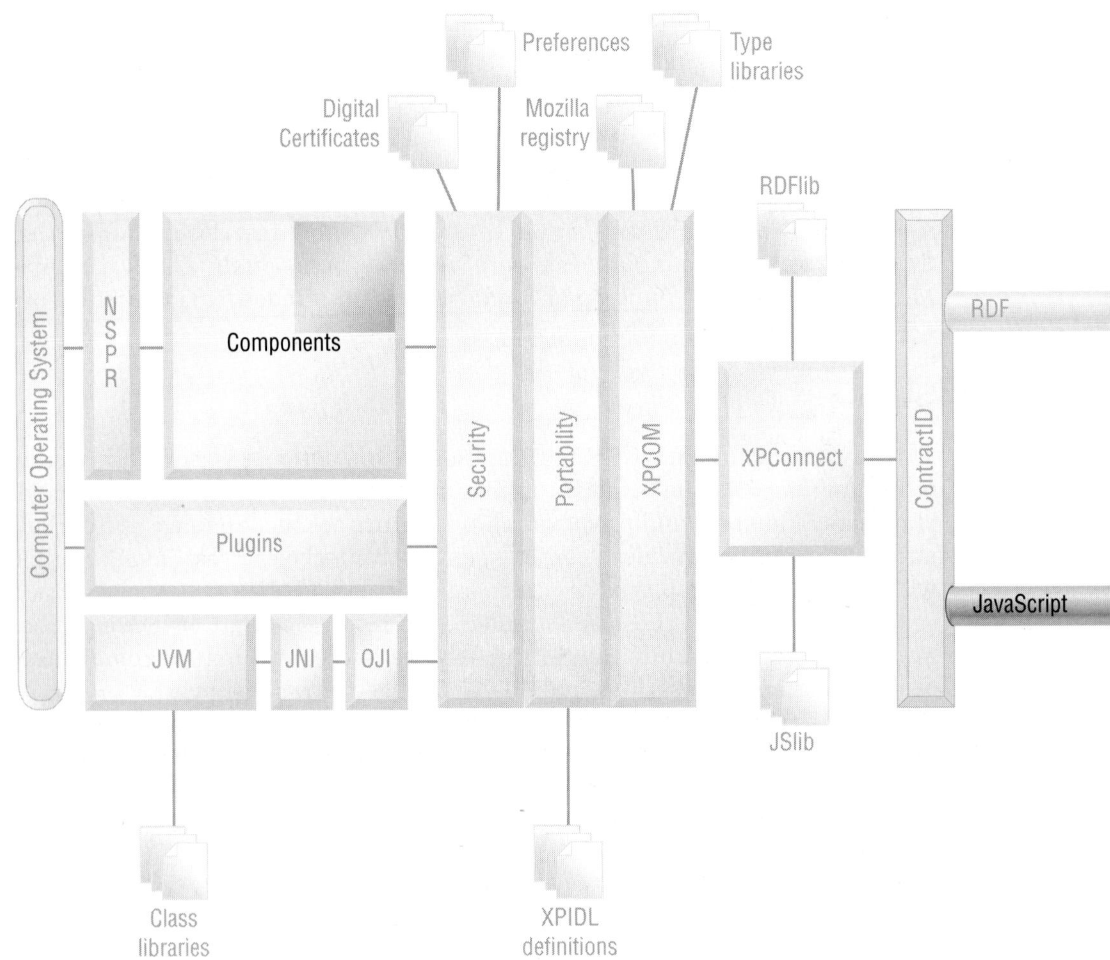

Preferences
Type libraries
Digital Certificates
Mozilla registry
RDFlib
Computer Operating System
NSPR
Components
Security
Portability
XPCOM
XPConnect
ContractID
RDF
Plugins
JavaScript
JVM
JNI
OJI
JSlib
Class libraries
XPIDL definitions

C H A P T E R 6

Events

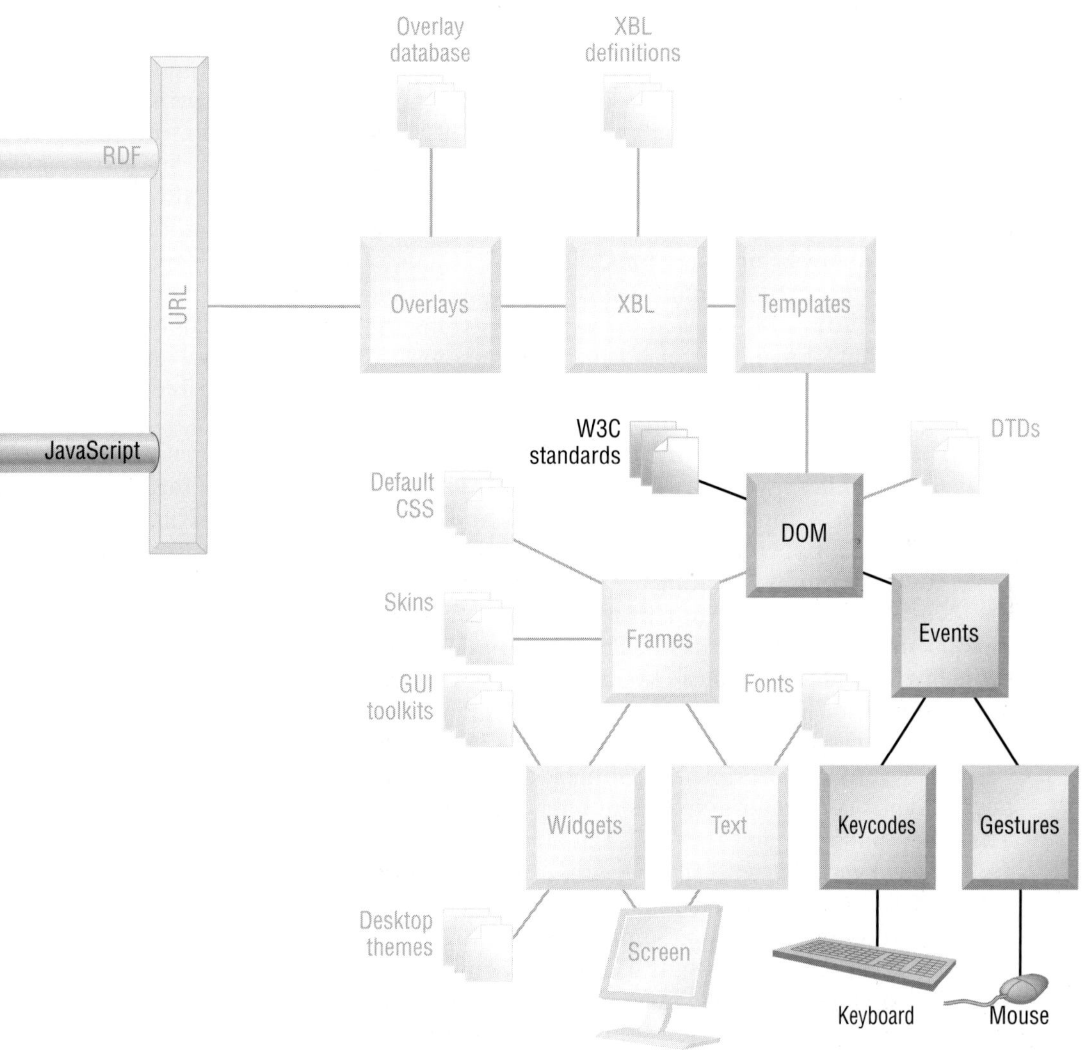

The Mozilla Platform is designed first and foremost for interactive applications. This chapter explains the basic features of Mozilla that build a bridge between a real live human and a software system. Such features are quite varied. They range from device drivers to single keystrokes to forms, menus, and toolbars. Underneath most of these possibilities is an event-driven input-processing system. This chapter covers that underlying raw, event-driven input.

In order to act, a user's raw input must first be boiled down into something more useful. This chapter also describes Mozilla's low-level collection systems for user input from the mouse, keyboard, and other sources. User input is deeply linked with Mozilla's event management systems, and the basics of these systems are carefully explored as well.

Traditional computer-user interfaces like keyboards, mice, and monitors are not very standard at all. These devices are connected to an operating system and a desktop, and those systems attempt to impose their own unique standards in order to make sense of it all. Such standards make the construction of cross-platform applications a challenge. Even the simplest standard makes portability a challenge: one mouse button for the Macintosh, two for Microsoft Windows, and three for UNIX.

On the other hand, most operating systems use Control-X, Control-C, and Control-V for cut, copy, and paste operations, respectively, except when keyboards don't have X, C, or V. The thing about standards is this: Not only are there many to choose from, but there are also many to be compatible with. Every standard is a little tyrant.

The Mozilla Platform must try to handle all these constraints gracefully, as well as find a way to set its own conventions. Users want their interaction with Mozilla to be familiar, obvious, simple, and reliable. Most user actions are repetitive, and users want to be able to perform those actions by reacting through habit, not by thinking.

The NPA diagram that precedes this chapter illustrates the areas of Mozilla that involve user input. The diagram is exactly as you would expect—most of the user input activity is on the user side of the diagram. The box labeled "Events" is of central concern to this chapter; it represents a system described in the DOM 2 Events and DOM 3 Events standards.

Now that JavaScript, XPConnect, and XPCOM have been introduced, a few relevant components from the back part of Mozilla are explored as well. These components, and the XUL tags that happen to complement them, provide several ways to express where an event should go after it appears.

Before proceeding, note this word of caution. Many of the concepts in this chapter are trivial to grasp. Some, however, are a little too subtle for readers with only HTML experience. If you are a beginner programmer, it's highly recommended that you experiment with the event concepts described, to gain experience. These event concepts recur throughout Mozilla and are an important step on the road to mastering the platform. The "Hands On" session in this chapter is a good starting point.

6.1 How Mozilla Handles Events

Figure 6.1 is a conceptual overview of the event-driven systems inside Mozilla.

All these approaches are briefly discussed here; most are extensively discussed here, but commands are discussed in Chapter 9, Commands, and content processing is a topic addressed in Chapter 16, XPCOM Objects.

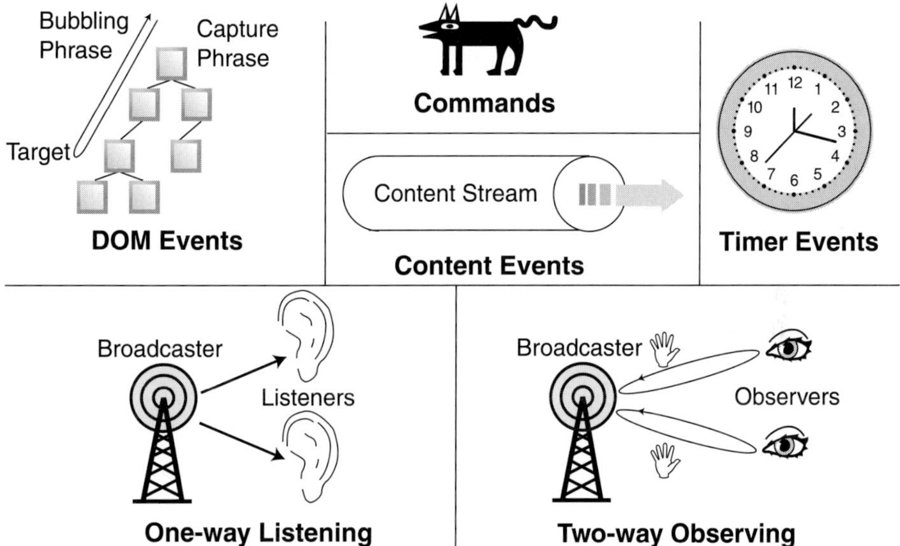

Fig. 6.1 Overview of event processing inside Mozilla.

6.1.1 Scheduling Input and Output

All programs need some form of input and output, and the Mozilla Platform is no exception. It can receive input from devices driven by human beings, from network and Internet connections, from the operating system, from other applications, and from itself. It can send output to most of those places. All together, that's a complicated set of possibilities to juggle. What if input arrives from several places at once? Won't something be missed? Mozilla's solution involves a simple event-driven scheduling system.

The problem with scheduling systems is that few programming languages have direct support for them, and simple-minded programs rarely use them. Some programmers never come into contact with such systems. A beginner's introduction is provided here. Experienced programmers note that this system is equivalent to a multithreaded environment and the `select()` kernel call.

"hello, world" might be the first program everyone attempts, but it only produces output. The second program attempted is likely to do both input and output. Listing 6.1 shows an example of such a second program, using JavaScript syntax. You can't run this program in a browser—it is just an imaginary example.

Listing 6.1 Example of a first input-output program.

```
var info;
while (true)
{
  read info;
  print info;
}
```

According to the rules of 3GL programming languages, this program has one statement block containing two statements, which are executed one after the other, over and over. This program never ends; it just reports back whatever is entered. It could be written in a slightly more structured way, as Listing 6.2 shows.

Listing 6.2 Example of a first structured input-output program.

```
var info;
function read_data()  { read info; }
function print_data() { print info; }

function run()
{
  while (true)
  {
    read_data();
    print_data();
  }
}

run();
```

Even though this second program performs only the single statement `run()`, it's clear that this is the same step-by-step approach used in Listing 6.1. Software based on scheduled systems doesn't work this way at all. The same program expressed in a scheduling system might appear as in Listing 6.3.

Listing 6.3 Example of a first scheduled input-output program.

```
var info;

function read_data() {
  if (!info)
    read info;
}
```

```
function print_data() {
  if (info) {
    print info;
    info = null;
  }
}

schedule(read_data, 500);
schedule(print_data, 1000);

run();
```

The schedule() function in this example takes two arguments: a function to run and a time delay in milliseconds. schedule() says that the supplied function should be run regularly whenever time equal to the millisecond delay has passed. run() tells the system to start looking for things to run. At time 0.5 seconds (500 milliseconds), read_data() will be run. At time 1.0 seconds (1,000 milliseconds, which is also 2 * 500 milliseconds), both functions will be run. At time 1.5 seconds (1,500 milliseconds = 3 * 500 milliseconds), read_data() will run for a third time, and so on. The run() function never finishes.

Such an arrangement can seem quite foreign, especially since the schedule() and run() functions aren't defined anywhere in the program. You just have to trust that they work as advertised. They are services provided by some existing scheduling system. Worse, read_data() and print_data() don't execute in any particular order. In fact, read_data() runs twice as frequently (every half second, compared to once a second for print_data()).

In order to work together, the two functions rely on a shared piece of data (the info variable). read_data() will not read anything until the last item in info is used by print_data(). print_data() will not print anything until read_info() puts something into info. The two functions are coordinated with each other via shared state information, even though they are otherwise independent.

In Mozilla, you can either create such a scheduler yourself or use an existing one and add your own scheduled items, but neither strategy is common practice. The Mozilla Platform takes care of all this for you. It has a built-in scheduler and scheduled functions that check for all possible forms of user input and output. A keypress is one kind of input, a JavaScript script to run is another, and a chunk of HTML content received from a Web server is a third. Scheduled items can be small (a mouse click) or very large (please redisplay this whole HTML document). Everything in Mozilla is a scheduled item, even if this fact is buried deeply underneath everyday features.

Occasionally this scheduled system is revealed to the programmer. Listing 6.4 closely matches Listing 6.3; however, it is a legal and runnable JavaScript script. Include it in any HTML or XML page, fill in the regularly appearing popup, and watch the text in the window's title to see the scheduling system at work. The example goes slowly so that you have time to shut the windows down with the mouse when you've had enough.

Listing 6.4 Example of function scheduling using `setInterval()`.

```
function read_data() {
  if (!window.userdata)
    window.userdata = prompt("Enter new title");
}

function print_data() {
  if (window.userdata) {
    window.title = window.userdata;
    window.userdata = null;
  }
}

window.setInterval(read_data, 5000);
window.setInterval(print_data, 100);
```

Even though the two functions run at very different frequencies, the system works. `print_data()` will do frequent checks for something to do; `read_data()` will less frequently ask the user for information.

This example could be simplified. The `read_data()` function could be made to write the title into the window as soon as it is read. If that were done, `print_data()` could be done away with entirely. Such a variation shows how bigger functions mean fewer scheduled items. The reverse is true as well. The number of items scheduled is just a programmer's choice at design time.

Listing 6.4 can be viewed from a different perspective. Rather than be amazed that two functions can run in a coordinated but independent manner, it is possible to think about the roles of those two functions inside the running environment. `read_data()` acquires new information and makes it available. From the perspective of the run-time environment, it is a producer of information. `print_data()` takes available information and puts it somewhere else, using it up in the process. It is a consumer of information.

Producers and consumers are very important design ideas, and they appear throughout Mozilla. The idea of a *producer-consumer pair* working together is a very common one, and the pair is tied together by a common purpose: the desire to process one kind of information. Sometimes the pair sits and does nothing. When some new stimulus occurs, the pair goes into action.

A further modification to Listing 6.4 might be to change the `setInterval()` calls to `setTimeout()` calls. `setTimeout()` schedules its function argument to run just once, not repeatedly. After that sole run, the scheduled item is removed from the schedule system, never to appear again. Items that appear just once in a schedule system are a very important special case.

Suppose that a schedule system consists of nothing but one-off items. Further, suppose that these items all have a time delay of zero. Lastly, suppose that these items are all producers—they will each produce one item of data when they run. In such circumstances, the schedule system is a simple event queue. When a producer in the queue runs, an event is said to be underway. In casual conversation, the producer in the queue is also called an event, but the data that the producer creates is called an event too. Since all the producers in an event queue have a zero delay, Mozilla will do its best to run them right away, which means they leave the queue almost immediately. Such a system is useful for reporting keystrokes, for example.

In Listing 6.4, the application programmer is responsible for creating both consumers and producers. An event queue can be arranged differently. The Mozilla Platform can be made responsible for adding the events to the queue. It can also be made responsible for finding a suitable consumer when a producer event occurs. The application programmer can be responsible for writing consumers that consume the created event data and for telling the Mozilla Platform that these consumers are interested in certain kinds of event data.

The application programmer calls these consumers event handlers, and Mozilla calls them listeners. A listener is a programming design pattern—a well-established idea that is a useful thinking point for design. Code designed to be a listener awaits information from other code and acts on it when it occurs. All JavaScript scripts are listeners that run in response to some event, even though no event appears to be at work.

This brief introduction has gone from a plain 3GL example to an event-driven system. This is how much of Mozilla works. In particular, this is how user input, for example, is processed. We have touched on the concepts of consumers, producers, scheduling, listeners, and timing along the way, and these concepts are all useful in their own right. When the moment comes to get dirty using XPCOM components, these concepts will become essential. For now, all you need to do is accept that events drive all processing in Mozilla, even if the thing to process is just one big script.

From Chapter 5, Scripting, you know that much of the Mozilla Platform is available as XPCOM interfaces and components, and that includes event queues. The two components

```
@mozilla.org/event-queue;1
@mozilla.org/event-queue-service;1
```

and the interface

```
nsIEventQueue
```

allow an event queue to be created, started, and stopped. These components are only useful for applications that deeply customize Mozilla.

Because the Mozilla event queue is so low-level, it is rarely used directly. Instead, Mozilla builds several higher-level systems on top that are easier to work with. These are the features that application programmers depend on heavily. They are still "below the surface" in the sense that they don't include much direct user input. They are like the middle layer of a cake, not the icing.

This overview of how Mozilla processes events is continued with a look at no less than five of these middle systems.

6.1.2 The DOM Event Model

The event handlers and events that Web developers use on a daily basis come from the W3C's DOM Events standards. Many of these events apply to any XML document, including XUL, and experience with these handlers can be directly applied to Mozilla. The DOM Event system sits on top of Mozilla's basic event queue. DOM Events are restricted to a single XML document.

Because the DOM Events standard has only recently been finalized with DOM level 3, Web browser support has some catching up to do. Cross-browser compatibility issues, nonstandard event behavior, and gaps have made the use of events in scripts something of a vexing issue. Generally, the "flat" event model of version 3.0 Web browsers, in which events do not propogate much, is all Web developers risk using for cross-platform HTML.

With the release of Mozilla, many of these problems have gone away. For application developers and for XUL documents, there are no cross-platform issues. Mozilla supports the full DOM 2 and DOM 3 Event flow for many common events. Both event capture and bubbling phases are supported.

Mozilla also supports the use of more than one event handler per event target, as per the standards. It is strongly recommended that you read sections 1.1 and 1.2 of the DOM 3 Events standard, if you haven't yet. That's a mere four pages of reading.

To briefly summarize those sections of the standard, events in an XML document can be handled with JavaScript scripts. A piece of script or a single function is an event handler, which the programmer installs against an event target. An event target is just a tag or the tag's DOM 1 `Element` object, plus an event type. When an event occurs as a result of user input or some other reason, an `Event` object is created. That object travels down the DOM hierarchy of tags, starting with the `Document` object and ending with the event target tag. This is the capture phase, and any tag along the way can process the event if it has a suitable event handler. Such an interposed handler can stop the event or allow it to continue to the event target tag.

After the `Event` object reaches the event target tag, the intended event handler is executed. This handler can stop the `Event` object from traveling and prevent the default action from occurring. The default action is what would happen if the event target tag had no installed handler at all. After the handler has finished running, the default action takes place (if it hasn't been stopped), and then the event enters the bubble phase. In the bubble phase, the `Event` object returns up the DOM hierarchy to the `Document` object, and again can be intercepted by one or more other handlers on the way. When it reaches the `Document` object, the event is over.

Events travel down and up like this to support construction of two types of interactive documents.

In one design, tags within a document are considered dumb objects that need to be managed. In this case, events need to be captured at the most abstract level (at the document level) so that high-level processing of the document's contents can occur. Examples of this type of design include window managers that receive input on behalf of the windows, desktops that receive input on behalf of icons, and rubber-banding (area-selection) operations. The capture phase supports this kind of design.

In another design, tags within a document are considered smart objects that can think for themselves. Input goes straight to the most specific object, which does its own processing. Examples of this type of design are ordinary application windows, forms, and graphical tools. This is the more common use of XUL. The bubbling phase supports this kind of design.

Table 6.1 shows events that Mozilla recognizes. This list is derived from the Mozilla source file `content/events/src/nsDOMEvent.cpp` and is organized according to the sections of the DOM 3 Events standard, plus two columns for Mozilla custom events. There are many XUL tags that support only a subset of these events.

Mozilla-specific events are discussed in the appropriate topic in this chapter. Here is a brief summary of these events. `dblclick` occurs on double-click of a mouse button. `contextmenu` occurs if the mouse or keyboard makes a context menu appear (e.g., right-click in Microsoft Windows). Events

Table 6.1 Implemented events in Mozilla

DOM mouse	DOM text	DOM HTML	DOM mutation	Mozilla	Mozilla
click	keydown	load	DOMNodeInserted	dblclick	popupshowing
mousedown	keyup	unload	DOMNodeRemoved	contextmenu	popupshown
mouseup		abort	DOMAttrModified		popuphiding
mouseover		error	DOMCharacterData-Modified	keypress	popuphidden
mousemove		select		text	
mouseout		change		command	dragenter
		submit		commandupdate	dragover
		reset		input	dragexit
		focus			dragdrop
		blur		paint	draggesture
		resize		overflow	
		scroll		underflow	broadcast
				overflowchanged	close

grouped with `keypress` are for keyboard actions or for actions that are typically initiated by the user. Events grouped with `paint` are for changes to document layout. `popup...` events are for menu popups and tooltips. `drag...` events are for drag-and-drop gestures with the mouse. `broadcast` supports the broadcaster-observer system that is a Mozilla-specific technology. `close` occurs when a user attempts to close a window.

These events all generate an `Event` object, as per the DOM Events standard. Mozilla's `nsIDOMEvent` interface is equivalent to the `Event` interface in the standard, and other interface names convert similarly.

Table 6.2 shows events that Mozilla does not recognize as of version 1.4. These events are also drawn from the DOM 3 Events standard.

Table 6.2 Unimplemented standard event names in Mozilla 1.2.1

DOM user interface events	DOM mutation name events	DOM text events
DOMFocusIn	DOMElementNameChanged	textInput (use keypress or text)
DOMFocusOut	DOMAttributeNameChanged	
DOMActivate	DOMSubtreeModified	
	DOMNodeInsertedIntoDocument	
	DOMNodeRemovedFromDocument	

The common way to specify an event handler is to use an XML attribute. Mozilla is case-sensitive, and all such attributes should be lowercase, unless uppercase is explicitly stated in these tables. A handler attribute has the same name as the event with a prefix of "on". Less popular, but more powerful, is the DOM system for setting event handlers. Listing 6.5 compares the syntax for these two systems.

Listing 6.5 Event handlers registration techniques.

```
<!-- the XML way -->
<button id="test" onclick="myhandler(event);">
  <label value="Press Me"/>
</button>

// The DOM way
  var obj = getElementById("test");
  obj.addEventListener("click", myhandler, false);
```

Traditional HTML would supply the handler function a `this` argument. In Mozilla, the current `Event` object is always available as an event property. That `Event` object's `currentTarget` property is equivalent to this, so use either name.

There are minor differences in the execution of these two variants. The scripted DOM approach is slightly more flexible for several reasons:

- More than one handler can be added for the same object using `addEventListener()`.
- `addEventListener()`'s third argument set to `true` allows a handler to run in the capture phase. That is not possible from XML.
- Handlers can be removed using `removeEventListener()`. In XUL, an inline event listener can only be replaced, not removed.
- The DOM method allows all event handlers to be factored out of the XML content. Handlers can therefore be installed from a separate `.js` file.

The XML approach has one advantage: It supports a script fragment smaller than a whole function. This capability might be useful for HTML, but for XUL, where structured programming is good practice, it is not much of a benefit. If your XML is likely to have a long life, it's recommended that you keep event handlers out of XML attributes.

6.1.2.1 XUL Support for Event Handlers According to Table 5.4, Mozilla does not support the `HTMLEvents` and `TextEvents` interfaces that are part of the DOM 3 Events standard. That is not the full story.

XUL is not HTML, so lack of support for `HTMLEvents` is not a surprise. The default actions for some HTML tags are substantial (e.g., form submission or link navigation), but default actions for XUL tags are less common. XUL tags, on the other hand, are frequently backed by XBL bindings and sophisticated styles. These bindings and styles add effects and handlers that might as well be counted as default actions. If a XUL tag has no programmer-installed event handlers, but something is still happening when the event occurs, the best place to start looking is in `xul.css` in the `toolkit.jar` chrome file. That is where default styles and bindings for tags are located. Chapter 15, XBL Bindings, describes how to add event support using XBL bindings.

TextEvents is a DOM standard term for events in which a character is sent to an XML document. In plain English, this means `keypresses`, but `TextEvents` could in theory originate from some other source. The `TextEvents` section of the Events standard is based on Mozilla's `nsIKeyEvents` interface, but it is slightly different in detail. In practice, Mozilla has almost the same functionality as the standard.

`TextEvents` do have one shortcoming in Mozilla. These events can only be received by the `Document` or `Window` object. There is no capturing or bubbling phase at all.

There is no exhaustive cross-reference yet that documents event support for every XUL tag. The easiest way to proceed is still to try out an event handler and note the results for yourself. The individual topics of this chapter provide some guidance on specific handlers.

Many XUL tags have XBL bindings attached to them, and XBL has a `<handler>` tag. This means that the default action for a given tag might be specified in XBL, rather than inside Mozilla's C/C++. This opens up some XUL default actions to study.

6.1.3 Timed Events

A second event system inside Mozilla is a simple mechanism for timed events. Listing 6.4 and its discussion use this system. Because Mozilla's event queue is such a fundamental feature of the platform, it is both easy and sensible to make a user-friendly version available to programmers. The four calls that make up this little system are shown in Listing 6.6.

Listing 6.6 Timed events API examples.

```
timer = window.setTimeout(code, milliseconds);
timer = window.setInterval(code, milliseconds);

window.clearTimeout(timer);
window.clearInterval(timer);

// examples of timed code
timer = setTimeout(myfunction, 100, arg1, arg2);
timer = setTimeout("myfunction();", 100);
timer = setTimeout("window.title='Go'; go();", 100);
```

The argument named `code` can be either a function object or a string containing JavaScript. If it is a string, it is evaluated with `eval()` when run. The timer return value is a numeric identifier for the scheduled item. Its only purpose is to allow removal of the item. The identifier has no meaning within JavaScript, other than being unique.

Timers have some restrictions: The timed event does not have the JavaScript scope chain of the code that called it; the window object is the first scope chain member; and the number of milliseconds must be at least 10.

Perhaps the biggest restriction is the single-threaded nature of both JavaScript and XPCOM. No timed event will occur until the current script is finished running. Only one timed event can be in progress at a given time. If a given piece of code takes a long time to complete, then all the due events will bank up and be executed late. Finally, some input and output operations must wait for an event handler to finish before they can take place. For example, style layout changes made by a `setTimeout()` event won't occur until the event is over. This is a major constraint on animated systems. In general, the JavaScript interpreter must release the CPU before other activities in the Mozilla Platform can proceed.

Mozilla's XPCOM system can also provide timed events. It has an API entirely separate from `setTimeout()`. The XPCOM pair required is

```
@mozilla.org/timer;1 nsITimer.
```

Such an object works with a second object that supports the `nsIOb-serves` interface. To use `nsITimer`, you must implement this second object yourself. Listing 6.7 illustrates.

Listing 6.7 Single `setTimeout()` call implemented using XPCOM components.

```
var observer = {
  // Components.interfaces.nsIObserver
  observe: function(aSubject, aTopic, aData)
  {
    alert("From: " + aSubject + " saw: " + aTopic + " data: " + aData);
  },

  // Components.interfaces.nsISupports
  QueryInterface : function(iid)
  {
    if ( iid.equals(Components.interfaces.nsIObserver) ||
 iid.equals(Components.interfaces.nsISupportsWeakReference)
 || iid.equals(Components.interfaces.nsISupports)
       )
       return this;
    throw Components.results.NS_NOINTERFACE;
  }
};

with(netscape.security.PrivilegeManager)
{  enablePrivilege("UniversalXPConnect");  }

var c, timer;

c = Components.classes["@mozilla.org/timer;1"];
timer = c.createInstance(Components.interfaces.nsITimer);

timer.init(observer, 5000, timer.TYPE_ONE_SHOT);
```

Most of this code simply creates an object that implements the `nsIOb-server` interface. How exactly this works isn't too important yet; it is just worth noting that the `observe()` method has the same name and arguments as the one defined in the `nsIObserver` interface, which you can find in the `nsIObserver.idl` interface file. Compare this object with the contents of `nsIObserver.idl` and `nsISupports.idl` in the source code, if you like. That created object will receive the timed event when it occurs.

The last few lines of Listing 6.7 create the `Timer` object, and set up the event. `init()` tells the timer what object should be used when the event comes due, when the event should be, and whether the event should run once or repeatedly. Just like `setTimeout()`, this script then ends. The event fires later on, causing `observer.observe()` to run. It's clear that this code achieves the same effect as a `setTimeout()` call that runs `alert()`.

The line of security code in the middle of this example is required if the script is not stored inside the chrome. The user must confirm that the script has permission to use XPCOM, for security purposes. It is shown here just to illustrate what is required for nonchrome XUL. Most XUL is stored in the chrome and doesn't require this line.

If you include this code in any HTML or XUL page, you'll see that a single alert box appears 5 seconds or so after the page loads. For everyday purposes, it's much easier just to use `setTimeout()` and `setInterval()`. Later on, this more formal system will seem much more convenient for some tasks.

6.1.4 Broadcasters and Observers

The third event system in Mozilla is based on the `Observer` design pattern. Recall that design patterns are high-level design ideas that, when implemented carefully, create powerful, flexible, and sometimes simple software systems. Mozilla's XPCOM components, which together look like an object library, make extensive use of the `Observer` design pattern. Any nontrivial use of XPCOM means learning this pattern. This pattern is used so much that it also appears directly in XUL tags.

Earlier in this chapter the concepts of event queues, producers and consumers, and listeners were outlined. All of these things are designed to bring some structure to input or, more generally, to notify that something, somewhere has changed. Recall that listeners are a kind of consumer that is notified when an event occurs. Observers are another kind of consumer that is notified when an event occurs.

The difference between listeners and observers is that listeners don't generally respond. A listener notes the information or event that it is advised of, perhaps does something with it, but usually ignores the system that supplied the event. An observer also notes the information or event that it is advised of and perhaps does something with it, but an observer is also free to interact with the provider of the event. Observers are somewhat interactive and, in less common cases, can even take on a supervisory role.

Observers work with a broadcaster. The broadcaster's role is to notify the observer when an event occurs. The broadcaster has the ability to notify any number of observers when one event occurs, hence its name. There is a one-to-many relationship between a broadcaster and its observers. Just as one DOM 2 Event can be handled by several event handlers on the same event target, one broadcast event can be handled by several observers.

An observer and a broadcaster are like a consumer-producer pair, except the broadcaster is a producer for many observer consumers. The pair's relationship doesn't end there, though. Initially, the observer does nothing but wait until the broadcaster acts, sending an event. After the event is sent, the roles are reversed. The broadcaster does nothing, and the observer can act on the broadcaster, if it so wishes. Both are free to act on other software that they are part of.

All that is a bit abstract, so here is some concrete technology.

6.1.4.1 XUL Broadcasters and Observers XUL supports the `<broadcasterset>`, `<broadcaster>`, and `<observes>` tags. It also supports the `observes` and `onbroadcast` attributes, which apply to all XUL tags. A related tag is the `<command>` tag. `<command>` is explored in Chapter 9, Commands.

These tags allow XML attribute value changes in one tag to appear in another tag. In other words, two tags are linked by an attribute. These changes are used as a notification system inside XUL. Syntax for these tags is shown in Listing 6.8.

Listing 6.8 Broadcasters and observers implemented in XUL.

```
<broadcasterset>
  <broadcaster id="producer1" att1="A" att2="B" ... />
  <broadcaster id="producer2" att1="C" ... />
</broadcasterset>

<observes element="producer1"
          attribute="att1"
          onbroadcast="alert('test1')"/>

<observes element="producer1"
          attribute="att1 att2"
          onbroadcast="alert('test2')"/>

<box observes="producer2"/>
```

`att1` and `att2` stand for any legal XML attribute names, except for `id`, `ref`, and `persist`. None of these tags have any visual appearance except possibly `<box>`. The last line could have used any XUL tag; there is no special reason for choosing `<box>`. An overview of these tags follows.

Recall that the `<stringbundleset>` tag was introduced in Chapter 3, Static Content. It is a nondisplayed tag with no special behavior. It is just used as a convenient container for `<stringbundle>` tags. `<broadcasterset>` has exactly the same role for `<broadcaster>` tags. It does nothing except look tidy in the source code; however, you are encouraged to follow its use convention.

The `<broadcaster>` tag has a unique id and a set of attributes. These attributes are just plain data and have no special meaning. The tag can have as many of these attributes as necessary. If any of these attributes change, the broadcaster will look for places to send an event.

The `<observes>` tag uses the element `attribute` to register itself with a `<broadcaster>` that has a matching id. The `<observes>` tag must also have an attribute `attribute`. This determines which of the `<broadcaster>`'s attributes it is observing. The second example in Listing 6.8 shows an `<observes>` tag observing two attributes. The value for this attribute can also be `"*"`, meaning observe all attributes.

The onbroadcast attribute applies only to the <observes> tag. It is optional. Broadcast events will occur even if such a handler is missing. If a handler is present, it will be fired before the attribute change takes place. In that way, the old value can be read from the tag, and the new value, from the event. The onbroadcaster handler is buggy in some Mozilla versions. It can fire twice, or not at all, which are both wrong. It works reliably if the attribute attribute has a value that is a single attribute name.

Finally for this example, the observes attribute allows any XUL tag to observe all the changes from a given broadcaster. This is the role that the <box> tag has. When observes is used, there is no way to restrict the observations to specific attributes. The tag with observes receives all attribute changes that occur on the broadcaster.

Listing 6.9 shows all this at work as a series of code fragments.

Listing 6.9 Processing order for a broadcast event.

```
<button label="Press Me" oncommand="produce('bar');"/>

function produce(str)
{
  getElementById("b").setAttribute("foo",str);
}

function consume1(obj)
{
  if (obj.getAttribute("foo") == "bar")
    getElementById("x1").setAttribute("style","color:red");
}

<broadcaster id="b" foo="default"/>

<observes id="o1"
          element="b"
          attribute="foo"
          onbroadcast="consume1(this)"/>

<box id="x1"><label value="content"></box>
```

In this example, the broadcast event starts and ends with the XUL tags <button> and <box>, respectively. This practice is common but not absolutely necessary. The two JavaScript functions produce() and consume1() are the real start and end points for the event.

produce() starts the event by changing a foo attribute on the broadcaster tag. The broadcaster then informs any observers of the change. In this case, there is only one observer. The observer's foo attribute then changes. The event could finish at this point, in which case some other script would have to come back and examine the observer's attribute. In this example, the <observes> tag finishes the event with a call to the consume1() function. It has some end-effect, in this case setting a style on the <box> tag. If there were more observers, consume2() and consume3() functions might exist as well. The consume1() function manipulates the observer tag, not the broadcaster tag. The foo attribute it manipulates is copied to the observer tag when it is changed on the broadcast tag—that is the origin of the broadcast event.

In this example, the button's handler could set the required style directly, saving a lot of tags and code. Even if there were more than one observer, each with a different effect, the button handler could still implement all these effects directly. Listing 6.9 is more sophisticated than a single button handler because the existing button handler has no idea what tags are observing the change it creates. This means that the <button>'s action is not rigidly connected to specific tags. The <button> tag provides a service, and any interested parties can benefit from it. This is particularly useful when overlays are used—they are described in Chapter 12, Overlays and Chrome. Overlays create an environment where even the application programmer is not sure what content might currently be displayed. In such cases, the observer pattern is a perfect solution: Just broadcast your event to the crowd, and those wanting it will pick it up.

There is a further use of <observes>. Any XUL tag may have an <observes> tag as one of its content tags. The parent tag of <observes> will then receive on broadcast whatever attributes of the broadcaster the <observes> tag specifies. The <observes> tag itself does not change in this case. If the broadcast event is just designed to change tag attributes, then this nested tag arrangement makes the general case in Listing 6.8 much simpler. The consume1() function can be done away with, and if attribute names are coordinated throughout the code, then Listing 6.10 shows how the <box> tag's attribute can be set without any scripting:

Listing 6.10 Processing order for a broadcast event.

```
<button label="Press Me" oncommand="produce('color:red');"/>

function produce(str)
{
  getElementById("b").setAttribute("style",str);
}

<broadcaster id="b" style=""/>

<box id="x1">
  <observes id="o1" element="b" attribute="style"/>
  <label value="content">
</box>
```

This example could be further shortened by using the observes attribute. To do this, remove the <observes> tag and add observes="b" to the <box> tag. The <box> tag now receives all broadcaster changes, not just those on attribute style, but less code is required.

Finally, a <broadcaster> tag also sends an event when its XUL page is first loaded. In this case, no broadcast-related event handlers fire.

Having covered the mechanics of <broadcaster> and <observes>, it's easy to wonder what it is all used for. The answer is that the application programmer adds a layer of meaning (semantics) on top of the basic system to achieve an end purpose. In Mozilla, informal but common naming conventions for the id attribute of the broadcaster are used to indicate different semantic purposes. Three example purposes follow:

1. **id="cmd_mycommand"**. The observer pattern can be used to send a command (like cmd_mycommand) to multiple destinations. The command might be a function attached to the broadcaster. When an event occurs, the observers all retrieve it and execute it. An example of this attribute at work is the closing of multiple windows in one operation.
2. **id="Panel:CurrentFlags"**. The observer pattern can be used to manage a resource or an object. This resource may or may not be exactly one XUL tag. In the simplest case, the <broadcaster> tag is effectively a record for the resource, holding many informational attributes. When those attributes of the resource change, the broadcaster sends updates to the observers, keeping them advised.
3. **id="data.db.currentRow"**. The observer pattern can be used as a data replication system. The id might exactly match a real JavaScript object or any other data item. When the data changes, the broadcaster tells all the observers. These observers can then grab the JavaScript object and update whatever subsystems asked them to observe the data.

These examples show that the observer design pattern is widely useful as a design tool.

When the observer concept was introduced, it was said that observers often interact with their broadcasters. This is less common for the XUL-based observer system, although there is nothing stopping an onbroadcast handler from digging into the matching broadcaster. It is far more common in Mozilla's XPCOM broadcaster system, discussed shortly.

6.1.4.2 JavaScript Broadcasters and Observers

Event handlers can be installed using an XML attribute or using a JavaScript method based on DOM standards. Both techniques were illustrated in Listing 6.8. The same is true of Mozilla's broadcasters and observers. The analogous methods apply only to XUL, however. Listing 6.11 compares the XUL and JavaScript DOM techniques for broadcast-observer pairs.

Listing 6.11 Linking broadcasters and observers using XUL JavaScript.

```
<!-- the XML way -->
<broadcaster id="bc"/>
<box id="x1" observes="bc" onbroadcast="execute(this)"/>
```

```
// the AOM way
<broadcaster id="bc"/>
<box id="x1"/>

var bc = getElementById("bc");
var x1 = getElementById("x1");
addBroadcastListenerFor(bc, x1, "foo");
addEventListener("broadcast", execute, false);

// also removeBroadcastListenerFor(bc, x1, "foo");
```

Both of these examples set up a broadcaster-observer relationship between the two tags. The new method `addBroadcasterListenerFor()` of the XUL window object sets up the connection in the JavaScript case. Note that the observer's `onbroadcast` listener needs to be installed as well.

6.1.4.3 XPCOM Broadcasters and Observers Like timers, broadcasters and observers can be created the quick, Web development way using XUL, or more slowly, but more flexibly using XPCOM components. Listing 6.7 illustrates a partial example of XPCOM component use. Recall that the observer object clearly follows the observer pattern, and that the `nsITimer` object is a broadcaster of sorts, although it is limited to accepting one observer for a given delayed event.

Listing 6.7 can be studied further. Figure 6.2 shows output from the single `alert()` call run in that example.

The three arguments passed to the `observe()` method are displayed in this dialog box. We didn't consider these arguments earlier, but they are now ripe for examination.

The third argument is data associated with the event. `nsITimer` supplies no data for this argument. Boring.

The second argument is equivalent to the `attribute` attribute in XUL's `<observes>` tag. It specifies what event is occurring. The value of "`timer-callback`" is the special value associated with an XPCOM `nsITimer` event. This value is specified in the C/C++ code of Mozilla, but it is not a standard DOM Event.

The first argument is the `nsITimer` object itself. In the alert box, it has been changed to a JavaScript String type. The only way to do this is to call the `toString()` method on that object. So the observer in this example is executing a method on the broadcaster for the trivial purpose of getting a string

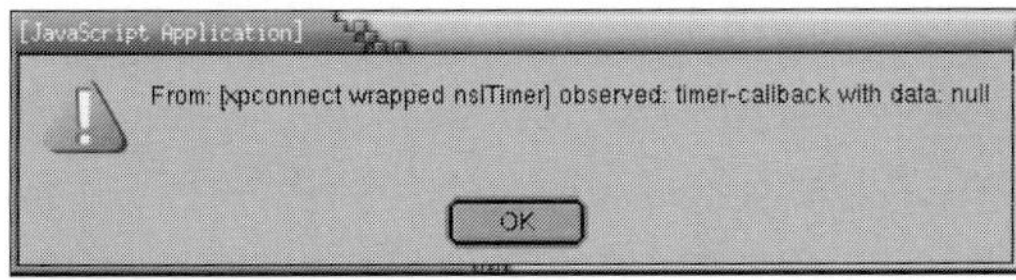

Fig. 6.2 `nsIObserver observe()` arguments from `nsITimer`.

back. This is an example of objects and broadcasters actively working together. The observer can in fact examine or use any of the properties that the broadcaster has, not just `toString()`.

Mozilla has more general support for broadcaster-observer systems than `nsITimer`. The simplest observer is

```
@mozilla.org/xpcom/observer;1 interface nsIObserver
```

This is a "do nothing" observer, a bit like `/dev/null`. It's `observe()` method just returns success. Mozilla has many specialist observer components, or you can make your own, as is done in Listing 6.7. Mozilla's XPCOM broadcaster is more useful. It is based on this XPCOM pair:

```
@mozilla.org/observer-service;1 interface nsIObserverService
```

This singleton object is a general-purpose broadcaster. It will broadcast to any observer object registered with it, regardless of the observer's window of origin. Listing 6.12 shows a typical use.

Listing 6.12 Example of an XPCOM broadcaster-observer pair.

```
var observer  = { ... as in Listing 6-6 ... };
var observer2 = { ... another observer ... );

var CC = Components.classes, CI = Components.interfaces;
var cls, caster;

cls = CC["@mozilla.org/observer-service;1"];
caster = cls.getService(CI.nsIObserverService);

caster.addObserver(observer,  "my-event", true);
caster.addObserver(observer2, "my-event", true);

caster.notifyObservers(caster, "my-event", "anydata");
```

The `caster` object is the single broadcaster. When observers are added, using `addObserver()`, the first argument is the observer object; the second is the event string to observer; and the third argument is a flag that indicates whether the observer is written in JavaScript. If it is, `true` must be used. If it is a C/C++ XPCOM component, `false`. `notifyObservers()` generates an event of the given type on the broadcaster; the third argument is a piece of arbitrary data in which arguments or parameters for the event can be placed. It will be received by the observer object.

That concludes this introduction to Mozilla's broadcasters and observers.

6.1.5 Commands

The fourth event system noted in this chapter relates to commands. In Mozilla, a command is an action that an application might perform. HTML's link navigation and form submission are roughly equivalent to the tasks that Mozilla commands implement.

Although the simplest way to think of a command is as a single JavaScript function, that is far from the only way. A command can also be a message sent from one place to another. This aspect of Mozilla commands is very event-like. Another set of event-like behaviors occurs on top of the basic command system. Change notifications are sent when commands change their state.

Overall, Mozilla's command system is quite complex. Chapter 9, Commands, not only examines this system in the context of a whole XUL window but also covers its nuts and bolts. For now, just note that Mozilla's command system is an extension of, or a complement to, the DOM 3 Events processing model.

6.1.6 Content Delivery Events

The final Mozilla event input system considered in this chapter is the content delivery system. This is the system responsible for accepting a URL and returning a document or for sending an email. It is a general system with several different uses.

DOM events, timed events, and observer events all deal with tiny pieces of information. The event that occurs may represent some larger processing elsewhere in the Mozilla Platform, but the event data itself is usually small. You might call these events lightweight events.

Content delivery events, by comparison, are typically big. They range from email download to a file delivered via FTP to a newsgroup update. Such events, furthermore, are likely broken into subevents: single emails, a partial chunk of an FTPed file, or individual newgroup headers. During the passing of these subevents, the producer and consumer have a long-term relationship. That relationship doesn't end until the last bit of the main job is complete.

Such a heavyweight event system has its own language. Producers are called content sources or data sources; consumers are called content sinks or just sinks. Detailed discussion of sources and sinks is left until Chapter 16, XPCOM Objects.

Having now covered Mozilla's internal event processing, it's time to see how those events can be created by the user.

6.2 How Keystrokes Work

Mozilla's XUL supports the `<keyset>`, `<key>`, `<commandset>`, and `<command>` tags. These tags are used to associate keys with GUI elements and to process keystrokes when they occur. These tags allow key assignments to be changed on a per-document or per-application basis. XUL also supports the `accesskey` attribute.

A key is a small bit of plastic on a keyboard, with some printing on it. Keys can be divided into two rough groups: those with an equivalent glyph and those without. A glyph is a visual representation, like A. The Unicode standard handles keys that have glyphs; for nonglyph keys, like Control-C, there is almost no standards support.

Mozilla's support for keypresses predates the DOM 3 Events standard. That standard defines only keys without glyphs. Mozilla's support includes additional keys that do have glyphs. Mozilla and the standard use different numbering systems, so values for keycodes are different in each. As noted under "XUL Support for Event Handlers" earlier, Mozilla only supports generic `keypress`, `keyup`, and `keydown` events on the `Document` object. These events are not supported on every tag.

Table 6.3 shows the keycode differences between the two definitions. VK stands for Virtual Key.

Table 6.3 Differences between Mozilla and DOM 3 event keycodes

Keycodes specific to Mozilla	Keycodes specific to Mozilla	Keycodes specific to DOM 3 Events
DOM_VK_CANCEL	DOM_VK_SEMICOLON	DOM_VK_UNDEFINED
DOM_VK_HELP	DOM_VK_EQUALS	
DOM_VK_CLEAR	DOM_VK_QUOTE	DOM_VK_RIGHT_ALT
	DOM_VK_MULTIPLY	DOM_VK_LEFT_ALT
DOM_VK_ALT	DOM_VK_ADD	DOM_VK_RIGHT_CONTROL
DOM_VK_CONTROL	DOM_VK_SEPARATOR	DOM_VK_LEFT_CONTROL
DOM_VK_SHIFT	DOM_VK_SUBTRACT	DOM_VK_RIGHT_SHIFT
DOM_VK_META	DOM_VK_DECIMAL	DOM_VK_LEFT_SHIFT
	DOM_VK_DIVIDE	DOM_VK_RIGHT_META
DOM_VK_BACK_SPACE	DOM_VK_COMMA	DOM_VK_LEFT_META
DOM_VK_TAB	DOM_VK_PERIOD	
DOM_VK_RETURN	DOM_VK_SLASH	
	DOM_VK_BACK_QUOTE	
DOM_VK_0 to 9	DOM_VK_OPEN_BRACKET	
DOM_VK_A to Z	DOM_VK_BACK_SLASH	
	DOM_VK_CLOSE_BRACKET	
DOM_VK_NUMPAD0 to 9		

Two further differences between the standard and Mozilla are worth noting:

- The DOM 3 Event `keyval` property matches the Mozilla `nsIDOMKeyEvent` interface's `charCode` property.
- The DOM 3 Event `virtKeyVal` property matches the Mozilla `nsIDOMKeyEvent` interface's `keyCode` property.

These differences are little more than syntax differences.

6.2.1 Where Key Events Come From

A key stroke is translated several times before it becomes a key event. The "Debug Corner" in this chapter explains how to diagnose that translation when it goes wrong. Here we just illustrate the process of collecting a key event.

Keypresses start at the keyboard. Each physical key in a keyboard has its own key number. This number does not match ASCII or anything else. This is the first number generated when a key is pressed.

A keyboard is not as dumb as you might think. It has two-way communication with its computer. Inside the keyboard firmware, a keypress, key release, or key repetition is converted into a scan code. A scan code is a single- or multibyte value. There is no absolute standard for scan codes, just well-known implementations like the IBM PC AT 101 keyboard. Scan codes don't match ASCII or anything else, and they are sent in both directions.

Some scan codes go directly to the hardware, like Delete when used to start BIOS firmware on PC hardware, or sometimes Pause or Control-Alt-Delete. Others are interpreted by the operating system of the computer. An attempt is made to turn interpreted scan codes into a character code—either an ASCII code, a Unicode code, or an internal representation. The Keyboard icon in the Control Panel comes into play in Microsoft Windows. On Linux, the operating system does this using a driver.

Some application software is quite sophisticated. Examples include X-Windows and East Asian (e.g., China, Korea, and Japan) word processors. If the application is sophisticated, almost-raw scan codes might be sent directly to it. In X-Windows, the `xmodmap` utility is responsible for mapping names associated with scan codes to X11's own internal character system. In countries where the character set is larger than the keyboard, a special system called an input method is used. This is a small window that appears when the user presses a "Character compose" key sequence. The window gives visual feedback as the character is created using multiple keystrokes. Non-Western versions of Mozilla have such an input method. An example is Japanese Hiragana, which has thousands of characters, all composed by a keyboard with less than a hundred keys.

6.2.2 What Keys Are Available

After conversion has been attempted, a standards-based character code (ASCII, Unicode, X11, or operating-system internal) holds the key. From that point on, the key itself is less interesting than so-called keyboard maps. These are use statements for individual character codes. Such maps can be added by the operating system, desktop, or individual application.

Some character codes are always interpreted by the operating system, desktop, or window manager keyboard maps. These keys never reach an application. An example is the ⊞ (Windows) key, used to pop up the Start menu on Microsoft Windows, or Alt-Tab. Pressing such a key is of no use to an application, so application programmers cannot readily implement these keys.

Of the keys that are sent to an application, some will be tied to application-specific functions, like "open addressbook window," and some will be tied to desktop or application keyboard map standards, like "save document." If the application programmer seeks maximum compatibility with desktop conventions, then the first group of keys is available for special tasks. The second group of keys must match existing desktop keyboard maps or else not be used at all.

Keyboard maps often use a modifier key like Control or Alt and another key. Such a modifier key is usually set by convention. This modifier key is not the same on all platforms. Mozilla solves this problem with an accelerator key. That key is bound to the modifier that best suits the current platform. The accelerator key and one or two others like it can be set as user preferences. See the URL *www.mozilla.org/unix/customizing.html* for details.

In the Mozilla Platform, character codes arrive via the native GUI toolkit and are converted into a `DOM_VK` keycode. These application keys are bound to tasks that a given Mozilla window performs. This can be arranged in one of several ways: by using a general keyboard mapping, by assigning keys directly, and by matching keys to an observer. Each of these techniques is described next.

At the highest level, what key does what action is a matter of design. A list of the current key allocation policy for Mozilla can be seen at *www.mozilla.org/projects/ui/accessibility/mozkeyplan.html*.
Click on any key in the top half of that page to get a report of uses for that key in the bottom half.

6.2.2.1 XBL Keyboard Maps Mozilla's generic keyboard mappings are done in XBL files. The existing examples are not in the chrome: they are platform resources stored under the `res/builtin` directory. There are two files: the general `htmlBindings.xml` and the specific `platformHTMLBindings.xml`. These files apply to the XUL and HTML in existing Mozilla windows and so are good starting points for any application bindings. XBL is described in Chapter 15, XBL Bindings, but a brief example of a keyboard binding is shown in Listing 6.13.

Listing 6.13 Implementing the Redo key command with XBL.

```
<bindings id="myAppKeys">
  <binding id="CmdHistoryKeys">
    <handler event="keypress"
             keycode="DOM_VK_Z"
             command="cmd_redo"
             modifiers="accel,shift"
    />
  </binding>
</bindings>
```

This fragment of XBL creates a group of binding collections called myAppKeys, presumable for a specific application. Each collection within the group sets keys for some part of the application. Collecting keys together into several collections encourages reuse. In this case, the CmdHistoryKeys collection specifies all the keys required for command history, that is, Undo and Redo operations. Only one such key is shown.

The handler tag is specifically an onkeypress event handler in this case. The command that the key is tied to is cmd_redo. For now, just note that this is a function implemented somewhere in the platform. The key and modifiers attributes together specify the keypresses required to make Redo occur just once. In this case, it is implemented with three keys: the platform accelerator, any Shift key, and the Z key. In Microsoft Windows notation, this combination is Control-Shift-Z, since the Control key is the accelerator key for Mozilla on Windows.

If the command attribute is left off, then plain JavaScript can be put between open and closing <handler> tags. In that case, the script is directly invoked for that keypress. keycode="DOM_VK_Z" can be replaced with just key="z" as well, since z has a character equivalent. If this is done without a modifiers attribute, both z and Z mean lowercase z.

6.2.3 <keybinding>, <keyset>, and <key>

The <keybinding>, <keyset>, and <key> tags are used to specify how a single XUL document will capture keystrokes. These tags are used more specifically than XBL bindings. The <key> tag is the important tag and supports the following attributes:

```
disabled keytext key keycode modifiers oncommand command
```

Except for the oncommand attribute, the <key> tag acts like a simple data record and has no visual appearance. It is not a user-defined tag because the Mozilla Platform specially processes its contents when it is encountered. Every <key> tag should have an id attribute, since that is how other tags reference the key.

The disabled attribute set to true stops the <key> tag from doing anything. keytext is used only by <menuitem> tags and contains a readable string that describes the key specified. The `key` attribute contains a single printable keystroke; if it is not specified, then the `keycode` character is examined for a nonprintable keystroke that has a `VK` keycode. *In XUL, such a key code starts with `VK_`, not with `DOM_VK_`.* `key` or `keycode` specify the keyboard input for which the `<key>` tag stands.

The `modifiers` attribute can be a space- or comma- separated list of the standard key modifiers and the cross-platform accelerator keys:

```
shift alt meta control accel access
```

Use of `accel` is recommended if the application is to be cross platform. The `access` modifier indicates that the user had pressed the shortcut key that exists for the tag in question.

The `oncommand` attribute is a place to put a JavaScript handler that will fire for the given keystroke. When used for the `<key>` tag, its meaning is different from the use in Chapter 9, Commands. For `<key>`, `oncommand` fires when the keystroke occurs, as you'd expect.

`<keyset>` is a container tag like `<stringbundleset>` and `<broadcasterset>`. It has no special properties of its own. Use it as a tidy container for a set of `<key>` tags.

`<keybinding>` is not a true XUL tag at all. Inside Mozilla's chrome, some key definitions are stored as separate `.xul` files. Rather than have `<window>` as the outermost tag in such files, `<keybinding>` is used instead. This is just a naming convention with no special meaning. These keybinding files are added to other XUL files and never display a window on their own.

The `<key>` tag is most often associated with formlike documents, and this shows. Once a `<key>` tag is in place, striking that key will fire the `oncommand` handler for that key, no matter where the mouse cursor is in the document window. There is, however, one restriction. There must be at least one form control in the document, and one of the form controls must have the current focus. This means that at least one of these tags must be present and focused before keys will work:

```
<button> <radio> <checkbox> <textbox> <menulist>
```

It is possible to bend this restriction a little by hiding a single, focused tag with styles so that it takes up zero pixels of space.

There are other XUL tags and attributes that relate to `<key>`. The `accesskey` attribute, described in Chapter 7, Forms and Menus, specifies a per-tag key for accessibility use. The `<key>` tag also works closely with the `<menuitem>` tag used in drop-down menus.

The following attribute names are used to lodge data with `<key>` tags, but they have no special meaning any more—if they ever did. They are listed here because they occasionally appear in Mozilla's own chrome. Don't be confused by them—ignore them:

```
shift cancel xulkey charcode
```

6.2.4 The XUL `accesskey` Attribute

XUL provides a feature that supports disabled access. The `accesskey` attribute can be added to many form- or menu-like tags, including `<button>` and `<toolbarbutton>`. It has the same syntax as the `keytext` attribute; in other words, it is specified with a printable character:

```
accesskey="K"
```

`accesskey` keystrokes are collected only if the access system is turned on. This access system is turned on either by custom accessibility equipment connected to the computer, like special input devices, or by pressing the Alt key. This system is described briefly in Chapter 8, Navigation, but is not a large theme of this book.

Individual XUL tags throughout this book note whether they support `accesskey`. Some tags provide a visual hint of the specified `accesskey`; others do not.

6.2.5 Find As You Type (Typeahead Find)

Find As You Type, formerly called Typeahead Find, is a Classic Browser feature in version 1.21 and later that makes extensive use of keystrokes. Its goal is to speed up Web navigation and to assist with accessibility goals. It works only in HTML pages.

Find As You Type is activated with the / key. From that point onward, any printable keys typed are gathered into a string. That string is matched against the text that appears in hypertext links on the page. Pressing Return/ Enter causes the currently matching link to be navigated to. This is similar to the search syntax used in UNIX tools like `more`, `less`, and `vi`.

Find As You Type affects state information in the document such as the current focus. This can have unexpected effects if navigation in your document is heavily scripted.

This feature picks up keystrokes during the bubbling phase of DOM Events processing. To stop it from running, call `preventDefault()` on the event after your own key handling code is finished with it.

Find As You Type is complemented by Find Links As You Type. This feature searches only the content of hypertext links. It runs if no / key precedes the search characters, or if the ? key is used instead of the / key.

6.3 How Mouse Gestures Work

Mouse gestures are button clicks, mouse movements, and scroll wheel rolls. Mozilla supports them all. Mozilla also supports graphic tablets and other devices that pretend to be mice.

Mouse gestures can be simple or complex. Just as keystrokes can be put together into a search word with the Find As You Type feature, so too can mouse clicks and movements be put together into a larger action that has its own special meaning. Such a larger action is a true mouse gesture. A simple click by itself is a trivial gesture. Nontrivial examples of gestures include drag-and-drop and content selection.

Trivial gestures are handled in Mozilla using DOM 3 Events. These events are the simplest (atomic) operations out of which larger gestures are built and are listed in Table 6.2 earlier in this chapter. Use them as for any DOM Event. More complex gesture support is examined in the following subtopics.

Why would you want complex gesture support? Users are well educated about several basic gestures, and some applications are expected to support them. The most common example is an image manipulation or drawing program with its bounding boxes and freestyle scribble. Novel or experimental uses of gestures must be handled carefully because there is a risk that the user will become confused.

In most cases, complex mouse gestures must be implemented in JavaScript. Although Mozilla can catch and process a stream of `mousemove` events in JavaScript impressively fast, such processing is also very CPU-intensive. Poorly implemented (or even well-implemented) JavaScript gesture support may be too CPU-intensive to run on older PC hardware.

6.3.1 Content Selection

Content selection is a mouse gesture that picks out a portion of a document, from a starting point to an ending point. Visual feedback, in which content is "blacked" or "highlighted" to indicate the extent of the current selection, is usually provided. Selections can be quite small, comprising a single menu or list item, or even just a few characters. Mozilla supports several types of content selection.

The simplest type is selection of whole data items. This applies to XUL widgets such as menus, listboxes and trees, and HTML equivalents, where they exist. Display any menu, and as you draw the mouse pointer down it, one item at a time is selected. This kind of selection is seen as part of the underlying widget's normal behavior, and the start and end points of the selected content are not generally user-definable. Selecting an item from a menu is something we do without thinking.

More significant content selection occurs where there is semistructured content and the user defines the start and end points of the selection with the mouse. Word processors and text editors are the places where this kind of selection is most common. In such systems, the selected content is separate from the gesture that selects it. A typical gesture for selecting content goes like this:

1. Left-click-press on the starting point.
2. Mouse move to the ending point.
3. Left-click-release on the ending point.

This is not an absolute rule, though. A different gesture with the same effect might be:

1. Left-click down and up on the starting point.
2. Mouse move to the ending point.
3. Right-click down and up on the ending point.

There are many such variations. For example, shift-click is also commonly used to extend a selection from an existing start point to a current point. Mozilla implements two kinds of content selection using one mouse gesture—the press-move-release gesture style. The first of these two selection types occurs inside textboxes. The second kind of selection occurs across all the content of a displayed document.

Textbox selection works inside HTML's `<input type="text">` and `<textarea>` tags and XUL's `<textbox>` tag. The DOM 1 Element for these tags contains properties and methods to examine and set this selected text:

- **value**. The whole content of the textbox.
- **selectionStart**. The character offset of the selection start point.
- **selectionEnd**. The character offset of the selection end point.
- **setSelectionRange(start,end)**. Set the offsets of the start and end points.

The CSS3 draft property `user-select` is also relevant.

General content selection outside widgets is only implemented for the user in HTML. A starting point for examining HTML's support is to look at the `document.getSelection()` method, which returns an object that includes an array of `Range` objects. `Range` objects are defined in the DOM 2 Traversal and Ranges standard.

By default, it is not possible for the user to select XUL content with a mouse gesture. Such a gesture-based feature can be added, though. A starting point is to examine the `createRange()` method of the XUL document object. This creates a DOM `Range` object, which can be manipulated to match any contiguous part of an XUL document tree. This object can be dynamically updated as the mouse moves, and styles can be applied to the subtree the range represents so that the content selected is visually highlighted.

In both HTML and XUL, this form of selection is restricted to visually selecting whole, contiguous lines of content (in other words line boxes; see Chapter 2, XUL Layout), except for the first and last lines, which may be partially selected. The exception to this rule is text that displays vertically, like Hebrew and Chinese, and HTML table columns (see "Multiple Selection").

If you decide to experiment with the DOM Range object, beware that although it is fully implemented, it is used only a little in Mozilla and has not had extensive testing.

6.3.1.1 Rubber Band Selection Rubber band selection is best known in desktop windows that display icons. By clicking on the background of the window and dragging, a small box with a dotted or dashed border appears. Any icon that falls within that expanding box is considered to be selected. Rubber-banding is a form of content selection, but it is not restricted to selecting whole contiguous lines. It can select any content in a given rectangular area.

Mozilla has no support for rubber band selection at all, but the platform has enough features to implement it. This can be done in HTML or XUL. The XUL case is discussed here.

Since XUL doesn't support layers or CSS2 `z-index` styles, the rubber band box itself is problematic to create. The solution is to ensure that all content inside the XUL document is contained in a single card of a `<stack>` tag (see Chapter 2, XUL Layout). The rubber band box is a `<box>` tag with no contents and a border style. It comprises the sole other card of the `<stack>`. In normal circumstances, this second card has style `visibility:none`.

When the user begins the mouse gesture, scripts makes the bordered box visible. As the drag part of the rubber band gesture proceeds, the width and height properties of the box are changed to match. At each `mousemove` update, a diagnostic routine walks the DOM tree and changes the styling of any tag that falls within the current edges of the rubber band box. Simple.

6.3.1.2 Multiple Selection Multiple selection is most familiar when it appears inside desktop windows that display icons. On Microsoft Windows or GNOME, for example, several icons can be selected by Control-left-clicking on each one in turn. This is different from rubber-banding, which is a form of single selection.

Mozilla supports multiple selection in `<listbox>` and `<tree>` tags. See Chapter 13, Listboxes and Trees, for a description of those tags at work. Multiple selection for those tags uses Control-left-click.

Mozilla also supports multiple selection in HTML for vertically oriented text. Support for this text, called BiDi text (bi-directional text) does not exist in XUL yet. The gesture for this form of multiple selection is the same as for normal content selection, but the data processing is different. When using the `getSelection()` factory method of the HTML document object, an array of `Range` objects, instead of just one object, is created. These ranges cover one vertical swath (one column of selected content) each. The `getRangeAt()` index method returns any one such range.

Desktop-style Control-left-clicking can easily be implemented in Mozilla. `keydown` and `keyup` events can be used to define the start and end of the gesture, which occur when the Control key is pressed and later released. Click events can be used to identify the items selected while the gesture is active.

Just because the mouse is completely released between clicks doesn't mean that the gesture ends. A gesture ends when the programmer says it ends.

6.3.2 Drag and Drop

Drag and drop is a gesture where a visual element is chosen and moves with the mouse cursor until it is released. An optional aspect of drag and drop is the use of target sites. A target site is a spot in the window where the drag-and-drop operation could successfully end. If target sites exist, they should be highlighted when the dragged object hovers over them. The classic example of a target site is the Trash icon on the Macintosh. The trash goes dark when a document's icon is dragged over it. When target sites are used, the dragged object usually disappears from view when the drop part of the drag-and-drop gesture occurs.

Drag-and-drop gestures can occur within an application window, between application windows, or between windows of different applications. Mozilla's support for drag-and-drop is designed for gestures that stay within one Mozilla window. This support can in theory be extended to gestures between Mozilla windows, but there is only basic support for dragging to or from the desktop or other applications. It is possible to detect when a desktop drag enters or leaves a Mozilla window and collect or send the resulting dragged data.

The major limitation of drag-and-drop gestures in Mozilla is that the item dragged does not follow the cursor. During the drag, Mozilla only provides alternate mouse cursors and occasional style information that hints when the dragged item is over a drop target. This limitation can be worked around using a stack as described in "Rubber Band Selection." Instead of the rubber band occupying a second card of the stack, that card contains a copy of the dragged item. This item can be animated to follow the mouse cursor using the techniques used in Dynamic HTML.

Mozilla's drag-and-drop support is a puzzle of several pieces.

The first piece of the puzzle is events and event handlers. Three events are required for simple drag and drop: `draggesture` (the start of the drag), `dragover` (equivalent to `mouseover`), and `dragdrop` (the end of the drag). Two additional events cover the more complex case where a desktop drag-and-drop operation enters or leaves a Mozilla window. Those two events are `dragenter` and `dragexit`.

The second piece of the puzzle is XPCOM objects. The most important component pair is

```
@mozilla.org/widget/dragservice;1 nsIDragService
```

This is the bit of Mozilla responsible for managing the drag-and-drop gesture while it is in progress.

The `invokeDragSession()` method of the `nsIDragService` interface starts the drag session. For special cases, it can accept an `nsIScriptableRegion` object. This object is a collection of rectangles stated in pixel coordinates.

It is used for the special case where the area dragged over includes a complex widget built entirely with a low-level GUI toolkit. The set of rectangles identify a set of "hotspots" (possible drop targets) on the widget that the widget itself should handle if the gesture tracks the cursor over any of them. This system allows the user to get drag feedback from a widget that can't be scripted, or from a widget where no scripts are present. This is mostly useful for embedded purposes and doesn't do anything in the Mozilla Platform unless a `<tree>` tag is involved. In most cases, use `null` for this `nsIScriptableRegion` object.

The `getCurrentSession()` method returns an `nsIDragSession` object. This object is a simple set of states about the current drag gesture and contains no methods of its own. At most, one drag operation can be in progress per Mozilla window.

The third piece of the puzzle is JavaScript support. Although management of the drag-and-drop gesture is implemented, the consequences of the gesture (the command implied) must be hand-coded. In the simple case, this means setting up the `nsIDragService` and `nsIDragSession` interfaces when the gesture starts, detecting the start and end points of the gesture, providing styles or other feedback while the gesture is in progress, and performing the command implied by the gesture at the end.

In the more complex case, the gesture might result in dragged data being imported to or exported from the desktop so that the scripting that backs the gesture must also copy data to or from an `nsITransferable` interface. This interface works with the desktop's clipboard (the copy-and-paste buffer).

In general, the scripting work for drag and drop is nontrivial. Two JavaScript objects are available to simplify the process.

The chrome file `nsDragAndDrop.js` in `toolkit.jar` implements the `nsDragAndDrop` object, which is installed as a property of the window object. This object provides methods that do most of the housekeeping described so far, including special support for the XUL `<tree>` tag. There is no XPIDL interface definition for this file—just what appears in the `.js` file. It has a method to match each of the drag-and-drop events.

The second object must be created by the application programmer. It is a plain JavaScript object and also has no published XPIDL interface. It must be created with the right methods. This object is a bundle of event handlers, one for each event. Regardless of what pattern it might or might not follow, an object of this kind is created and assigned to a variable, usually with a name like `myAppDNDObserver`.

Together, these two objects reduce each required drag-and-drop handler to a single line of script. The event first passes through the generic code of `nsDragAndDrop` and then into any specific code supplied by `myAppDNDObserver`. To examine this system at work, look at the simple example in Mozilla's address book. Look at uses of `abResultsPaneObserver` (which could be called `abResPaneDNDObserver`) in `messenger.jar` in the chrome.

Table 6.4 shows the equivalences between these handy methods and the basic events.

Table 6.4 Equivalences between Drag events and Script methods

Event	nsDragAndDrop method	-DNDObserver method
Draggesture	startDrag()	onDragStart()
Dragover	dragOver()	onDragOver()
Dragdrop	drop()	onDrop()
dragexit	dragExit()	onDragExit()
dragenter	dragEnter()	onDragEnter()

6.3.3 Window Resizing

Window resizing is a consequence of a mouse gesture that is built into the C/C++ code of Mozilla. See the discussion on the `<resizer>` tag in Chapter 4, First Widgets and Themes.

6.3.4 Advanced Gesture Support

Mouse gestures can be less formal than the examples discussed so far. Like an orchestra conductor waving a baton, specific movements and clicks with the mouse might cause the Classic Browser to execute menu and key commands such as Bookmark This, Go Back, or Save. Support for these kinds of gestures is being considered for the Mozilla Browser as this is written.

In the simplest case, such gesture support consists of chopping mouse movements up into a number of straight strokes. The strokes are identified by dividing the window into an imaginary rectangular grid, with each cell some pixels wide and high. A stroke is considered complete when `mousemove` events indicate that the mouse cursor has left one cell in the grid and entered another. Such strokes form a set of simple instructions that together make a distinctive pattern that is the gesture. After the instruction set is complete, the gesture is identified, and the matching command is executed.

The Optimoz project is such a gesture system and is implemented entirely in JavaScript. It can be examined at *www.mozdev.org*. The code for this extension is small and not difficult to understand. Like Find As You Type, this gesture system grabs events during the bubbling phase, thus avoiding competition with other consumers of the same events.

6.4 Style Options

There are no Mozilla-specific styles that affect event handling. Some of the CSS2 pseudo-styles, like `:active`, are activated by changes to the currently focused and currently selected element.

6.5 HANDS ON: NOTETAKER USER INPUT

In this session, we'll add key support and a few event handlers to the NoteTaker dialog box. There is further discussion on event handlers in "Hands On" in Chapter 13, Listboxes and Trees. There, a systematic approach is considered. This session contains simple introductory code only.

The key support we want comes in two parts: We want the user to have a hint at what keys can be pressed and we want the actual keystrokes to do something.

To add key hints, we use the accesskey attribute. This attribute serves as the basis for disabled use of the application, but we're not designing for disabled users at this point. Instead, we're just exploiting the fact that this attribute underlines a useful character of text for us.

To do that, we change all the buttons in the dialog box, as Listing 6.14 shows.

Listing 6.14 Addition of accesskeys to NoteTaker.

```
// old
<toolbarbutton label="Edit" onclick="action('edit');"/>
<toolbarbutton label="Keywords" onclick="action('keywords');"/>
<button label="Cancel"/>
<button label="Save"/>

// new
<toolbarbutton label="Edit" accesskey="E" onclick="action('edit');"/>
<toolbarbutton label="Keywords" accesskey="K"
          onclick="action('keywords');"/>
<button label="Cancel" accesskey="C"/>
<button label="Save" accesskey="S"/>
```

We can go further than that one set of changes. We can also highlight keys in the body of the edit area using the <label> tag. This means changing content that reads

```
<description>Summary</description>
```

to

```
<label value="Summary" accesskey="u"/>
```

In this case, the key for Summary can't be S because we've used that already for "Save". When this change is made to all four headings, the resulting window looks like that in Figure 6.3.

After these changes, pressing the underlined keys still has no effect. To change that, we need to add some <key> tags, as shown in Listing 6.15.

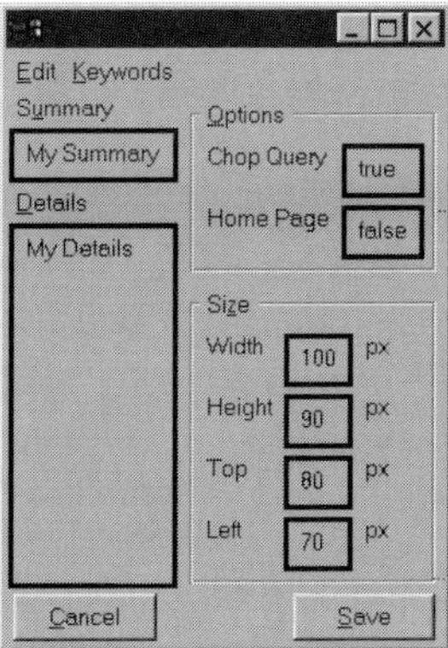

Fig. 6.3 NoteTaker dialog box with available keys highlighted.

Listing 6.15 Tying NoteTaker keys to actions.

```
<keyset>
  <key key="e" oncommand="action('edit')"/>
  <key key="k" oncommand="action('keywords')"/>
  <key key="c" oncommand="action('cancel')"/>
  <key key="s" oncommand="action('save')"/>
  <key key="u" oncommand="action('summary')"/>
  <key key="d" oncommand="action('details')"/>
  <key key="o" oncommand="action('options')"/>
  <key key="z" oncommand="action('size')"/>
</keyset>
```

The `key` attribute is not case-sensitive; if we explicitly want a capital S, then we would add a `modifiers="shift"` attribute. If we wanted to use F1, then we'd use the `keycode` attribute and a `VK` symbol instead of `key` and a printable character. We're able to reuse some code from previous chapters because the function `action()` accepts a single instruction as argument. If `action()` is modified to include a line like this

```
alert("Action: " + task");
```

then it is immediately obvious whether pressing a given key has worked. We'll defer the cancel and save instructions to a later chapter. To practice event handling in a bit more depth, we'll experiment with the other four keys. In later chapters, this experimentation will become far easier.

It would be convenient if the user didn't need to consider every detail of this dialog box. Perhaps there are some defaults at work, or perhaps some of the information is not always relevant. Either way, it would be nice if the user could de-emphasize some of the content, with a keystroke or mouse click. That is what we'll implement.

Our strategy is to deemphasize content using style information. When we pick up the user input, we'll change the class attribute of the content so that new style rules are used. When the user repeats the instruction, we'll toggle back to the previous appearance. We intend to apply this rule to the boxed content only. The deemphasizing style rule is

```
.disabled {
  border : solid; padding : 2px; margin : 2px;
  border-color : darkgrey; color : darkgrey
}
```

There are four areas on the edit panel (Summary, Details, Options, and Size) and a total of eight displayed boxes, each of which might need an update. We can group the eight back into four using broadcasters and observers. We add the broadcasters in Listing 6.16, which specify nothing to start with.

Listing 6.16 Broadcasters for disabling NoteTaker dialog subpanels.

```
<broadcasterset>
  <broadcaster id="toggle-summary"/>
  <broadcaster id="toggle-details"/>
  <broadcaster id="toggle-options"/>
  <broadcaster id="toggle-size"/>
</broadcasterset>
```

We add `observes=` attributes on all eight boxes, tying each one to one of the four broadcasters, so

```
<box id="dialog.top" class="temporary">
```

becomes

```
<box id="dialog.top" class="temporary" observes="toggle-size"/>
```

If any broadcaster gains a `class="disabled"` attribute, that attribute will be passed to the boxes observing it, and those boxes will change style. We can test this system by temporarily hand-setting the `class="disabled"` attribute on any broadcaster. If that is done for the last broadcaster (`"toggle-size"`), then the dialog box displays as in Figure 6.4.

Now that this code is working, we can hook it up to the user input. The keystrokes are first. For those, we update the `action()` method. Listing 6.17 shows the new code.

Listing 6.17 Code to toggle gray-out state of NoteTaker dialog subpanels.

```
function action(task)
{
  if ( task == "edit" || task == "keywords" )
  {
    var card = document.getElementById("dialog." + task);
    var deck = card.parentNode;
```

```
    if ( task == "edit" )    deck.selectedIndex = 0;
    if ( task == "keywords") deck.selectedIndex = 1;
  }

  if ( task == "summary" || task == "details" || task == "options" || task
          == "size" )
  {
    var bc = document.getElementById("toggle-" + task);
    var style = bc.getAttribute("class");

    if ( style == "" || style == "temporary" )
      bc.setAttribute("class","disabled");
    else
      bc.setAttribute("class","temporary");
  }
}
```

This code modifies the broadcaster tags only, and the platform takes care of the rest. If necessary, we can test this code by directly calling the `action()` method, perhaps from the `onload` handler of the `<window>` tag. It's just as easy to test by pressing the correct key.

Supporting the mouse is a little trickier. Exactly where in the dialog box is a user click supposed to have an effect? We could install an event handler on every tag, but that isn't very clever. Instead we'll use the XUL layout model and the DOM Event model. We'll make sure that each of the subpanels is contained in a single XUL tag—that's the layout part. And, at the top of the document tree, we'll install an event handler that will catch any `onclick` events and figure out which of the subpanels applies—that is the DOM Event part.

First, we will look at the XUL layout part. The Summary and Details subpanels aren't contained in a single box, so we'll just wrap another `<vbox>` around each `<label>` plus `<box>` pair. That's unnecessary from a display

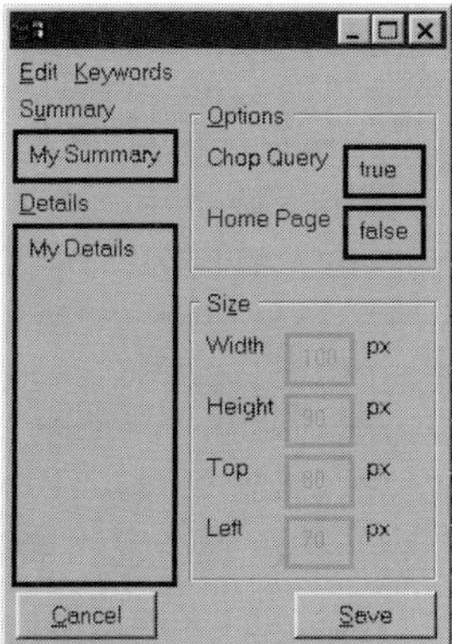

Fig. 6.4 NoteTaker dialog box with content grayed out.

point of view, but it's convenient for our code. Now we have two subpanels contained within <vbox> tags and two within <groupbox> tags. We'll add a subpanel attribute with the name of the subpanel to each of these four tags:

```
<groupbox subpanel="size"/>
```

This attribute has no special meaning to XUL; we just made it up. It's a conveniently placed piece of constant data.

Second, we'll write an event-handling function to catch the mouse click. We want to catch it right at the start, which means during the capture phase. The XUL `onclick` attribute is good only for the bubbling phase, so we'll have to use `addEventListener()` from JavaScript. The handler function and handler installation code is shown in Listing 6.18.

Listing 6.18 Code to capture click events and deduce the action to run.

```
function handle_click(e)
{
  var task = "";
  var tag = e.target;
  while ( (task = tag.getAttribute("subpanel")) == ""
          && tag.tagName != "window" )
    tag = tag.parentNode;

  if ( task != "")
    action(task);
}

document.addEventListener("click", handle_click, true);
```

Since this handler is installed on the `Document` object (the `<window>` tag) and set for the capture phase, it will receive `onclick` events before anything else. It looks at the passed-in DOM 2 Event object and determines what the target of the event is. That target is the most specific tag that lies under the user's click. The code then walks up the DOM tree from that target, looking for a tag with a subpanel attribute. If it finds one, it runs the action in that attribute. If it doesn't find one, nothing happens. The event then continues its normal progress through the tree.

Because the actions are the same for each of the subparts of the dialog box, the resulting code is very general. Instead of four, eight, or more event handlers, we've succeeded with only one. Again, savings have resulted from the passing of command names into a general routine. We can't expect these savings all the time, but good design should always yield some. We've used four tag names, three attribute names, and two functions to achieve all of this.

That concludes the "Hands On" session. We won't keep all the experiments we've made here, but in general terms, they are valuable practice.

6.6 Debug Corner: Detecting Events

Detecting events is a trivial process in Mozilla.

First, ensure that you have the preference browser.dom.window.dump.enabled set to true. Start the platform with the -console option. Second, write a one-line diagnostic function:

```
function edump(e) { dump(e.type+":"+e.target.tagName); }
```

Third, install this function as a handler on the window object for every event that interests you. Install it via addEventListener() if you want to see the events during the capture phase as well. Finally, start the browser from the command line, and watch the flood of events appear in that command-line window as you click and type.

To diagnose broadcast events, install handlers for the oncommand event, or just add diagnostic observers to the nsIObserverService object. Currently, there is no way to observe all the topic names that are broadcast from this global broadcasters in the standard platform.

In a debug version of the platform, it is possible to create a log file of all broadcasts using these environment variables (see the source file prlog.h for more details):

```
set NSPR_LOG_MODULES=ObserverService:5
set NSPR_LOGFILE=output.log
```

6.6.1 Diagnosing Key Problems

Nothing is more frustrating than a key that doesn't work. The application, whether Mozilla or something written on top of it, often receives the blame because it is the intended destination of the keystroke. Some problems, however, have nothing to do with Mozilla.

At the lowest level, a physical key can be damaged or its contact ruined. Test the key in some other application (e.g., in vi enter insert mode ('i'), press Control-V, and then type the key desired).

The software drivers in the keyboard firmware and in the operating system can be updated and, on rare occasions, may be incorrect. Read the Linux Keyboard HOWTO document for more details on keyboard technology.

To test if the operating system is receiving the key correctly, start Windows in DOS-only mode or login to Linux from the console without starting X11. On Windows, the Edit character-mode editor can be used to test non-ASCII keys.

To test foreign language keyboard issues, it is best to ask a native speaker for help. The soc.culture USENET newsgroups are good places to put a polite request. Some languages receive less support than others, and users of those languages are occasionally keen to help out. The Mozilla bugZilla bug database (*http://bugzilla.mozilla.org*) has captured many discussions on the topics of internationalization, compatibility, and localization.

To test if a desktop application is receiving a key, test the key using a terminal emulator (e.g., a DOS box, `xterm`, or `gnome-terminal`) in “raw” mode. Raw mode exists when an editor like Edit or `vi` runs in that terminal. That terminal emulator relies on the desktop (or at least the windowing system) for input.

To test if Mozilla is receiving a key, just add an event listener for that key to the document object of a chrome window.

6.7 Summary

Programmers can’t get access to user-typed data by admiring a widget; they need some kind of internal structure to work with. The Mozilla Platform is built on an event-oriented architecture from the very beginning and provides several different event models for the programmer to work with.

The most powerful and obvious of these systems is the DOM 3 Event model and associated HTML events, most of which are applicable to Mozilla’s XUL. This event system is sufficient for the programmer to capture raw user keypresses and mouse gestures.

Mozilla also supports less obvious event processing. From the world of software design patterns, there are several models that allow the programmer to handle input and change notifications. Generally speaking, these systems have at their cores the producer-consumer concept for data processing. The most noteworthy of these systems is the observer-based system that allows several tags (or programming entities) to be advised of changes that occur at one central place. This system lays the foundation for understanding the more sophisticated command system that is at the heart of Mozilla applications.

Raw processing of events is fairly primitive. Most events occur in association with a useful widget. In the next chapter, we look at Mozilla’s most useful widgets—forms and menus.

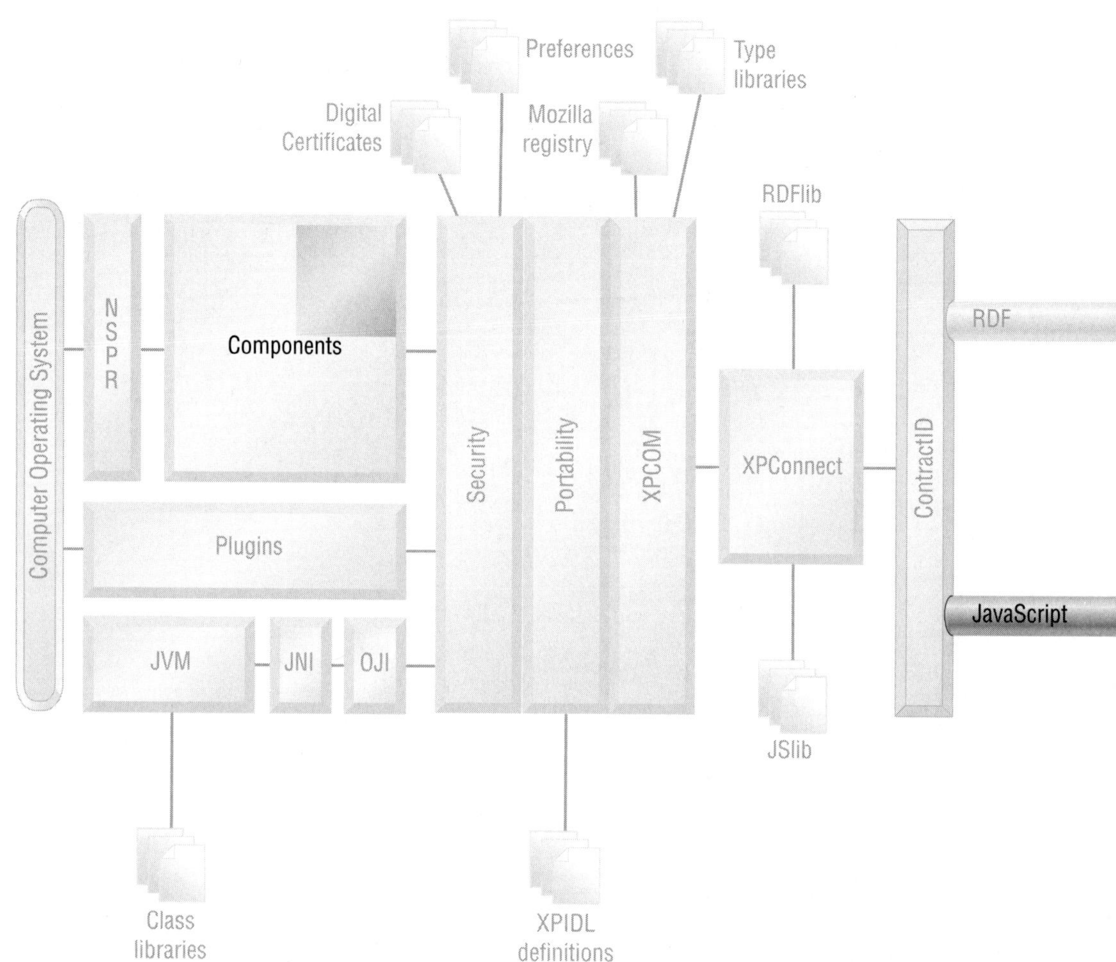
Preferences
Type
libraries
Digital
Certificates
Mozilla
registry
RDFlib
Computer Operating System
N
S
P
R
Components
Security
Portability
XPCOM
XPConnect
ContractID
RDF
Plugins
JavaScript
JVM
JNI
OJI
JSlib
Class
libraries
XPIDL
definitions

CHAPTER 7

Forms and Menus

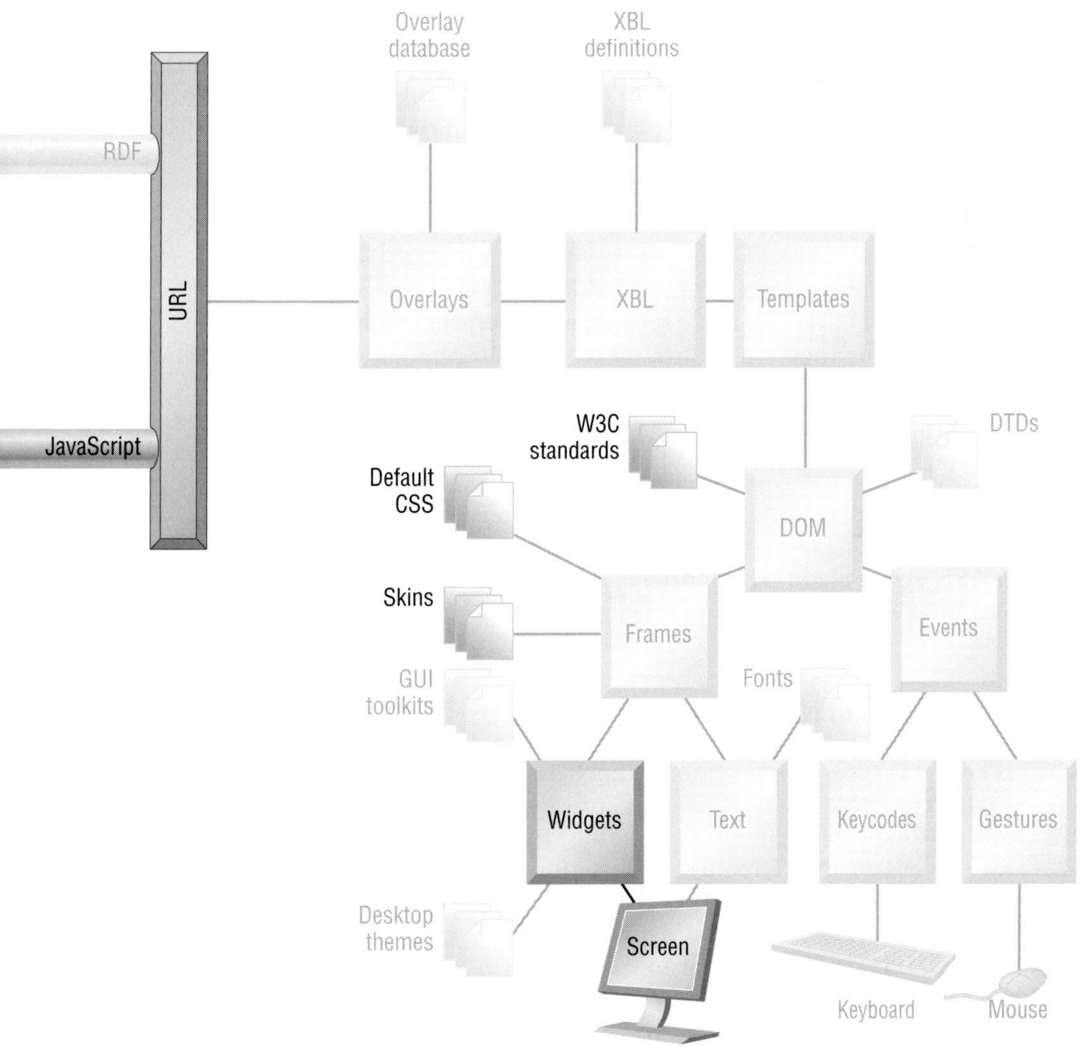

This chapter describes most of the XUL tags used for data entry. It also explains how to submit forms over the Web. Widgets and tags more concerned with user movement are covered in Chapter 8, Navigation.

The best way to assist users with their input is with guidance and feedback. For paper-based systems, this means using a particular style of layout called a form. GUI toolkits provide widgets that are electronic versions of paper forms. In Chapter 4, First Widgets and Themes, buttons were considered at length. This chapter describes the other basic form controls that go with buttons: menus, check boxes, text boxes, and so on. Each of these controls, plus the various menu controls, expresses either a uniquely new widget or a unique combination of widgets.

The NPA diagram that precedes this chapter shows where in Mozilla form and menu technology sits. Unsurprisingly, XUL form and menu tags are heavy users of the desktop's GUI toolkit. Each widget must contribute something new and unique to XUL, and that new functionality is best found in the features the desktop provides.

Forms and menus have the same constraint as the `<button>` tag: They must look like forms and menus to be recognized. Style information, therefore, plays an important part in these widgets. The NPA diagram also notes the importance of XBL definitions (bindings). Form and menu tags are usually manipulated extensively by scripts, and the programmer needs to have XBL definitions for those tags at hand in order to remember what properties and methods are available.

Finally, the NPA diagram shows that some XPCOM components are relevant to the forms environment. Submitting a form to a Web server is a classic use of the Mozilla technology, and the first example of using the platform as client software to some server.

HTML's form tags have been wildly successful. XUL forms are similar to HTML, so we begin with a brief comparison of the two. After that, we will look at all the XUL tags involved.

7.1 XUL AND HTML FORMS COMPARED

HTML/XHTML has a `<FORM>` tag. This tag collects `<BUTTON>`, `<SELECT>`, `<INPUT>`, and `<TEXTAREA>` tags into a group. The `<FORM>` tag's DOM object has methods that combine the values of the form members together into an HTTP GET or POST request. This automates the process of permanently capturing form data by sending it to some Web server. As a result, Web-based HTML-based applications are now common.

XUL has no equivalent to the `<FORM>` tag. XUL form control equivalents are not bound into groups (except via `<radiogroup>`). There is no equivalent to `<INPUT TYPE="reset">` or `<INPUT TYPE="submit">` in XUL, and XUL has no semiautomatic form submission process. If a plain XUL document is presented to the user, then nothing happens to the data the user enters.

This means that if a XUL application is to behave like an HTML form, then form submission must be added by hand. This is done with scripts, which are added to each XUL document that is to be formlike. Fortunately, such scripts are trivial to write.

On the other hand, XUL form controls are more varied than HTML ones. The `<button>`, `<textbox>`, and `<menu>` tags are all more flexible than the HTML equivalents. In addition, XUL has many high-end tags, such as `<menubar>`, `<listbox>`, and `<tree>`, that are far more sophisticated than anything HTML has to offer. These better-than-forms tags are discussed in later chapters.

Table 7.1 lists the tags in XUL that are closest to HTML's form and menu tags.

Table 7.1 HTML and XUL form and menu tags compared

HTML tag	XUL tag	Notes
<FORM>	none	Use XMLHttpRequest object.
<BUTTON>	<button>	
<INPUT TYPE="button">	<button>	
<INPUT TYPE="text">	<textbox>	
<INPUT TYPE="radio">	<radio>	Or use <button type="radio">.
<INPUT TYPE="checkbox">	<checkbox>	Or use <button type="checkbox">.
<INPUT TYPE="password">	<textbox type="password">	
<INPUT TYPE="submit">	none	Use <button> and a script.
<INPUT TYPE="reset">	none	Use <button> and a script.
<INPUT TYPE="file">	none	Use the FilePicker object.
<INPUT TYPE="hidden">	none	Use a plain JavaScript variable.
<INPUT TYPE="image">	<button>	Use a script for any form submit.
<SELECT>	<menulist> or <listbox>	
<OPTGROUP>	none	Use <menuseparator> instead.
<OPTION>	<menuitem>	
<TEXTAREA>	<textbox multiline="true">	Supports rows and cols attributes.

Table 7.1 HTML and XUL form and menu tags compared (Continued)

HTML tag	XUL tag	Notes
<LABEL>	<label>	See discussion on accessibility.
<FIELDSET>	<groupbox>	
<LEGEND>	<caption>	
<INPUT TYPE="radio" NAME=>	<radiogroup>	

7.2 Where to Find Information on Menus

Forms and menus tend to appear together in GUI-based applications. XUL's support for menus is nearly as varied as its support for buttons. Unlike the overview of buttons in Chapter 4, First Widgets and Themes, menus are described in several different places in this book. There is a brief comparison of all menu types in "Menu Variations" in this chapter. Otherwise, look here:

- This chapter describes drop-down menus used as form controls. These controls are based on the `<menulist>` tag. `<menulist>` is built from `<menupopup>`, `<menuitem>`, and more, and those tags are discussed here, too.
- Buttons that are menulike are discussed in Chapter 4, First Widgets and Themes.
- Menus that do not drop down appear flat inside a document as a multi-line box. They are called listboxes in HTML and XUL. XUL's `<listbox>` is described in Chapter 13, Listboxes and Trees.
- Menus that appear in menu bars using the `<menu>` tag are described in Chapter 8, Navigation. `<menu>` used as a submenu is discussed here.
- Context menus based on the `<menupopup>` tag are described in Chapter 10, Windows and Panes.

The only real distinction between menus in XUL is between `<listbox>` and `<menulist>`. `<listbox>` is the far more sophisticated tag of the two. All the other tags and uses noted are variations on `<menulist>`. All popup menus are implemented using the `<menupopup>` tag.

7.3 Forms

The form, in which a number of user-modifiable items are collected into a structured group, is central to both HTML and XUL. HTML is hypertext, and the hypertext concept doesn't really include the idea of a form, but forms are so useful that their addition to HTML is just a matter of history. XUL, on the other hand, is meant for forms from the beginning. If XUL achieves widespread acceptance, then the forms module of future XHTML standards might be no more than a reference to part of XUL.

Mozilla's HTML and XUL forms are quite similar. The simplest of the form elements are nearly identical. Event handlers and navigation work much the same in both. Any HTML primer that contains a little JavaScript is good preparation for XUL forms. Don't, however, expect every fine detail to be identical. The two form systems are implemented separately, although they share some common code.

The simplest of XUL's form tags are discussed here. This set of simple tags is

```
<button> <checkbox> <radio> <radiogroup> <textbox> <label>
```

7.3.1 Form Concepts

One form widget is called a form control (from Microsoft terminology) or a form element (originally from graphic design, adopted by Netscape and the W3C). Such elements might interact with the user in different ways, but they are united by some common design.

7.3.1.1 Navigation If the user is to enter anything into a form, then interacting with one form widget at a time is a simple approach. Both XUL and HTML allow one widget to be selected at a time. Interactive form widgets are also ordered within a document. In W3C terms, this is called the *navigation order*. In Mozilla, the ordered collection of these widgets is called the *focus ring* because stepping one beyond the last widget leads back to the first one. All form elements are members of the focus ring.

The focus ring is discussed in more detail in Chapter 8, Navigation.

7.3.1.2 Common Properties of XUL Form Elements In the process of developing the CSS3 standard, the W3C produced a draft document, "User Interface for CSS3." Although old, it is still available at *www.w3.org/TR/1999/WD-css3-userint-19990916*. This document is an early attempt at some of the newer features that CSS3 hopes to support. It is at least ironic and coincidental that this part of CSS3 is (1) the part most similar to Microsoft's .NET and (2) one of the slowest parts of CSS3 to be finalized.

Mozilla implements many features of this draft document. In particular, it implements four style properties that represent the interactive potential of the simple XUL form elements. In Mozilla, the `nsINSDOMCSS2Properties` interface implements these styles. They appear as `-moz` styles in the stylesheet system. The four style properties are

```
user-input user-modify user-select user-focus
```

These style properties are somewhat independent of each other and are important because they make understanding the user input system easier.

Such an understanding has been hard to come by in the past because the results of applying event handlers like `onclick` and DOM methods like `focus()` tend to depend on many of these four states at once. Now that these states are identified, it is easier to understand what effect form element handlers have. You can take a set of four states and an event and write down new states that will result if a form element with those states gets that event.

Beyond these four styles, form elements share two other concepts. The first such concept is private state. All simple form elements are stateful and share at least the disabled attribute, which can be set to `"true"`. Figure 7.1 illustrates disabled and nondisabled form controls.

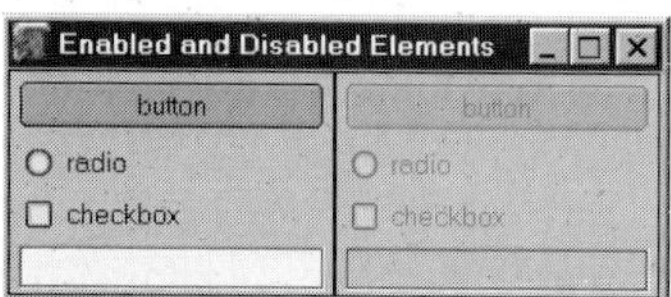

Fig. 7.1 Enabled and disabled simple form controls.

Finally, all simple form elements share a bundle of event handlers and matching object methods for interactive events like focus and blur.

7.3.1.3 Accessibility Accessibility is a feature of software designed to make it usable for those with disabilities. HTML hypertext content, links, and XUL application windows can be made accessible. Form elements are of particular interest because governments want to provide services over the Internet that supply equity of access to disabled citizens and other minorities.

In all discussion to date, the XUL `<label>` tag has appeared to be identical to the `<description>` tag, except that it can be reduced to a label attribute. In the area of accessibility, the `<label>` tag first differs from the `<description>` tag. The `<label>` tag can provide the alternate content that is needed for an accessibility system.

If a form element has a label attribute, Mozilla will present its content as the guide information that the accessibility system expresses to the user. If the form element doesn't have such an attribute, then Mozilla will look for a child tag that is a `<label>` tag and will use that tag. If no suitable child tag exists, it will look for a `<label>` tag whose id matches the id stated in the form element tag's control attribute. If that isn't found, then there is no accessibility information to supply.

Mozilla has accessibility support for all the simple XUL form elements. The `<menuitem>`, `<menulist>`, and `<tab>` tags also have accessibility support.

How accessibility works is discussed in more detail in Chapter 8, Navigation.

7.3.2 Simple XUL Form Tags

Figure 7.2 shows the simple form tags with additional styles applied so that their structure is clearer. Dashed lines indicate `<label>` tags, thick solid lines indicate `<box>` tags, and thin solid lines indicate `<image>` tags. The middle two sections are `<radiogroup>` tags, of which the second one contains `<button type="radio">` tags.

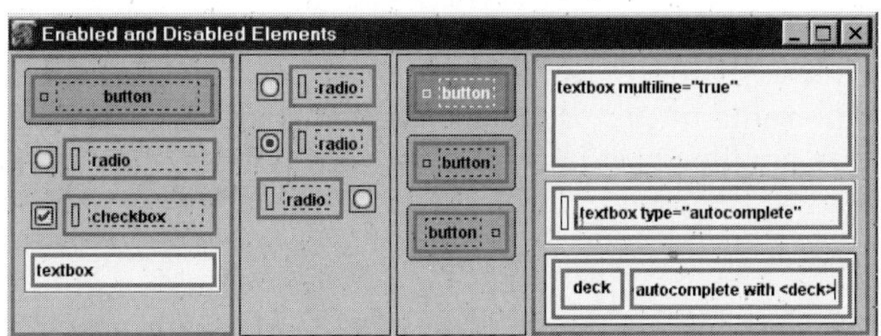

Fig. 7.2 Simple XUL form elements with internals exposed.

It's easy to see from Figure 7.2 that all simple form tags contain at least one other tag, even if that other tag is a contentless `<image>`. All these form tags are defined in XBL.

Inside Mozilla there are special event handlers written in C/C++. These are installed on the XUL document object with the C/C++ version of `addEventListener()`. These event handlers capture and process some of the event information associated with these simple controls. This is how the non-XBL form element functionality is implemented. There is no simple way to interact with these embedded handlers from JavaScript and no need to do so.

These tags have DOM interfaces that closely match the equivalent HTML interfaces. The XPCOM interface names all start with `nsIDOMXUL` prefixes.

7.3.2.1 `<button>` The `<button>` tag is discussed extensively in Chapter 4, First Widgets and Themes. Recall that the `type` attribute allows it to act like a checkbox, radio button, or menu start point if required.

7.3.2.2 `<checkbox>` The `<checkbox>` tag is made out of plain XUL content tags. It has an XBL definition. The checkbox graphics that appear when this widget is displayed are formed from ordinary images. They can be styled larger or smaller, or they can be replaced. `<checkbox>` has the following custom attributes:

```
src label crop checked disabled accesskey
```

`src` is passed to an optional `<image>` that appears between the checkbox and the text. `crop` is passed to a `<label>` containing the text. `checked` is the boolean state of the <checkbox>, and `disabled` grays out the checkbox completely if it is set to `true`. The checkbox label can appear on the left of the checkbox if `dir="rtl"` is specified. Checkbox states are independent of other checkboxes. If the text (the <label>) of a checkbox is mouse-clicked, that is the same as clicking the Checkbox icon itself.

Using the command system described in Chapter 9, Commands, the <checkbox> tag sends a `CheckboxStateChange` event when its state changes. This event can be observed by application code if that is desired.

7.3.2.3 <radio> The <radio> tag is made out of plain XUL tags. It has an XBL definition. The radio button icons are formed from ordinary images and can be styled larger, smaller, or differently. The <radio> tag has the following custom attributes:

```
src label crop selected disabled accesskey
```

These attributes are the same as for <checkbox> except `selected` substitutes for `checked`. If the <radio> tag is in a <radiogroup>, only one such tag may have `selected` set. The bottom <radio> tag in the first <radiogroup> in Figure 7.2 has `dir="rtl"` set. Both the <label> text of a radio button and the button itself may be clicked.

Until very recent Mozilla versions, the <radio> tag occasionally became confused about when it should have focus. Look for recent reports in Mozilla's bug database to clarify the status of <radio> in your version.

7.3.2.4 <radiogroup> The <radiogroup> tag binds a set of <radio> or <button type="radio"> tags together into one unit. If any radio tag in the unit is selected, the others in the unit are deselected. The <radiogroup> tag supports the following attributes:

```
disabled selectedItem focusedItem selectedIndex
```

`disabled` grays out the whole radio group. `selectedItem` and `focusedItem` report the radio item in the group that is currently selected or focused. `selectedIndex` reports the number of the radio item in the group that is currently selected, starting with 0.

Using the command system described in Chapter 9, Commands, the <radio> tag sends a `RadioStateChange` event and a `selected` event when its state changes. These events can be observed by application code if that is desired.

7.3.2.5 <textbox> The <textbox> tag allows the user to enter text. It is four tags in one: normal, password, multiline, and autocompleting. <textbox> has an XBL definition. The <textbox> tag is implemented using the HTML <input type="text"> or <textarea> tags. The standard <textbox> tag has the following special attributes:

```
value disabled readonly type maxlength size multiline
```

These attributes match the HTML `<input type="text">` tag's attributes, except for `multiline` and `type`. `Multiline` can be set to `true`, and `type` can be set to `password` or `autocomplete`. If set to `password`, `<textbox>` acts like HTML's `<input type="password">` tag; however, they are the same otherwise. If the `multiline` attribute is set to `true`, then `<textbox>` has an alternate set of attributes:

```
value disabled readonly rows cols wrap
```

These attributes match the attributes of HTML's `<textarea>` tag. Because XUL has no anonymous content, initially displayed text cannot be included between start and end tags as it is for HTML's `<textarea>`.

For all these first three variants, an initial value for the textbox can only be set if the textbox is not multiline. For multiline textboxes, an initial value must be set from JavaScript using the `value` property of the matching object. An example for a `<textbox id="txt"/>` tag is

```
document.getElementById("txt").value = "initial text";
```

The fourth `<textbox>` variant occurs if `type` is set to `autocomplete`. It is a complicated tag, with a great deal of application-specific functionality. After substantial testing, this book recommends against using the `<textbox type="autocomplete">` tag as a basic tool for your own application. This is because it is not general enough yet.

Where this last tag excels is within the Classic Browser. A simple declaration as follows is enough to provide easy access to the browser's history, email address, and LDAP address mini-databases:

```
<textbox type="autocomplete" searchSessions="addrbook"/>
```

Because none of these mini-databases are available to a standalone application, this use of `<textbox>` is rather limited. It is possible, however, to apply it to any mini-database, even one as simple as a JavaScript array of values. To do so is to struggle with an interface that isn't all that clean or even intended for reuse. With about a day's work, you can analyze the `autocomplete.xml` XBL definition for this tag and come up with some workarounds and hacks for your data. This might do for a one-off use, but you might as well create your own autocomplete XBL definition from scratch if you have a serious application in mind.

7.3.3 Form Submission

XUL does not tie form elements to a target URL the way HTML does, and yet the purpose of filling in a form is to have the information go somewhere. In Mozilla, the options for storing data are as general and as wide as for any programming environment. That is not much comfort if you are trying to produce a quick prototype. Fortunately, two options in Mozilla allow XUL form data to be submitted to a Web server efficiently.

7.3.3.1 HTML Submission of XUL Forms The first XUL form submission method, which is very quick and dirty, is to use XML namespaces. It is possible to create a document that starts with XUL but that includes all of HTML's features. Listing 7.1 shows such a document.

Listing 7.1 Mixing of HTML and XUL forms.

```
<?xml version="1.0"?>
<!DOCTYPE window>
<window
  xmlns=
"http://www.mozilla.org/keymaster/gatekeeper/there.is.only.xul"
  xmlns:html="http://www.w3.org/1999/xhtml">
<vbox>
  <script>
    function copy()
    {
      var getID = document.getElementByID;
      getID("h1").value = getID("x1").value;
      getID("h2").value = getID("x2").value;
      return true;
    }
  </script>
  <html:form action="test.cgi" method="GET"
             enctype="application/x-www-form-urlencoded">
    <html:input id="h1" type="hidden"/>
    <html:input id="h2" type="hidden"/>
    <radiogroup>
      <button id="x1" label="Button 1" type="radio"/>
      <button id="x2" label="Button 2" type="radio"/>
    </radiogroup>
    <html:input type="submit" onsubmit="return copy();">
  </html:form>
</vbox>
</window>
```

This document displays a form consisting of two XUL buttons and one XHTML submit button. It's not possible to put buttons in a radio group in plain XHTML, but that is done here because Mozilla supports mixing XUL into HTML. The XHTML form elements are linked to the form submission process, but the XUL form elements aren't. A simple JavaScript function copies the required data to hidden fields before the submission occurs.

It is possible to create a legal XHTML + XUL document without resorting to `xmlns` namespaces. To do that, start with a "pure" XHTML (or XUL) document, and add DTD entities for the XUL (or XHTML) application to the `<!DOCTYPE>` declaration. Such a document does not include the special `xmlns` triggers that Mozilla uses to detect the document type. That means that no special processing (support) for those extra tags will be used. This lack of detection is the reason why adding an `<A>` tag to a XUL document does not result in an XHTML link being rendered.

7.3.3.2 `XMLHttpRequest` Object The second XUL form submission technique uses the `XMLHttpRequest` object. This is a scriptable AOM object available to all XML documents, much like the `Image` object that is available to HTML documents. It allows HTTP requests to be submitted directly from JavaScript. A server response to such a request does not replace the currently displayed document. Such a response document is just read in as a big string. This `XMLHttpRequest` object is based on the following XPCOM component:

```
@mozilla.org/xmlextras/xmlhttprequest;1
```

This component implements the `nsIXMLHttpRequest` and `nsIJSXMLHttpRequest` XPCOM interfaces, which are well explained in their definition files. These interfaces allow an HTTP request to be submitted synchronously or asynchronously. Synchronous submission means that the script halts until the full response is received. Asynchronous submission is a "fire and forget" system, except that progress can be tracked, and the final result can be recalled. Listing 7.2 shows synchronous requests at work.

Listing 7.2 Examples of synchronous `XMLHttpRequests`.

```
var req    = new XMLHttpRequest(); // Request
var res    = null;                 // Response
var params = encodeURI("param1=value1;param2=value2");

// -- GET request

req.open("GET", "test.cgi" + "?" + params);
req.send("");
if ( req.status / 100 == 2 )  // HTTP 2xx Response?
  res = req.responseText;

// -- POST request

req.open("POST", "test.cgi");
req.send(params);
if ( req.status / 100 == 2 )  // HTTP 2xx Response?
  res = req.responseText;
```

The function `encodeURI()` is the ECMAScript version of `escape()`; both are supported. The second argument to `open()` is any valid URL. Because `send()` doesn't return until the HTTP request-response pair is complete, the programmer should provide the user with some kind of "waiting ..." indicator just before `send()` is called so that the user knows that the application hasn't locked up.

Asynchronous form submissions are useful when multiple HTTP requests are needed. It is more efficient to schedule all the requests at once and then to check back later on progress. The simplest way to perform an asynchronous submission is to put a synchronous submission into a function and to schedule the function with `setTimeout()`. Listing 7.3 shows a more formal and structured approach using the `nsIXMLHttpRequest` interface.

Listing 7.3 Example of an asynchronous `XMLHttpRequest`.

```
var req = new XMLHttpRequest(); // Request
var res = null;                 // Response
var url = "test.cgi?text1=value1";

// Stuff specific to the async case

function finished() { res = req.responseText; }

function inprogress() {
  if ( req.readyState != req.COMPLETED ) {
    res = "Waiting ...";
    setTimeout(inprogress, 100);
  }
}

req.COMPLETED = 4;           // from the interface
req.onload = finished;

// -- GET case (POST is similar)

req.open("GET", url, false);  // false == asynchronous
req.send();

// next statement executes immediately.
setTimeout(inprogress,100);
```

In this example, the `send()` method returns almost immediately, leaving the HTTP request still in progress. The function `finished()` is installed as an event handler that fires when the response finally does complete. In between those two times, `setTimeout()` is used in a simple way to check the request progress regularly. The user might not require progress reports when such an asynchronous request is sent. Nevertheless, the programmer must take care to ensure that actions taken by the user subsequently don't confuse the handling of the response when it arrives. For example, users buying stocks shouldn't be able to empty their bank accounts while the stock purchase is in progress.

7.4 Menus

Menus and forms go together like wine and cheese. Mozilla's menu tags are built out of simpler XUL tags, just like most other XUL tags discussed so far. Menus, however, are a bit more complicated for several reasons:

- ☞ Popup menus don't fit into the normal flow of a two-dimensional XML document.
- ☞ Menus contain many separate values (menu items), not just one value.

- ☞ Menus have complex internal structure.
- ☞ Menus can be used separately from forms, but they still need to fit in with the constraints imposed by other form elements.

Mozilla does not use XUL menus for so-called listboxes, which lie flat inside an XML document. The `<listbox>` tag fills that role. XUL menus are only used for popup-style menus. Mozilla's menus follow the design rules that apply to simple form elements and so can be considered a simple form element of sorts.

This topic describes XUL's menu support, starting from the smallest tag. Tags that an application programmer might use for simple popup menus include

```
<menulist> <menupopup> <menuitem> <menuseparator> <menu> <button>
     <toolbarbutton>
```

The following additional structural tags might be used by an application programmer who needs to examine the XUL menu system closely. Generally, they do not have to be stated in an XUL document.

```
<dropmarker> <arrowscrollbox> <scrollbox> <autorepeatbutton>
```

Figure 7.3 illustrates the structure of a fully featured but simple XUL menu with two menu items.

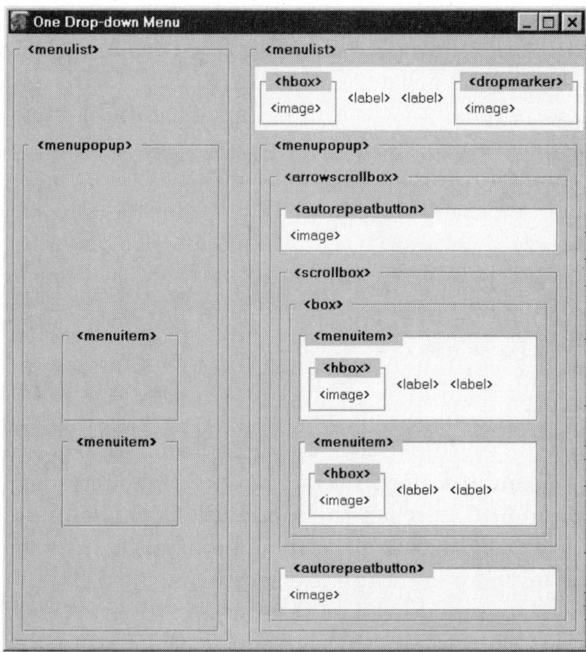

Fig. 7.3 Full structure of an XUL menu.

This figure shows two aspects of the same menu. The left-hand breakdown is the tags that the application programmer specified. The right-hand menu is made up of the tags actually created by the XUL/XBL system inside Mozilla. It's obvious that there are many tags at work. The menu system is designed so that it is always built from a full set of menu content, but the parts that aren't needed are hidden. For example, the `<autorepeatbutton>` tags are hidden when the list of menu items is small enough to appear all at once. A second example is the various labels and images. Each menu item can have an icon and a shortcut key, as well as the ordinary text of the menu item, for a total of one `<image>` and two `<label>` tags. These tags are exposed by tag attributes supplied by the programmer and by the circumstances of the menu display.

The complex tag structure of menus does not translate into complex event handling. The `command` event and `oncommand` event handler are all you need to hook up simple menus to your application logic.

Various tag-level customizations of XUL menus are also possible. On the inside, the `<menuitem>` tags can be replaced with `<menuseparator>` or `<menu>` tags. On the outside, the tags that surround the `<menupopup>` tag can be reorganized by changing the `<menulist>` tag to something else.

7.4.1 `<menuitem>`

The `<menuitem>` tag stands for a single menu option. It has several XBL definitions, of which just one is applied. Attributes with special meaning to `<menuitem>` are

```
type disabled
image validate src checked
label accesskey
acceltext crop
value
```

The `type` attribute is not used in the simple case, but it can be set to "`radio`" or "`checkbox`". These options will cause the menu item to look and act like the equivalent form control. The `disabled` attribute grays out the menu item so that it can't be selected.

The next row of attributes relates to the icon for the menu item. When specified, this icon appears by default on the left, but standard box alignment attributes like `dir` can change this. Both `image` and `src` specify the URL of the icon's image. For a standard `<menulist>` menu, the currently selected item appears on the menu button when the menu is not popped up. If `src` is used, the menu item's icon will be carried to the menu button if its menu item is selected. If both `type` and `src` or `image` are set, the Radio or Checkbox icon takes precedence over the specified icon. `validate` has the same meaning as for the `<image>` tag; `checked` has the same meaning as for the `<radio>` and `<checkbox>` tags.

The third row of attributes is related to the normal text of the menu item. This text can be missing. label provides that text. accesskey provides an accessibility key for the item, as described in Chapter 8, Navigation.

acceltext and crop apply only to menus based on the <menu> tag. crop acts on the menu item text as it does on a <label>. acceltext provides text to the right of the menu text that states what key combination selects that menu item. It is never cropped. Normally this text spells out a keyboard shortcut, like "Shift-A." If acceltext is stated, its value is displayed. If it is not present, and a key attribute is present, then the text will come from the matching <key> tag. That key tag will provide text from its keytext attribute or, failing that, from its key attribute or, failing that, from its keycode attribute. In all three cases, the text will be modified by the contents of the <key>'s modifier attribute. This simply reminds the user how any keystroke matches the menu item and links that keystroke to the menu.

The value attribute sets an internal data value for the menu item. This value may be used to provide an identifier for the menu item because the item's label may have been translated into another language by the platform's locale system.

Figure 7.4 shows many of these menu options at work. It is built out of several bits of real code. Note that it's not possible to drop down two menus in real life (occasionally technical writing gets an edge on programming).

It appears from Figure 7.4 that <menuitem> is quite flexible. This tag also has an armory of styles that can be used to modify its appearance further.

7.4.2 <menuseparator>

The <menuseparator> tag is a near-anonymous XUL tag with some style rules associated with it. It provides a horizontal line that provides visual separation between menu items. Look at the Mozilla menu toolbar for many examples. Use it in place of the <menuitem> tag. This tag has no specialist attributes, but it is occasionally useful to give it an id.

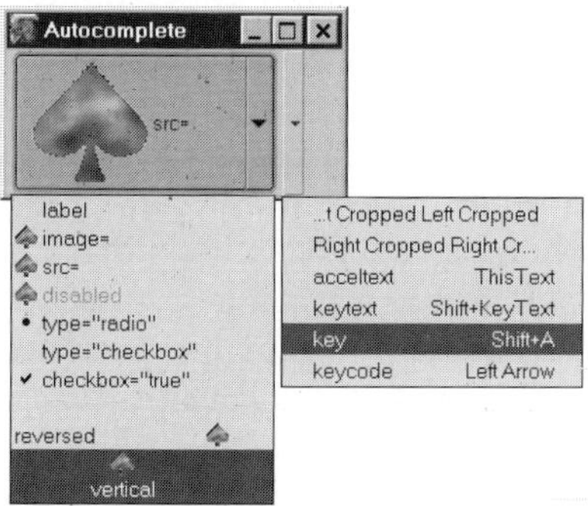

Fig. 7.4 Examples of <menuitem> variations.

The Mozilla Platform recognizes this tag when dealing with menu operations.

7.4.3 <arrowscrollbox> and <scrollbox>

The <arowscrollbox> and <scrollbox> tags allow the user to navigate a rectangle of content that won't easily fit on the screen. Both are discussed in Chapter 8, Navigation, but they also have applications to menus. One of each is created automatically when a menu is specified.

The <arrowscrollbox> tag is used to display a menu that is too long to fit on the screen. If the menu is lengthy, then the <autorepeatbutton>s that are part of that tag automatically appear. The easiest way to see the scrolling at work is with the Personal Toolbar of Mozilla's Navigator.

To see this scrolling, make sure that a bookmark folder appears on this toolbar, and that the folder contains many bookmark items. There should be enough items to take up more than half the screen's height. Move the navigator window so that the Personal Toolbar is about halfway down the screen, and press the bookmark folder button for the folder that contains many items. A list of bookmarks with <arrowscrollbox> icons at top and bottom should appear. They will also appear if you set the maxheight attribute on the <menupopup> tag to something small, like 200px.

The <scrollbox> tag implements the moving area inside the <arrowscrollbox>. It shows scrollbars only when they are used inside a <textbox type="autocomplete"> tag. When used inside the <arrowscrollbox>, it has no style class and generally should be left alone.

The buttons on the <arrowscrollbox> can be styled. <arrowscrollbox> cannot scroll sideways, only up and down.

7.4.4 <menupopup>

The <menupopup> tag is the heart of XUL's menu system. It is responsible for creating a window that is outside the normal flow of the XUL document's layout and that might extend outside the borders of the whole Mozilla window. In order to do this, it uses features of the native GUI toolkit. <menupopup> has significant support from the C/C++ side of Mozilla. It also has an XBL definition.

The <menupopup> tag is quite general. Within the small window it creates, it acts like a <vbox>, and most simple XUL content can be put inside. Reasons for doing so are obscure, but this feature does allow for very decorative menus. The only content that is selectable within a <menupopup> are <menuitem> and <menu> tags. A <menupopup> tag may be specified without any content. That content can be added later via JavaScript, templates, or other XUL techniques.

When creating a menu, the application programmer must specify this tag. The attributes with special meaning to <menupopup> are

```
popupanchor popupalign position allowevents
onpopupshowing onpopupshown onpopuphiding onpopuphidden
```

popupanchor chooses the corner of the parent tag that the <menupopup> will appear near—the so-called anchor point. popupalign chooses the corner of the popup menu that will be fixed in position over the anchor. Thus, the popup is aligned corner to corner with its parent tag. Both of these attributes may take on one of these values:

```
topleft topright bottomleft bottomright none
```

The position attribute is an older, less flexible way of specifying this alignment and should be avoided. It is obsolete.

The allowevents attribute can be set to true, but this is not recommended in ordinary uses. The Mozilla Platform has special event processing for menus. Figure 7.4 illustrates the complex set of tags that make up a menu. If the full DOM Event model were to apply to these tags, then selecting a menu item would generate many events. The Mozilla Platform reduces these many events down to a single, manageable command event.

The remaining four attributes are event handlers for the DOM Events noted earlier. They are paired event targets. The showing and shown variants fire at the start and end of the process that reveals the popup. The hiding and hidden variants fire at the start and end of the process that takes down the popup. The display process works in three stages, and the Mozilla code marks each stage by setting one of these three temporary attributes to true:

```
menutobedisplayed menugenerated menuactive
```

The first indicates that something is going to happen but hasn't happened yet. The second indicates that the content has been assembled for the menu. The third indicates that the menu is revealed and has the focus.

7.4.5 <menu>

The useful content that a <menupopup> can hold consists of three tags: <menuitem>, <menuseparator>, and <menu>. <menu> is very similar to <menuitem> except that it generates a new menu to the side of the existing one. The attributes specific to <menu> are

```
label accesskey crop acceltext disabled
```

These attributes have the same meaning as they do for <menuitem>. A <menu> tag cannot contain an icon representing the menu's action as content, but an icon can be sneaked in with a suitable style. It does contain an automatically supplied arrow-like icon that provides a hint that a submenu exists. The only tag that can appear inside a <menu> tag is a <menupopup>.

The <menu> tag is also used in menu bars:

```
<menulist id="foo" editable="true"/>
```

7.4.6 <menulist>

The <menulist> tag is the top-level tag for simple XUL menus. It is the wrapper around a <menupopup> tag. It gives the user something to look at and interact with when the popup is not displayed. It displays a button-like widget showing the currently selected menu item, and a dropmarker used to reveal the menu. <menulist> always has a currently selected menu item. The <menulist> tag can only contain a <menupopup> tag. The attributes with special meaning to <menulist> are

```
src label crop accesskey disabled editable value
```

The attributes are all the same as for <menuitem>, except that disabled set to true disables the whole menu popup, and editable is new.

The editable attribute is something of a misnomer. If set to true, the label on the <menulist>'s button is replaced with an HTML <input type="text"> textbox. The user can then type in a string. When focus leaves the <menulist>, this string will be compared to the existing menu items. If it matches the main text of one such item, that item will be the currently selected one. All the menu items are treated as though they had type="checkbox" applied. The editable attribute does not provide insertion, deletion, or update of menu items.

7.4.7 Menu Variations

The <menulist> tag is a wrapper for the <menupopup> tag. There are other wrappers. For completeness, the entire list is

```
<menulist>
<menulist editable="true">
<menu>
<button type="menu">
<button type="menu-button>
<toolbarbutton type="menu">
<toolbarbutton type="menu-button">
<textbox type="autocomplete">
<menubutton>
```

Except for <textbox>, using any of these tags means adding a <menupopup> tag as the sole content. The <menubutton> tag is an anonymous tag used to hold styles and handlers for menus that appear in toolbars (see Chapter 8, Navigation).

Under MacOS, it is possible to add a Preferences menu item and submenu to the MacOS Application menu. To do this, ensure that a suitable <menuitem> tag has the special id of id="menu_preferences".

7.5 Style Options

As for static content and buttons, Mozilla duplicates much of the information about forms and menus in the style system.

Perhaps the most powerful style features are style rules that affect which XBL binding applies to which XUL tag. The `type` attribute (for `<button>`, `<toolbarbutton>`, and `<textbox>`) and the editable attribute (for `<menulist>`) are all specified in style rules. Those rules direct the basic XUL tag to a specific binding, which ultimately affects its content, appearance, and behavior. After you have learned XBL, it is possible to add more such bindings and style rules. The `type` attribute can then provide more widget variants.

7.5.1 CSS Styles from HTML Forms

Some standard HTML form styles are available for use in XUL forms. Table 7.2 lists them. See the CSS3 draft document at *www.w3.org/TR/1999/WD-css3-userint-19990916* for details of the newer styles.

Table 7.2 XUL style extensions that follow HTML forms

Property or selector	Values	Use
:-moz-drag-over	(selector)	Any element under the drag item when dragging with the mouse
:-moz-selection	(selector)	Near complete support for CSS3 ::selection, as of version 1.21
-moz-key-equivalent	See draft	CSS3 draft key-equivalent
-moz-outline-radius	As for margin, but use px	These attributes mimic the margin attribute, except that they dictate the roundness of the corners of a border or outline
-moz-outline-radius-topleft -moz-outline-radius-topright -moz-outline-radius-bottomleft -moz-outline-radius-bottomright	Px	Roundness of a single outline corner; 0 for square
-moz-outline	As for outline	Near-complete CSS2 outline
-moz-outline-color	As for color	Near-complete CSS2 outline-color
-moz-outline-style	As for border-style	Near-complete CSS2 outline-style
-moz-outline-width	As for border-width	Near-complete CSS2 outline-width
-moz-user-focus	See draft	CSS3 draft user-focus
-moz-user-input	See draft	CSS3 draft user-input
-moz-user-modify	See draft	CSS3 draft user-modify
-moz-user-select	See draft, plus -moz-all	CSS3 draft user-select

The outline-related styles follow to a degree the border styles (see "Style Options" in Chapter 2, XUL Layout, for an example). The `-moz-all` values for the `-moz-user-select` style allows more than one form element to be selected at once. This is useful if you are developing a visual IDE for XUL and need to be able to group form elements with a select action.

7.5.2 Custom Widget Display Types

The <menupopup> tag relies on the following style:

```
display: -moz-popup
```

The `-moz-appearance` style property makes a given tag take on the appearance of the native theme. These native theme appearance types work for the widget-like tags described in this chapter:

```
radio checkbox textfield menulist menulist-button menulist-text
    menulist-textfield checkbox-container radio-container
```

7.6 Hands On: NoteTaker Events and Forms

After many chapters laying the groundwork, we've now got some useful widgets. In this session on the NoteTaker tool, we'll clean out some of the oddments the dialog box has accumulated and replace them with normal XUL form elements. We'll get rid of the properties file and submit the entered data to a Web server. If the dialog box appears as the result of an HTTP GET request, we'll populate it with parameters from that request as well.

Cleanup comes first. We'll throw away the `subpanel` attribute and the `handle_click()` code. If we still choose to disable any of the content, it now makes sense to use the form tags' own disabling features. That means all the broadcasters and half of the actions and keys can also be cleaned out. The task that `load_data()` performs will still be needed, but we'll throw away the current implementation.

Finally, we'll throw away the `boxes.css` / `boxesTemp.css` diagnostic styles and their horrid placeholder <box> tags. Instead of those, we'll have

1. A single line `<textbox>` for the Summary subpanel
2. A multiline `<textbox>` for the Details subpanel
3. Two `<checkbox>` tags for the Options subpanel
4. Four small `<textbox>` tags for the Size subpanel

As shown in Listing 7.4, the matching tags are trivial.

Listing 7.4 New form element tags for the NoteTaker dialog box.

```
<textbox  id="dialog.summary"/>
<textbox  id="dialog.details multiline="true" flex="1"/>
```

```
<checkbox id="dialog.chop-query" dir="rtl" label="Chop Query"
          checked="true"/>
<checkbox id="dialog.home-page" dir="rtl" label="Home Page"
          checked="true"/>
<textbox  id="dialog.width" value="100" maxwidth="3" size="3"/>
<textbox  id="dialog.height" value="90" maxwidth="3" size="3"/>
<textbox  id="dialog.top" value="80" maxwidth="3" size="3"/>
<textbox  id="dialog.left" value="70" maxwidth="3" size="3"/>
```

This cleanup, together with a little layout adjustment, yields a dialog box similar to that in Figure 7.5.

Before replacing `load_data()`, we can experiment briefly. The DOM objects for XUL formlike tags are very similar to the DOM objects for HTML formlike tags. Either by looking at the DOM 2 HTML standard, or the XBL bindings for `<checkbox>` and so on, or just repeating from memory tricks used in Web pages, we can get a long way. Suppose that we replace this code in `load_data()`

```
desc  = document.createElement("description");
desc.setAttribute("value",value);
box   = document.getElementById("dialog." + names[i]);
box.appendChild(desc);
```

with this

```
if (box.value) box.value = value;
```

Since most form "elements" have a value property, we've succeeded in loading most of the properties file into the form with a trivial effort.

Having cleaned up the form, we would like to process the data the user enters, which is the description of a note. Until now, we have used a read-only properties file for that description. Now we want to read and write the form. There are any number of places to put the information, but we'll try using a Web server. Perhaps one day we'll be able to access that note from any Mozilla Browser in the world.

To save the NoteTaker note, we use the code described in this chapter, which we'll slightly customize and put in the `action()` method. We also keep

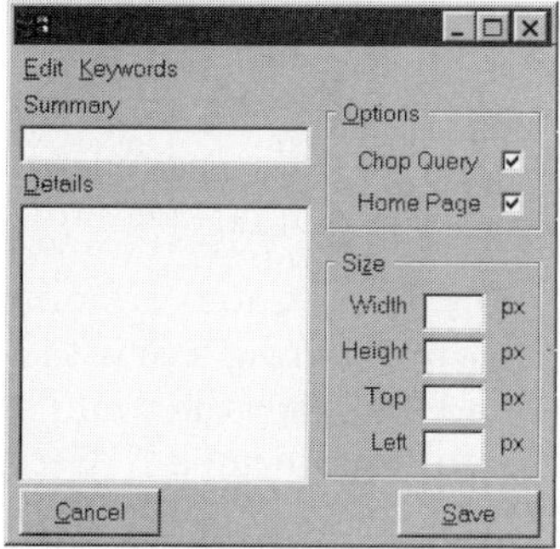

Fig. 7.5 Form-based dialog box.

the names array, formerly local to `load_data()`, but now it's a global array. Listing 7.5 shows this new logic.

Listing 7.5 Posting a NoteTaker note to a Web server.

```
if (task == "save")
{
  var req    = new XMLHttpRequest(); // Request
  var params = "";

  var i = names.length -1;  // build up params
  while (i>=0)
  {
    var widget = document.getElementById("dialog." + names[i]);
    if (widget.tagName == "checkbox")
      params += names[i] + "=" + widget.checked + ";";
    else
      params += names[i] + "=" + widget.value + ";";
    i--;
  }

  params = encodeURI(params);
  req.open("POST", "test.cgi");
  req.send(params);
  if ( req.status / 100 != 2 )  // HTTP 2xx Response?
    throw("Save attempt failed");
}
```

Of course, we also need a `test.cgi`, or some equivalent on the Web server. If we're running from the chrome, `test.cgi` can be replaced with any URL for any Web server.

The NoteTaker tool works with the Classic Browser, so it's unlikely to be loaded from a remote URL. Nevertheless, it's possible that arguments could be passed to it when the window is created. Since it shares the same programming environment as all the rest of the chrome, those arguments could be passed in any number of imaginative ways. One simple way is to append HTTP GET–style parameters to NoteTaker's URL. Instead of using

```
chrome://notetaker/content/editDialog.xul
```

the same document can be loaded using

```
chrome://notetaker/content/editDialog.xul?top=440;left=200
```

This information can be examined at any subsequent time using the `window.location` AOM property. We'll do that by creating a new task for the `action()` method: This one will be called `'load'`. Rather than matching any element of the GUI, `'load'` is a task that is only performed by scripts. The new `onload` handler of the <window> tag will be

```
onload="action('load')"
```

The logic added to the `action()` method is shown in Listing 7.6. The `window.location` object is one of very few AOM objects that exists in both HTML and XUL documents. It provides an object with the `nsIDOMLocation` interface and is useful in XUL only as used here.

Listing 7.6 Reading form parameters from a GET-style URL.

```
if (task == "load" )
  {
    var pair, widget;
    params = window.location.toString();
    if ( params.indexOf("?") == -1 )
      return;
    params = params.replace(/.*\?/,"");
    params = params.split(/[;&]/);
    i = params.length - 1;
    while (i >=0 )
    {
      pair = params[i].split(/=/);
      pair[0] = decodeURI(pair[0]);
      pair[1] = decodeURI(pair[1]);

      widget = document.getElementById("dialog."+ pair[0])
      if (widget.tagName == "checkbox")
        widget.checked = ( pair[1] == "true" );
      else
        widget.value = pair[1];
      i--;
    }
  }
```

This code uses the regular expression support in ECMAScript 1.3. The `replace()` method is used to chop off all the characters leading up to the `?` symbol, which starts the parameter string. `split()` divides the remaining string into an array of strings, with the separation points everywhere that a regular expression match occurs. In this case, the match occurs on each `;` or `&` character. Finally, each `param=value` pair is split again, and the two halves are used to find a form element with a matching id. That element is then updated.

7.7 Debug Corner: Diagnosing Events and Forms

Forms and events aren't that challenging, unless you are in the business of constructing your own widgets. A few standard techniques can make life easier.

7.7.1 Unpopping Menus

The `<menupopup>` tag only appears when you click on its associated button. This can be a nuisance if you just want to see that the constructed contents are correct. You can embed the popup in the normal flow of the XUL document by changing its display style as follows:

```
menupopup { display: -moz-box ! important }
```

If you do this, the popup won't work interactively any more, but at least you can see its contents easily. Figure 7.6 shows the same document as in Figure 7.3, but with this style added.

Doing this is not recommended as an implementation strategy, or even as a stable testing technique; it just happens to work and is convenient.

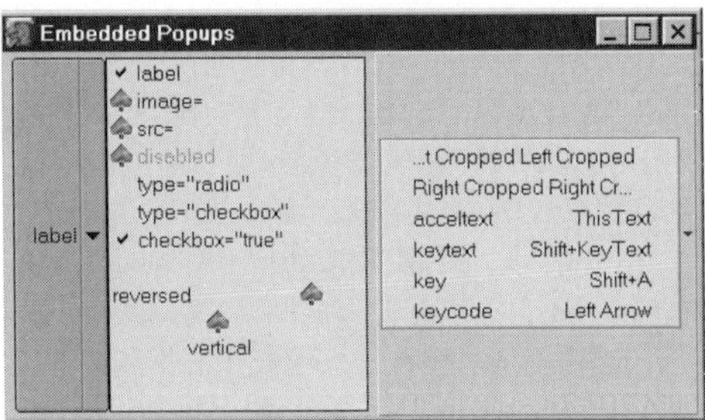

Fig. 7.6 Examples of embedded <menupopup> contents.

7.7.2 Picking Apart Complex Widgets

Complex widgets like `<menulist>` take some work to understand, particularly if you don't like the default content, appearance, or behavior. It always helps if you can see the unseen.

The simplest strategy is to analyze a given tag with the DOM Inspector. This tool reveals tag content, tag ids, and tag style classes at the touch of a button. It's so easy you'd be crazy not to experiment with it.

Another strategy used in this chapter and elsewhere in this book is to use a diagnostic stylesheet. Some of the examples in this book are enhanced with simple styles that provide a few extra visual hints. Listing 7.7 shows these informal styles.

Listing 7.7 Example of an asynchronous `XMLHttpRequest`.

```
label { border: dashed thin; padding: 2px; margin: 2px;}
image { border: solid thin; padding: 2px; margin: 2px; }

.radio-check { width:20px; height:20px;}
.checkbox-check { width:20px; height:20px;}

vbox, hbox, box, deck
{ border: solid; padding: 2px; margin: 2px; border-color: grey;}

* { font-family:Arial; font-weight: bold;}
```

This is pretty simple stuff, except possibly for the checkbox styles, which had to be dug out of the DOM Inspector. Without these two styles, the check icons are reduced to tiny sizes by the padding added in the other rules.

7.7.3 Finding Object Properties for Forms and Menus

This chapter has covered the XUL interface to Mozilla's forms and menus but not the JavaScript interfaces to those tags' DOM objects. To find AOM and DOM properties and methods, there are several approaches.

- **Guess**. Many of the XUL interface properties exactly mimic those of HTML forms. `selectedIndex`, `focus()`, and `blur()` all work as you might expect. They're also documented in the DOM 1 Core standard, under HTML.
- **Use the DOM Inspector**. Select a tag in the left panel, and choose JavaScript Object from the toolbar menu at the top left in the right panel. All property and method names are revealed. To find values for object properties, consult this book or the CSS2 and CSS3 standards.
- **Examine XBL definitions**. The XBL bindings for each form or menu widget are located in the chrome in `toolkit.jar`. It's easy to treat those definitions as a form of help after a quick read of Chapter 15, XBL Bindings. XBL definitions list the parameter names for each method, which the DOM Inspector does not yet do.

7.8 SUMMARY

Form and menu widgets are a vital first access point for users needing to interact with Mozilla-based applications. XUL supports all the simple form controls (or elements) with which users of Web browsers are familiar. XUL's support, however, is flexible and only begins with simple form and menu controls. That support goes much further, and it is not bound rigidly to user actions as HTML forms are.

Unlike HTML, XUL applications can only submit forms across the Web via a script. Such a submission, however, can be tailored more flexibly than any HTML form submission can.

Forms and menus are all interesting enough, but fiddling with such things won't allow the user to go anywhere or explore other parts of a possibly complex application. Support for such navigational activities is the subject of the next chapter.

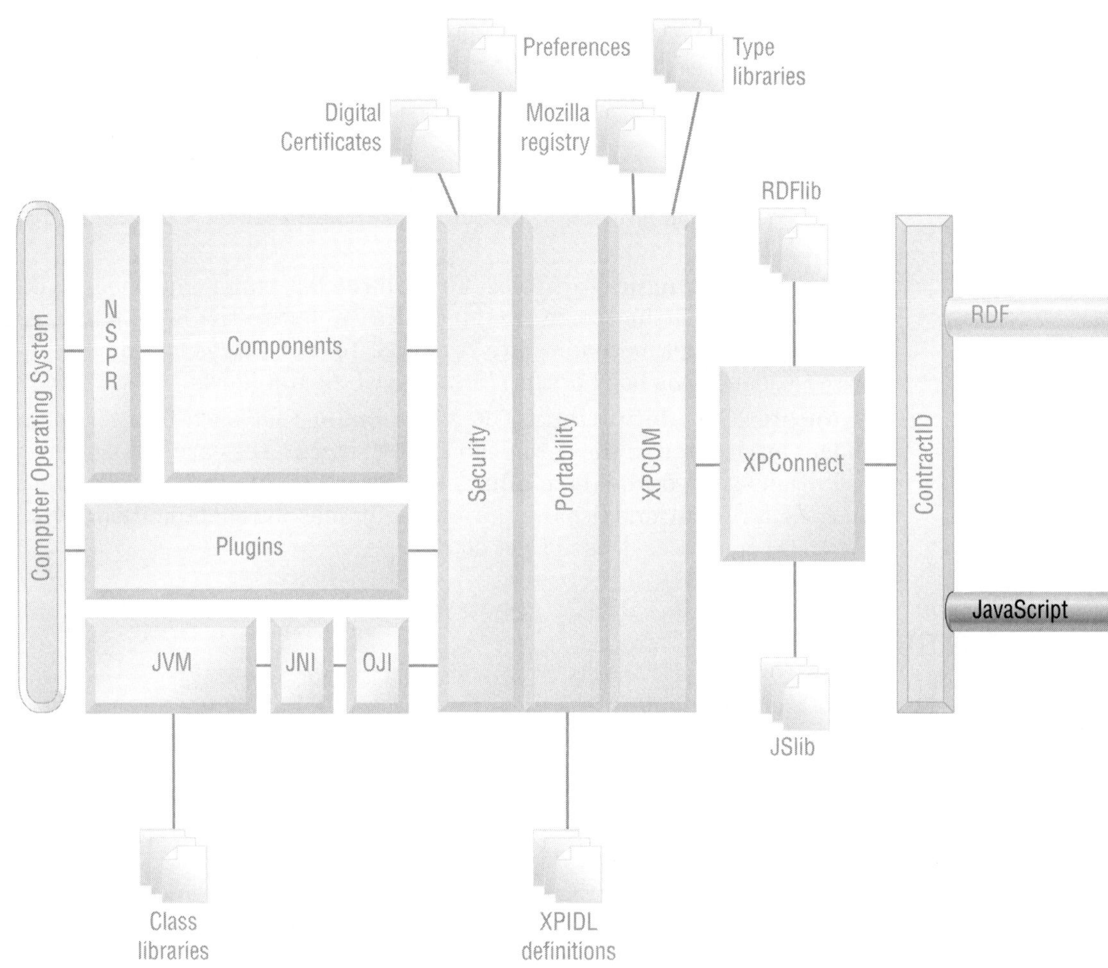

Preferences
Type libraries
Digital Certificates
Mozilla registry
RDFlib
Computer Operating System
NSPR
Components
Security
Portability
XPCOM
XPConnect
ContractID
RDF
Plugins
JavaScript
JVM
JNI
OJI
JSlib
Class libraries
XPIDL definitions

CHAPTER 8

Navigation

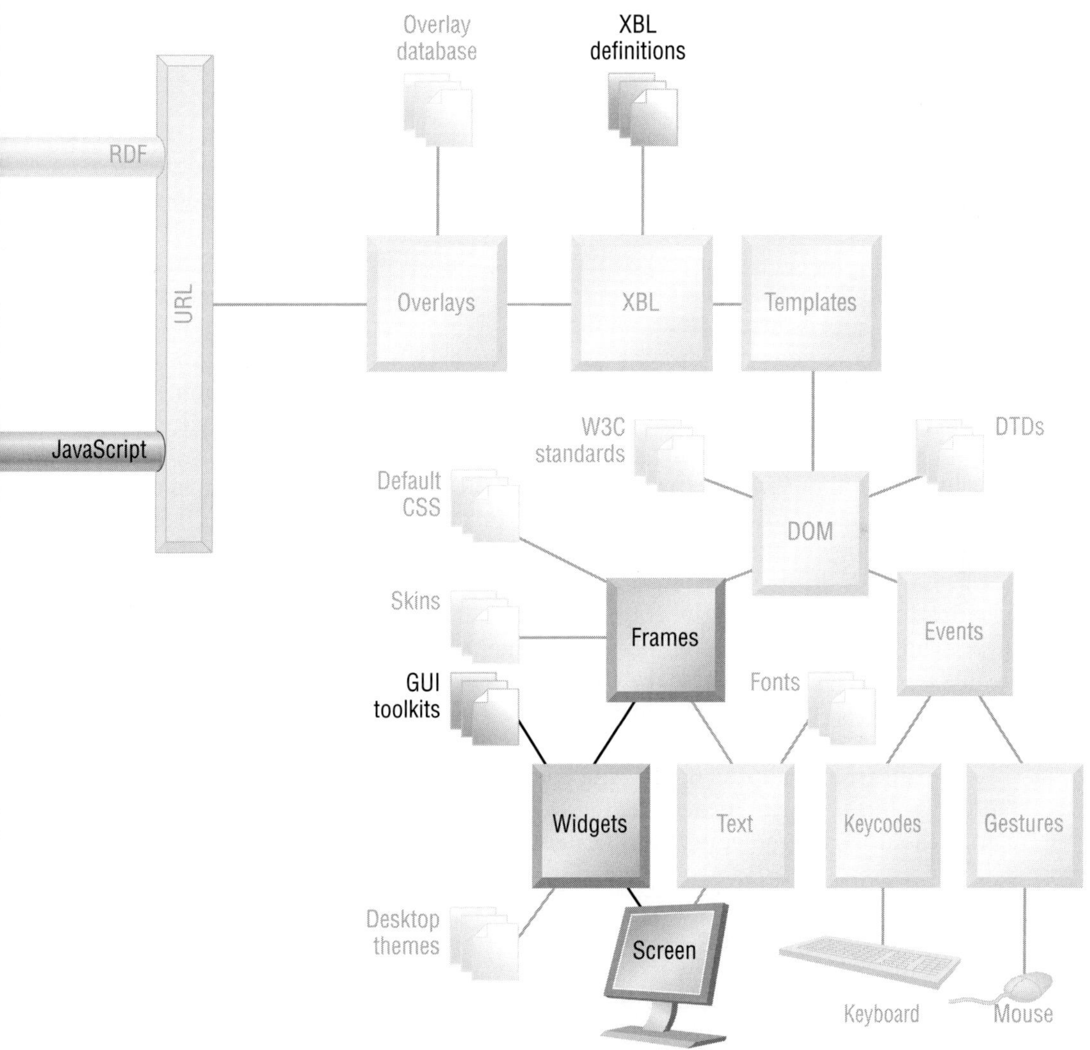

An application window should not be a random collection of text, boxes, and widgets, no matter how beautifully it is presented. A window should impose some order on the features that it provides. That order makes moving around in the application easier. This chapter describes the XUL tags and related design that can impose such order.

The end user, whether competent and impatient or lost and confused, should have free will to move around within an application. That movement is navigation. The number one rule of navigation is: Don't frighten the user off. Navigation strategies should always use familiar hints and feedback and should never surprise or challenge. XUL provides navigation tags that are the same as the widgets of most GUI-based applications. That means scrollbars, toolbars, and menus. Like all XUL tags, naming conventions for these new tags are straightforward:

```
<scrollbar orient="horizontal"/>
```

These navigation widgets are separate from any application logic, so a window made of these widgets is no more than a mockup. Application logic can be added later.

XUL applications are more structured than those in HTML. In a traditional Web environment, the user is free to cast his or her eye across any information that is presented. Graphic design techniques can impress some order on that browsing behavior, but the user is always in window-shopping mode. In a XUL application, there is much less of this unstructured navigation. Users tend to repeat the same tasks over and over (if the application is heavily used), and sometimes the application constrains what the user can do quite tightly. This busier and more structured style of interaction means that there is a high expectation that application use will flow smoothly. Navigation in XUL therefore needs some design attention if the application is to have a polished feel.

The NPA diagram at the start of this chapter highlights the bits of Mozilla involved. From the diagram, navigation builds on top of platform pieces that by now are quite familiar. Navigation is mostly XUL tags, and that means more screen display, more widgets based on the underlying GUI toolkit, and more frames. As for the simple form tags, the XBL bindings that lie behind these tags are vital for scripting purposes.

Recall from Chapter 6, Events, that Mozilla's focus ring links form elements so that they can be accessed via the keyboard. The focus ring and other complementary technologies are further explored in this chapter.

8.1 NAVIGATION SYSTEMS

The Mozilla Platform contains several pieces of design that tie together the existing navigable XUL widgets. Each of these pieces provides a basis for communication between the user and the platform. Each piece is a high-level concept built on top of the event infrastructure discussed in Chapter 6, Events.

8.1.1 Visual Versus Recipe Navigation

We live in a world that is visually rich and full of memories. We are well designed to process both kinds of information. It is no surprise that software systems use both sight and memory to assist users with navigation, but sometimes one of these helps more than the other does.

Visual navigation is in the art of a graphic designer. A well-designed and well-layed-out display makes it easy for users to find what they're looking for. A classic example of an application that is visually oriented is Adobe Photoshop. Although that tool has a menu system, menus are secondary to navigating the palettes and the canvas with the cursor. A Photoshop user knows that by right-clicking on the current selection with the Flood Fill tool (which is over *here*), the current background color (shown over *there*) will be applied to that selection's content.

Visual navigation is particularly important when a user is interacting with something for the first time.

Recipe navigation occurs when the user calls on habit and memory to complete a task. It is something of a black art. A well-designed sequence of key-driven commands makes it easy for a user to remember how to do things. An obvious example of a recipe-oriented navigation tool is a command line. If the user has a good memory for commands, then the command line is a very expressive, efficient, and direct way to get things done. Window-based tools also support recipe navigation. Under Microsoft Windows, most applications will respond to the keystroke sequence Alt-F-S (File | Save) by saving the current document. Reusing remembered keystroke sequences is a very fast navigation technique, perhaps the fastest.

Recipe navigation is very important when the user performs a repetitive action.

Traditional non-Web applications do not have much room for clever layout when displayed inside a window or on a monitor. Menu bars, toolbars, and scrollbars are examples of the little strips of layout that are now familiar features of such applications. Keystroke support in such traditional applications is usually much more extensive than layout.

The success of the Web has resulted in HTML being used as the foundation for many applications. HTML is very weak on recipe navigation because of slow response times and browser compatibility problems. That is why visual cues and graphic design support have become very important for those applications.

With XUL, Mozilla moves back toward the recipe style of use that is efficient for power users. XUL provides extensive support for keylike navigation. Any nontrivial visual design required is left to the application developer. Regarding traditional applications, XUL still provides visual navigation support in the form of menu bars and scrollbars.

What all this means is that Mozilla technology makes creating memory-driven systems easy. Complex visual arrangements are left to the application programmer and have no support beyond the basics of CSS2 (which is still extensive) and XUL.

8.1.2 The Focus Ring

The focus ring is Mozilla's system for small navigation movements within a document. In XUL and HTML, those movements must be between user-modifiable elements, like form fields.

If a user is to enter something into a form, then interacting with one form element at a time is a sensible approach. Like HTML, XUL brings such widgets to the fore one at a time. The widget currently available for user input is said to have the current focus.

Any such set of widgets have an order. In the W3C standards, this order is called the navigation order. In Mozilla, the ordered collection of these widgets is called the focus ring because stepping out beyond the last widget leads back to the first widget.

All widgets in Mozilla's focus ring can be visited. The simplest way to see this visitation order is to step around the ring with the Tab key. Try that in any Mozilla window displaying a XUL or HTML document. In addition to the Tab key, a focusable widget can be given the focus with a mouse click. There is one focus ring per Mozilla window.

Some formlike widgets are not members of the focus ring. Examples are `<toolbarbutton>` and `<menu>`. This is because the focus ring's main purpose is to support the user's data-entry activities. Widgets that are more about controlling the application, like menus, do not participate.

Mozilla's focus ring is quite sophisticated. It can step inside an XBL binding and focus specific pieces of content in the binding. This allows the user to interact with small parts of a given binding. So a binding, which normally builds a single whole widget out of pieces, can be invaded by the focus ring. The focus ring also steps inside embedded content. A XUL document can contain `<iframe>` tags that display other documents inside the main one. The focus ring reaches down into those other documents and includes all focusable elements in the focus ring. It also adds those whole documents to the ring. To see this, load an HTML document that contains a form into any Mozilla Browser. As you tab around the focus ring, both the individual form elements and the whole HTML document, as well as the XUL parts of the browser window, take a turn at being focused.

Because the focus ring includes whole embedded documents, there is also a hierarchical aspect to the ring. To see this, imagine that the Google home page (*www.google.com*) is displayed in a browser, and that the cursor is in the search field of that home page. All these items are focused: the search field, the HTML document that is Google's home page, and the window holding the XUL document that is the Web browser application. In XML terms, the focused items are HTML's `<INPUT TYPE="text">` tag, the XUL `<iframe>` and HTML `<HTML>` tags, and the outermost XUL `<window>` tag.

This hierarchical aspect of the focus ring is meant for the user's benefit, but it is also used by Mozilla's command system, described in Chapter 9, Commands. There, the `commandDispatcher.getControllerForCommand()` method scans up through the focus ring hierarchy looking for a usable controller.

Most focusable XUL tags have `focus()` and/or `blur()` methods for scripts to use. Until very recently, the focus ring has had some subtle bugs. These issues occasionally confuse the state of XUL windows. With version 1.4, the focus ring is now quite reliable.

8.1.2.1 Hyperlinks When Mozilla displays HTML pages, any hyperlinks on the page are included in the focus ring. XUL has no hyperlinks. If XUL and HTML share the same document (via use of `xmlns` attributes), then XUL tags and HTML hyperlinks can coexist in the one focus ring.

8.1.3 The Menu System

A navigation system separate from the focus ring is Mozilla's menu system. This system is initiated by pressing the Alt key (or Control or Meta on older UNIX systems) or by hovering over or clicking an item on the menu bar.

The menu navigation system is not just a series of `<key>` tags. It is a fundamental part of the platform's support for XUL. For the menu system to be enabled, the XUL document displayed must contain a `<menubar>` tag. Only menus in the menu bar can be navigated to using this system.

Individual items in the menu system may also be accessed directly, separate from the menu system. To do this, just decorate the menu items with keys. That process is described in Chapter 6, Events. Support for specific tags is noted in this chapter.

8.1.4 Accessibility

Accessibility is a feature of software designed to make it usable for those with disabilities. Mozilla has accessibility support on Microsoft Windows and Macintosh, and its UNIX/Linux version will have it when support for the GTK2 libraries is complete.

All XUL widgets contributing to the focus ring and to the menu system can be made accessible. HTML form elements and links can also be made accessible. Form elements are of particular interest because governments want to provide services that disabled citizens can access over the Internet.

Accessibility support can be implemented a number of ways. The simplest way involves no programming at all. Various devices and software utilities that can magnify a visual display until it is readable exist; other devices are easier-to-handle substitutes for traditional keyboards and mice.

At the other extreme, a complex solution is to provide an API and let other programmers hook their accessibility software and devices into it.

Mozilla provides such an API in the form of many XPCOM interfaces, all prefixed with `nsIAccessible`. Use of these interfaces is nearly, but not quite, an embedded use of the Mozilla Platform. These interfaces are not recommended for applications where the users are able.

Between these extremes is a solution that uses simple XML markup techniques. This solution consists of CSS2 `@media` style declarations, the XHTML and XUL `accesskey` attribute, and the XUL `<label>` tag. `@media` and `accesskey` are well documented in the relevant standards—`accesskey` works the same for XUL as it does for HTML.

At a technical level, these features must be implemented so that they use the accessibility features of the underlying GUI toolkit. If this is done, the problem of expressing the content to the user is the GUI toolkit's problem, not the application's problem. This is how Mozilla works. The `nsIAccessible` interfaces expose information from the XML document to the GUI toolkit.

In all discussion to date, the XUL `<label>` tag has appeared identical to the `<description>` tag, except that it can be reduced to a `label` attribute. The `<label>` tag first differs from the description tag in the area of accessibility. The `<label>` tag provides the alternate content that is needed for an accessibility system.

If a form element has a `label` attribute, Mozilla will present its content both to the screen and to the GUI toolkit as guide information that should be expressed to the user. Expressed to the user might mean that the guide information is spoken by the computer.

If a form element doesn't have such an attribute, then Mozilla will look for a child tag that is a `<label>` tag and use that. If no suitable child tag exists, it will look for a `<label>` tag whose `id` matches the `id` stated in the form tag's `control` attribute. If that isn't found, then there is no accessibility information to supply.

Mozilla has accessibility support for all the simple XUL form elements. The `<menuitem>`, `<menulist>`, and `<tab>` tags also have accessibility support. Accessibility support is connected to XUL tags in the XBL bindings for each such tag.

8.2 Navigation Widgets

Figure 8.1 illustrates all XUL's navigation tags in one screenshot.

Figure 8.1 diagram is special in several ways. First, diagnostic styles are turned on so that you can see some of the internal structure of the tags. Second, this screenshot is taken with Mozilla version 1.02. That version includes support for toolbar grippys, support that is not present in version 1.21. Third, some `<description>` tags have been added where no tags are meant to be. These tags, the text of which appears inside braces and is surrounded by a light background, show the position of the nondisplayed container tags.

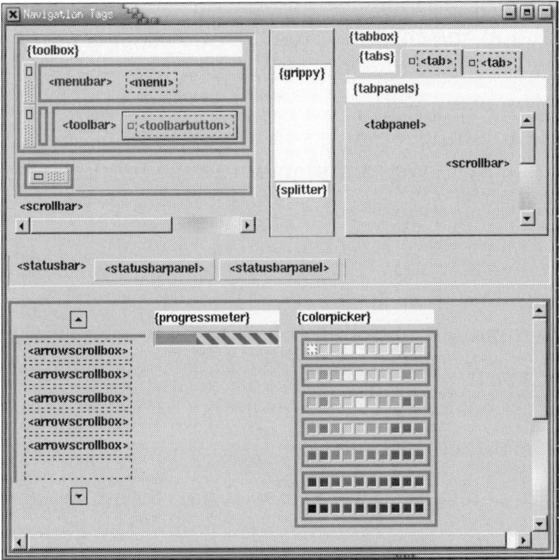

Fig. 8.1 XUL Navigation tags with diagnostics.

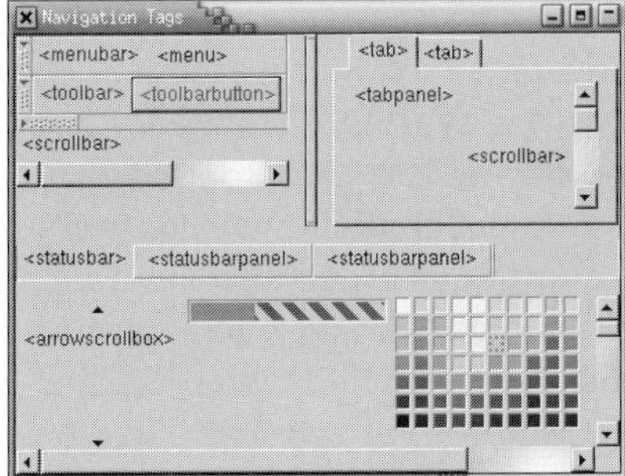

Fig. 8.2 XUL Navigation tags.

All the tags illustrated in this diagram have XBL definitions. Figure 8.2 shows the same content as Figure 8.1 without the diagnostic extras.

8.2.1 Scrolling Widgets

XML content that exceeds the current window or the screen in size can be created. Such content is usually clipped to the border of the current window. HTML and XUL provide scrollbars that allow the user to move the content inside the clip region. This is a command to pan the current view based on a mouse gesture or keypresses. Such panning actions are implemented directly by both HTML and XUL. XUL has the following tags available for panning actions:

```
<arrowscrollbox> <scrollbar> <nativescrollbar> <scrollbox>
```

Mozilla's implementation of HTML supports the <MARQUEE> tag, whose XBL definition can be found in the chrome. This tag allows for animated scrolling of the tag's contents.

XUL also supports the `overflow:scroll` and `overflow:auto` CSS2 style properties. These are the quickest ways to provide simple content scrolling. Some CSS2 extensions, however, complement these features (see "Style Options" later in this chapter).

8.2.1.1 <scrollbox> The <scrollbox> tag might sound like all the solution you need for scrolling, but that is not true. The <scrollbox> tag provides no user-interface elements. It acts like the <box> tag, except that it also implements the `nsIScrollBoxObject` interface. Like the <box> tag, it supports these layout attributes:

```
orient align pack dir maxwidth maxheight minwidth minheight
```

This tag is similar to <box> because it has a narrow purpose. It is the first tag discussed in this book that is a specialization of the generic <box> object.

Recall from Chapter 2, XUL Layout, that boxes are implemented on top of a lower-level concept called a frame. A frame is just an area of the screen that is managed independently. <scrollbox> is designed to display its content so that it is offset from the frame by a given *x*- and *y*-amount. That is all.

<scrollbox> has no special features available from XUL, but it does supply some scriptable object methods. The `nsIScrollBoxObject` interface adds these methods. Each method call moves the displayed contents to a new position inside the frame. Raw pixel amounts or other units can be specified. For example, methods with "line" in their names move the content vertically by the specified number of whole lineboxes. Methods with "index" in their names move content vertically by the height of a set number of content tags. If these methods are used repeatedly, the content will appear to scroll in a given direction (up and down, back and forth, or any other animated movement).

These extra methods are not present on the <scrollbox>'s DOM object. Every boxlike XUL tag has a `boxObject` property. This `boxObject` property is an object containing all the states that apply to a box tag (e.g., position and size). It also contains the `QueryInterface()` method, which is used for retrieving XPCOM interfaces. If the tag is a <scrollbox>, then this method can be used to retrieve the `nsIScrollBoxObject` interface methods. It is the only way to get this interface.

All this means that the <scrollbox> tag must be controlled by some programmer's bits of script if it is to do anything. It is only really useful to programmers creating their own widgets.

A simple example can be seen in the chrome file `scrollbox.xml` inside `toolkit.jar`. The XBL binding named `autorepeatbutton` extracts the `nsIScrollBoxObject` interface from nearby <scrollbox> content and manipulates that content via the interface so that it scrolls up or down. A fragment of that code is shown in Listing 8.1.

Listing 8.1 Example of an XUL tab box.

```
<handler event="command"><![CDATA[
  ... some code removed ...
  var dir = this.getAttribute("scrolldir");
  var bx =
          this.mScrollBox.boxObject.QueryInterface(Components.interfaces.n
          sIScrollBoxObject);
  bx.scrollByIndex(dir == "up" ? -1 : 1);
]]>
</handler>
```

This code says that a command event on an <autorepeatbutton> results in an (assumedly nearby) <scrollbox> tag being scrolled one line. Because that kind of button continuously fires events when it is pressed, the scrollbox is scrolled repeatedly. The <autorepeatbutton> is a visual tag and manages the <scrollbox> tag's special nsIScrollBoxObject.

You can study this binding if you want to make your own widget based on <scrollbox>. Beware, though, that <scrollbox> is unusual in one respect. The tag expects to have a single <box> as its content, with all other content inside that box. That is more complex than the simple case, in which the boxObject property belongs to the topmost tag's DOM object.

To summarize, <scrollbox> is a fundamental tag that needs to be surrounded with other tags and some scripting before it provides a final solution. Fortunately, there are other, better ways of quickly providing a scrolling box.

8.2.1.2 <arrowscrollbox>

The <arrowscrollbox> tag is a building block used to create the <menupopup> tag and is, in turn, built on other tags. Listing 8.2 shows the hierarchy of tags that make up an <arrowscrollbox>. Note that this is not a piece of literal XML, just a breakdown of tag contents.

Listing 8.2 Breakdown of the <arrowscrollbox> tag.

```
<arrowscrollbox>
  <autorepeatbutton>
    <image>
  <scrollbox>
    <box>
      <anything>
      <anything>
      ...
  <autorepeatbutton>
    <image>
```

If the <box> contents exceed the size of the <arrowscrollbox>, then the two <autorepeatbutton> tags are visible. If the content all fits within the outermost tag, then the two button-like tags are hidden. This is the normal case for menus, and so there is no indication that an <arrowscrollbox> exists in every menu, even though that is the case. This tag can also be used by itself, separate from any menus. It has a particularly simple XBL definition that is easy to experiment with.

8.2.1.3 <scrollbar> The <scrollbar> tag provides a single vertical or horizontal scrollbar that is completely independent of surrounding content. If the scrollbar is to scroll anything, it must be coordinated with that other content by JavaScript. Listing 8.3 shows a breakdown of the structure of the <scrollbar> tag.

Listing 8.3 Breakdown of the <scrollbar> tag.

```
<scrollbar>
  <scrollbarbutton>
    <image>
  <scrollbarbutton>
    <image>
  <slider>
    <thumb>
      <gripper>
  <scrollbarbutton>
    <image>
  <scrollbarbutton>
    <image>
```

The <scrollbar> tag contains four buttons in total. Because two are for vertical scrollbars and two are for horizontal scrollbars, two are always hidden by CSS2 styles. This is done by the XBL definition for <scrollbar>. The DOM Inspector can be used to reveal this structure.

<scrollbar> supports the orient attribute, which can be set to vertical or horizontal. Other XUL attributes specific to <scrollbar> match the attributes of the <slider> tag. The <slider> tag should never be used outside the <scrollbar> tag. These shared attributes are

```
curpos maxpos pageincrement increment
```

These four attributes model the current position of the slider as a single number. This number represents the position of the center of the thumb, and it is a relative position. Stretching the window won't alter the value of the slider, unless the amount of visible content changes as well. The range of values is from 0 to maxpos, with a current value of curpos.

Sometimes curpos is exposed as a scriptable DOM property, but this is buggy and should not be relied on—always use setAttribute() and getAttribute(). increment is the largest change caused by clicking a <scrollbarbutton>; pageincrement is the largest change caused by clicking the tray that the <slider> draws around the thumb. These two actions might cause a smaller increment if the thumb is near one end of the scrollbar.

Other aspects of the <scrollbar> tag are all managed by styles. To make the thumb of the slider larger or smaller, apply CSS2 styles to it. You must do your own calculations if you want the size of the thumb to reflect the portion of the content that is visible. To get this effect for free, either keep maxpos small relative to the scollbar's size, which provides some thumb-styling, or use a CSS-based scrollbar instead of a <scrollbar> tag. See "Style Options" for the later option. The size of the thumb is not particularly meaningful for a <scrollbar> used the default way.

8.2.1.4 <nativescrollbar> XUL divides a scrollbar widget up into a number of parts, but that is only one way to implement such a widget. Many GUI toolkits can supply a scrollbar widget as a single whole object, rather than supply pieces that the application must put together. The <nativescrollbar> tag is intended to display a whole native scrollbar as a single widget. Its use is restricted to the Macintosh at the moment, and applies only when native themes are at work.

Ignore the <nativescrollbar> tag unless you are doing extensive work with native themes or embedding Mozilla in some other GUI application.

8.2.2 Toolbars

A bar is a rectangular section of a window covered in user controls. Toolbars and menu bars typically appear along the edges of an application window, primarily along the top edge. They provide a convenient place from which users can launch commands. To see toolbars in Mozilla, just open a Classic Browser window and look at the top part. The Classic Browser has extra functionality that collapses and redisplays toolbars. Try playing with the options on the View | Show/Hide submenu.

Mozilla's XUL toolbar system, which includes menu bars, is simple but can be made complex when used expertly. This complexity is the result of how overlays and templates are used to build up a single toolbar from several different documents. This chapter considers only the basic toolbar tags; overlays and templates are treated in later chapters.

Mozilla's toolbars are not sophisticated. By default, they are not draggable or dockable as Netscape 4.x's toolbars were, or as toolbars in Microsoft applications are. They cannot be pinned or torn off either. In fact, Mozilla toolbars cannot be layed out vertically. Mozilla's toolbars do not provide the "more items" icon that appears on Internet Explorer toolbars. Nearly all these features can be added to the basic toolbars provided, if you have the will and the time.

Mozilla's toolbars have a few advantages. The collapsible toolbar grippys of Netscape 4.x are available, but not in version 1.2. When they are present, the toolbars can be locked in place by hiding the grippys using style information. When toolbar grippys aren't supported, the toolbars are always locked in place. Locked toolbars are a concept from Internet Explorer 6. Mozilla's toolbars can also appear anywhere in the content of an application window, and being XUL they are very simple to create.

Figure 8.3 is a screenshot of the Mozilla Composer, with the Modern theme applied. Note the horizontal line that separates text from icons in the main toolbar. This line appears throughout the Modern theme, but it has nothing to do with toolbar functionality. It is merely a background image. Don't be confused by it.

In addition to toolbars and menu bars, Mozilla also supports status bars.

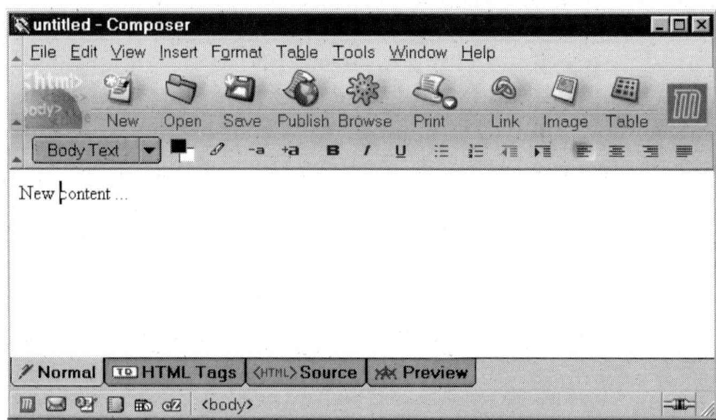

Fig. 8.3 Toolbar tricks applied by the Modern theme.

8.2.2.1 `<toolbox>` The <toolbox> tag is a container for a set of toolbars. Its XBL binding is in `toolbar.xml` in the chrome. When there are no toolbar grippys (Mozilla 1.21), it acts like a <vbox>. In both earlier and newer versions, where grippys are supported, the tag's internal content is as shown in Listing 8.4.

Listing 8.4 Breakdown of the <toolbox> tag.

```
<toolbox>
  <vbox>
    <toolbar or menubar>
    <toolbar>
    ... more toolbars ...
  <hbox>
    <hbox>
    <spacer>
```

Although more than one <menubar> can appear in a given <toolbox>, that is not a recommended practice because of the confusion it creates when key-navigation is attempted.

The application programmer specifies only the <toolbox> tag and its <toolbar> and <menubar> contents; all the rest is automatically generated.

The <vbox> contains the toolbars; the <hbox> contains an empty <hbox> and a <spacer> that provides flex. This empty <hbox> holds images that represent grippy-collapsed toolbars. The image tags are not precreated and hidden with CSS2 styles because there might be any number of toolbars present. They are instead created dynamically by the JavaScript `onclick` handlers in the XBL definition.

Where there are no grippys, <toolbox> is little more than a target for style information. Any tag can be contained inside a <toolbox>, but <toolbar> and <menubar> tags should be its immediate children.

8.2.2.2 <toolbar> The <toolbar> tag is the first of two options for <toolbox> content. It provides a single horizontal toolbar that acts like a <hbox> and is unremarkable. It can contain any type of content. The only XML attributes of particular interest are

```
collapsed grippyhidden grippytooltiptext
```

`collapsed` set to `true` will collapse the toolbar as for any tag, `grippyhidden` set to `true` will lock the toolbar in place by hiding any <toolbargrippy> that appears by default. `grippytooltiptext` sets the tooltip text for the grippy. This text appears when the toolbar is collapsed and the mouse hovers over the remaining grippy.

Setting the `collapse` attribute is not the same as clicking a grippy. To emulate that user action, call the `collapseToolbar()` method of the parent <toolbox> tag, with the <toolbar>'s DOM object as the sole argument.

Early versions of Mozilla included a lead-in image or icon for the whole toolbar, but that has been removed in more recent versions. A lead-in icon or image can still be added using the CSS2 `list-style-image` property.

A restriction on the <toolbar> tag is that it does not always lay out reliably. Problems can occur if it occupies less than the full width of a XUL window. If tags appear to the right of the enclosing <toolbox>, and the window is narrow, then <toolbar> contents can be incorrectly truncated. Sometimes this works; sometimes it doesn't. For best results, just give <toolbar> the full width of the application window.

There is some discussion on the toolbar grippy, implemented with <toolbargrippy>, in Chapter 4, First Widgets and Themes. The grippy is based on a simple image, reminiscent of Sun Microsystem's OpenLook desktop environment.

Because toolbars can be dynamically created, it is best to give their content a simple structure. Make all items on the toolbar immediate children of the <toolbar> tag.

8.2.2.3 <toolbaritem>, <toolbarbutton>, and <toolbarseparator> The <toolbaritem>, <toolbarbutton>, and <toolbarseparator> tags are used as <toolbar> content. <toolbaritem> is an anonymous tag. <toolbarseparator> is an anonymous tag styled to provide extra space and a further destination for style information. <toolbarbutton> is a button. The last two are described in Chapter 4, First Widgets and Themes.

Although two of these tags have no special capbilities, they do have a purpose. When templates are used to construct toolbars, the template system decides how to generate content based on tag names. Even though <toolbaritem> has no particular meaning of its own, a template system can recognize the name and ignore it. This allows the tag to be used as a container for generic content that shouldn't be manipulated.

Tooltips for toolbuttons, and floating help in general, are described in Chapter 10, Windows and Panes.

8.2.3 Menu Bars

Mozilla's XUL supports menu bars, which are a specialized form of toolbar. By common convention, a menu bar should be the first toolbar in a <toolbox> so that it appears at the top of the toolbar area.

8.2.3.1 <menubar> This tag acts like a plain <hbox> and can appear inside or outside a <toolbox> tag. More than one <menubar> can appear inside a <toolbox>. That is the general case.

The Macintosh Platform, both MacOS 9 and X, is a special case. That platform has a single menu bar that is dynamically shared between all running applications. That special menu bar exists outside the basic windowing system. A <menubar> tag has its contents applied to that Macintosh menu bar, and that content appears only on that special menu bar. Only one <menubar> tag is examined, and only the <menu> tags inside that <menubar> are applied to the special bar. The menu items appear on that bar when the Mozilla window gains focus. They do not appear inside the Mozilla window as well.

On other platforms, <menubar> can be filled with any content.

<menubar> supports Mozilla's accessibility features. <menubar>'s special attributes are the same as for <toolbar>:

```
collapsed grippyhidden grippytooltiptext
```

These attributes do nothing on the Macintosh. Mozilla's XBL definition for <menubar> appears in toolbar.xml in the chrome.

8.2.3.2 <menu> The <menu> tag is the sole tag that should appear inside a <menubar>. It implements a button-like label that displays a dropdown menu when pressed. It is a wrapper for the <menupopup> tag, similar to the other menu wrapper tags described in Chapter 6, Events. The <menu> tag can also be used outside of <menubar> as a form element (although <menulist> is a better approach) or as a submenu inside another menu. If the <menu> tag inside a <menubar> has no content, it acts much like a <toolbarbutton>; use <toolbarbutton> instead.

The <menu> tag supports Mozilla's accessibility features and has the following special attributes:

```
disabled _moz-menuactive open label accesskey crop acceltext image
```

`disabled` set to `true` grays out the menu. `_moz-menuactive` set to `true` applies a style that highlights the menu title as though it were a button. `open` set to `true` might apply a further style to the menu title and also indicate that the drop-down menu is displayed. The other attributes apply to the <label> content tags that hold the menu title, except for `image`, which applies to an optional content icon that is sometimes available. Any automatically generated content tags are described in "Menu Variations."

The `_moz-menuactive` attribute is passed through the <menu> tag from the parent <menubar> tag all the way to the <menuitem> tags that are the contents of the menu. Many styles are based on this attribute. These styles provide visual feedback to the user when navigating through the menu structure. `_moz-menuactive` would be called `-moz-menuactive`, except that XML attributes may not start with a "-". The name of this attribute is not yet final, so check the XBL in your version to see if this name has changed.

<menupopup> and <template> are the only tags that can be put inside the <menu> tag as content. With respect to toolbars, menu bars can have the content generated by XUL's template or overlay systems. Menu bars can also have the content of individual menus generated in this way.

<menu> can also be used inside a <toolbar> tag, but this is not particularly recommended.

8.2.3.3 Menu Variations Various formlike XUL tags, such as <button> and <textbox>, have variants that are determined by a `type` attribute. The <menu> tag also has variants, but they are determined by the `class` attribute. The value of this attribute maps to standard style rules that determine which XBL binding will apply to the <menu> tag. Several bindings are available, and each one provides different default content.

There are five minor menu variations in total. These variations only affect the initial presentation of the <menu> tag, not the subsequent dropped-down <menupopup> tag. The `class` attribute can be unset; set to `"menu"`; or set to `"menu-iconic"` (three options). The <menu> tag can be inside or outside a <menubar> (two options). $2 \times 3 = 6$ variations, but two of these variations are the same. Figure 8.4 illustrates these variations with some diagnostic styles.

Fig. 8.4 Variations on the <menu> tag.

The top row of this screenshot is a <menubar>. The bottom row is an <hbox>. The accesskey and acceltext attributes are varied trivially to illustrate some combinations. The important thing to note is the presence and absence of <label> and <image> content, marked out with dotted black and solid, thin black borders, respectively.

In this example, all <menu> tags have maxwidth="150px" applied to show the alignment. Tags inside a menu bar are left-aligned, but those outside are right-aligned. The words "no class," "menu," and "menu-iconic" are the titles of each of the six displayed menus and match the value of the class attribute on that <menu> tag. Any second <label> to the right holds the text of the acceltext attribute.

It is a small challenge to add icons to <menubar> menus. Set class="menu-iconic" to start with. The image attribute can be used if the <menu> is outside a menu bar, but it has no effect if the menu is inside. To get an icon to appear for a menu that is inside, set the class attribute on the <menu> tag and add a custom style like this to the document:

```
.menubar-left#X {list-style-image: url("icon.png");}
```

X is the id of the <menu> tag needing an icon. Add one style rule per <menu> needing an icon. This is not perfect, but it is a workaround for now.

8.2.4 Statusbars

Mozilla's XUL supports statusbars. Such a bar usually appears at the base of a XUL window where it reports state information and progress messages. It might also provide clickable icons. Whether statusbars are really any different from toolbars is a matter of debate. In Mozilla, statusbars are a separate system.

XBL definitions for the tags supporting statusbars are stored in the chrome file general.xml in toolkit.jar.

8.2.4.1 <statusbar> The <statusbar> tag is a horizontal region like a <toolbar>, except that a <statusbar> does not act like an <hbox>. Therefore, further content can appear to the right of such a bar. In the normal case, a <statusbar> should extend the full width of the Mozilla window. <statusbar> can contain any content. The <statusbar> tag exists as a convenience for the Mozilla Browser. It is almost an application-level tag rather than a fundamental building block. It provides styles and a little special-purpose content. It has no special-purpose attributes.

Looking back at Figure 8.3, a <statusbar> appears as a recessed tray to which content can be added. The appearance of the tray is entirely the result of styles. If you expect your XUL window to be resizable on the Macintosh, then including a <statusbar> tag at the bottom of the document is the simplest way to ensure that it is because the right-hand end of the statusbar contains a <resizer> tag.

It is tempting to put <statusbar> tags next to each other, but this will look odd on the Macintosh. More than one <resizer> icon would appear in that case. Don't do it.

8.2.4.2 <statusbarpanel> Any content can appear in a <statusbar>, but an orderly approach is to cluster it into a set of <statusbarpanel> tags. This tag mimics the styles of the <button> tag, but it is not a button and is not ordinarily clickable. This tag just divides the statusbar into visual sections at the bottom of any Mozilla Browser window. It is all done with styles; <statusbarpanel> has no special widget-like behavior and acts like an <hbox>.

A <statusbarpanel> can contain any XUL content. It can alternately have its appearance determined by attributes. Attributes specific to <statusbarpanel> are

```
src label crop
```

There are two variants on this tag. If class="statusbarpanel-iconic", then the content is a single image, specified by the src attribute. Otherwise, the content is a single label to which the label and crop attributes are passed. If <statusbarpanel> contains user-defined content, that content overrides these attributes.

Use <statusbarpanel> to highlight a control area in a XUL document's display. This tag can appear outside a <statusbar>, but such uses are obscure.

8.2.5 Title Bars

Mozilla's XUL provides a tiny bit of support for title bars. In most cases, the title bar is part of the window decorations added by the desktop window manager. XUL has little control over such bars. The title bar is not a frame.

The simplest way to specify the content of a title bar is with the window.title property. Whatever it is set to will appear in the main part of the bar. Other elements of the bar are not configurable, although a window based on a <dialog> tag can remove some controls. A window can be opened with no title bar at all, using options to window.open() (see Chapter 10, Windows and Panes, for details).

The Mozilla chrome contains an XBL definition of a <titlebar> tag. It is occasionally used in other XBL definitions, but it has no real status as a XUL tag. It is no more than an <hbox> containing a <label> and an <image>. It is intended to simulate the title bar added to a window by the desktop window manager. It is a building block of the <floatingview> tag described next. Explore its use if you wish.

The <dialogheader> tag has nothing to do with title bars, it is plain content.

window.open(), <dialog>, <dialogheader>, and <page> are described in Chapter 10, Windows and Panes.

8.2.6 Displaying Multiple Panels

What do you do if all your XUL content won't fit on the screen at once? XUL provides several techniques for addressing such a problem, based on the idea of squeezing more into a single window. Each subpart of the window is called a panel, although that term is not a particularly technical one. Some aspects of panels are covered in Chapter 10, Windows and Panes. All such techniques are easily overused, so first let's look at a brief analysis.

The easiest way to display extra content is to use scrollbars, but scrollbars are a simplistic fix. A better solution is to examine the design of your application window. Most windows should have a simple purpose or purposes, and users should not need to do extensive navigation. No one should ever need to scroll down an application window to reveal "extra" form elements. That may be common in Web pages, but in the end it is bad design. Forms should always fit into the initially visible window.

Some applications are desktop-like. Those applications typically have power-users who don't want dumbed-down design. If simplifying the design fails, then XUL provides splitters and tab boxes to break up the content into bits. Both splitters and tab boxes divide the window content into sections, leaving the user responsible for navigating around those sections by hand. The benefit of such a division is a more sophisticated arrangement of content; the cost is the appearance of extra navigational controls that are peripheral to the core purpose of the application.

Some applications are not desktop-like. For repetitiously used applications, like data-entry screens, splitter and tab box divisions can get in the way of performance. Only use these techniques if you expect that the users will exercise some discretion over what they do with the window or how they arrange it. Don't use these techniques for hardened applications or point-solution applications. Don't use them as a substitute for proper design. It is better to make the application support the true task rather than make a Swiss-army knife flexible enough for any need. That advice doesn't apply to a competitive sales environment, however. In a sales environment, it's more important to amaze the audience with nifty features than produce something that is usable and issue-free. That's life.

If there is a risk that users will have a small screen resolution, then splitters and tab boxes may help. Such a risk should be seen as a high-level design constraint. It should not be addressed by pouring extra splitters and tab boxes into the window.

Chapter 10, Windows and Panes, contains further discussion on managing content too big for a single window. Another XUL technique for multi-panel display is the `<wizard>` tag, which is described in Chapter 17, Deployment.

8.2.6.1 `<splitter>` The `<splitter>` tag acts like a blend of the `<button>`, `<resizer>`, and `<spacer>` tags. The example shown in Figure 8.3 is a little atypical because `<splitters>` are usually quite narrow so that they take up minimal screen space. One XUL document can contain many <splitter> tags. Splitters are used extensively in Mozilla's JavaScript Debugger and separate the sidebar from the Web page content in the Navigator window. The purpose of a splitter is to separate content into two panels, one on either side.

The <splitter> tag usually contains a single <grippy> tag. As noted in Chapter 4, First Widgets and Themes, the <splitter> tag can be dragged or clicked via its <grippy> tag. The <grippy> tag provides a place to store event handlers and styles; that's all it does. Its use is very simple:

```
<splitter><grippy/></splitter>
```

The <grippy> tag can be left out if required.

The <splitter> tag works as follows: It and its sibling tags are contained in some <vbox>, <hbox>, or boxlike tag. When users click and drag on the splitter, the splitter recalculates its position, based on each tiny drag offset. It then orders its sibling tags to squeeze up or stretch out. The splitter itself stays the same size, and in the normal case, the parent <vbox> or <hbox> stays the same size. How the siblings are stretched or squeezed depends on the attributes used for the <splitter> tag. If more than one <splitter> exists inside the parent tag, then each one acts as though the others were just simple content.

The attributes with special meaning to the <splitter> tag are

```
orient disabled collapse state resizebefore resizeafter fixed
```

The `orient` attribute determines if the splitter is `vertical` or `horizontal`. `disabled` set to `true` stops the splitter from responding to user input. `collapse` indicates which side of the splitter, `before` or `after`, should disappear if the splitter is collapsed. `state` may be set to `open`, `dragging`, or `collapsed`. `open` means that content on both sides of the splitter is visible. `dragging` means that the user is in the middle of a mouse gesture started on the splitter, and `collapsed` means that content on one side of the splitter is entirely hidden, giving all of the space to the splitter's other panel.

For splitter collapse to work, the <splitter> must have one sibling tag on the side to be collapsed. The easiest way to do this is to use a <box> on that side. The collapse action occurs only when the `state` attribute is set, which is done using JavaScript that is part of the <grippy> implementation. Note that `state="collapsed"` and `collapse="..."` are different from the standard `collapsed="true"` attribute usable on all XUL tags. `collapsed="true"` used on the <splitter> tag will make the splitter itself disappear.

The remaining attributes set the resizing policy for sibling content. If `resizebefore` or `resizeafter` is set to `farthest`, then a shrinking panel will rob space from the sibling most remote from the <splitter> first. If set to `closest`, then a shrinking panel will rob space from the sibling closest to the <splitter> first. If the panel that is shrinking contains a single <box>, then the content of that box will shrink evenly and ignore the `resizebefore` or `resizeafter` hint. `resizeafter` can also be set to `grow`. In this last case, the content after the splitter will not shrink when the splitter is dragged toward it. Instead, it will be moved across so that it overflows and is clipped by the containing box or the window boundaries. Setting `fixed` to `true` overrides the other settings and prevents the grippy from being dragged. It may still be collapsed.

This set of arrangements means that the `state` and `resizebefore/resizeafter` attributes cannot all work at once because they require a different layout for the sibling content. Mixing resize policies with the `flex` attribute, and window resizing can yield a wide range of slightly different stretching effects.

`<splitter>` has one variant: It is also responsible for the resizing of columns in a `<tree>` tag. In that case, it has `class="tree-splitter"` and has no visible appearance. See Chapter 13, Listboxes and Trees.

8.2.6.2 `<tabbox>` XUL's tab box system is Mozilla's way of providing a multidocument interface (MDI), and the `<tabbox>` is the topmost tag. Such an interface allows several documents to be visible from a single window. In Mozilla's case, those documents can be as small as a single XUL tag or, by adding tags like `<iframe>`, as large as a whole document. `<iframe>` is discussed in Chapter 10, Windows and Panes; here the basic tab box arrangement is described.

A typical use of a XUL tab box appears in Listing 8.5. The application programmer must supply most of the content for a tab box as in `<arrowscrollbox>` and `<scrollbar>`. As discussed earlier in the chapter, this is not the case for tags.

Listing 8.5 Example of a XUL tab box.

```
<tabbox>
  <tabs>
    <tab id="t1" label="First" selected="true"/>
    <tab id="t2" label="Second"/>
  </tabs>
  <tabpanels>
    <tabpanel>
      <description>Panel 1 content</description>
    </tabpanel>
    <tabpanel>
      <description>Panel 2 content</description>
    </tabpanel>
  </tabpanels>
</tabbox>
```

The number of `<tabpanel>` tags should match the number of `<tab>` tags if everything is to be coordinated properly. Any XUL tag can substitute for `<tabpanel>`, although that tag is the clearest way to design the tab box. Figure 8.5 shows how the standard `dir` and `orient layout` attributes can be used on `<tabbox>` and `<tabs>` tags to vary the standard appearance of the box.

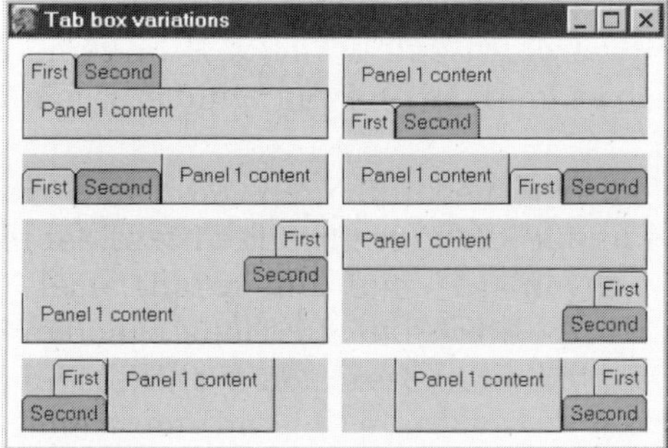

Fig. 8.5 Variations on tab-box orientation.

Clearly, Mozilla's tab boxes aren't as flexible as you might hope; only the most common, normal orientation looks correct. Extensive additional style rules can be used to clean up the appearance of the other orientations, but the effort required is only justified for special cases. Special cases can be found in the Classic Composer and in the Classic Chat client.

The `<tabbox>` tag is a plain box tag. It has accessibility support and many keystroke handlers for the keys used to navigate around the box. Its XBL definition as well as those for all the tab box–related tags can be found in `tabbox.xml` in `toolkit.jar` in the chrome. It has no attributes with special meanings, but the following JavaScript properties are available:

```
selectedIndex selectedTab selectedPanel accesskey
```

`selectedIndex` is the tab number currently selected, with 0 (zero) for the first tab. `selectedTab` and `selectedPanel` point at the DOM objects for the `<tab>` and `<tabpanel>` matching the currently selected index. `accesskey` provides accessibility support for the whole tab box.

The DOM object for `<tabbox>` also has a range of useful methods. Look at the `<method>` tags for the `"tabbox"` binding in the XBL file for `<tabbox>` to see their names, parameters, and uses.

`<tabpanels>` is a form of the `<deck>` tag; otherwise, none of the tags associated with the tab box feature of Mozilla have any special meaning as widgets. They are all constructed out of plain boxes, styles, and XBL definitions.

8.2.6.3 `<tabs>` and `<tab>` The `<tabs>` tag is a plain box tag. It contains a set of `<tab>` tags, plus some hidden `<spacer>` tags that are used at each end for styling. In the standard Mozilla themes, the tabs cannot overlap (as, for example, the spreadsheet tabs in Microsoft Excel do), but complex and probably pointless style rules can be created to make this happen if necessary.

The `<tab>` tag is a plain box tag as well. Its rounded corners are the result of Mozilla-style extensions for borders as described in Chapter 2, XUL

Layout. The content of such a tab can be any content. If no content is supplied, then the following special attributes can be used to specify an icon and a label:

```
image label accesskey crop disabled
```

These attributes work the same as for the <button> tag. The <tab> DOM object has a Boolean `selected` property, which is `true` if the tab is the currently selected tab.

The <tabs> and <tab> tags can be specified outside of a <tabbox>, but there is little reason to do so, and they won't function properly without extra programming effort.

8.2.6.4 <tabpanels> and <tabpanel> The <tabpanels> tag is a <deck>. Each <tabpanel> is one card in the deck and is exposed when the matching <tab> tag is clicked. These tags have accessibility support and some XBL handlers for keyboard navigation; otherwise, they are unremarkable.

XUL is not HTML, and it is possible to hide form elements completely by putting them in a tab that is not the top tab. In HTML, form elements always have the highest possible CSS2 `z-index` and are impossible to cover over.

8.2.6.5 Custom Panel Systems The combination of XUL, JavaScript, and XBL provides plenty of scope for creating display systems that hide and display panel-like content. In addition to the XUL tags discussed so far, the Classic Browser includes some purpose-built panel-display systems.

The <multipanelset> and <multipanel> are tags specific to the DOM Inspector. They are programmer-defined XBL-based tags. The matching XBL definitions are stored in the DOM Inspector chrome, not in the general-purpose chrome. Figure 8.6 shows these tags at work.

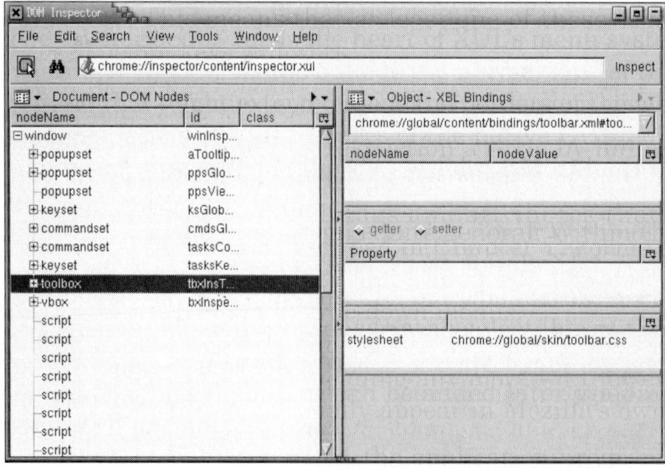

Fig. 8.6 DOM Inspector's <multipanelset> content.

This screenshot shows the DOM Inspector displaying the "XBL bindings" version of its right-hand panel. Look carefully at that panel in this screenshot. All the content beneath the <textbox> displaying the chrome://global/... URL is the <multipanelset> content, which takes up the remainder of the right panel. Inside that content area are spread six plain, thin horizontal bars. Each of these bars looks a bit like a <splitter>; they have been slightly darkened in the screenshot to make them stand out. Look at the content of that right panel: There is one bar at the top, one near the bottom, and two groups of two bars partway down. Each of these bars is a <multipanel>, and each bar may have its own user-defined content. That content appears below the bar in a panel of its own. By clicking on one of the bars, the associated content is hidden or revealed. In the screenshot, three <multipanel> tags are showing their content, and three aren't. These bars cannot be dragged.

The <floatingview> tag is a programmer-defined tag even more sophisticated than <multipanelset>. It is used in the JavaScript Debugger. It also has an XBL definition specific to the content of that application. This can also be copied and reused if required. Figure 8.7 illustrates this tag.

This screenshot shows the debugger displaying four <floatingview> tags. Three are stacked vertically on the left (with two <splitter> tags), and one fills the whole right-hand panel. This tag also consists of a header bar (e.g., "Loaded Scripts") plus user-defined content in a panel below. The icon on the right end of the header is used to hide the whole <floatingview> panel. The icon on the left end of the header hides the panel but creates a new, small window in which the same <floatingview> tag is displayed. The header bar of the <floatingview> can also be dragged over another <floatingview> tag, which allows the position of the tag to be changed.

Both <multipanelset> and <floatingview> are better suited to power users or desktop-like applications.

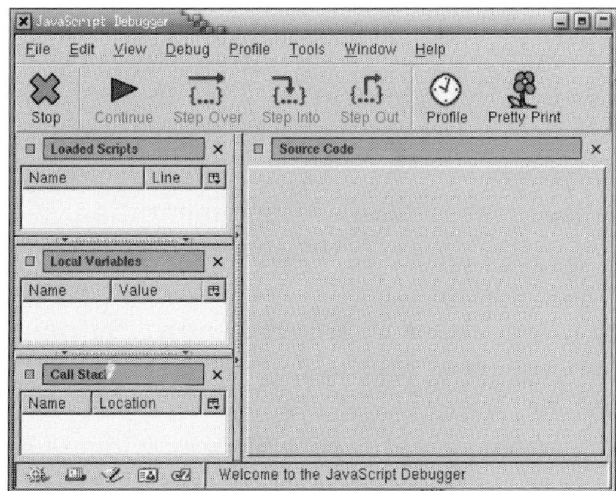

Fig. 8.7 JavaScript Debugger's <floatingview> content.

8.2.7 Special-Purpose Widgets

XUL has a few tags that defy categorization. Because they have some small relationship to navigation, they are discussed here.

8.2.7.1 `<progressmeter>` The `<progressmeter>` tag is a read-only tag with accessibility support. It provides a bar graph of one bar that gives an indication of progress. It is a `<progressmeter>` tag that you watch when waiting for a Web page to download, or when waiting for a large file to download. Special attributes for `<progressmeter>` are

```
mode value label
```

`mode` specifies the type of `<progressmeter>`. If set to `undetermined`, then the progress meter represents a task that is either underway or finished. It is similar in purpose to a "Waiting ..." message. Using Mozilla themes, this is indicated with an animated image that looks like a barber's pole. If `mode` is set to `determined`, then the meter is split crossways into two parts. One part is styled in width to match the "progress complete" fraction of the task; the other is styled in width to match the "yet to go" fraction of the task. Together they make 100% of the task. The `value` attribute (and property) specify how much of the task is completed so far, as a percent. The `label` attribute is used for accessibility and provides no visual content.

The `<progressmeter>` tag is no more than two styled `<spacer>` tags set next to each other. The UNIX version of `<progressmeter>` gets a little confused if both `mode="undetermined"` and `value` are specified as attributes, as the example in Figure 8.3 shows. The meter can also be layed out vertically with the `orient` attribute, but it looks ugly, needs extra styles to repair its appearance, and confuses the layout of the page. Avoid doing this.

To make a `<progressmeter>` physically larger, use `minheight` and `minwidth` attributes.

8.2.7.2 `<colorpicker>` The `<colorpicker>` tag is a feature of Mozilla invented for the Composer tool and the Appearance tab of the Preferences dialog box. It allows the user to select a CSS2 color from a color swatch. Both of these uses wrap other logic around the basic tag to make it more complete. `<colorpicker>` does not have a neatly modular implementation.

If you want to experiment with this tag, then a starting point is to note that the color property of the tag's DOM object is set to a value whenever one of the color patches displayed in the picker is clicked. Features beyond that are mixed up with the application uses of the tag. Examine the `colorpicker.xml` XBL definition if you wish.

`<colorpicker>` contains no special functionality or widgets except for generating a `DOMMenuItemActive` event to support accessibility requirements.

8.2.7.3 Nontags Although Mozilla's source code suggests that there might be a <fontpicker> XUL tag, there is no such thing as of version 1.21.

The Mozilla chrome contains an XBL definition of a <titlebar> tag. It is occasionally used in other XBL definitions but has no real status as a XUL tag. It is no more than an <hbox> containing a <label> and an <image>. It is intended to simulate the title bar added to a window by the desktop window manager. Explore its use if you wish.

The `FilePicker` dialog box is a XUL application that can be created by an object, not a tag of its own.

That brings to an end XUL's most obvious tags for user navigation.

8.3 Style Options

Navigation widgets benefit from a few of Mozilla's style extensions.

The `-moz-appearance` style extension supports native themes for stylable widgets. Some values are applicable to the XUL tags described in this chapter:

```
toolbox toolbar statusbar statusbarpanel progressbar progressbar-
     vertical progresschunk progresschunk-vertical tab tab-left-edge
     tab-right-edge tabpanels tabpanel scrollbartrack-horizontal
     scrollbartrack-vertical
```

Mozilla supplies the CSS2 overflow style property with some very handy alternatives as shown in Table 8.1.

Mozilla also supports `scrollbar : auto`.

Table 8.1 CSS2 overflow: scroll style extensions

Value for overflow property	Content layout	Scrollbar appearance
scroll	clipped inside a scrollable box	Scrollbars always appear.
-moz-scrollbars-none	clipped inside a scrollable box	Scrollbars never appear.
-moz-scrollbars-horizontal	clipped inside a scrollable box	Horizontal scrollbar appears.
-moz-scrollbars-vertical	clipped inside a scrollable box	Vertical scrollbar appears.

8.4 Hands On: NoteTaker Toolbars and Tabs

In this "Hands On" session, we add navigation to the NoteTaker tool. If NoteTaker were a full application window, like the Classic Browser, then a central menu bar and a set of toolbar icons would be an obvious starting point. NoteTaker, however, is an add-on tool, and its navigation is mixed up with the navigation of the host application. We have no choice but to design it as a set of pieces.

A problem with this design task is that we don't yet have enough technology to see how the NoteTaker pieces will connect to the host application. For now, we'll just create those pieces separately and wait until a later chapter to integrate them.

The pieces that make up NoteTaker's navigation system follow:

1. The dialog box we've worked on so far.
2. A note management toolbar in the main application window.
3. A menu item on the Tools menu of the main application.
4. The small, inset window that displays a note on the content of a given Web page.

One day there might also be a Note Manager item to add to the Tools menu, but not in this book. The small inset window requires special treatment. It is handled in Chapter 10, Windows and Panes. We'll address the other three points here.

The dialog box needs only limited improvement. We'll replace the clumsy `<toolbarbutton>`s, `<deck>`, and some `action()` logic with a simple `<tabbox>`. Listing 8.6 shows this new code, which is straightforward.

Listing 8.6 `<tabbox>` control for the NoteTaker Edit dialog box.

```
<tabbox id="dialog.tabs">
  <tabs>
    <tab id="dialog.tab.edit" label="Edit" accesskey="E" selected="true"/>
    <tab id="dialog.tab.keywords" label="Keywords" accesskey="K"/>
  </tabs>
  <tabpanels>
    <tabpanel>
      ... Edit pane content goes here ...
    </tabpanel>
    <tabpanel>
      <description>Content to be added later.</description>
    </tabpanel>
  </tabpanels>
</tabbox>
```

The result of this change is shown in Figure 8.8.

We must also update the `action()` function because the individual tabs can still be selected using keypresses. We need to control the `<tabbox>` from JavaScript. Looking in `xul.css` in `toolkit.jar` in the chrome, we see that there are bindings for all of `<tabbox>`, `<tabs>`, `<tab>`, and `<tabpanel>`. Examining the `tabbox.xml` file (again in the chrome) that contains these XBL bindings, we note that `<tabbox>` has a `selectedIndex` property, and that `<tab>` has a `selected` property. Again, those names match the XML attributes and standard DOM 2 HTML properties in their use. We'll use the

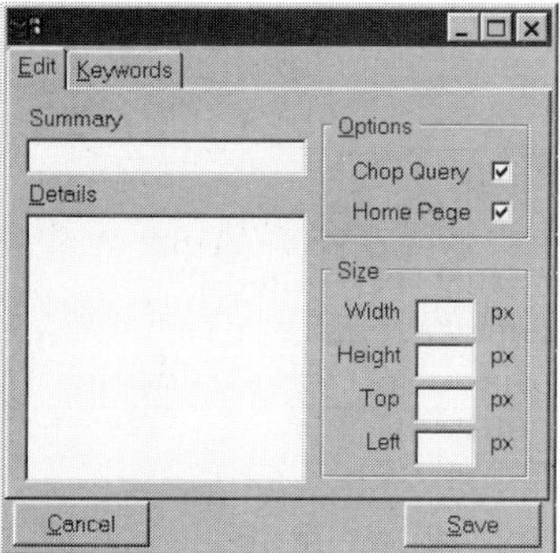

Fig. 8.8 NoteTaker dialog implemented with a `<tabbox>`.

`<tabbox>` `selectedIndex` property. The changes required for the `action()` function are shown in Listing 8.7.

Listing 8.7 New NoteTaker panel changes using `<tab>`.

```
// old code

var card = document.getElementById("dialog." + task);
var deck = card.parentNode;

if ( task == "edit" )     deck.selectedIndex = 0;
if ( task == "keywords") deck.selectedIndex = 1;

// new code

var tabs = document.getElementById("dialog.tabs");

if ( task == "edit" )     tabs.selectedIndex = 0;
if ( task == "keywords") tabs.selectedIndex = 1;
```

Clearly `<tabbox>` and `<deck>` operate in a similar manner, but `<tabbox>` has a slightly better user interface. That concludes the changes to the dialog box.

The NoteTaker toolbar is a XUL `<toolbar>` tag that will appear in the main Classic Browser window. It provides an Edit button that allows users to navigate to the main NoteTaker Edit dialog box. It also provides form items that can be used to create or delete a NoteTaker note quickly. The toolbar creates exactly the same note as the Edit dialog box, except it provides default values for nearly everything. It is a shorthand alternative like the "Google bar" toolbar sometimes used to add a search engine to the Classic Browser toolbox. When displayed by itself, the NoteTaker toolbar appears as in Figure 8.9.

Eventually this toolbar will reside in a XUL file with other GUI elements, but for the purposes of this chapter, we'll just create it by itself. Listing 8.8 shows the code required.

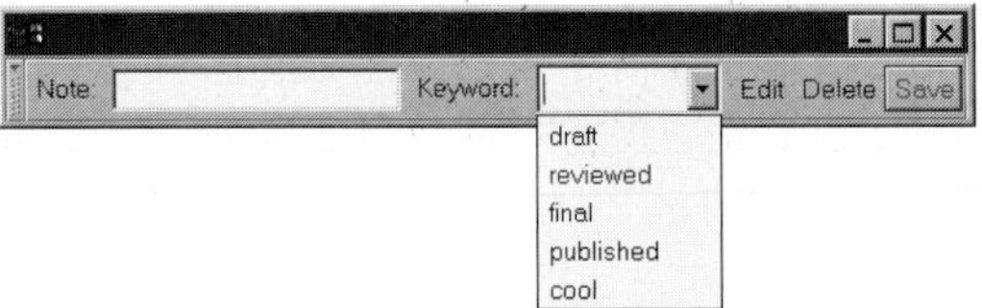

Fig. 8.9 NoteTaker note creation and navigation toolbar.

Listing 8.8 NoteTaker toolbar mock-up.

```
<?xml version="1.0"?>
<?xml-stylesheet href="chrome://global/skin/" type="text/css"?>
<!DOCTYPE window>
<window xmlns="http://www.mozilla.org/keymaster/gatekeeper/
          there.is.only.xul">
  <toolbox>
    <toolbar id="notetaker-toolbar">
      <description value="Note:"/>
      <textbox/>
      <description value="Keyword:"/>
      <menulist editable="true">
        <menupopup>
          <menuitem label="draft"/>
          <menuitem label="reviewed"/>
          <menuitem label="final"/>
          <menuitem label="published"/>
          <menuitem label="cool"/>
        </menupopup>
      </menulist>
      <toolbarbutton label="Edit"/>
      <toolbarbutton label="Delete"/>
      <toolbarbutton label="Save"/>
    </toolbar>
  </toolbox>
</window>
```

In the final NoteTaker version, the keywords listed in the dropdown menu will be dynamically created. For now, we display a fixed set. There are many questions to overcome if this toolbar is to be completed, and those questions are addressed in future chapters.

The final change for this chapter is to add an item to the Tools menu of the Classic Browser window, so that users can still open the Edit dialog box if the toolbar isn't installed. That requires only a `<menuitem>` tag, which will accompany the toolbar changes at a later date.

Adding navigation widgets is obviously easy and painless.

8.5 Debug Corner: Navigation Problems

XUL's navigation tags are so straightforward that few thorny problems exist. For difficulties with individual tags, see the text for those tags.

In more general terms, layout is the main source of problems with these navigational tags. If you push the use of these tags too far, they will not lay out properly. Use them as they are intended to be used. An alternative is to study the XUL layout mechanics behind these tags very closely and then to patch their behavior with extra style information.

The sole other problem you might encounter is difficulties with widget focus and selection. Although this system recently improved in 1.4, it is sometimes possible to confuse the window, the running platform instance, and even the Microsoft Windows desktop if the XUL code is poorly expressed. A symptom of this problem is a window that has two or more of the input cursor (used for `<textbox>` tags), the current focus and the current selection in disagreement. To test if this is caused by buggy behavior, reboot the computer and determine whether the display and the behavior of the exact same page have improved.

8.6 Summary

A professional application contains much functionality, and that is a challenge for the user to master. Application developers must exert a considerable amount of control at the design stage if the application is to be both comprehensible and efficient.

Mozilla provides a number of navigational aids at the user interface level. XUL tags like `<tabbox>`, `<toolbar>`, and `<splitter>` bring structure to the user interface, but at the expense of a more demanding interactive environment. The `<scrollbox>` tag is an early example of a powerful tag with its own custom box object.

The focus ring allows the user to move around inside a document, and the menu system lets the user break out of the document. If the user is disabled, most navigation elements are accessibility enabled to compensate.

Provided that the navigational aspects of a given window are thought through, these tools can smooth the flow of work and can compress much functionality into a given window. Using poorly conceived navigation widgets can be intrusive, cluttered, and confusing.

Navigation gives the user power to move around an application. Such freedom is complemented by the Mozilla command system, which allows users to do something after they've moved. That system is discussed in the next chapter.

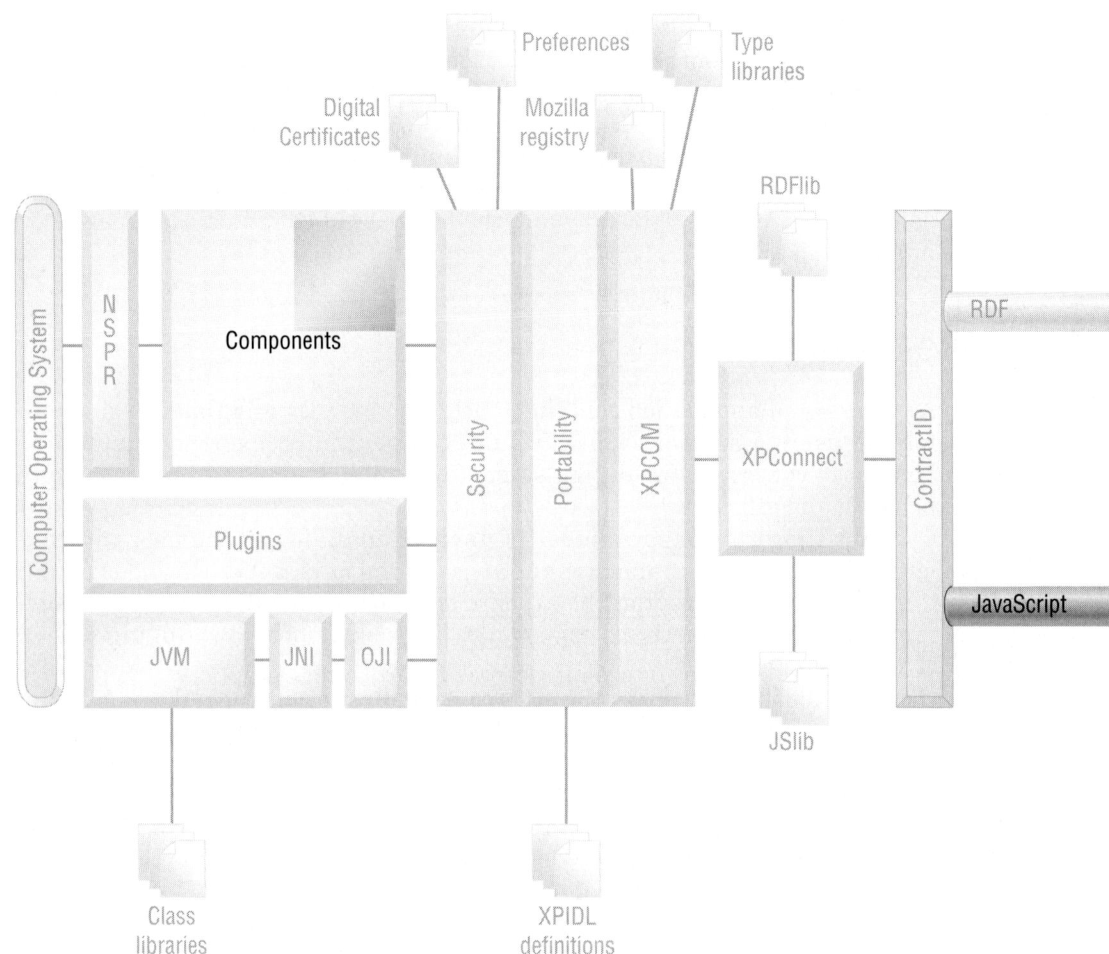
Preferences
Type libraries
Digital Certificates
Mozilla registry
RDFlib
Computer Operating System
NSPR
Components
Security
Portability
XPCOM
XPConnect
ContractID
RDF
Plugins
JavaScript
JVM
JNI
OJI
JSlib
Class libraries
XPIDL definitions

CHAPTER 9

Commands

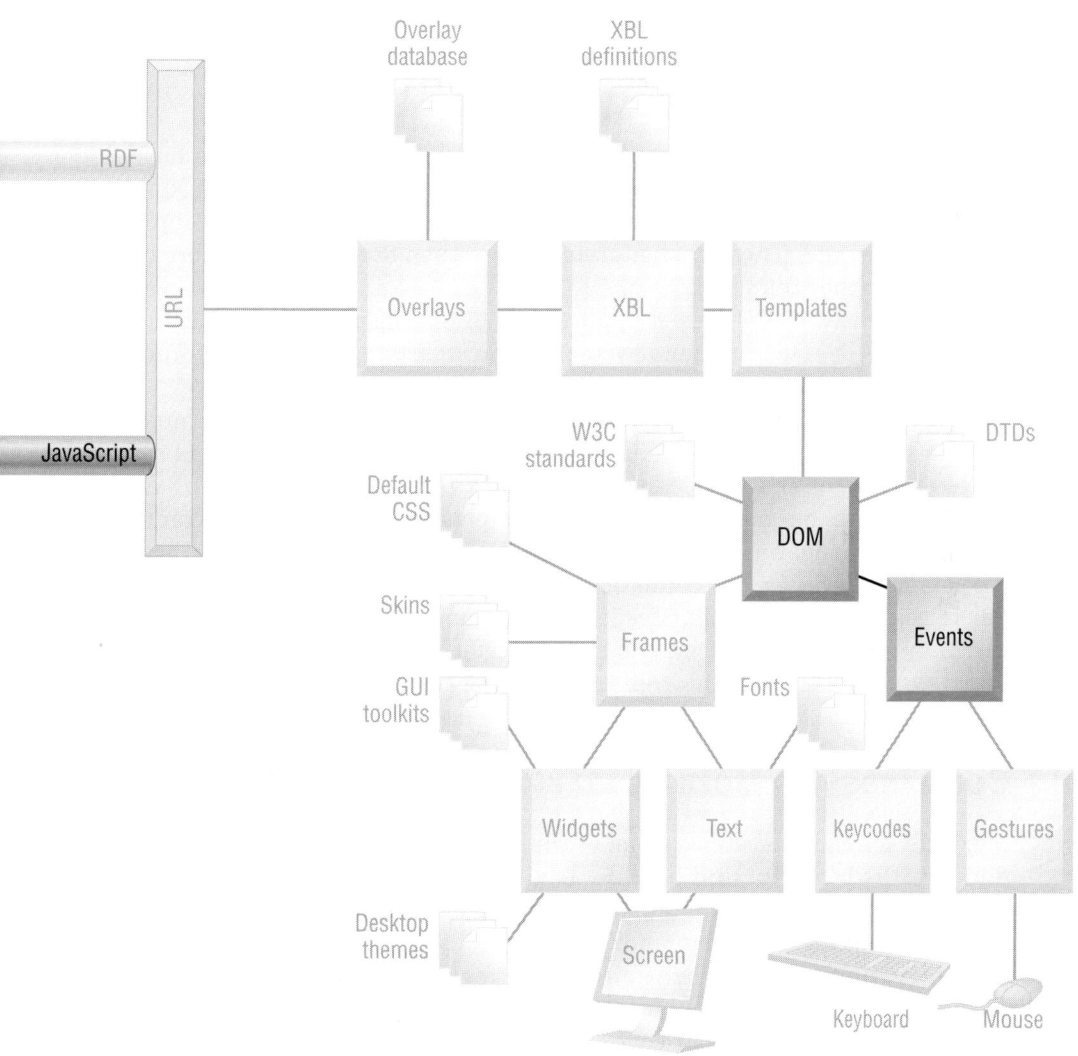

This chapter explains the Mozilla command system. The command system is used to separate the functionality of an application from its appearance. It is separate from the DOM Events model, although events and commands can interact a little.

It is critical that somehow, somewhere, the tasks that an application window performs are separated from their user interfaces. One reason for this separation is that XUL user interfaces are highly changeable, both at design time and at run time. Such interfaces are a demanding constraint on application architecture. A second reason is that many existing software engineering techniques can be applied to application tasks if they can be expressed by themselves. Use cases and functional hierarchy diagrams are examples of such techniques. Separately defining tasks also make reuse more likely. Overall, such a separation strategy is an attractive and flexible design environment.

A professionally built application will have all its commands formally identified at design time. Identifying to-be-implemented commands is part of the design breakdown process and can be used to detect convoluted, duplicate, and messy actions. These design problems can then be addressed before implementation rather than afterward.

Traditional HTML-based applications often consist of a spaghetti pile of JavaScript code. The command system is also an attempt to get away from this unstructured approach.

The NPA diagram that precedes this chapter illustrates the pieces of Mozilla that implement commands. From the diagram, the command system builds on top of the DOM and the DOM Events subsystems, but it also requires access to a number of XPCOM components. The most important components also appear as AOM objects. The XUL language has tags that support the command system, but those tags have no visible appearance; they are similar to the `<key>` tag in that respect. The command system goes further than the `<key>` tag because it has no user interface of any description. The command system is entirely internal to the platform.

9.1 Commands and Mozilla

Mozilla's command system is one of the less obvious aspects of the platform, and yet it is powerful and flexible. It allows the application programmer to think of application functionality as a set of messages. Each message is either a command or about a command. Used correctly, the command system acts as an integration and organizational point for application functions. Classic Mozilla's own use of its command system is fairly organized, but it is also buried in an abundance of other code.

The Mozilla command system is designed to support complex applications. Trivial applications do not need a command system; they can get by with simple event handlers. For complex applications, Mozilla's design goals are to provide a system where

- ☞ User interface widgets can share a command, even across source files.
- ☞ Commands can have their own state, which can be changed and reported on.
- ☞ Commands and widgets can be added or changed independently.
- ☞ All kinds of programmers, not just application programmers, are catered to.
- ☞ Useful default behavior exists.
- ☞ Simple uses are supported with trivial syntax.
- ☞ The existing DOM Event system is reused where possible.

In Mozilla, a command is very easy to find. Simple operations such as Save File, Add Bookmark, Select Content, Bold, Scroll One Page, and Undo are all commands.

It is not so easy to pin a command down in terms of code. The most obvious programming signature a command has is a simple string whose name is the command name. Such names can be predefined by the platform, or they can be programmer-defined. Unfortunately, the rest of the command infrastructure is rather spread out. Bits of the command system exist in XUL, JavaScript, XPCOM, existing chrome files, and the platform's internals.

9.1.1 Hello, World

A simple example of the command system at work is shown in Listing 9.1.

Listing 9.1 hello, world implemented as a Mozilla command.

```
<?xml version="1.0"?>
<!DOCTYPE window>
<window
  xmlns= "http://www.mozilla.org/keymaster/gatekeeper/there.is.only.xul">
  <command id="hello" oncommand="alert('hello, world');"/>
  <button label="Say It" command="hello"/>
</window>
```

The `<command>` tag implements a command, in this case a simple event handler that calls `alert()`. The `<button>` tag identifies that command by name. When the button is pressed, a DOM 2 Event with the special type command is generated, and the identified command traps this event and runs. The result is that an `alert()` box is thrown up.

Commands are not always so simple, and they do not always involve events. If a command is implemented in JavaScript, then the effect achieved in Listing 9.2 is the same as that in Listing 9.1.

Listing 9.2 hello, world implemented as a Mozilla JavaScript command.

```
<?xml version="1.0"?>
<!DOCTYPE window>
<window
  xmlns= "http://www.mozilla.org/keymaster/gatekeeper/there.is.only.xul">
  <script>
    var control = {
      supportsCommand   : function (cmd) { return true; },
      doCommand         : function (cmd) { alert(cmd + ", world"); },
      isCommandEnabled  : function (cmd) { return true; },
      onEvent           : function (event_name) {}
    };
    window.controllers.appendController(control);

    function execute(cmd) {
      var disp = document.commandDispatcher
      var cont = disp.getControllerForCommand(cmd);
      cont.doCommand(cmd);
    }
  </script>
  <button label="Say It" onclick="execute('hello')"/>
</window>
```

This code makes a custom object named `control` that implements the command; in fact, this object can implement several commands. The command is implemented in the `doCommand()` method. This object needs to be installed into the platform's command infrastructure as well. It is retrieved again when the command to be run is required. Finally, using this approach, the command can be run from any point in the XUL document that calls the `execute()` function. In this case, it is convenient to use an `onclick` handler.

This second example requires and explanation, and that is where this chapter begins. Obviously this second example is more complex than the first, and there are good reasons why using a more complex approach is sometimes better.

9.2 Command Concepts

The Mozilla command system is a command delivery system. Actual commands are implemented by the application programmer. Creating and running commands is straightforward compared to understanding how they are invoked, found, and executed.

This delivery system is very different from a traditional client-server architecture. In such an architecture, servers implement commands that are entirely separate and remote from client GUIs. They often run silently and only report when finished. For example, HTTP GET and POST requests ignore browser GUIs entirely; they merely return a status code, and possibly a new document.

Mozilla commands are not like client-server commands. Mozilla commands are close to the GUI and are likely to operate on it extensively. An example is the Bold operation in the Classic Composer (or similarly in any word processor). Bold applies a style to the current selection, which is usually on display. The Mozilla command delivery system must allow commands to be executed close to the GUI, not buried in some server. Of course, those commands can use server-like features if they so choose.

This last point means that commands are not "distant" from the application programmer. They are part of the content that the application programmers create and are loaded into the XML document environment like other content.

Mozilla uses a common piece of design called the Command pattern to separate command names from command implementations. Most modern GUI toolkits include technology based on the Command pattern. The next few topics build up a picture of how this pattern works.

9.2.1 The Functor Pattern

The Functor pattern is a well-known piece of design that is the lowest level of a command system. A functor can be implemented as an object. That object represents a single function. Listing 9.3 illustrates a functor and a normal function. Both provide an implementation of a "halve" command that calculates half of a supplied number:

Listing 9.3 Function versus functor object for a single operation.

```
// Plain function
function halve_function(num) { return num / 2.0; }

// Functor
var num = null;

var halve_functor = {
  enabled : true,
  exec : function () { num /= 2.0; return true; }
}

// Examples of use
num = halve_function(23);   // sets num = 11.5

num = 23;
halve_functor.exec();       // sets num = 11.5
```

The functor object not only seems unnecessarily complex compared with the simple function, but it also has a loose global variable to deal with. The functor, however, is far more flexible than a function because it has a standardized interface. All functor objects have a single `exec()` method that executes the implemented command and reports success or failure. All functor objects therefore look the same to an application programmer.

The example functor object also contains some state information about the command. In Listing 9.3, the very common example of an `enabled` state is illustrated. In fact, most command systems, including Mozilla's, explicitly provide support for the `enabled` state. Application code can check this state to see whether the command is available and then react appropriately. A functor can store any kind of state information about a command that seems convenient, not just an enabled state. Other states that might be stored include the command name; a unique id for the command; flags to indicate whether the command is ready, blocked, or optimized; or the language the command is implemented in or its version. Anything is possible.

In this example, the functor object modifies global data (the `num` variable) when the command executes. This keeps the `exec()` method free of parameters so that all functor objects are alike. `num` could be a property of the functor, but that is a bad design choice. It is a bad choice mostly because the functor should be stateless with respect to the command's execution. Although it contains state information about the command (the enabled property), the command's implementation does not use any of that state information when it executes. That state information is used only by those that need the functor object.

The example functor also presents an opportunity. The `exec()` method could be changed to this:

```
exec: function () { return really_halve_it(); }
```

In this alternative, the `really_halve_it()` function does all the actual work for the command and is implemented somewhere else in the application, perhaps in a library.

This last change means that the functor object contains none of the command implementation. Instead, it is the programmer's point of access to the command and its state. It is a proxy object, or a handle, or a façade. It is a representative for the real functionality. This proxy object provides part of the separation required for the Mozilla command system. Application programmers only need to know where the proxy object is, not where the final command implementation is. This is simple abstraction, similar to the design of file descriptors, symbolic links, network mapped drives, and aliases.

In non-Mozilla literature on the Functor pattern, `exec()` is often called `execute()`. In Mozilla, a proxy object (a functor) for a command is called a *command handler*. Application programmers do not use command handlers much because the higher-level concept of a controller is more convenient.

9.2.2 The Command Pattern and Controllers

The command pattern is a well-known piece of design that builds on the functor pattern. It is responsible for separating the GUI side of an application from a command's implementation. A functor removes the need to know the exact location of a command's implementation. A command pattern removes the need to know whether a command exists.

In reality, application code generally assumes that the commands that it relies on do exist. This is just a matter of forward planning, and peeking "behind the scenes."

To implement the command pattern, create an object that holds a set of functor objects. When the user supplies a command name to that object, execute the matching functor object. That is the command pattern. Listing 9.4 is an example of such an object, called a *controller* in Mozilla. This example implements a simple traffic light.

Listing 9.4 Controller object implementing a stop sign.

```
// functors
var stop = { exec: function () { top.light = "Red"; };
var slow = { exec: function () { top.light = "Amber"; };
var go   = { exec: function () { top.light = "Green"; };

// controller containing functors

var controller = {
  _cmds: { stop:stop, slow:slow, go:go },

  supportsCommand : function (cmd) {
    return (cmd in this._cmds);
  },
  doCommand : function (cmd) {
    return _cmds[cmd].exec();
  },
  isCommandEnabled : function (cmd) {
    return true;
  },
  onEvent : function (event_name) {
    return void;
  }
};

// set the light to green
controller.doCommand("go");
```

The controller object contains an object `_cmds` that maps property names to functors. In a language with full information hiding, like C++, this inner object would be private. The three functions supplied are convenience functions that take a single command name as a string and work on the stored information. `supportsCommand()` reports whether the controller knows about a particular command; `doCommand()` executes the functor for a given command. `onEvent()` is passed any event name that might be relevant to the command.

The final `isCommandEnabled()` method cheats a little. It should check the enabled property of the matching functor, but this controller knows that all three lights on the traffic light always work, so it never checks—it just returns `true`. That is just as well because none of the functors implement the enabled property shown in Listing 9.4. This choice means that the controller and the functors are dependent on each other. They appear to implement three complete functors, but in fact those three functors only implement what the controller really needs.

This last point is important. Because the controller completely hides the command implementations (functors) from the user, those implementations can be done in any way. In Mozilla, it is common for simple controllers written in JavaScript to avoid functors altogether and to implement the command states and command implementations directly. This would not be possible if the controller had a `getFunctor(cmd)` method because then the functor would be exposed to the application programmer, requiring it to be complete. Happily, the controller has no such method, at least in its simplest form, and so implementation shortcuts can be taken. Listing 9.5 shows how Listing 9.4 can be stripped down even further.

Listing 9.5 Controller object with no separate functors.

```
var controller = {
  supportsCommand : function (cmd) {
    return (cmd=="red" || cmd=="amber" || cmd=="green");
  },
  doCommand : function (cmd) {
    if ( cmd == "red"   ) top.light = "Red";
    if ( cmd == "amber" ) top.light = "Amber";
    if ( cmd == "green" ) top.light = "Green";
  },
  isCommandEnabled : function (cmd) {
    return true;
  },
  onEvent : function (event_name) {
    return void;
  }
};

// set the light to green
controller.doCommand("go");
```

In this example, the controller still acts as though three functors are present, but none are actually implemented.

Complex controllers can also benefit from direct implementation. Sometimes commands have coordination problems that are best solved in the controller. An example is implementing Undo in an editor like the Classic Composer. The controller is responsible for executing the individual commands, so it might as well be responsible for maintaining the Undo history too. If the command to execute is Redo or Undo, then the controller can read the top item from the history and can call the correct command implementation to fill the Redo/Undo request. Any such state machine should first be implemented without a controller and then hidden inside the controller so that the controller's main purpose (controlling) is still clear. Controllers are also good places to hide macro languages, synchronization, and other artifacts that are made out of commands.

9.2.3 Controller Sites

Mozilla does not stop at a single static controller. It is possible to create as many controllers as you want. This is done, for example, in Mozilla's Composer, where there are three controllers, each of which looks after a different subset of the implemented commands.

Any and all controllers created must be placed where the platform can find them. Controllers can be lodged in several places.

- Controllers can be lodged on the window object of a chrome (XUL) window.
- A few XUL tags are suitable sites. Allowed tags are `<button>`, `<checkbox>`, `<radio>`, `<toolbarbutton>`, `<menu>`, `<menuitem>`, and `<key>`.
- The XUL `<command>` tag is like a functor when it directly implements a command using an event handler. If such a tag is created, the platform effectively adds that functor to a permanent controller that it maintains internally.

Use of these sites is discussed later when command syntax is explored.

If more than one controller is lodged at a particular site, then the set of such controllers at that site is called a controller chain. Such a set of controllers is ordered, and when it is consulted, it is searched in order. This means that the first controller in a chain that can fill a request for a command implementation will be the controller that runs that command.

9.2.4 Dispatchers and Dispatching

Controllers hold a set of commands each; controller sites hold zero or more controllers each; and a command dispatcher works with a set of controller sites. Fortunately, it stops there. A command dispatcher has the job of finding and executing a particular command.

Mozilla has one dispatcher designed for HTML documents and one dispatcher designed for XUL documents. The HTML dispatcher is not visible or available to scripts under any circumstances. The XUL dispatcher can be scripted. Each XUL application window has one dispatcher object at its document root, and that object is always present and available.

The dispatcher has a getControllerForCommand() method. This method accepts a command name as a string and returns a controller that can execute that command. The dispatcher and the returned controller must be explicitly coded by an application script—they do not do any anything automatically. In the chrome files of Classic Mozilla, calls to the dispatcher are hidden inside a custom-made JavaScript function called goDoCommand(). That function is included in every Classic Mozilla window and is used in most.

The dispatcher uses state information about the current focus to work out what controllers it should provide for a given command. This state information consists of the window focus, any XUL <iframe> focus, plus any DOM element in the focus ring that is the currently focused member of the ring. In other words, the dispatcher uses all the focus hierarchy information. The dispatcher starts at the most specific item currently in focus (usually a form or menu item) and works its way up the DOM tree to the outermost window. At each focused DOM element it finds, it examines the element's controller chain for controller objects. The dispatcher then checks support for the given command by testing each controller in the chain using that controller's supportsCommand() method. The first controller object the dispatcher encounters that implements the dispatched command is returned. If none match, the dispatcher moves further up the focus hierarchy. If the dispatcher reaches the top of the focus hierarchy without finding a suitable controller, it returns null.

A XUL window and its contents are not fully initialized with the focus when that window first appears. Even though the window is the current desktop window, it can still be missing the focus. This means that installed controllers are not necessarily available, even if they are installed at the top of the current window. The application programmer must explicitly give the window focus if these window-level controllers are to be made available. The simplest way to do this is with a single line of script:

```
window.focus();
```

It is very important that focus is explicitly set both before and after a command is dispatched. If this is not done, the focus ring can become confused, and problems can occur from that point onward. This constraint has been fixed to a degree with the 1.4 release, but explicit focusing is still recommended practice.

The dispatcher does not search everywhere for a command implementation. If a focused widget has a command attribute, the dispatcher will not consider that attribute. The dispatcher only examines controllers.

9.2.5 Change Notifications

One important enhancement to the command system is a change notification system for the commands themselves. This change notification system is also called command updates.

Commands can be created and managed, commands can be found and executed, but what if commands change? Suppose a command's `enabled` state changes from `true` to `false`. How can the pieces of an application that use the command find out that it is no longer available? Change notification is the solution to this problem.

Chapter 6, Events, introduced the observer-broadcaster pattern. Mozilla uses that pattern for command state changes. Instead of one or more XUL tags observing an attribute on another XUL tag, one or more XUL tags observe the proxy functors of particular commands. If a command's state changes, the dispatcher broadcasts change notifications about its functors, and the observing XUL tags catch those notifications. Even when the functor objects are merged in with the ordinary controller code for simplicity, change notifications are still generated. Therefore, imagining that command functors are always there is convenient because it explains neatly the change notifications that are observed.

The dispatcher keeps a list of observer XUL tags in the form of DOM element objects. These are normal DOM objects but are called command updaters when used for this purpose. Methods are provided on the dispatcher for adding and removing such updaters.

A DOM Event is created and inserted into the event system using the `dispatchEvent()` method. A command change notification is inserted into the broadcaster-observer system using the `UpdateCommands()` method of the dispatcher or of the window. This causes all the observers watching the single specified event to receive a `commandupdate` event. This event acts like any event that a XUL tag might receive.

`commandupdate` events work in XUL, but not in HTML. The syntax and use of these events is covered shortly.

9.3 How Commands Are Started

Mozilla commands can be started a number of ways. Here are all the possibilities:

- If a functor or controller object is available, its methods can be called directly from JavaScript. This approach ignores the command system and treats the object like any other object.
- The dispatcher's `getControllerForCommand()` method can be called directly from JavaScript. This method is a first step toward resolving a command name into actionable code. In this case, the dispatcher searches for a suitable command implementation.
- The `doCommand()` method of a focusable XUL tag can be called directly from JavaScript. If this is done, then any `<command>` specified as a value of the `command` attribute will be executed. This method does not use the dispatcher or any controllers.

- If a key with a suitable <key> tag is pressed, or if a focusable XUL tag is clicked or stimulated with a key press, then any <command> specified as a value of the command attribute will be executed. This is the same as the doCommand() example, except that the tag or key first generates a command event. Special processing in the platform is responsible for checking both the event type and any command attribute to see if a command needs to be run.
- If a DOM Event that is a command event is created, then the dispatchEvent() method can be called on any XUL tag. If that tag is a focusable tag, then that method call is the same as the user input generating a command event. It is therefore the same as the previous case.

In any of the previous three cases, the <command> executed might elect to call the dispatcher. This links the <command> tag to a controller.

- Finally, if the UpdateCommands() method of the dispatcher is called, any outstanding change notifications will be sent to all XUL tags observing such changes. This means that a commandupdate event will be sent to all command updaters.

The Classic Mozilla applications include a function called goDoCommand(). This function manipulates the dispatcher. It is the starting point for commands in those applications. It is located in globalOverlay.js in toolkit.jar in the chrome.

9.3.1 A Virtuous Circle

A summary of the Mozilla command system reveals a convenient twist for the application programmer. A command implementation can begin and end in a single XUL document, as the earlier "hello, world" examples illustrate.

- Commands can enter the command delivery system from an ordinary piece of JavaScript. That script might itself be an event handler, perhaps for a more traditional DOM event like the click or select event. In that case, the script must be associated with a XUL tag.
- Commands can leave the command delivery system from an ordinary piece of JavaScript that implements the command. A command functor, or better still a controller, can be written to contain that implementation. That controller can also be attached to a particular XUL tag.
- Finally, a XUL tag can get feedback if a command's state changes, via the command update system.

Altogether, this means that a command can begin and end in XUL (or in XUL and JavaScript). For example, a <toolbarbutton> that initiates a command can also observe the command to see if it should stay enabled. That <toolbarbutton> can also supply the command's implementation with a controller. The dispatcher and standard event processing are the only pieces of the puzzle supplied by the platform.

9.4 Using Commands Via XUL

XUL provides the <command> tag for Mozilla commands. The tags <commandset> and <commands> are also used, but they are user-defined tags with no special meaning of their own. A <commandset> tag is used to contain a set of <command> tags and acts like the other XUL container tags, like <keyset>.

XUL also contains a number of XML attributes that can be applied to any tag. They are

```
command events targets commandupdater
```

and two event handlers:

```
oncommand oncommandupdate
```

Outside of XUL, the Mozilla Platform also has many predefined command names, but we'll discuss those in more detail later.

9.4.1 <command> and command=

The <command> tag is used to define a Mozilla command, just as the <key> tag is used to define a Mozilla keypress. It represents the command and can embody the concrete aspects of the command. In terms of a virtuous circle, the <command> tag represents both an identifier to use when invoking a command and an implementation to use when the command executes. The <command> tag has the following special attributes:

```
disabled oncommand
```

The disabled attribute can be set to true, in which case the command does nothing. oncommand is set to JavaScript code that will be used in place of any controllers that might exist. Other attributes, such as disabled, label, accesskey, and checked are sometimes added to <command>. The command update system, discussed next, uses them, but they have no special meaning to the <command> tag.

An example of <command> use is

```
<command id="test-command" oncommand="alert('executed');"/>
```

The id attribute names the command. The oncommand event handler provides an implementation for the command—it is a command handler. If this tag generates a DOM Event named command, then this handler will run. Because the <command> tag has no interactive features (no widget), it is rare that this tag ever generates a command event.

The command attribute allows other tags to be extended by the <command> tag in the same way that the key attribute allows other tags to be extended by a <key> tag. For example,

```
<mytag id="myAppTag" command="test-command"/>
```

If the <mytag> tag generates a command event of the right type, then the alert() specified earlier by the oncommand handler of the <command> tag will execute. Only the following tags can be used in place of "mytag":

```
<button> <checkbox> <radio> <toolbarbutton> <menu> <menuitem> <key>
```

When one of these tags has the focus, user interaction generates a command event automatically. The oncommand handler can be usefully added to these tags, but doing so is poor practice. It is better to record all known commands centrally in <command> tags than to fragment the commands across all the application's widgets.

The oncommand handler can also be fired directly from JavaScript:

```
var target = document.getElementById("mytag-id");
target.doCommand();
```

If the oncommand attribute is specified, then the command system's dispatcher is not used, and no controllers are consulted. Only the code in the handler is executed. If the handler code wishes, it can call the dispatcher, which then operates as it always does.

There is one further use of the command attribute. The XBL tag extension system has a <handler> tag, which allows an ordinary DOM Event like click to be translated into a specified command. The command attribute is used to do this in the XBL <handler> tag.

In the XBL case, there is no matching <command> tag for the <handler> tag. The value of the command attribute is sent straight to the dispatcher as the sole argument of getControllerForCommand(). Therefore, command in XBL is different from command in XUL.

9.4.2 commandupdater="true" and oncommandupdate=

If a XUL tag contains this attribute, then it is a command updater and will receive change notifications about commands. These change notifications are received through a broadcaster-observer arrangement. When the platform's XUL parser discovers the commandupdater attribute, it automatically registers the tag holding that attribute as an observer of a broadcaster inside the dispatcher. This broadcaster causes commandupdate events to be placed on all its observers when the UpdateCommands() method of the dispatcher is run. In summary, if a commandupdate event occurs, this tag's oncommandupdate event handler will fire. An example of this code is simply

```
<mytag commandupdater="true" oncommandupdate="update_all()"/>
```

The update_all() function is any custom script that is knowledgeable about the current application. It does whatever work is required to identify the commands that have changed. It also performs any consequential actions. For example, there is such a function in Classic Mozilla. The file globalOverlay.js in toolkit.jar in the chrome contains goUpdateCommand() (and other go... functions). That function performs some standard processing associated with command updates. It sets the disabled attribute of a <command> tag by checking the isCommandEnabled() method of the controller for a command that is passed to it as an argument.

A further example of command update is discussed in "How to Make a Widget Reflect Command State."

A filter can also be applied to a command updater tag:

```
<mytag commandupdater="true" events="focus blur" targets="*"
     oncommandupdate="update_all()"/>
```

The events attribute restricts the events that will cause a commandupdate event. It can be a space- or comma-separated list of events and can include command names. The targets attribute has the same syntax, except the list of names consists of tag ids. It is rarely used and is not recommended. It restricts the events reported on to those whose event target (tag) is in the supplied list of ids. The default for both events and targets is "*", meaning all.

Even if the targets attribute is specified, the commandupdate event only goes to the commandupdater's tag, not to the target tags. We're still waiting to see what this functionality finally evolves into.

A commandupdate event can be synthesized from JavaScript, just as a command event can be. To do this, call the UpdateCommands() method of the dispatcher. In the case of XUL-defined commands, this is not a very flexible or useful arrangement because the simple event handlers used in oncommand have no state. Only when JavaScript is used to construct commands (using controller objects) do commandupdate events start to make sense.

9.4.3 <commandset> and <commands>

The <commandset> tag is an user-defined tag with no special meaning. It is sometimes used to group commands.

Sometimes a XUL application is built from a number of separate definition files. In that case, the <commandset> tag often has an id that allows those separate definitions to be merged, as described in Chapter 12, Overlays and Chrome.

The second use of <commandset> is to be a command updater. Such a tag is well placed to handle command updates because all its direct children are typically <command> tags. When a commandupdate event occurs, the oncommandupdate handler of a <commandset> tag can iterate through its children and get each one to check its status. This strategy is used throughout the Classic Mozilla's chrome.

Finally, the `<commands>` tag is also a user-defined tag with no special meaning. It is used just to group `<commandset>` tags. It is also exploited by Mozilla's use of the overlay system. Matters can be arranged using overlays so that all `<commandsets>` distributed across an application's files end up as children of the `<commands>` tag.

9.5 Using Commands Via the AOM

Direct use of XUL is a convenient way to implement simple commands, but it doesn't allow for imaginative designs. Such designs require scripting, and such scripts can work with several objects.

Every XUL tag in the document hierarchy can be an event target, and so every tag supports the `dispatchEvent()` method. Which implementation of a command is executed ultimately depends on what DOM element the `dispatchEvent()` method is called on.

The `document` object in a XUL document contains a `commandDispatcher` property. This property is the sole command dispatcher. It contains the `UpdateCommands()` method and is also used to add command updaters. The command dispatcher also provides an interface that allows the application programmer to move the focus of the document through the widgets in the focus ring.

Every XUL tag in the document hierarchy also has a `controllers` property. This property is an object that is a collection of controllers. This set of controllers is the set that the dispatcher will look through for a controller that can execute the command dispatched. Because only some tags fully support the command system, and because all commands instigated by the user start with a `command` event, it is important to choose the correct DOM object for a command. If you choose the wrong object, the dispatcher will look through the wrong set of controllers.

- ☞ In XUL, this `controllers` array is empty for all tags except `<textbox>`. `<textbox>` has one controller item because it is constructed from HTML's `<input type="textbox">`.
- ☞ The `window.document` property is not a tag and does not have a `controllers` property.
- ☞ The window object itself is not a XUL tag, but it has a `controllers` property, whose array contains a single controller. This single controller is called the focus controller and is responsible for managing window focus and focus ring events.

Individual, application-specific controllers are the objects that application programmers are most interested in. No such controllers exist by default. Even after creation they are not accessible outside the chrome. It is up to the application programmers to create these objects, which may be built with or without functors.

Command functors managed by controllers can be created directly in JavaScript. Such functors must support the `nsIControllerCommand` interface, which looks like this when implemented in JavaScript:

```
var functor = {
  isCommandEnabled        : function (cmd) { … },
  getCommandStateParams : function (cmd) { },
  doCommandParams         : function (cmd) { },
  doCommand               : function (cmd) { … }
}
```

Normally a functor implements only one command, but in Mozilla a functor may implement many commands at once. This is just an extra feature in case it is efficient to implement several commands with one functor. The single argument of each method of the functor states which command implemented by the functor should be acted on.

In the ordinary case, the `Param`-style methods are never used, and so do nothing. Such a functor is then registered with a command controller object.

If a controller exists, functor registration can easily be done using the interfaces available, for example:

```
controllers.getControllerAt(2).registerCommand(cmd,functor);
```

In practice, only one reusable controller exists, and it is not immediately available in the AOM (it must be created via XPCOM). Therefore, controllers are also made from scratch using JavaScript. Such a controller object must implement the `nsIController` interface. In JavaScript:

```
var controller = {
  supportsCommand  : function (cmd) { … },
  isCommandEnabled : function (cmd) { … },
  doCommand        : function (cmd) { … },
  onEvent          : function (event) { … }
}
```

The functors can then be used, declared, or even implemented inside the body of the controller object, as illustrated earlier. If a more structured approach is desired, the controller can also implement the `nsIController-Context` interface. In that case, the functor objects can be added and removed from the controller at run time, after the controller is initialized with an `nsIControllerCommandTable` object. Such an object can also be created in JavaScript.

After the controller is complete, the next task is to add it to the appropriate tag's DOM element object. This DOM element can only be one of a few tags.

```
aNode.controllers.appendController(controller);
```

The onEvent() method only fires if application code calls it explicitly. It does not fire automatically.

The window object's controllers collection is the best place to put general-purpose commands.

In the case of a pure XUL window, the final implementation step is to initialize the focus so that the dispatcher has at least a focused window to examine when a command is invoked. The simplest way to do this is to focus the whole window, using the window AOM object:

```
window.focus()
```

If this is not done, then you must rely on some other piece of script (or the user) setting the focus before any commands are run.

The Addressbook of the Mozilla Messenger client is a good example of the command system at work. Two controllers are created there, one for each <tree> tag in the Addressbook dialog box. The file abCommon.js in the chrome file messenger.jar is a good starting point for study.

9.5.1 How to Make a Widget Reflect Command State

One of the main goals of the command system is to allow user-visible widgets to change dynamically. For example, a menu offering Cut, Copy, and Paste operations should have the Paste operation grayed out (disabled) if nothing has been cut or copied yet. Any state information responsible for such changes should rest with the command that implements Paste, not with the GUI widget. This is because the Paste action might be offered to the user by several different widgets, such as a menu item and a toolbar button.

The command and command update systems support this design. Listing 9.6 shows a XUL fragment that is half of such a system.

Listing 9.6 Controller object with no separate functors.

```
<updater commandupdater="true" oncommandupdate="update()">
  <command id="paste" oncommand="doPaste()"/>
</updater>
<button label="Paste1" command="paste" observes="paste"/>
<description value="Paste Enabled" observes="paste"/>
```

The <updater> tag is a user-defined tag, which could alternately be called <commandset>—that tag name is not so important. The <button> and <description> tags represent two places that reflect the state of the Paste command. Since <description> does not have special support for the command attribute, it does not act as a user-input widget, it acts as a read-only status indicator.

The doPaste() function is the implementation of the Paste operation. This function might or might not require the dispatcher, depending on how it is implemented. The update() function is responsible for reflecting the state of the command into the GUI. It also could be implemented with or without the dispatcher, but if good design is used, it will look for a controller or functor representing the command and extract required state from there.

The second half of this system is JavaScript. Listing 9.7 shows the `update()` function.

Listing 9.7 Controller-based command updater.

```
function update()
{
  var cont, node;
  cont = document.commandDispatcher.getControllerForCommand('paste');
  node = document.getElementById('paste');

  if ( !cont || !node ) return;

  if ( cont.isEnabled(cmd) )
  {
    node.removeAttribute("disabled");
    node.removeAttribute("value");
  }
  else
  {
    node.setAttribute("disabled", true");
    node.setAttribute("value", "Paste Disabled");
  }

  if ( cont.clipboardEmpty() )
  {
    node.setAttribute("value", "Nothing to Paste");
  }
}
```

This function is tied to certain commands: It knows only about the Paste command. It seeks out the implementation for that command and then examines it with `isEnabled()` and `clipboardEmpty()`. `isEnabled()` is a standard method of a controller, but this controller must have extra features because `clipboardEmpty()` is new. This particular command has two states: whether it is enabled, and whether there is anything in the clipboard. If there is nothing in the clipboard, then there is nothing to paste.

Based on the analysis of these states, the `update()` function loads the `<command>` tag with extra XUL attributes. None of these attributes is meaningful for `<command>`. They are put there only so that the widgets observing the `<command>` tag can pick them up. Both the `<button>` and the `<description>` tags pick up attributes `disabled` and `value`, but `disabled` only has special meaning for `<button>`, and `value` only has meaning for `<description>`.

The net result is that the widget tags are updated, and their appearance changes. All this is in response to one call to the `UpdateCommands()` method of the dispatcher, which starts the change notification/command update process.

Note that there are two broadcaster-observer systems at work in this example. The first is the automatic registration of the `<updater>` tag as a command updater with the dispatcher. The second is the application-specific `observes` attribute put onto the two widget tags. This second system is just a design choice; it is equally possible to update the widget tags directly from the `update()` method, perhaps using ids or, in fact, any other approach.

9.6 Commands and XPCOM Components

Although functors and controllers can be created entirely in JavaScript, XPCOM equivalents also exist. The simple combination of functor, controller, and dispatcher can also be enhanced in a number of ways. These enhancements allow command implementations to be added or removed from controllers dynamically. They also allow extra information to be associated with a given command. None of these enhancements is required for ordinary use of the command system.

If these enhancements are considered, then Mozilla has enough command-related XPCOM objects and interfaces to make your head swim. A naming policy that concatenates and reuses descriptive keywords does not help; instead, it tends to make the different interfaces blend into each other until they all look very similar.

The only way to proceed is to try to characterize each interface until it stands out a little. That is the strategy adopted here. Table 9.1 is based on Mozilla 1.4. Beware that a few of these interfaces are not "frozen" for that version; they may have minor changes in later versions.

Table 9.1 XPCOM components that contribute to Mozilla command infrastructure

Interface name	Useful in scripts?	Existing XPCOM implementations	Purpose
nsICommand		Although it seems a logical name, no such interface exists	
nsICommandHandler		@mozilla.org/embedding/browser/nsCommand-Handler;1	Lowest-level command implementation—not intended for JavaScript use.
nsICommandHan-dlerInit		@mozilla.org/embedding/browser/nsCommand-Handler;1	Used to initialize nsICommandHandler objects.
nsIController	✓	@mozilla.org/embedcomp/base-command-controller;1	A basic controller, with command table support.

Table 9.1 XPCOM components that contribute to Mozilla command infrastructure (Continued)

Interface name	Useful in scripts?	Existing XPCOM implementations	Purpose
nsIControllerContext	✓	@mozilla.org/embedcomp/ base-command-controller;1	Used to initialize a controller.
nsIController-CommandTable	✓	@mozilla.org/embedcomp/ controller-command-table;1	A mutable collection of commands.
nsICommandController		@mozilla.org/embedcomp/ base-command-controller;1	Poorly named interface that adds parameterized command calls (commands with arguments) to a basic controller.
nsIController-CommandGroup		@mozilla.org/embedcomp/ controller-command-group;1	A mutable collection of commands used to give a set of commands group identity.
nsIControllerCommand	✓	None	A basic functor.
nsICommandManager		@mozilla.org/embedcomp/ command-manager;1	Exposes intermediate features of a functor object.
nsICommandParams		@mozilla.org/embedcomp/ command-manager;1	A data structure used as a parameter list for parameterized command execution.
nsIControllers	✓	None	The controllers collection that is a property of DOM elements.
nsIDOMXULCommand Dispatcher	✓	The dispatcher is not an XPCOM component.	The XUL command dispatcher.
nsPICommandUpdater		Internal interface of no use to applications	
nsISelectionController		Nothing to do with command delivery at all	
nsIEditorController		@mozilla.org/editor/composercontroller;1 @mozilla.org/editor/editor-controller;1	Two controllers used in the Mozilla Composer tool.
nsITransaction nsITransactionList nsITransaction-Manager	✓	@mozilla.org/transaction-manager;1	Three interfaces useful when controllers become complicated. Use these data structures to implement undo/redo, macros, history, auditing, and other advanced controller functionality.

Several interfaces that are used to implement the command-line syntax also exist; they can be used to start platform windows. Those interfaces have nothing to do with the command delivery system.

9.7 Existing Commands

So far this discussion has covered XUL, AOM, and XPCOM aspects of command delivery in the Mozilla Platform. Mozilla, however, is a finished application (Classic Mozilla) as well as a platform. Some application commands are provided with the platform. Application programmers sometimes reuse or exploit these platform features. There are several opportunities to do so.

The focus controller is a very simple example of reusing existing technology. This controller is always available in a XUL window. The command dispatcher contains `advanceFocus()` and `rewindFocus()` methods that automate Tab-style navigation that the user normally does. These methods effectively send commands to the focus controller. The controller can also be exploited for command updates. A command updater tag can receive change notifications as a result of focus events from the focus controller. Why the controller sends two `commandupdate` events for each navigation step through the focus ring is not clear at this point.

Another kind of reuse is theft. The file `globalOverlay.js` in the chrome file `toolkit.jar` contains handy function for managing commands and controllers. The command architecture used in the Messenger Addressbook and in the three-controller system used in the Composer are good enough to use as guides. Some of the keyboard-command bindings are modular enough that you can reuse the overlay files that hold them.

Beyond that, reuse of existing Mozilla commands is a little harder to achieve. There is one special case where a great deal of reuse is possible.

Classic Mozilla's Composer, Messenger, and Navigator tools implement about a hundred commands. A moment's thought reveals that even trivial user actions must ultimately be some kind of command because even trivial actions make changes to the user interface. This means that everything from the minor (e.g., "Select Current Word") and the ordinary (e.g., "Delete Message") to the substantial (e.g., "Load URL") must have an implementation inside the Web application suite. Many of these commands are implemented efficiently in C++, and many are available directly in JavaScript in the chrome.

If your application is similar to Classic Mozilla's in purpose (perhaps another browser variation), then these commands may be reused. If your goal is to customize the existing Mozilla application deeply, then familiarity with these commands is essential. If your application is an add-on to a browser, it is also important to avoid clashing with the names of existing commands. Unfortunately, these names are not centralized. This is partly because different programmer teams worked on different parts of the Classic suite. Classic Mozilla does attempt to use the same names for the commands that have the same purpose in several applications.

A readable example of Classic Mozilla commands can be seen in `ComposerCommands.js` in the `comm.jar` chrome file.

It is easy to get excited about the availability of all these commands, but reuse of them is somewhat limited. In the end, the success of a new application depends on its unique value, not on how well it mimics something that has gone before. If your application works the same as an existing application, why did you bother building it? Most new applications should contain at least some new commands. If you manage a little reuse along the way, more power to you.

This last kind of reuse is required in a minor way with the `<textbox>` XUL tag. It is possible to do simple editing operations inside this widget. Such operations are implemented by Mozilla commands that contribute toward Mozilla's finished HTML browser. If all of Mozilla's commands are stripped away from your application, then at least this much must be re-implemented if form elements are to be supported properly.

9.8 Style Options

There are no styles that apply to Mozilla's command system.

9.9 Hands On: Command Design

To date, the NoteTaker example has relied on a simple `action()` function to implement all the tasks that need scripting. NoteTaker is a small project and doesn't require heavy engineering, but for the sake of experience we use this session to wrap those actions up in commands. In order to do this, we need to

1. Design the commands.
2. Implement the commands.
3. Install the command implementations.
4. Invoke commands from wherever they are needed.

The first step is design. The NoteTaker tool has fixed functionality, so there is a fixed and known list of commands. Furthermore, none of the NoteTaker commands can be disabled. Together, these two statements mean that the controllers that handle the commands won't ever change or change state, and so there will be no `commandupdate` events. We therefore have the simple case where the required command system is entirely static after it is set up.

The command names we choose to implement are an issue. By using the command system, we're sharing the command name namespace with everyone else's code. In the Edit dialog box, this is a lesser issue because there is no other application code present. In the main browser window, however, the NoteTaker toolbar and Tools menu item must share the command system with the rest of the browser application. The command names we choose shouldn't clash with that application.

To prevent clashes, there are two solutions. One solution is to choose carefully command names that have the same spelling and meaning as existing commands. When a "save" command is issued, all interested parties, including NoteTaker, might receive this command. This solution is a very complex integration task. A second solution, chosen here, is to go it alone and make sure that the command names implemented don't clash with any other names. To that end, we'll prefix all our commands with "`notetaker-`". That is a little verbose, but recall that NoteTaker is a unique package name.

In the last chapter, we had four possible arguments to the `action()` function:

```
edit keywords cancel save
```

These tasks could be designed better. `save`, for example, both saves the note and closes the dialog box; those two steps could be separate commands. `edit` and `keywords` are really navigation instructions and don't match the intended purpose of the Edit button on the toolbar, which is to open the Edit dialog box. A better list of commands is

1. Open the dialog box. Used by the Tools menu item and the Edit button on the toolbar.
2. Close the dialog box. Used by the Cancel button and the Save button on the dialog box.
3. Load the current note. Used by the onload handler in the Edit dialog box.
4. Save the current note. Used by the Save button on the toolbar and on the Edit dialog box.
5. Delete the current note. Used by the Delete button on the toolbar.
6. Navigate to the Edit tab. Used by a keyboard shortcut in the Edit dialog box.
7. Navigate to the Keywords tab. Used by a keyboard shortcut in the Edit dialog box.

No doubt we'll find more commands as more chapters pass. So far, our new commands are

```
notetaker-open-dialog notetaker-close-dialog notetaker-load
     notetaker-save notetaker-delete notetaker-nav-edit notetaker-
     nav-keywords
```

Any syntax convention could be used; here we're just following a convention of dash-separators sometimes used by the platform itself. So we're now finished designing the commands.

To implement the commands, we need to use the <command> tag and command= attribute, or we can create a command controller on some DOM object, or we can do both. We choose to use a command controller to start with because it clarifies the discussion earlier, and because it can be used as a debugging aid.

Although we could control everything from one sophisticated controller instance, it's neater and cleaner to use more than one. We'll create one controller that handles all the NoteTaker commands and then use it several times. Just for fun we'll add a second controller implementation; it will pick up any stray commands we haven't planned for.

Our `action()` function has served us well, and there's no need to remove it. We'll create controller objects that call the `action()` method when commands arrive. In design pattern language, the command functors will be aggregated into the controller objects, which will delegate the execution of the actual command to the `action()` function. In short, Listing 9.8 shows the controller we need.

Listing 9.8 NoteTaker command controller.

```
var notetaker = {
  _cmds : { "notetaker-open-dialog":true,
            "notetaker-close-dialog":true,
            "notetaker-load":true,
            "notetaker-save":true,
            "notetaker-delete":true,
            "notetaker-nav-edit":true,
            "notetaker-nav-keywords":true
          },
  supportsCommand   : function (cmd) { return (cmd in this._cmds); },
  isCommandEnabled  : function (cmd) { return true; },
  doCommand         : function (cmd) { return action(cmd);},
  onEvent           : function (cmd) {}
};
```

Clearly this object is just a big wrapper around the `action()` function, one that makes it fit the command infrastructure of the platform. It is particularly simple because (1) no commands can be disabled, and (2) commands cannot be added dynamically. The second just-for-fun controller we'll create looks like Listing 9.9.

Listing 9.9 NoteTaker command detective.

```
var detective = {
  supportsCommand   : function (cmd) { return true; },
  isCommandEnabled  : function (cmd) { return true; },
  doCommand         : function (cmd) {
    throw("NoteTaker detective called on command: " + cmd);
    return true;
  }.
  onEvent           : function (cmd) {}
};
```

This controller is a fake; it accepts and pretends to run all commands, and reports what it sees to the JavaScript console. It can be used to detect all command requests. So both controllers are now implemented, except for the little matter of the action() function.

Finally, these controllers must be installed on some DOM object. We choose to install these commands on the DOM object for the <window> tag (the window AOM object). We can install on one of two windows: the main browser window (for the toolbar and Tools menu item) and the Edit dialog box. We'll install both the notetaker and the detective controllers in both cases, for a total of four controllers installed. Both windows will have support for all seven commands, but each window will use only a selection of that support. Here is a simple function that installs controllers for one window.

```
function install_controllers()
{
  window.controllers.appendController(notetaker);
  window.controllers.appendController(detective);
}
```

Since the detective controller is added second, it will only pick up what the notetaker controller misses. These two controllers, the install_controllers() function, and a call to that function can all be put into one JavaScript file. If we include it with a <script src="controllers.js"> tag in all relevant windows, then each window will get separate but identical controller objects.

Invoking the commands is also easy. A simple function holds the required logic:

```
function execute(cmd)
{
  window.focus();
  try {
    var disp = window.document.commandDispatcher;
    var ctrl = disp.getControllerForCommand(cmd);
    ctrl.doCommand(cmd);
  }
catch (e) {
    throw (" Command Unknown: " + cmd + ". Error: " + e);
  }
  window.focus();
}
```

This execute() function sets a command on its way; it will throw an error if the dispatcher can't find a suitable controller. The window.focus() calls that precede and follow the command dispatch are critical; they ensure that the dispatcher has something to work with, and that the window returns to a sensible state when the dispatcher is finished.

In the browser window, we could instead use an existing function: goDoCommand(). That function is provided in globalOverlay.js in toolkit.jar in the chrome. It is almost the same as execute() but allows an unknown command to be submitted. In our case, we want an error rather than silence if an unknown command appears. The `globalOverlay.js` file contains many short functions used by Mozilla Classic.

This `execute()` function is put everywhere that a command might occur. We replace all calls to the `action()` function with calls to `execute()` in the dialog box. That means the <key> tags change like so:

```
<key key="e" oncommand="action('edit')"/>
<key key="e" oncommand="execute('notetaker-nav-edit')"/>
```

Previously we didn't implement anything for the buttons at the base of the dialog box. Now we can at least call the right command. We can call `execute()` from an `onclick` handler on each button, or we can send the button events to a <command> tag. Let's do the latter. The Cancel button goes from

```
<button label="Cancel" accesskey="C"/>
```

to

```
<button label="Cancel" accesskey="C" command="dialog.cmd.cancel"/>
```

The command= attribute requires a matching <command> tag, which is

```
<command id="dialog.cmd.cancel"
         oncommand="execute('notetaker-close-dialog')"/>
```

Let's review the way this works: The user generates events that include a "command" DOM 2 Event by clicking the button. The <command> tag is the listener for that event, which is a result of the `command` attribute on the <button> tag. When that event occurs, the <command> tag takes over, and its `oncommand` handler then fires. That is the end of the event's influence. When the `oncommand` handler fires, it runs `execute()`, which sends a named command to the controller that the dispatcher finds for it. The controller runs the command using the `action()` function and then finishes. After that, the `command` event (and other events like click) begins its bubbling phase. Since there are no bubbling phase handlers installed, no further event processing occurs.

Using <command> tags for both the Save and Cancel buttons yields this XUL:

```
<commandset>
  <command id="dialog.cmd.save"
     oncommand="execute('notetaker-save');execute('notetaker-close-
     dialog');"/>
  <command id="dialog.cmd.cancel"
     oncommand="execute('notetaker-close-dialog');"/>
</commandset>
```

The Save button causes two commands to be run. We could collapse these two commands into one, but it's worth making the point that any number of commands can be run at a given opportunity. By using <command> and <key> tags, we've managed to confine all the event handlers for the dialog to the top of the XUL document. We can do exactly the same thing for the toolbar buttons, except three `<command>` tags are required instead of two.

Everything is in place now except for an updated `action()` function. We can write two versions of this function—one for each window that gains a `notetaker` controller. That saves the function from having to work out what window it is being run in. We'll just include a different `.js` file in the toolbar XUL and in the Edit dialog box XUL.

For the Edit dialog box, all we need to do is update the `action()` logic to use the new command names. For the toolbar, we're not sure what to do yet, so the `action()` function just reads:

```
function action(cmd) {};
```

That ends our experimentation with commands for now.

9.10 Debug Corner: Catching Unexpected Commands

When the command system and the focus system of the Mozilla Platform interact, some very subtle problems can occur. It is very important that the focus is correctly set up when a XUL window first appears. This means a call to `window.focus()`, or `window.content.focus()`. Such a call is less necessary in recent versions, but it remains good defensive programming.

If this is not done, and an application that has or acquires focus problems is run, then it is possible for both the Mozilla Platform and the desktop environment to become confused. Just shutting down the platform is not always enough. On Microsoft Windows at least, sometimes it is also necessary to reboot in order to clean out problems that result from poorly organized focus.

In the end, commands are just strings, and a string can contain anything. When working with commands, it is important to remember that those strings form a simple namespace that should be managed properly. Do not be tempted to send randomly named commands from random places in the code, just because they're easy to dispatch.

There are numerous examples of code in the Mozilla Platform and Mozilla applications where lazy checking of data values is done. A very common example is XML attributes that can be set to boolean values. The platform typically checks for `"true"`, and assumes that anything else must be false. This is a quick way to do development, but it makes debugging harder because many invalid values are accepted or ignored by the systems that read them. This is especially true for commands, which include a layer of complexity (the dispatcher) between the command invocation and the command implementation.

When developing an application, command strings should always be strictly evaluated, and there should be no default or unmatched case. Such a case is a bottomless pit for accidental typos and other small mistakes, which would otherwise yield a useful error. When commands are scheduled from timed scripts and other asynchronous tasks, it is even more important that they are properly recognized. You should always know all the commands that are being dispatched to your code.

This strict evaluation is not implemented in the Mozilla Classic because of that application's desire to be open to enhancements. For applications that are point solutions, there is no reason to leave this strict evaluation out. Only in rare cases (like extensible text adventures such as MUDs [Multi-User Dungeons—text games], IRC, and online games) should the command set be left open.

The "detective" controller, illustrated in "Hands On" in this chapter, is one way of ensuring that nothing slips past you. This controller should never receive a command; if it does, something is wrong, and it needs to be fixed.

Note that unexpected commands and unexpected events are different issues. It is not necessary to block or catch unexpected events. Such events can be produced by the global observer service discussed in Chapter 6, Events.

9.11 Summary

Mozilla provides a command specification and delivery system. This system encourages functional analysis of applications. Such functional analysis allows the application programmer to separate application tasks from the visual appearance of the application. That separation encourages a clean design. It protects implemented commands from most changes in the fragile and fashion-conscious GUI of the application. The command system can automatically sort out where a command is implemented, perform that command, and pass on advice about command changes.

The command system is an example of Mozilla-specific functionality that is entirely nonvisual. It is also separate to the W3C standards–based DOM Event system. The mechanics of the command system support the visual appearance of an application, but it contributes nothing to that appearance directly.

The command system is also flexible. For custom applications it provides a small framework on which application-specific commands can be hung. For minor enhancements to existing Mozilla applications, the command system provides a large collection of ready-to-use commands.

Like the focus ring of the last chapter, each instance of the command system is limited to a single platform window. The next chapter explores in general terms the use of more than one window at a time.

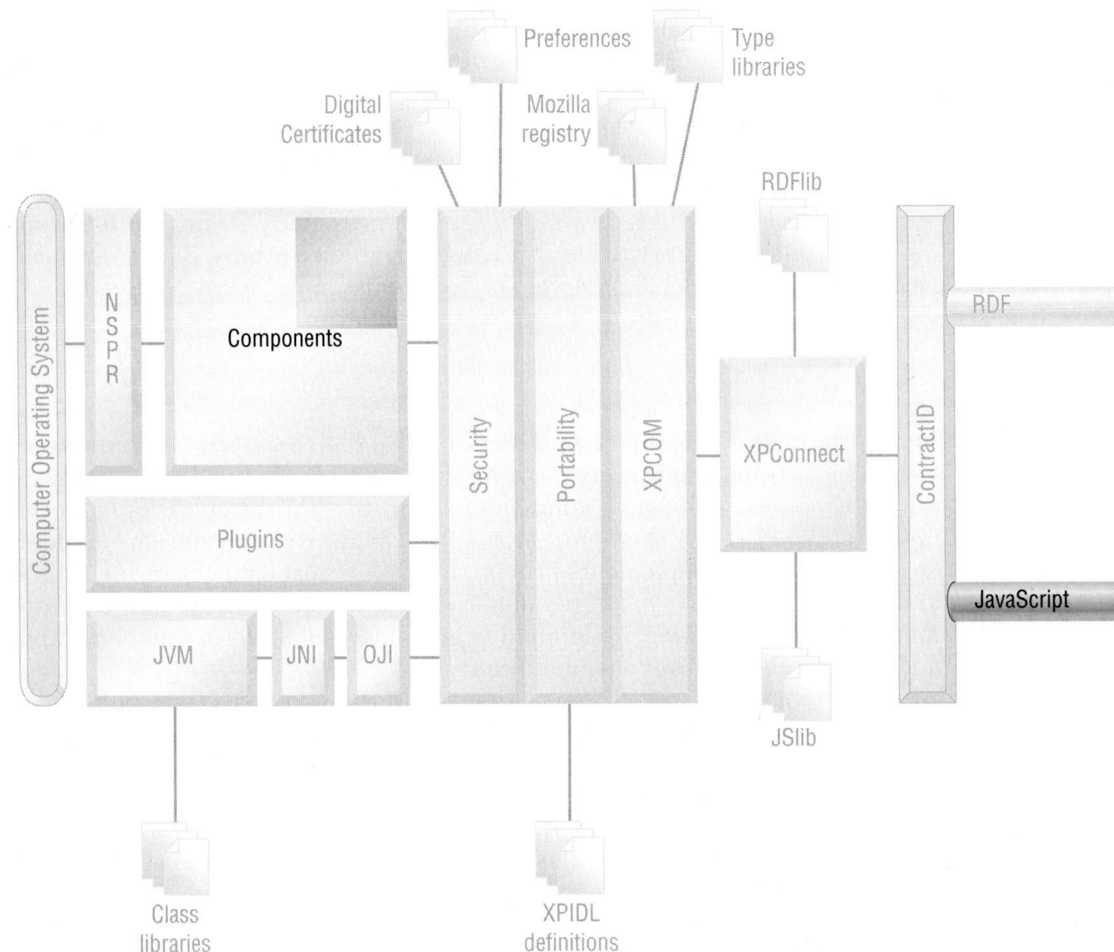

Preferences
Type libraries
Digital Certificates
Mozilla registry
RDFlib
RDF
Computer Operating System
NSPR
Components
Security
Portability
XPCOM
XPConnect
ContractID
Plugins
JavaScript
JVM
JNI
OJI
JSlib
Class libraries
XPIDL definitions

C H A P T E R 10

Windows and Panes

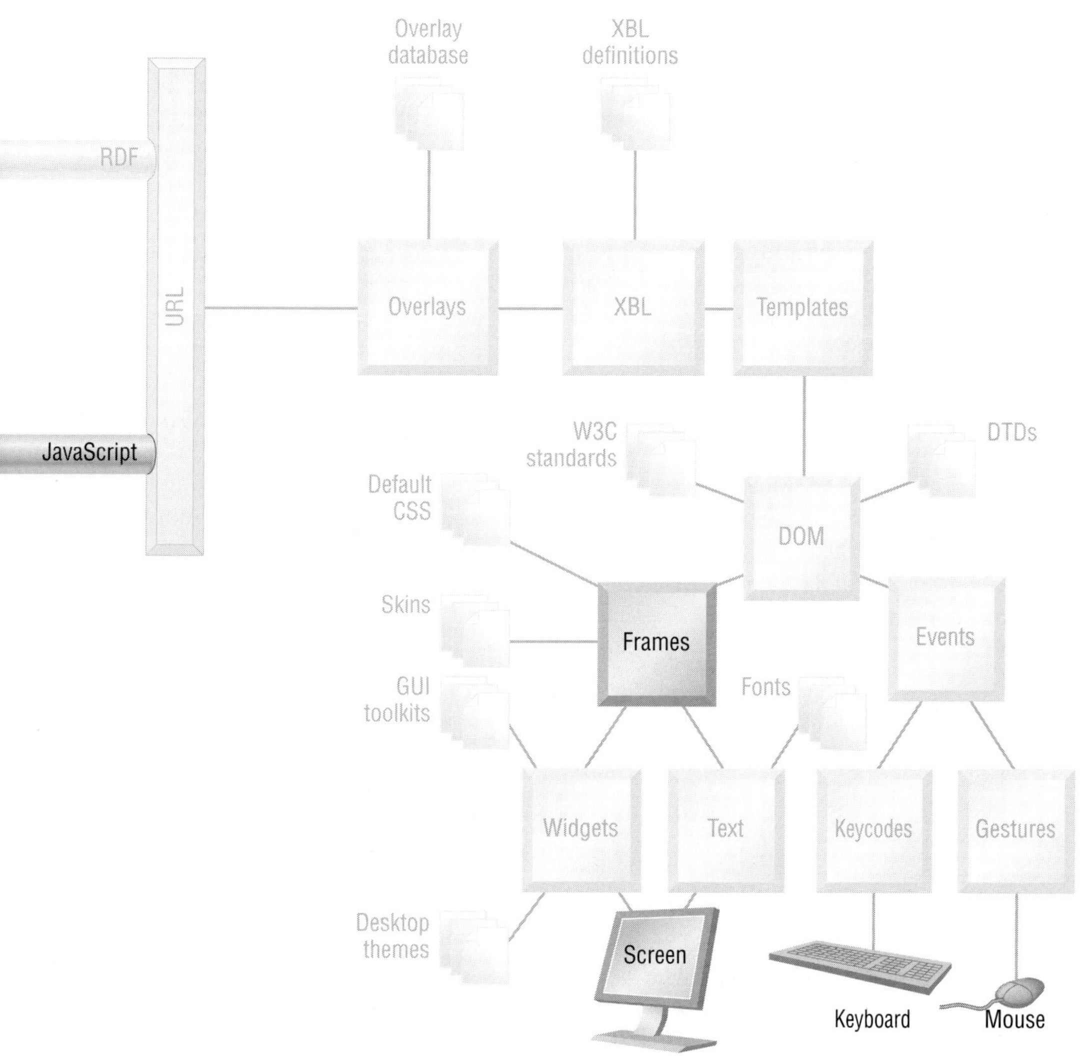

Only the most trivial of applications will fit a single window. Eventually, either part of the current window's content will need to be replaced, or a second window will be required. This chapter explains how to do both.

Some aspects of Mozilla are complicated; some aspects are simple. Working with windows is pretty simple. The tools available to XUL applications are much like the tools used in traditional Web development. If you've used the DOM method `window.open()` before, then this chapter will just be a review. Mozilla's XUL (and HTML) have a few new features to consider, but little described here is groundbreaking. Working with windows is just a matter of a few lines of code.

Mozilla provides a wide range of external windows ranging from tiny flyover help boxes (called tooltips by Microsoft and Mozilla) to large and complex application-specific XUL tags. Mozilla also provides internal (or inset or embedded) windows that appear as content inside other documents. Here these windows are called *panes*. Security hobbles devised for HTML browsers restrict these window types, but not when the application is installed in the chrome or is otherwise secure.

Mozilla's windows do contain a few surprises. XML namespaces can be employed to mix content types. There are improved tools to manage existing windows. Perhaps the most significant enhancement to window content is overlays. That subject is important enough to be covered separately in Chapter 12, Overlays and Chrome.

The NPA diagram at the start of this chapter shows the bits and pieces of Mozilla that have a little to do with window management. From the diagram, windows are a little about JavaScript and a little about frames. An object that exists outside the normal content of a document needs a container more complex than an ordinary `<box>` tag's frame, so there are several frame types to consider. There is also an XPCOM component or two worth considering. Overall, it's simple stuff.

10.1 Ordinary <window> Windows

Before looking at new XUL tags, we briefly revisit the `<window>` tag. The window tag supports the following special attributes:

```
sizemode windowtype screenX screenY width height
```

`sizemode` applies only to the topmost `<window>` (or `<dialog>`) tag. It records the appearance of the matching window on the desktop. It can be set to `normal`, `minimized`, or `maximized`.

`windowtype` is used to collect windows of like type. This attribute can be set to any programmer-defined string. This attribute takes effect when two or more windows with the same `windowtype` are displayed. Mozilla will make an effort to ensure that when the second or subsequent windows are opened, that they are offset from the existing windows of the same type. This assists the user by preventing exact overlap of two windows.

screenX and screenY locate the window's offset from the top-left corner of the desktop in pixels.

width and height state the window's horizontal and vertical dimensions on the desktop, in pixels.

None of screenX, screenY, width, or height can be modified to affect the window's position once the window is displayed.

A dialog box can be built from a <window> tag, as described under the window.open() topic. On UNIX, it is not yet common for dialog boxes to be modal, so those semantics are not yet necessary. In general, it is nearly pointless to use a <window> tag for a dialog box when the <dialog> tag exists specifically for that purpose.

10.2 Popup Content

XUL content in a given window can be covered by additional content from the same document using these tags:

```
<tooltip> <menupopup> <popup> <popupgroup> <popupset>
```

Not all of these tags are recommended, however. <menupopup>, for example, should generally be used only inside a <menu> or <menulist> tag. The following XML attributes can sometimes be applied to other XUL tags:

```
tooltiptext grippytooltiptext popup menu context contextmenu
    contentcontextmenu
```

Not all these attributes are recommended either. The <menupopup> tag is discussed in Chapter 7, Forms and Menus. The other bits and pieces are discussed here.

The <deck> tag can also be used for visual effects. It is discussed in Chapter 2, XUL Layout.

10.2.1 Defining Popup Content

Mozilla's popup system has a little history associated with it. This history affects which tags are used to define popup content. It is best to use the XUL tags that are forward looking, rather than linger over the tags that were used in the past but that are now out of favor. Even so, older tags are still robust and unlikely to be desupported for any 1.x version of Mozilla.

There are three kinds of popup content: flyover help (tooltips), context menus, and ordinary menus.

When using the most modern XUL tags, state flyover help and context menu content inside the <popupset> tag. This is a user-defined tag with no special meaning, in the style of <keyset>. There may be more than one <pop-

upset> if required. Flyover help should be stated with the <tooltip> tag, and context menus, with the <menupopup> tag. Ordinary menus can also be stated inside the <popupset> using <menupopup>, but it is recommended that ordinary menus be stated elsewhere, using tags like <menu> and <menulist>.

Well-established but old-fashioned practices involve stating context menus with the <popup> tag. The <context> and <popupset> tags are rarely seen and even older than <popup>. These tags (and others) can be contained in a single very old <popupgroup> tag. <popupgroup> can only be used once per document. Do not use any of these three tags, even though <popup> is still common in the Mozilla chrome. They are deprecated and part of the past.

10.2.2 Flyover Help/Tooltips

Flyover help is a small window that appears over a GUI element (a XUL tag) if the mouse lingers in place more than about a second. The design intent is to give the user a short hint about the element in question, which might be cryptic (badly designed) or partially hidden. Tooltips can be fully styled, so the default yellow color is not fixed.

The <tooltip> tag supports the following attributes:

```
label crop default titletip
```

If the <tooltip> tag has no content, it acts like a label. The `label` attribute supplies label content, and `crop` dictates how the tooltip will be truncated if screen space is short.

If `default` is set to `true`, then the tooltip will be the default tooltip for the document. If `titletip` is set to `true`, then the tooltip is for a GUI element that is partially hidden. These two attributes apply only to tooltips that appear on the column headings of a <tree> tag.

The <tooltip> tag can contain any content—it acts like a <vbox>. Filling it with content is of limited value because the user cannot navigate across the face of the tooltip with the mouse pointer. Tooltips can be sized with `minwidth` and `minheight`, but that can confuse the layout of the parent window. Those attributes are not recommended.

To associate a tooltip with another tag, set the `tooltip` attribute of the target tag to the id of the <tooltip> tag. A shorthand notation that requires no <tooltip> tag is to specify the tooltip text directly on the target tag with the `tooltiptext` attribute. A further alternative is to include a <tooltip> tag in the content of the tag requiring a tooltip. If this is done, the parent tag should have an attribute `tooltip="_child"` set.

The `grippytooltiptext` attribute applies only to the <menubar> and <toolbar> tags and provides a tooltip for the <toolbargrippy> tag, when one is implemented.

The `contenttooltip` attribute applies only the <tabbrowser> tag and provides a tooltip for the embedded content of that tag.

A tooltip will also appear over the title bar of a window if the title text does not appear in full.

The currently visible tooltip's target tag can be had from the `window.tooltipNode` property.

10.2.3 Context Menus

Context menus are a form of dropdown menu. They appear the same as other menus, except that they are exposed by a context click (apple-click in Macintosh, right-click on other platforms). When the context click occurs, the context menu appears at the point clicked, not at some predetermined point in the document.

Context menus should be defined with the `<menupopup>` tag described in Chapter 7, Forms and Menus. Such a menu is associated with a target tag by setting an attribute on that tag to the `<menupopup>`'s id. The attribute set should be `contextmenu` for most tags and `contentcontextmenu` for the `<tabbrowser>` tag.

In the past, other attributes such as `popup`, `menu`, and `context` filled the role of the `contextmenu` attribute. They should all be avoided, even `context`, which still works.

The `popupanchor` and `popupalign` attributes apply to `<menupopup>` context menus, just as they do to normal `<menupopup>s`.

The currently visible context menu's target tag can be had from the `window.popupNode` property.

10.3 Dialog Boxes

If new content to be displayed is more than trivial, then a dialog box is a simple design solution. Dialog boxes are no more than XUL windows with a very narrow purpose. Normally they are not standalone but operate in the context of (using the resources of) some other more general window.

Dialog boxes have two design purposes. The first is to expose complexity. When a user performs a command, the ideal result is that the command completes immediately and silently. Introducing a dialog box causes the user to deal with a set of further choices before their command completes. In terms of usability, this is an obstacle to the smooth flow of an application. The second design purpose is to focus the user on a specialist task. Such dialog boxes typically bring the application to a halt while the users tidy up the task thrust upon them by so-called modal dialog boxes. This second use is a disruption to the normal user navigation of the application.

Neither of these design goals is particularly compatible with a high-performance application. In a perfect world, there would be no dialog boxes at all. A well-designed application keeps dialog boxes to a minimum and avoids displaying meaningless configuration options. Too much configuration is a symptom of poor process modeling at design time. If extensive configuration is required, it should be designed as an application in itself, like the Mozilla preference system.

When dialog boxes are required, Mozilla has plenty of support.

10.3.1 <dialog>

The <dialog> tag is the main building block for dialog boxes. It is a replacement for the <window> tag and adds extra content and functionality to a standard XUL window. The <dialog> tag does not create a modal dialog box (one that seizes the application or desktop focus) unless additional steps are taken.

To use the <dialog> tag, just replace <window> with <dialog> in any XUL document. Beware that the <dialog> tag is designed to work from within the chrome, and using it from a nonchrome directory on Microsoft Windows can freeze Mozilla completely. No such problems occur on UNIX. Figure 10.1 compares the different uses of <dialog>.

In this example, standard diagnostic styles are turned on, and the word *Content* is a <description> tag that is the sole content of the document. In the top line of the image, the same content is displayed, first with the <dialog> tag and then with the <window> tag. The <dialog> tag adds extra structural <box> tags to the document plus two <button> tags. In the second line of the image, the buttons attribute of the <dialog> tag has been used to turn on all the buttons that <dialog> knows about. In the last line, extra content has been added to the document in the form of six buttons. These buttons override the standards <dialog> buttons, and so those standard buttons don't appear in the bottom box where they otherwise would. Note that the button text in the Full and Modified cases differs. Let's examine how all this works.

The <dialog> tag has an XBL definition that supplied boxes and buttons as extra content. In the normal case, four of these buttons are hidden.

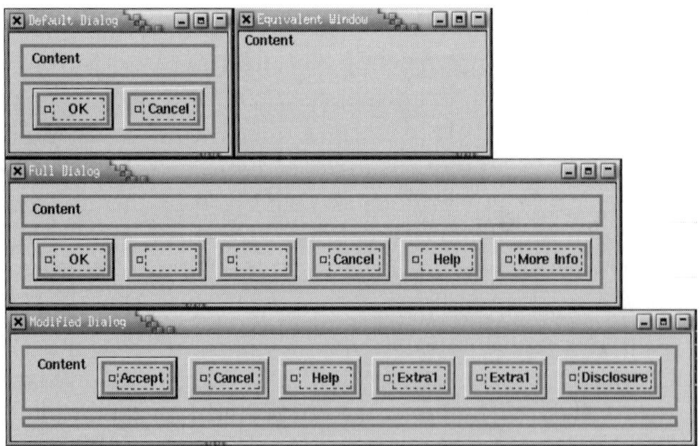

Fig. 10.1 Variations on the use of the <dialog> tag.

The tag also relies on a properties file in the chrome. That file contains button label text suitable for the current platform. Access to this properties file is one good reason for installing dialog boxes in the chrome. The `<dialog>` tag supports the following attributes:

```
buttonpack buttondir buttonalign buttonorient title buttons
```

The `buttons` attribute is a comma-separated list of strings. Spaces are also allowed. It is a feature string, similar to the *feature string* used in the `window.open()` method, but it's simpler in syntax. Allowed values are

```
accept cancel extra1 extra2 help disclosure
```

These values do not need to be set to anything. An example of their use is

```
<dialog buttons="accept,cancel,help"/>
```

The following event handlers, plus those of the `<window>` tag, are also available:

```
ondialogaccept ondialogcancel ondialogextra1 ondialogextra2
     ondialoghelp ondialogdisclosure
```

The `title` attribute sets the content of the title bar of the window, as for the `<window>` tag. `buttonpack/dir/align/orient` serve to lay out the `<hbox>` at the base of the dialog window as for the standard `pack/dir/align/orient` attributes. The `buttons` attribute states which of the standard dialog buttons should appear.

These standard buttons appear with standard content and standard behavior. For example, the `cancel` button shuts down the dialog box. The `extra1` and `extra2` buttons are available for application use, but they must include a replacement for the properties file if those buttons are to have labels. The event handlers noted earlier match the buttons one-for-one and fire when the buttons receive a command event (when they are clicked).

These `<dialog>` attributes are sufficient to explain the first three variations in Figure 10.1, but not the bottom one. That last variation depends on the `dlgtype` attribute, which typically appears on a `<button>` tag.

The `dlgtype` attribute can be set to any one of the standard button types:

```
accept cancel extra1 extra2 help disclosure
```

The `dlgtype` attribute has no meaning to the `<button>` tag itself, or to whatever tag it appears on. Instead, the `<dialog>` tag is quite smart. It searches all the content of the dialog window for a tag with this attribute, and if it finds one, it uses that tag instead of the matching dialog button. This brings flexibility to the dialog by allowing the application programmer some control over the placement of the dialog window controls. Only tags that support a `command` event may be used as replacement tags. If the replacement tag does not have a `label` attribute, it is supplied one by the `<dialog>` tag from the standard set of property strings.

A <dialog>-based window can be opened the same way as any other window. To add modal behavior, use the `window.openDialog()` method discussed shortly.

A <dialog> tag should not be explicitly sized with `width` and `height` attributes.

10.3.2 <dialogheader>

Although this tag is defined in the chrome, it is simple content only. It provides the heading area inside the Preferences dialog box, but it's no more than a <box> and some textual content. It has no special meaning to dialog boxes.

10.3.3 <wizard>

The <wizard> tag is an enhancement of the <dialog> tag. It and <wizard-page> are discussed in Chapter 17, Deployment.

10.3.4 Java, JavaScript, and Others

For completeness, note that dialog windows can also be created from Java, using standard Java techniques. The JVM and standard class libraries can be used to create windows that have nothing to do with the semantics of the Mozilla Platform. Such dialog boxes can exist outside the rectangular browser area occupied by HTML-embedded applets and can survive the destruction of the window that created them. They can appear in their own windows as the Java Console does. A starting point for such dialog boxes is to create a canvas.

Dialog windows can also be created from JavaScript using XPCOM and AOM/DOM resources. Some techniques for doing so are discussed next.

Embedded programmers can use languages such as Perl and Python to drive all the windows that an application based on the Mozilla Platform creates. Such uses are not documented here.

10.4 JavaScript Window Creation

New application windows can be created from JavaScript.

Recall that the JavaScript interpreter environment supplies the application programmer with a global object. In a XUL document, that global object has a property named `window` that is effectively the global object. This object supports many methods useful for creating windows.

The Mozilla hierarchy of JavaScript properties is a constructed system that is separate from the many XPCOM interfaces. Although some JavaScript properties, like `window` and `window.document`, appear to be identical to XPCOM components, these properties are just convenient fakes hiding the real components that make up a Mozilla window.

This last point is important. It is easy to become convinced that AOM JavaScript properties exactly match a particular Mozilla component, but this is not always true. Deep inside Mozilla, a number of separate abstractions make up a window displaying document content. It is best to view window and document as separate systems that closely match a few of the XPCOM interfaces rather than as direct replicas of some unique platform object.

The DOM Inspector, while very useful for examining content nodes like DOM elements, is not as revealing for the window and document JavaScript objects. For these objects, available JavaScript properties should be compared against the XPCOM XPIDL interfaces so that differences can be seen.

The window object reports its type as `ChromeWindow`. There is no such XPCOM object, although there is an `nsIDOMChromeWindow`. Interfaces more relevant to the features of the `ChromeWindow` object are `nsIJSWindow` and `nsIDOMWindowInternal`.

10.4.1 Navigator Versus Chrome Windows

JavaScript access to windows is designed with the traditional Web developer in mind. By default, a new window means a new Navigator window. A Navigator window is a XUL window that contains a standard set of XUL content that supplies all the features of a Web browser. This includes toolbars, other window decorations, bits of the DOM 0 document object model, a pane in which to display Web pages, and security. The alternative to a Navigator window is a chrome (plain XUL) window.

Navigator windows present a restricted interface to Web developers. The `window` and `window.document` objects apply only to the content loaded into the content pane. Web developers cannot access the XUL content that surrounds that pane; to such a developer, the XUL Navigator controls are a black box. The only options available to Web developers are a few flags that can be supplied to the `window.open()` method. These flags allow a new Navigator window to hide some of the XUL content, like toolbars.

To a XUL programmer, such Navigator windows are either a blessing or a nuisance. If the programmer is making minor enhancements to the existing Navigator system (such as overlays), then a Navigator window provides a great deal of functionality for free. If, however, the programmer is building a new application, all the Navigator functionality is just unwanted junk. In that case, simple steps (like the `-chrome` option) must be taken to avoid that content.

10.4.2 `window.open()`

The `window.open()` method opens an independent window. It is a DOM 0 interface commonly used in Web development. Its signature in Mozilla is

```
target = window.open(URL, name, features);
```

- URL is a valid URI and can be set to a zero-length string or "about:blank" for empty content. It does not need to be URL encoded.
- name is an identifier for the new window. It can be set to null or to "_blank" for a nameless window.
- features is a comma-separated list of feature keywords (a feature *string*) that controls the appearance and behavior of the new window.
- Finally, the returned value is a reference to the global (window) object of the target window. The target window's AOM can be accessed from the window that keeps this reference, provided that any security restrictions are obeyed.

The feature string is widely used but poorly documented, so here is a full discussion.

Each feature stated is a name=value pair. It is case insensitive. Such pairs are either boolean flags or a scalar. In the boolean case, the =value part can be left off or set to "=yes" for a value of true. Anything else is a value of false. In the scalar case, the =value part is a number, and any trailing characters are ignored. The features must be separated by commas and may have additional spaces, although spaces present portability problems for HTML documents displayed on older browsers. To summarize in an example:

```
"toolbar,location=yes, menubar=no,top=100, left=100px,width=100cm"
```

This example turns the Navigation toolbar on, the Location toolbar on, and the menu bar off. It positions the window 100 pixels from the top and the left, making it 100 pixels wide (cm is ignored).

The feature string dictates whether a window will be a Navigator browser window (the default) or a plain XUL chrome window. Navigator is the default. A plain chrome window requires this feature:

```
chrome
```

chrome defaults to false. If it is left off, then the following features are specific to a Navigator window:

```
toolbar location directories personalbar status menubar scrollbars
     extrachrome
```

These features default to true if no feature string at all is provided.

The extrachrome feature is a boolean value that determines whether a new Navigator window will load and display user-defined content (called the sidebar in the Classic Browser). In technical terms, this feature enables or disables the loading of programmer- or user-defined overlays installed in the chrome. The other features are standard Web options.

The following features apply to both Navigator and chrome XUL windows:

```
resizable dependent modal dialog centerscreen top left height width
     innerHeight innerWidth outerHeight outerWidth screenX screenY
```

If stated without a value, `resizable` and `centerscreen` default to `true`; `dependent` and `modal`, to false. An exception is that if the current window is `modal`, then the new window is made to be `modal=true`. The remainder are scalars and so must have a value supplied.

`resizable` enables the resize drag points supplied to the window by Microsoft Windows and X11 window managers. These resize drag points are separate from any `<resizer>` tag.

`dependent` ensures that the new window will be closed if the parent window is closed. The new window will always be on top of the invoking window.

`modal` ensures the original window cannot get focus until the new window is closed.

`dialog` tells the window manager to strip all buttons, except the Close button, from the new window's title bar.

`centerscreen` positions the new window in the middle of the desktop.

The remaining options are scalars that affect the position and size of the new window. If just one of `top`, `left`, `screenX`, or `screenY` is set, the other direction will be set to zero. The sizing and positioning features for a Navigator window are overridden if the `persist` attribute is used, which it is for Classic Browser windows.

Some features work only if the window is created with security privileges, for example from the chrome. These features are

```
titlebar close alwaysLowered z-lock alwaysRaised minimizable
```

`titlebar` and `close` default to `true`; the others, to `false`.

`titlebar` enables the decorations added by the window manager: the title bar and window frame borders. `close` enables the Close window button on the title bar. `alwaysLowered` and `z-lock` keep the new window behind all other windows when it gets the focus; `alwaysRaised` keeps the window in front of other windows when it loses the focus. `minimizable` appears to do nothing.

If the `close` feature is turned off, the window can still be closed by the user using the window manager. For example, on Microsoft Windows, the Windows icon in the task bar retains a close menu item on its context menu.

10.4.3 `window.openDialog()`

The `window.openDialog()` method is available only when the document calling this method is secure. Installed in the chrome is a secure case. It takes nearly the same arguments as the `window.open()` method and produces nearly the same result.

```
win = window.openDialog(URL,name,features,arg1, arg2, …);
```

`arg1`, `arg2`, and so on are arbitrary JavaScript function arguments passed to the `window.arguments` array of the new window.

The `openDialog()` method is equivalent to adding the feature string "`chrome=yes,dialog=yes`". If either of those features is set to `false` by the feature string, the values supplied override the `openDialog()` defaults. `openDialog()` also supports this feature keyword:

```
all
```

The `all` attribute turns on all features that grant the user control over the window. That means the Close and Minimize icons on the title bar and so on.

10.4.4 window.content, id="content" and loadURI()

In a Classic Browser window, the XUL tag with `id="content"` is a `<tabbrowser>` tag that represents the content panel. This tag is invisible to Web developers, but highly useful for application developers who are customizing browsers. It is heavily loaded with scriptable functionality and is worth exploring with the DOM Inspector.

If the window is a standard XUL-based browser window, then this `<tabbrowser>` object is available as the `content` property of the `window` object. In addition to implementing the `nsIWebNavigation` interface, that `content` property has a `document` property that points to the HTML (or XML) document that appears in the current tab.

The `nsIWebNavigation` interface provides all the methods used to control the in-place loading, reloading, and navigating of content in a single browser content pane. The `<tabbrowser>` AOM object has a `webNavigation` property that exposes this interface. The most useful method is `loadURI()`. `loadURI()` is similar to the `XmlHttpRequest` object discussed in Chapter 7, Forms and Menus. The main difference is that the `XmlHTTPRequest` object returns an HTTP request's response as pure data, whereas `loadURI()` also stuffs the response document into the display so that it is visible and integrated with other Classic Browser features like history. `loadURI()` has this signature:

```
void loadURI(uri, flags, referrer, postData, headers)
```

- ☞ `uri` is the Web resource to display.
- ☞ `flags` (default `null`) is a set of bitwise ORed flags that modify the load behavior. These flags are supplied as `webNavigation` properties prefixed with `LOAD_FLAGS` and provide options to bypass the browser cache, reload the page, and so on.
- ☞ `referrer` (default `null`) is the HTTP referrer for the load request. The programmer may override the referrer the Mozilla Platform supplies with this argument.
- ☞ `postData` (default `null`) is a string of HTTP POST request data.
- ☞ `headers` (default `null`) is a string of additional HTTP headers.

The last two options are rarely used from JavaScript. If you require them, then the string supplied must be specially crafted to match the `nsIInputStream` interface. To do so, use XPCOM as shown in Listing 10.1.

Listing 10.1 Construction of a string-based `nsIInputStream`.

```
var str, C, obj, iface, arg;

str   = "put data here";
C     = Components;
obj   = C.classes["@mozilla.org/io/string-input-stream;1"];
iface = C.interfaces.nsIStringInputStream;

arg = obj.createInstance(iface);
arg.setData(str, str.length);

loadURI("page.cgi", null, null, arg, null);
```

10.4.5 `alert()`, `confirm()`, and `prompt()`

These three methods of the window object are basic user feedback windows in the style of Microsoft's `MessageBox` functionality. They are specialized, modal dialog boxes. `alert()` is also the simplest way to put a breakpoint in your JavaScript code: Execution halts until the alert is dismissed. See any Web development book.

The small dialog windows created by these methods have been redesigned for Mozilla. In Netscape 4.x and earlier, and in Internet Explorer, these windows hold the output of a single C-like `printf()` statement. There was no support for Unicode characters, only ASCII. In Mozilla, these windows are full XUL windows, as Figure 10.2 reveals.

Dotted boxes in this diagram represent `<description>` tags. To see this structure, apply diagnostic styles to the `userChrome.css` file in your Mozilla user profile directory and restart the platform. This screenshot was produced with this line of code:

```
alert("Line 1\nLine2");
```

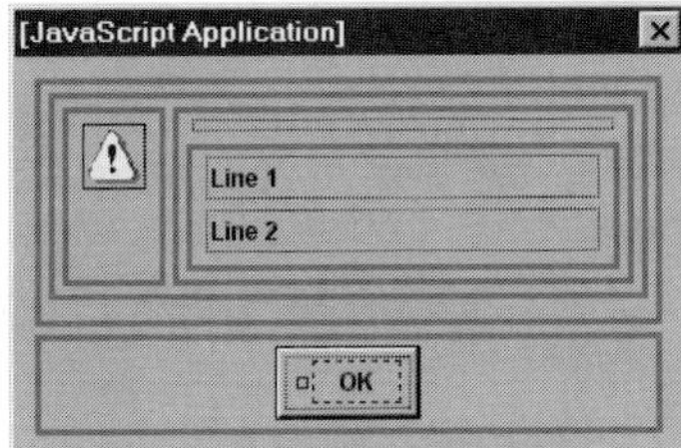

Fig. 10.2 XUL structure of an `alert()` dialog box.

Mozilla takes the string supplied to `alert()`, `confirm()`, and `prompt()` and splits it on all end-of-line characters supplied. Each split piece is allocated a `<description>` tag and, therefore, can wrap over multiple lines if required. Each `<description>` tag has a `maxwidth` of `45em`. An empty description tag at the top can be styled by the application programmer and has `id="info.header"`.

These dialog boxes originate in the chrome, in files prefixed `commonDialog` in `toolkit.jar`. The same XUL document is used for all three dialog boxes.

10.4.6 nsIPromptService

This XPCOM pair is the technology behind the `alert()`, `confirm()`, and `prompt()` dialog boxes:

```
@mozilla.org/embedcomp/prompt-service;1 nsIPromptService
```

An object can be created by this pair only when the document has full security access, but such an object can create a wide variety of small dialog boxes. Table 10.1 lists these boxes.

The `nsIPromptService` interface contains extensive documentation on the arguments for each of these methods. Use this interface when building a chrome-based application, rather than the simpler `alert()`. `alert()` is really intended for HTML.

Table 10.1 Mozilla CSS2 font name extensions

Method name	Dialog box created
alert()	Same as the AOM alert().
alertCheck()	Same as the AOM alert(), but with an extra line containing a checkbox and a text message.
confirm()	Same as the AOM confirm().
confirmCheck()	Same as the AOM confirm(), but with an extra line containing a checkbox and a text message.
confirmEx()	A fully customizable dialog box with up to 3 buttons, each with custom or standard text, and an optional checkbox and message.
prompt()	Same as the AOM prompt().
promptUsernameAndPassword()	A dialog box showing a user name and password field, and an optional checkbox and message.
promptPassword()	A dialog box showing a password field, and an optional checkbox and message.
select()	A dialog box showing a `<listbox>` from which a single item may be selected. Each item is plain text.

10.4.7 Special-Purpose XPCOM Dialog Boxes

Mozilla provides several special-purpose dialog boxes, all of which are located in `toolkit.jar` in the chrome. The following dialog boxes are implemented: Ask the user to specify a file; assist the user with printing; assist the user when searching content in pages; and report progress for a file being downloaded.

All of these special-purpose dialog boxes have a matching XPCOM component and must be controlled via XPCOM interfaces, not via the URLs of their chrome components.

Two of these dialog boxes are briefly examined next.

10.4.7.1 FilePicker The FilePicker is an XPCOM component and interface. It is also a set of dialog windows. Sometimes these dialog windows are Mozilla windows containing XUL, and sometimes they are standard file dialog windows provided by the operating system. Such native dialog windows cannot be inspected with the DOM Inspector.

The following XPCOM technology is used to implement the FilePicker:

```
component @mozilla.org/filepicker;1 interface nsIFilePicker
```

The `nsIFilePicker` interface has very straightforward methods for customizing the dialog box, as a brief examination of the XPIDL file will reveal. To use the dialog box, proceed as follows:

1. Create a FilePicker object using XPCOM.
2. Initialize it with the `init()` method.
3. Add filters and choose which one is selected.
4. Set any other defaults required.
5. Call the `show()` method, which blocks until the user responds.
6. Extract the user's response from the object.

The last stage, extracting the user's response, is not as straightforward as it might seem. Files nominated by the user cannot be specified with a string containing a simple path. This is because some operating systems require a volume as well as a path in order to specify a file's location fully. The Macintosh (and VMS, mainframes, and others) are examples. Chapter 16, XPCOM Objects, describes the objects and interfaces Mozilla uses to manage files. That is recommended reading before attempting to use the FilePicker.

Listing 10.2 is an example of the FilePicker used to ask the user for a file that is to be the location of written-out content.

Listing 10.2 Acquiring an `nsILocalFile` using the FilePicker dialog box.

```
var Cc = Components.classes;
var Ci = Components.interfaces;
var fp;
```

```
fp = Cc["@mozilla.org/filepicker;1"];
fp = fp.createInstance(Ci.nsIFilePicker);
fp.init(window, "Example File Save Dialog", fp.modeSave);
fp.show();

// fp.file now contains the nsILocalFile picked
```

10.4.7.2 `PrintingPrompt`

Mozilla provides XPCOM objects that interface to the native printing system, objects that provide native printing dialog boxes, and some print dialog windows that are built from XUL. In very recent versions of Mozilla, XUL documents can be printed as for HTML documents. Just load the XUL content in a browser window and print. Before version 1.3 or thereabouts, only HTML documents could be printed.

The printing system is nontrivial and is not covered in detail here. Starting points for exploring the printing system are the `nsIPrintingPromptService` and `nsIWebBrowserPrint` XPCOM interfaces.

10.5 Embedding Documents in Panes

The alternative to putting content in a new window is to create a pane in an existing window whose content can be flexibly managed. A traditional television is such a device, with many channels but only a single pane for display. In this book, a *pane* is different from a *panel*. A panel is an area of a window that displays related information in one spot. A pane is a panel whose related information is sourced from a document that is separate from the rest of the window.

Mozilla's XUL allows unrelated content to appear in part of an existing window. Several tags that can achieve this exist.

10.5.1 `<iframe>`

The `<iframe>` tag is at the core of all Mozilla's document embedding solutions. It has the same purpose as an HTML `<iframe>`, but it is less flexible. No content can be specified between start and end `<iframe>` tags, and it cannot float beside other content. A XUL `<iframe>` allows focus to enter the content in the `<iframe>`'s area. XUL `<iframe>`s can be sized and resized as for any boxlike tag:

```
<iframe minwidth="100px" flex="1" src="about:blank"/>
```

The `<iframe>` tag has only one special attribute: `src`. This can be set to the URL of the document to be displayed in the `<iframe>`. Since the contents are often HTML, it is useful to set the name attribute as well so that the window to which the content belongs has a name that can be used from inside the content.

In Chapter 8, Navigation, it was remarked that the `<scrollbox>` tag represents a special case of a boxlike tag, with its own interface. The `<iframe>` tag is another such special case. It is the sole example of a component named

```
@mozilla.org/layout/xul-boxobject-iframe;1
```

The AOM object for the `<iframe>` tag has a `boxObject` property as for all XUL tags that are boxlike. Like `<scrollbar>`, `<iframe>`'s `boxObject.QueryInterface()` method can be used to retrieve a special-purpose interface. In this case, it is called `nsIIFrameBoxObject`. Although this interface has only one property, `docShell`, that property in turn reveals the `nsIDocShell` interface, which is extensive.

DocShell stands for "Document Shell." A DocShell is a shell for documents in the same way that `ksh`, `bash`, or `DOS` is a shell for a set of operating system commands. It is used to manipulate whole documents, just as DOS is used to manipulate whole files and programs.

The extensive properties and methods of the `nsIDocShell` interface provide all the basic operations required to load and manage a document retrieved by the Mozilla Platform. This interface can also be used to access all the other interfaces that are handy for document management. The `nsIDocShell` interface is therefore something like the driver's seat of a car—most of the controls are within easy reach of it. This interface is well commented and worth looking over. The downloadable files described in the Introduction include this interface.

In simple cases, an application programmer merely uses an `nsIDocShell` that appears as a result of some content being loaded. Only in ambitious projects does an application programmer need to hand-create a document shell and drive the loading of documents through scripts.

Since the `<iframe>` tag supports this interface, its contents must have the status of a full XML document. Most boxlike tags only have the status of a single DOM element object and its children. The `<iframe>` tag is the fundamental tag required to create a Mozilla Browser window: It implements the pane in which the downloaded content appears. It is the heart of the Browser window.

To summarize, the `<scrollbar>` tag has a simple box-object enhancement that allows its content (an XML document fragment) to be moved within the tag's display area. The `<iframe>` tag's box-object enhancements are far more complicated: Its content (a whole XML document) can be extensively managed within the tag's display area. In both cases, the display area is an undecorated plain rectangle. Clearly, `<iframe>` is an extensive enhancement on a plain <box>.

`<iframe>` has an XBL definition in `general.xml` and in `toolkit.jar` in the chrome. This definition provides properties that are shorthand for commonly used parts of `nsIDocShell`:

```
docShell contentWindow webNavigation contentDocument
```

- docShell is the starting point for management of the content.
- contentWindow is the equivalent of the JavaScript window property for the content.
- webNavigation is the window.webNavigation property for the content.
- contentDocument is the window.document property for the content.

The commandDispatcher that is supplied with every XUL document has an advanceFocusIntoSubtree() method that can move the focus into an <iframe>'s content, if that content is capable of receiving the focus.

If an <iframe>'s content is taller or wider than the clipping area of the frame, and the pane's content is not XUL, then scrollbars will appear. Any XUL document displayed in an <iframe> should start with a <page> tag. <iframe> tags may be nested, provided that each level of nesting is contained in a complete document.

10.5.2 <page>

The <page> tag is an alternative to the <window> tag. The <page> tag should be used when the XUL document is to appear inside an <iframe>, rather than in its own window. The <page> tag has no special attributes.

A document that uses <page> can still be displayed in a window by itself, but that use is not recommended. <page> is intended for documents that only appear inside <iframe> tags.

10.5.3 <editor>

The <editor> tag is a specialist box-object tag like <iframe>. It displays an entire document as <iframe> does. The only special attribute for <editor> is src, which holds a URL for the displayed content. Some versions of Mozilla support an editortype="html" or "text" attribute. There is also the type="content" or "content-primary" attribute; the latter makes the window.content property refer to the editor's contentWindow. <editor> is an example of the XPCOM pair:

```
@mozilla.org/layout/xul-boxobject-editor;1 nsIEditorBoxObject
```

The nsIEditorBoxObject interface has the DocShell functionality present in the <iframe> tag, plus the very extensive functionality of the nsIEditor interface, hanging off an editor property. This second interface provides all the technology required to implement visual editing of an HTML document, like selection, insertion, and so on. The <editor> tag is the heart of the Classic Composer tool, just as the <iframe> tag is the heart of the Classic Browser tool.

The <editor> tag provides no controls for the displayed edit pane.

10.5.4 <browser>

The <browser> tag is a custom tag like <iframe>. It displays an entire document as <iframe> does and supports the src attribute as for <iframe>. <browser> is a boxlike tag and an example of the component

```
@mozilla.org/layout/xul-boxobject-browser;1
```

This component implements the nsIBrowserBoxObject interface, which is nearly identical to the nsIIFrameBoxObject interface. <browser> and <iframe> are identical at heart.

The <browser> tag differs from the <iframe> tag in its XBL definition. That definition is in browser.xml in toolkit.jar in the chrome. The XBL binding for <browser> is very extensive with many methods and properties. Implementing simple tasks with the <iframe> tag means digging through a few interfaces, finding the right properties, and making a few method calls. The <browser> tag provides a range of convenient methods that do this digging for you. The <browser> tag's XBL definition also adds and coordinates history, security, and drag-and-drop support.

The <browser> tag also adds caret browsing functionality. Caret browsing occurs if F7 is pressed: The user can then navigate a read-only HTML page by moving the insertion point around the page, as though it were an editor session.

<iframe> is more efficient than <browser> when the document displayed is static and never changes. <browser> is more convenient when the document in the pane might be replaced several times or when basic navigation is needed.

10.5.5 <tabbrowser>

Just as <browser> is an enhancement of <iframe>, <tabbrowser> is an enhancement of <browser>. Unlike the other two tags, <tabbrowser> has no XPCOM component identity; it is just one very large XBL definition in tabbrowser.xml in toolkit.jar in the chrome.

<tabbrowser> is a combination of <tabbox> and <browser> tags. Each <tabbox> tab is a <browser>, and tabs can be dynamically added. <tabbrowser> is ultimately used to implement the content display area of the Classic Browser window.

<tabbrowser> supports the following special attributes:

```
onnewtab contenttooltip contentcontextmenu
```

onnewtab is an event handler that fires when the user creates a new tab by pressing the New Tab button, or by using the menu system. contenttooltip and contentcontextmenu are stripped of the prefix content and passed to the <browser> tags inside the <tabbox> tabs.

Although it is possible to automate the actions of the <tabbrowser> through its many methods, there is little point in doing so because the tag is designed for user viewing of multiple read-only documents. The most an application programmer might do is examine the current state of the tab system.

10.5.6 <IFRAME>,<iframe> and <FRAME>,<frame>

These HTML or XHTML tags are used to place documents inside a frame in an HTML page. A XUL document can be displayed inside such a frame.

10.5.7 Non-Tags

When embedding documents, there are several do-nothing combinations.

By default, the <html> tag does nothing in a XUL document. It acts like any user-defined tag. It can be made more useful with an XML Namespace, as described in "Mixing Documents."

The <window> tag does nothing when embedded in other XUL content, so <window> tags do not nest, and neither do <dialog> or <page> tags. Outermost tags only nest when they are in separate documents and an <iframe> is between them.

The `chromehidden` attribute of the <window> tag does nothing for the application programmer. It is set by the `window.open()` method, or by toolbar logic in the Classic Browser, or by the toolbar toggle widget on MacOS X, on the Macintosh only. The `windowtype` attribute of the <window> tag takes a string and is used for window management (see "Managing Existing Windows"). It has no special meaning to <window>.

If there was ever a <package> tag, then it is gone now. It occasionally appears in older Mozilla documentation.

10.6 Mixing Documents

It is possible to combine documents so that their individual tags are mixed together, without isolating one document in an <iframe>.

10.6.1 Mixing XML Document Types

A very powerful yet complex feature of Mozilla is the capbility to render a document that contains tags from several standards. This means that a document can contain HTML, SVG, MathML, and XUL content, all mixed together. This is done simply by adding XML namespaces. All tags from the added namespace are then available. Mozilla, however, will only recognize XUL content from a `.xul` file extension or from the correct XUL MIME type, so that much is mandatory if XUL is involved. This system was touched on in Chapter 7, Forms and Menus, where HTML and XUL forms were mixed.

There is a distinction between deeply mixing and lightly mixing types of content. The distinction is that layout is harder to perfect for deeply mixed content.

When different content is lightly mixed, a few large chunks of different content are put together. An example of light mixing is an HTML document that contains a few equations, each written in a chunk of MathML.

When different content is deeply mixed, individual tags from different content types sit side by side. This usually occurs when the document author naïvely assumes that any tag from any standard can be used anywhere.

Lightly mixing content generally works. Deeply mixing content doesn't always work. HTML and MathML is the least problematic deep mixture. Deeply mixing XUL and HTML or MathML requires care. Deeply mixing SVG with something else doesn't work because SVG content requires its own dedicated display area.

Mixing standards can be useful, but it is also something to be wary of. There are several reasons for caution:

- ☞ The layout models for different standards are not identical. A precise set of rules for laying out mixed content is very difficult to find. You can spend much time fiddling with styles.
- ☞ Mixed standards are not well tested. The number of tests required to conclude that two standards are fully compatible is huge. By the grace of a good internal design, mixing does work. If you press hard, though, you'll find effects that no one has thought of or tested yet.
- ☞ The renderable standards in Mozilla do not share the same document root. This means that the C/C++ object that implements the DOM 1 document interface is different for each standard. The set of features available depends on what the root document is. XUL embedded in HTML is not the same as HTML embedded in XUL. For heavily scripted documents, like XUL and DHTML, the right interfaces are very important.

It's very tempting to add an HTML `<A HREF=>` tag to XUL so that your splash or help screen includes a link back to the vendor's Web site. It's very tempting to add an HTML `<FORM>` tag and auto-submit forms from XUL. Both of these tasks, however, can be done without any HTML. It is better to keep your XUL clean.

The more recent DOM standards include interface methods like `createElementNS()` and `getAttributeNS()`. NS stands for Namespace. These methods let you specify the namespace of content items in a given merged document.

10.6.2 Mixing XUL Documents

The `<overlay>` tag is similar to a sophisticated version of C/C++'s `#include` directive. It allows several XUL documents to be merged seamlessly, using the `id` attribute. It is described in Chapter 12, Overlays and Chrome.

10.7 Managing Existing Windows

After windows are created, the application may wish to manage them. A simple example is the File | Inspect a Window menu option of the DOM Inspector, which picks up a window for study. An even simpler example is the bottom half of the Window menu in most Mozilla applications, which moves the focus between windows.

Trying to juggle multiple windows can lead to very bad design. In most cases, the user can close a window at any time. This wipes out all the state of that window (except possibly for Java applets and shared XPCOM objects). It is difficult to maintain a rational design when state can disappear arbitrarily. Generally speaking, an application should have one master window, with any other required windows being dependent on that master. The dependent and modal features of `window.open()` are the simplest way to coordinate windows. If a desktop metaphor is required, then either all windows must be independent of each other, or a registration system must be implemented to track who is still available.

Mozilla provides several components and interfaces for managing windows. The simplest pair is

```
@mozilla.org/appshell/window-mediator;1 and nsIWindowMediator
```

This interface provides a list of the currently open windows. It is not finished (frozen) as of version 1.2.1 and may change slightly. The list has several forms, depending on which method is used. Listing 10.3 illustrates how to get a static list of currently open windows.

Listing 10.3 Retrieval of currently opened windows using `nsIWindowMediator`.

```
var C, obj, iface, mediator, enum, windows;
C     = Components;
obj   = C.classes["@mozilla.org/appshell/window-mediator"];
iface = C.interfaces.nsIWindowMediator;

mediator = obj.createInstance(iface);
enum     = mediator.getEnumerator(null);
windows  = [];

// record all windows using nsISimpleEnumerator methods
while ( enum.hasMoreElements() )
   windows.push(enum.getNext());

// do something with the first window
windows[0].document.GetElementById …
```

The `getEnumerator()` method can be passed a string that will filter the list of windows retrieved. Only windows with an `<html>`, `<window>`, `<dialog>`, or `<wizard>` tag whose `windowtype` attribute matches the string will be returned.

To return only XUL windows, use `getXULWindowEnumerator()` instead. The interface can also report stacking order for the currently open windows. Iconized (minimized) windows are at the bottom of the stacking order.

Windows open and close all the time, and an application might want to track this dynamically, as the menus noted earlier do. One way to do this is to add a listener to the window mediator object. This listener (an object implementing `nsIWindowMediatorListener`) is advised if a window opens, closes, or has its title changed. A more advanced solution, which requires little code, is to use the `rdf:window-mediator` data source directly in XUL. RDF and data sources are described in Chapter 11, RDF.

10.8 Style Options

The windowing aspects of XUL and HTML benefit from both trivial and systematic Mozilla enhancements to the CSS2 style system.

The trivial enhancements are as follows.

The `<tooltip>` tag displays `-moz-popup`, as for the `<menupopup>` tag discussed in "Style Options" in Chapter 7, Forms and Menus. It is less useful to display tooltips inline than menus, although that does provide a quick eyecheck that all visual elements have such tips.

The `-moz-appearance` style property, used to support native (desktop) themes, also supports the following values:

```
window dialog tooltip caret
```

Systematic enhancements also exist for native theme support. It is useful for windows, and for dialog windows in particular, to appear exactly like windows created by the native desktop (e.g., Windows or GTK). Dialog boxes are disruptive enough for the user, without including bizarre colors and shapes. Mozilla includes color name and font name extensions designed to help dialog boxes (and other content) mimic the dialog boxes that the desktop would produce. These color and font names can be used anywhere in a style rule that a normal color or font name would appear.

In addition to these custom colors and fonts, Mozilla supports the desktop-oriented colors and fonts specified in the CSS2 standard, section 18.2.

Extensive and careful use of these styles in a XUL application can remove every hint that the application is Mozilla based. Well-styled applications designed this way may appear to be no different than traditional desktop applications, such as Visual Basic Applications on Windows, or GTK-based applications on UNIX.

Additional native-matching color names supported by Mozilla are noted in Table 10.2. Recent updates to these colors can be found by examining the source code file `nsCSSProps.cpp`.

Table 10.2 Mozilla CSS2 color name extensions

Native color name	Matches this native item	Additional Macintosh-specific color names
-moz-field	Background of a form field	-moz-mac-focusring
-moz-fieldtext	Foreground of text in a field	-moz-mac-menuselect -moz-mac-menushadow
-moz-dialog	Background of a dialog box	-moz-mac-menutextselect -moz-mac-accentlightesthighlight
-moz-dialogtext	Foreground of text in a dialog	-moz-mac-accentregularhighlight -moz-mac-accentface
-moz-dragtargetzone	Highlighted color of a drag target when dragged over	-moz-mac-accentlightshadow -moz-mac-accentregularshadow -moz-mac-accentdarkshadow
-moz-hyperlinktext	Clickable link text, such as Windows Active Desktop links	-moz-mac-accentdarkestshadow
-moz-visitedhyperlinktext	Clickable link text for a visited link	

Similarly, Mozilla supports the font name extensions listed in Table 10.3, but these font names don't appear to do anything as of version 1.4.

The special font name `-moz-fixed` does provide a real font and can be used to ensure that a fixed-width font is displayed. It has the special property

Table 10.3 Mozilla CSS2 font name extensions

Native font name
-moz-window
-moz-document
-moz-workspace
-moz-desktop
-moz-info
-moz-dialog
-moz-button
-moz-pull-down-menu
-moz-list
-moz-field

that it can be rendered at all point sizes, so text in that font is guaranteed to appear regardless of the value of the `font-size` CSS2 property.

10.9 HANDS ON: NOTETAKER DIALOGS

In this "Hands On" session, we'll take advantage of the windowing aspects of XUL to clean up the NoteTaker Edit dialog box some more. We'll also coordinate the application window and the Edit dialog window a little so that they work together. These two items consist of a number of tiny jobs:

1. Replace `<window>` with `<dialog>` in the Edit dialog box.
2. Replace plain `<button>` handlers with `<dialog>` button handlers.
3. Implement the `notetaker-open-dialog` command on the main browser window so that `window.openDialog()` is used to display the Edit dialog box.
4. Implement the `notetaker-close-dialog` command.
5. Find and implement a strategy for handling data that is used by more than one window.
6. Work out what kind of window a NoteTaker note is.

First, we look at the Edit dialog box. Replacing the `<window>` tag is trivial. The new dialog tag could do with a title as well. That new tag will be

```
<dialog xmlns="http://www.mozilla.org/keymaster/gatekeeper/
     there.is.only.xul"
    id="notetaker.dialog"
    title="Edit NoteTaker Note"
    onload="execute('notetaker-load')">
```

Unfortunately, we gain a little but also lose a little on the handler side. We don't need to hand-create `<button>` tags any more because `<dialog>` supplies them, but at the same time we can't easily use `<command>` tags with `<dialog>` because there's more than one possible command attached to that tag. If we desire, we could suppress the buttons that `<dialog>` shows us and keep our existing buttons. Instead, we'll do it the way `<dialog>` suggests, which is to use that tag's own buttons. This gives us standard buttons on each platform. We also might add these handlers:

```
ondialogaccept="execute('notetaker-save');execute('notetaker-close-
     dialog');"
ondialogcancel="execute('notetaker-close-dialog');"
```

In fact, the `notetaker-close-dialog` command is not needed in some cases because `<dialog>` will automatically close the window when Cancel is pressed, or when the Close Window icon on the title bar is pressed. We might as well get rid of it from the code since `<dialog>` does everything for us. We can use an `onclose` handler at a later time if necessary. So only the `ondialogaccept` handler needs to be added.

That leaves the `-open-` and `-close-` commands to implement. We don't yet have a fully integrated toolbar, but we can use the fragment of XUL that we do have to test the command's implementation. The `action()` function used by the toolbar needs a very simple enhancement:

```
if ( task == "notetaker-open-dialog" )
{
  window.openDialog("editDialog.xul","_blank","modal=yes");
}
```

We use `modal` because the Edit dialog box isn't a full manager window like many of Mozilla's windows. We want the main browser window to freeze while the user is working on the dialog box. In that way, we don't need to worry about focus jumping back and forth between the two windows, or worse, between form fields on different windows.

Similarly, the `action()` function for the Edit dialog box requires a trivial enhancement:

```
if (task == "notetaker-close-dialog")
  window.close();
```

Penultimately, there is the matter of managing data. The NoteTaker tool is designed to maintain one note at most per URL, and the user is expected to work on one note at a time. But the tool spans two windows so far. Both the toolbar and the dialog box contain form fields that the user can enter information into. Which window holds the temporary state of the current note?

The answer depends on how that state is stored. In later chapters, the information will be stored in RDF, which is independent of a given XUL or HTML window. In this chapter, we'll store the data as a simple JavaScript object. Such an object originates in a single window. We choose the browser window to store the state because it's the window that displays the Web page to which the note is attached.

```
var note = {
  url : null;
  summary : "",
  details : "",
  chop_query : true, home_page : false,
  width : 100, height : 90, top : 80, left : 70
}
```

This object is automatically available to JavaScript in the Edit dialog code using the simple syntax:

```
window.opener.note
```

Each browser window will have one such object. This object can be further enhanced at any point with methods that perform updates to or from the form fields on the toolbar or in the dialog box. In this way, processing is centralized. If the dialog box were more complicated, it might have its own state and its own set of objects, but that is unnecessary in this case.

If we use the `opener` object, we must be very careful. Even though the data are being put into a different window, the current JavaScript context resides in the window that the script started in. Calls to `setTimeout()`, `setAttribute()`, or other trickery will always run against the current window, not the window being manipulated, even if the call is made through a function that is defined in that other window. Listing 10.4 shows logic for the dialog box's `action()` function, which is implemented in the dialog box window.

Listing 10.4 Save and load of NoteTaker dialog box data to the main window.

```
if (task == "notetaker-save")
{
  var field, widget, note = window.opener.note;

  for (field in note)
  {
    widget = document.getElementById("dialog." + field.replace(/_/,"-");

    if (!widget) continue;

  if (widget.tagName == "checkbox")
    note[field] = widget.checked;
  else
    note[field] = widget.value;
  }
}

if (task == "notetaker-load" )
{
  var field, widget, note = window.opener.note;

  for (field in note)
  {
    widget = document.getElementById("dialog." + field.replace(/_/,"-");

    if (!widget) continue;

    if (widget.tagName == "checkbox")
      widget.checked = note[field];
    else
      widget.value = note[field];
  }
}
```

These two routines are the inverse of each other. The `continue` statements let the dialog box ignore properties of the note object that the dialog box doesn't know about. With a bit more organization, we could make the object property names and the form field name the same (even though "-" is not a valid character for literal property names), which would slightly shorten the code, but we haven't bothered. The Edit dialog box now "saves" and "loads" its information back to the main window, so the toolbar logic must be expanded (later) to do a real save from the running platform to the external world. The note object is now our official record of the current note.

Last of all is the question of the NoteTaker note itself. The purpose of the note is to annotate a Web page with a comment from the viewer, so the note must appear on top of the Web page somehow. The note's data will be stored locally, and its display will be generated locally, but the Web page may come from any Web site. Because NoteTaker is installed in the chrome, and is therefore trusted, it has permission to obscure or alter any displayed Web page without restriction, including covering part of the site with note content.

One implementation strategy for the note is to use pure XUL, XBL, and JavaScript. A Web page in a browser window is displayed inside an `<iframe>` that is part of a `<tabbox>` that is part of a `<tabbrowser>`. If the `<iframe>` were wrapped in a `<stack>`, then the second card of the `<stack>` could be the Web page, and the first card of the stack could be the note. That note could be positioned using relative styles, and the Web page would "show through" everywhere except where the note was located. The note could then be any simple XUL content, like a simple `<box>` with some borders, background, and content. Think of a message written on a window pane—the garden can still be seen even though part of the glass has writing on it.

This strategy would require changes to the `<tabbox>` tag, which is defined in XBL. We can do that, but replacing the standard `<tabbox>` tag is a big move because it requires much testing. We would need to integration test all the changes we make with every application installed on the platform. That includes the browser itself. We'd rather not do that much work.

An alternate strategy is to implement the note in HTML and CSS. From the chrome-installed NoteTaker, we could reach down into the displayed Web page. Using DHTML techniques, we could add a `<span>` tag and its content. That `<span>` tag would be styled to be absolutely positioned and to have a high `z-index` so that it's always on top. There's a one-in-one-billion chance that this will clash with existing content on the page, but that's small enough for us to live with. This strategy has the benefit that it doesn't affect the rest of the chrome. This is the strategy we'll use.

A NoteTaker note will appear as shown in Figure 10.3. That figure is an ordinary Web page.

We must use the lowest-common denominator HTML because we don't know what standard the Web page will be written to. That means valid XML and valid HTML, just in case the page is displayed in strict mode. We are free, however, to use any of Mozilla's HTML enhancements because we know

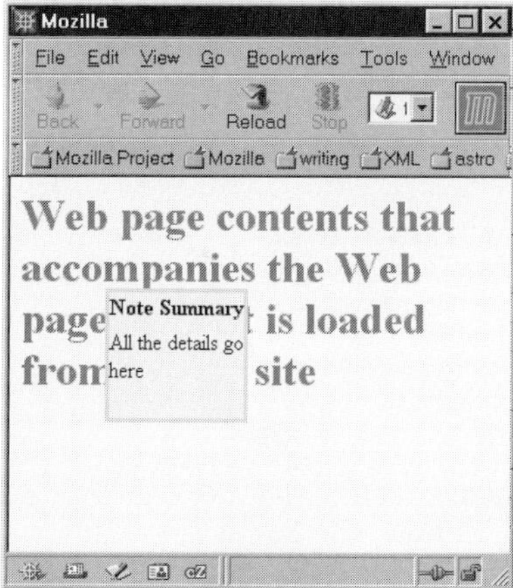

Fig. 10.3 Sample NoteTaker note constructed from HTML.

the browser will always be Mozilla. Compared with normal browser compatibility issues, that's a little unusual. HTML for the previous note is given in Listing 10.5.

Listing 10.5 HTML construction of a NoteTaker note.

```
<span id="notetaker-note">
  <span id="notetaker-note-summary">
    Note Summary
  </span>
  <span id="notetaker-note-details">
    All the details go here
  </span>
</span>
```

In fact, we should go to some extra trouble to make sure that the `xmlns` prefix for the tags is always correct, but we won't bother here. This HTML code has styles shown in Listing 10.6.

Listing 10.6 CSS style construction of a NoteTaker note.

```
#notetaker-note {
    display : block;
    position : absolute;
    z-index : 2147483646; /* one less than menu popups */
    overflow : auto;

    background-color : lightyellow;
    border : solid;
    border-color : yellow;
```

```
    width  : 100px;
    height : 90px;
    top    : 80px;
    left   : 70px;
}
#notetaker-note-summary {
    display : block;
    font-weight: bold;
}
#notetaker-note-details {
    display : block;
    margin-top : 5px;
}
```

Sometime in the future, this Web note technology could get an upgrade. Each note could be draggable, resizable, and iconizable, using the mouse. Each one could be directly editable. Most of these additions are standard DHTML tricks and aren't pursued here. Such changes would also need to be detected by the NoteTaker tool, which is not hard either.

To get a basic note in place, we can capture these two pieces of HTML and CSS code in JavaScript strings. Instead of hard-coded values, we can use placeholders so that

```
"… width : 100px …"
```

is stored as

```
"… width : {width}px …"
```

Using JavaScript regular expressions, we can substitute the values entered by the user in the toolbar or Edit dialog box into this string. After we have a finished string, we can create the note as shown in Listing 10.7.

Listing 10.7 Dynamic HTML creation of NoteTaker note.

```
function display_note()
{
  var style = generate_style();
  var html = generate_html();
  var doc = window.content.document;

  var stree = doc.getElementById("notetaker-styles");
  if ( !stree )  // add the topmost <style>
  {
     stree = doc.createElement("style");
     stree.setAttribute("id","notetaker-styles");
     var head = doc.getElementsByTagName('head').item(0);
     head.appendChild(stree);
  }
  stree.innerHTML = style;

  var htree = doc.getElementById("notetaker-note");
```

```
    if ( !htree )  // add the topmost <span>
    {
      htree = doc.createElement("span");
      htree.setAttribute("id","notetaker-note");
      var body = doc.getElementsByTagName('body').item(0);
      body.appendChild(htree);
    }
    htree.innerHTML = html;
}
```

The code uses `getElementByTagName()` to locate the <head> and <body> tags in the HTML page—the `id` for those tags in unknown by us. It then creates the topmost tag for the styles or the content and appends it to the <head> or <body> tag's existing content. Mozilla's special `innerHTML` property inserts the rest of the content from a string. For this simple system, we assume that the displayed page is not a frameset, and that it contains a <head> and a <body> tag. These assumptions can be lifted, but the result is just more DHTML code, which doesn't teach us much about Mozilla. The `generate_html()` function looks like Listing 10.8 and is trivial; the `generate_style()` function is analogous.

Listing 10.8 Insertion of NoteTaker data into Dynamic HTML content.

```
function generate_html()
{
  var source =
   '<span id="notetaker-note-summary">{summary}</span>' +
   '<span id="notetaker-note-details">{details}</span>';

  source = source.replace(/\{summary\}/, note.summary);
  source = source.replace(/\{details\}/, note.details);

  return source;
}
```

These changes are not so easy to test because they require integration with the Web browser. A complete testing solution is to read about overlays, which are two chapters in the future. A temporary solution is to hack the browser code, which we'll do here.

To hack the browser, make a copy of `navigator.xul` and put it in your `notetaker/content` directory in the chrome. The original is in `comm.jar` in the chrome. If we start Mozilla using this file:

```
mozilla -chrome chrome://notetaker/content/navigator.xul
```

then, voilà, a perfectly normal browser window appears. We'll modify *the copy* of this file. First, we add `<script src=>` tags for all the scripts needed for the toolbar code. Second, we find this line:

```
<toolbar id="nav-bar" …
```

This is the main navigation toolbar. Immediately after that opening tag, we add a `<toolbarbutton>` like so:

```
<toolbarbutton label="Test" onclick="display_note()"/>
```

When we save and load this file, a test button appears on the navigation bar. Pressing it makes a note appear—provided an HTML page is loaded. We can install any `onclick` handler we want on this button, including calls to `execute()`, `action()`, and anything else. In fact, we could put the whole NoteTaker `<toolbar>` content into this file (temporarily) if we wanted to.

This testing requires that the tester wait for a given HTML page to load before pressing the Test button. In the final, automated NoteTaker tool, we won't have that luxury. Instead, we'll need to detect the loading page. An unsophisticated solution is simply to poll the contents regularly to see if anything arrived.

```
function content_poll()
{
  if ( !window.content ) return;
  var doc = window.content.document;
  if ( !doc ) return;
  if ( doc.getElementsByTagName("body").length == 0 ) return;
  if ( doc.location.href == "about:blank" ) return;
  if ( doc.visited ) return;

  display_note();
  doc.visited = true;
}
setInterval("content_poll()", 1000);
```

This code examines the currently displayed HTML page to see if a note needs to be displayed. If there's no document, or the document doesn't have a body yet, or it's blank, or it already has a note, do nothing. Otherwise, find the note and add it.

To summarize this "Hands On" session, we now have the windows that make up the display portion of the NoteTaker tool. We have a memory-resident version of the current note in the form of a JavaScript object. We have some coordination between windows and some logic tying the note object to the displayed note. We even have a way to store and load the note on a Web server. With a little more work tying the user input to the JavaScript note object, this tool could be finished. The note even reloads when the Web page reloads.

The major thing missing is proper treatment of the Web page's URL. Each Web page is supposed to support a unique note. With the current arrangement, we need to submit a form request to a server to get the note back—that's rather inefficient. Our only alternative so far, and that is merely hinted at, is to write all the notes to a flat file. There's a better way, and that way is to store the notes as RDF. We discuss that option in the second half of this book.

10.10 Debug Corner: Diagnostic Windows

Before exploring window diagnostics, let's consider a cautionary remark about Microsoft Windows. When you are in the middle of constructing a still-buggy XUL application on Windows, the Mozilla Platform can occasionally become confused. The result of this confusion is that the platform remains in memory even when the last Mozilla window is shut down. When subsequent windows are started, they attach to the existing, confused instance of the platform. The most obvious symptom of this problem is that, no matter how hard you try, your changes to source files never appear in newly displayed windows.

To detect this problem, note that the splash screen only appears when the platform is first started: no splash screen + no existing windows = confused platform. To confirm the problem, use Control-Alt-Delete to review the list of running processes, and do "End Task" on any Mozilla processes.

Fortunately, this problem is less frequently seen as the platform matures. Being mindful of it can save hours of fruitless testing, though. There are many sources of defects, and this behavior is only one. For the rest, you must look to your own code.

When analyzing a complex application, nothing beats real-time information about the state of the application, delivered neatly in a controllable window. Mozilla provides a number of alternate ways to achieve this.

The simplest method is to use the `dump()` method described in Chapter 5, Scripting. Its output appears in the Mozilla window that appears when the platform is started with the `-console` option.

Nearly as simple to use are the many windows supplied by the JavaScript Debugger. To enable the debugger, first open a debugger window by hand. Turn on all the subwindows listed under View | Show/Hide as an experiment. At the first scripting opportunity in the XUL or HTML page to be diagnosed, add this line:

```
debugger;
```

When this line of script is executed, control will be thrown to the debugger, and you can step through the page's scripts from that point on. Use the big buttons in the debugger window and examine the content of each of the small subwindows as you go.

In HTML, the `document` object has `open()`, `close()`, and `write()` methods and a progressive rendering system that displays content before the document is completely loaded. This system can be used as a logging system. An HTML window can be opened from another window using `window.open()` and diagnostic content logged to it with `document.write()` as required.

XUL does not support HTML-style incremental display, but a similar system is still possible. Load a simple, empty XUL document into the window destined for logging, using `window.open()`. That document should have no content other than `<window orient="vertical">`. Use a sequence of statements as in Listing 10.9 to insert new content into that page:

Listing 10.9 Insertion of diagnostic messages into a new XUL window.

```
var win = window.open( …new window …);

function logger(message)
{
 var obj = win.document.createElement("description");
 var txt = win.document.CreateTextNode(message);
 obj.appendChild(txt);
 win.document.appendChild(obj);
}
```

Note that the document elements are created using the document in the new page, not the document in the existing page. Such a system can be enhanced with scrollbars and other controls. If the application is secure (e.g., installed in the chrome) it is just as easy to use the JavaScript Console. This is shown in Listing 10.10.

Listing 10.10 Logging messages to the JavaScript Console.

```
// Find the console
var C     = Components;
var obj   = C.classes["@mozilla.org/consoleservice;1"];
var iface = C.interfaces.nsIConsoleService;
var cons  = obj.getService(iface);

// Log a message
cons.logStringMessage("test message");
```

A similar system can be used for logging to the Java Console. This console has the advantage that it is not a XUL window and doesn't require a debug build of the browser or command-line display (which `dump()` needs). Messages can be logged to it without disturbing the normal state of any XUL windows. The Java Console does not appear in any list of windows retrieved using the earlier window mediator code either. This old-fashioned but familiar line from Netscape 4.x days can be used to write directly to the Java Console (it is a static class method):

```
window.java.lang.System.out.println("my message");
```

The console itself can also be exposed from code. The process is simple and shown in Listing 10.11, but it requires a secure application.

Listing 10.11 Revealing the Java Console window from a script.

```
var C = Components;
var obj   = C.classes["@mozilla.org/oji/jvm-mgr;1"];
var iface = C.interfaces.nsIJVMManager;
```

```
var cons  = obj.getService(iface);

if (cons.JavaEnabled) cons.showJavaConsole();
```

Before exposing the window, the whole Java subsystem must be checked to ensure that it is not disabled by the user.

10.11 Summary

Managing windows in Mozilla is heavily inspired by technology used in traditional Web browsers. Much can be achieved with the `window.open()` method and a few highly customized XUL tags. These tags are only of interest to application developers whose applications are browser-like.

Mozilla's XPCOM architecture reveals many interesting objects used to manage documents retrieved by the platform, not the least of which is the idea of a DocShell. These objects are saturated with functionality needed for ambitious content-oriented applications.

Mozilla's highly customizable windows also benefit from styles. Using style information, application programmers can integrate a window with the standard desktop appearance, which prevents the application from appearing foreign.

Many of the XUL tags discussed so far in this book are content-like and static. Software applications, however, are often data-centric and dynamic rather than content-centric and static. Mozilla caters to these nonbrowser needs with novel support for data-oriented processing tasks. That support is the topic of the next few chapters, starting with the RDF language.

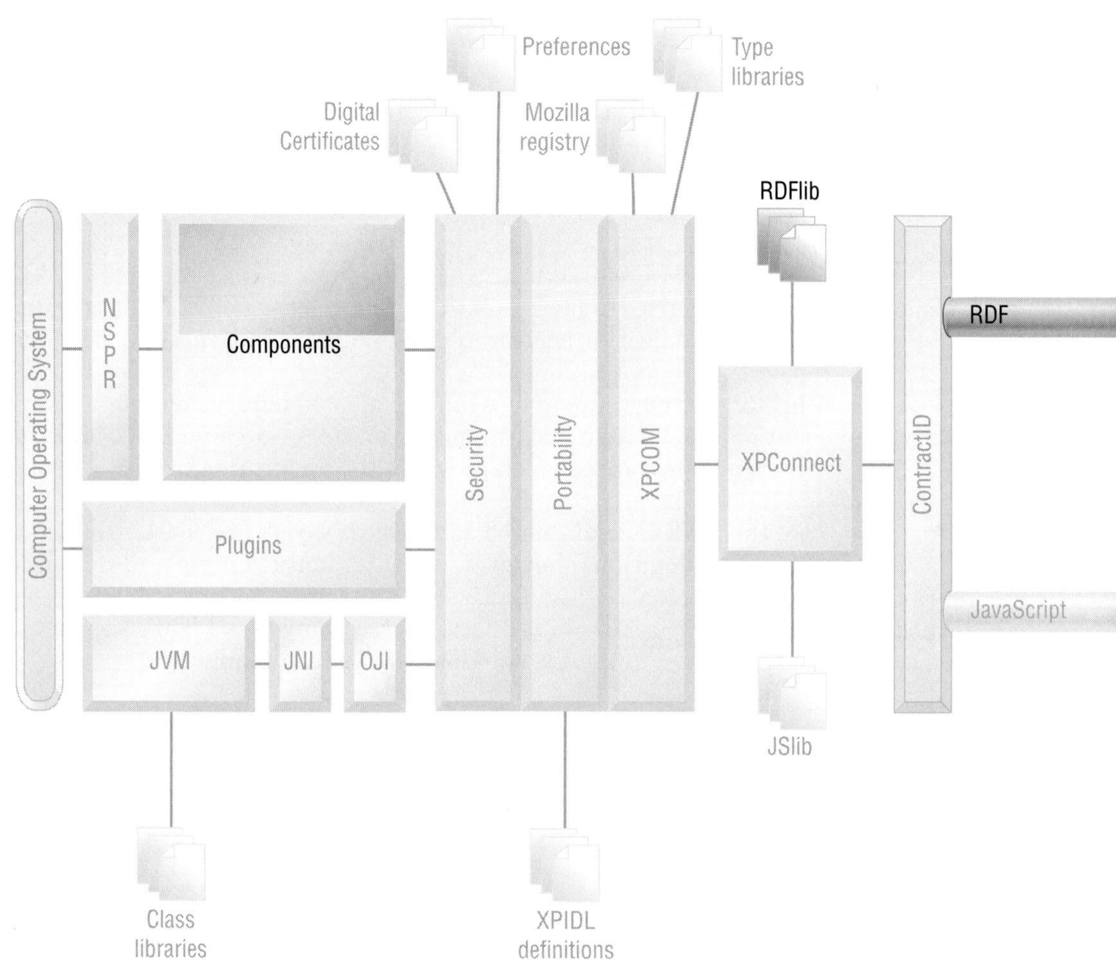
Preferences
Type libraries
Digital Certificates
Mozilla registry
RDFlib
Computer Operating System
NSPR
Components
Security
Portability
XPCOM
XPConnect
ContractID
RDF
JavaScript
Plugins
JVM
JNI
OJI
JSlib
Class libraries
XPIDL definitions

CHAPTER 11

RDF

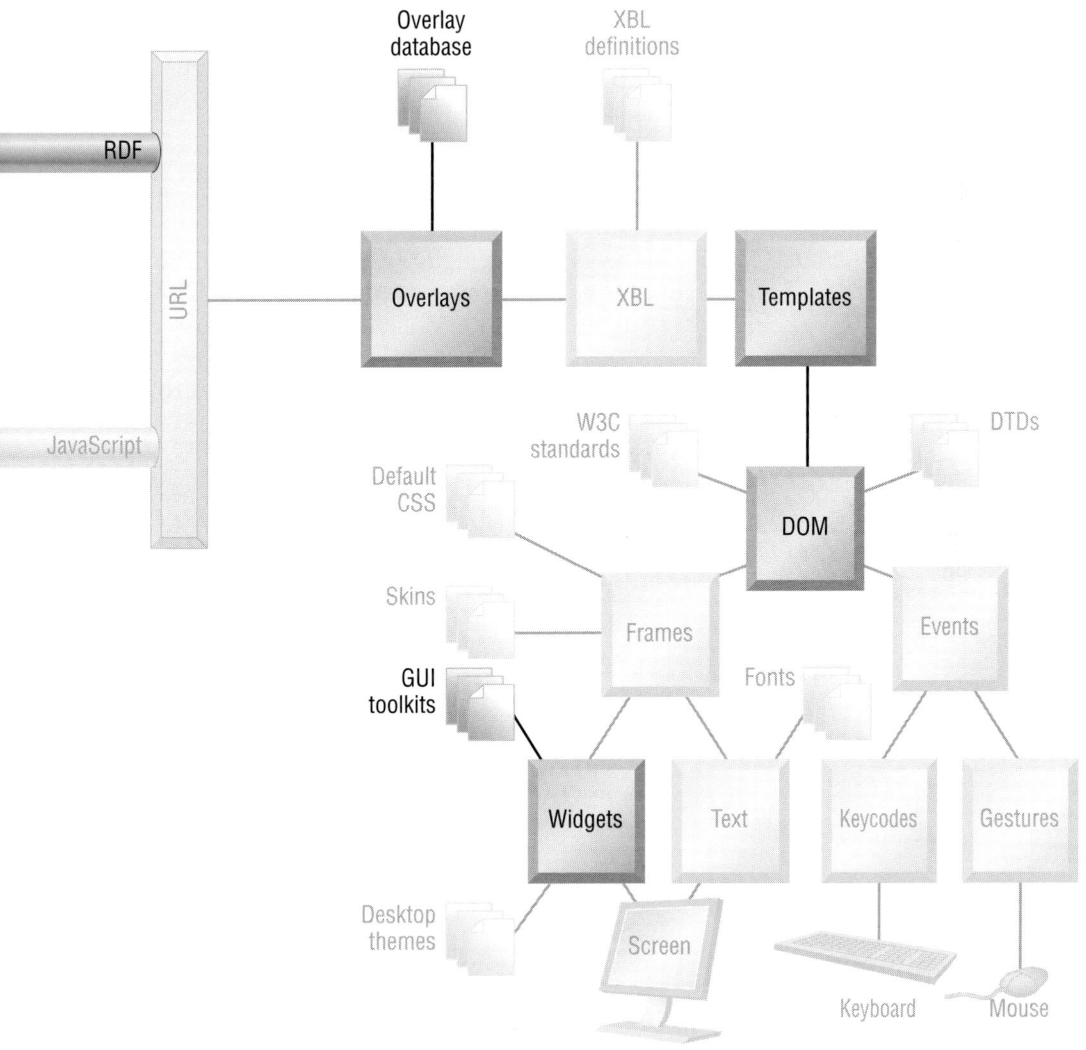

This chapter explains the basics of RDF—a significant information format used by the Mozilla platform. RDF is a W3C XML standard. It is one of the more unusual technologies in Mozilla, but correctly applied it is both powerful and convenient.

Few applications can do useful work without externally supplied information, and Mozilla applications are no different. RDF is a good way to supply small amounts of reusable information. The Mozilla platform can process that RDF information. The Mozilla platform is also partially built out of RDF information. The everyday operation of most Mozilla-based applications depends on RDF building blocks.

This chapter explains the underlying concepts, syntax, and a little about platform support. That is quite a lot by itself. This chapter is mostly RDF introduction, just as Chapter 5, Scripting, introduced JavaScript. Chapters 12, Overlays and Chrome; Chapter 14, Templates; and Chapter 16, XPCOM Objects, expand greatly on applications of RDF.

Most computer technologies can be picked up with a few glances. That strategy doesn't work if you meet something that is a bit new and unusual. In such a case, you need to slow down and absorb the material more systematically. RDF is such a technology. It is also a gateway to all the fancier features of Mozilla. Pull up a comfy chair, pour your drink of choice, and discover this technology carefully. RDF can be fascinating, expressive, and thought-provoking.

What is RDF? Well, there are many kinds of information. One arbitrary set of information categories might be *content*, *data*, and *facts*. Each is processed in a different way. Content-like information tends to be processed as a whole: Display this HTML page; play that music. Datalike information tends to be processed piecewise: Add this record to a database; sort this list of objects. Factlike information is less commonly seen. Facts are statement-like data items. Facts are used by ordinary humans in their daily lives, by specialist academics, and by technologists called knowledge engineers. Some everyday examples of facts are

I went to the shop.

The moon is made of green cheese.

Tom, Dick, and Harry are brothers.

This function is never used.

Every person must find their own path through life.

It is not important whether these facts are true when tested against the real world. It is not important where they came from or whether anyone agrees with them. The important thing is that it is possible to write them down in some useful and general way (in this case, in English). Writing facts down moves them from your head to a formal specification where they can be used. It is only *after* they are captured that you might reflect on their importance or correctness. The modeling in the "Hands On" session in this chapter shows one way that facts can be scrutinized.

The world, including computer technology, is soaked with factlike information. Nearly all of it is expressed in ways that are not specifically designed for fact processing. Generalist programmers rarely deal with specialist fact-processing systems, even though their code is full of implied facts. That implied information is merely used to get other things done. RDF, on the other hand, is an explicit fact-writing system.

A very primitive, trivial, and non-RDF example of a factlike system is the Classic Mozilla bookmarks file, stored in the user profile. Here is a snippet of that file:

```
<A HREF="http://www.mozilla.org/"
   ADD_DATE="961099870"
   LAST_VISIT="1055733093"
   ICON="http://www.mozilla.org/images/mozilla-16.png"
   LAST_CHARSET="ISO-8859-1">
  The Mozilla Organization
</A>
```

This code states information about a URL: the date added; the date last visited. These XML attributes can be seen as plain data or as facts about a URL. Although facts can be expressed in plain XML (or ancient semi-HTML, as shown), there is no hint in those syntaxes what a standard form of expression should be. RDF exists to provide that formality. The bookmarks file is not written in RDF because of backwards-compatibility issues.

In this bookmark example, many industries call the stated information *metadata*. The term metadata is supposed to help our minds separate the data a URL *represents* (content) from the data that is *about* a URL (a description). Unfortunately, if a programmer writes code to process the bookmark file, the only interesting information is the so-called metadata—the substance of that file, which is its content. To the programmer, the metadata is therefore the data to be worked on. This is a very confusing state of affairs when trying to learn RDF. One person's metadata is another's data.

In short, the term *metadata* is overused. To a programmer, the only thing in RDF that should be considered metadata is type information. Everything else is just plain data or, preferably, plain facts. No facts are special; no facts have any special "meta" status.

RDF has its own terminology. For example, here is a fact expressed in RDF:

```
<Description about="file:///local/writing/" open="true"/>
```

In simple terms, this line says that the folder `/local/writing` is open. A more precise RDF interpretation is: "There exists a subject (or resource) named `file:///local/writing`, and it has a predicate (or property) named open, whose object (or value) is the anonymous literal string `"true"`. That is rather awkward language, and we need to explore what it all means.

Finally, RDF is not a visual language. Mozilla cannot lay it out as for HTML or XUL. If display is required, RDF must be hooked up to XUL. RDF itself is silently processed inside the platform. Some of this internal processing happens automatically without any programmer effort. The concept of a *data source* is central to all that processing.

The NPA diagram at the start of this chapter shows that RDF support extends from the very front to the very back of Mozilla's architecture. At the back are the precious XPCOM components that the application developer can use for power manipulation of RDF content. A convenient set of scripts also exists to make this job easier. Those scripts are called RDFlib here, but they are really part of the JSLib library. RDF technology acts like a bridge between front and back ends of the platform. This is because there is direct support for RDF in both XUL and in the scriptable AOM objects. The two ends are automatically connected. The template and overlay systems, both of which manipulate XUL, also depend on RDF.

Unfortunately, Mozilla is only version 1 and RDF processing could be faster. Don't use RDF for data with millions of records; it is not a database. Performance is more than adequate for small data sets.

11.1 Mozilla Uses of RDF

Here is a taste of what RDF can be used for.

Classic Mozilla uses RDF extensively in the construction of the Classic application suite. Some of those uses involve RDF files stored in the file system, and some do not. Uses that do create RDF files are

- ☞ User choices for window arrangement and position
- ☞ Content of the Mozilla Sidebar
- ☞ Manifest files for JAR archives, chrome packages, skins, and locales
- ☞ Overlay database for application overlays
- ☞ Search types for the Smart Browsing Navigator feature
- ☞ Searching and Viewing states in the DOM Inspector
- ☞ The Download Manager
- ☞ MIME types

In addition to these uses, Netscape 7 creates and uses many custom RDF files. Enhancements to the Classic Browser, such as those at *www.mozdev.org*, might also manipulate RDF files.

RDF is a data model as well as a file format. Mozilla's platform infrastructure uses RDF facts in a number of places, without necessarily reading any RDF documents. This infrastructure might convert a non-RDF source into RDF for internal processing. Some places where the RDF model is important are

- The XUL Overlay system described in Chapter 12, Overlays and Chrome
- The XUL Template system described in Chapter 14, Templates
- Directories and files in the local file system
- Bookmarks
- Web page navigation history
- Downloadable Character Set support
- The Mozilla registry
- The What's Related feature of the Sidebar
- Currently open windows
- The address book
- Email folders
- Email folder messages
- Email SMTP message delivery
- Email and Newsgroup accounts
- Sounds to play when email arrives

RDF is not used for any of the following tasks: permanent storage of Internet connections and subscriptions; databases of newsgroups and of newsgroup headers; databases of email folders and of email items; or the platform's Web document cache.

11.2 Learning Strategies for RDF

Learning RDF is like flying. It's tricky to get off the ground, but once you're away, it's great. Why should this be so, and what can be done to make it easier? Here are some thoughts.

XML syntax is quite verbose. By the time your eye and brain absorb all the text and punctuation in an example RDF file, it's hard to focus on the bigger picture. Even the W3C RDF standards people have acknowledged this problem. Use an informal syntax at design time, and only use the official RDF syntax during code and test. This chapter uses informal syntax everywhere except in real code.

RDF itself is frequently confused with its applications. The nature of RDF is one thing; a purpose to which RDF is put is another thing entirely. Reading about content management when trying to learn RDF is of no use. That's like trying to understand a database server by learning an accounting package. It's best to learn the fundamental technology first.

Well-known explanations of RDF are aimed at many different audiences. When reading someone else's explanation, ask yourself: Was that explanation suited to me? Don't frustrate yourself with an explanation that doesn't suit your purpose or your mindset.

RDF in its full glory is also quite big, even though it only has about ten tags. It is equal to several XML standards all at once. RDF runs all the way from simple data to schemas and meta-schemas. That is too much to absorb in one quick reading. To experiment with RDF, practice with very simple tasks to start with. Gain confidence with the basics before trying to compete with Einstein. It's just like any big technology—don't get run over.

Finally, RDF presents an unusual learning trap for those who need absolute certainty. The concepts behind RDF are very open-ended. The RDF philosophy goes on forever with many subtleties and twists. Questions about the meaning of advanced features in RDF have few real answers. Take it at face value, and just use it.

Even given all that, RDF is no big deal. There are tougher XML standards, like OWL. If you have any Prolog or AI training, then RDF will be trivial to pick up.

11.3 A Tutorial on Facts

The basic piece of syntax in XML and RDF is the element, which is frequently expressed as a tag. The basic concept unique to RDF is the fact. A fact does equal one element, but only sometimes equals one tag. What is a fact, and what can you do with one? That is first up. Experts on deductive predicate logic need only glance though this material.

A programmer can glimpse the world of facts through familiar technologies that are a little factlike. Two examples are SQL and `make`. Manipulating records (rows) in a relational database via SQL's INSERT, DELETE, and particularly SELECT is a little factlike. Retrieving rows with a query is like retrieving facts. Alternatively, stating file dependencies in a `make(1)` makefile and letting `make` deduce what is old and needs re-compilation is a little factlike. A makefile dependency rule is like a fact about files or targets. Another example of a configuration file that is factlike is the rather unreadable UNIX `sendmail.cf` configuration file.

What these systems have in common is that the preserved data items are stated independently and are multivalued—each fact has several parts (columns/targets/patterns in the respective examples). Working with a fact means working with some processing engine, like a database server, `make` program, or email routing system. That processing engine presents or crunches facts for you.

11.3.1 Facts Versus Data Structures

Facts are used to describe or model data. Programmers typically model data using data structures. Programmers who are also designers might also model data using tools like data dictionaries or UML diagrams.

Perhaps the easiest way to see how facts differ from traditional data is to write one down. Suppose a boy is at the beach with a dog and a ball. Those four real-world objects (boy, beach, dog, ball) can be stored together as a data structure, or as a fact. Consider first traditional data structures. In JavaScript, this information could be stored as an object:

```
{ boy:"Tom", dog:"Spot", ball:"tennis", beach:"Waikiki" }
```

This is also near the syntax for a suitable C/C++ `struct`. Alternately, this information could be stored in a JavaScript array:

```
[ "Tom", "Spot", "tennis", "Waikiki" ]
```

Fortunately, all the data items consist of strings, which suit the array concept. This syntax can also be used for a C/C++ array. Perl, on the other hand, has lists:

```
( "Tom", "Spot", "tennis", "Waikiki", )
```

In general, there are many ways to write the same bits of data, and each way has its benefits and restrictions. Using an *object* or *class* implies that all the data items (object properties) share the same owner and have a type each. Using an *array* implies that the data items are numbered and of the same type. Using a *list* implies that the items are ordered. Programmers choose whichever is best for a given problem.

This information can also be written as a fact, using a *tuple*. A tuple is a group of N items, where N is any whole number. The number of items is usually fixed per tuple, so a tuple can't grow or shrink. The word tuple comes from the ordered set of terms: single, double, triple, quadruple, quin*tuple*, sex*tuple*, sep*tuple*, oc*tuple*, and so on. Few computer languages support tuples directly (SQL's INSERT is one), so mathematical notation is used as syntax. There are many different mathematical notations. For example, one briefly used in the RDF standards is

```
< Tom, Spot, tennis, Waikiki >
```

That notation, and many others that are similar, can be easily confused with XML tag names. We use

```
<- Tom, Spot, tennis, Waikiki ->
```

Each of the four words in the tuple is called a *term*. Later on, these "crow's feet" brackets will remind you that certain tuples should have three terms only. No quotes are required because this is not a programming language. The terms in a tuple are ordered (like a list) but not numbered (unlike an array) and do not have fixed types (unlike a `struct` or class). The meaning of a tuple is just this: These terms are associated with each other. How they are associated is not important in the general case.

The use of angle brackets < and > hints at the big difference between tuples and other data structures. That difference is that a tuple is a declaration and a statement, like an XML tag or a class definition. The data structure examples are merely expressions. An expression can be calculated and put into a variable. You can't put a statement into a variable. A statement just exists.

When a tuple statement is processed, it simply makes the matching fact true. If a tuple for a fact exists, the fact is said to be true. If the tuple doesn't exist, the fact is said to be false. This truth value is not stored anywhere; it is calculated as required. This arrangement lets the programmer imagine that all possible facts can exist. This is convenient for computer programming because you can process what you've got and conclude that everything else is untrue (false).

The example tuple we created makes this fact true: "Tom, Spot, tennis, and Waikiki are associated with each other." It is true because we've managed to write it down. Note that the tuple we've created contains most, but not all, of the original statement. For example, it doesn't state that Tom and Spot were at Waikiki at the same time. It is normal for any information-gathering exercise to capture the most important details first.

This example tuple has four terms in it. It could have any number of terms. To keep the example simple, we'll now reduce it to just a boy, his dog, and a ball—three terms. Where they happen to be (at a beach or otherwise) is no longer important.

Suppose that this simpler example needed to be captured more completely. A standard modeling approach is to start by identifying the nouns. From there, objects, classes, entities, tables, or types can be inferred. This can also be done for facts. A JavaScript example using objects is shown in Listing 11.1.

Listing 11.1 Objects modeling boy and dog example.

```
var boy = { Pid:1, name:"Tom", Did:null, Bid:null };
var dog = { Did:2, name:"Spot", Pid:null, Bid:null };
var ball = { Bid:5, type:"tennis", color:"green" };

boy.Did = dog;    // connect the objects up
boy.Bid = ball;
dog.Pid = boy;
dog.Bid = ball;
```

`Pid`, `Did`, and `Bid` are short for Person-id, Dog-id, and Ball-id, respectively. These ids are used to make each person unique—there might be two different dogs, or Tom might have five green tennis balls. In addition to the base objects, some effort is made to link the data. Both Tom and Spot are concerned with the same ball; Spot is Tom's dog, Tom is Spot's person.

This modeling can be repeated using tuples, as shown in Listing 11.2.

Listing 11.2 Tuples modeling boy and dog example.

```
<- 1, Tom, 2, 5 ->
<- 2, Spot, 1, 5 ->
<- 5, tennis, green ->
```

As for relational data, links (relationships) between nouns are represented with a pair of identical values. Here we use numbers as identifiers instead of the object references used in Listing 11.1. In Listing 11.2, there is a pair of 1s, a pair of 2s, and two pairs of 5s (the 5 in the third tuple is matched twice). Tuples obviously have a compact notation that is simpler to write than 3GL code. That is one of their benefits. Basic tuples have a naming problem though—there are no variable names to give hints as to what each tuple is about. So the tuple syntax is sometimes harder to read. Nevertheless, both relational databases and facts are based on the tuple concept.

These two modeling attempts, object-based and fact-based, have their uses, but overall they are not very good. The starting scenario is: "Tom and his dog Spot play with a ball." The results of the two modeling attempts are shown in Table 11.1.

Table 11.1 Example information held by object and tuple models

Object model	Tuple model
There is an object for Tom.	There is a tuple for Tom.
There is an object for Spot.	There is a tuple for Spot.
There is an object for a green tennis ball.	There is a tuple for a green tennis ball.
Tom uses-a Spot.	Tom, 1, 2, and 5 are associated.
Spot uses-a Tom.	Spot, 1, 2, and 5 are associated.
Tom uses-a green tennis ball.	Green tennis ball and 5 are associated.
Spot uses-a green tennis ball.	
(More information can be deduced.)	(More information can be deduced.)

Table 11.1 cheats a bit because the purpose of each tuple and object is assumed. The problem with both of these models is that priority is given to the *things* in the scenario (the nouns). The *relationships* between the things are a far distant second. Both models have lost a lot of relationship information. It is not captured that Tom *owns* Spot, or that Spot *plays* with the ball.

The traditional solution to this loss is to add more objects, or more tables, or more whatever. In the world of facts, the solution is to make every existing relationship a term in a tuple. Such a tuple is called a *predicate.*

11.3.2 Predicates and Triples

A special group of tuples are called predicates. Since all tuples are facts, predicates are also facts. Predicates contain terms holding relationship information as well as terms holding simple data items. The naïve way to add this relationship information is shown in Listing 11.3, which updates Listing 11.2.

Listing 11.3 Addition of relationships to boy and dog tuples.

```
<- 1, Tom, owner, 2, plays-with, 5 ->
<- 2, Spot, owned-by, 1, plays-with, 5 ->
<- 5, tennis, green ->
```

In this example the relationships have the same status as the other information. It is almost possible to read the first tuple as though it were a sentence: "Id one (Tom) is owner of id two (Spot) and plays with id five (a ball)." Clearly there is more specific and complete information here than in either of the attempts in Table 11.1. This process is similar to database entity-relationship modeling.

Here is some technical jargon: Tuples containing relationship information are called predicates because one or more terms in the tuple *predicates* a relationship between two other terms in the tuple. The relationship term by itself is also called a predicate because it is responsible for the predication effect. This is confusing unless you work out the context in which "predicate" is used. Either it refers to a whole tuple, or just to a particular term in a tuple. Here we try to use it only for the particular term. We use tuple, triple, or fact for the set of terms.

Listing 11.3 is still not ideal because some tuples have more than one relationship term. If a tuple contains more than one predicate term, then the processing of facts is not simple. Some repair of this example is therefore needed. Listing 11.4 splits the tuples up so that there is at most one predicate term per tuple.

Listing 11.4 Single predicate boy and dog tuples.

```
<- 1, Tom, owner, 2 ->
<- 1, Tom, plays-with, 5 ->
<- 2, Spot, owned-by, 1 ->
<- 2, Spot, plays-with, 5 ->
<- 5, tennis, green ->
```

At the cost of a little duplication, the predicates are now separated, and the tuples are perhaps even simpler to read. In database design, an equivalent process is called normalization. In software design, it is called factoring. In all cases, it is a divide-and-conquer information-reduction strategy. This refinement process is not complete, however. More can be done. These tuples can be cleaned up so that every tuple has exactly three items ($N = 3$). Listing 11.5 does this cleanup.

Listing 11.5 Predicate triples for boy and dog example.

```
<- 1, is-named, Tom ->
<- 1, owner, 2 ->
<- 1, plays-with, 5 ->
<- 2, is-named, Spot ->
<- 2, owned-by, 1 ->
```

```
<- 2, plays-with, 5 ->
<- 5, type-of, tennis ->
<- 5, color-of, green ->
```

All these tuples are now triples. Triples with a predicate item are a well-understood starting point for all factlike systems. Using predicate triples is like using first normal form for a database schema ("every table has a unique key ...") or identifying nonvalue classes in an OO design ("All classes with identity..."). When thinking about facts, start with predicate triples ("A fact has three terms ..."), not with general tuples.

Note that it is easy to get carried away with predicates and relationships. The last two triples in Listing 11.4 have very weak relationships. *Tennis* and *green* are more like simple descriptive properties than first-class data items like persons and dogs. Just as you can have too much normalization or too many trivial objects, you can have too many trivial facts. If trivial facts are the interesting part of your problem, however, then use them freely.

Because triples are so widely used, their three data items have formal names. The relationship-like item is called the predicate, as before. The first data item is called the *subject*, and the third data item is called the *object*. This use of the term "object" derives from the grammar of spoken language not from technology engineering. The answer to the question "Which of these three is a triple about?" is a matter of personal philosophy. The most common answer is that it is about the subject. In Listing 11.5, the predicate data items have been chosen so that the subject always comes first. That is a convention you should always follow.

Finally, facts that are predicates can be written in a number different ways. For example, in the Prolog computer language, they can be written:

```
predicate(subject, object)
plays-with(1,5)
```

Alternately, in Lisp or Scheme, they can be written:

```
(predicate subject object)
(plays-with 1 5)
```

Predicates can also be written in English:

```
subject predicate object
1 plays with 5
```

And, of course, using RDF, predicates can be written in XML. One of several options is to use a single tag:

```
<Description about="subject" predicate="object"/>
<Description about="1" plays-with="5"/>
```

To write down a predicate in convenient shorthand, the informal tuple notation of this chapter can also be used, or the punctuation can be stripped away, leaving the simple *N*-Triple syntax used by some RDF experts:

```
   tuple: <- subject, predicate, object ->
N-Triple: subject predicate object
```

If you prefer to stick to real-language syntax, then the simplest and clearest notations are those of Prolog and Lisp, which have been used for decades for fact-based processing. The alternative is RDF itself.

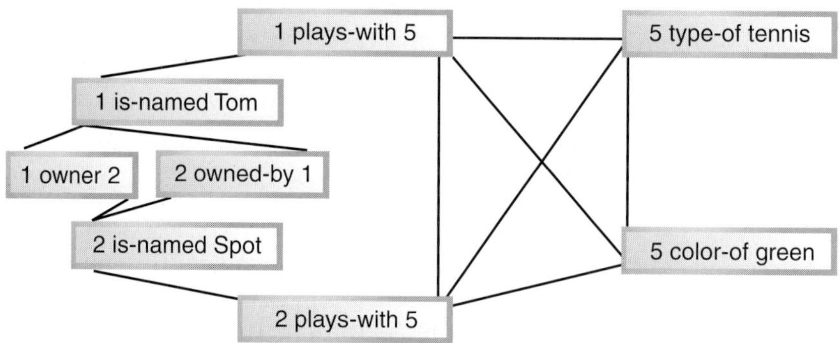

Fig. 11.1 Graph of boy-dog tuple links.

11.3.3 Three Ways to Organize Facts

So far, all that has been achieved in this tutorial is to identify what a good format for a fact is. How are you to store such facts in a computer? There are several ways to do so.

The first way to store facts is as a set of independent items. In relational technology that means as separate rows in a three-column table; in object technology, as a collection of items, say in a Bag or Set; and in plain data structure technology, as a simple list. Listing 11.5 is a written version of such a simple set.

Such a simple approach is very flexible. More facts can be added at any time. Facts can be deleted. There is no internal structure to maintain. Such a solution is like an ordinary bucket (a pail). You can pour facts into and out of the bucket as you please.

One of the chief benefits of using a bucket is that fact sets can be trivially merged. You can pour facts into the bucket from several sources. The result is just one big collection of facts. When facts are poured out of the bucket, all facts appear together, regardless of origin. This is just a simple union of two sets.

The second way to store facts is to recognize that there are links between them that create an overall structure. This structure can be stored as a traditional data structure, with pointers or references between the tuples. Because the links are quite general, the structure is a graph, rather than a simple tree or list. Recall that a graph is the most general way to represent data. Graphs have edges (lines) and vertices (junction points or nodes), and that's all. Both edges and vertices might be labeled. Such a graph can also be displayed visually. Figure 11.1 shows the links between facts from Listing 11.5.

This is a rather complex diagram for a system consisting of only a boy, a dog, and a ball. In fact, this diagram is six lines short; there should be three more "1" lines and three more "2" lines, for a total of 18 lines. A simplification strategy is to add intersection points by breaking out the ids from the tuples. Figure 11.2 shows this improved diagram, which reduces the total line count from 18 to 12.

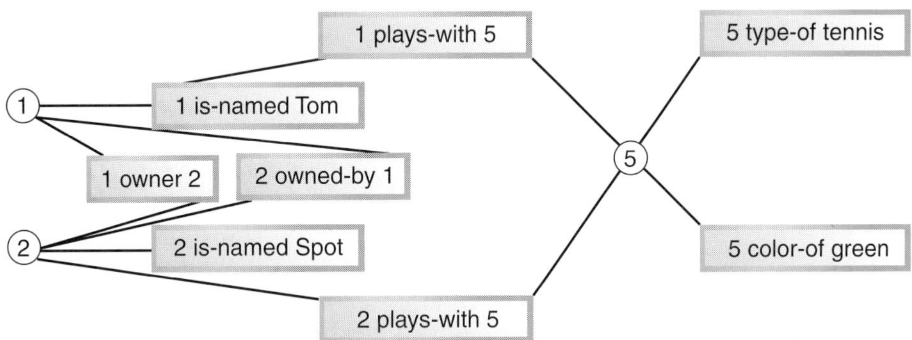

Fig. 11.2 Reduced graph of boy-dog tuple links.

The strategy of breaking out items from the tuples seems to have worked a little, so let us continue it. All of the items can be broken out, not just those with identifiers. Furthermore, it can be seen that some tuples are opposites (`owner` and `owned-by`, in this example). Such duplication can be removed by giving a line a direction. Follow an arrow one way for one predicate; follow it the reverse way for the opposite predicate. Figure 11.3 shows these improvements.

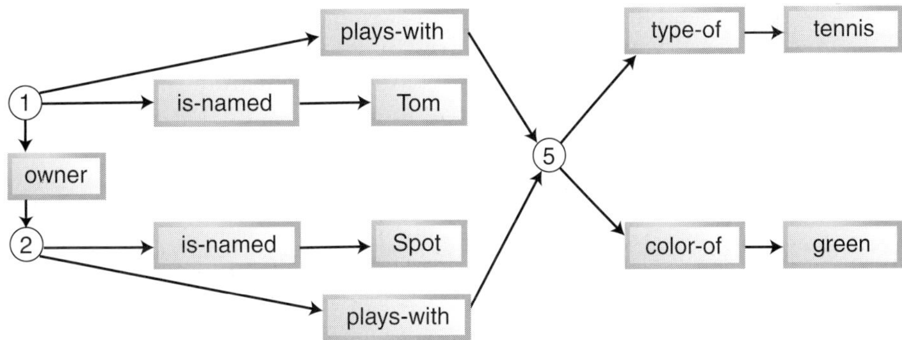

Fig. 11.3 Much reduced graph of boy-dog tuple links.

As a final improvement, note that every predicate has exactly one arrow in and one arrow out. The predicate might as well be used as a label for the arrow that passes through it, and save some boxes. That last step is done in Figure 11.4, which also slightly reorganizes the left side of the diagram.

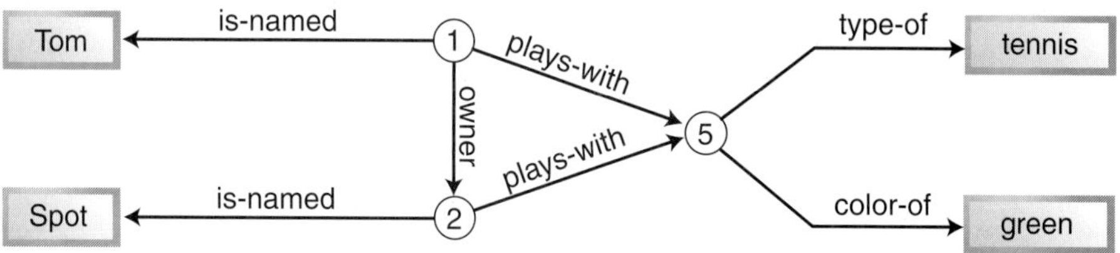

Fig. 11.4 RDF graph of boy-dog tuple links.

The predicate relationships in Figure 11.4 are very clear. There are peripheral predicates that merely add information to a given identifier (`is-named`, `type-of`, `colour-of`), and more critical predicates (`plays-with`, `owner`) that say something about the relationships between the identifiers under scrutiny. The decision to use an identifier for each real-world thing being modeled (decided in Listings 11.1 and 11.2), and to focus on the identifier in the diagram (done in Figure 11.2) have both paid off. Those identifiers have turned out to be vital for diagramming purposes.

The graph in Figure 11.4 follows the official RDF graph notation. Circles or ellipses are used for identifiers, and squares are used for literal values. A better system for identifier and predicate names is needed, though. We can use URLs as identifiers. That will come shortly.

The benefit of a graph representation of RDF data is that scripts can navigate intelligently through the set of facts, using or ignoring each connection, as the need determines.

There is a third way to organize facts, which is often used in Mozilla RDF documents. Drop all the facts onto a kitchen table randomly. Now take a needle and thread and run the thread through any terms that are relevant to a given topic. If you need to know about that topic, just pick the thread up and those terms and their related facts are lifted out from the full set. Continuing the boy and dog example, Figure 11.5 shows an imaginary line that connects all the number identifiers.

There is no syntax in RDF for implementing such lines. Instead, this effect is achieved with special RDF tags called *containers*. Since RDF can only represent facts, containers are made out of facts. Any term of a fact can appear in one or more containers, although the subject term is the common choice. The other fact terms are stored as usual. Figure 11.6 is the same as Figure 11.5, except that it shows the container expressed in the same way as the other facts.

The term holding the word `Container` is the start point for the container. The only thing that distinguishes a container from other facts is the way predicates are named. Each fact that represents one contained item is automatically given a number as a name. Unlike the numbers the example has used as placeholders for subject and object identifiers, the numbered predicates used by a container really are expressed using numbers in the RDF syntax.

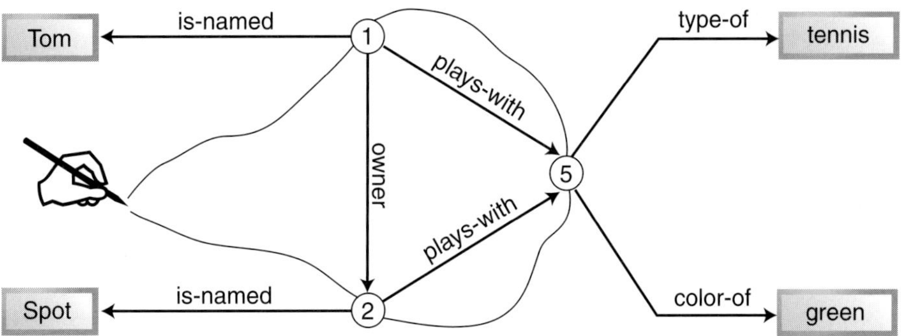

Fig. 11.5 RDF graph showing like terms connected by a line.

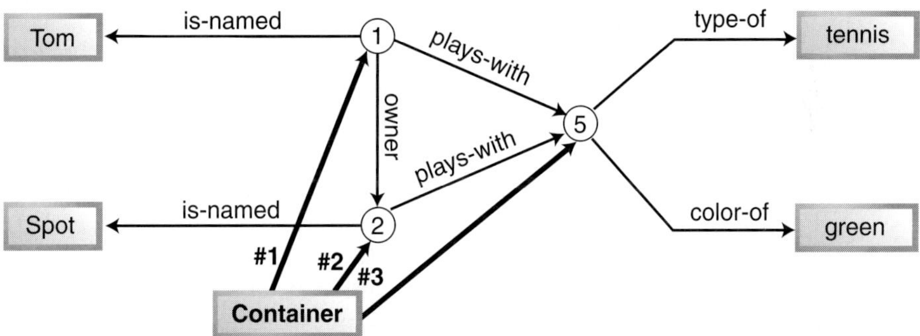

Fig. 11.6 RDF graph showing like terms connected by a container.

Containers are simple structural mechanisms. They also support querying a fact set. An application programmer can use a container as a partial index, or as an iterator, or as a relational view. A given RDF document can have unlimited containers.

To summarize, facts can be stored as a simple set of triples or as a complex graph that revolves around identifiers. In between is the partial structure of a container, which is like drawing a travel route on a map. A set of facts is called a fact store. Complex fact stores are called knowledge bases, just as a data collection is a database. Simple RDF documents are fact stores; RDF documents that include RDF schema tags are knowledge bases.

11.3.4 Facts About Facts

Facts can describe other facts. Knowing this is sometimes useful, but only for special applications. Most of the time it's better to ignore it. Some of the more standard effects are described here. If your brain is full by now, skip this section, take a break, and resume with the next section. Otherwise, onward.

In the boy and dog example, many extra facts that could be stated explicitly are implied by the stated facts. Some of these extra facts are the result of design observations, and some are almost automatically true. The following examples are based on this single fact:

```
<- 1, is-named, Tom ->
```

One set of design observations that yields extra facts is type information. A programmer developing a fact set can choose to add types. For example, these facts might follow from the preceding single fact:

```
<- 1, is-type, integer ->
<- Tom, is-type, string ->
```

These facts give a type to the subject and object data items in the earlier fact. These facts provide extended information about another fact. They are equivalent to a data dictionary or a schema. Unlike database and OO design, these facts are not separate in any sense to other "plain" facts. They can be stored with any other facts. Such facts might be used by a Mozilla/RDF application that is a data modeling tool, which needs to manipulate schemas.

To repeat the remarks at the start of this chapter, many industries call this stated information *metadata*. The term *metadata* is supposed to help our minds separate the data the URL *represents* from the data that is *about* the URL, as in the example. Unfortunately, if a programmer writes code to process a file of so-called metadata, the only interesting information is the metadata itself—the contents of that file. To the programmer, the metadata is the data. This is a very confusing state of affairs, not only because one person's metadata is another person's data but also because RDF is about facts, and not really about plain data at all.

In short, the term *metadata* is overused. To a programmer, the only thing in RDF that should be considered as metadata is type information. Everything else is just plain data or, preferably, plain facts. No facts are special; no facts have any special "meta" status.

A second set of facts are these three, which are automatically true:

```
<- example-fact, subject, 1 ->
<- example-fact, predicate, is-named ->
<- example-fact, object, Tom ->
```

Here, `example-fact` means the preceding example fact. The `subject` predicate says that 1 is the subject for that fact. The `predicate` predicate says that `is-named` is the predicate for that example fact. In other words, these facts are facts about the example fact. This process is called *reification* (from *reify*), which loosely means "exposing the facts about this fact so that we can work on it."

Reification is similar to extracting metadata, but far messier. To see why, consider this problem. Earlier it was said that all stated facts are true, and all unstated facts are false. Does an example fact without the first reification fact above have a subject or not? If the reification fact doesn't exist, then the answer should be false. But the example fact exists, so assumptions about its composition are surely true. There is an apparent contradiction (but the logic is flawed). Such thinking gets a practical person nowhere. Neither does asking whether the reification facts should themselves be reified. These kinds of facts might be used by a Mozilla/RDF application interested in textual analysis or natural language processing, but that's all.

A further set of design observations that yields extra facts is the matter of names. A programmer developing a fact set might choose to name features of the fact set. Using the same single example fact, one might name the subject and object data items, perhaps if data are to be presented in columns with column headings, or if some King is handing out titles to his nobles.

```
<- 1, is-named, person-id ->
<- Tom, is-named, person-name ->
<- example-fact, is-named, person-definition ->
```

This is also very messy. The original fact states that there is a person named Tom. But according to the first fact here, the string "Tom" is named (has the type) `person-name`, and the name of the string "1" used to recognize Tom is `person-id`. Also, the whole initial fact that states "a person exists named Tom with identity 1," is itself named `person-definition`. To summarize, Tom's name is `"Tom"`, `"Tom"`'s name is `person-name`, and "Tom is named `"Tom"`" is named `person-definition`. This subtle thinking is not of practical use to programmers.

Next, note that most aspects of most data modeling systems can be expressed as predicate facts. For example, you can use the following predicates to state facts describing an OO model:

```
is-a has-a uses-a instance-of
```

These other predicates might instead assist a relational model:

```
has-key has-foreign-key one-to-many one-to-one has-optional
```

Using such predicates, it is possible to add complex layers of meaning (like object-orientedness) over the top of the basic fact system. This is very messy and not for beginners. RDF includes a few features like this itself, but for ordinary use they should be avoided. Use of these predicates might appear to be metadata, but metadata should use "is-a" (and other relationships) as an object term, not as a predicate term. A correct metadata example fact is "*UML arrow 5* has-feature *is-a*." A messier, layered solution is just to state directly "*UML entity 3* is-a *UML entity 2*."

Finally, new facts can be derived from existing facts. In the boy and dog example, this fact might be implied because of the other facts stated:

```
<- Tom, plays-with, Spot ->
```

Whether this fact is implied depends on what assumptions are made about the safety of leaping to such conclusions. After all, Tom and Spot are playing with the same ball, so they're probably playing with each other. Such derived facts are the responsibility of deductive systems, and neither RDF nor Mozilla does any real deduction.

When facts are collected together for processing, they are held in a *fact store*. A fact store is the fact equivalent of a database, and is usually memory-based rather than disk-based.

To summarize this tutorial on facts, predicate triples are a useful subset of simple tuples. Facts are expressed in such triples. RDF documents contain facts. Facts are statements, not data, and when stated are true. Complex aspects of facts are easily revealed, but they are not that useful. Using facts as information about other, named, nonfact information (like URLs) is normal. Using facts as information about other facts should wait until simpler uses are mastered.

11.3.5 Queries, Filters, and Ground Facts

Storing facts in a fact store is useless if you can't get them out. Programmers need a way of extracting important facts and ignoring the rest.

RDF documents are XML content and therefore can be navigated by hand, or queried. The simplest way to navigate XML by hand is to use the DOM standards. The simplest way to query an XML document is to use a search method like `getElementById()`, or something fancier like XML Query or XPath. None of these approaches is used for RDF.

Instead, RDF documents are read or produced as a stream of facts. A programmer would rather receive only the content that is needed, not everything under the sun. For RDF, that means only the facts that are needed. To restrict the supplied stream of facts, a matching process is required, one that throws away irrelevant information. Such a process is a kind of query or filtering system, like SQL or `grep(1)`.

Query systems aren't explored in this chapter, but they rely on the concept of a *ground fact*. A ground fact (sometimes called a concrete fact) is a fact that is fully known. All the facts discussed so far in this chapter are ground facts.

As an example, consider this statement: "Tom is the owner of Spot." It is easy to identify a subject (Tom), object (Spot), and predicate (owner). Everything is known about the statement, and so the statement is said to be *ground*. This means it has a solid basis. An equivalent ground fact can be written down right away:

```
<- Tom, owner, Spot ->
```

By comparison, a trickier statement might be: "Tom owns a dog." The subject, object, and predicate can still be identified so the statement is ground. An equivalent fact is

```
<- Tom, owner, dog ->
```

If, in this case, you happen to know that there are many dogs, then the question "Which dog does Tom own?" is left unanswered. In that case, "Tom owns a dog" is not ground because no object (a particular dog) can be identified. A lawyer would say, "That statement is groundless because you can't produce a specific dog that Tom owns." That is his way of saying that you are too vague to be trusted. In such a case, the best fact you can write down is

```
<- Tom, owner, ??? ->
```

The question marks just indicate that something is missing; they are not special syntax. There is very little you can do if handed such an incomplete fact. The opposite of ground is *not ground*, so this fact is not ground.

This partial-fact problem can be turned on its head. If the computer knows which dog Tom owns, but you don't, then the incomplete fact can be given to the computer to fix. The computer runs some code that compares the incomplete fact (called a *goal*) against all the available facts and returns all the facts that would ground it. This is called *unification*; in Mozilla's simple system, it's a matching process. You would find out all the dogs that Tom owns, or even all the pets that Tom owns, or possibly everything that Tom owns. How much you get back just depends on what facts are in the fact store. Mozilla's query and filtering systems do this for you.

RDF ground facts are queried or filtered by programmers using a fact or facts that are not ground and that are called a goal. RDF itself can state both ground and not ground facts, but facts that are not ground are rare and generally bad design. Mozilla-specific features are required to support goals.

To summarize, facts can be stored like data and examined with a matching system that unifies a goal against ground facts. That is all the ground facts about facts.

11.4 RDF Syntax

RDF's syntax is based on several standards and nonstandards.

The core standard at work is, of course, RDF. This W3C standard consists of two main parts and has evolved in two stages.

The first stage of standardization consisted of draft standards developed in 1999 and 2000. There are two main documents:

- *http://www.w3.org/TR/1999/REC-rdf-syntax-19990222.* This document is the "RDF 1.0 Model and Syntax Final Recommendation." Model just means underlying conceptual design.
- *http://www.w3.org/TR/2000/CR-rdf-schema-20000327.* This document was not finalized for several years. It provides complex schema operations on RDF tags and is different from XML Schema.

The second stage of RDF standardization consisted of expanding and completing the existing documents. These newer documents were finalized in 2003:

- *http://www.w3.org/TR/rdf-syntax-grammar/*, "RDF/XML Syntax Specification (Revised)," is an update to the preceding 1999 document.
- `http://www.w3.org/TR/rdf-schema/`, "RDF Vocabulary Description Language 1.0: RDF Schema," is a completion of the earlier RDF schema document.
- There are also several explanatory documents at `http://www.w3.org/RDF/` that analyze RDF from different points of view.

Of these five items, Mozilla implements nearly all the first item (the 1999 recommendation) and a little of the new features of the third item (the Revised recommendation).

Other standards that work closely with RDF are XML Namespaces and XML Schemas. Mozilla implements XML Namespaces and XML Schema, but the XML Schema support is not used in any way for RDF processing. Mozilla's XUL also has some syntax support for RDF.

These standards provide a set of XML tags from which facts can be constructed. Fact subjects and fact objects can be expressed as attribute values, or (for objects) as text nodes enclosed in start and end tags. The standards, however, provide only a few special-purpose predicates. All the rest of the predicates must be supplied by the application programmer. This means that names for extra XML tags and/or extra XML attributes must be defined.

These extra names form a vocabulary. Such a set of names can be specified in an XML Schema document or in an RDF document. Some existing vocabularies have well-known URLs and specifications to encourage their reuse. The most famous example is the Dublin Core, which is a set of keywords. It is used primarily by librarians and archivists for catalogues, and consists of predicates like "Title" and "Author."

Mozilla does not use the Dublin Core for its vocabulary. It does not allow XML Schema to be used to specify a vocabulary. Instead, a few vocabularies are built into the platform directly. The RDF processing that Mozilla does also allows the application programmer to make up names on the spot without any formal definition existing. So predicate names can be made up in the same way that JavaScript variable names can be made up.

11.4.1 Syntax Concepts

An RDF document is an XML document, and RDF is an application of XML. The XML Namespace identifier used for RDF in Mozilla is

```
http://www.w3.org/1999/02/22-rdf-syntax-ns#
```

RDF documents should have an `.rdf` suffix. The MIME types Mozilla recognizes for RDF are

```
text/rdf
text/xml
```

The official MIME type is not yet supported as of 1.4. That type is

```
application/rdf+xml
```

11.4.1.1 Tags The primary goal of RDF is to provide a syntax that allows facts to be specified. XML facts could be represented a number of ways. Listing 11.6 illustrates some imaginary options:

Listing 11.6 Potential XML syntax for facts.

```
<fact subject="…" predicate="…" object="…"/>

<fact>
  <subject …/>
  <predicate …/>
  <object …/>
</fact>

<subject … predicate="…" object="…"/>
```

None of the forms in Listing 11.6 is used for RDF. RDF syntax uses this form instead:

```
<fact subject="…">
  <predicate>object</predicate>
</fact>
```

This is conceptual syntax only, not actual RDF. A syntactically correct RDF fact matching the conceptual syntax is

```
<Description about="http://www.mozilla.org/">
  <NC:LastVisited>10 January 2004</NC:LastVisited>
</Description>
```

This syntax choice provides options for nesting facts inside other facts. It makes a number of syntax shortcuts possible. It mimics some technical aspects of the Web environment. Unfortunately, terminology is a real challenge for beginners. The words in this conceptual syntax are not used in RDF. Worse, the different bits of this syntax are described with RDF-specific ideas, not with the fact concepts that appear earlier in this chapter. That is a very confusing state of affairs.

RDF uses different ideas because it attempts to reuse thinking from Web technologies; RDF was originally created to address issues in the Web environment. On the one hand, this reuse does create a somewhat familiar environment for developers. On the other hand, RDF is still about facts, and no amount of clever naming can hide that. Table 11.2 compares these RDF names with fact concepts and Web terminology.

The recommended way to handle this is to wear two hats. When thinking very generally, RDF syntax is best seen as a set of facts, so use the fact con-

Table 11.2 RDF terminology

Fact concept	RDF term	Web terms borrowed from	RDF syntax
Fact	Description	Description of a document or record	<Description>, <Seq>, <Alt>, <Bag>
Subject	Resource	URL	about=, id=
Predicate	Property (and resource)	Object property, CSS property, XML attribute	user-defined
Object	Value (or resource)	Property value, attribute value	resource=, plain text

cepts. In specific examples where the set of facts forms a simple tree, it is best to see it as a hierarchy of resources and properties, so use RDF terms. Because most RDF documents are small or highly structured or both, this simpler case is easy to get away with.

We can practice this thinking on the simple `<Description>` tag stated earlier. In fact terminology, it is interpreted as follows. The `<Description>` tag defines the subject term of a fact. If that tag has any contents, that content represents the remaining terms of one or more facts. The `<NC:LastVisited>` tag is a predicate term, and the plain string "`10 January 2004`" is an object term. By comparison, in RDF terminology, the `<Description>` tag is interpreted this way. The `<Description>` tag identifies a resource. That resource may have properties, given by other tags. The `<NC:LastVisited>` tag is one such property, and it has the value "`10 January 2004`".

An advantage of the RDF terminology is that most predicate names in Mozilla's RDF are property-like. Although `color` (or any word) can be used as a predicate, `color` sounds more like a DOM or CSS property name than a predicate relationship. Even so, in RDF, the terms *predicate* and *property* are harmlessly interchangeable.

The complete list of basic RDF tags is as follows:

```
<RDF> <Description> <Seq> <Bag> <Alt> <li>
```

The last four tags are redundant and can be expressed using `<Description>`, so RDF has a very small number of tags. Although predicate tags are application-specific, RDF does predefine some predicates. These predicate tags are named

```
<Statement> <subject> <predicate> <object>
```

These tags are used for reification of facts. `<Statement>` reifies a fact. The other three reify one term each of a triple. Mozilla does not support any of these four tags.

11.4.1.2 Containers RDF supports containers. Containers are a lazy person's way of writing and collecting repetitious facts. A container consists of a <Bag>, <Seq>, or <Alt> tag. The container and its content together make a collection. Such a collection can be put where the object appears in a fact. Such a container looks like this:

```
<Description>
  <Bag>
    <li>object 1</li>
    <li>object 2</li>
    <li>object 3</li>
  </Bag>
</Description>
```

In a normal fact, there is a one-to-one mapping between the fact's subject and object (between resource and property value). That means one object per subject. Containers change this so that there can be a one-to-many mapping. That means at least zero objects per subject. Containers are the RDF equivalent of a list or an array. If a container is used, it is up to the application to know about it or to detect it and react appropriately.

An obvious use of a container is to track the empty seats in a theatre or plane booking system. Each seat is a resource; such a system needs to manage all the seats, whether full or empty. A list of yet-to-be allocated seats can be maintained in a container separate from the facts about the seats themselves. An example RDF fragment is shown in Listing 11.7.

Listing 11.7 Two facts specified with a single RDF <description> tag.

```
<Description id="seat:A1">
  <aisle>true</aisle>
</Description>
<Description id="seat:A2">
  <booked>Tim</booked>
  <aisle>false</aisle>
</Description>
<Description id="seat:A3">
  <aisle>false</aisle>
</Description>

<Description id="seat:vacancies">
  <Bag>
    <li resource="seat:A1"/>
    <li resource="seat:A3"/>
  </Bag>
</Description>
```

This example states whether each seat is an aisle seat, and if the seat is booked, it adds the name of the person booked. The `seat:` syntax is an imaginary application-specific URL scheme. Only seat A2 is booked. The <Bag> container holds references to the two unbooked seats. The syntax used for the <li> tag is one of the several shorthands that RDF supports.

So containers are also used to give programmers access to subsets of facts. A container's held items are the subjects of another set of other facts, and those other facts can be accessed by grabbing the container and looking through it. Containers can be viewed as a simple data structure for facts and as a simple navigation mechanism. In the booking system, the programmer can book a seat by first checking it is in the vacancies container, then adding a `booked` predicate to the seat's `<Description>`, and then removing it from that container.

In object-oriented terms, the container has a uses-a relationship with each collected item. The collected items are not in any way hidden inside the container.

Container tags and their collection of items can always be replaced with an equivalent set of plain facts. See the specific tags.

11.4.1.3 Identifiers The boy and dog example discussed earlier in this chapter made some effort to provided identifiers for each significant item modeled by the set of facts. This emphasis on identifiers is much stronger in RDF than it is in most XML applications. Identifiers are critical to RDF and are used two ways.

The first use of identifiers identifies whole facts. This is achieved by adding an id attribute to the tag holding a particular fact. The RDF document's URL, plus #, plus the id's value uniquely identifies that fact worldwide. According to IETF RFC 2396, such a URL represents a document fragment, not a complete resource. RDF breaks that rule—such a URL is considered a whole resource even though it is part of a larger document. RDF documents therefore can be viewed as a bundle of resources—a resource collection. Each resource is a single fact. This is very different from HTML. In HTML, an id is just a single tag, and `<A>` without HREF just marks progress points inside a single document. An example of an RDF identifier is

```
<Description ID="printEnabled" … />
```

This RDF file might store information about the printing subsystem, and the `ID` makes this specific fact locatable via a meaningful name.

The second use of RDF identifiers is to replace local literals in a given RDF file. The example facts so far noted generally work with information stored right in that fact. For example, "tennis" (for tennis ball) is a piece of information stored directly in one fact in Listing 11.5.

Such immediacy does not need to be the case. For example, several facts have been considered about Tom. Tom's physical body does not appear in the fact—just a number (1) used to identify him. It's understood that this number stands in for him. RDF provides a better identifier for Tom than a simple number; a URL can be used instead. This URL represents Tom just as a simple number can. Perhaps it's a `mailto:` address or a URL that retrieves a personnel record. Any facts whose subject is a string matching that URL are about Tom. In Web terms, Tom is a resource, and a URL locates him.

RDF goes further, though. The fact's object can be a URL, just as the subject can. For subject and object, this is straightforward. Tom's dog has a URL and so does Tom's ball.

More subtly, RDF allows the fact predicate/property to have a URL. The URL of a predicate is just a pointer to a location where that predicate is fully described. The URL is the predicate's identifier and stands in for the actual predicate, which might be held by some regulatory body, a standards organization, or even an MIS server. Actually, RDF insists that the predicate part of a fact be represented with an id, and that id must be a URL. For readability, the URL of a predicate usually contains a word that expresses its general meaning, like *www.example.com / #Owner.*

Facts can therefore be expressed entirely in URL identifiers if necessary. This is really no more than using pointers to the terms the facts are composed of. This kind of RDF document is one source of confusion for beginners because such a file seems to have some direct interaction with the Web. The URLs in such a document are no more significant than strings that hold a street address. There is no automatic Web navigation or other magic, unless the software processing the RDF file adds it. Mozilla does not add any such processing. RDF documents do not need access to the Web. URLs are just data items in RDF.

There is one complexity, however. Any URL in an RDF document might be a fact in another RDF file. Facts in documents can therefore refer to each other. In ordinary applications, this is a bad idea because it creates a spaghetti mess of fact dependencies. In specialized cases, like authentication protocols, it might be more necessary. It makes sense for facts in one document to contain URLs to metadata facts or schema items in some other, authoritative resource, but that's about as far as it should go.

These stand-in URLs can have the more general syntax of a URI (Universal Resource Identifier). A URI is a URL or URN (Universal Resource Name). The benefits of this broader possibility are explored shortly. The example of a URL has only been used because it is familiar.

It is possible for a fact to have a missing term in an RDF document. This happens when a container or `<Description>` tag with no identifier is used. The container tag represents an extra subject in the graph of facts and without some identification; it is anonymous. An RDF document with no anonymous facts is ground. For query purposes, it is highly recommended that all RDF documents be ground. Therefore, container tags should not be left without identifiers.

11.4.2 `<RDF>`

The `<RDF>` tag is the container tag for a whole RDF document and is required. Because RDF documents contain several namespaces, it is common to always use a namespace prefix for RDF. Thus,

```
<rdf:RDF xmlns:rdf="http://www.w3.org/1999/02/22-rdf-syntax-ns#">
```

This tag has no special attributes of its own. The only things that appear in it are XML namespace declarations, which add a vocabulary (additional tags) to the RDF document. These namespace declarations assist RDF in the same way the DTDs assist HTML. Table 11.3 shows all the namespaces used in the Mozilla Platform.

Table 11.3 XML Namespaces Used for RDF Vocabulary

URL of Namespace	xmlns Prefix	Defined Where?	Use
http://www.w3.org/1999/02/22-rdf-syntax-ns#	RDF	www.w3.org	Core RDF support
http://home.netscape.com/WEB-rdf#	Web	Hard-coded	Bookmarks and timestamps
http://www.mozilla.org/rdf/chrome#	Chrome	Hard-coded	Managing chrome packages and overlays
http://home.netscape.com/NC-rdf#	nc	Hard-coded	General purpose
http://www.mozilla.org/LDAPATTR-rdf#	ldapattr	JavaScript, based on LDAP properties	email LDAP support in Mail &News client
http://www.mozilla.org/inspector#	ins	JavaScript	DOM Inspector

Except for the first entry, none of these URLs exists as documents. The URLs containing "netscape" are a legacy of Netscape Communicator 4.x. Prefixes are suggestions based on existing conventions. Of these prefixes, `web`, `chrome`, and `nc` are used the most in Mozilla. To use a namespace, you must know the keywords it supplies. Those keywords are remarked on under "Predicate Tags." An application programmer is free to add namespaces as needed because namespaces are just arbitrary `xmlns` strings.

The contents of the `<RDF>` tag is a set of child tags. Each of those child tags must be either `<Description>` or one of the collection tags `<Seq>`, `<Bag>`, or `<Alt>`.

11.4.3 <Description>

The `<Description>` tag is the heart of RDF. A `<Description>` tag represents one or more facts and can contain zero or more child tags. Each child tag is a predicate (RDF property). Each child tag implies one complete fact, with the `<Description>` tag as subject in each case. An example of two facts is layed out in Listing 11.8.

Listing 11.8 Two facts specified with a single RDF <description> tag.

```
<fact subject="...">
  <property1 ...>object1</property1>
  <property2 ...>object2</property2>
</fact>
```

This is pseudo-code, not plain RDF. In this example, *property* has been written instead of predicate, since they are interchangeable. The example makes it clear why RDF uses the term property: the fact appears to hold two properties for its subject. In reality this syntax just states two different facts with the same subject. It just saves some typing.

Because the role of the `<fact>` pseudo-code is taken by the RDF `<Description>` tag, that tag is therefore like a container. It is not like other RDF containers because it has no special semantics at all and contains predicates/properties, not subjects or objects.

`<Description>` has the following special attributes.

```
ID about type
```

Every `<Description>` tag should have an `ID` or an `about` attribute. If both are missing, the subject of the stated fact will be anonymous. It will not be visible to the rest of the world, and inside the document it represents a term that is not ground.

The `ID` attribute has a name as its value; this name is appended to the RDF document's URL to create a unique URL for the whole fact. That constructed URL is also the URL of the stated fact's subject. Applying an `ID` to `<Description>` only makes sense when the `<Description>` tag has exactly one property. A fact subject stated with `ID` is visible to the whole Web.

The `about` attribute specifies the subject of the stated fact. It takes a full URI as its value. If the `about` attribute is used instead of the `ID` attribute, the whole fact has no URL of its own. A fact subject stated with `about` is not visible to the Web.

The `type` attribute records the type of the fact's object (its value). The value/object normally appears as XML content between the property start and end tags. The `type` attribute states what kind of thing the value/object is. If it is present, its value should be a URI. Mozilla does nothing with the `type` except store and retrieve it. It is not integrated with any schema definition. The `type` attribute has one additional role. It is also a property or predicate. Its use as shown here is really a shorthand notation, as described below.

Mozilla does not support these attributes:

```
aboutEach aboutEachItem bagID
```

All but `bagID` are deprecated in the most recent RDF standards. `bagID` is used for reification of RDF facts. Mozilla does not do this.

11.4.3.1 Shorthand Notation The <Description> tag and its contents can be reduced to a single <Description/> tag with no contents. This can be done by treating the property/predicate and value/object as an XML attribute.

This RDF fragment is a single fact stating that Tom owns Spot:

```
<Description about="www.test.com/#Tom">
  <ns:Owns>Spot</ns:Owner>
</Description>
```

The subject and predicate are defined by URLs; the object is defined by a literal. The predicate belongs to a declared namespace with ns as prefix, so the full URL of the predicate is not obvious. This example can be shortened to a single tag:

```
<Description about="www.test.com/#Tom" ns:Owns="Spot"/>
```

Note the namespace prefix before the Owns attribute name. That is standard XML but is not often seen in practical examples. This shorthand can be used only if the value/object is a literal. It does not work if the value/object is a URI.

11.4.4 Predicate/Property Tags

Predicate or property tags must be supplied by the application developer. The easiest way to do this is to find an existing set of tags useful for your purpose. For informal use, it is possible to make up tags as you go, but properly defining the namespace that you use is a sign of good design and ensures that the purpose of your RDF content is clear.

RDF supplies XML attributes that can be added to property tags. Just as the observes attribute turns any XUL tag into an observer, so too do RDF custom properties affect application-defined property tags. The list of such special attributes is

```
ID parseType
```

The ID attribute has the same purpose for the predicate tag that it has for the <Description> tag. It is used when the parent <Description> tag has more than one predicate tag, and therefore represents more than one fact. The ID on a specific predicate tag identifies the matching fact globally.

The parseType attribute provides a hint to the RDF parser. It is different from the type predicate, discussed in the next topic. It states how the XML text string holding the value/object should be interpreted. It can be set to one of these four values:

```
Literal Resource Integer Date
```

Literal means the value is an arbitrary string; it is the default. Resource means that the value is a URI. Those two options are standard. Integer and Date are Mozilla enhancements. Integer reads the string as a 32-bit signed integer. `Date` reads the string to be a date. Such a date can be in any of several formats, but Mozilla's support is incomplete. The safest format is to use the UTC output of the UNIX `date(1)` command, and change "UTC" in the resultant string to "UT" or "GMT." The `Date` option does not accommodate Unicode characters, only ASCII ones.

11.4.4.1 Existing Predicates RDF itself provides the `type` predicate. This predicate matches the `type` attribute of the `<Description>` tag. Its use in that tag is actually shorthand for

```
<rdf:type>value</rdf:type>
```

where `rdf` is the prefix used for the RDF namespace. Because `type` is a predicate, it can be applied to all fact subjects. Such a use can extend the basic type system of RDF, either with application-specified facts, or with RDF Schema, if that were implemented. It is not much used in Mozilla applications.

The namespaces noted in Table 11.3 also provide sets of predicates. Because predicates are ultimately just data items, these names do not "do" anything by themselves.

In Chapter 9, Commands, we noted that many command names exist in the Mozilla Platform, but those commands are all tied to specific application code, such as the Navigator, Messenger, and Composer clients. The same is true of predicates. Many exist, but their uses are all tied to specific application code.

These predicates are not centrally listed anywhere, not even in the source code. Since it is easy to make new predicates up (just add them to the `.rdf` and to the code), it is a matter of curiosity to track down the ones that Mozilla uses. Some examples of their use appear in Chapter 12, Overlays and Chrome.

A new Mozilla application that uses RDF should have a formal data model, and/or a data dictionary that states the predicates used in the application. The application programmer might look to the existing Mozilla predicates as a source of inspiration or to ensure the new application is similar, but there is no need to use the same names.

The only time predicate names must be followed exactly is when RDF files in existing formats are to be created, like `mimeTypes.rdf`. In such cases, it is enough to create a sample file using the Classic Browser, and then to examine the predicates generated. A more thorough alternative is to look at the source code.

11.4.4.2 Shorthand Notation The RDF `resource` attribute can be added to predicate tags. It works like the `about` attribute on the `<Description>` tag, except that it specifies the value/object of the fact. When the `resource` attribute is added, no XML content is required for the object, and the object must be a URI, not a literal. An unshortened example is

```
<ns:Owns parseType="Resource">www.test.com/#Spot</ns:Owns>
```

and the equivalent shortened form is

```
<ns:Owns rdf:resource="www.test.com/#Spot"/>
```

This use of the resource attribute is straightforward. The resource attribute has a further use which is more complicated.

In the simple case, the object/value specified with the resource attribute participates only in one fact—the current one. The URI of that object might, however, be specified as a subject in another fact. In that case, the URI's resource has two roles: It is both subject and object. A very confusing shorthand syntax rule says this: If XML attribute-value pairs appear in the predicate tag, and the resource attribute is also specified, then those attribute-value pairs act as though they appeared in the <Description> tag where the URI is a subject.

This means that the final shorthand technique noted for the <Description> tag can also be used inside predicate/property tags. However, another <Description> tag, elsewhere in the document, is affected as a result.

This is messy and complex, and not worth exploring unless your application is ambitious. It is designed to reduce the total number of tags required in a set of nested tags. In theory, this makes the RDF document more human-readable, but that is debateable. For more on this subject, read section 2.2.2 of the original RDF standard.

11.4.5 <Seq>, <Bag>, <Alt>, and <li>

<Seq>, <Bag>, and <Alt> are RDF's three container tags.

- <Seq> is a sequence or ordered list. The contained items are ordered. One possible use is history information, like a list of commands recently executed.
- <Bag> is a simple collection. There are no restrictions on contained items.
- <Alt> stands for alternative. It is a simple collection with no restrictions except that the contained items are all considered equivalent to each other in some application-specific way. One possible use of <Alt> is support for a message stated in multiple languages.

These container tags provide a way to organize objects and subjects into groups and to write many similar facts in a compact notation. All three containers can contain duplicate terms.

Containers contain items. Each item in a container is enclosed in an RDF <li> tag, just as each item in an HTML <UL> or <OL> list is enclosed in an HTML <LI> tag. Each item in a container is an object. Therefore, <li> is a delimiter for an object. Because <Description> tags or container tags can substitute for objects, containers can be nested. Listing 11.9 shows a single container.

Listing 11.9 Example of an RDF container.

```
<Description about="www.example.com/#Tom">
  <ns:Owns>
    <Bag ID="Dogs">
      <li>Spot</li>
      <li>Fido</li>
      <li>Cerberus</li>
    </Bag>
  </ns:Owns>
</Description>
```

Tom owns Spot; Tom owns Fido; Tom owns Cerebus. That should be three facts. Containers are easy to write down. Unfortunately, containers are slightly ugly to implement. The equivalent facts are shown in Listing 11.10.

Listing 11.10 Equivalent facts for ownership of three dogs.

```
<- "www.example.com/#Tom", ns:Owns, "Dogs" ->
<- "Dogs", rdf:_1, "Spot" ->
<- "Dogs", rdf:_2, "Fido" ->
<- "Dogs", rdf:_3, "Cerberus" ->
```

RDF can only state facts, so containers must be implemented with facts. This is accomplished by manufacturing an extra term to stand for the container itself. The `<Description>`'s fact has this subject as object. Whole facts are also manufactured. In turn, these facts tie the manufactured subject term to each of the container items. These new facts are therefore one-to-one, as all facts really are. These manufactured facts and terms are automatically added to the fact store created when the RDF document is read.

Two things are missing from this manufacturing strategy: The manufactured subject needs an ID, or at least a literal value, and the new facts need predicate or property names.

The first gap is filled easily: The container tag must be supplied with an ID or an about attribute by the document creator. If it isn't, it remains anonymous, and the RDF document is not ground. Anonymity should be avoided because it prevents Mozilla templates from working.

The second gap is filled when the RDF document is interpreted by software. If that software meets the RDF standard, then it will generate predicates for these new facts as it goes. These predicates will be named _1, _2, _3, and so forth. They exist in the RDF namespace, so they will be called `rdf:_1`, `rdf:_2`, and so forth, assuming `rdf` is the prefix selected for that namespace. That is the origin of those names in Listing 11.10.

Listing 11.11 shows facts equivalent to Listing 11.9 after that RDF fragment has been read. The RDF standard has some diagrams showing graphs for container-style facts and is worth glancing at.

Listing 11.11 Equivalent RDF facts to a container of three items.

```
<Description about="www.test.com/#Tom">
  <ns:Owns resource="Dogs"/>
</Description>
<Description about="Dogs" rdf:_1="Spot"/>
<Description about="Dogs" rdf:_2="Fido"/>
<Description about="Dogs" rdf:_3="Cerberus/>
```

Shorthand can be used for the `<rdf:_1>` predicate tag because its object value is a literal. Full shorthand cannot be used for the id of `Dogs` in the first fact because it is a URL fragment, not a literal. Whether you do or don't use containers is a design choice, but they are somewhat neater than the equivalent `<Description>` tags.

Because the container items and the `<Description>` subject are sorted into separate facts, they are not directly connected. An application cannot find a single fact in Listing 11.11 that states that Tom owns Spot. This means that an application looking for such a fact must either know the structure of the fact graph and navigate through it, including knowing where the containers are, or make an extensive analysis of the content. The former strategy is obviously far more efficient.

The following attribute applies to container tags:

```
ID type
```

The `ID` attribute has the same purpose as for `<Description>`.

The `type` attribute is not set by the document creator. It is set automatically to the name of the container tag (e.g., `rdf:Bag`), which is the type of that tag. This attribute is a predicate and value pair for the `<Description>` subject and is, thus, a fact in its own right. That extra fact is stated not with type as predicate, but with the special value `instanceOf`. For the example of three dogs, that fact is

```
<- "Dogs",
   http://www.w3.org/1999/02/22-rdf-syntax-ns#instanceOf,
   http://www.w3.org/1999/02/22-rdf-syntax-ns#Bag
->
```

That fact can be used by the application programmer to detect the existence and kind of the container tag. In Mozilla, such direct detection is not usually necessary because the platform supplies utility objects that do the job for you.

Container tags can also use the general property = value shorthand that applies to `<Description>` tags. The following attributes apply to `<li>` tags:

```
parseType resource
```

These attributes act the same as they do for predicate/property tags, and support the same shorthand forms.

That concludes the discussion on RDF syntax.

11.5 RDF EXAMPLES

Several examples are presented to show how the syntax and concepts work together.

11.5.1 A URL Example: The Download Manager

Classic Mozilla's Download Manager presents a clean example of an RDF document that manages Web-based resources. The Download Manager is available only in version 1.2.1 and greater. It tracks progress and completion of downloaded files. It is turned on with a preference under Edit | Preferences | Navigator | Downloads.

The Download Manager consists of a single XUL window and an RDF file. The window appears when saving a URL to the local file system, perhaps with File | Save Page As .. from the Navigator menu system. It can also be opened directly with Tools | Download Manager. The RDF file is called downloads.rdf and is stored in the user's profile directory. The code for the Download Manager is in the chrome file comm.jar. The GUI is implemented with a XUL <tree> tag.

To see this at work, open the Download Manager and remove all listed items by selecting them and clicking the "Remove From List" button. Using a text editor, open the downloads.rdf file. It contains nothing but namespace declarations and an empty collection which is a <Seq> tag. Listing 11.12 shows this file.

Listing 11.12 "Empty" downloads.rdf file.

```
<?xml version="1.0"?>
<RDF:RDF
  xmlns:NC="http://home.netscape.com/NC-rdf#"
  xmlns:RDF="http://www.w3.org/1999/02/22-rdf-syntax-ns#"
>
  <RDF:Seq about="NC:DownloadsRoot">
  </RDF:Seq>
</RDF:RDF>
```

Next, view any remote Web page such as *www.mozilla.org*. Save the page to a local file. Using a text editor, reopen the downloads.rdf file when the save operation is complete. A <Description> tag and contents, and an <li> collection item have been added. The <Description> tag states eight facts (spot them) about the locally downloaded file. The <li> item states a further fact: The fact subject that is the downloaded file is also an object in the sequence collection. This sequence is used to find all the files recorded in the document.

After a single file has been downloaded, the RDF appears as in Listing 11.13.

Listing 11.13 `downloads.rdf` file after a single complete download.

```
<?xml version="1.0"?>
<RDF:RDF
  xmlns:NC="http://home.netscape.com/NC-rdf#"
  xmlns:RDF="http://www.w3.org/1999/02/22-rdf-syntax-ns#"
>
  <RDF:Seq about="NC:DownloadsRoot">
    <RDF:li resource="C:\tmp\test_save.html"/>
  </RDF:Seq>
  <RDF:Description about="C:\tmp\test_save.html"
                   NC:Name="test_save.html"
                   NC:ProgressMode="none"
                   NC:StatusText="Finished"
                   NC:Transferred="1KB of  1KB">
    <NC:URL resource="http://www.mozilla.org/"/>
    <NC:File resource="C:\tmp\test_save.html"/>
    <NC:DownloadState NC:parseType="Integer">1</NC:DownloadState>
    <NC:ProgressPercent NC:parseType="Integer">100</NC:ProgressPercent>
  </RDF:Description>
</RDF:RDF>
```

If you are using Microsoft Windows, don't be confused by path names prefixed with `C:` (or any drive letter). This is just a variation on URL syntax invented by Microsoft that Mozilla supports. Such things are equivalent to a `file:///C|/` prefix and are still URLs.

Try viewing and saving any Web page, and then deleting entries with the Download Manager. It is easy to see how the RDF data file and XUL window are coordinated. Shut down the Download Manager and carefully hand-edit the `downloads.rdf` file so that one sequence item and the matching `<Description>` is removed. Restart the Download Manager to see the effect.

When downloading Internet files to local disk, there is sometimes a long pause before the FilePicker dialog box appears. This is a bug and occurs when the Download Manager's RDF file has grown large. Delete or empty the file to improve response times.

The Download Manager could be implemented without using RDF. RDF is used because it means that only a small amount of code is needed. The extensive RDF infrastructure inside the Mozilla Platform makes retrieving and storing information in RDF format easy.

11.5.2 Using URNs for Plain Data

The whole point of using RDF is to get some perhaps fact-driven processing done in an application. Although URLs have their uses, most applications work on traditional data. Traditional data are also expressible in RDF.

Why use RDF for traditional data? The RDF infrastructure in Mozilla allows data stored in RDF to be pooled and dynamically updated. This pool of data can be used from several points in an application at once, or even from several different applications. The RDF infrastructure also provides extensive automatic parsing and management of RDF content. The application programmer's script does not have to perform any low-level operations. Most importantly, RDF is the basis for Mozilla's XUL Template system, which provides automated display of RDF content.

11.5.2.1 Summary of Useable Types in Mozilla RDF To complete previous remarks on RDF types, the available types include the following:

- **Literal types**. `Literal`, `Resource`, `Integer`, `Date`, `Blob`. `XMLLiteral` is not supported.
- **Fact component types**. `Property`, `Bag`, `Seq`, `Alt`. List is not supported.
- **Fact types**. `Statement` is not supported.
- **Reification types**. Subject, predicate, and object are not supported.

The `Blob` type holds an array of binary data. It cannot be specified in an RDF document or from JavaScript. It is a Mozilla extension that can only be used from C/C++ code. One use of the `Blob` type occurs in the Classic Mail & News client. There, attachments are treated as fact objects of type `Blob`.

Types that are supported in RDF are specified with the `<Description>` tag's type attribute, which is the same as the built-in `rdf:type` predicate.

None of the type features of RDF Schema are supported. In general, an application programmer should store content in RDF as a plain XML string and do any necessary conversion in application code.

11.5.2.2 URNs When identifiers were discussed earlier, all the examples used URLs. URLs are useful if the stored facts are about Web or Internet resources. For more ordinary applications that only work with plain data, URNs are recommended instead of URLs.

Identifiers in RDF are actually URIs, not URLs. Recall that a URI (a Uniform Resource Identifier) is either a URL (a Uniform Resource Locator) or a URN (a Uniform Resource Name).

A URL ties a resource to a particular access point and an access method such as HTTP. The resource at that point might change over time, like a Web page. A URN, on the other hand, is just a name for an unchangeable thing that exists as a concept. If that concept has a real-world equivalent, that is at most convenient.

To a programmer, a URN is a variable name for a constant piece of data. Although URNs are supposed to be globally unique, you can make up your own provided your application is isolated from the rest of the world. This is like making up your own domain name or your own IP address. See IETF RFC 2611 for the URN registration body. In Mozilla, URNs are short, which suits programmers. Their syntax is

```
urn:{namespace}:{name}
```

where {namespace} is a string, and {name} is a string. {namespace} cannot be "urn" and cannot contain colons (:). {name} can be anything, including colons, which can be initially confusing. RFC 2141 describes the exact syntax, which allows for an ASCII, alphanumeric, case-insensitive namespace and an ASCII-punctuated case-insensitive name. {name} is optional in Mozilla. There are no "relative" URNs. Some punctuation marks are banned. See also RFC 2379. Two examples of URNs are

```
urn:myapp:runstate
urn:myapp:perfdialog:response
```

In the second URN, the {name} part is constructed to look like a second namespace plus a final name. In standards terms, this is just an illusion, but in programming terms it is a useful way to divide up a large number of URNs into subcategories. This kind of subdivision can have as many levels as necessary.

URNs are useful in RDF. They turn a verbose, Web-specific document with a worldwide focus into a general-purpose document about local information. An example of a URN fact is

```
<Description about="urn:mozilla:skin:modern/1.0"
    chrome:author="mozilla.org"/>
```

Here, chrome: is an XML namespace, "mozilla.org" is a literal, and "skin:modern/1.0" is the name of the thing the URN describes. Although this is a fact, not data, such a simple arrangement can be compared to a line of JavaScript code:

```
mozilla["skin:modern/1.0"].author = "mozilla.org";
```

It can also be compared to a more verbose line like this:

```
urn.mozilla.skin["modern/1.0"].chrome.author = "mozilla.org";
```

Of course, this simple code does not match all the behavior that facts have; it just reflects one possible use of a particular fact.

There is a URL scheme called data URLs. It is documented in IETF RFC 2397. This scheme offers a tempting way to pretend that raw data are also a URL. It might seem that this is a way to name a resource after its own contents. Data URLs are not useful in RDF, except possibly as objects, because they are not unique identifiers. Avoid them.

11.5.3 A URN Example: MIME Types

MIME types (and file suffixes) are used in the Classic Browser to handle foreign documents to the correct application for viewing. An example is a Microsoft Word .DOC document, which on Microsoft Windows is handed to winword.exe for display. MIME types are configured under Edit | Preferences | Navigator | Helper Applications.

As for the Download Manager, the MIME types system has a GUI and a file component. The GUI component is a panel in the Preferences dialog box; the file component is the file `mimeTypes.rdf` stored in the Classic Browser's profile directory. Code for this system is in `comm.jar` in the chrome, in files prefixed `pref-application`.

This subsystem of Mozilla can be exercised in a similar way to the Download Manager. The significant difference is that the RDF data model uses URNs instead of URLs. That data model is a set of facts, whose subjects are a hierarchy of URNs. An example of that hierarchy, for a configuration of two types only, is shown in Listing 11.14.

Listing 11.14 Hierarchy of URNs for a two-type MIME configuration.

```
urn:mimetypes
urn:mimetypes:root
urn:mimetypes:text/plain
urn:mimetypes:application/octet-stream
urn:mimetypes:handler:text/plain
urn:mimetypes:handler:application/octet-stream
urn:mimetypes:externalApplication:text/plain
urn:mimetypes:externalApplication:application/octet-stream
```

Because these URNs are just names, their apparent hierarchy has no technical meaning. It just serves to tell the reader that something is going on. There is also real hierarchy at work, one that is made of facts. If you draw the RDF graph for a `mimeTypes.rdf` file (try that), you will see that the facts make up a simple hierarchy, with a little bit of cross-referencing. This hierarchy is very much like the `window.navigator.mimeTypes` DOM extension used by Web developers. In fact, that array is populated from the `mimeTypes.rdf` data.

As for the Download Manager, a `<Seq>` container captures the full set of MIME types in an easy-to-retrieve structure. If multiple Classic Browser windows are open, and content of several special types is downloaded, then all those windows will use a single pool of RDF MIME type data to determine how to display that content.

11.5.4 RDF Application Areas

Mozilla uses RDF as an implementation technology for a number of features, but those features could have been created without it. Why does RDF exist, really? The answer is that there are some application-level problems for which RDF is a supposed solution.

According to the RDF specification, the primary application use of RDF is library catalogs. Such catalogs need a formal and flexible data model that everyone agrees on because such catalogs are increasingly Web-enabled and interconnected.

The most visible result of this application area is the Dublin Core. This is a data model broadly agreed to by the library industry and suitable for storing information about any kind of publication, including Web pages. In RDF terms, it is a list of predicate names that should be used for this type of application. See *www.purl.org* (that's P-URL not Perl).

A second use of RDF, according to the RDF specification, is Content Management. This is the process of adding review-generated information to content so that management decisions can be made about it. Simple examples of review information are secrecy ratings and maturity ratings. RDF is an obvious way to attach such information to content URLs via facts. A software system can then choose to supply or not supply the content, depending on the clearance or age of the reader.

In practice, there are many mechanisms for managing Web content, and RDF is not yet a clear winner, or even a major player.

A more successful use of RDF is to maintain information hierarchies. The volunteer-run Web catalog *www.dmoz.org* stores its entire subject hierarchy, including individual URL entries, as a single large RDF file.

RDF has not yet broken out as a vital piece of Internet infrastructure; at the moment it is just a useful tool. When developing Mozilla applications, consider RDF in that light.

That concludes the discussion of RDF examples.

11.6 Hands On: NoteTaker: Data Models

This "Hands On" session gives you an example of the modeling process required to create a set of RDF facts.

We've experimented extensively with GUI elements of the NoteTaker tool, and with the scripting environment, but now its time to go back to the design phase. We have no clear statement yet what data NoteTaker manipulates. We choose RDF as the final storage format for that data. We need a data model that tells us what RDF facts are needed. Facts are the modeling language we'll use.

In Mozilla, RDF is strongest when it is used inside the platform's own install area, although it can be passed across the Internet as well. It is also strong when the amount of data is small. Those strengths suit us because the NoteTaker tool will store the few notes that the user creates in their Mozilla user profile, on the local disk. No Internet access will be required.

The choice of facts as a modeling language is not a casual choice. We could as easily have chosen an object-oriented approach, or a relational approach like SQL. But facts have one clear advantage over those other systems: They map directly to RDF syntax. UML is good for objects; Entity Relationship Modeling is good for relational databases; facts are good for RDF.

The process we use to find, build, and implement the model follows.

1. Write down everything about the data.
2. Pick out the significant words (terms).
3. Construct some useful facts.
4. Ensure that those facts are about resources.
5. Consider how those facts need to be accessed.
6. Arrange the facts into structures that support that access.
7. Translate the results into pure RDF.

Data modeling usually requires several drafts, but here we'll get it mostly right to start with, and highlight a few common pitfalls and blind alleys as we go.

The NoteTaker data model is very simple for us to state in words. Each note is associated with one URL. It has a short and a long description (summary and details). It has a position on the screen (top, left, width, height). It also has keywords associated with it.

Keywords are just descriptive words added by the user that classify the URL to which the note belongs. If two keywords appear on the same note, those two keywords are said to be related. This "relatedness" goes beyond a single note. After two keywords appear together somewhere, that is evidence that they are related in a general sense. Related keywords can give the user guidance. When the user picks a keyword for a note, any related keywords are displayed at the same time. The user can then check if any of those other keywords should be added to the note at the same time.

This keyword system is used only a little by the NoteTaker tool. It is merely a reminder system for the user and an exploration of XUL and RDF technology. A version of NoteTaker created after the example in this book will support a Note Manager window. Such a window is used to list all existing notes, order and manage those notes, search for notes by keyword, and retrieve and display URLs for specific notes.

In the NoteTaker GUI, two other pieces of data exist. They appear as checkable boxes in the Edit dialog box under "Chop Query" and "Home Page." These items are not properties of the note, but rather control how the note is created.

If "Chop Query" is ticked, then a new note's URL will have any HTTP GET parameters removed. For example,

```
http://www.test.com/circuits.cgi?voltage=240V;amps=50mA
```

would be reduced to

```
http://www.test.com/circuits.cgi
```

The constructed note would appear on any page whose URL is prefixed with this shorter URL. If "Home Page" is ticked, then the URL will be reduced even more, to

```
http://www.test.com/
```

In this case, the note will only appear on the home page. If the URL contains an individual user's directory like this example:

```
http://www.test.com/~fred/mytests/test2.htm
```

then ticking "Home Page" will reduce this URL to

```
http://www.test.com/~fred/
```

For both of these options, only the most specific note for a given URL will be shown when that URL is displayed. In summary, after these choices are made in the GUI, the results are implicit in the URL for the note. Therefore, they add no further data to the model.

That concludes our descriptive overview of the data.

This overview of the data needs to be reduced to the three components of facts. Step 2 involves picking out the significant terms. Because facts include relationship information, we need to spot that as well, not just the nouns (entities, objects, or resources). Finding the nouns is a useful beginning point, though. Our first guesses in this case are as follows:

```
note keyword URL summary details top left width height
```

To these noun-like items, we add some relationship guesses:

```
related-keyword note-data note-for-a-url
```

Now to assemble these terms into facts—step 3. Facts can be viewed as subject-predicate-object triples (the general terminology) or as resource-property-value triples (the RDF terminology). Here we will see how both of these views are useful. First, we test each of the found terms for useful meaning by asking three questions:

1. Could this term be a thing of its own (a subject or resource)?
2. Could this term be a relationship (a predicate)?
3. Could this term be a descriptive feature of something else (a property)?

Question 3 will help us separate out the "weaker" terms so that we set a reasonable limit on what we model. Table 11.4 shows the early results of these questions.

Table 11.4 XML namespaces used for RDF vocabulary

Term	Thing?	Relationship?	Feature?
note	✓		✓ 3.
keyword	✓		1.
URL	✓		✓ 3.
summary	2.		✓

Table 11.4 XML namespaces used for RDF vocabulary (Continued)

Term	Thing?	Relationship?	Feature?
details	2.		✓
top	2.		✓
left	2.		✓
width	2.		✓
height	2.		✓
related-keyword		✓	✓
note-data		✓ 4.	
note-for-a-url		✓	✓

After this initial guesswork, we have some results and some outstanding issues. First the results: keyword is a thing; note-data is a relationship; and summary, details, top, left, width, and height are all descriptive features. We're sure of these results because each relevant row in the table has one tick only.

Next, the issues:

1. We suspect that a keyword can't be a feature of another term because that would make it a property in RDF (a fact predicate). Although there's nothing legally wrong with that, properties are generally expected to have well-known names, like "color." We know that there can be zero or more keywords per note, each with a different user-entered name. That means there is no single well-known name. Keyword is therefore not a good example of a feature. We would have this problem with any data item that has a many-to-one relationship with another data item.
2. These terms have no features of their own, so we can't see any reason to elevate them to the status of a thing. It seems pretty obvious that they're properties of something else, like a URL or a note.
3. We're still a bit confused about note and URL. Which belongs to which, or are they separate? We'd better assume they're both things for the minute.
4. Note-data sounds a bit uncertain. It doesn't identify the data or its relationship. In fact, it's not a concrete piece of information at all; it's vague. We've accidentally introduced a metadata concept: "notes have data." Summary, by comparison, is a concrete piece of data for a note. We'll throw note-data away. Metadata is never required for simple applications.

Out of this analysis, the facts we've identified are shown in Listing 11.15.

Listing 11.15 Starting facts for NoteTaker data model.

```
<- note, ?, URL ->
<- URL, ?, note ->
<- note, URL, ? ->
<- URL, note, ? ->

<- keyword, ?, ? ->
<- note, summary, ? ->
<- note, details, ? ->
<- note, top, ? ->
<- note, left, ? ->
<- note, width, ? ->
<- note, height, ? ->
<- ?, related-keyword, ? ->
<- ?, note-for-a-url, ? ->
```

The first four facts are possibilities that reflect our uncertainty about how notes and URLs are related. We need to fill in the unknowns, using our knowledge of the application's needs. We'll come back to these, after we've done the easy bits.

The six facts from `summary` to `height` are easy. They will hold a simple value each, so their object component is not a URI. It must be one of the types that Mozilla supports (`Literal`, `Integer`, `Date`, `Blob`). We'll just choose `Literal` (which is a string). So an example is

```
<- note, top, Literal ->
```

The related-keyword fact relates two keywords together. It seems obvious that the subject and object of this fact should be a keyword. We'll reduce the spelling `related-keyword` to `related`, for brevity:

```
<- keyword, related, keyword ->
```

The keyword fact presents us with a naming problem. We know that a keyword must be named by a URI because it's a thing (a resource). Unless some server specifies all the keywords in the world (not our case, and not even practical), it must be a URN rather than a URL. What is that URN? We haven't got one. We'll have to construct it out of the data the user supplies. We'll make it by prefixing the keyword string with `urn:notetaker:keyword:`. For example, the keyword `foo` will have URI:

```
urn:notetaker:keyword:foo
```

We also need access to the keyword string itself. It's not obvious now, but in later chapters we'll see that it's hard to extract a substring out of an RDF URI. So we'll have a property named label, and we'll hold the keyword as a separate string in it:

```
<- urn:notetaker:keyword:{keystring}, label, "{keystring}" ->
```

Finally, there is the complexity of a note and a URL. Each note has one URL, and each URL has one note. We need to know if they're separate. If they are separate, we'll need some kind of cross-table relationship between them. If they're not separate, then one will probably be a property of the other.

If note and URL are separate, then both will have a URI, so let's test that possibility. The URI for a URL is obvious—it's just the URL itself. What is the URI for a note? It will have to be a URN (it could be a file: URL, but that would be unusual). What will that URN be? Ultimately, we don't have a name for the note, we'd have to manufacture an arbitrary one (how?), or make the note anonymous (but then the final RDF document wouldn't be ground). Both of those options are ugly.

The truth is that the note lacks identity of its own and must therefore be dependent on the URL. Because it has no identity, it can't appear as a subject or object in any fact. Since a note doesn't have an "own value," it can't be a literal either. The whole concept of a note as a thing collapses to nothing. We throw it out of the model, leaving only the URL that the note is for. That resolves most of our issues with the first four facts in Listing 11.13.

This last point may seem very surprising, especially if you've done any object-oriented or relational modeling before. Aren't notes central to the whole NoteTaker application? Aren't we at liberty to create whatever objects/entities we like? The answers are Yes to the former and No to the latter. Yes, notes are a concept of the application, but as it turns out, not of the data model. No, we're not at liberty to create whatever entities we like because we're not working with a pure fact system like Prolog or Lisp, we're working with RDF. In RDF, one concept exists already before modeling starts: the concept of a URI-based resource. We're not free to create first-class objects; we're only free to create things with URIs, or else plain literals. Although we have a concept of a note in the NoteTaker application, in the RDF data model everything significant must be a URI. The only reason we managed to keep "keyword" as a data model concept is because we found a URI for each one.

The moral of this modeling process is simple: If you are not modeling a URL, you must make a URN for it, treat it as a literal, or forget it.

Listing 11.16 shows what's left when all of these changes are made:

Listing 11.16 Completed data facts for the NoteTaker data model.

```
<- URL, summary, Literal ->
<- URL, details, Literal ->
<- URL, top, Literal ->
<- URL, left, Literal ->
<- URL, width, Literal ->
<- URL, height, Literal ->
<- keyword, label, Literal ->
<- keyword, related, keyword ->
```

The obvious missing fact is some link between keyword and the note-laden URL. In Table 11.4 we put off thinking about this link because it wasn't clear how a keyword could be related to another fact when it's a many-to-one relationship. We can't use a keyword as a property/predicate because it's URN changes for each keyword. We could try either of these:

```
<- URL, keyword, keyword-urn ->
<- keyword-urn, note-url, URL->
```

Each URL (and note) would have zero or more instances of the first fact; alternately (or also), each keyword would have zero or more instances of the second fact.

In this proposed solution, there are multiple "keyword" properties per note (per URL). Could we store those keywords in an RDF container, like `<Seq>`? The answer is: not easily. If we did, there would be one such container for each URL with a note defined. What would those containers have as names? Such names would need to be URNs, and so we would need to construct them. We would need to do something like concatenating the URL for the note to the end of some prefix. That is possible, but messy, and we would run into string-processing problems in later chapters. We are better off sticking to a simple solution. We avoid `<Seq>` because such sequences would be repeated. We stick with the proposed solution, but we'll be lazy and only use the first fact:

```
<- URL, keyword, keyword-urn ->
```

We have now finished step 4 of our seven-step modeling process—we have captured all the necessary information for the data model. An example of the facts we'll store for one note with two keywords "test" and "cool" is shown in Listing 11.17.

Listing 11.17 Example facts for one NoteTaker note.

```
<- http://saturn/test.html, summary, "My Summary" ->
<- http://saturn/test.html, details, "My Details" ->
<- http://saturn/test.html, top, "100" ->
<- http://saturn/test.html, left, "90" ->
<- http://saturn/test.html, width, "80" ->
<- http://saturn/test.html, height, "70" ->
<- http://saturn/test.html, keyword, urn:notetaker:keyword:test ->
<- http://saturn/test.html, keyword, urn:notetaker:keyword:cool ->

<- urn:notetaker:keyword:test, label, "test" ->
<- urn:notetaker:keyword:cool, label, "cool" ->

<- urn:notetaker:keyword:test, related, urn:notetaker:keyword:cool ->
```

The last fact is the sole "relatedness" between keywords. We could also store a fact that is the reverse of the last fact, since `test` is also related to cool. If we do that, we'll have many extra facts for notes with many keywords. Here we'll just describe the minimum facts necessary to link the keywords.

Steps 5 and 6 of the modeling anticipate Chapter 14, Templates. Eventually, we'd like to extract these facts from an RDF document efficiently. This means adding extra structure to the basic facts. Scripts and templates will be able to exploit this structure. The only such structures that RDF provides are container tags, a little type information, and the capbility to add facts without restriction. Looking at the NoteTaker tool, scripts and templates will want to:

1. Find out if a note exists for a given URL, so that NoteTaker knows whether to display one or not.
2. Extract the details of a note, including keywords, using a URL. That is for display in the dialog box, for both the Edit and the Keywords panes.
3. Extract just the summary and details of a note using a URL. This is for the toolbar textboxes and for the content of the HTML-based note.
4. Extract a list of all the existing keywords. That is for the drop-down menu in the toolbar.
5. Somehow extract all the related keywords for a given keyword, and all their related keywords, and so on. That is for the user's information in the Keywords pane of the dialog box.

In addition to these fact extractions, we want to be able to add, remove, and update notes easily. Those tasks are generally easy, so we'll address only the preceding list. That list is effectively a set of queries.

Mozilla can find facts in an RDF document no matter how they are arranged, but some arrangement makes it faster, and some arrangements make the RDF easier to read. We'll do two things:

☞ Put all the URLs for existing notes into a <Bag> RDF container with URI urn:notetaker:notes. Queries 1, 2, and 3 can use this container to find a note and its content.

☞ Put all the URNs for existing keywords into a <Bag> RDF container with URI urn:notetaker:keywords. Query 4 can use this container to get its list.

Query 5 is quite difficult because it requires extensive exploration of the keyword-laden facts. We'll just say that there is no obvious help we can add at this stage. Whatever system handles query 5 will probably have to search the whole set of facts, or a large subset.

Because RDF documents are supposed to use <Bag> tags as fact subjects, we'd better add a topmost <Description> tag with resource urn:notetaker:root. Our two <Bag> tags can be property values of that tag.

That is all the modeling we need. In step 7, the last step, it is purely mechanical to turn the data model into an RDF document. A skeleton document based on our RDF container choices, and containing no notes, is shown in Listing 11.18.

Listing 11.18 Example facts for one NoteTaker note.

```
<?xml version="1.0"?>
<RDF xmlns="http://www.w3.org/1999/02/22-rdf-syntax-ns#"
     xmnls:NT="http://www.mozilla.org/notetaker-rdf#>
  <Description about="urn:notetaker:root">
    <NT:notes>
      <Seq about="urn:notetaker:notes"/>
    </NT:notes>
    <NT:keywords>
      <Seq about="urn:notetaker:keywords"/>
    </NT:keywords>
  </Description>
</RDF>
```

If this document is populated with the note of Listing 11.18, then the final RDF document is shown in Listing 11.19.

Listing 11.19 Example NoteTaker database in RDF—one note only.

```
<?xml version="1.0"?>
<RDF xmlns="http://www.w3.org/1999/02/22-rdf-syntax-ns#"
     xmnls:NT="http://www.mozilla.org/notetaker-rdf#>
  <Description about="urn:notetaker:root">
    <NT:notes>
      <Seq about="urn:notetaker:notes">
        <li resource="http://saturn/test.html"/>
      </Seq>
    </NT:notes>
    <NT:keywords>
      <Seq about="urn:notetaker:keywords">
         <NT:keyword resource="urn:notetaker:keyword:cool/>
         <NT:keyword resource="urn:notetaker:keyword:test/>
      </Seq>
    </NT:keywords>
  </Description>

<!-- one note -->
  <Description about="http://saturn/test.html">
    <NT:summary>My Summary<NT:summary/>
    <NT:details>My Details<NT:details/>
    <NT:top>100<NT:top/>
    <NT:left>90<NT:left/>
    <NT:width>80<NT:width/>
    <NT:height>70<NT:height/>
    <NT:keyword resource="urn:notetaker:keyword:test"/>
```

```
    <NT:keyword resource="urn:notetaker:keyword:cool"/>
  </Description>

<!-- values for each keyword -->
  <Description about="urn:notetaker:keyword:test label="test"/>
  <Description about="urn:notetaker:keyword:cool label="cool"/>

<!-- all related keyword pairings go here; one so far -->
  <Description about="urn:notetaker:keyword:test">
    <NT:related resource="urn:notetaker:keyword:cool">
  </Description>
</RDF>
```

Some of the `<NT:keyword>` tags are duplicated in this file. There's always a balance between keeping data simple and keeping systems that query that data simple. In our case we've chosen a little duplication of data so that most of the data querying work (described in Chapter 14, Templates) is straightforward.

Thus we are now finished with the data model for NoteTaker's notes. The file format that we'll eventually use to store those notes is set at the same time. The only reason we're using RDF is because NoteTaker is a client-only tool (no server), and the amounts of data are likely to be small.

11.7 Debug Corner: Dumping RDF

RDF data are processed silently so there's not much feedback to be had. A few tricks exist.

RDF documents usually contain whitespace that hint at the purpose of the facts stated. You can strip that whitespace out and view such a document as plain, hierarchical XML. To do this, just change the file extension to `.xml` (or use a shortcut or a link) and load it directly into a Navigator window.

There is no need to restart Mozilla every time you read an RDF document, or even every time you modify that document by hand. The document is managed by the Mozilla cache. If you modify the fact store extensively (and get lost), then you should restart Mozilla entirely.

The RDF diagram (as in Figure 11.5) for a given document is not easy to produce automatically. It is possible to write a graph-drawing routine for a graph of known, familiar, or simple structure. Such a graph can be displayed by an SVG-enabled version of Mozilla—you can use DOM operations on an SVG document to create such a graph dynamically. What you can't easily do is write a general-purpose function that analyzes and arranges an unknown RDF graph in a guaranteed readable way—there are theoretical constraints. It is a hard task and not worth attempting on limited time. The RDF page at the W3C (*www.w3.org*) contains a massive list of RDF software tools.

If you are not sure of the state of your fact store, then the easy way to inspect it is to write it out. The code in Listing 11.20 achieves this end.

Listing 11.20 `downloads.rdf` file after a single complete download.

```
// preparation ..
var Cc = Components.classes;
var Ci = Components.interfaces;
var comp  = Cc["@mozilla.org/rdf/rdf-service;1"]
var iface = Ci.nsIRDFService;

var svc = comp.getService(iface);
var ds  = svc.GetDataSource("file:///C|/tmp/test.rdf");
var rds = ds.QueryInterface(Ci.nsIRDFRemoteDataSource);

// .. normal processing of the fact store here ..

function dumpRDF()
{
    // one change must be made before a store is writable
    var sub  = svc.GetResource("urn:debug:subject");
    var pred = svc.GetResource("DebugProp");
    var obj  = svc.GetResource("urn:debug:object");
    ds.Assert(sub, pred, obj, true);

    rds.Flush(); // write it out
}
```

This code does nothing more than create a data source for the file `C:/tmp/test.rdf`. The function `dumpRDF()` can be called anytime after the source has finished loading, which can be detected with the `rds.loaded` flag or with an observer object. The `dumpRDF()` function just adds a fact to the fact store and writes the whole fact store out. One fact is added so that the data source knows that the file is out of date. If the written file is subsequently viewed, the extra fact appears like this:

```
<RDF:Description about="urn:debug:subject">
    <DebugProp resource="urn:debug:object"/>
  </RDF:Description>
```

`DebugProp` and `debug` are plain strings and have no special meaning.

11.8 Summary

Fact-based systems are a little different from normal data processing. There's plenty of new concepts to pick up: fact, tuple, triple, subject, object, predicate, fact store. When those are finished, there's RDF-specific terminology as well: description, resource, property, value, container, URL, URN. RDF is a not-so simple application of XML, but at least it has a core of sensible design.

In addition to standards- and theory-based concept, Mozilla has a number of concrete, heavyweight internal structures that can pump information around. These are different from simple event-processing systems because the processing content takes time. Channels and data sources are heavyweight structures that are intimately tied to RDF.

Inside Mozilla, RDF is used all over the place. There are many data sources, components, and interfaces that an application programmer can take advantage of, and a fair chunk of the finished browser application uses RDF to store state permanently. If only RDF processing were a little faster, it might be useable as a general message exchange format, but at the moment it's best for nonperformance critical tasks.

After digesting RDF, something lighter would be most welcome. In the next chapter, Mozilla's overlay and chrome systems are examined. It requires only XML and XUL tags. Just to keep the discussion honest, the RDF system underneath is examined as well.

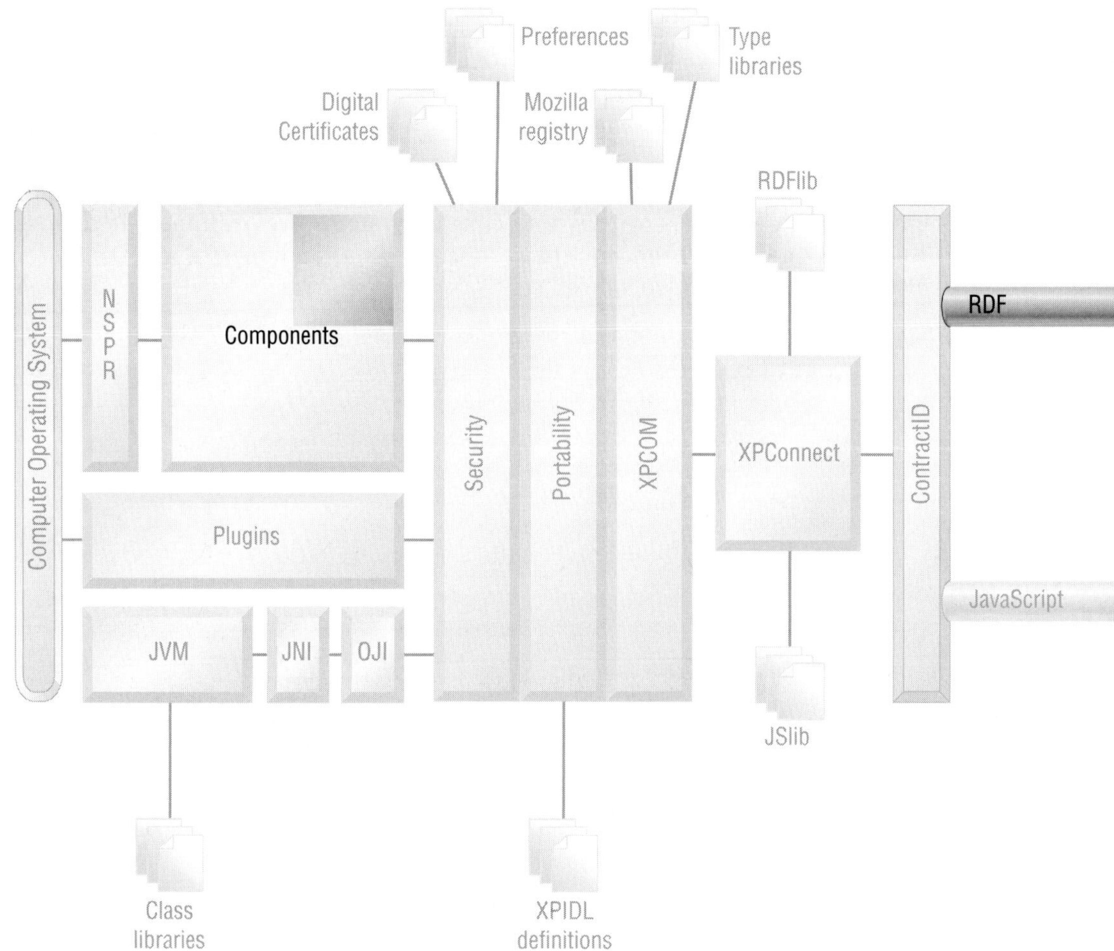
Preferences
Type libraries
Digital Certificates
Mozilla registry
RDFlib
Computer Operating System
NSPR
Components
Security
Portability
XPCOM
XPConnect
ContractID
RDF
Plugins
JavaScript
JVM
JNI
OJI
JSlib
Class libraries
XPIDL definitions

CHAPTER 12

Overlays and Chrome

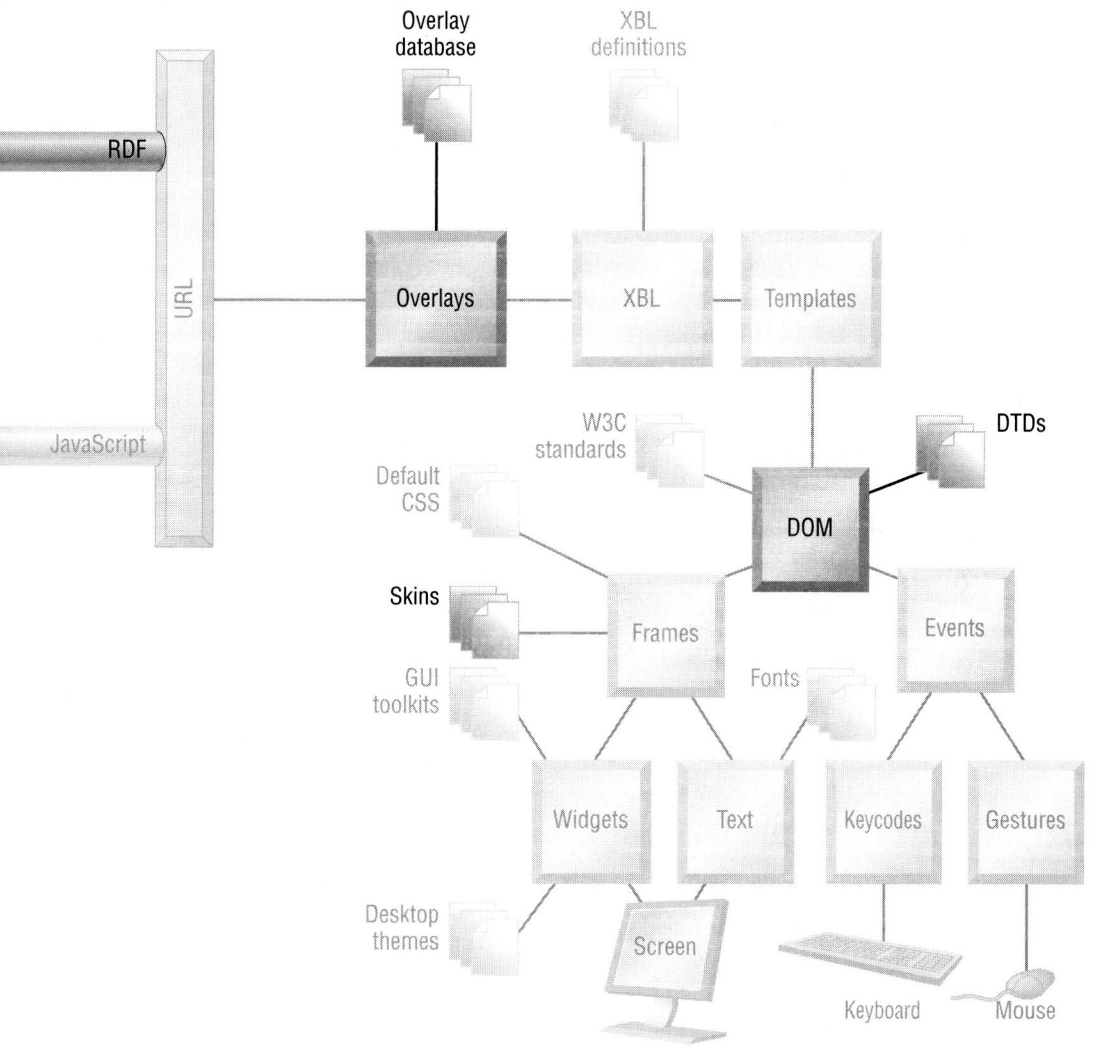

This chapter describes the overlay and chrome infrastructure of the Mozilla Platform. That infrastructure provides mechanisms for modular development of XUL applications. Both overlays and chrome depend heavily on data files expressed in RDF.

The overlay system allows a single, final XUL document to be constructed from one or more other XUL documents. It is a merging process that can be set up in several different ways. The overlay system is a component technology designed for larger Mozilla applications. It allows large source files to be split up into pieces.

An example of a document that uses the overlay system is shown in Listing 12.1.

Listing 12.1 Simple XUL document with two overlays.

```
<?xml version="1.0"?>
<?xul-overlay href="chrome://test/content/overlayA.xul"?>
<?xul-overlay href="chrome://test/content/overlayB.xul"?>
<window xmlns="http://www.mozilla.org/keymaster/gatekeeper/
          there.is.only.xul">
  <description id="start">Anything</description>
</window>
```

This single document collects content from the two files `overlayA.xul` and `overlayB.xul`. With minor differences, those files also hold XUL content. That collected content is added to the content of the present file. The result is displayed for the user. None of the source files is changed.

The chrome registry is also a component technology. It tracks and records components called packages, skins, and locales. These components are just groups of files stored in the chrome part of the platform install area. There they benefit from full access to the platform and from special processing of URLs. The chrome registry may be used to manage information about those files. It is somewhat related to the installation systems described in Chapter 17, Deployment.

The NoteTaker running example in this book has exploited that chrome directory structure since Chapter 1, Fundamental Concepts, but much of that system have been glossed over in the process. In this chapter, the RDF model that underlies the chrome is examined more carefully.

The NPA diagram at the start of this chapter shows the small parts of the platform affected by chrome and overlays. Overlay processing occurs early in the document load cycle. That processing sits between URL requests and the assembly of content into a final DOM hierarchy. The chrome registry is all but invisible, except for the automatic selection of theme-driven skins and locale-driven DTDs. An XPCOM component that implements the chrome registry is always at work, so most overlay and chrome processing is automatic.

Overlays and the chrome registry also represent a chance to practice RDF. This chapter examines both the `overlayinfo` overlay database and the `chrome.rdf` chrome database. We also take a brief look at persistence.

12.1 OVERLAYS

The overlay system is quite simple. One XUL document is the master document. This document provides a starting point for the final content. Any other XUL documents are overlays. Overlay content is merged into, or added to, the master document's content. This happens in memory when those documents are loaded and has no effect on the original files.

An overlay is a XUL document based on the `<overlay>` tag instead of the `<window>` tag. Such a file has a `.xul` extension and is well-formed XML, but it isn't meant to be displayed alone. Mozilla can display an overlay file by itself, but that is only useful for testing purposes.

Mozilla also supports *stylesheet overlays*. These are plain Mozilla CSS2 files with a `.css` file extension. They must be stored in a skin directory in the chrome. They do not use the `<overlay>` tag.

The chrome of Classic Mozilla also contains so-called *JavaScript overlays*. These files are not overlays in the strict sense; they are ordinary JavaScript scripts with `.js` file extensions. They are associated with overlay files by placing a `<script>` tag anywhere in the overlay content. This is no different from normal XUL.

Both XUL master and XUL overlay documents can contain syntax specific to the overlay system.

The overlay system has two file discovery methods, which are used to decide what files should be merged. These methods are called the *top down* and *bottom up* methods because one is driven by the master document (top down) and the other is driven by a separate database of overlays (bottom up).

The overlay system uses a single algorithm for merging content. That algorithm is based on the XUL id attribute and has a few minor variations.

Here is an example of overlays at work. Irrelevant syntax has been removed for clarity. Suppose that a master document appears as in Listing 12.2.

Listing 12.2 Example content that acts as an overlay master.

```
<window>
  <box id="one"/>
  <box id="two">
    <label value="Amber"/>
  </box>
</window>
```

Further, suppose that two overlay documents exist as in Listing 12.3.

Listing 12.3 Example content that acts as two overlays.

```
<overlay>
  <box id="one">
    <label="Red"/>
  </box>
```

```
  <box id="three">
    <label="Purple"/>
  </box>
</overlay>

<overlay>
  <box id="two">
    <label value="Green"/>
  </box>
</overlay>
```

If these two overlays are merged into the master document, then the in-memory final document will be as shown in Listing 12.4.

Listing 12.4 Merged document resulting from a master and two overlays.

```
<window>
  <box id="one">
    <label="Red"/>
  <box id="two">
    <label value="Amber"/>
    <label value="Green"/>
  </box>
</window>
```

If an `id` attribute in the master document matches an `id` attribute in an overlay document, then the child tags of that `id` are copied from the overlay to the master. They are merged in with the content of the master under that id, if any. If no id match is found (the Purple case), then nothing is added to the master. Except for some finer points, that is all the overlay system does.

12.1.1 Overlay Tags

The overlay system adds `<?xul-overlay?>` and `<overlay>` to the set of tags that Mozilla understands. The merging process also discusses four new attributes.

12.1.1.1 `<?xul-overlay?>` `<?xul-overlay?>` is an extension to XML that is allowed by the XML standards. It is a processing instruction that is specific to Mozilla. This process instruction states: Please merge the contents of a specified document into this document. This tag has one special attribute:

```
href
```

`href` can be set to any valid URL, which is the overlay to merge in.

This tag is used in master documents by the top-down file discovery system. It can also be put in overlay documents, in which case they also act as master documents. A series of documents can therefore be formed into a hierarchy using this processing directive.

Mozilla does not support `<?xul-overlay?>` for HTML files.

12.1.1.2 `<overlay>` The <overlay> tag is used in place of <window> in an overlay document. Like <dialog> or <page>, <overlay> represents a special use of XUL content. Unlike those other tags, <overlay> implies a document that is incomplete. An example is shown in Listing 12.5.

Listing 12.5 Skeleton of an overlay document.

```
<?xml version="1.0"?>
<overlay
      xmlns="http://www.mozilla.org/keymaster/gatekeeper/
          there.is.only.xul"
  id="style-id"
>
  <description>Sample content</description>
</overlay>
```

The `xmlns` attribute is always required. The <overlay> tag has three attributes with special meaning:

```
id class style
```

All three have the same meaning and use as in XUL and HTML.

CSS2 styles based on these attributes can behave unusually. When an overlay document is merged into a master document, the <overlay> tag can be consumed completely and then disappear. If this happens, any CSS2 rules based on the <overlay> tag will not be applied.

It is a convention to add an `id` to <overlay> anyway. Such an attribute is useful only if one of these points is true:

- The overlay includes other overlays in turn (nesting of overlays).
- The merging process succeeds in matching that `id`.
- The overlay should not be appended by default if the `id` fails to match.

These three conditions are all consequences of the merging process, which is discussed shortly.

The <overlay> tag does not necessarily act like a boxlike tag. Adding layout attributes like `orient` only have an effect if the <overlay> tag is merged with a suitable tag in the master document.

12.1.1.3 `<overlaytarget>` The <overlaytarget> tag is sometimes used to hold an id that matches an id in an overlay document. It is a user-defined tag with no special meaning.

12.1.2 Overlay Discovery

Before the overlay system can merge anything, it must work out what files might have content to merge.

The first file discovery method is called the *top-down* method. The top-down method requires that the programmer state inside the master document all other files that are to act as overlays. This method is equivalent to textual inclusion techniques provided by many computer languages. C/C++ has #include, Perl has `use` and `require`, and XUL has the `<?xul-overlay?>` processing instruction.

The top-down method gives an application programmer the ability to break a XUL document into a hierarchy of separate files.

The second file discovery method is called the *bottom-up* method. The bottom-up method requires that the programmer state in a database any overlay files and the master files those overlays should be merged into. That database, called `overlayinfo`, is consulted when the platform first starts up. This method is equivalent to a linking system like `make(1)` and `ld(1)` on UNIX. It is similar to the project concept in IDE programming tools like Visual Basic.

The bottom-up method gives an application programmer the ability to add to the content of existing XUL documents without modifying those documents.

One master document can benefit from both the top-down and bottom-up methods. Listing 12.1 uses the top-down method. It is not possible to tell by looking at any XUL document whether the bottom-up method is used. You need to look at the `overlayinfo` database instead.

The Classic Mozilla application suite includes many overlays, and more can be added. If you do so, you are enhancing that application suite. The NoteTaker tool relies on this system, as do most of the browser experiments at *www.mozdev.org*. Similarly, Classic Mozilla overlays can be added to a separate Mozilla application. Either way, this is an example of reuse of XUL content.

12.1.2.1 Top Down Overlays can be specified directly in a master XUL document. This can be done in any XUL file. It does not require access to the chrome.

To state use of an overlay the top-down way, include one line in the master document:

```
<?xul-overlay href="chrome://mytest/content/Overlay.xul"?>
```

This line is normally put at the top of the master document, after the `<?xml?>` header. If more than one such tag is added, then the specified files are merged in the same order. If the same file is specified twice, it is merged twice. The overlay file specified does not need to be located in the chrome.

A simple example of top-down overlays can be found in the code for the JavaScript Console. See the file `console.xul` in `toolkit.jar` in the chrome. A more complex example is `navigator.xul` in `comm.jar` in the chrome. That is the master document for the whole Classic Browser. Not all overlays finally included in these examples are specified top-down, but a fair number are.

If `<?xul-overlay?>` is used to load a nonoverlay document, then Mozilla can become confused and freeze or crash.

12.1.2.2 Bottom Up The bottom-up approach to overlays does not use the `<?xul-overlay?>` processing instruction. Instead, Mozilla decides what documents to merge by consulting a database in the chrome. The bottom-up system requires that both master and overlay documents be installed in the chrome.

This alternative exists to make Mozilla applications extensible. Mozilla application packages that are added to the chrome can contribute content to other packages that already exist.

The most common example of bottom-up design is the Classic Browser, which includes a package named navigator installed in the chrome (in `comm.jar`). Many programmers are aware of this package. When they develop browser add-ons, they include overlays that the bottom-up system will merge with the Classic Browser window. These overlays contain GUI elements that appear prominently in that window. Those add-ons are then exposed to the user as part of a familiar interface.

A simple example is the DOM Inspector. It is available by default in Classic Mozilla, but not in Netscape 7.0. In Netscape 7.0, there is no DOM Inspector menu item anywhere in the Netscape Navigator browser. The DOM Inspector can, however, be installed later. After it is installed, a menu item appears on the Tools | Web Development menu in the Navigator window. This menu item is the content of a new overlay, one delivered with the DOM Inspector application.

It is not mandatory to integrate overlays with the Classic Mozilla application suite. Any known XUL window can act as a master document and be the integration point.

To use the bottom-up approach, work with RDF facts, as follows.

12.1.2.3 Reading the Overlay Database The overlay database is a set of directories and RDF files. The database lives in the `chrome/overlayinfo` directory under the platform install area. This directory is generated from other files and may be deleted if the platform is shut down. Mozilla reads this directory every time it starts up, re-creating it if it doesn't exist.

This generated database is a set of subdirectories. Each one is the name of a chrome package that has overlays defined the bottom-up way. For example, `editor` is the name of the package that contains the Classic Composer, and so the `overlayinfo/editor` directory contains information on all overlays specified for that tool. This information does not include any top-down overlays.

Inside each `overlayinfo` package is a `content` subdirectory, and inside there is an `overlays.rdf` file. This file is equivalent to a `make(1)` makefile for a single package. It acts like a set of `<?xul-overlay?>` processing instructions for that package. It is a set of facts about each chrome URL that has bottom-up overlays. For example, the overlayinfo/editor/content/overlays.rdf file might have the set of facts in Listing 12.6.

Listing 12.6 RDF overlay facts for the Mozilla Composer.

```
<?xml version="1.0"?>
<RDF xmlns="http://www.w3.org/1999/02/22-rdf-syntax-ns#">
  <Seq about="chrome://editor/content/editor.xul">
    <li>
      chrome://messenger/content/mailEditorOverlay.xul
    </li>
    <li>
      chrome://cascades/content/cascadesOverlay.xul
    </li>
  </Seq>
</RDF>
```

This file says that when the URL chrome://editor/content/editor.xul is loaded, it will have two overlays automatically merged into it. They are named mailEditorOverlay.xul and cascadesOverlay.xul.

In many cases, the master document quoted in this file is itself an overlay, one that is included in the real master document the top-down way. This is a grouping technique designed to keep the many ids used for the overlay content out of the main document's XUL. Instead, those ids merge into an intermediate overlay that is built specifically for the purpose. That intermediary is the document sometimes specified in overlays.rdf. The whole intermediate overlay can then be included in the master XUL using a single id. When merged, it drags in all the other overlay content with it.

Separate from the overlayinfo database, but still in the chrome, is the chrome/chrome.rdf file. That file is maintained by the chrome registry, which is responsible for the overlay system. It can contain a couple of overlay-specific configuration items in the form of facts. The three overlay-specific predicates are

```
hasOverlays hasStylesheets disabled
```

hasOverlays and hasStylesheets are used to indicate that overlay XUL and overlay CSS files exist for that package. disabled is used to indicate that this package should not accept overlays from outside the package. In other words, overlays cannot be imported into any of the package's documents from another package.

Facts using these predicates must have as subject a package name URI, like urn:mozilla:package:editor, and as object the literal value "true". None of these properties can have subjects of "false". To make them false, the matching fact must be removed entirely. An example fact is

```
<- urn:mozilla:package:editor, hasOverlays, "true" ->
```

So a typical line in the chrome.rdf file might read:

```
<Description about="urn:mozilla:package:editor" hasOverlays="true"/>
```

12.1.2.4 Changing the Overlay Database Mozilla's overlay database is designed to support automated detection of new overlays. It works very closely with the XPInstall installation system described in Chapter 17, Deployment. Even so, it is easy to use this system by hand.

A forward look at XPInstall reveals the following:

- Application packages add lines to the chrome file named `installed-chrome.txt` when they are installed.
- Mozilla must be restarted after packages are installed.
- When Mozilla restarts, it reads the file `installed-chrome.txt`, but only if its last-modified date is more recent than that on the chrome `overlayinfo` directory, or that on `chrome.rdf`.
- If `installed-chrome.txt` is read, Mozilla collects up all the files called `contents.rdf` from all the installed packages. The `overlayinfo` directory is then refilled from the facts in those `contents.rdf` files.

This process means that any hand-made changes to the overlay database will disappear if a package is installed. Hand-made changes are good for testing purposes only.

To add a new overlay to the database by hand, shut down the platform and edit the `overlays.rdf` file for the package that owns the master document. The master document should be the subject of a fact that has a `<Seq>` tag as its object. The examples in Listing 12.6 are all that are required.

A more permanent way to proceed is to create a `contents.rdf` file in the package under development. This file will then add to the `overlayinfo` database the next time it is rebuilt. Note that the RDF containers used in the `contents.rdf` files are different from the containers used in the `overlays.rdf` files. When the platform creates the `overlayinfo` database, it also re-sorts all the facts it finds according to package names.

To add a new overlay permanently, the `contents.rdf` file for a suitable package should contain two extra facts. The first fact states that the required master document now has a bottom-up overlay. In other words, that master document requires special treatment from now on. The second fact states what new overlays exist for that master document. In both cases, these facts must be added to the right container if everything is to work:

```
<!-- State the document that receives the overlay -->
<Seq about="urn:mozilla:overlays">
  <li resource="chrome://package1/content/master.xul"/>
</Seq>

<!-- state the overlay that applies to the target -->
<Seq about="chrome://package1/content/master.xul">
  <li>chrome://package2/content/overlay.xul</li>
</Seq>
```

The `<Seq about="urn:mozilla:overlays"/>` container is the official list of chrome documents with bottom-up overlays. Note that the second fact states the overlay file as a literal, not as a URI. That is very important (see "Debug Corner" for an explanation of why this is true).

To change the `chrome.rdf` overlay configuration information, either edit it by hand (temporary) or use the `nsIXULChromeRegistry` interface discussed under "XPCOM Objects" in Chapter 17. This file can also be modified using the XPInstall system, or by adding extra facts to one of the `contents.rdf` files.

12.1.3 The Merging Process

Overlays are merged based on the XUL id attribute. If ids are absent, then a simpler system is used. Other special cases depend on attributes that modify the way ids are processed.

In this discussion, *source id* is an id in an overlay document. *Target id* is an id in a master document.

12.1.3.1 Simple Merging In the simplest case, an overlay document is merely appended to the master document. If several overlays are merged into the master document, then they are appended in the order that they are stated in. This case requires that no ids appear in the overlay.

If the master document's `<window>` or `<dialog>` tag has `dir="rtl"` set, then overlay content will appear at the start rather than the end, but in reverse order. If the master document has `orient="horizontal"`, then overlay content will appear to the right, and so on.

12.1.3.2 Id-Based Merging The power of the overlay system comes from XUL tag ids. Ids can be used to merge an overlay document into a master document piece by piece. This is done as follows.

Suppose a master document has content that includes a tag with a target id. That tag is a container for any other tags inside it, or for no content at all, if it happens to be empty. Further, suppose that an overlay document has a tag with the same id (a source id). The tag with the source id has some content tags of its own.

When the two documents are merged, this processing occurs:

1. The source id tag and target id tags are matched up.
2. The source id tag's content is appended to the target id tag's content.
3. Any XML attributes from the source id tag are copied to the target id tag, overriding any attributes on the target id tag with the same names.
4. The source id tag is thrown away.

The first and second points add content to the master document. The third point affects layout, styles, and any other attribute-driven behavior. The last point is just convenience.

The beauty of this system is that it can be used repeatedly. An overlay can have several document fragments, each labeled with an id. These fragments will be inserted at different points in the master document, wherever the matching ids are. Therefore, overlays are a more powerful system than C/C++'s `#include` or Perl's `use`. Those systems only insert content (code) at a single point.

Here is an example. Listing 12.7 is a master document with two target ids. Listings 12.8 and 12.9 show two overlays that exploit those sites. Stylesheets have been left out for brevity:

Listing 12.7 Master document that includes two overlays.

```
<?xml version="1.0"?>
<?xul-overlay href="part1.xul"?>
<?xul-overlay href="part2.xul"?>

<window xmlns="http://www.mozilla.org/keymaster/gatekeeper/
          there.is.only.xul">
  <vbox id="osite1">
    <description>Main Box A</description>
  </vbox>
  <vbox id="osite2">
    <description>Main Box B</description>
  </vbox>
</window>
```

The master document has two boxes, each of which contains a single tag.

Listing 12.8 First overlay containing two fragments for inclusion.

```
<?xml version="1.0"?>
<overlay     xmlns="http://www.mozilla.org/keymaster/gatekeeper/
          there.is.only.xul">
  <box id="osite1">
    <description>Box C</description>
  </box>
  <box id="osite2">
    <description>Box D</description>
  </box>
</overlay>
```

This overlay has two ids matching the master document (`osite1`, `osite2`). Listing 12.9 is exactly the same except that the content reads "Box E, Box F," instead of "Box C, Box D," and the box with `id="osite2"` has an extra attribute: `orient="horizontal"`.

Listing 12.9 Second overlay containing two fragments for inclusion.

```
<?xml version="1.0"?>
<overlay     xmlns="http://www.mozilla.org/keymaster/gatekeeper/
          there.is.only.xul">
```

```
  <box id="osite1">
    <description>Box E</description>
  </box>
  <box id="osite2" orient="horizontal">
    <description>Box F</description>
  </box>
</overlay>
```

Figure 12.1 shows the master document both with and without these two overlays included.

The content from each overlay has been appended to the content in the master document. Each overlay has been appended in turn to each target id. The second target id has had its layout changed to horizontal by an overlay-supplied attribute. It doesn't matter that the master document has <vbox>es or that the overlays have <box>es. The tag names in the overlays are not important. Use of matching names does reduce confusion.

This example can be made slightly more complex. The master document can have some of its content changed from this:

```
<vbox id="osite1">
  <description>Main Box A</description>
</vbox>
```

to this:

```
<vbox id="osite1">
  <description>Main Box A</description>
  <box id="innersite"/>
</vbox>
```

Either of the overlays can then contain this content as a child of the <overlay> tag:

```
<box id="innersite">
  <description>Inner Content</description>
</box>
```

It doesn't matter where in the overlay this content appears—it can even be nested inside other tags. The result of these two additions is shown in Figure 12.2.

The new content is appended at the new site. It appears before the other appended content in the first box, because it is inside existing content from the master. It is appended to the content of the master's <box> tag, not to the content of the master's <vbox> tag.

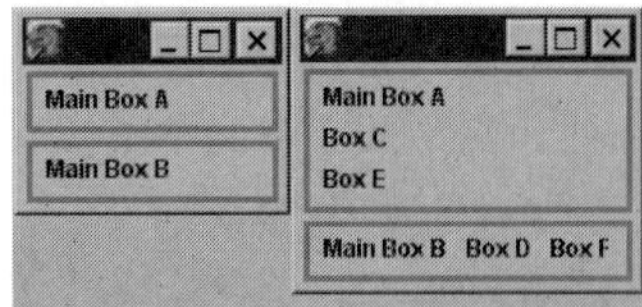

Fig. 12.1 Master document with and without overlay content.

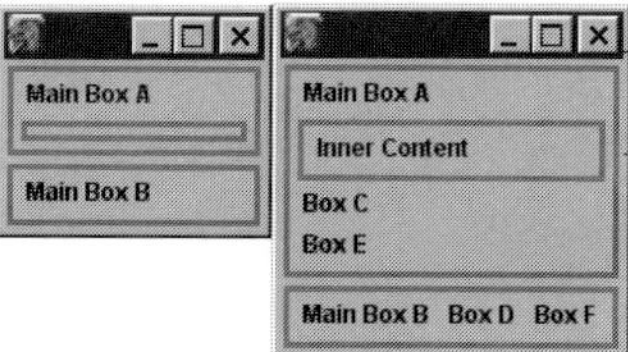

Fig. 12.2 Master document with extra overlay content.

This example, which adds extra content to boxes, is quite trivial. In application terms, there are many XUL tags that are container tags to which it is sensible to add extra content. `<commandset>` might acquire extra commands. `<deck>` might acquire extra cards. `<menupopup>` might acquire extra `<menuitem>`s. `<toolbar>` might acquire extra `<toolbarbutton>`s.

12.1.3.3 Merging Options The id-based system for merging content can be modified slightly. Overlay content does not always have to be appended to the master content. XML attributes can modify where it is put. The following attributes provide those further options:

```
position insertbefore insertafter removeelement
```

`position` is used in addition to the `id` attribute. It accepts a number index as its value and is placed on one or more of the content tags inside the tag with the source id. That content tag will then be inserted at that position in the target id tag's content. So `position="3"` puts that content tag after the first two content items in the target id tag. There cannot be clashes in position between overlays because overlays are added one at a time.

`insertbefore` and `insertafter` are used instead of id on an overlay tag. They each take an id as their value. Instead of the source id tag's content being added into the master document, the source id tag itself (and its content) is added. That is one extra tag inserted. `insertbefore` puts that content before the supplied id in the master document. `insertafter` puts that content after the supplied id in the master document. In both cases, the content is a sibling DOM node of the supplied id.

`removeelement` can be set to `true` and is used with the `id` attribute. If the overlay tag has this attribute set, the matching tag in the master document is removed. It makes no sense to specify overlay content when this attribute is used.

Listing 12.10 illustrates all this syntax.

Listing 12.10 Overlay showing merge options syntax.

```
<?xml version="1.0"?>
<overlay xmlns="http://www.mozilla.org/keymaster/gatekeeper/
         there.is.only.xul"
  >
```

```
  <box insertbefore="Box1">
    <description>insertbefore="Box1"</description>
  </box>
  <box insertafter="Box2">
    <description>insertafter="Box2"</description>
  </box>
  <box id="Box3">
    <description position="3">position="3" in content item</description>
  </box>
  <box id="Box4" removeelement="true"/>
</overlay>
```

Figure 12.3 shows each of these options at work on a simple master document. The top screenshot is the master document without overlays. The bottom screenshot is the resulting document after all merging has occurred.

Note that Box 4 is missing because of the use of the `removeelement` attribute.

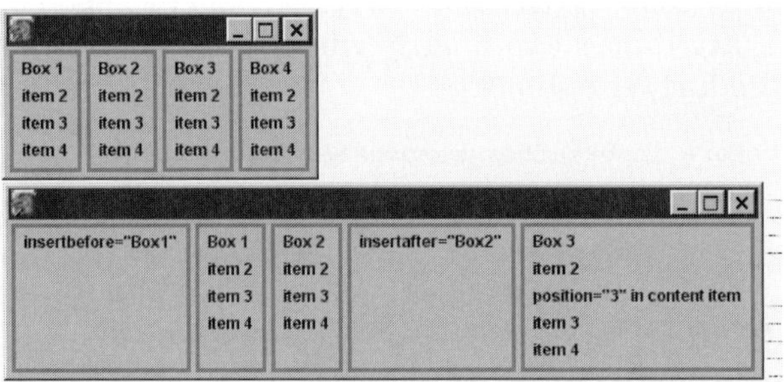

Fig. 12.3 Master document showing the effect of overlay merge options.

12.2 The Chrome Registry

Mozilla's chrome registry is a set of RDF facts that describes the packages that exist in the chrome. The chrome is used to support `chrome:` URLs and to apply some simple restrictions to packages. It is automatically used when XUL documents are loaded, and when new packages are installed.

Use of the term *registry* is unfortunate because Mozilla has several registries, all in different formats. The chrome registry is more accurately a database of information and a processing system. The chrome registry is used at the XUL application level inside the platform. The Mozilla registry, which is separate, is used lower down at the platform functionality level.

Without the chrome, the platform would have to perform searches of the file system hierarchy under the chrome directory. These searches would be required to find packages, skins, and locales for each XUL document displayed. With the chrome in place, an in-memory database of RDF information (a fact store) can be consulted, and the exact files identified before the disk is touched. This in-memory fact store can also be used to switch the current theme and the current locale and to add new packages. In theory those changes can be made without restarting the platform, but in practice the current implementation still requires a restart.

The main use of the chrome registry is simply to map a `chrome:` URL for a specific package to another URL. In normal circumstances, a `chrome:` prefix is mapped to a `resource:/chrome/` prefix. This in-memory mapping has two little-used features that illustrate the role of the registry. First, a package can be installed under a Mozilla user profile instead of under the platform install area. Second, a package can be installed anywhere on the file system. In both cases, the chrome registry ensures that the URL for that package still starts with

```
chrome://package-name/content/
```

Like the overlay system, the chrome registry translates a set of application-programmer-supplied source-generated files into generated files. Both sets of files use RDF syntax. The source files consist of all the `contents.rdf` manifest files that accompany packages, skins, and locales. The chrome registry ignores information in those files about overlays. There is only one generated file; it is called `chrome.rdf` and has the URL *resource:/chrome/chrome.rdf*.

The "Hands On" sessions in Chapters 2, 3, and 4 provide examples of this RDF chrome information for packages, locales, and skins, respectively. Here we consider the overall data model into which those examples fit.

The `chrome.rdf` file contains a fully populated copy of the chrome registry data model. Look in that file for the features noted in the remainder of this section. A `contents.rdf` file contains only a slice of the data model. That slice is just the pieces of information specific to a particular package, locale, or skin.

Chrome RDF information is based on a data model consisting of a set of URNs. These URNs start with three RDF `<Seq>` containers:

```
urn:mozilla:package:root
urn:mozilla:locale:root
urn:mozilla:skin:root
```

Each container states what packages, locales, or skins are available to the platform. Although some variation is possible, the URN names for the individual packages, locales, or skins, which are the contents of the container, should have the form

```
urn:mozilla:package:{package-name}
urn:mozilla:locale:{locale-name}
urn:mozilla:skin:{skin-name}/{skin-version}
```

Some example URNs are, therefore,

```
urn:mozilla:package:navigator
urn:mozilla:locale:en-US
urn:mozilla:skin:classic/1.0
```

These URNs can be decorated with RDF property/value pairs. In other words, they can be the subjects of facts. The predicates for those facts must come from this namespace:

http://www.mozilla.org/rdf/chrome#

The available predicates are listed in Table 12.1.

Table 12.1 Chrome registry top-level predicates

Predicate name	Applies to	Value	Purpose
accessKey	skin	A character	A menu shortcut key used in the Classic Browser for changing themes
author	package, locale, skin	Any text	Originator of the package
baseURL	package	URL	Location of the package; do not use the chrome: scheme
disabled	package	"true"	Prevents external overlays; do not set to "false"
displayName	package, skin	Any text	Readable text name for the item
hasOverlays	package	"true"	XUL overlays exist; do not set to "false"
hasStylesheets	package	"true"	CSS2 overlays exist; do not set to "false"
name	package	Package name	Name of the package should match a directory name
name	skin	Any text	Name of the skin; may be any text
image	skin	URL	An image that illustrates what the skin looks like; do not use the chrome: scheme
localeVersion	package	Version number	Minimum locale version the package requires
locType	package, skin	Install, profile	Where the package or skin is installed
packages	locale, skin	URN	The <Seq> holding package-specific implementations
previewURL	locale	URL	A document that illustrates what the locale looks like; do not use the chrome: scheme
selectedLocale	package	URN	The current locale; applies only to the global package

Table 12.1 Chrome registry top-level predicates (Continued)

Predicate name	Applies to	Value	Purpose
selectedSkin	package	URN	The current skin; applies only to the global package
skinVersion	package	Version number	Minimum skin version the packages requires

In addition to these main containers are two sets of secondary containers. They are accessible from each locale and skin URN via its packages predicate. These additional containers state the existence of package-specific implementations of skins and locales. They are also `<Seq>` containers and have the following names:

```
urn:mozilla:locale:{locale-name}:packages
urn:mozilla:skin:{skin-name}:packages
```

Each of these containers holds a list of package-specific implementations of locales or skins. The URNs for a given implementation should be one of

```
urn:mozilla:locale:{locale-name}:{package-name}
urn:mozilla:skin:{skin-name}/{skin-version}:{package-name}
```

So if the navigator package (the Classic Browser) has an implementation of the French locale (FR), then this URN is required to state that the locale is implemented and available:

```
urn:mozilla:locale:FR:navigator
```

Each specific skin or locale resource so stated can also be decorated with RDF property/value pairs. The available predicates are listed in Table 12.2.

The newer Mozilla Browser slightly enhances Tables 12.1 and 12.2 with additional predicates.

Table 12.2 Chrome registry implementation predicates

Predicate name	Applies to	Value	Purpose
allowScripts	skin	"true"	Skin may run scripts; do not set to "false"
baseURL	locale, skin	URL	Location of the implementation; do not use the chrome: scheme
localeVersion	locale	Version number	The version of this implementation
package	locale, skin	URN	The owning package of this implementation
skinVersion	skin	Version number	The version of this implementation

12.3 Persisting Window State

Similar to the overlay system and chrome registry, but far simpler, is Mozilla's GUI persistence system. This system allows the desktop position and location of Mozilla windows to be remembered after the application is shut down. It can also be used to store any kind of noncritical information, for any application. All such information is stored on the local computer.

The persisting system consists of one RDF file, one XUL attribute, and some automatic processing by the Mozilla Platform. It records the state (the value) of one or more attributes for specific XUL tags. Sometimes this is done automatically, and sometimes it requires a hint from the application programmer. Because an attribute can contain an arbitrary string, information can be stuffed into an attribute for later. For XUL programmers, this is an alternative to using cookies, although no network information is automatically available.

The persisted RDF file is called `localstore.rdf` and is stored in the user's profile. It is written to every time a window is closed. For each attribute persisted, there are two facts. One fact states that the XUL document (subject URL) is persisting (the predicate) something in the specific tag (the object). This fact occurs only once for all attributes persisted in a given tag. In the second fact, the tag (subject URL) has a predicate/property equal to the attribute name, and a subject literal equal to the attribute value. Listing 12.11 shows these facts for a tag in the `editor.xul` document that has `id="editorWindow"` and a width attribute.

Listing 12.11 Example of persisted facts in `localstore.rdf`.

```
<RDF:Description about="chrome://editor/content/editor.xul">
  <NC:persist resource="chrome://editor/content/editor.xul#editorWindow"/>
</RDF:Description>

<RDF:Description about="chrome://editor/content/editor.xul#editorWindow"
         width="884"/>
```

No attributes are persisted by default. Some attributes are persisted by the chrome files that make up Classic Mozilla. Each such attribute may or may not be persisted for a given window or dialog box. A selection of commonly persisted attributes is

```
checked collapsed height hidden moz-collapsed open offsetX offsetY
     ordinal screenX screenY sizemode state width
```

In the end, whether an attribute is persisted is a matter of application design, not platform capability.

The value persisted for each attribute is the value currently held by that attribute. In the cases where an attribute isn't set in the XUL, like window dimensions, the current value is written out.

A hint added to XUL content by the application programmer ensures that an attribute is remembered. Such a hint is given with this XUL attribute:

```
persist
```

`persist` can contain a comma- or space-separated list of attributes for that tag. This example preserves the layout direction for a window, in addition to the automatically saved positional attributes.

```
<window dir="ltr" orient="vertical" persist="dir orient"/>
```

If the persist attribute is to be used, then the tag it is added to must have an id.

12.4 Related AOM and XPCOM Objects

The overlay and chrome registry systems are implemented using these XPCOM features:

```
@mozilla.org/chrome/chrome-registry;1 nsIXULChromeRegistry
```

A few methods on this interface allow simple operations on the overlay system, but they don't allow the programmer to drive the overlay merging system by hand. There is little reason to use this interface, unless you are building a tool like the DOM Inspector or a custom install system.

To persist an attribute from JavaScript, use this method call:

```
document.persist(tagid, attname);
```

This will persist the value of the `attname` attribute for the tag with id equal to `tagid`.

12.5 Hands On: The NoteTaker Toolbar

In this short "Hands-On" session, we'll convert the NoteTaker toolbar from a XUL fragment to an overlay that merges correctly into the Mozilla Browser window. The steps to do this are straightforward.

- ☞ Find an id that can be used to merge the NoteTaker toolbar into the Classic Browser window.
- ☞ Find an id that can be used to merge the Tools NoteTaker menu item into the Classic Browser window.
- ☞ Review the toolbar content for any other content that might need a merge id.
- ☞ Update the toolbar content to include the Tools menu NoteTaker item, suitable ids, and an `<overlay>` tag.
- ☞ Update the chrome registry to record the existence of the overlay.
- ☞ Delete the existing overlay database and restart the platform to see the result.

To find ids, we need to know the master XUL document for the Classic Browser application (that is, the document that contains the `<window>` tag for the browser).

Looking through the chrome directory, the only file that could possibly contain the browser application is comm.jar. 'comm' is an abbreviation of Communicator (the Netscape Communicator suite). This .jar file contains a large number of XUL files spread over many subdirectories, but if we look through these files, it's soon clear that many of them are <dialog>, <page>, or <overlay> documents. In the content/navigator subpart of the .jar is the file navigator.xul with this useful-looking beginning:

```
<window id="main-window" … >
```

We can test if this navigator.xul file is the starting point for the Classic Browser, by loading it directly:

```
mozilla -chrome "chrome://navigator/content/navigator.xul"
```

If we do that, we discover that this file is the correct starting point for the browser application. The id needed is either in this file or in one of the overlays merged into this document. We can either use the DOM Inspector on the final merged document to find a suitable id, or we can examine the source code directly, which requires a full list of overlays used. To get a full list of those overlays, add together:

- Overlays declared directly in navigator.xul with the <?xul-overlay?> tag.
- Overlays declared for chrome://navigator/content/navigator.xul in the file chrome/overlayinfo/navigator/contents/overlays.rdf under the platform install directory.
- Repeat both previous points for all overlay files discovered on the first and subsequent passes.

In our case, however, such a list is unnecessary because the navigator.xul file itself contains suitable ids.

For the NoteTaker toolbar, we find

```
<toolbox id="navigator-toolbox" class="toolbox-top"
     deferattached="true">
```

For the NoteTaker Tools menu item, we find

```
<menu id="tasksMenu">
  <menupopup id="taskPopup">
```

The <menupopup> tag is a suitable site for a single, extra menu item. It may not be the ideal site for the new item, but here we're just trying to get something working.

After glancing at our toolbar code, we also see that our <commandset> content will need to be merged in. For that we find in navigator.xul

```
<commandset id="commands">
```

<script> content is interpreted immediately and doesn't need to be merged.

We rename `toolbar.xul` to `browserOverlay.xul` for consistency with existing file naming conventions, and change its content. That file's final structure will be as shown in Listing 12.12.

Listing 12.12 Overlay structure of NoteTaker toolbar.

```
<?xml version="1.0"?>
<!DOCTYPE overlay>
<overlay xmlns="http://www.mozilla.org/keymaster/gatekeeper/
          there.is.only.xul">

<script src="controllers.js"/>
  <script src="toolbar_action.js"/>

<commandset id="commands">
    … existing commands go here …
  </commandset>

<menupopup id="taskPopup">
    <menuitem label="Edit Note" command="notetaker.toolbar.command.edit"/>
  </menupopup>

  <toolbox id="navigator-toolbox">
    <toolbar id="notetaker-toolbar">
      … existing toolbar content goes here …
    </toolbar>
  </toolbox>
</overlay>
```

If we use the bottom-up approach to overlays, then we don't need to modify the Classic Browser at all. We'll do it that way, which means no more XUL changes. All that remains is to register the RDF document with the chrome registry, using the `chrome://navigator/content/contents.rdf` file. In Chapter 2, XUL Layout, the `contents.rdf` was created with the content in Listing 12.13.

Listing 12.13 Chrome registration file for a package without overlays.

```
<?xml version="1.0"?>
<RDF
  xmlns="http://www.w3.org/1999/02/22-rdf-syntax-ns#"
  xmlns:chrome="http://www.mozilla.org/rdf/chrome#">

<Seq about="urn:mozilla:package:root">
    <li resource="urn:mozilla:package:notetaker"/>
  </Seq>

<Description about="urn:mozilla:package:notetaker"
    chrome:displayName="NoteTaker"
    chrome:author="Nigel McFarlane"
    chrome:name="notetaker">
  </Description>

</RDF>
```

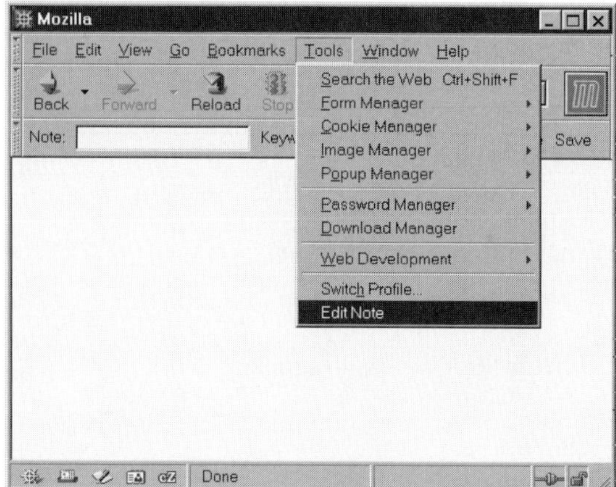

Fig. 12.4 Master document with extra overlay content.

This existing file states that the NoteTaker package exists. Now we must tell it that the overlay URL and the target URL exist. The target URL is the document to which the overlay will be added. The extra facts required are shown in Listing 12.14.

Listing 12.14 Registration content required for a single overlay.

```
<!-- State the document that receives the overlay -->
<Seq about="urn:mozilla:overlays">
  <li resource="chrome://navigator/content/navigator.xul"/>
</Seq>

<!-- state the overlay that applies to the target -->
<Seq about="chrome://navigator/content/navigator.xul">
  <li>chrome://notetaker/content/browserOverlay.xul</li>
</Seq>
```

In the distant past, overlay names were plain strings, not URLs. This history is responsible for the restriction that the last `<li>` tag cannot use the `resource=` attribute. This is true up to at least version 1.4.

After all these changes are made, the Classic Browser is decorated as shown in Figure 12.4. To see this change, we must shut down the platform, delete the existing `chrome.rdf` file and the existing `overlayinfo` directory, and restart the platform. Note that part of the NoteTaker toolbar is covered by the exposed menu.

That concludes the "Hands On" session for this chapter.

12.6 Debug Corner: Overlay Tips

Overlays are very simple and need little debugging, but there are one or two serious potholes to avoid.

The most subtle problem with overlays is caused by the contents.rdf file that sits inside the contents directory of a package. When the URL of an overlay is specified, it must be specified as plain XML text, not as a URI. This is wrong:

```
<li resource="chrome://package/content/overlay.xul"/>
```

This is right:

```
<li>chrome://package/content/overlay.xul</li>
```

If the package also acts as a master document (because it includes its own overlays), then it should be written as a resource when it is registered as a master. It should still be written as XML text when it is registered as an overlay. This stumbling block is a defect in the chrome system.

If an overlay document has illegal XML syntax and is registered in the overlayinfo database, then any application that includes that overlay may not load. In versions from 1.3 onward, the faulty overlay will result in a yellow syntax error message at the bottom of the incomplete final document. To fix this, shut down the platform and delete the RDF overlay information for that file, or fix the original syntax. To delete the overlay information, delete the whole overlayinfo database and delete any facts in contents.rdf files that refer to the problem document.

A useful feature of overlays delivered the bottom-up way involves popup windows generated by Web sites. When those sites attempt to pop up windows without toolbars, any custom toolbar or other overlay content will still appear. That is quite convenient if you are a Web developer who likes to examine the source of other people's pages. The source of popup windows is normally not accessible if the window has lost all its decorations.

12.7 Summary

Mozilla's overlay system provides a programming-in-the-large, or at least in-the-medium, component technology for programmers. It is a component technology for XML-based GUI systems, but in Mozilla only works with XUL. Overlays can be added directly into XUL content. Alternatively, platform features can be exploited to drive the inclusion process automatically.

Overlays, the chrome registry, and persisted data make very passive use of RDF. RDF files are read and written automatically, without the programmer even trying. That is hardly an opportunity to see the application power of RDF. In the next chapter, we return to XUL to see the two power tags: <listbox> and <tree>. In addition to being indispensable in their own right, these tags will bring us one step closer to full programming of RDF.

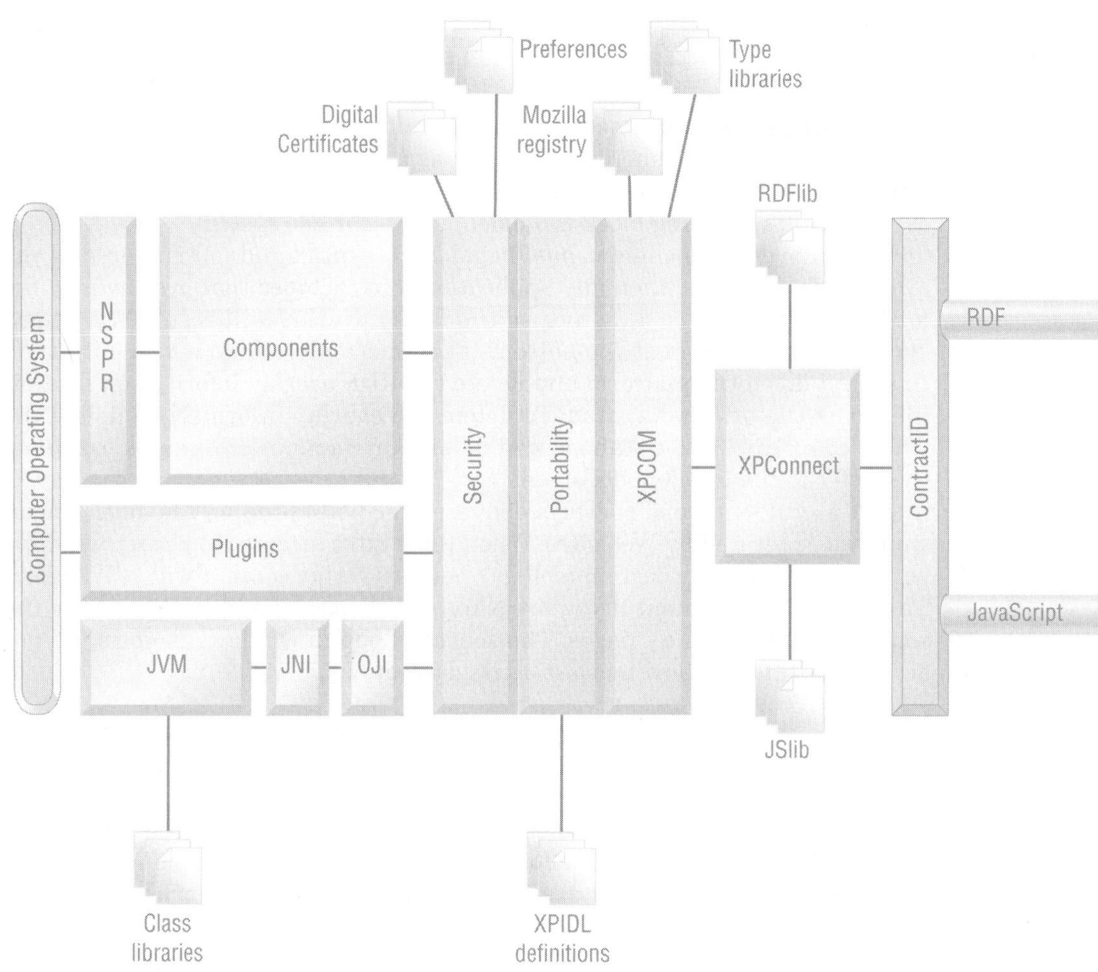

Preferences
Type libraries
Digital Certificates
Mozilla registry
RDFlib
Computer Operating System
NSPR
Components
Security
Portability
XPCOM
XPConnect
ContractID
RDF
Plugins
JavaScript
JVM
JNI
OJI
JSlib
Class libraries
XPIDL definitions

C H A P T E R 13

Listboxes and Trees

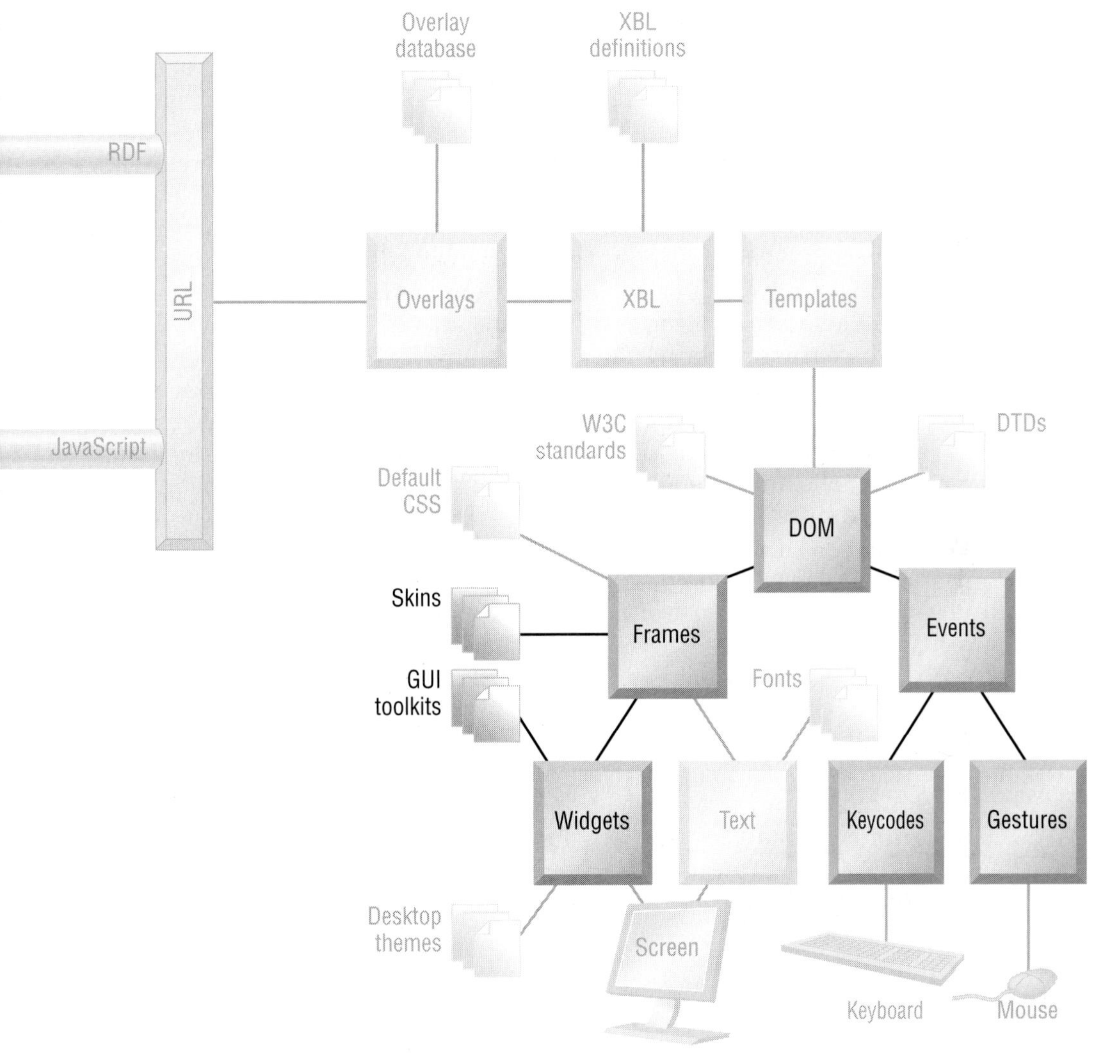

This chapter describes the construction of XUL's most powerful widgets: <listbox> and <tree>. These tags are designed for data-intensive applications.

The <listbox> tag provides an inline, scrollable, multirecord list, similar to a menu, but it may contain more than one column. The <tree> tag provides a flat or hierarchically indented list of tree-structured records. <tree> is similar to Windows Explorer on Microsoft Windows, or better yet, the Finder in the Macintosh. <tree> can do everything that <listbox> does, and more, but <listbox> has a simpler and more direct syntax. The syntax of <tree> can become quite complex.

To see a <tree> in action, just open the Classic Mail & News client. The three-pane arrangement consists of three <tree> tags, one per pane. A similar example is the Bookmark Manager, which displays all the available bookmarks in a single <tree>. Spotting a <listbox> is harder because that functionality can also be provided by <tree>. The Appearance, Themes panel of the Preferences window in Classic Mozilla is an example of a <listbox>.

Applications focused on data entry or data management are more tightly designed than Web pages. They tend to pack an available window full of information. They don't waste space on graceful layout. A packed display needs widgets that can economically organize the display of structured data. <listbox> and <tree> have this design constraint in mind. Both tags manage content in a scrollable window that is highly interactive.

Another feature of data management applications is multirecord (or record set) displays. Applications as diverse as email clients, order-entry, point-of-sale, and network management can all display several records at once. Traversing through a set of structured data items is data browsing in the same way that clicking through hypertext links is Web browsing. The interactive, scrolling nature of <listbox> and <tree> is perfect for such uses.

These final XUL widgets require that we visit the GUI of the Mozilla Platform yet again. The NPA diagram at the start of this chapter shows the bits of Mozilla engaged by simple use of these XUL tags. Both <listbox> and <tree> are very fully featured tags. They extend right across the user-interface features of the platform, as well as extending up into the DOM, frame, and CSS2 styling infrastructure. Both tags have features that allow scripts to pry further into the frame system than any other XUL tag. Their other novel feature is support for multiple selection. This chapter covers all that, but leaves the equally complex matter of data-enabling these widgets to Chapter 14, Templates.

Mozilla presents many options for displaying structured data, such as the humble form. Before turning to <listbox> and <tree>, we briefly consider another simple system—the text grid.

13.1 Text Grids

Text input tags can be arranged into a text grid. A text grid is an informal term for a two-dimensional array of editable boxes. An obvious example of a text grid is a spreadsheet, with its columns and rows. Small text grids are also ideal for the detailed part of master-detail forms and for working with sets of records. XUL has no direct support for text grids, but such things are easy to design using the `<textbox>` tag.

The Web tends to ignore the flexibility of textboxes. On the Web, it is customary to see data-entry forms designed so that individual fields are spaced well apart. Requests for contact details or for purchase order details are often displayed so that there is one form element per line. This makes text boxes appear to be bulky and spacious things.

In fact, the HTML `<INPUT>` tag and the XUL `<textbox>` tag can be styled to be quite slim. Only simple styles are required:

```
textbox {
  border : solid thin;
  border-width : 1px;
  padding : 0px;
  margin : 0px;
}

input:focus { background-color : lightgrey; }
```

The second style serves to ensure that the field with the current focus is background-highlighted when it has the focus. Recall from Chapter 7, Forms and Menus, that `<textbox>` also contains an `<html:input>` tag. Figure 13.1 shows an example application using these thinned-down textboxes.

Each `<textbox>` is the contents of one cell in a `<grid>`. The XUL code is routine. XUL's navigation model and focus ring ensures that each `<textbox>` can be tabbed into in turn, and that each field is background-highlighted when it receives the focus. This results in the look and feel of traditional data management applications, which are fast and efficient for data entry operators to use. Properties dialog boxes, typically accessed from content menus, can't possibly compete for speed.

A collection of `<textbox>` tags is hardly a complete solution—the whole back end of the application needs to be added. Such a XUL page could end up with many event handlers whose only purpose is to coordinate data against the user's navigation. There is significant scripting design work required for such a window (called a screen in older jargon).

Web-based systems do not follow this kind of look and feel for many reasons. There is the difficulty of POSTing multiple records at once; the need to

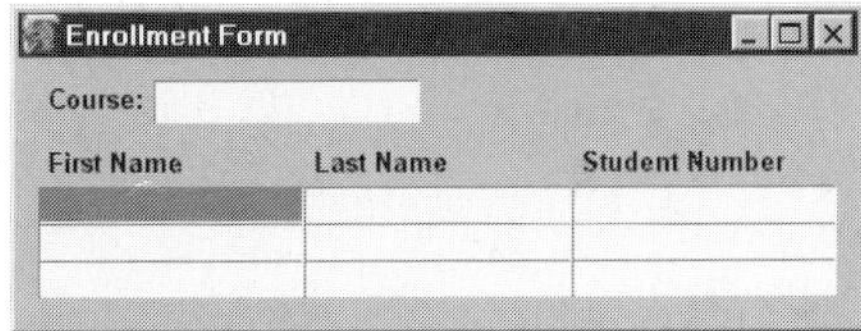

Fig. 13.1 A simple text grid using the `<textbox>` tag.

provide accessibility support; the complexity of implementation; and the likelihood that the sizes of browser windows will vary greatly. XUL applications, built to be vertical solutions, are not always so constrained, and the performance gains delivered to users may be tempting.

Both `<listbox>` and `<tree>` improve on and specialize the concept of a text grid. A text grid made out of XUL tags is the most general arrangement possible. It may also be the most useful if a lot of data entry is required.

13.2 Listboxes

The `<listbox>` tag is similar in construction to the `<grid>` tag, but in appearance and behavior it is more like the `<menulist>` tag. A listbox is a vertically arranged set of records or rows, where each record has one or more subparts.

HTML's `<SELECT rows= >` tag has a similar implementation to `<listbox>`. That HTML tag produces an inline menu rather than a popup one. The `<SELECT>` tag is both robust and standard, but the `<listbox>` tag is not yet either. In Mozilla versions up to 1.4 at least, `<listbox>` is somewhat fragile, so tread carefully when using it. Despite that weakness, it is a powerful tool when used properly.

13.2.1 Visual Appearance

To see a `<listbox>` at work, open the Mozilla Preferences dialog box (Edit | Preferences) and look at the `Appearance`, `Themes` panel on the right. That white panel displaying theme names like Classic and Modern is a listbox.

Figure 13.2 shows two listboxes with most of the available features visible.

The listbox on the left is a one-column listbox. This format is used for HTML's `<SELECT>`. The listbox has height and width style rules that have defaults of `200px` each. If the box area is forced smaller by layout issues, then a vertical scrollbar will appear, and any contained `<label>` text might be cropped. Each row can also contain a leading icon and a leading checkbox, as shown. In a real application, all rows would be iconized or checkboxed, not just a few sample rows. In this example, row 4 was checked by clicking on the row, and then row 3 was selected as the current row.

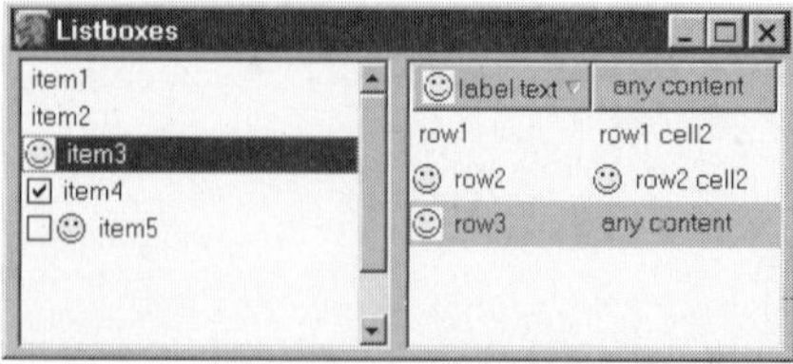

Fig. 13.2 Two listboxes showing popular features.

The listbox on the right of Figure 13.3 is a multicolumn listbox. It has two columns, but any number of columns is possible. The top row is an optional row of column headings. The first column heading has an icon on both left and right of its text. The left icon is an arbitrary image, added using a style. The right icon is a special-purpose image that shows the sort order of the rows underneath that heading, and therefore of all rows. That right icon is placed with an XML attribute. The other rows (also called *items*) of this listbox contain two cells each. Icons can be placed in these cells, although it is not very meaningful to do so. Checkboxes can also be placed in these cells, but there is no automated means of checking them, and it is almost meaningless to put them in. In the screenshot, the third row of the second listbox is selected (it appears light gray) but the second listbox doesn't have the focus. The listbox on the left-hand side has the focus—its focussed row is dark gray (blue normally).

The contents of a cell can be a simple `<label>` or a boxlike tag that holds arbitrary content. If arbitrary content is used, layout becomes more of a challenge, and the listbox doesn't neatly crop its content when resized. This can cause CSS2 overflow and other messy effects, so simple labels are the safest kind of content. A multicolumn listbox can have a row with fewer cells than there are columns, and that will work (including checkboxes), but that use is not recommended.

If a multicolumn listbox gains a vertical scrollbar, then that scrollbar does not include the optional header row.

13.2.2 Construction

Figure 13.3 repeats Figure 13.2, but with diagnostic styles turned on.

As before, thin dotted lines are labels, thin black boxes are images, and thick gray lines are boxes. Smileys are slightly squashed on the left only because extra border styles have distorted the layout slightly. The right-hand listbox is quite confusing with all its boxes revealed, but a bit of study reveals

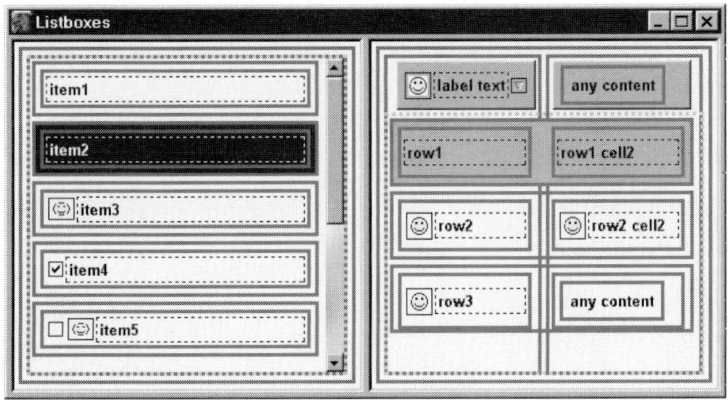

Fig. 13.3 Two listboxes with their internal structure exposed.

that those boxes are very similar to the <grid> boxes discussed in Chapter 2, XUL Layout. A grid is used as the core of a <listbox>'s layout strategy, with <button> tags for column headers and <label> tags for the default cell content. The column 2 header and the right half of row 3 show that such a label can be replaced with an arbitrary box of content. The two dark rows (one in each listbox) show the extent of the highlighting that results from selecting a row. This highlighting is just a background style applied to something equivalent to the <grid> tag's <row> subtag.

Figure 13.4 also reveals a box specific to the layout of <listbox>. This is the gray, thick, dotted line in both of the listboxes displayed. This box surrounds all the list items or rows. This box is used extensively in the implementation of the <listbox> system. It makes the <listbox> layout system unique and separate from <grid>.

The <listbox> tag, and its related tags, has XBL definitions stored in the file `listbox.xml` in `toolkit.jar` in the chrome. The Mozilla Platform has extensive C/C++ support for listboxes as well.

Which listbox tags exist depends on your perspective. The tags an application programmer uses are different from the tags used by the platform to generate the final XUL. Table 13.1 describes all the listbox tags in Mozilla and their status as of version 1.4.

<listbox> uses the pair <listcols> and <listcol> to identify list columns, but it uses <listrows> and <listhead> or <listitem> for rows. The <grid> tags, therefore, do not have exact matches for <listbox>. The special dotted box noted in Figure 13.3 is the border of the <listboxbody> tag. It is a key part of Mozilla's listbox scrolling support.

Table 13.1 Mozilla's listbox tags

Tag name	Useable tag?	Must use?	Internal use only?	<grid> Rough equivalent
<listbox>	✓	✓		<grid>
<listcols>	✓			<columns>
<listcol>	✓			<column>
<listhead>	✓			<row>
<listheader>	✓			one child of <row>
<listheaditem>			✓	one child of <row>
<listboxbody>			✓	
<listrows>			✓	<rows>
<listitem>	✓	✓		<row>
<listcell>	✓			one child of <row>

Listing 13.1 Basic <listbox> containing three items.

```
<listbox>
  <listhead>
    <listheader label="Sole Column">
  </listhead>
  <listitem label="first item"/>
  <listitem label="second item"/>
  <listitem label="third item"/>
</listbox>
```

Listing 13.1 specifies a single-column listbox of three items, with a header that reads "Sole Column." No icons or checkboxes are present. It is similar to many of the boxes present in the Preferences dialog box; for example, in the `Appearance`, `Themes` panel, or in the `Navigator`, `Languages` panel. Those examples have no header, however.

The XML that Mozilla constructs from this listbox contains many additional tags, as illustrated in Figure 13.4.

In this fully expanded tag tree, the darker tags match Listing 13.2. The lighter tags with `xul:` prefixes are extra content generated by listbox XBL definitions. This is a complete breakdown of a listbox, except that if there were two columns, the `<xul:listcol>`, `<xul:listheaditem>`, and `<xul:listcell>` tags would appear twice in each tree position, rather than just once.

This tree shows that Listing 13.2 is a specification that uses very condensed syntax—many tags in the final listbox are implied rather than stated. It also shows the similarities and differences between `<listbox>` and `<grid>`. While both have columns and rows, a `<listbox>` has at most two

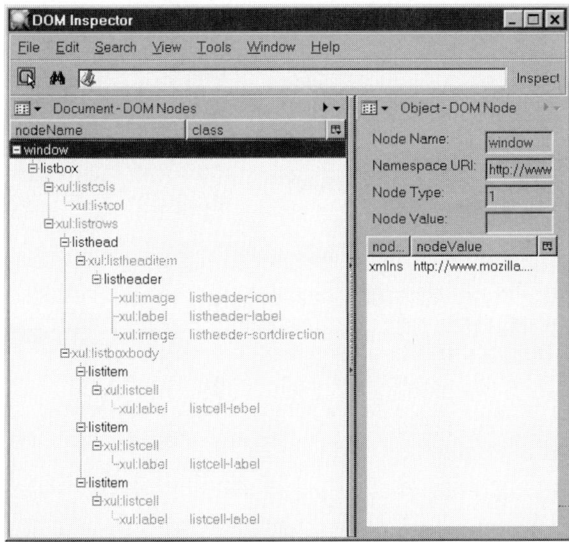

Fig. 13.4 DOM Inspector view of three-item `<listbox>`.

immediate rows, whereas a <grid> can have any number. The items displayed in the listbox are nested within the second row, as though that row were a <vbox>. The first row, which contains the header line, is left out if no header is specified.

Some basic rules of <listbox> construction follow:

1. For each <listbox>, there should be at most one <listcols> and at most one <listhead>.
2. For a <listcols>, if it is present, there should be at least one <listcol>
3. For a <listhead>, if it is present, there should be at least one <listheader>.
4. Items per <listitem> should equal the number of <listcols>, or be one if no <listcols> exists.
5. Do not ever state <listrows>, <listboxbody>, and <listheaditem> explicitly. These tags are for internal use only.

This complex construction process has its pitfalls. The main pitfall is that XUL cannot handle the combination of tags that it in turn generates for <listbox>. If you create a piece of explicit XUL that matches the tags and structure shown in Figure 13.5, it will not work as a listbox, and Mozilla will probably crash. This means that the XML specification of a listbox and its XML implementation are separate and different.

Mozilla may also crash if you use any of the tags in construction rule 5. It will crash if you specify any content for the <listcol> tag. It may become confused, do poor layout, or possibly crash if you deviate much at all from the assumptions that the XUL/XBL processor makes once it sees a <listbox> tag.

Listing 13.2 shows the most extended listbox specification that XUL supports.

Listing 13.2 Extended <listbox> showing all options.

```
<listbox>

  <listcols>       // tag and content optional
    <listcol/>     // can be repeated
  </listcols>

  <listhead>       // tag and content optional
    <listheader>   // can be repeated
    </listheader>
  </listhead>

  <listitem>       // can be repeated
    <listcell>     // can be repeated
    </listcell>
  </listitem>

</listbox>
```

The open and close tags for <listitem>, <listcell>, and <listheader> can be collapsed into singleton <tag/> tags, and attributes can be used in place of the removed tag content. These attributes are discussed under the individual tags. All these tags have XBL definitions in `listbox.xml` in `toolkit.jar` in the chrome.

13.2.3 <listbox>

The <listbox> tag has the following special attributes:

```
rows size seltype suppressonselect disableKeyNavigation
```

`rows` and `size` dictate the height of the listbox in number of line items. The `size` calculation is based on the tallest line item that exists, multiplied by the value of the attribute. This is the same as setting the `minheight` attribute to a fixed number of pixels for each line item. Each line item will be expanded to the height of the tallest item, and so line items are always equally sized. The `size` attribute is deprecated for XUL; use `rows` instead. A <listbox> may be dynamically resized by setting the `rows` attribute from JavaScript.

The `rows` attribute (and `size` and `minheight`) are passed internally to the <listboxbody> tag for processing, so the space any header row takes up is not included in the calculations.

The <listbox> tag works poorly with the `maxheight` attribute. If <listbox> tags are inside an <hbox>, and sibling tags of the <listbox> have a `maxheight` that is less than the <listbox>'s `maxheight`, then the content can overflow downward, resulting in messy layout. The recommended approach when <listbox> has large siblings is to set the <listbox>'s height with `height` and avoid setting `rows` entirely.

The `seltype` attribute determines if multiple rows of a listbox can be user-selected. If it is set to `multiple`, then that is possible. If it is set to anything else, only a single row will be selected. The dynamics of this arrangement are discussed in section 13.2.11.

The `suppressonselect` attribute can be set to `true`. When a user selects an item in a <listbox>, the XBL code for that tag fires a `select` DOM event, which can be picked up by an event handler on the <listbox> tag. This attribute prevents that event from being created.

The `disableKeyNavigation` attribute can be set to `true`. This prevents alphabetic keypresses from changing the current selection when the <listbox> tag has the input focus.

See the "AOM and XPCOM Interfaces" section for a discussion of JavaScript access to <listbox>. <listbox>'s support for templates is discussed in Chapter 14, Templates.

13.2.4 <listcols>

The <listcols> tag is a container for <listcol> tags and has no other purpose. It does not have any special attributes and is not displayed. The <list-

cols> tag should appear before all other content inside a <listbox>, if it appears at all.

If this tag is omitted from a <listbox>, then that is the same as

```
<listcols>
  <listcol flex="1"/>
</listcols>
```

This tag is also a possible site for template-based sort attributes.

13.2.5 <listcol>

The <listcol> tag is never displayed and should never have any content. This tag has no special attributes of its own. In a well-formed <listbox>, the number of columns is determined by the number of <listcol/> tags.

The <listcol> tag has two other purposes. It can be used to give an id to the column, and it can control the layout of the column it stands for. This can be done by adding `flex` and `width` attributes or by setting `hidden` or `collapsed` to true.

This tag is a possible site for template sort attributes.

13.2.6 <listhead>

The <listhead> tag is a container tag for <listheader> tags. If <list-head> is not present, then there will be no header row for the listbox. It has no special attributes or purpose. This tag wraps all the <listheader> tags in a single <listheaditem> tag. This ensures that each column header has a box-like tag.

13.2.7 <listheader>

The <listheader> tag is based on the <button> tag, meaning that it is itself a <button>. There should be one <listheader> tag per column. From the XBL definition, if no content is supplied, then this tag is equivalent to

```
<button>
  <image class="listheader-icon"/>

  <label class="listheader-label"/>
  <image class="listheader-sortdirection"/>
</button>
```

The first <image> tag can only be set using a style. The <label>'s `value` and `crop` attributes are set from the <listheader>'s `label` and `crop` attributes. The second image is styled into place according to <listheader>'s only special attribute:

```
sortDirection
```

A value of "ascending" yields an up arrow. A value of "descending" yields a down arrow. A value of "natural" (or anything else) results in no arrow.

If content is supplied, that content appears inside the displayed button.

This tag is also a possible site for template sorting.

13.2.8 <listitem>

The <listitem> tag is used to specify a row in a <listbox>. Use of any other tag to specify a row can cause Mozilla to crash. A <listitem> tag with no user-supplied content is given a single <label> as content. You can alternately specify your own content as one or more child tags of this tag. In that case, there should be one child tag per column, and <listcell> is the obvious choice for that content.

<listitem> supports these special-purpose attributes:

```
label crop flexlabel disabled type checked image selected current
     allowevents value
```

All of these attributes work only for <listbox>es that are single column, unless otherwise stated.

label, crop, and disabled are passed to the interior <label>. The value of flexlabel is passed to the <label>'s flex attribute. A row with disabled set to true can still be selected, but is grayed-out.

The type attribute can be set to checkbox, in which case a checkbox appears to the left of the row. The position of this checkbox cannot be changed with dir. disabled set to true will gray out the checkbox and stop the user from ticking or unticking it.

If the <listitem> has the class listitem-iconic, it can contain an icon. This icon's URL can be set with the image attribute.

The remaining attributes apply to both single- and multicolumn listboxes.

The current attribute is set internally to true by <listbox> processing during selection. If it is true, that means that the <listitem> is the currently selected <listbox> item, or the item just selected in the case where multiple item selection is allowed.

The plain selected attribute is also set to true if this item is selected.

The allowevents attribute, which can be set to true, allows DOM mouse events to pass through the <listitem> tag and into the content that makes up the item. Normally, those events are stopped from propagating when <listitem> receives them. If this attribute is set, then the current row cannot be selected.

The value attribute states the data value that the <listitem> represents. This is for programmer use and is not displayed anywhere.

13.2.9 <listcell>

The <listcell> tag is used to specify a single column entry (a cell) for a row in a <listbox>. Column entries can be specified with a user-defined tag, but the Mozilla Platform checks for <listcell> in a number of places, so it is the right thing to use. The default XBL content of a <listcell> is a single <label>, unless user content is substituted.

The <listcell> tag supports all the attributes that <listitem> supports, except for current, selected, and allowevents. To add an icon to a <listcell>, use the class listcell-iconic. If the <listbox> is multicolumn, then checkboxes will not work when set on a single <listcell>.

The checkbox, icon, and label in a listbox can be reversed with dir="rtl". Other box layout attributes like orient can also be applied to <listcell>, if it makes sense to do so.

That concludes the <listbox> tags.

13.2.10 RDF and Sorting

<listbox> and its related tags can be connected to an RDF document. If this is done, the content of a <listbox> derives from the content of the RDF document. Under such an arrangement, the data in a <listbox> can then be sorted. See Chapter 14, Templates, for detailed instructions.

13.2.11 User Interactions

Listboxes allow for more user interaction than simple XUL form tags. They are at least as versatile as menus.

Listboxes support both keyboard and mouse navigation and have accessibility support. Navigation keys include Tab, Arrow, Paging, Home, and End keys and the spacebar. Mouse support includes clicks, key-click combinations, and the use of scroll wheels. To use the accessibility support, specify the <listitem> contents as label attributes or <label> tags.

Listboxes are members of the focus ring for the currently displayed page. If a <listbox> does not have a currently selected row, then navigating into the listbox from the last member of the focus ring does not provide any visual feedback, but the listbox still has the focus.

The selection of listitems is a flexible matter. If only single item selection is enabled, then selection is much the same as for a menu. If, however, seltype is set to multiple, then multiple list items can be picked. With the mouse, this is done by shift-clicking, to select a contiguous range of items, or by control-clicking, to pick out individual list items not necessarily next to each other. A range of items can also be selected with the keyboard, using shift-arrow combinations. The keyboard cannot be used to pick out multiple separate list items. Only the mouse can do that.

A single row of a listbox can also be selected by typing a character. The `<listbox>` must first have the input focus. The single typed character is matched against the `label` attribute of the `<listitem>` tags in the `<listbox>`. If the label starts with the same character, there is a match. This system selects one row only and works as follows. The `<listitems>` are treated as a circular list of items, like a focus ring. The starting point is either the currently selected `<listitem>` or the first `<listitem>` if no selection yet exists. The list is scanned until a match for the character is found. This allows the user to cycle through the list multiple times.

The user cannot resize the columns of a multicolumn listbox, unless the application programmer enhances the listbox widget with extra event handlers. The same is true of hiding or collapsing columns.

13.2.12 AOM and XPCOM Interfaces

A `<listbox>` can be used for more than just display; it can be used to manage the data it contains. The need to insert, update, and delete that data, or to get and set it, means that robust interfaces are needed from the programming side.

The XBL definition for the `<listbox>` tag makes a number of properties and methods available to the JavaScript programmer. Many of these features mimic the actions of the DOM 0 and DOM 1 standards. Table 13.2 documents them. This table is drawn from the version 1.4 XBL binding named `listbox`.

Table 13.2 Properties and methods of the DOM object for <listbox>

Property or method	Description
accessible	The XPCOM accessibility interface for <listbox>
listBoxObject	The specialized boxObject for <listbox>
disableKeyNavigation	Turn alphabetic keyboard input on (true) or off (null)
timedSelect(listitem, millisec delay)	Select a single <listitem> with a pause that allows page layout (scrolling) to keep up, and the selection to be paced at user speed
selType	Same as attribute seltype
selectedIndex	Get or set the current selected item, starting from 0; returns -1 if multiple items selected
value	Current value of the sole selected item, or fails if more than one item is currently selected
currentItem	The <listitem> most recently selected
selectedCount	The number of <listitem>s selected
appendItem(label, value)	Add a <listitem> to the end of the <listbox>

Table 13.2 Properties and methods of the DOM object for <listbox> (Continued)

Property or method	Description
insertItemAt(index, label, value)	Add a <listitem> at position index
removeItemAt(index)	Remove the row at position index
timedSelect(listitem, millisec delay)	Select a single <listitem> with a pause that allows re-layout (scrolling) to keep up
addItemToSelection(listitem)	Add this DOM <listitem> to the currently selected items (and select it)
removeItemFromSelection(listitem)	Deselect this DOM <listitem>
toggleItemSelection(listitem)	Reverse the selection state for this <listitem>
selectItem(listitem)	Deselect everything and then select this sole <listitem>
selectItemRange(startItem, endItem)	Deselect everything and then select all <listitem>s including between these two items
selectAll()	Select all rows in the <listbox> except the header row
invertSelection()	Flip the select state of all rows in the <listbox>
clearSelection()	Deselect everything
getNextItem(listitem, offset)	Go offset <listitem>s forward from the supplied item and return the item found
getPreviousItem(listitem,offset)	Go offset <listitem>s backward from the supplied item and return the item found
getIndexOfItem(listitem)	Return the index of this <listitem> within the <listbox>
getItemAtIndex(index)	Return the <listitem> at index in the <listbox>
ensureIndexIsVisible(index)	Scroll the listbox contents until the <listitem> with this index is visible
ensureElementIsVisible(listitem)	Scroll the listbox contents until this <listitem> is visible
scrollToIndex(index)	Scroll the listbox content to the <listitem> with this index
getNumberOfVisibleRows()	Return the number of items currently visible
getIndexOfFirstVisibleRow()	Return the index of the <listitem> that currently appears at the top of the <listbox>
getRowCount()	Return the total number of rows; unreliable at this publication date

These properties and methods are listed here because <listbox> widgets generally benefit from scripting, and these interfaces are different from standard Web development experiences. These properties and methods should be used instead of the DOM 1 Node and Element interfaces, or else the internals of the <listbox> can become confused. In general, a basic understanding of XBL allows these properties and methods to be read straight out of the XBL binding for <listbox>. There is nothing new in this table; it is just reformatted XBL and comments.

One critical feature of this interface is the use of an index argument. This index refers to any viewable item in this listbox. The viewable items are those rectangular boxes of content inside the listbox that can be scrolled into view. The index does not refer to any list of tags in the listbox's construction. For a listbox, this difference is trivial, because each visible rectangle of content has exactly one <listitem> tag. Later we'll see that a similar index used with the <tree> tag matches nothing but the rectangles of content displayed.

In Chapters 7, 8, and 10, we noted that the <menupopup>, <scrollbox>, and <iframe> tags (amongst others) are special kinds of boxlike tags. They are special because they support additional processing on their box contents. These tags' DOM objects contain a `boxObject` property that can yield up a specialist interface. This specialist interface gives access to that additional content processing.

<listbox> is another example of such a specialist boxlike tag. It supports the `nsIListBoxObject` interface. That interface provides traversal and scrolling operations on the listbox contents. It can also be had from the component

```
@mozilla.org/layout/xul-boxobject-listbox;1
```

One of the reasons that Table 13.2 is so big is because most (but not all) of the features of `nsIListBoxObject` are exported by the <listbox> XBL definition. They appear as the bottom third of Table 13.2. In object-oriented design pattern terms, the <listbox> XBL definition is a façade for this special interface.

In fact, most of the methods and properties in Table 13.2 match a published XPCOM interface. Interface `nsIDOMXULSelectControlElement` is also implemented by menu lists, radio groups, and tab controls. The `nsIDOMXULMultiSelectControlElement` is only implemented by the object that XBL creates for <listbox>.

That concludes the discussion of <listbox>. XUL trees, covered next, can do just about everything the <listbox> tag can do, and more.

13.3 TREES

If the <listbox> tag is a blend of <grid> and <menulist> concepts, then the <tree> tag is a blend of <listbox> and <iframe>. A <tree> widget is a vertically arranged, scrollable set of records like <listbox>. <tree> allows a simple containment hierarchy to be imposed on the displayed rows so that rows are indented different amounts and decorated with graphical hints. When this hierarchy is not imposed, <tree> looks much like <listbox>.

<tree> gives the user room to control the display of the records presented. The user can collapse and expand subparts of the tree interactively. Columns can be reordered, hidden, and resized, and their contents can be sorted and selected.

<tree> gives the application programmer many data processing options. Sort and view features give the programmer direct control over data presentation. When integrated with overlays or templates, the tree widget provides a highly dynamic panel in which data can be managed. Trees can be extensively styled.

If whole-of-document widgets like <iframe> are ignored, then <tree> is the most complex widget that XUL provides.

13.3.1 Visual Appearance

To see a <tree> at work, look at any of these Classic Mozilla windows: The Preferences dialog (left panel); the Messenger window (two panels); the Manage Bookmarks window; the Download Manager. All these windows contain <tree> tags. In fact, there are dozens of trees used throughout the Mozilla application.

Figure 13.5 is a tree that shows the features that XUL trees support. This screenshot uses the Modern skin.

From the diagram, a <tree> appears as a set of columns, much like a <listbox>. Unlike a <listbox>, there is a dropdown menu under the icon in the top-right corner. This menu (not shown) is a set of checkboxes that can be used to hide or redisplay any column.

A <tree> has several kinds of special-purpose columns. Column A in Figure 13.5 is a primary column. A primary column shows the hierarchical organization of the rows in the tree. Looking at this column closely, there are four top-level rows: rows 1, 2, 7, and 9 (so this tree is a "forest" of trees). The second of these has a subtree that is revealed for display—it is open. The small downward-pointing triangle (a *twisty*) also indicates that the subtree row is open. That subtree has four child rows, and one of those rows has its own sub-

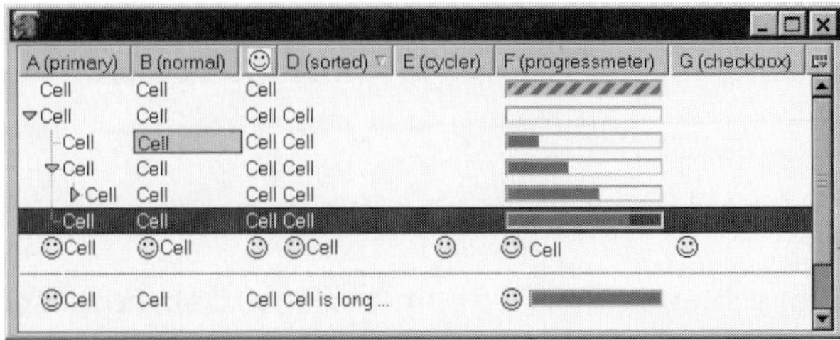

Fig. 13.5 <tree> example showing most features.

tree, which is also open. Finally, that second subtree has a single child row that again has a subtree. This final subtree is closed (the twisty icon points right), so the display doesn't show how many rows are in that final subtree. Twisties can be clicked open or closed by the user. The short lines between twisties and rows just indicate the level of the tree to which the current row belongs. Finally, the column A cells are indented to match their tree level.

The remaining columns in the diagram are less complex. Column B is an ordinary column. Column C is an ordinary column whose column header text has been replaced with an image. Column D is sortable: The column can be used to force the order of rows in the tree, breaking the normal tree structure. This sorting is indicated by the small arrow in the column header. Technology discussed in Chapter 14, Templates, needs to be added to a `<tree>` before sorting will work; in Figure 13.5, it is just present for the sake of completeness. Column E is a cycler. Such a column contains a clickable image only and has a special interaction with the user. Column F holds a `<progressmeter>` tag. Column G is designed to hold a checkbox, but that functionality is not finished and does not work in versions 1.4 and less.

The parentheses in the column names are not specially constructed; they are just part of the column name text. The scrollbars on the right of the tree appear and disappear as required, based on the amount of tree content. The scrollbar in Figure 13.6 is part of the `<tree>` tag, not some other part of the chrome window. Trees do not support horizontal scrollbars.

Figure 13.5 can also be examined row by row. The first interesting row is row 3. One cell of that row has an alternate background color and a border. Mozilla has a special styling system for trees, which is described under "Style Options" in this chapter. Row 6 is the currently selected row so the tree has the input focus. Row 7 shows that cell contents can have an image prepended to the cell content; this is not a `list-style-image` style. Row 7 also shows how an image replaces all the cell content in a cycler column and how a progress-meter column's cell content can be overridden with ordinary content. Row 8 (a single horizontal line) is a `<treeseparator>`; it acts as `<menuseparator>` does for menus. Row 9 shows that cell content is cropped if there isn't room to display it. If very little space is available in the cell, then not even ellipses will be displayed. Finally, the last row is completely empty. This is probably a bad idea in a real application, but it is technically possible.

A tree cell cannot contain arbitrary XUL content. It can only contain a line of text and the few variations noted previously. It cannot contain a `<box>`.

13.3.2 Construction

Figure 13.6 repeats Figure 13.5 with diagnostic styles turned on.

Little of the tree's internal structure is revealed with these styles. Only the column heading bears some resemblance to other widgets like buttons and labels. Obviously, `<tree>` is not based on a gridlike structure and is very different from `<listbox>`. Something unusual is going on.

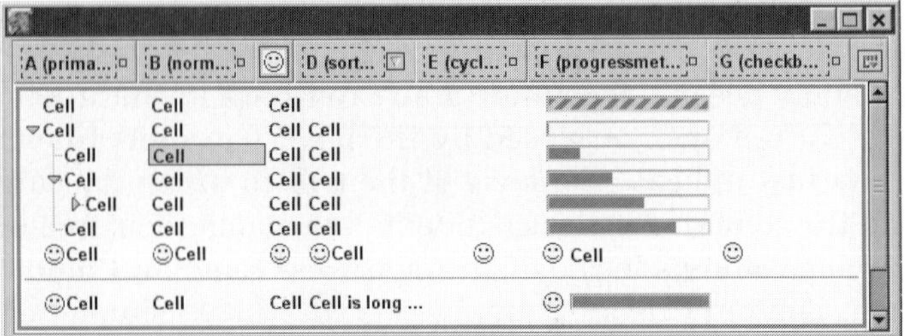

Fig. 13.6 <tree> example with diagnostic styles.

In fact, the content area of a <tree> is a little like an <iframe>. It is a rectangular area in the XUL document whose content is stored separate from the rest. In an <iframe>, the <iframe> content comes from a separate XUL document. In the <tree> case, the <tree> content has no separate XUL document, but it is still held apart from the other content.

It is not possible to style part of a tree using normal CSS2 styles. A special style system exists instead. The reason is that the individual cells and rows of a tree have frames that are not fully exposed to the styling system. This just happens to be the way <tree> is designed and implemented.

Figures 13.5 and 13.6 require over a hundred lines of XUL, so Figure 13.7 shows a simpler example with just two rows.

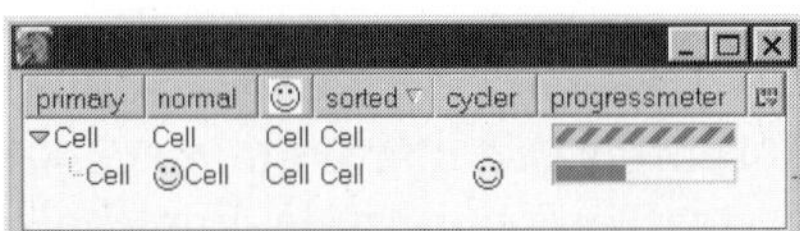

Fig. 13.7 Simple two-row <tree> example.

This tree is constructed in a XUL document as for all XUL content. The content fragment required for this tree is shown in Listing 13.3.

Listing 13.3 Basic construction of <tree> content.

```
<tree flex="1">
  <treecols>
    <treecol flex="1" id="A" label="primary" primary="true"/>
    <treecol flex="1" id="B" label="normal"/>
    <treecol flex="1" id="C" label="icon" class="treecol-image"
          src="face.png"/>
    <treecol flex="1" id="D" label="sorted" sortDirection="ascending"/>
    <treecol flex="1" id="E" label="cycler" cycler="true"/>
    <treecol flex="1" id="F" label="progressmeter" type="progressmeter"/>
  </treecols>
```

```
  <treechildren id="topchildren" flex="1">
    <treeitem container="true" open="true">

      <treerow>
        <treecell label="Cell"/>
        <treecell label="Cell"/>
        <treecell label="Cell"/>
        <treecell label="Cell"/>
        <treecell label="Cell"/>
        <treecell label="Cell" mode="undetermined"/>
      </treerow>

      <treechildren>
        <treeitem>
          <treerow>
            <treecell label="Cell"/>
            <treecell src="face.png" label="Cell"/>
            <treecell label="Cell"/>
            <treecell label="Cell"/>
            <treecell src="face.png" label="Cell"/>
            <treecell label="Cell" mode="normal" value="40"/>
          </treerow>
        </treeitem>
      </treechildren>

    </treeitem>
  </treechildren>
</tree>
```

The <tree> tag has a <treecols> child, in which the columns are defined, and a <treechildren> child. Column ids are very important for trees. The top-level <treechildren> tag is a little like <listbox>'s <listboxbody>, except that it is specified by the application programmer and can be nested inside other tags. A tree "item" is a whole subtree of the tree; therefore, a list item appears as a series of rows. This example code has a single top-level <treeitem> tree item. The container attribute says that this item is not just a row but also the top of the subtree. open says that the next level of the subtree is visible. If a second or third top-level <treeitem> were to appear, it would appear after the bottom </treeitem> tag. The sole top-level tree item has two parts: the row content and the subtree children. That is all it can hold. The subtree started with the second <treechildren> tag also has a single tree item, but this time it is not a subtree, it is just a row. If it were to have a second tree item, that would appear after the inner </treeitem> tag.

XBL definitions for <tree> are stored in tree.xml in toolkit.jar in the chrome.

There are other structural aspects to trees: RDF, sorts, views, builders, and templates. An overview of each is provided after the XUL tree tags are explained.

13.3.3 <tree>

The <tree> tag surrounds all of a tree's content. More than one tree can be specified in a given XUL document. The <tree> tag has the following special attributes:

```
seltype hidecolumnpicker enableColumnDrag disableKeyNavigation
```

- seltype set to multiple (the default) allows the user to select multiple items at once in the tree. Set to single, only one item at a time can be selected.
- hidecolumnpicker set to true collapses the <treecolpicker> tag in the top right corner of the tree.
- enableColumnDrag set to true allows a user to reshuffle the order of columns.
- disableKeyNavigation set to true prevents the user from selecting rows using alphabetic keystrokes.

The <tree> tag and many of the other <tree>-like tags also support RDF and templates. The attributes relevant to those features are discussed in Chapter 14, Templates.

A maximum display height for <tree> can be set with the standard box layout attribute height. <tree> does not support a rows attribute.

13.3.4 <treecols>

The <treecols> tag encloses the column definitions for a tree. This tag has no special attributes. It might be assigned an id if the tree is partially built from overlays. The <treecols> tag is a simple container tag. This tag must be the first child tag inside <tree>. It is not optional.

<treecols> can contain two types of tag: <treecol> and <splitter>.

The number of <treecol>s inside a <treecols> tag gives the number of columns in the tree. At least one <treecol> tag must be present. At most, one <treeecol> tag per tree can have primary="true" set.

A splitter represents a drag point that can be moved by the user. If a <splitter> tag is specified, it must appear between two <treecol> tags. If all possible <splitter> tags are supplied, <treecol> and <splitter> tags must alternate across the tree header. The net result of such a drag is that the columns on either side of the splitter are resized. The XBL definition for <tree> includes logic that supports such <splitter> tags and drag gestures.

Any <splitter> tags in a tree should be styled with class="tree-splitter" so that the tags have zero width. If this is not done, the column headings and columns may not line up. Because of the way Mozilla identifies the current tag under the mouse cursor, the <splitter> tag can be the current tag even when it has no visible area. It can still be dragged when of zero size.

13.3.5 <treecol>

The <treecol> tag defines a single column of a tree. It cannot contain any tags. Each <treecol> tag must have a unique id. This id is used internally by the Mozilla Platform. The column header for the tree is a <button> containing a <label> and an <image>, or just an <image> for a column header with the treecol-image class. Column headings can be styled with list-style-image if an additional image is required.

The attributes with special meaning to <treecol> are

```
label display crop src hideheader ignorecolumnpicker fixed
     sortDirection sortActive sortSeparators cycler primary
     properties
```

- ☞ label specifies the text to appear in the column header for that column. A <label> tag cannot be used as content.
- ☞ display specifies the text to appear in the column picker for that column.
- ☞ crop applies to the <label> content of the column.
- ☞ src replaces the column label with an image. The style class="treecol-image" must also be applied to the <treecol> if this is to work.
- ☞ hideheader="true" removes the button-like appearance of the column header. The space for the header still exists—the header is neither collapsed nor hidden. If this attribute is used, the label for the column should be removed as well. This attribute can be used on all headers and, when coordinated with the hidecolumnpicker attribute, can completely collapse the column header area.
- ☞ ignorecolumnpicker="true" prevents the dropdown menu from hiding or showing this column.
- ☞ fixed="true" prevents this column from feeling the effects of dragging any splitter next to it. In other words, this specific column cannot be resized unless the whole tree is resized. This is a consequence of the <splitter> tags in the tree header.
- ☞ If sortActive="true", then this column is sorted. sortDirection can be set to ascending, descending, or normal. If sortSeparators is set to true, then special sorting occurs that keeps rows between the <treeseparator> tags that they started between. Sorting only occurs automatically when RDF and templates are used—see Chapter 14, Templates.
- ☞ cycler="true" means that this column is a cycler column and will contain only an icon. That icon can be made button-like by adding onclick handlers. If a cycler column is clicked, the row under the mouse pointer is not selected.

- ☞ `primary="true"` means that this column id is the primary column for the tree and should show a hierarchical view of the tree items. This attribute can only be applied to one `<treecol>` tag per tree.
- ☞ The `properties` attribute supports Mozilla's special tree styling system. See "Style Options" in this chapter.

A column can be hidden or collapsed using standard XUL attributes.

13.3.6 <treechildren>

The `<treechildren>` tag is both the ultimate container tag for all of a tree's rows and the container tag for each subtree in the tree. It has no special attributes.

The `<treechildren>` tag can contain only `<treeitem>` and `<treeseparator>` tags.

This tag has two uses. A `<tree>` tags second child *must* be a `<treechildren>` tag. A `<treeitem>`'s optional second child tag can *only* be a `<treechildren>` tag. If used in the second way, then the `<treechildren>` tag should always have at least one `<treeitem>` content tag. If it does not, the twisty icon for that subtree will act strangely.

The `<treechildren>` tag is the tag used for style rules that exploit Mozilla's special tree styling system.

13.3.7 <treeitem>

The `<treeitem>` tag represents one horizontal item in a tree. An item is one of

1. A single row of cells without any subtree.
2. A single row of cells with a subtree that is displayed.
3. A single row of cells with a subtree that is hidden.

This tag can contain either a `<treerow>` tag (case 1) or a `<treerow>` tag followed by a `<treechildren>` tag (cases 2 and 3). `<treeitem>` cannot contain multiple `<treerow>` or `<treechildren>` tags.

The attributes with special meaning to `<treeitem>` are

```
container open properties
```

If `container` is set to `true`, then the item has a subtree and should contain a `<treechildren>` tag as its second content tag. If open is set to `true`, then the items' subtree is displayed (case 2). By default, neither attribute is set. `properties` is used by the style system that is described under "Style Options."

The `<treeitem>` tag also supports template-related attributes such as `uri`. See Chapter 14, Templates, for more on that.

13.3.8 <treeseparator>

The <treeseparator> tag draws a horizontal line across the tree. It can control sort behavior, as described in Chapter 14, Templates. This horizontal line is not indented, so <treeseparator> is only useful as a substitute for a top-level <treeitem> tag. It has one special attribute:

```
properties
```

This is used by the special style system described under "Style Options." <treeseparator> is meant to be a visual cue only.

13.3.9 <treerow>

The <treerow> tag holds the contents of a single row in the tree. It can contain only <treecell> tags. There should be <treecell> content tags equal to the number of columns. Specifying fewer <treecell> tags is also possible, but it is not very meaningful and is not recommended. Doing so reduces the number of cells visible in that row. The only attribute special to `treerow` is

```
properties
```

This attribute has the same use as it does for <treeitem>.

13.3.10 <treecell>

The <treecell> tag is responsible for the content of a single cell in a tree. In a primary column, it is not responsible for the indentation, twisty, or any connecting lines.

<treecell> cannot have any content, except for the special case of the column that holds <progressmeter> content. In that case, a single <progressmeter> tag is automatically added. <treecell> cannot contain a <label> tag.

The attributes with special meaning to <treecell> are

```
label src value mode allowevents properties
```

- `label` sets the displayed content for the cell. Text content cannot wrap lines as <label> can.
- `src` can be used to prepend an image to the content of the cell.
- mode can be set to `normal` or `undetermined`, provided the matching column has `type="progressmeter"`. It provides the mode attribute for a <progressmeter> tag.
- `value` is the percent value of any `mode="normal"` progress meter that is present.
- If `allowevents="true"`, then clicks that would normally select the row go through to the cell for handling. The row is not selected in this case.
- `properties` is used by the system described in "Style Options."

<treecell> also supports RDF template attributes like resource and ref. See Chapter 14, Templates, for these.

13.3.11 <treerows> and <treecolpicker>

These tags are used only inside XBL definitions. They are used automatically to construct the contents of the <tree> tag. <treerows> holds all the rows of the tree. It plays the same role for <tree> that <listboxbody> plays for <listbox>. <treecolpicker> holds the image and dropdown menu for the column picker. The dropdown menu is generated dynamically when the tree is first created. <treecolpicker> has an ordinal attribute that is set to a very high number. This ensures that it always appears to the right of the tree columns.

The <treecolpicker> tag can be styled as for any XUL tag. Its icon has class tree-columnpicker-icon.

There is no need to use these tags directly in a XUL document. The XBL code that implements <treecolpicker> is a useful guide for applications needing a similarly dynamic widget.

13.3.12 Nontags

<tree> was once called <outliner>, but no longer. The <outliner> tag does not exist any more. When <tree> was called <outliner>, <listbox> was called <tree>, but that <tree> was different from the contemporary <tree> tag. Beware of these ancient names in very old documentation that sometimes appears on the Mozilla Web site, in newsgroups, or in the bug database.

The <treecolgroup> tag is an old name for <treecols>. It lingers in a few Mozilla chrome files but should never be used. Use <treecols> instead.

The <treecolpicker> tag is part of the XBL definition for <tree>. It is meant for internal use only and shouldn't be specified in a XUL document.

The <treeindentation> and <treeicon> tags have no meaning as XUL tags. The <treehead>, <treecaption>, <treefoot>, and <treebody> tags have no meaning as XUL tags. All these tags are old and experimental at best. They are not supported.

13.3.13 RDF and Sorting

As for <listbox>, <tree> and its related tags can be connected to an RDF document. If this is done, the content of a <tree> derives from the content of the RDF document. Under such an arrangement, the data in a <tree> can then be sorted. See Chapter 14, Templates, for more detailed instructions.

13.3.14 User Interactions

Trees have all the user interactivity options that listboxes have, and more.

The most important user interactions that XUL trees support are more about application semantics than they are about keystrokes or mouse gestures. When a tree displays hierarchical structure, it allows the user to participate in drill-down, summarizing, and classification actions. These tasks should be properly supported. Drilling down bears some further thought.

When the user clicks a twisty to reveal a subtree, that is a drill-down action. In such an action, the user is asking for more detail on a given subject. Data displayed in a hierarchy should always support this kind of exploration with data that is an answer to the user's request. The rows exposed should not be irrelevant: They must be about the parent row.

Studies have shown that users cannot handle drilling down many levels—they get lost and it is inefficient navigation. It is better to have a wide, shallow tree that scrolls a lot, than a very structured and deep tree whose subtrees easily fit the window.

The lower-level interactions that trees support closely match those of the listbox and are noted as follows.

Trees support keyboard and mouse navigation and have accessibility support. Navigation keys include the Tab, Arrow, Paging, Home, and End keys, and the spacebar. Mouse support includes clicks, key-click combinations, and the use of scroll wheels. Accessibility follows automatically because `<treecell>` tags always require labels.

Trees are members of the focus ring for the currently displayed page. If a `<tree>` does not have a currently selected row, then navigating into the tree from the previous member of the focus ring does not provide any visual feedback, but the tree still has the input focus. This behavior may be improved after version 1.4, using a workaround in Classic Mail & News that relies on styles.

The selection of tree items is a flexible matter. If only single-item selection is enabled, then selection is much the same as for a menu. If, however, `seltype` is set to `multiple`, then multiple list items can be picked. With the mouse, this is done by shift-clicking, to select a contiguous range of items, or by control-clicking, to pick out individual list items not necessarily next to each other. A range of items can also be selected with the keyboard, using shift-arrow combinations. The keyboard cannot be used to pick out multiple separate list items. Only the mouse can do that. If a `<treeitem>` that contains a subtree is selected, then only the row at the root of the subtree is selected, even if the subtree is collapsed.

A single row of a tree can be selected by typing a character, as for `<listbox>`. The `<tree>` must first have the input focus. The single typed character is matched against the `label` attribute of the `<treeitem>` tags in the `<tree>`. If the label starts with the same character, there is a match. This system selects one row only and works as follows. The `<treeitem>`s are treated as a circular list of items, like a focus ring. The starting point is either the currently selected `<treeitem>`, or the first `<treeitem>` if no selection yet exists. The tree is scanned until a match for the character is found. This allows the user to cycle through the tree multiple times.

If `enableColumnDrag` is set, then tree columns can be reordered using a mouse gesture. Just drag the column header across the face of the tree. The column picker icon cannot be moved.

If `<splitter>` tags are used between `<treecol>` tags, then these splitters can be used to resize the columns with a drag gesture on the splitter tag. The column picker icon cannot be resized.

The column picker, if it is not disabled or ignored, can be used to hide or show any of the columns of a tree. Hidden columns are persistent across Mozilla application sessions if `persist="hidden"` is set.

Finally, sorting is implemented with a simple mouse click on a column header.

13.3.15 AOM and XPCOM Interfaces

The scriptable features of XUL trees are quite complex. This topic provides a concept overview of these features and a detailed look at the interfaces that apply to simple trees. A simple tree is a tree that doesn't involve RDF or templates. All the examples of trees in this chapter are simple trees. More complex trees are covered in Chapter 14, Templates.

`<tree>` is an example of a specialist boxlike tag, just like `<listbox>`, `<iframe>`, and `<scrollbox>`. `<tree>` is a boxlike tag and so the DOM object for `<tree>` has a `boxObject` property. That property supports a tree-specific interface. That interface provides scrolling, navigation, selection, and data extraction methods for the tree content. Like `<listbox>`, the XBL definition for `<tree>` makes this special interface immediately available. This interface can also be had from the component and interface:

```
@mozilla.org/layout/xul-boxobject-tree;1 nsITreeBoxObject
```

This interface is similar in many ways to the `nsIListBoxObject` interface. Unlike the `<listbox>` tag, few of the features of this interface are exported to the `<tree>` tag's XBL binding. That means you must work on the `nsITreeBoxObject` object directly. That object is exposed as the `treeBoxObject` property of the `<tree>` tag's DOM object.

Table 13.3 shows the precise control that this interface gives over the screen area taken up by the tree.

Table 13.3 Properties and methods of the nsITreeBoxObject interface

Property or method	Description
view	Any nsITreeView view associated with the tree
focussed	True if the <tree> has the focus
treeBody	The <treebody>'s DOM element

Table 13.3 Properties and methods of the nsITreeBoxObject interface (Continued)

Property or method	Description
selection	An nsITreeSelection object that understands which rows are currently selected
rowHeight	The height in pixels of a row (all rows are the same height)
getColumnIndex(id)	The ordinal number of the column with id="id"
getColumnId(index)	The id of the column with ordinal number index
getKeyColumnIndex()	The ordinal number of the primary column
getFirstVisibleRow()	The row index of the topmost visible row
getLastVisibleRow()	The row index of the bottommost visible row
getPageCount()	Total rows divided by the number of rows that fit the tree area; equals the number of pages of displayable rows
ensureRowIsVisible(index)	Scroll the tree content until the index'th row is visible
scrollToRow(index)	Scroll the tree content until the index'th row is at the top
scrollByLines(count)	Scroll down (>0) or up (<0) count lines; stop scrolling as soon as there is no more to scroll
scrollByPages(count)	Scroll down (>0) or up (<0) count number of pages; a page is the number of rows that fit inside the tree's area
invalidate() invalidateColumn(id) invalidateRow(index) invalidateCell(index, id) invalidatePrimaryCell(index) invalidateRange(index1, index2) invalidateScrollbar()	Tell Mozilla to redisplay (repaint) the stated part of the tree; index is a row index; id is a column id
getRowAt(x,y)	Return the index of the row under the given relative (x,y) coordinates, or return -1
getCellAt(x,y,r,c,type)	Return the row index, column id, and type of the cell at relative (x,y) coordinates; r, c, and type must be empty objects: {}; each object gains a value property that contains the returned data
getCoordsForCellItem(index, id, type, x, y, w, h)	Return the x-, y-, width-, and height- layout for the element with type held in the index'th row in column id; type may be "cell," "twisty," or "image." x, y, width, and height must be empty objects: {}; each object receives a value property
isCellCropped(index, id)	Return true if the index'th row in column id

Table 13.3 Properties and methods of the nsITreeBoxObject interface (Continued)

Property or method	Description
rowCountChanged(index, total)	Rows equal to total starting from the row at index have changed, so redisplay
beginBatchUpdate()	Tell the tree to stop re-laying out and repainting the tree after every little change
endUpdateBatch()	Tell the tree to catch up on changes that require layout or repainting
clearStyleAndImageCache()	Remove all style information in the tree in preparation for a theme change

XUL trees also have very flexible implementation options. Not only are there familiar interfaces, but there are some important design concepts to understand as well.

XUL trees are built around the design pattern called Model-View Controller but use different terms for each of these things. To recap, in this design pattern, the Model holds the data; the View displays the data; and the Controller coordinates the other two based on input from the outside world.

A XUL tree implements this design pattern with a graphical widget, seminal data, a builder, and a Mozilla view. A Mozilla view is a piece of code that provides an arrangement of the seminal data that is suitable for display. In MVC terms, the seminal data, assisted by the Mozilla view, makes up the MVC model, *not* the MVC view. The widget is part of the MVC view, which is completed by the builder. The builder can take the role of MVC controller as well. There is only one tree widget; it is shown in Figure 13.6. When constructing a tree, an application programmer has choices in each of the other three areas: the builder, the Mozilla view, and the seminal data.

Some of these new tree concepts require templates. In the following discussion, the parenthetical remark (Chapter 14, Templates) means that concept is discussed in detail in the next chapter.

13.3.15.1 Seminal Data *Seminal data* are the data that the content of a tree comes from. Seminal data is not a technical term; it is just a descriptive term that avoids reusing other technical terms. The `<tree>` tag is always required for a XUL tree, but the data that make up the tree items, rows, and cells can come from one of three places: XUL, JavaScript, or RDF.

Listing 13.4 is an example of tree data specified in XUL. The content of the tree is stated literally and directly in the document containing the `<tree>` tag. This is a straightforward way to specify tree content. Even if overlays are used to contribute content from other documents, this is still a pure XUL solution.

Tree content can also be specified directly in JavaScript. There are two ways to do this. The first way is to use the DOM 1 interfaces to create DOM 1

Element objects with calls to document.createElement(). By modifying the DOM tree, plain XUL-based trees can be dynamically added to. This is no different from any other use of the DOM. Listing 13.4 is an example of adding a row to the tree in Listing 13.3. This is routine DOM 1 manipulation, with the new tags being created and added bottom-up.

Listing 13.4 DOM manipulation of a XUL tree.

```
var doc = document;
var tree = doc.getElementById("topchildren");
var item = doc.createElement("treeitem");
var row  = doc.createElement("treerow");

for (var i=1; i!=7; i++)  // there are six columns
{
  var cell = doc.createElement("treecell");
  cell.setAttribute("label","NewCell"+i);
  row.appendChild(cell);
}
item.appendChild(row);
tree.appendChild(item); // item, row and cells now appear
```

The other way to use JavaScript as seminal data for a tree is to create a custom view. Views are described shortly, but to look ahead, a set of JavaScript methods can be used to serve up all the tree's content.

Finally, seminal data can come from an RDF document. This is achieved using XUL templates and a little ordinary XUL content (Chapter 14, Templates).

13.3.15.2 Builders Builders are a somewhat confusing topic in XUL, mostly because they are obvious only when trees are used. When used with a tree, special cases distract from the core reason that builders exist. We first consider what a builder is in the ordinary case.

Any XUL tag starts life as a simple textual string. If it is a visual tag, like <button>, it must end up as pixels on a display. The Gecko styling, layout, and rendering engine inside Mozilla is responsible for that transformation. If the tag is relatively simple, like <box>, then the tag's information might be sent directly to that engine.

There are only a few simple XUL tags. <button>, for example, can end up as a collection of tags that might include <label> and <image>. The XBL definition for <button> generates these tags and sends the results to the display engine. So XBL processing is an extra preparatory step before the display engine gets something to work with.

Some XUL tags require preparation beyond what XBL can provide. <menulist> is an example. Some part of the platform must construct and destroy the popup menu of a <menulist> when it is used. XBL does not do that work. A piece of functionality that is built into the platform must do it.

Such a piece of functionality is called a builder, merely because it assembles and disassembles content that is to be displayed (or undisplayed).

Every XUL tag has a builder, at least conceptually, but in most cases the builder is trivial. In nearly all cases, the builder is invisible to applications and runs automatically. Only the most complex tags might have a builder sophisticated enough to be exposed to applications. `<listbox>` has a sophisticated builder, but it is invisible. Only `<tree>` and `<template>` tags have visible builders, but even those builders are visible only part of the time. Mozilla contains two different tree builders.

The XUL *content builder*, or *default tree builder*, is used to construct plain XUL trees and trees constructed via the DOM. No programming effort is required to use this builder. This builder creates a tree using a batch process, and the whole tree is created in one step. If DOM operations change the content of a plain XUL tree, the builder is not involved. Instead, the pieces of the already built tree are intelligent enough to absorb those changes directly.

This tree builder is an invisible builder. It has no XPCOM component or interface. It is not scriptable. It is given a name merely to separate it from the *template builder*, which does have some visibility. The content builder, or default tree builder is the bit of Mozilla that acts like a builder, when no specialist builder is present.

The XUL template builder (Chapter 14, Templates) is used to construct all template-driven content, including templated trees. It is chosen automatically when templates are used. It has a specialized version specifically for building trees, called the *tree builder*. The tree builder should really have a more descriptive name, like builder-for-special-combination-of-template-and-tree. The tree builder can construct a tree "lazily," which means that parts of the tree are left unbuilt (and undisplayed) until needed later on. The tree builder can also be accessed and controlled by the application programmer. To do its job, that builder may use the content builder. Alternately, it may do part of the building work itself and rely on a separate object for the rest of the work.

This builder also supports application-programmer-specified observers, which further assists the building work. It has a scriptable component:

```
@mozilla.org/xul/xul-tree-builder;1
```

The builder interfaces (Chapter 14, Templates) on this object are

```
nsIXULTemplateBuilder nsIXULTreeBuilder
```

The second interface is part of the customization process. If a builder exists for a given tree, then the builder property on the tree's DOM Element will contain that builder.

13.3.15.3 Views A builder might do all the work required to create a tree out of seminal data. Or, it could hand part of the work to a subcontractor who specializes in making the data ready to use. The builder would then be free to spend most of its energy overseeing the process. Such a specialist subcontractor is in this case called a view. It provides a view of the seminal data, not a view of the graphical (GUI) result. In object-oriented terms, this approach is called delegation. Without the view, the builder is incomplete and can't do any work. Without the builder, the view is ready to use, but has no boss telling it where to do work.

A view is used by a builder, but it can also be used by an application programmer. In some cases, the view can also be created by a programmer. In all cases, the view created must have these interfaces:

```
nsITreeView nsITreeContentView
```

Table 13.4 shows the properties that the XBL definition of `<tree>` creates to support views.

Table 13.4 JavaScript <tree> properties that are the result of views

Property name	Related to other properties?	Contents
treeBoxObject.view	Yes	View object exposing nsITreeView
view	Yes	View object exposing nsITreeView
contentView	Yes	View object exposing nsITreeContentView
builderView	Yes	View object exposing nsIXULTreeBuilder

If a view is replaced with another, in theory all these properties should be updated. In practice, it is enough to update the `treeBoxObject.view` property or the `view` property and avoid using the other properties afterwards. Table 13.5 shows the interface that such a view provides.

Table 13.5 Properties and methods of TreeView interfaces

Property or method	Useable in XUL content builder?	Description
nsITreeContentView		
root		Points to the <tree> tag's DOM object
getItemAtIndex(index)	✓	Returns the <treerow> at the index'th visible row in the tree; rows count if they can be scrolled into view, but not if they require a hidden subtree to be revealed; counts from 0
getIndexOfItem(treerow)	✓	Returns the index position of the <treerow> in the tree

Table 13.5 Properties and methods of TreeView interfaces (Continued)

Property or method	Useable in XUL content builder?	Description
nsITreeView		
canDropBeforeAfter(index)	✓	True if a dropped item can be inserted before or after this row
canDropOn(index)	✓	True if the given row can be a drop site for a drag-drop operation
cycleCell(index, id)		Fires when a cell (in row index, column id) in a cycle="true" column is clicked
cycleHeader(id, element)		Fires when the element tag in the column with this id is clicked
drop(index, where)		Fires when a dragged row is dropped; index is the row, where indicates the drop target and is 0, 1, or 2
getCellProperties(index, column_index, array)	✓	Fills the nsISupportsAarray with the values found in the cell's properties XML attribute and returns the array
getCellText(index, id)	✓	Returns the label= value in the cell at row index and column id
getCellValue(index, id)	✓	Returns the value= value in the cell at row index and column id
getColumnProperties(index, column-id, array)	✓	Fills the nsISupportsAarray with the values found in the column's properties XML attribute
getImageSrc(index, id)	✓	Returns the URL for any image prefixed to the cell with row index and column id
getLevel(index)	✓	Returns the depth of this row in the tree
getParentIndex(index)	✓	Returns this row's parent row index, or -1 if there is no parent
getProgressMode(index,id)	✓	Returns the type of <progressmeter> in the cell with row index and column id (returns 1, 2, or 3)
getRowProperties(index, array)	✓	Fills the nsISupportsAarray with the values found in the row's properties XML attribute and returns the array
hasNextSibling(index, start_index)	✓	True if the first sibling of this row after start_index
isContainer(index)	✓	True if the row has container="true" (has a subtree of zero or more elements)

Table 13.5 Properties and methods of TreeView interfaces (Continued)

Property or method	Useable in XUL content builder?	Description
isContainerEmpty(index)	✓	True if the row has container="true" and zero child nodes of <treechildren>
isContainerOpen(index)	✓	True if the row has open="true" and container="true"
isEditable(index, id)	Always false	Returns true if the cell at row index and column id is editable
isSeparator(index)	✓	True if the row is a <treeseparator>
isSorted()	Always false	True if any column in the row is sorted
performAction(command) performActionOnRow(command, index) performActionOnCell(command, index, column id)		Send the given command to the whole tree, to the row alone, or to a single cell
rowCount	✓	Reports the total rows in the tree
selection	✓	Returns an nsITreeSelection object containing details of the current selection
selectionChanged()		Fires when the selected row(s) in the tree changes
setCellText(index, id, value)		Sets the cell text at row index and column id to value
setTree(nsITreeBoxObject)		Used during initialization—avoid
toggleOpenState(index)	✓	Fires when a subtree container is opened or closed; can be called direct

Mozilla has half a dozen existing views written in C/C++, and about a dozen views written in JavaScript. One specific view belongs to the XUL content builder. It is called simply the "tree content view" and is the view that gives access to trees based on plain XUL content. This simple view is not a full XPCOM component; it is just a subpart of the XUL content builder. It does, however, support the preceding interfaces properly.

When the XUL content builder builds a tree, an object with this interface is attached to the view property of the `<tree>`'s DOM object. This view is available to the application programmer. It is used by the XUL content builder during tree construction, and it can be used by the application programmer after the tree is displayed.

There is one restriction to use of this view. It is a read-only system. The `isEditable()` view method reports back false, which means that the `set-`

CellText() view method does nothing. The methods that "fire" can only be called internally by the tree system, not by the application programmer. Also, because of the way this system is hooked up to the tree, the methods of this interface can't be replaced with user-defined ones. All that can be done with this view interface is extract information about the tree.

If a view is to be read-write, or if a view is to be created by the application programmer, then the tree must be the base tag of a template (Chapter 14, Templates).

In addition to the tree content view, many application-specific XPCOM components have nsITreeView interfaces and can be used as ready-to-go views. They, however, are highly specific components. Using these components requires extensive study of existing applications such as the Messenger. At version 1.4, the components with tree views are

```
@mozilla.org/addressbook/abview;1
@mozilla.org/filepicker/fileview;1
@mozilla.org/inspector/dom-view;1
@mozilla.org/messenger/msgdbview;1?type=quicksearch
@mozilla.org/messenger/msgdbview;1?type=search
@mozilla.org/messenger/msgdbview;1?type=threaded
@mozilla.org/messenger/msgdbview;1?type=threadswithunread
@mozilla.org/messenger/msgdbview;1?type=watchedthreadswithunread
@mozilla.org/messenger/server;1?type=nntp
@mozilla.org/network/proxy_autoconfig;1
@mozilla.org/xul/xul-tree-builder;1
```

To use any of these components except for the last (the default), it is recommended that their existing uses within the chrome files be studied carefully first.

The Classic Mozilla chrome also contains many pure JavaScript implementations of nsITreeView, whose implementation can be casually studied. The Navigator View | Page Info functionality has five views (in pageInfo.js in comm.jar in the chrome) and is the easiest to understand—see also pageInfo.xul. The DOM Inspector has two (in jsObjectView.js and stylesheets.js), the XUL <textbox type="autocomplete"> functionality has one (in autocomplete.xml), and the Navigator about:config URL functionality has one (in config.js). The JavaScript Debugger and several other tools such as the Component Viewer implement JavaScript-based views as well.

Several of these JavaScript applications have created reusable prototype objects for custom views. These objects attempt to reduce the work required to create a view.

13.4 Style Options

Mozilla has a special styling system for <trees>. <listbox>, on the other hand, is mundane.

13.4.1 <listbox>

The listbox system has no Mozilla extensions unique to the CSS2 style system. It does, however, have an extensive set of style rules and id'ed tags to which styles can be applied. These rules appear in xul.css in toolkit.jar and in listbox.css in the global skin (e.g., in classic.jar). All those files are in the chrome.

13.4.2 <tree>

XUL has some unique and specific style functionality. This functionality is used for trees, which are styled differently than all other tags. All the body of a given tree, specified as content of the <treechildren> tag, can be styled directly from a treechildren selector. A style extension makes this possible.

Styling of trees is done using new pseudo-classes. Here is an example style, based on a tree that represents a company organization chart. If a staff member has been hired recently, then his or her entry is yellow:

```
treechildren:-moz-tree-row(hired)
  { background-color : yellow };
```

The -moz-tree-row pseudo-class identifies what is to be styled, in this case the rows of the tree. This selector is passed a list of zero or more parameters. Each of these parameters is a text string. Such a text string appears in some content tag of the tree as an argument to the properties keyword. For example,

```
<row properties="hired,causeNewDept,dateJune">...</row>
```

Any and all tags within a tree's body that have a property of hired are styled according to the given rule, so that includes the example <row> tag. If the rule appeared thus

```
treechildren:-moz-tree-row(hired,dateJuly)
  { background-color : yellow };
```

then the example row would not be styled because it does not contain both properties listed in the style rule.

Three pieces of information are required to make a style built with this system work:

1. The right pseudo-class name needs to be chosen.
2. A suitable property name needs to be decided.
3. The style properties available for the pseudo-class need to be reviewed.

Each of these items is covered in turn here.

13.4.2.1 Tree Pseudo-Classes Table 13.6 lists the tree pseudo-selectors that are Mozilla extensions to the CSS2 standard.

Table 13.6 CSS2 pseudo-class extensions for XUL trees

Pseudo-selector name	Matching part of the displayed tree
:-moz-tree-row	A whole row, but without leading indentation
:-moz-tree-cell	One cell in a row
:-moz-tree-column	A whole column
:-moz-tree-cell-text	Text within a cell
:-moz-tree-twisty	The icon (twisty) clicked on that controls subtree expansion
:-moz-tree-indentation	Blank space to the left of an indented row
:-moz-tree-line	The small lines connecting parent, child, and sibling rows in the primary column
:-moz-tree-image	An image that prefixes a cell's contents
:-moz-tree-separator	<treeseparator>
:-moz-tree-drop-feedback	The line that appears between rows when dragging a row around
:-moz-tree-progressmeter	A cell whose column is type="progressmeter"

13.4.2.2 Built-in Property Names CSS2 uses keywords rather than literal strings for most purposes. It's important to remember that special tree-styling properties are just arbitrary strings of text that the application developer makes up. They are application-specific and have no meaning to the style system.

Some of the property-naming work is done for you. Special property names are automatically applied to a tree's contents when it is created and when the user interacts with it. These names still have no meaning to the style system. They are meaningful only in terms of the structural arrangement of a tree, and for use in custom pseudo-selectors. These names are automatically added to properties lists by Mozilla and can be selected just like user-defined properties. Table 13.7 lists them.

Table 13.7 Style pseudo-selector automatic properties for XUL trees

Property string	Meaning
container	The thing to style is part of an internal node.
leaf	The thing to style is part of a leaf node.
open	The thing to style is part of an internal node, and that node is uncollapsed so that any subtree contents are showing.

Table 13.7 Style pseudo-selector automatic properties for XUL trees (Continued)

Property string	Meaning
closed	The thing to style is part of an internal node, and that node is collapsed so that any subtree contents are hidden.
selected	The thing to style is part of a selected row.
current	The thing to style is part of the currently selected row.
focus	The tree is the currently focused document element.
sorted	The tree rows are sorted.
primary	The thing to style is part of the primary tree column.
progressmeter	The thing to style is part of a <treecol type="progressmeter">.
progressNormal	The thing to style is a part of a progress meter that reports progress as it occurs.
progressUndetermined	The thing to style is part of a progress meter that only reports when it's underway or finished.
progressNone	The thing to style is part of a progress meter that doesn't report progress.
dragSession	The user is dragging a tree element with the mouse.
dropOn	The user's dragged object is over the thing to style.
dropBefore	The user's dragged object is just above the row that the thing to style is in.
dropAfter	The user's dragged object is just below the row that the thing to style is in.

Recall that simple tree structures are built from internal nodes, which contain other nodes, and leaf nodes, which contain data. XUL tree nodes are either leaf nodes or internal nodes, but not both.

There is a second group of automatically available properties. All ids of all tree columns are available as properties. You should therefore ensure that those ids are legal CSS2 names.

Regardless of whether automatically available properties are used, you are always free to make up new property names.

13.4.2.3 Matching CSS2 Properties The third aspect of this custom styling system is quite tricky. Each of the pseudo-classes supports only a small number of the CSS2 style properties. If you choose a property that isn't supported, then nothing will happen. Table 13.8 sketches out which CSS2 properties are available for each pseudo-class.

Table 13.8 CSS2 properties supported by new pseudo-selectors

Pseudo-selector	Tag to use for properties attribute	Types of CSS2 sstyle property supported
:-moz-tree-row	<treerow>	Backgrounds, borders, margins, outlines, padding, display, -moz-appearance
:-moz-tree-cell	<treecell>	Backgrounds, borders, margins, outlines, padding, visibility
:-moz-tree-column	<treecol>	Margins, text styles, visibility
:-moz-tree-cell-text	<treecell>	Foreground color, fonts, visibility
:-moz-tree-twisty	<treecell>	Margins, padding, borders, display, -moz-appearance, list styles, positioning
:-moz-tree-indentation	<treeitem>	Positioning
:-moz-tree-line	<treeitem>	Borders, visibility
:-moz-tree-image	<treeitem>, <treecell>	List styles, margins, positioning
:-moz-tree-separator	<treeseparator>	Display, borders, -moz-appearance
:-moz-tree-drop-feedback	<treerow>	Margins, visibility
:-moz-tree-progressmeter	<treecell>	Foreground color, margins

Putting together Tables 13.6, 13.7, and 13.8 yields the following example, which is entirely constructed out of names that Mozilla is aware of:

```
treechildren:-moz-tree-cell(leaf,focus)
  { background-color : red; }
```

This says that any row in the tree that is a leaf row and that has the current input focus will have its cell background changed to red. Because background styles are supported for tree cells, this style rule both is sensibly constructed and will have the desired effect. Compare that with the earlier examples of this system which use custom styles consisting of known targets and known pseudo-selectors but use application-specific property strings.

13.4.3 Native Theme Support

As of version 1.4, trees do not have native theme support on Microsoft Windows XP.

Where native themes are supported, the `-moz-appearance` style property can be set to these values:

```
listbox listitem treeview treeitem treetwity treetwistyopen treeline
     treeheader treeheadercell treeheadersortarrow
```

13.5 Hands On: NoteTaker: The Keywords Panel

This "Hands On" session is about using standard, scripted XUL to master <listbox> and <tree>. First, we'll build a static page out of pure XUL, and then we'll enhance it to include scripting effects. We'll also experiment a little.

At last it's time to complete the layout and XUL content of the NoteTaker dialog box. Until now the Keywords panel of the displayed <tabbox> has contained only a placeholder. We'll fix that by adding a listbox, a tree, and some other form elements.

The Keywords panel allows the user to add keywords to, and delete keywords from, the current note. It also lists the current keywords. Finally, it displays keywords related to the current keyword, which provides a memory jogger to the user.

To design this pane, we must go back to Chapter 2, XUL Layout, and start with a rough diagram and then work on layout, static content, form elements, and so on. Rather than repeat that process here, we'll just summarize the important results.

- ☞ A <textbox> will allow the user to enter a keyword.
- ☞ A <listbox> will display the current set of keywords.
- ☞ An Add <button> will copy the <textbox> contents into the <listbox> as a new item.
- ☞ A Delete <button> will remove the <textbox> contents from the list box if it already exists.
- ☞ Clicking on a <listbox> item copies it to the <textbox>.
- ☞ A <tree> will display the keywords related to the keywords in the <listbox>.

Both the <listbox> and <tree> tags will have dynamically changing content. In this chapter, we'll implement those with JavaScript, the DOM, and tree views. For now, the related keywords we'll use will come from a small, fixed set. In the next chapter, we'll replace part of this system with a better solution based on templates. We're not going to use the RDF model designed in the last chapter. We'll do that in the next chapter.

Altogether, this result will be a dialog box as shown in Figure 13.8.

13.5.1 Laying Out <listbox> and <tree>

Without further ado, the structure of the Keywords panels is shown in Listing 13.5.

Listing 13.5 New panel content for the NoteTaker Edit dialog box.

```
<tabpanel>
  <vbox>
    <hbox>
```

```
      <vbox>
        <description value="Enter Keyword:"/>
        <textbox id="dialog.keyword"/>
        <hbox>
          <button id="dialog.add" label="Add"/>
          <button id="dialog.delete" label="Delete"/>
        </hbox>
      </vbox>
      <vbox>
        <description value="Currently Assigned:"/>
        <listbox/>
      </vbox>
    </hbox>
    <description value="Related:"/>
    <tree/>
  </vbox>
</tabpanel>
```

The panel is made of two boxes stacked vertically. The top box has a left and right half. In this listing the `<listbox>` and `<tree>` tags are not filled in, for brevity. The `<listbox>` content is shown in Listing 13.6.

Listing 13.6 Static `<listbox>` content for current NoteTaker keywords.

```
<listbox id="dialog.keywords" rows="3">
  <listitem label="checkpointed"/>
  <listitem label="reviewed"/>
  <listitem label="fun"/>
  <listitem label="visual"/>
</listbox>
```

In the completed version of NoteTaker, these keywords will come from an RDF file that will be composed from user input. Here we're starting out with some fixed keywords. Similarly for the `<tree>` tag, we start with some fixed related keywords. The content of the `<tree>` tag appears in Listing 13.7.

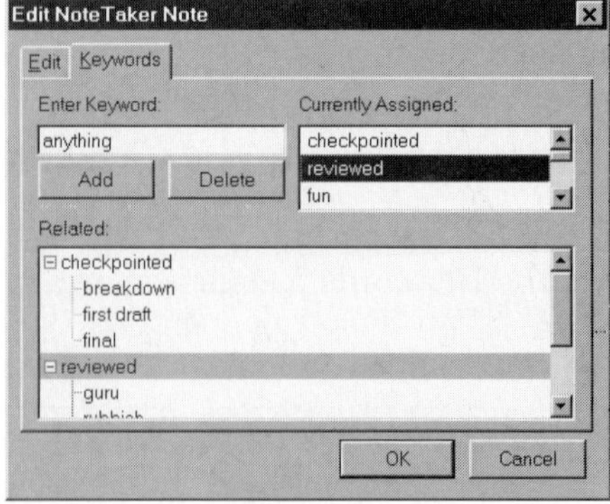

Fig. 13.8 NPA diagram showing `<list>` and `<tree>` technology.

Listing 13.7 Static <tree> content for related NoteTaker keywords.

```
<tree id="dialog.related" hidecolumnpicker="true" seltype="single"
          flex="1">
  <treecols>
    <treecol id="tree.all" hideheader="true" flex="1" primary="true"/>
  </treecols>
  <treechildren flex="1">
    <treeitem container="true" open="true">
      <treerow> <treecell label="checkpointed"/> </treerow>
      <treechildren>
        <treeitem>
          <treerow> <treecell label="breakdown"/> </treerow>
        </treeitem>
        <treeitem>
          <treerow> <treecell label="first draft"/> </treerow>
        </treeitem>
        <treeitem>
          <treerow> <treecell label="final"/> </treerow>
        </treeitem>
      </treechildren>
    </treeitem>
    <treeitem container="true" open="true">
      <treerow> <treecell label="reviewed"/> </treerow>
      <treechildren>
        <treeitem>
          <treerow> <treecell label="guru"/> </treerow>
        </treeitem>
        <treeitem>
          <treerow> <treecell label="rubbish"/> </treerow>
        </treeitem>
      </treechildren>
    </treeitem>
    <treeitem container="true" open="true">
      <treerow> <treecell label="fun"/> </treerow>
      <treechildren>
        <treeitem>
          <treerow> <treecell label="cool"/> </treerow>
        </treeitem>
      </treechildren>
    </treeitem>
  </treechildren>
</tree>
```

The keywords in this tree are displayed as a hierarchy, but it's not implied that child keys are subtopics of parent keys. That is a tempting way to think of them. They're just related concepts. A Web page could receive a note with the "guru" keyword, but not the "reviewed" keyword if the user decided that "guru" meant the page author was well-known, rather than that the page contained well-thought-out information.

A hierarchical display such as the <tree> tag lends itself well to hierarchically broken-down material, but it can be applied to other problems as well.

We're using it to show relationships that form a simple network. Instead of viewing the network as a whole, we're discovering parts of it from a set of starting points. That's not unlike the RDF queries in Chapter 14, Templates, but here it's familiar XUL and JavaScript technology.

13.5.2 Systematic Use of Event Handlers

Here is how this dialog box will work. The top-left part of this box is where the user enters new keywords. Clicking Add puts the typed-in keyword into the list at top right; clicking Delete removes it from the list. Clicking an item in the list copies that item to the textbox. If a list item is selected, then the matching item in the tree is selected and scrolled to. If an item in the tree is clicked, it is copied to the textbox.

All these actions could be implemented as commands. Some of these actions, however, are fairly trivial. It can be overkill to make every fragment of script a command. None of these actions sound like formal "transactions," "instructions," or "operations." They're just GUI tweaks. We'll use plain event handlers to implement them.

We could add these event handlers to individual `<listbox>` and `<tree>` content tags (`onclick= ...`), but we won't. Tree views also support custom actions, which are like localized commands (see the tree view methods prefixed with `performAction`). We're not doing that either. For our plain events, we'll need:

- `onclick` on the Add `<button>`
- `onclick` on the Delete `<button>`
- `onselect` on the `<listbox>`
- `onselect` on the `<tree>`

Rather than use XUL syntax, we'll choose a more interesting option. We'll use the DOM 2 Events "`EventTarget`" interface, in particular, the `addEventListener()` method. This method is available on every DOM Element object, which means most XUL tags. Using just scripts, we'll install all the event handlers when the Edit dialog box first loads. Listing 13.8 shows how this is set up.

Listing 13.8 Event handler installation for NoteTaker Keywords panel.

```
var ids = {};

function init_handlers()
{
  var handlers = [
    // id                event     handler function
    ["dialog.add",      "click",  add_click],
    ["dialog.delete",   "click",  delete_click],
    ["dialog.keywords", "select", keywords_select],
    ["dialog.related",  "select", related_select]
  ];
```

```
  for (var i = 0; i < handlers.length; i++)
  {
    var obj = document.getElementById(handlers[i][0]);
    obj.addEventListener(handlers[i][1], handlers[i][2], false);
    ids[handlers[i][0]] = obj;
  }
  // also spot this final tag
  ids["dialog.keyword"] = document.getElementById("dialog.keyword");
}

window.addEventListener("load",init_handlers, true);
```

The `init_handlers()` function is installed as a handler that runs when the document is first loaded. When it runs, it installs five more handlers, using the tag ids, event names, and functions supplied in the handlers array. Those handler functions all accept a single argument, which is an Event object. In the case of this simple pane, each handler is used in only one place, so the Event object is not that useful. The function also stores in the `ids` object the DOM objects for each handler. This is just a performance optimization that saves retrieving those objects over and over later on in the handlers.

Each of these handlers is described in turn. The listbox and tree widgets are more complex than a simple button, so we'll need to roll our sleeves up a bit—there's plenty of code. Other programming environments have their headers, libraries, and modules; Mozilla has documentation on XBL, XPIDL, DOM, and this book. We'll need to use all that documentation to do a professional job.

Listing 13.9 shows the `add_click()` handler's code:

Listing 13.9 `add_click()` handler for NoteTaker keywords.

```
function add_click(ev)
{
  var listbox = ids["dialog.keywords"];
  var textbox = ids["dialog.keyword"];

  // getRowCount() workaround
  var items = listbox.childNodes.length;

  if ( textbox.value.replace(/^ *$/,"") == "" )
    return;      // don't add pure whitespace

  for (var i = 0; i < items; i++)
  {
    if ( listbox.getItemAtIndex(i).label == textbox.value )
      return;    // already exists
  }

  listbox.appendItem(textbox.value, textbox.value);
  listbox.scrollToIndex(items > 1 ? items - 2 : items);
}
```

This function adds the typed keyword to the listbox of existing keywords. It looks through the `<listbox>` items to see if the new item is already there, and if not, that item is added and the listbox scrolled to it so that the user can see it.

Most of the method calls in this function come from Table 13.2, but we also had to peek at the XBL definition for `<listitem>` and `<textbox>` to find the `label` and `value` properties.

Nothing is perfect, and as this book goes to press, the `<listbox>` `getRowCount()` XBL method has a bug, which will probably be fixed by the time you read this. That function returns the total number of existing list items (when it works properly). As a workaround, we go underneath the AOM widget level, which means using basic XML methods from the DOM 1 Core. The third line of the code returns a DOM 1 Core `NodeList` object, whose length property is the number of direct children of the `<listbox>` tag. That works for us because we know there's no `<listcols>` tag in our listbox.

Listing 13.10 shows the code for the `delete_click()` handler.

Listing 13.10 `delete_click()` handler for NoteTaker keywords.

```
function delete_click(ev)
{
  var listbox = ids["dialog.keywords"];
  var textbox = ids["dialog.keyword"];
  var items = listbox.childNodes.length;

  for (var i = 0; i < items; i++)
    if ( listbox.getItemAtIndex(i).label == textbox.value )
    {
      listbox.removeItemAt(i);
      return;
    }
}
```

This handler is a very minor variation on the `add_click()` handler. It deletes the textbox item from the listbox.

Listing 13.11 shows the code for the `keywords_select()` handler.

Listing 13.11 `keywords_click()` handler for NoteTaker keywords.

```
function keywords_select(ev)
{
  var listbox = ids["dialog.keywords"];
  var textbox = ids["dialog.keyword"];
  var tree    = ids["dialog.related"];
  var items   = document.getElementsByTagName('treecell');
  var item = null, selected = null;

  try { listbox.currentItem.label; }
  catch (e) { return; }

  textbox.value = listbox.currentItem.label;
```

```
    var items = document.getElementsByTagName('treecell');
    for (var i = 0; i < items.length; i++)
    {
      if (items.item(i).getAttribute("label") == textbox.value)
      {
        item = items.item(i).parentNode.parentNode;
        break;
      }
    }

    if ( item )
    {
      selected = item;
      if ( tree.view.getIndexOfItem(item) == -1 )
      {
        while (item.tagName != "tree")
        {
          if (item.getAttribute("container") != "")
            item.setAttribute("open","true");
          item = item.parentNode.parentNode;
        }
      }
      // tree.currentIndex = tree.view.getIndexOfItem(selected);
      // only supplies the focus,not the selection.
      i = tree.view.getIndexOfItem(selected);
      tree.treeBoxObject.selection.select(i);
      tree.treeBoxObject.ensureRowIsVisible(i);
    }
  }
```

This function copies the label of the currently selected listbox item to the textbox. That takes one line of code. The rest of the function seeks and highlights the same keyword in the tree, if it exists. The tree view interfaces described in Table 13.4 work only on the currently rendered rows of the tree (including rows hidden by the surrounding scrollbox). If a keyword isn't displayed, the view interfaces won't find it. So we must use the DOM to search through the tree. After we find a matched item, we can work through the tree view to manipulate the display of the tree.

When grabbing the selected keyword, we have a second awkward problem with `<listbox>`. The `currentItem` XBL property isn't maintained correctly; specifically it is poorly created when the listbox has no currently selected elements. Although this is not obvious, it will spew errors to the console if we don't do something. These errors occur because our `onselect` handler also happens to be invoked when the listbox is scrolled. The `try {}` block catches this special case and aborts the handler, since there's nothing to do in that case.

To find the keyword in the tree, we use the very heavyweight DOM 2 Core method `getElementsByTagName()`. It searches the whole DOM for a given tag and returns all instances as a collection. We happen to know the only

<treecell> tags in the document are in the required tree, so it is safe and convenient to use this method. The actual keyword is stored in a <treecell> inside a <treerow> inside the <treeitem> tags returned. So we use the DOM 1 Core parentNode attribute to reach up to the <treeitem> tag, which we'll need to manipulate the visual appearance of the tree.

If we find a keyword, we need to expose the item displaying it in the tree. We start at the <treeitem> and reach up the tree, opening any containers we find by marking the <treeitem> tags with open="true". Again this is done with the DOM 1 Core. After the treeitem with the keyword is displayed, it will be visible to the tree view interface.

To finish up, we select the row of the tree with the keyword. The user will see this and can then easily see other keywords that might be relevant, both above and to a single level below in the hierarchy. To do this we use the tree view interface, which is exposed by the XBL property tree.view. We could have just as easily (but slightly more verbosely) acquired the view by using the AOM tree.treeBoxObject property, but we would've also had to use XPCOM's QueryInterface() method to extract the correct interface on that object. So we've done it the quick way.

We can't use the tree.currentIndex XBL property to select the tree row because that property records only the row that's focused, not the row that's highlighted. If you experiment with it, note the dotted line that appears around the correct row, indicating that the focus is present. Instead we use the AOM treeBoxObject.selection object, which implements the interface nsITreeSelection. The simple method select() highlights the row in question. Finally, we go back to the AOM treeBoxObject to scroll the tree view so that the selected row is not clipped by the scroll box that surrounds the tree.

Listing 13.12 shows the code for the related_select() handler.

Listing 13.12 related_select() handler for NoteTaker keywords.

```
function related_select(ev)
{
  var textbox = ids["dialog.keyword"];
  var tree    = ids["dialog.related"];

  textbox.value = tree.view.getCellText(tree.currentIndex, "tree.all");
}
```

After keywords_select(), related_select() is a very simple job. It picks out the currently selected keyword from the tree view and copies its value to the textbox. No DOM operations are used at all.

That concludes the event handler logic for the Keywords panel. Some commands, like notetaker-save and notetaker-load, need an update to accommodate this new pane. We'll put off doing that, because we're going to change everything to RDF in the next chapter.

13.5.3 Data-Driven Listboxes and Trees

We have now created the dialog box so that most of its trivial interactivity is in place, but the initial keywords are restricted to a statically defined set of XUL tags. Our ultimate solution is to feed content into these widgets using RDF, but as a brief experiment, we'll feed content to these widgets from plain JavaScript.

A sufficient reason for this experiment is the problem of related keywords. If A is related to B, then surely B is also related to A. Even though hierarchical XML is not so good at handling these two-way relationships, we'd like the tree widget to show related keywords in both directions. The tree display will still be organized hierarchically (that's all it can do), but our custom processing will feed a better set of information to the widget.

To feed content to `<listbox>`, the only option we've encountered so far is to use the raw DOM operations. This is sometimes called a dynamic listbox. To feed content to `<tree>`, we can use a tree view. Because we'll create that *view*, it is a *custom tree view*, or *custom view*.

There are several ways to create these things. For example, existing JavaScript libraries inside the `cview` and DOM Inspector tools provide JavaScript objects that are designed to make custom tree views easier. Also some treelike data, such as IMAP and SNMP data, place performance or functionality restrictions on how that data can be accessed. Here we'll stick to a from-scratch, basic approach.

In terms of the Model-View Controller design pattern, we'll implement the MVC model as a simple JavaScript data structure for both `<tree>` and `<listbox>`. The View will be built on top of (a) Mozilla's fundamental layout system, (b) the DOM hierarchy, and (c) the specialist box objects for `<listbox>` and `<tree>`. In the `<listbox>` case, the standard DOM interfaces are the meat and drink that our MVC view will be based on. In the `<tree>` case, we only need to create a special view object to implement the MVC view. Finally, the MVC in the `<listbox>` case is up to us to write, but in the `<tree>` case, it's the tree's existing builder, and so we don't need to do anything there.

Before exploring this functionality, we'll turn off the event handlers created previously. They're not part of this experiment:

```
// window.addEventListener("load",init_handlers, true)
```

We also need to remove the existing, static content for the `<listbox>` and `<tree>` tags in the XUL document. Those tags will be reduced to these XUL fragments:

```
<listbox id="dialog.keywords" rows="3"/>

<tree id="dialog.related" hidecolumnpicker="true" seltype="single"
      flex="1">
  <treecols>
```

```
        <treecol id="tree.all" hideheader="true" flex="1" primary="true"/
        >
      </treecols>
      <treechildren flex="1"/>
    </tree>
```

As usual, we have some initialization code to set everything up. Listing 13.13 shows this code.

Listing 13.13 Setup for data-driven NoteTaker keyword widgets.

```
var listdata = [ "checkpointed", "reviewed", "fun", "visual" ];

var treedata = [
  [ "checkpointed", "breakdown" ],
  [ "checkpointed", "first draft" ],
  [ "checkpointed", "final" ],
  [ "reviewed", "guru" ],
  [ "reviewed", "rubbish" ],
  [ "fun", "cool" ],
  [ "guru", "cool" ]
];

function init_views()
{
  var listbox = document.getElementById("dialog.keywords");
  var tree = document.getElementById("dialog.related");

  listbox.myview     = new dynamicListBoxView();
  listbox.mybuilder = new dynamicListBoxBuilder(listbox);
  listbox.mybuilder.rebuild();

  tree.view = new customTreeView(tree);
}

window.addEventListener("load",init_views, true);
```

The `listdata` and `treedata` arrays hold the seminal data for the listbox and tree content. In this example, that content is still static, but this code is easy to modify so that dynamic changes to that data are also pushed to the widgets. The pairs of values in the `treedata` variable are related pairs of keywords. If the first such pair were expanded a little, it could almost pass for a fact:

```
<- "checkpoint", related, "breakdown" ->
```

This approach, therefore, is slowly leading us in the direction of RDF. There's no RDF in this experiment, however.

The `init_views()` function creates three custom JavaScript objects—two for the listbox and one for the tree. There is less to do for the tree because it has a built-in builder that automatically goes to work when the `<tree>` tag is displayed. Listbox also has a builder, but it is not exposed to the application programmer until we learn about templates. We've used properties myview and mybuilder to emphasize that in the listbox case we're not overriding anything that the platform already has. This initialization step is done when the document loads, and there are no other event handlers that run later; but see the section "Custom Tree Views."

13.5.3.1 Dynamic Listboxes A dynamic <listbox> has all its displayed rows generated from a script. The script needs to implement both a view and a builder. Not only do these two objects create a working effect, they also give us some insight into the harder <tree> case. In the <tree> case, the builder (and sometimes the view) is hidden inside the platform's own code. The <listbox> case fully exposes these objects (because we create them), and we can imagine how the <tree> case works by analogy.

The first object, shown in Listing 13.14, is the view object for the listbox.

Listing 13.14 JavaScript object for the dynamic listbox View.

```
function dynamicListBoxView() {}

dynamicListBoxView.prototype = {
  get rowCount ()
  {
    return listdata.length;
  },
  getItemText: function (index)
  {
    return listdata[index];
  }
};
```

This object is a simple case of data-abstraction. The original data for the interface is hidden behind the view's interface. This object does more than that, however. It provides an interface that is expressed in terms of displayed rows in the <listbox>—rows or items. This association with the visible rectangular rows of the listbox is what makes it a view. It is convenient that the object uses an array of data, and that each member of that array exactly matches one listbox item. If, however, the underlying array were replaced with some other, more complex, data structure, the object would still be a view. This is because, to the outside world, its unchanged interface would still make the set of listbox items look like a simple list of viewable rows.

By itself, the View does nothing. It is the builder object that exploits that view. It appears in Listing 13.15.

Listing 13.15 JavaScript object for the dynamic listbox builder.

```
function dynamicListBoxBuilder(listbox) {
  this._listbox = listbox;
}
```

```
dynamicListBoxBuilder.prototype = {
  _listbox : null,
  rebuild : function () {
    var rows, item;

    while (_listbox.hasChildNodes())
      _listbox.removeChild(_listbox.lastChild);

    rows = _listbox.myview.rowCount;

    for (var i=0; i < rows; i++)
    {
      item = document.createElement("listitem");
      item.setAttribute("label", listbox.myview.getItemText(i));
      _listbox.appendChild(item);
    }
  }
}
```

The builder is also simple—it contains one method: `rebuild()`. When `rebuild` is called, the object goes to work on the `<listbox>`'s DOM 1 Core Element object. First, it removes all the existing listbox rows; then it adds back in a full set of up-to-date rows. Assumptions are made that the `<listbox>` has only `<listitem>` children and no column specifications, and for our case that is true. Again, it is convenient, but not necessary, that each displayed row equals exactly one DOM Element (a `<listbox>` element).

When the builder goes to work, it relies entirely on the view object. The only thing the builder knows about the content to be displayed is what the view tells it.

Both the view and the builder objects could be enhanced so that the listbox can be changed after it is built. In the current implementation, updating the listbox requires that (a) the array be changed and then (b) the builder's `rebuild()` function be called. Each such change is a 100% update of the listbox. To make only partial changes, extra methods would need to be added to the builder object, and some system would need to be put in place so that the builder knows when to make those partial changes, and what those changes are.

13.5.3.2 Custom Tree Views A customized tree is more complicated to understand than a dynamic listbox. Several pieces are in place already: Trees have an existing builder and view, and both are advised when a user's clicking opens or collapses part of a tree, or scrolls the tree's viewport. When parts of trees are opened or closed (but not when they are scrolled), the number of rows in the tree's display changes, even if the data underlying the displayed tree does not. So ordinary XUL trees are inherently more dynamic than listboxes because the number of viewable rows can change, whereas ordinary listboxes have a fixed number of viewable rows.

To proceed, we intend to fit in with the existing tree content builder and override the existing tree content viewer with our own view. That means creating an object with the nsITreeView interface. Such an object is quite large, so we attack it a piece at a time. The overall structure of this object is shown in Listing 13.16.

Listing 13.16 Skeleton of a JavaScript Custom Tree View object.

```
function customTreeView(tree) {
  this.calculate();
  this._tree = tree;
}

customTreeView.prototype = {
  // 1. application specific properties and methods
  calculate : function () { ... },
  ...
  // 2. Important nsITreeView features
  getCellText : function (index) { ... },
  ...
  // 3. Unimportant nsITreeView features
  getImageSrc : function (index) { ... },
  ...
 }
```

Here is a breakdown of this object. The customTreeVew() constructor is specific to our application. It calculates some information held internally in the object and retains a reference to the <tree> object. That is just preparation work. The prototype for the object contains all the ordinary properties and methods. We're free to add whatever features we want, as long as we also implement the nsITreeView interface. Part 1 of the prototype is these additional features, which the tree builder knows nothing about and doesn't need or use. Part 2 of the prototype is a portion of the nsITreeView interface. That interface has methods for many different aspects of <tree> content: drag and drop, styles, specialist content like progress meters, and so on. Some aspects of the interface are critical—either for the builder or for our own purposes—and that portion of the interface we will implement properly. Part 3 is the other part of the nsITreeView interface. For this other part, we'll provide stub routines that do nothing or almost nothing.

In fact, it's possible to omit some of the less-used methods of the nsITreeView altogether. If the builder decides to call those missing methods, which it might or might not do, then an error will appear in the JavaScript console. It's better to provide a minimal implementation of everything than gamble that something will never be needed.

Let's now address the three parts of this custom view object.

The first part, the application-specific part, is by far the most complicated. It is complicated because in this example we're going to design most of the requirements of the builder into this part. It's also complicated because our initial data (the treedata array) is nothing like a hierarchical tree. We must fix that.

Our overall goal is to transform the raw data into other data structures. The first data structure is a hierarchy that will match the hierarchy that the tree displays. This data structure might represent all the possible data, or just the currently open-for-display subtrees. In our case, it's the open subtrees only. The second data structure is an indexed list of the displayed items in the tree. Even though a primary column of a <tree> can be hierarchical, the rectangular tree items of the tree form a simple ordered list. It is the index numbers of this simple list that are passed as arguments from the builder to the view and back again, and that make the view a view. This is the same as the dynamic listbox case. The custom view we make must be able to handle these indexes.

Our tactics for these data structures follow:

☞ Create a relatedMatrix data structure that represents all the keyword-to-keyword pairs. This will be handier to use than the simple list we are given and has nothing to do with custom views.

☞ Create an openTree data structure so that we can keep track of what the tree looks like. We need to stay synchronized with the user's actions on the tree.

☞ Create a viewMap data structure. This is a collection in the form of an array that maps from the tree item index to the openTree data structure.

These data structures are created in Listing 13.17, which is Part 1 of the custom view object's prototype.

Listing 13.17 NoteTaker specific part of a custom view object.

```
_ relatedMatrix : null,
 _openTree : null,
 _viewMap : null,

 calculate : function () {
   this.calcRelatedMatrix();
   this.calcTopOfTree();
   this.calcViewMap();
 },

 calcRelatedMatrix : function () {
   this._relatedMatrix = {};
   var i = 0, r = this._relatedMatrix;
   while ( i < treedata.length )
   {
     if ( ! (treedata[i][0] in r) )
         r[treedata[i][0]] = {};
     if ( ! (treedata[i][1] in r) )
         r[treedata[i][1]] = {};

     r[treedata[i][0]][treedata[i][1]] = true;
```

```
      r[treedata[i][1]][treedata[i][0]] = true;
      i++;
    }
  },

  calcTopOfTree : function () {
    var i;
    this._openTree  = [];

    for (i=0; i < listdata.length; i++)
    {
      this._openTree[i] = { container : false,
                            open : false,
                            keyword : listdata[i],
                            kids : null,
                            level : 0
                          };
      if ( listdata[i] in this._relatedMatrix )
        this._openTree[i].container = true;
    }
  },

  calcViewMap : function () {
    this._viewMap = [];
    this.calcViewMapTreeWalker(this._openTree, 0);
  },

  calcViewMapTreeWalker : function(kids, level) {
    for (var i=0; i < kids.length; i++ )
    {
      this._viewMap.push(kids[i]);
      if ( kids[i].container == true && kids[i].open == true )
        this.calcViewMapTreeWalker(kids[i].kids, level + 1);
    }
  },
```

That's a lot of code, but it's straightforward. First, there are three properties, all prefixed with underscore to indicate that they shouldn't be touched by users of the object. They will hold the view's internal data structures. Then there's the `calculate()` method, which builds these data structures, using a specific method in each case. The rest are those three specific methods.

The `calcRelatedMatrix()` makes a better-organized copy of the raw data. For the raw data in Listing 13.13, it makes the data structure of Listing 13.18.

Listing 13.18 Example keyword-to-keyword relationship matrix.

```
_relatedMatrix = {
  "checkpointed" : { "breakdown" : true,
                     "first draft" : true,
                     "final" : true },
  "reviewed" :     { "guru" : true,
```

```
                         "rubbish" : true },
  "fun" :              { "cool" : true },
  "guru" :             { "cool" : true,
                         "reviewed" : true },
  "breakdown" :        { "checkpointed" : true },
  "first draft" :      { "checkpointed" : true },
  "final" :            { "checkpointed" : true },
  "rubbish" :          { "guru" : true },
  "cool" :             { "fun" : true,
                         "cool" : true }
};
```

Every keyword in the original list of pairs appears as a property of the `_relatedMatrix` object, and every keyword that is related to it has a property on a subobject for that keyword. With this arrangement, both the forward- and backward-related cases are recorded, and it's easy to test if a given keyword is related to another one. This data structure is our official keyword reference in the view.

The next step is to create a hierarchical version of this related data. Each tree item can have zero or more children, and any such children are ordered. This means that each node of the tree (a data structure node, not a DOM node) is a list of children (a bucket). We'll use an array for each node. The `calcTopOfTree()` starts this data structure off. It appears in Listing 13.19.

Listing 13.19 Creation of the root node in a tree data hierarchy.

```
calcTopOfTree : function () {
  var i;
  this._openTree  = [];

  for (i=0; i < listdata.length; i++)
  {
    this._openTree[i] = { container : false,
                          open : false,
                          keyword : listdata[i],
                          kids : null,
                          level : 0
                        };
    if ( listdata[i] in this._relatedMatrix )
      this._openTree[i].container = true;
  }
},
```

This method creates an array of keyword records as the top-level node and puts into it the keywords that appear in the listbox—the ones in the listdata array. So the listbox keywords are all at the top level of the displayed tree. Each keyword record is an object that holds the keyword string, a reference to the immediate children of this node, and some housekeeping information. The housekeeping information is: whether this item is a container (`container="true"` in XUL), whether this container is open in the tree display (open="true" in XUL), and the depth of this node in the tree. When the time comes, other methods of the view will add to this tree.

Finally, we need to maintain an indexed list of the rows visible in the tree. Listing 13.20 shows how this is done.

Listing 13.20 Creation of the root node in a tree data hierarchy.

```
calcViewMap : function () {
  this._viewMap = [];
  this.calcViewMapTreeWalker(this._openTree, 0);
},

calcViewMapTreeWalker : function(kids, level) {
  for (var i=0; i < kids.length; i++ )
  {
    this._viewMap.push(kids[i]);
    if ( kids[i].container == true && kids[i].open == true )
      this.calcViewMapTreeWalker(kids[i].kids, level + 1);
  }
},
```

The calcViewMap() method is the starting point for constructing this list. It merely passes the root of the tree hierarchy to calcViewMapTreeWalker(), which is a recursive function. This function walks through the open parts of the tree left-to-right, which is the same order as the top-to-bottom order displayed in the <tree> tag. At each found keyword, it adds a reference to that keyword's record to the index item list. So each keyword record is tracked by both the tree and this list.

Altogether, these routines create data structures that are otherwise not yet used. These data structures are created inside the view object. The relatedMatrix structure is entirely static, unless it is re-created. The other two structures change over time.

Let's turn to the important parts of the nsITreeView interface. Listing 13.21 shows most of these methods. The tree's built-in builder will call these methods when it needs to access the data that the view provides. If any custom scripts are needed later, they can call these methods, too.

Listing 13.21 Most important methods of the nsITreeView interface.

```
get rowCount() {
    return this._viewMap.length;
  },

  getCellText: function(row, column) {
    return this._viewMap[row].keyword;
  },

  isContainer: function(index) {
    return this._viewMap[index].container;
  },
```

```
isContainerOpen: function(index) {
  return this._viewMap[index].open;
},

isContainerEmpty: function(index) {
  var item = this._viewMap[index];
  if ( ! item.container ) return false;
  return ( item.kids.length == 0); // empty?
},

getLevel: function(index) {
  return this._viewMap[index].level;
},

getParentIndex: function(index) {
  var level = this._viewMap[index].level;
  while ( --index >= 0 )
    if ( this._viewMap[index].level < level )
      return index;
  return -1;
},

hasNextSibling: function(index, after) {
  var level = this._viewMap[index].level;
  while ( ++index < this._viewMap.length )
  {
    if ( this._viewMap[index].level < level )
      return false;
    if ( this._viewMap[index].level == level && index > after )
     return true;
  }
  return false;
},
```

These methods and the `rowCount` property show how important the `viewMap` is—we can directly read out the needed results. This is because of our early design effort with data structures. Because keyword records contain a precalculate level value, the more complex of the methods, like `hasNextSibling()`, are still easy to implement. We need only look up or down the `viewMap` until the level changes to find the required row. In the case of `getParentIndex()`, this means looking up the list until the level decreases by one. In the case of `hasNextSibling()`, this means looking down the list for an item at the same level, but with no intervening items at lesser levels.

A final important method is the `toggleOpenState()` method. It is called when the user opens or closes a subtree. That action is unusual because it changes the number of rows in the list of items displayed by the tree. The implementation of `toggleOpenState()` must keep the view's data structures up to date when this happens, and it must also tell the underlying layout system to redraw (repaint and re-layout) the tree. If these two things are not done, the view will be out-of-date in its understanding of the currently displayed view, and the tree display won't change until the mouse cursor leaves the tree's XUL box. Listing 13.22 is the code for this method.

Listing 13.22 The important `toggleOpenState()` method of `nsITreeView`.

```
toggleOpenState: function(index) {
  var i = 0;
  var node = this._viewMap[index];
  if ( ! node.container )
    return;
  if ( node.open )
  {
    node.open = false;
    node.kids = null;
    i = index + 1;
    while ( this._viewMap[index].level > this._viewMap[i].level)
      i++;
    i = i - index;
  }
  else
  {
    node.open = true;
    node.kids = [];
    for (var key in this._relatedMatrix[node.keyword])
    {
      node.kids[i] = { container : false,
                       open : false,
                       keyword : key,
                       kids : null,
                       level : node.level + 1
                     };
      if ( typeof(this._relatedMatrix[key]) != "undefined" )
        node.kids[i].container = true;
      i++;
    }
  }
  this.calcViewMap();
  this._tree.treeBoxObject.rowCountChanged(index,i);
},
```

This function aborts if the item supplied is not a container; otherwise, it handles both the open closed subtree and close opened subtree cases. In each case, it performs these tasks: updates the keyword record to match the new toggle state, updates the `openTree` hierarchy by trimming a closed subtree or adding a set of children records, and calculates the number of rows added or deleted using the `viewMap`. In the open case, the `relatedMatrix` is consulted to see how may children (related keywords of the current keyword) need to be added. After either operation, the `viewMap` is entirely recalculated to bring the view's understanding of the displayed rows up to date. The final step is to tell the tree to refresh its display. To do that, we need to interact with the tree's special box object. Normally we only use that box object to scroll, but its `rowCountChanged()` method (from the `nsITreeBoxObject` interface) is exactly what we need. It accepts an index and a number of rows from that index as a hint that describes the part of the tree that needs to be re-painted.

In a simple tree with a custom view, such as this case, opening or closing a subtree is the only way to change dynamically the list or rows currently displayed. If, however, event handlers are added to the tree, then those handlers might also make dynamic changes. An example is a mouse click on a tree row that deletes that row. For this to work, the handler must manipulate the view's data structures and call `calcViewMap()` and `rowCountChange()` just as `toggleOpenView()` does. The cleanest way to arrange that is to add extra methods to the view that do the work and then to call those methods from the handler.

Having covered the application-specific methods of the view, and the important `nsITreeView` methods, what remains of the custom view's object prototype are the unimportant `nsITreeView` methods. For another application, some of these methods might be critical, but they're not in our case. Listing 13.23 shows our implementation of them.

Listing 13.23 Less important methods of `nsITreeView`.

```
  canDropBeforeAfter: function(index, before) { return false; },
  canDropOn: function(index) { return false; },
  cycleCell: function(row, column) {},
  cycleHeader: function(col, elem) {},
  drop: function(row, orientation) { return false; },
  getCellProperties: function(row, prop) {},
  getCellValue: function(row, column) {},
  getColumnProperties: function(column, elem, prop) {},
  getImageSrc: function(row, column) {},
  getProgressMode: function(row, column) {},
  getRowProperties: function(row, column, prop) {},
  isEditable: function(row, column) { return false; },
  isSeparator: function(index) { return false; },
  isSorted: function() { return false; },
  performAction: function(action) {},
  performActionOnCell: function(action, row, column) {},
  performActionOnRow: function(action, row) {},
  selectionChanged: function() {},
  setCellText: function(row, column, value) {},
  setTree: function(tree) {}
}; // end of customTreeView.prototype
```

These methods either say "No" or do nothing. Our custom view doesn't support drag-and-drop anywhere on the tree. There are no properties on cells, rows, or columns, and no cell values, images, progress meters, editable fields, or implemented actions. We have no sorted columns or `<treeseparator>`

tags, and we don't care if the user selects rows. The `setTree()` method is run at tree initialization, and there's nothing for us to do there; although we could call `calculate()` in that method if we wanted. As it stands, we call `calculate()` when the view object is created.

After a fair amount of code, our experiment with custom views is complete. This experiment has several noteworthy results.

The first result is obvious: Using a custom view we can base a `<tree>` on non-XML content using JavaScript. That might be preferable to manipulating the DOM, especially for examples like ours where the original data for the tree are not hierarchical.

The second result is not so obvious: Using our custom view the resulting tree is *infinite* in size. If A is related to B, then B is related to A, and so opening a subtree on one always reveals a further subtree on the other. Such infinite trees clearly can't be created with static XUL. In the next chapter, we'll see how partially constructed (and therefore possibly infinite) trees are a common feature of the template system.

Our final result is that we've seen some of the inside mechanics of the `<tree>` tag. That tag is backed by several platform-supplied interfaces and structures (like a builder), and it pays to appreciate what's going on in such a powerful widget.

We've now finished the UI and the data model for the NoteTaker tool. In the following "Hands On" sessions, we'll finish it using RDF and templates. That will be the last set of changes we'll make to the way data are stored in the tool.

13.6 Debug Corner: Making <listbox> and <tree> Work

The `<listbox>` and `<tree>` tags are more complex than form elements and can be very frustrating to use if the wrong approach is used. `<listbox>` is still fragile and a little tricky, and that situation demands an element of caution. No matter how it may look, the `<tree>` tag is not fragile. It works properly, and if nothing displays inside the tree, then it must be the application code at fault. As Mozilla matures, these two tags will no doubt become more user friendly as well as more robust.

The main problem with `<listbox>` and `<tree>` stems from XUL. There are no detailed run-time syntax or layout checks that can act as a compiler, although debug features of the platform can spew out some diagnostics if required. This means that success with these widgets requires good programmer habits—in particular structured testing.

The recommended way to proceed is to always, always start with the simplest possible static widget and to work toward the desired end point using a series of simple increments. Test every change to ensure that it builds up the widget as you intend. If unexpected results occur, you can retreat one step to the last safe position. Under no circumstances should you dump a screen full of new code into a tree or listbox. Always start with a `<listbox>` or `<tree>` that has a single, static row, even if you've made it all work before.

Many specific problems with these widgets are the result of simple oversights. Some of the more common oversights include the following:

- Lack of `flex="1"` attributes. The tags surrounding `<tree>` and `<listbox>`, those two tags themselves, and column specifier tags all benefit from flex.
- Using shorthand syntax for `<tree>`. `<tree>` and its content tags have no shorthand or abbreviated syntax. All tags are required and must be fully stated. `<listbox>` does have some shorthand.
- Missing column ids. If your `<treecol>` tags are missing column ids, you can't select anything in the tree.
- No height for `<tree>`. The `<tree>` tag has no default height. One must be implied by the surrounding layout, or that tag must be given a height.
- Not enough homework. It's a fact of life that the AOM, XBL, DOM, and XPIDL documentation types are all stored in separate formats, plus this book. They take some exploring before you can claim to have the landscape mapped out. Try examining a `<tree>` and a `<listbox>` with the DOM Inspector, or review the content of this chapter.
- Confusion about "item indexes." In the tree view interface, item indexes represent the series of vertically stacked rectangles in the tree that each displays a row. That set of rectangles is clipped by the tree viewing area. "Item indexes" do not represent the tags that make up the content of the tree, or even all the rows that might be displayed by the tree. These indexes only represent the currently open subtrees and their exposed rows. The same is true for listboxes, but in that case, there is a one-to-one correspondence between viewable rectangles and listbox rows.

Overall, `<tree>` and `<listbox>` can't always be used as trivially as `<button>` can, so take care. Until `<listbox>` has a long track record of robustness, beware of laying it out in the same horizontal space as other XUL tags. Layout and behavior can be unusual in that case. Always try to arrange matters so that `<listbox>` dictates the size of its layout area, not its sibling, parent, or other nearby tags.

13.7 Summary

`<listbox>` and `<tree>` are powerful widgets in the XUL bestiary. They are like form elements on steroids. `<listbox>` is a little fragile, and `<tree>` a little complicated, but they are both flexible display systems for serious data-oriented applications.

Even so, you can only go so far displaying static data. The alternative of scripting up content changes using the DOM is bulky, slow, and awkward. For dynamic data, something new is required. Templates are that new technology, and they are discussed next.

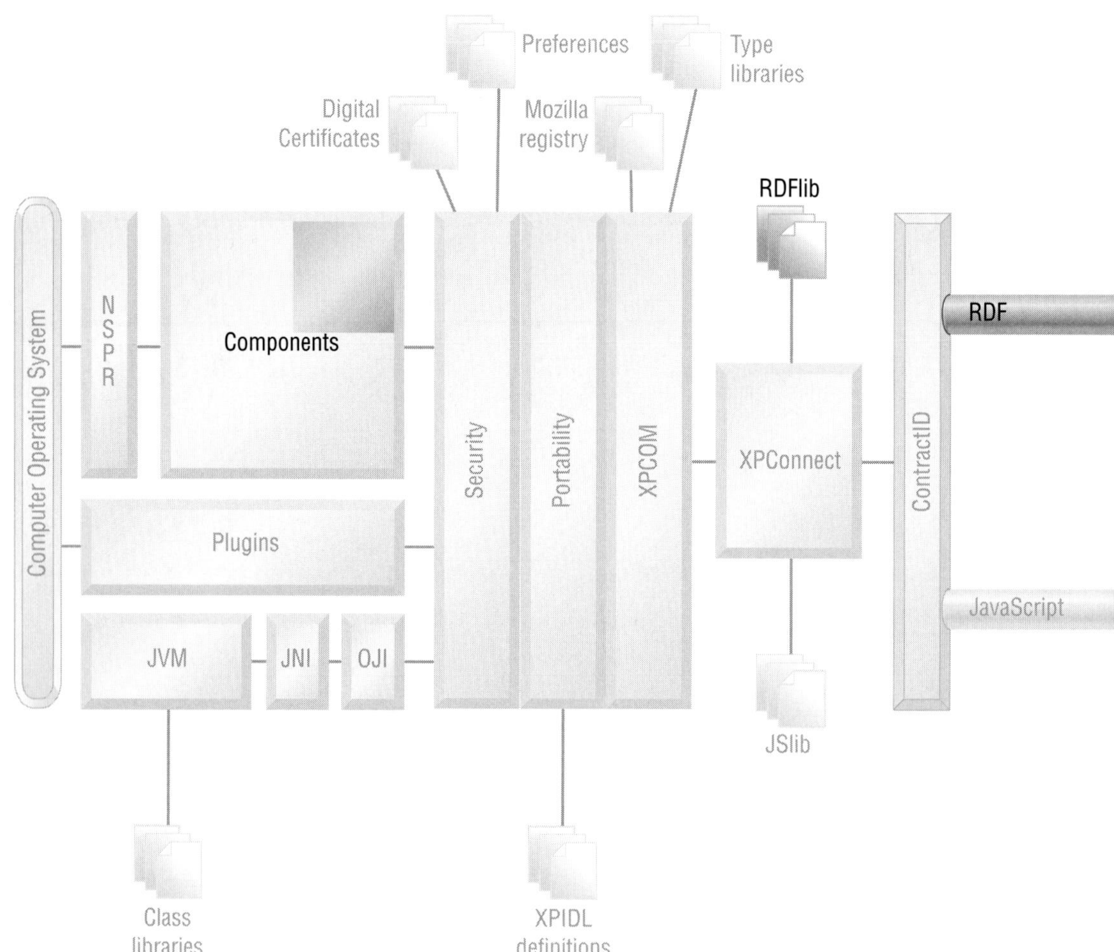

Preferences
Type
libraries
Digital
Certificates
Mozilla
registry
RDFlib
Computer Operating System
NSPR
Components
Security
Portability
XPCOM
RDF
XPConnect
ContractID
Plugins
JavaScript
JVM
JNI
OJI
JSlib
Class
libraries
XPIDL
definitions

C H A P T E R 14

Templates

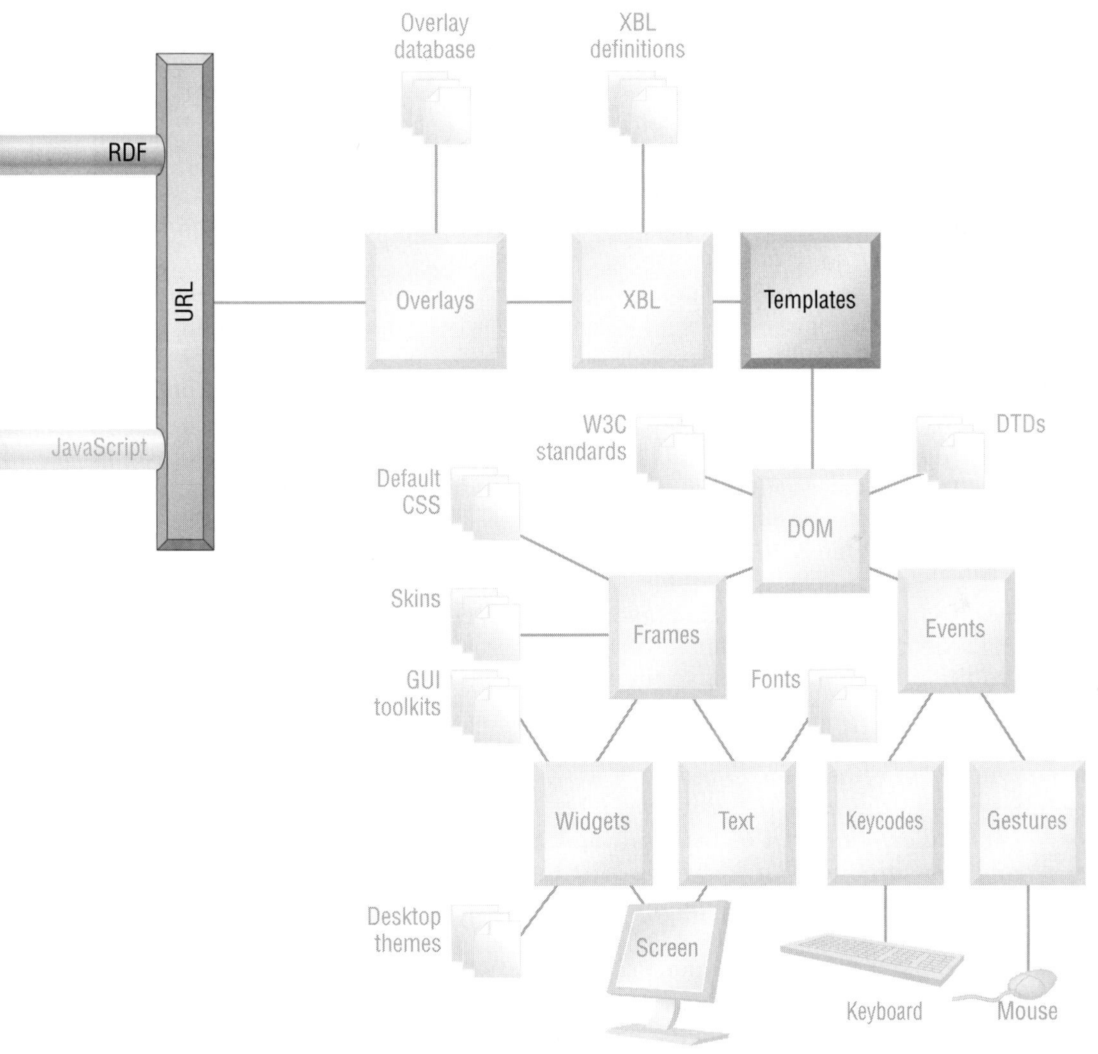

This chapter describes how to specify content for a XUL document using a stream of RDF data. This is done with a combination of ordinary XUL tags, XUL template tags, and RDF tags.

Mozilla's template system is a subset of XUL's tags. These tags are used to create a document whose content is not fixed. Such a document is the basis for display of data that varies over time, either because of user interaction, or because of its origin. It is also the basis for applications whose UI depends on external information. That external information might be as simple as a file, as complex as a database, or as remote as a network device. In all cases, such a document has an appearance that varies according to the viewing occasion.

The template system enables many classes of application. When the template-based information is updated by equipment, the user interface acts like a telemetry application, such as a network manager or environmental control system. When the template-based information is updated by the end user, the user interface acts like a data management application. The template system is particularly good at supporting drill-down data management activities, like category analysis, work breakdowns, content and document management systems, and network visualizations. It can also be used for the more traditional data entry style of application.

In the traditional Web application environment, an HTML document with dynamic appearance can be achieved in two ways. HTML can be generated by a program installed behind a Web server (like a CGI program), or existing HTML can be heavily scripted (Dynamic HTML). In either case, 3GL code has to be written to produce the desired results.

Mozilla's template system requires no 3GL code and no Web server. It is, of course, specific to Mozilla. All that is required is an RDF document and a set of rules that state what to do with that RDF. These rules are expressed as XUL tags. The Mozilla Platform automatically pumps the RDF facts into the XUL template document when it is being loaded. The set of rules is used to modify the final content displayed, as directed by the pumped-in facts. The XUL template system is therefore a data-driven system. Some templates require full security access to the platform, such as is provided by the chrome area.

The RDF content consumed by templates has two possible origins. Content might come from an ordinary RDF document stored as a file on some file system. In this case, the content can be RDF facts on any topic. The NoteTaker running example in this book ultimately does that. Alternately, that content might be produced "live" by the Mozilla Platform. In that case, the content consists of RDF facts on a platform-specific topic. An example is window management within the Mozilla Platform. The DOM Inspector consults that internal RDF information in order to build the File | Inspect a Window... menu. This menu consists of currently open windows.

Understanding templates means understanding the template rules system. Sets of rules can be trivial or complex. In the most trivial case, the rules are implicit and not stated directly. In the complex case, rules are a bit like a database query and a bit like JavaScript `switch` statements. Both cases have the use of special template variables.

Like many aspects of XUL, the template system starts with direct and obvious syntax:

```
<template>
  <rule> ... </rule>
  <rule> ... </rule>
</template>
```

Templates are as complex as trees, and this basic syntax doesn't last long—it has a number of subtle points.

Templates do not carry any content of their own: None of the template tags are boxlike tags. Template tags are more like macro processing instructions and the `#ifdef` features of C's preprocessor. These tags are always used inside some other XUL tag; they are not top-level tags like `<window>`.

The NPA diagram at the start of this chapter shows the extent of the template system. From the diagram, templates are a small system of their own, somewhat separate from the rest of Mozilla's processing. They are the final step in the content assembly process when a XUL document is loaded. Templates have nothing to do with presentation of XUL content. Because templates work intimately with RDF, both RDF files and URL/URI names are heavily used by templates. As for most features of the platform, a few XPCOM objects are responsible for much of the template functionality.

14.1 An Example Template: Hello, World

Listing 14.1 is a XUL document containing a trivial template that implements "hello, world" one more time.

Listing 14.1 XUL application showing "hello, world" use of template technology.

```
<?xml version="1.0"?>
<window xmlns="http://www.mozilla.org/keymaster/gatekeeper/
          there.is.only.xul">

  <vbox datasources="test.rdf" ref="urn:test:seqroot">
    <template>
      <label
         uri="rdf:*"
         value="Content: rdf:http://www.example.org/Test#Data"/>
    </template>
  </vbox>

</window>
```

From the listing, the template system consists of its own tags, like `<template>`, and special-purpose attributes like `ref` that are added to other tags.

Mozilla provides several syntax options for rules that make up the template query system. In this example, the most trivial syntax of all is used. Only one template rule exists, and it is implied. That rule says: Process all facts in the nominated RDF container, and generate content to represent those facts. The nominated container has URI `urn:test:seqroot`, and the content to represent the facts is a `<label>` tag. Note that there are nontemplate XUL tags both outside and inside the `<template>` tag.

Listing 14.2 is an RDF file that matches the RDF graph structure that this template expects:

Listing 14.2 Trivial example of an RDF file used for templates.

```
<?xml version="1.0"?>
<RDF
  xmlns:Test="http://www.example.org/Test#"
  xmlns="http://www.w3.org/1999/02/22-rdf-syntax-ns#"
>
  <Description about="http://www.example.org/">
    <Test:Container>
      <Seq about="urn:test:seqroot">
        <li resource="urn:test:welcome"/>
        <li resource="urn:test:message"/>
      </Seq>
    </Test:Container>
  <Description about="urn:test:welcome" Test:Data="hello, world"/>
  <Description about="urn:test:message" Test:Data="This is a test"/>
</RDF>
```

This RDF file has no special features other than a `<Seq>` tag whose resource name is used in the XUL template code in Listing 14.1. This URN is used as the starting point for the template. `Test` is an `xmlns` namespace. `Data` and `Container` are made-up property (predicate) names for that namespace. The URNs and the `"http://www.example.org/Test"` URL are all equally made up. No formal process is required to allocate these names; just make good design choices. The `Data` property also appears in the `<label>` tag in Listing 14.1, where it is quoted with its full URL.

If these two listings are saved to files, and Listing 14.1 is loaded into the platform, then Figure 14.1 is the result. Diagnostic styles have been turned on to show the structure of the resulting window.

This screenshot shows that two `<label>` tags have been generated in the final XUL. The value of each tag consists of both fixed content ("`Content: `") and a string that matches one of the two `<Description>` facts in the RDF doc-

Fig. 14.1 XUL document created by a template and two facts.

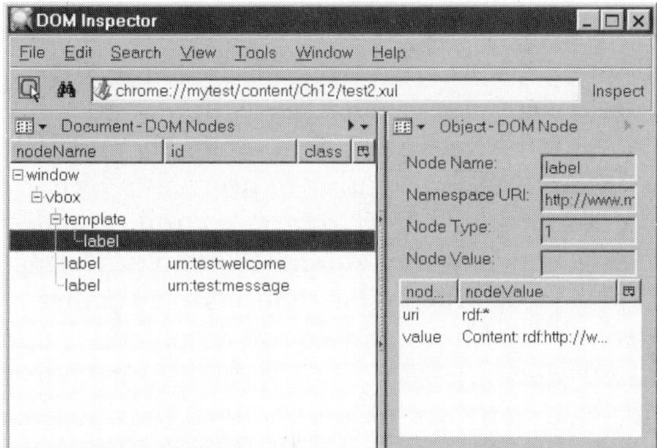

Fig. 14.2 DOM Inspector view of a template-generated document.

ument. By comparison, the <vbox> tag appears only once. The structure of this final document can also be examined using the DOM Inspector. Figure 14.2 shows a full DOM Inspector breakdown of Figure 14.1.

This screenshot shows that the template system has indeed added two tags to the document, one for each RDF fact in the `<Seq>` tag. The highlighted `<label>` tag is the original template label; the other two `<label>` tags are the template-generated content. So the final document contains two subtrees—one for the specification of the template, and one for the generated content. The subtree starting the `<template>` tag contributes no visual content to the document. When the template system generated the tags in the other subtree, it gave them ids equal to the URN of the resource in the matched RDF fact.

The XUL for this template can be made far more complex by using the extended features of the template rule system.

Before diving into the XUL syntax of the template system, we first take a big step back and consider what it all means from the point of view of facts. After all, templates require RDF content to work on, and that means fact processing.

14.2 Template Concepts

Mozilla's template system extends all the standard features of Mozilla applications: XUL, JavaScript, and RDF. There is also the matter of data sources. These extensions are explained and then tied together with an example.

14.2.1 RDF Queries and Unification

The XUL template system is a query system. It searches through data and returns the items that match the search specification. The data searched through is a set of RDF facts. A template query is therefore an RDF-specific piece of processing.

The queries that XUL templates do are often described as a pattern-matching system. In the most general computer science sense, this is true, but pattern matching also has a simple, everyday meaning. That everyday meaning is used for file name masks like `*.txt` and for regular expressions like "`^[a-zA-Z]*66$`". Tools like command line shells, Perl, `grep`, `vi`, and even JavaScript use everyday pattern matching, which is very similar to simple filtering. In simple filtering, a large list of items (or characters) is reduced to a smaller list.

XUL template queries are not filters and do not do pattern matching in the everyday sense. If an RDF document contains a certain fact, then a XUL template that queries that document can do much more than just choose or ignore that fact. Template queries are not just simple filters.

Instead of simple filtering, template queries do *unification*. Unification is where a set of data items is combined into a final result. Solving a jigsaw puzzle is a real-world example. When all the jigsaw puzzle's pieces are fitted together, the result (a finished picture) is achieved. If there are more puzzle pieces than are needed (perhaps several puzzle sets have been mixed together), then some pieces will be discarded as irrelevant. Unification can have more than one outcome. If there are enough jigsaw pieces, then several pictures might be put together at once, not just one. If the jigsaw pieces are similar shapes, then even more pictures might be possible because of the many possible arrangements of pieces.

In Mozilla, the jigsaw puzzle pieces are the subjects, predicates, and objects of a set of RDF facts. The desired result is stated by a XUL template's query. Any combination of pieces that fits the query specification (the rules in the template) is returned as a number of pieces of information—a new tuple. If more than one combination of pieces fits, more than one tuple is returned.

Such a system might sound familiar. The SELECT statement in SQL acts exactly like this when it contains a join—that is, a FROM clause with two or more tables. The column names in the returned rows are drawn from all the joined tables. The set of returned columns does not exactly match one table row; instead, it matches pieces of rows from several tables. More than one row can be returned in a SELECT query's result set.

In fact, XUL template queries are examples of relational calculus, just as SQL queries are examples of relational algebra. University researchers have shown that these two relational approaches are fundamentally the same, even though they are programmed differently and have little syntax in common.

The XUL syntax for templates is unusual and best avoided to start with. To learn about template queries, let's return instead to the boy, dog, and ball example of Chapter 11, RDF.

Recall that example was used to describe a "pure" fact system, free of any RDF or XML syntax. It is used again here to show "pure" examples of fact queries and fact unification. The example facts from Chapter 11, RDF, are repeated in Listing 14.3.

Listing 14.3 Predicate triples for boy and dog example, from Chapter 11.

```
<- 1, is-named, Tom ->
<- 1, owner, 2 ->
<- 1, plays-with, 5 ->
<- 2, is-named, Spot ->
<- 2, owned-by, 1 ->
<- 2, plays-with, 5 ->
<- 5, type-of, tennis ->
<- 5, color-of, green ->
```

The information modeled is "Tom and his dog Spot play with a green tennis ball," and each thing in the model has an identifying number. We can query this set of facts using a single- or multi-fact query.

14.2.1.1 Single-Fact Queries In Chapter 11, RDF, we noted that facts (and RDF documents) are often ground. Ground facts are a good thing because every piece of a ground fact is just a literal piece of data, with no unknowns. Literals are easy to work with. A fact that isn't ground was also shown in Chapter 11, RDF. That fact, slightly changed, is repeated here:

```
<- 1, owner, ??? ->
```

Because the object part of this triple isn't known, this fact is not ground. It is useless as a piece of data, but it is useful as a starting point for a fact query. Let's use a placeholder variable for the unknown part. Such variables start with a question mark (`?`) just as DOS variables start and end with `%`, or just as UNIX shell variables start with `$`. A variable cannot be in the ground state, or else it wouldn't be a variable—it would be a literal again. We say that the process of turning a variable with unknown value into a variable with a known value is "grounding the variable" or that it is done "to ground the variable":

```
<- 1, owner, ?dogId ->
```

When a query is run, unification causes all variables to be turned into literals from the set of available facts. That is a very fancy way of saying, "Ground All Variables, Please." For this simple example, the second fact stated in Listing 14.3 matches this variable-laden query:

```
<- 1, owner, 2 ->
```

`?dogId` has no value, and if the value `2` were to replace it, a fact matching an existing fact would be constructed. The variable `?dogId` can therefore be ground to the value `2`. This is a trivial example of a query that returns one resulting fact.

Suppose that Tom has a second dog, called Fido. These additional facts would then exist:

```
<- 1, owner, 3 ->
<- 3, is-named, Fido ->
```

If the fact containing ?dogId is again treated as a query, then there are two facts that can fit the query:

```
<- 1, owner, 2 ->
<- 1, owner, 3 ->
```

?dogId can be ground to either 2 or 3, so there are two solutions. We can say the result set contains two facts, two rows, or two items.

The preceding fact that acts like a query can also be expanded. It might read:

```
<- ?personId, owner, ?dogId ->
```

In this case, a match requires a combination of values that satisfies both variables at once (?personId is ground *and* ?dogId is ground). If we use the existing facts, the result set is still two rows: either (?personId is ground to 1 *and* ?dogId is ground to 2), yielding one fact, or (?personId is ground to 1 *and* ?dogId is ground to 3), yielding the other fact. Adding extra variables does not always mean more facts will appear in the results. It just means that more things need to match correctly.

Suppose that Jane (with person id = 4) also owns Fido, but not Spot. Fido is shared, but Spot is exclusively owned by Tom. There are then two more facts in the fact store:

```
<- 4, is-named, Jane ->
<- 4, owner, 3 ->
```

If the last query is posed again, then three solutions result:

- ?personId ground to 1 (Tom) *and* ?dogId ground to 2 (Spot)
- ?personId ground to 1 (Tom) *and* ?dogId ground to 3 (Fido)
- ?personId ground to 4 (Jane) *and* ?dogId ground to 3 (Fido)

Even though ?personId can be set to 4 (Jane) and ?dogId can be set to 2 (Spot), no fact results from this combination because no such fact (Jane owning Spot) appears in the fact store. When a fact is matched against a query fact, there must be a complete fit, not a partial fit.

Finally, note that the information to be ground in this last single-fact query has an alternate notation. It can be written as a collection of unknowns that need to be solved. That collection can be written as a tuple. In this example, such a tuple is a double, not a triple. That tuple-to-be-ground can be stated like this:

```
<- ?personId, ?dogId ->
```

This tuple doesn't describe the query at work. It merely explains what unknowns are involved and therefore what variables will be set when the query returns solutions. That is useful information for programmers, and somewhat similar to the INTO clause of Embedded SQL's SELECT. If someone else is responsible for creating the query, then such a tuple is all you really need to know to grab the results returned.

In the last example, the three solutions found fill this tuple like so:

```
<- 1, 2 ->
<- 1, 3 ->
<- 4, 3 ->
```

The tuple of two variables neatly collects the unknown information together. The query processor still needs information that matches the structure of the facts in the fact store. That is why queries are always posed using the longer syntax shown earlier.

If the query processor isn't given enough information, it can't guess what to do. It is not enough to say, "Smart computer, please fill these variables for me somehow." The query must tell the query processor what to look at. In a single-fact query, the prescription given is very simple: "Dumb computer, examine all triples for a match against this query triple."

Mozilla's template system supports single-fact queries. Single-fact queries can be specified using the template extended query syntax. Single-fact queries cannot be specified using the template simple query syntax.

Looking ahead slightly, to query a single fact, the `<conditions>` tag of the query must be arranged one of two ways. If the facts sought are RDF container containment facts, with predicates `rdf:_1`, `rdf:_2`, and so on, then `<conditions>` should hold a `<content>` and a `<member>` tag. If the facts sought have well-known predicates, then the `<conditions>` tag should hold a `<content>` and a `<triple>` tag. Template queries that are single-fact queries are discussed further under "Common Query Patterns."

In summary, a single-fact query tries to ground a query fact against a real fact, and when it succeeds, the ground results are called solutions.

14.2.1.2 Multifact Queries The XUL template system supports multifact queries. A multifact query is a bit like an SQL join, and a bit like navigating a tree data structure.

A multifact query poses a question that requires two or more whole facts to be combined. In other words, it requires some deduction. Mozilla's support for deduction is like simplistic Prolog predicate calculus, except the similarity is heavily disguised by syntax. We consider "pure" multifact queries first, before examining the XUL syntax.

Using the boy and dog example, suppose that a needed query is: "What is the name of the dog that Tom owns?" Using variables, that query could be stated as three facts to be unified:

```
<- ?personId, is-named, Tom ->
<- ?personId, owner, ?dogId ->
<- ?dogId, is-named, ?dogName ->
```

Forming a multifact query such as this takes a little practice. It is the same kind of practice required to learn how to do multitable SQL joins or multivariable regular expressions. The core problem is that you are required to write the query straight down direct from your brain.

This particular query was constructed as follows. First, the things we already knew were identified ("Tom"). Next, the things we didn't know, but wanted to know, were noted: dogName. We looked at the available tuples to see where these known and unknown things might fit in. That gave us two tuples, the first and third in the final query. Looking at those tuples, we saw what some of the predicates must be: is-named is the useful predicate for both tuples. To ground those tuples fully, some other unknowns (the tuple subject terms) would have to be found: personId and dogId. So we added those variables to the list of unknowns. We noticed that these two tuples don't share any unknowns, so they weren't "connected." We then looked again for more tuples that might connect the ones we really need together. We discovered the second tuple, which links personId and dogId. With that addition, we were satisfied that all required unknowns were present, and that the set of tuples was connected so that the tuples formed a single query.

If these three facts are submitted as a single query to the query processor, then all variables must be ground at once if a solution is to be found. Because ?personId and ?dogId appear in two triples each, whatever value they take on must simultaneously match both triples. In this way, triples with data items in common can be linked (or joined or tied) together. The only possible solution in the example fact store (without Fido or Jane) is:

```
<- 1, is-named, Tom ->
<- 1, owner, 2 ->
<- 2, is-named, Spot ->
```

Compare these three facts with the preceding query. This solution unifies the unknown variables

```
<- ?personId, ?dogId, ?dogName ->
```

to a single set of possibilities

```
<- 1, 2, Spot ->
```

The value Spot is the value sought; the other variables are just used to tie the facts together. So Spot is the name of the dog that Tom owns, and the query has been answered. The other variables can be examined or ignored according to need. This multifact query shows why variables undergo "unification" rather than simply being "set": They must all be matched at once before a solution is found.

How does the Mozilla query processor find this solution? There are many possible techniques. The simplest technique is to go though every combination of three facts in the fact store and compare each combination against the query. That is a "brute force" solution and very inefficient. It is not done in Mozilla. Mozilla uses a narrower approach, which involves exploring part of the fact graph structure only. We'll see more on that shortly.

If Fido and Jane are put back into the fact store, then the same query would report two solutions:

```
<- 1, is-named, Tom ->
<- 1, owner, 2 ->
<- 2, is-named, Spot ->

<- 1, is-named, Tom ->
<- 1, owner, 3 ->
<- 3, is-named, Fido ->
```

The values that the unknown variables are ground to are thus

```
<- 1, 2, Spot ->
<- 1, 3, Fido ->
```

Note how the query is designed to match the particular facts in the fact store. Subject and objects are matched up using variables like `?personId`. The results, on the other hand, are just a set of ground variables that make up one tuple per solution. In this example, there are three variables, so the result tuple is a triple. Any number of variables might be used, though.

This example is equivalent to a three-table join in SQL. Listing 14.4 shows an imaginary `SELECT` query that does the same job as the last fact query. Each of the three imaginary tables matches one of the facts in the preceding three-fact query.

Listing 14.4 SQL `SELECT` analogous to a three-fact query.

```
SELECT p.personId, d.dogId, d.dogName
FROM   persons p, owners o, dogs d
WHERE  p.personName = "Tom"
AND    p.personId   = o.personId
AND    o.dogId      = d.dogId
```

Just as the join in the SQL query links tables (relations) together, the variables in a factual query link facts together. Compare the use of `personId` in the two types of query, and you should be able to see a little similarity, even though the syntax is vastly different.

In the general case, this example shows how a big bucket of facts can be examined using a carefully constructed query that contains variables. If the bucket of facts is an RDF document, then clearly Mozilla's templates can do simple but general-purpose queries on that document.

The template system supports multifact queries in two ways. The simple template syntax automatically performs a two-fact query, provided that the RDF data is organized correctly. The extended template syntax allows multifact queries of any length to be created by stringing together one `<content>` tag, any number of `<member>` and `<triple>` tags, and any number of `<binding>` tags. Each such tag (except for `<content>`) represents one fact in the query.

14.2.1.3 Query Solution Strategy Chapter 11, RDF, explains how a collection of facts can be viewed in one of three ways: as a simple unstructured set of items, as a complex graph-like data structure, or as a simple set that has useful subsets of items identified with RDF containers like `<Seq>`. Mozilla uses a combination of the RDF graph (the second view) and containers (the third view) to get its XUL template queries done.

To the application programmer, it appears that Mozilla uses a drill-down algorithm to solve queries. This drill-down process is equivalent to a depth-first tree traversal. This algorithm requires that the query have a starting point that is known—the *root* of the query. In the preceding example, `Tom` is a known starting point. In practice, the starting point in Mozilla should be a fact subject, as well as a fact object. Such a fact subject is always a URI (a URL or URN).

After this starting point is known, the Mozilla query processor navigates through the graph of the RDF facts from that starting point. Each fact in the query equals one arc (one predicate or property) traversed. So for a three-fact query, the processor will penetrate only three hops into the graph from the starting point. It will only look that far for solutions to the query.

This query system can be visualized using actual RDF graphs. We return to a variation of the boy and dog example. In this variation, the dog Spot has discovered that he can play by himself. He has also managed to get ownership of a softball, which is entirely his. Figure 14.3 shows the graph that results from these additional facts, with a particular query highlighted.

In Figure 14.3, all facts are part of the fact store. The query illustrated is a two-fact query that starts at Tom's identifier, which is one (1). Perhaps the query is something like "What things do Tom's pets play with?" The dark lines on the graph show fact terms that are reached by the query—a two-fact query must traverse exactly two arrows. The pale lines are not reached. There are three initial solutions to this query. Each one matches a unique path that starts from the (1) identifier: path 1-2-Spot, path 1-2-7, and path 1-2-5. To be more specific, we might require that the first fact have an owner predicate (a

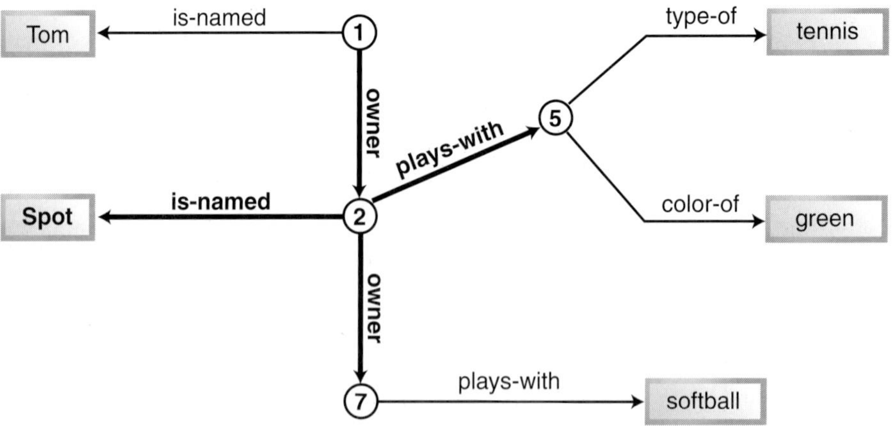

Fig. 14.3 Enhanced boy and dog graph showing a query path.

pet of Tom's) and the second fact have a plays-with predicate. In that case, the 1-2-Spot combination would no longer be a solution, and just two solutions would be found: "Tom's dog Spot plays with a softball" and "Tom's dog Spot plays with a tennis ball."

We can experiment a little further with this example. Figure 14.4 shows a different query on the same graph of facts.

This is again a two-fact query, but this time it starts at Spot's identifier (2). There are again three solutions. This time, note that the path 2-1-Tom is not a solution. This is because the arrows point the wrong way in that path. Rather than 2 being a fact subject and 1 being an object, it is the other way around. The query system can't go in reverse like that. Even for the solutions possible, this second query probably doesn't make much sense. The predicates in the possible solution paths are all quite different. If this query seemed necessary, it would be fair to guess that either the data model behind the facts was wrong, or the query was poorly thought up.

The disadvantage of this system is that not all the facts in the fact store are looked at. In theory, a query might miss some of the solutions. The advantage of this system is speed. In practice, if the RDF facts are neatly ordered, a quick search from a known starting point is sufficient to provide all answers.

This drill-down approach is part illusion; the template system is actually more complicated than that. It is, however, a good enough approximation and is a recommended way to interpret XUL template code.

The way to organize an RDF document so that this system works is to use an RDF container: a `<Seq>`, `<Bag>`, or `<Alt>`. The known starting point provided to the query system could be the URI of the fact holding the container. The sought-after data should be facts within that container. The query then drills down into the container, retrieving the required facts. This is an indexing strategy.

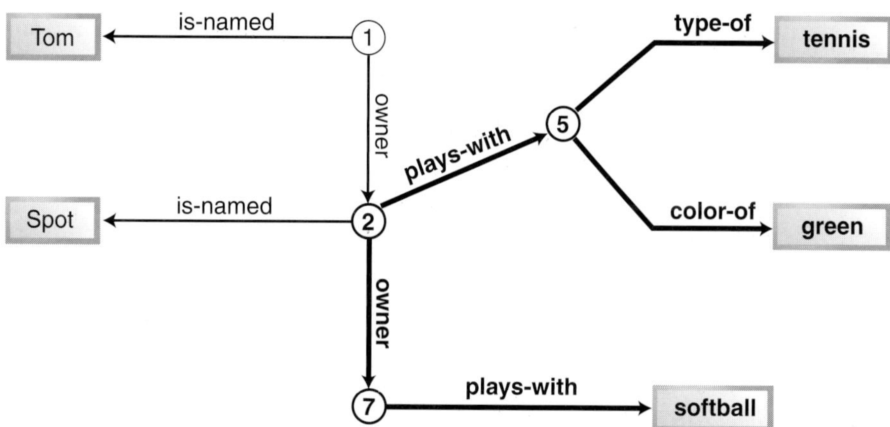

Fig. 14.4 Enhanced boy and dog graph showing second query path.

Listings 14.5 and 14.6 show an RDF fragment and a matching query.

Listing 14.5 Example RDF fragment useful for a multi-fact query.

```
<Description about="http://www.example.org/">
  <NS:Owns>
    <Bag about="urn:test:seq">
      <li resource="urn:test:seq:fido"/>
      <li resource="urn:test:seq:spot"/>
      <li resource="urn:test:seq:cerebus"/>
    </Bag>
  </NS:Owns>
</Description>
<Description about="urn:test:seq:fido" NS:Tails="0"/>
<Description about="urn:test:seq:spot" NS:Heads="1"/>
<Description about="urn:test:seq:cerberus" NS:Heads="3"/>
```

NS in Listing 14.5 stands for some namespace, presumably declared with `xmlns` elsewhere in the code. The namespace would have some URL like *www.test.com/#Test*. Listing 14.6 uses the NS namespace to identify the fact items equivalent to those in Listing14.5. Use of NS in Listing 14.6 has no particular meaning because the facts stated in that listing are neither XML nor code.

Listing 14.6 Example RDF query for drilling into an RDF container.

```
<- http://www.example.org/, NS:Owns, ?bag ->
<- ?bag, ?index, ?item ->
<- ?item, NS:Heads, ?heads ->
```

In this query, the first fact to be ground drills down to the RDF fact with the bag as subject (one fact only). The second fact drills further down to facts with bag *items* as subject (three facts for the sole bag). The third fact drills down to the fact stating how many heads that bag item has (zero or one fact per bag item, depending on whether the Heads property exists). The end result is that two solutions are found. The set of variables to be unified are

```
<- ?bag, ?index, ?item, ?heads ->
```

and the two solutions found are

```
<- urn:test:seq, rdf:_2, urn:test:seq:spot, 1 ->
<- urn:test:seq, rdf:_3, urn:test:seq:cerberus, 3 ->
```

Recall that RDF automatically assigns predicate names starting with `rdf:_1` to each of a container's children. The first container child was not reported by this query because the last of the three query facts couldn't be matched to a fact with `NS:Tails` instead of `NS:Heads`.

Support for this kind of query is the first priority of Mozilla's template query system. This is the most reliable and useful way to work with templates.

In the preceding example, the `?index` variable is used to stand in for the predicate of a fact. Mozilla's query system cannot use a variable for a predicate term, but it has a <member> tag that can achieve a similar but more limited effect.

In summary, by poking into an RDF graph of facts from a certain point, a set of query facts can be tested for matches against a neatly ordered collection of facts near that point.

14.2.1.4 Stored Queries The queries that XUL templates specify live as long as the document they are contained in. They do not run once and are then thrown away. They are useable until the window that they are displayed in is torn down.

A collection of RDF facts (perhaps loaded from a file) can be modified anytime after it is created because such a collection is stored in memory in a fact store. Facts can be added to the store, removed, or changed. The template query system can be advised of these changes.

When fact changes occur, each template's query can update its understanding of what solutions exist for that query. If new solutions are possible, they are added to the set of results. If some solutions are no longer possible, they are removed from the result set. Updates to existing solutions are also possible.

The net result is that the solution sets can change over time. Template queries are not always passive "read consistent views" (to use RDBMS jargon). They can be live and fully up-to-date actively changing "event lists" (to use telemetry jargon).

This live updating requires a little scripting assistance from the application programmer. In the end, the query must repeatedly poll (check) the fact store if the solutions are to be kept up to date. Scripts can be written so that this is done in an efficient way, and only when required.

In a XUL document, template queries hang around.

14.2.1.5 Recursive Queries The drill-down strategy used by Mozilla template queries can be applied recursively. Each drill-down end point for a query can be reused if it yields a solution. That end point can be used as the new starting point for a repeat of the same query. This allows the query system to drill down further into the RDF graph structure, possibly finding another solution or solutions. Only when no additional facts exist to consider is the end point of the recursion reached.

This recursive use of queries is useful for treelike data structures. Such structures can have any depth, which equals any number of arc hops in an RDF graph. Without recursion, it wouldn't be possible to retrieve the whole of a tree because the depth searched by a query equals the number of facts in the query.

In a XUL document, template queries inside <tree> tags do extra work.

14.2.1.6 Query Lists The Mozilla template system allows a number of queries to be put together into a simple list.

When query processing starts, all queries in such a list are run at the same time. Any solution found that fits more than one query will be assigned to just one of those queries. The query chosen will be the one nearest the head of the list.

The way this is done is simple: For each drill-down hop into the RDF graph, the query processor examines the query list for queries that are part-solved by the facts found so far. Those queries that are part-solved are considered again after the next hop, while the rest are ignored from that point on. When the query processor has finished drilling down, only those queries completely solved by the found facts remain.

This system allows a set of facts to be assessed according to one set of criteria (one query) and, if that fails, to be reconsidered according to another set of criteria (a second query). This is much like the boolean conditions in a series of `if` ... `else if` ... statements.

Query lists in Mozilla allow several completely different sets of content to be generated from the one set of facts. Each query can provide fact solutions for one such set.

That concludes template queries. After the query succeeds, something needs to be done with the solution.

14.2.2 XUL Content Generation

In the ordinary case, all a XUL template does with retrieved RDF data is display it.

A template does this by mixing the retrieved data with ordinary XUL content. It acts like a simple pretty-printer or like a report-writing tool. The output content is contributed to the XUL document and appears for the user's consumption, just like any XUL content.

If the XUL tag surrounding the template is a `<menupopup>`, `<listbox>`, `<toolbar>`, `<tree>`, or even `<box>`, then the contents of that XUL tag (the menu items, toolbar buttons, tree or listbox rows) can be generated entirely by the template. This means that interactive interfaces can derive directly from an RDF file, rather than be hard-coded.

A simple example illustrates this generation process. Listing 14.7 is an RDF file containing two facts inside a container. Each fact has a single property/value pair. These pairs are usually the interesting part of an RDF document, and they are usually displayed as XUL content.

Listing 14.7 Simple RDF document used to illustrate displayed content.

```
<?xml version="1.0"?>
<RDF xmlns:Test="http://www.test.com/Test#"
     xmlns="http://www.w3.org/1999/02/22-rdf-syntax-ns#">
  <Description about="urn:test:top">
    <Test:TopSeq>
      <Seq about="urn:test:seqroot">
        <li resource="urn:test:message1"/>
```

```
      <li resource="urn:test:message2"/>
    </Seq>
  </Test:TopSeq>
</Description>

<Description about="urn:test:message1" Test:Foo="foo"/>
<Description about="urn:test:message2" Test:Bar="bar"/>
</RDF>
```

The two properties can be dug out of this file and displayed using a template. Figure 14.5 shows two sets of template-generated content from the same RDF file. This requires two templates in the same XUL document.

Fig. 14.5 Output from two templates using the same RDF data.

The two templates are side by side in this screenshot. Only the final results of the template content generation are visible. The template on the left generates `<description>` tags with a border style applied. Those tags are contained inside a `<vbox>`. The template on the right generates `<treeitem>` tags, each with `<treerow>` and `<treecell>` content. Those tags are contained inside `<tree>` and `<treechildren>` nested tags. It is easy to see that the content extracted from RDF is the same in both cases, but the structure, appearance, and use of the data are different. For example, the tree items are user-selectable but the plain text on the left isn't.

In summary, templates merge separately stored solution data with other content that determines how the data are to be presented.

14.2.2.1 Template and Content Subtrees The XUL tags that make up a template are not displayed in the final, displayed document. The content tags generated by the XUL system are displayed. Both types of tags exist in the XUL document at the same time, but the template tags are styled to have no display.

The template tags form one DOM subtree of the XUL document. After the template has generated its content, these tags exist only for reference purposes. The template system might reread them at a later point if the application programmer adds scripts that make this happen.

The generated content tags form one DOM subtree for each solution found by the template query. Three solutions mean up to three subtrees. These subtrees occur where any user interaction or scripting support ultimately occurs.

Each of these generated subtrees has a topmost tag. That tag acquires a unique id attribute that matches the URI of a fact subject from the query results. This id acts as a unique key and is used to identify each generated subtree. This id comes from the `uri` attribute, described under content tags.

The "hello, world" example at the start of this chapter shows these different subtrees in a screenshot.

14.2.2.2 Dynamic Content Templates can change over their lifetimes. The content generated by a template can also change over the template's lifetime. Both effects require the use of JavaScript, and both might require a template rebuild. Templates can also delay the generation of content.

Rebuilding a template requires a line of JavaScript code. No document or page needs to be fetched or reloaded. The portion of the XUL document containing the template and its results is changed in-place. Surrounding content is unaffected, except possibly for changes to layout. A typical line of code that does this is

```
document.getElementByTagName('tree').database.rebuild();
```

The template tags themselves can be altered using DOM 1 operations like `removeChild()` and `appendChild()`. If this is done, then the next time the template content is rebuilt the displayed content will be replaced with content generated by the changed template.

If the template is not altered, the content displayed can still change. This occurs when the RDF data that the template uses is changed. If the template content is rebuilt, then content associated with new query solutions will be added, and content associated with old solutions that are no longer relevant will be removed. The template system does these content changes itself using DOM 1 operations.

In a XUL document, the queries not only hang around but also can be reused anytime.

14.2.2.3 Lazy Building Content generation can be delayed until later. This is only possible for recursive queries. When this system is used, only the topmost, most immediate solutions to a template query are sought. These immediate solutions yield content. Later on, if an indication comes from the user or the platform that more content is needed, further solutions are sought. Any extra content generated from those further solutions is added to the displayed results.

Lazy building only works if the template content tag that holds the `uri` attribute is one of these tags:

```
<menu> <menulist> <menubutton> <toolbarbutton> <button> <treeitem>
```

The children of these tags, like the `<menu>` tag in a `<menulist>`, are the pieces built lazily.

Templates that use <tree>s or <menu>s can put off some of the recursive query work until later.

14.2.2.4 Common Source Content Two or more templates can use the same RDF data. If the RDF data changes, then those changes can be reflected in all the templates simultaneously. The templates must be rebuilt for the changes to appear. Each template can be like a big observer of the RDF fact data.

This feature of templates is very powerful and useful. It allows multiple views of a set of data to be displayed at the same time, and all are kept up to date. This is particularly useful for applications that use a desktop metaphor. Examples are design tools and Integrated Development Environments (IDEs). These applications have power users who appreciate being able to visualize the data they work with in several different ways. This is also used in the Classic Mozilla/Netscape browser suites, in the bookmarks system, address book, and elsewhere.

To see this coordination at work, perform the following test:

1. Start the Classic Brower so that a Navigator window appears.
2. Make sure that the Personal Toolbar and Navigation Toolbar both appear (View | Show/Hide).
3. Create a bookmark on the Personal Toolbar by dragging any URL onto that toolbar (drag the bookmark icon to the left of the Location textbox).
4. Display the Bookmark Manager window (Bookmarks | Manage Bookmarks).
5. Make sure that the new bookmark is visible in both the Bookmark Manager and the Personal Toolbar at the same time.
6. In the manager, delete the new bookmark by selecting it and choosing Delete from the right-click context menu.
7. The new bookmark disappears from both the toolbar and manager at the same time.

The Bookmark Manager window contains a template based on a <tree> tag. The Personal Toolbar contains a template based on a <toolbar> tag. The Delete menu item runs a script that deletes the facts that hold information for the new bookmark. That script then causes both templates to rebuild themselves. The piece of content associated with those deleted facts (a <treeitem> in one case, and a <toolbarbutton> in the other) disappears everywhere as a result.

14.2.3 JavaScript Access

The template system adds objects to the AOM of the XUL document. The template system also uses a number of XPCOM components and interfaces, particularly RDF ones. These can be manipulated from JavaScript. JavaScript can perform any of the following tasks:

- ☞ Use the `database` AOM object property to manipulate facts and the sources of the RDF data used by the template.
- ☞ Use the `builder` AOM object property to control the template build process.
- ☞ Create a custom view for a template.
- ☞ Fill a template with facts when it has none to start with.
- ☞ Add observers to the template system.
- ☞ Control sorting of `<tree>`- and `<listbox>`-based templates.
- ☞ Use the DOM 1 standards to modify template tags (occasionally done) and template-generated tags (unwise).

These tasks are all described under "Scripting" in this chapter. These tasks often require working with the XPCOM components that support RDF. Those RDF components are discussed in Chapter 16, XPCOM Objects.

14.2.4 The Data Source Issue

A final technical aspect of templates is *data sources.*

The RDF data that templates use can come from an ordinary RDF document or from a preexisting source inside the Mozilla Platform. In both cases, an object called a data source sits between the template processing code and the true origin of the RDF facts.

Mozilla templates can draw facts from more than one data source at a time. This means that facts from several RDF files (for example) can contribute to the content generated by a single template. There is a many-to-many relationship between data sources and templates.

Data sources are discussed extensively in Chapter 16, XPCOM Objects. Here we simply note that the choice of data source for a template is absolutely critical. If the wrong data source is chosen, very little will work. Know your data sources.

Here is a brief overview of the main points. Each template has a composite data source. To work on the template's data source from a script, it is often necessary to find and use one of the data sources that contribute to the composite data source. Such a data source gives the programmer access to the fact store containing the RDF facts of that source. In principle, a full range of database-like operations is possible. In practice, only the data sources associated with RDF files and with the bookmark system are highly useful. The bookmark system has the drawback that it is cryptic. Of the other internal data sources, some are easily read and some are not. The `rdf:null` data source is a convenient choice when the programmer wants to start with an empty set of facts and fill it by hand. It is often used when a custom view is built.

The scripting topic in this chapter describes some of the common template manipulations that require data sources. Chapter 16, XPCOM Objects, is also recommended.

14.3 TEMPLATE CONSTRUCTION

This discussion explains how templates are put together, and describes the individual tags. The overall composition of a template is shown in Listing 14.8, which is pseudo-code, not pure XUL:

Listing 14.8 Basic containment hierarchy for template tags.

```
<top>
  <stuff/>
    <template>
      <rule>
        ... simple or extended rule info goes here ...
      </rule>
      ... zero or more further <rule> tags go here ...
    </template>
  <stuff/>
</top>
```

The tag named <top> can be any ordinary XUL tag—<top> is not a special tag. Although the template proper starts with the <template> tag, some attributes specific to templates must also be added to the <top> tag. Other XUL content can precede, follow, or surround the <top> tag, whatever it is. Typical candidates for <top> are <tree>, <toolbar>, <menulist>, and <listbox>, but <top> could be a <box> or even a <button>.

The tags named <stuff> can also be any ordinary XUL tag—<stuff> is not a special tag. These tags are optional and can be repeated and nested as much as required. The tags between <top> and <template> are copied and generated only once for each template, and they are all displayed before the template content, even if they appear after the <template> tag in the XUL.

The <template> tag is a real XUL tag. Any content within this tag is generated once per query solution found. The <template> tag surrounds all content that might be repeated.

The <rule> tag is a real XUL tag. It is the only content allowed inside <template>. There can be one or more rule tags, and there is a shorthand notation that allows for zero rule tags. Each rule tag is one template query, as described under "Query Lists" earlier. Each rule tag also holds content. This content is duplicated each time a solution for the rule query is found.

The template system has several different syntaxes for the content of the <rule> tag.

The most flexible and powerful syntax is the *extended template syntax*. This syntax requires that template query variables be defined in one spot and then applied later in another spot. This system uses variables called *extended template variables*. The extended syntax requires that each <rule> contain a set of specialist template tags as part of its content.

A convenient and short syntax is the *simple template syntax*. This syntax is designed for the special but common case where the query is looking through an RDF container for data. The "hello, world" example in Listings 14.6 and 14.7 uses this syntax. This syntax uses variables called *simple template variables*. The simple syntax requires that each `<rule>` contain only plain XUL content. That content might contain simple template variables. The simple system generates that content when a query solution is found, replacing the variables with fact data in the process.

If a template has only one rule, then the simple syntax has a shorthand version. The `<rule>` and `</rule>` tags can be left out. This shorthand version is otherwise the same as the simple syntax.

See the `<rule>` tag for more detail on rules.

14.3.1 Special XUL Names

The XUL template system uses a number of special literal values. Template variables are used nowhere except inside the `<template>` tag.

14.3.1.1 Extended Template Variables Mozilla's extended template variables are the variables used to create single fact queries and flexible multifact RDF queries. Such variables always appear inside XML strings.

Extended template variables start with a question mark ("?") and can contain any character. They are case-sensitive. They end with either a space (" ") or a caret or circumflex ("^") or by the termination of the string that they are embedded in. The space or caret is not part of the variable name. If a space is detected, it is left as the first nonvariable name piece of content. If a caret is detected, it is silently consumed, and has no further role.

The following ordinary names are identical. The third example has an XML character entity reference for space.

```
"?name " "?name^" "?name&#x20;"
```

These further names are also valid variable names. Meaningful names are always recommended over unreadable names, though.

```
"?name_two" "?nameThree" "?name-four" "?name66" "?66name" "?$%@$z+"
```

14.3.1.2 Simple Template Variables The simple template notation for rules (see "`<rule>`") has its own "variables." These variables are really just the URIs of fact predicates. Such variables always appear inside XML strings.

Simple template variables have the format:

```
rdf:URI
```

Such variables end with either a space (" ") or a caret ("^"), or by the termination of the string they are embedded in. The space or caret is not part of the variable. If a space is detected, it is left as the first nonvariable piece of content. If a caret is detected, it is silently consumed, and has no further role.

The URI part of a simple template variable should be a valid URI. If it is to be processed meaningfully, it should be constructed to suit the context in which it is used.

Examples of meaningful URIs are

```
"rdf:urn:test:example:more"
"rdf:http://www.test.com/Test#Data"
```

14.3.1.3 Variable Interpolation Both extended and simple variables are used only inside XML attribute values. In the content part of a template rule, variable names are replaced with content when content is generated.

If a rule's query finds a solution, content generation will follow. When that happens, variable names are simply replaced with their values in the strings they contain. If the variable name has no ground value as a result of the query (possible if a `<binding>` tag is used), then it is replaced with a zero-length string.

14.3.1.4 Special URIs and Namespaces The template system uses a few special URIs and namespaces. The URI scheme `rdf` is used to represent RDF data that originates from inside the Mozilla Platform itself. The currently implemented URIs in this scheme are

```
rdf:addressdirectory rdf:bookmarks rdf:charset-menu
rdf:files rdf:history rdf:httpindex rdf:internetsearch
rdf:ispdefaults rdf:local-store rdf:localsearch
rdf:mailnewsfolders rdf:msgaccountmanager
rdf:msgfilters rdf:smtp rdf:subscribe
rdf:window-mediator
```

There are two special values for this `rdf` URI scheme. The URI

```
rdf:null
```

means use a data source that contains zero facts. Such a data source usually has facts added later via JavaScript. The URI

```
rdf:*
```

is Mozilla-specific notation that means "match any and all predicates." The use of asterisk ("`*`") is inspired by the use of asterisks in CSS2—in CSS2, * also means "match all." This URI should be seen as a special case of a simple template variable. It does not identify one fixed resource. There is also an old notation for this special URI:

```
...
```

This notation is identical to the ellipses (three dots) character, except that it consists of three separate, single, full-stops (periods). This old notation means the same thing as `rdf:*`, but it should not be used any more.

Table 11.3 lists a set of XML namespaces that Mozilla uses for the RDF facts managed by the platform. If templates use Mozilla-internal data sources, then these namespaces can be used to identify predicates/properties within those data sources.

It is common in XML to use the xmlns attribute to provide a shorthand alias for a long namespace URL. Within the template system, in nearly all cases, the full URL, not an alias, must be used. This is not a consequence of any XML standard; it is just the way the Mozilla Platform works. XML namespaces do not perform alias substitution inside attribute values, so there is no help from XML itself. That leaves detection of those names up to the platform. Mozilla does not know how to detect or expand xmlns aliases or relative URLs inside an attribute value, so full URLs are required. The only place where an xmlns alias can be used is as an attribute of the <rule> tag. In that case, the alias is used in the attribute name, not in the attribute's value, where it is handled by standard XML parsing.

14.3.2 The Base Tag

The topmost template tag is the parent tag of a <template> tag. It is called the base tag of the template. It is an ordinary XUL tag like <tree> or <box>. This tag must carry part of the template configuration information if the template is to work.

The special attributes that can be added to such a topmost tag are

```
datasources flags coalesceduplicatearcs allownegativeassertions
    xulcontentgenerated ref containment
```

The datasources attribute states what RDF data are to be used in the template. It is a space-separated list of RDF file names like test.rdf, and named data sources like rdf:bookmarks.

Because the datasources attribute takes one or more arguments, it is always a composite data source (with interface nsIRDFCompositeDataSource).

If the XUL document is installed in the chrome, or is otherwise secure, then the internal data source rdf:local-store is automatically added to the start of the data sources list. This data source adds the current user profile's localstore.rdf configuration information. This is important because it is common to work on the data sources of a template from a script, and so the application programmer must remember that this data source is present.

The flags attribute is used to optimize the performance of the template query process. It applies only to recursive queries and accepts a space-separated list of keywords. Two keywords are currently supported:

- dont-build-content. This keyword is specific to tree-based templates. It tells the standard template builder to drop responsibility for sending generated content to the display. Instead, the tree builder is responsible for that. The template-building system still generates RDF-based content, but it acts as a view that the tree builder uses. Chapter 13, Listboxes and Trees, describes the different builders. The benefit of this system is that generating content is put off until it needs to be displayed.

This is efficient for systems where generating content is expensive, such as querying a directory server. It also prevents the template system from "flashing" content to the screen once before the query has generated its own content.

☞ `dont-test-empty`. This keyword tells the query processor not to examine containers to see if they are empty. This is a performance optimization that saves doing a test that can be expensive. It also allows the template system to handle specialized hierarchical data where testing for empty is impossible. Dynamic network discovery is a practical case where such a situation might exist. In that field, it is impossible to answer the question: "Is the number of network elements out there zero?" It is impossible because the code must wait forever to be sure that no answer arrives. `dont-test-empty` is a good choice for templates based on the `rdf:null` data source.

`coalesceduplicatearcs`, `allownegativeassertions`, and `xulcontentgenerated` are also performance tweaks and further modify how queries work.

☞ The `coalesceduplicatearcs` attribute, when set, affects the facts that can be extracted from a template's set of data sources. Most flaglike attributes in Mozilla are set to `true` when specified, but this attribute is set to `false`. It affects JavaScript access to facts, not the results of template queries. If this attribute is not set, identical facts inside the template's data sources will be reported only once, not once for each copy. If it is set to `false`, then all facts are reported, duplicate or not. Template data sources go faster if this attribute is set.

☞ The `allownegativeassertions` attribute, when set, also affects the facts that can be extracted from a template's set of data sources. Most flaglike attributes in Mozilla are set to `true` when used, but this attribute can also be set to `false`. It also affects JavaScript access to facts, not the results of template queries. If this attribute is not set, a fact that is stated (*asserted*) both positively and negatively will never be reported because the two facts cancel each other out. RDF documents contain only positively asserted facts. Negatively asserted facts can be made using JavaScript only. If this attribute is set, no cancelation is done, and all facts are reported. Template data sources go faster if this fact is set.

The `xulcontentgenerated` attribute is applied to any content tag in the template, or any generated content tag produced by the template. It is listed here because it is also a performance optimization. Experiment with this attribute only after you have a full understanding of templates.

☞ The `xulcontentgenerated` attribute can be set to `true`. It affects when template query and content generation occur. If a template does lazy building, then at any time, some of the possible content will be generated and some may not. If a DOM operation (like adding a child tag) were attempted on a tag with incomplete lazy content, confusion could result. Where would such a child tag be put when the final set of children is yet to be determined by the query? Mozilla handles this by forcing the template to build that tag's children completely before starting the DOM operation. The `xulcontentgenerated` attribute is a programmer-supplied hint that advises there is nothing to rebuild at this point in the XML tree. This speeds up DOM operations and saves unnecessary processing.

The `ref` attribute states the starting point for the template query. It holds the full URI of a fact subject. That subject should be the name of an RDF `<Seq>`, `<Alt>`, or `<Bag>` container.

`ref` and `containment` are also discussed in the following subtopic.

14.3.2.1 `ref` and `containment`: Container Tests The `ref` and `containment` attributes can be used to specify a starting point for a template query that doesn't use an official RDF container tag. This is useful for plain RDF facts that form a simple hierarchy but that don't use `<Seq>`, `<Bag>`, or `<Alt>`. Such pretend containers require a little explanation.

Consider a normal RDF container. An example is shown in Listing 14.9.

Listing 14.9 RDF container fragment equal to three facts.

```
<Description about="urn:eg:ownerA">
  <prop1>
    <Seq about="urn:eg:ContainerA">
      <li>
        <Description about="urn:eg:item1" prop2="blue"/>
      </li>
    </Seq>
  </prop1>
</Description>
```

The predicates in this example are deliberately kept simple. Listing 14.9 is equivalent to three facts:

```
<- urn:eg:ownerA,      prop1,  urn:eg:containerA ->
<- urn:eg:containerA, rdf:_1, urn:eg:item1 ->
<- urn:eg:item1,       prop2,  blue ->
```

The first fact has the RDF container as its subject. This is the fact that "owns" the container. The second fact states that `item1` is a member of the container. The third fact records some useful color information about `item1`. This is all normal RDF. These three facts result directly from the `<Seq>` syntax in Listing 14.9.

Suppose that a program was presented with these three facts rather than with the RDF markup. How could it tell if a container were present? In this simple example, detecting the predicate `rdf:_1` is enough to tell that containerA is an RDF container. Inside Mozilla, a different test is used (involving the `rdf:instanceOf` predicate), but in this example, testing for `rdf:_1` will do.

Now suppose that a single change is made to these three facts. Suppose that the predicate `rdf:_1` is changed to `rdf:member` (or anything else). Then the three facts would be

```
<- urn:eg:ownerA,      prop1,  urn:eg:containerA ->
<- urn:eg:containerA, rdf:member, urn:eg:item1 ->
<- urn:eg:item1,       prop2,  blue ->
```

Listing 14.10 shows an RDF fragment that could produce these slightly different facts. This fragment is just a series of nested facts.

Listing 14.10 RDF non-container fragment equal to three facts.

```
<Description about="urn:eg:ownerA">
  <prop1>
    <Description about="urn:eg:ContainerA">
      <rdf:member>
        <Description about="urn:eg:item1" prop2="blue"/>
      </rdf:member>
    </Description>
  </prop1>
</Description>
```

Is there still a container in these three facts? After all, the three facts are very similar in both before and after cases. Purists would argue that the answer is *No*. Mozilla says that the answer is *Maybe*.

It is easy to argue that a container does exists. First, the organization of the three facts hasn't changed. Second, the choice of `rdf:member` as a predicate suggests that `item1` belongs to *something*. Third, any query built for a `<Seq>` tag might work just as well with the new predicate as it did with the old.

The point is this: When RDF markup is boiled down to simple facts, whether containers exist or not is just a matter of opinion. It is easy to create an RDF document with no RDF container tags, but still think of containers as being present. There is no reason why Mozilla should work with one arrangement but not with the other. Mozilla and templates work with both arrangements.

That brings us back to the `ref` attribute. It can be set to "`urn:eg:ContainerA`", and that resource will be used as a starting point for a template query, regardless of whether the original RDF looks like Listing 14.9 or 14.10. An RDF `<Seq>`, `<Bag>`, or `<Alt>` is not necessary.

There is one catch to this flexible use of `ref`. Mozilla must still determine whether the `ref` URI can act like a container. By default, there are three ways that the `ref` URI can pass this test:

1. The URI is a `<Seq>`, `<Bag>`, or `<Alt>` tag's `about` value.

2. A fact exists with `ref` as subject and `http://home.netscape.com/NC-rdf#child` as predicate.
3. A fact exists with `ref` as subject and `http://home.netscape.com/NC-rdf#Folder` as predicate.

These tests are the Mozilla equivalent of testing for `rdf:_1`.

If you don't want to use the `child` or `Folder` predicates in your facts, then you don't need to. You can use your own predicate. To do that, create the RDF content as you see fit, and in the XUL template code, add the `containment` attribute to the template's base tag.

The `containment` attribute can be set to a space-separated list of predicates. These predicates will be added to the list of container tests. These predicates will be tested for just like the items in the preceding list. For example, setting

```
containment="http://www.test.com/Test#member"
```

means that the RDF `<Description>` tag in this code will be considered a container by Mozilla, provided that `xmlns:Test="http://www.test.com/Test#"` is declared somewhere:

```
<Description about="urn:foo:bar">
  <Test:member resource="urn:foo:bar:item1"/>
<Description>
```

In summary, template queries work even if official RDF container tags aren't present, but in that case, you must tell the template system what predicates are used to implement the unofficial container.

14.3.2.2 Attributes Specific to `<tree>` If the `<tree>` tag is used for a template, then some extra attributes apply:

```
flex="1" statedatasource flags="dont-build-content"
```

Trees do not have a default height. If a `<tree>` template does not have `flex="1"`, the template content often does not appear. Always use `flex="1"` on a `<tree>` template.

The `statedatasource` attribute is set to a named data source that is used to store the current state of the displayed tree. If the user has opened or closed a number of subtrees in the display, then information about which subtrees are open or closed will be persisted to the nominated data source. Currently, this is used only in the Classic Mail & News client, in the pane where the Mail and Newsgroup folders are listed.

If `statedatasource` is not set, then the data source named in the `datasources` attribute is used instead.

The "`dont-build-content`" value for the `flags` attribute is also tree-specific. It is described under "The Base Tag."

14.3.2.3 Sort Support for `<template>` Siblings

The template system allows a column of data to be sorted. This feature works with XUL menus, listboxes, and trees.

The sorting process uses several attributes. These can be set either on the base tag of the template or on an individual `<listcol>` or `<treecol>` tag. These attributes are

```
resource resource2 sortActive sortDirection sortResource
     sortResource2
```

- `resource` holds a template variable. This attribute is set by the XUL document author on the column to be sorted. The data that are used for the sort key is specified by this attribute. The template variable it names represents a fact predicate/property associated with each row's solution to the template query. The data used as the sort key are the object/value of that predicate. In other words, this attribute specifies a property whose value per-row is to be sorted.
- `sort` is an alternate syntax for resource. It is also used to detect the sort column in a tree or listbox. Use `resource` and `sortActive` instead of this attribute.
- `resource2` is a secondary predicate for the sorting system. The sort performed on the resource values is not a stable sort. This means that after sorting, a secondary column of information might be very disordered. The `resource2` attribute causes a second column to be sorted if values in the primary column are equal. A third or subsequent column may still be disordered.
- `sortActive` can be set to `true` and indicates whether the data are currently sorted. Mozilla automatically sets this attribute on the specific column and on the tree or listbox. It can be set by the application programmer as well. It is also used to detect the column to be sorted, so it should always be set if `sort` is not set.
- `sortDirection` may be set to `ascending`, `descending`, or `natural`. This attribute may be set by the XUL document author or automatically by Mozilla after a sort. Mozilla will set it on both the specific column sorted and on the base tag.
- `sortResource` and `sortResource2` are the same as `resource` and `resource2`. Mozilla sets these attributes. The secondary sort criteria can be specified by the application programmer using JavaScript, but not directly using XUL.
- `sortSeparators` can be set to `true`. If that is done, then special processing occurs for bookmarks. A sort will not move an item across a bookmark separator if this attribute is set and the `rdf:bookmarks` data source is used.

14.3.3 <template>

The <template> tag holds all the details of a template that are not specified in the base tag. It holds a set of rules, each of which is a query-content pair. The <template> tag has no special attributes of its own. The only tag that the <template> tag can hold is the <rule> tag. It can have any number of <rule> tags as children.

If no <rule> tags appear in the template, but other content does, then the content is assumed to be the content of a single rule that uses the simple-rule syntax.

A <template> tag can contain simple and extended rules.

14.3.4 <rule>

The <rule> tag defines a single template query and the content that is generated to pretty-print the results of the query. A set of <rule> tags makes a query list, so the first <rule> in the list that is satisfied by a set of facts will pretty-print the template variables ground to those facts.

A rule can be expressed in either simple syntax or in extended syntax. If the first child tag of the <rule> tag is a <conditions> tag, then the rule is in extended syntax. In all other cases, simple syntax applies. A <rule> tag may be a singleton tag with no content.

14.3.4.1 The Standard Fact Arrangement All simple syntax queries and many extended syntax queries rely on the facts in an RDF file being arranged a particular way. This arrangement is used repeatedly. It is the case where the RDF data has a three-step, two-fact arrangement. These steps consist of a container term, its item terms, and their property-value terms. Listings 14.1 and 14.2 and the accompanying discussion gives an example of this arrangement.

This standard arrangement also has an equivalent in JavaScript:

```
var container = {item1:{p1:v1,p2:v2}, item2:{p1:v1,p3:v3} }
```

In this literal, container collects two items. item1 and item2 are objects, each with a set of properties pN. Each property has a value vN. There can be any number of items, each with any number of properties. The whole point of this structure is just to make a set of objects and their interesting properties easy to get at. In RDF, Listings 14.2, 14.5, 14.7, and 14.9 are all correct examples of this structure. An RDF equivalent to this JavaScript is shown in Listing 14.11.

Listing 14.11 Required RDF structure for an RDF rule using simple syntax.

```
<Seq about="container">
  <li resource="item1"/>
  <li resource="item2"/>
</Seq>
<Description about="item1" p1="v1" p2="v2"/>
<Description about="item2" p1="v1" p3="v3"/>
```

To make the RDF syntax neat, the `<Seq>` tag is usually wrapped up inside a `<Description>` tag, not shown in Listing 14.11. RDF has flexible syntax, and there are several other ways of expressing this same structure. Also, `<Seq>` can be replaced with `<Bag>` or `<Alt>`. A `<Description>` tag that acts like a container can be used instead.

All facts processed with simple syntax queries must have this standard arrangement.

14.3.4.2 Simple Syntax for <rule> The simple rule syntax has no special-purpose tags.

All the content of the `<rule>` tag is generated each time the rule's query finds a solution. The content of the `<rule>` tag can contain simple template variables embedded in any XML attribute value. The content is generated out as for the `<action>` tag, except for two minor differences: The simple syntax requires that the `uri` attribute be set to `rdf:*`, and the simple syntax cannot use the `<textnode>` tag.

When simple syntax is used, the `<rule>` tag has several special attributes:

```
type iscontainer isempty predicate="object" parsetype
```

All these attributes determine whether the rule's query will be successful. Part of the rule's query comes from the assumption that the RDF facts are in the standard fact arrangement. These attributes make up the rest of the query.

The `type` attribute comes from the official RDF XML namespace `http://www.w3.org/1999/02/22-rdf-syntax-ns#`. It is usually quoted as `rdf:type`, with that namespace included somewhere in the XUL document using `xmlns`. `rdf:type` can be set to a full predicate name, such as `http://home.netscape.com/NC-rdf#version`. This attribute is used to test for the existence of a predicate. `rdf:type` therefore tests to see if any objects in the container have a given property. If they don't, the rule fails for that query solution candidate.

The `iscontainer` attribute can be set to `true` or to `false`. The default is don't care., which cannot be set explicitly. It tests to see if a given fact subject is a container, using the container tests described earlier under "`ref` and `containment`: Container Tests." If the test fails, the rule fails for that query solution candidate.

The `isempty` attribute can be set to `true` or to `false`. The default is don't care, which cannot be set explicitly. It tests to see if a given URI has any kind of content. In the `true` case, it tests to see if container-like URIs have any contained items, or if item-like URIs have no properties. If the test fails, the rule fails for that query solution candidate.

The *`predicate="object"`* attribute stands for any pair of predicate and object names. Because predicate names are often long, they are usually shortened by adding an `xmlns` declaration at the top of the XUL document. If that is done, then a *`predicate="object"`* pair like

```
NC:version="0.1"
```

will test whether a fact exists with a version predicate in the NC namespace (perhaps `http://home.netscape.com/NC-rdf#`) and whether it has an object literal of "`0.1`"—in other words, whether an object in the container has a version property set to "`0.1`". The following reserved names cannot be used for the predicate part because they have other uses:

```
property instanceOf id parsetype
```

These three attributes, plus any number of *`predicate="object"`* tests, can be stated in the one `<rule>` tag. They are boolean ANDed together and make up all the query of the rule. If none of these attributes is present, then every fact in the container is a solution to the rule's query. If any of these attributes is present, then the rule fails for a given solution candidate if any of these attributes does *not* match.

The final attribute, `parsetype`, can be set to `Integer`. If this is done, all *`predicate="object"`* pairs in the `<rule>` tag will have their object part interpreted as an integer during the query. Any values that are not integers will cause the whole rule to be ignored. If this attribute is not used, all such parts will have their object part treated as a string. The query system has no support for integer mathematics like addition. It just performs comparisons on a string or integer basis.

The query of a simple rule can usually be expressed as an extended rule. Listing 14.12 is an example of simple syntax that uses several of the special attributes:

Listing 14.12 Simple template query showing all options.

```
<rule iscontainer="true"
      isempty="false"
      rdf:type="http://home.netscape.com/NC-rdf#version"
      NC:title="History"
>
```

The equivalent extended syntax rule is shown in Listing 14.13.

Listing 14.13 Simple template query showing all options.

```
<rule>
  <conditions>
    <content uri="?uri"/>
    <member container="?uri" child="?item"/>
    <triple subject="?item
            predicate="http://home.netscape.com/NC-rdf#version"
            object="?version"/>
    <triple subject="?item"
            predicate="http://home.netscape.com/NC-rdf#title"
            object="History"/>
  </conditions>
```

The extended syntax can do everything the simple syntax can do, except for the options `iscontainer="false"` and `isempty="true"` (the opposites of the preceding example). These two options are not possible in the extended syntax. The extended syntax can check for the existence of facts but not for the absence of facts. These simple tests can still be done with extended syntax by stating two rules instead of just one. The first rule tests for particular facts, but generates no content; the second rule catches the remaining cases, where that content is missing, and generates whatever content is required.

14.3.4.3 Extended Syntax for `<rule>` When extended rule syntax is used, the `<rule>` tag has no special attributes. This syntax is the most flexible and powerful template syntax. "Common Query Patterns" later in this chapter provides recipes for most common uses. This topic covers the syntax options.

The extended rule syntax consists of a `<rule>` tag with two or three immediate children. The `<conditions>` tag must be the first child and contains the query of the rule. The `<bindings>` tag is the optional middle child and allows extra variables to be created. The `<action>` tag holds the content to generate each time the query finds a solution. These tags are described under their individual headings.

The extended rule syntax uses extended syntax variables, and these variables may be used in siblings of the `<template>` tag. A common use is to put them in the column definition tags of listboxes and trees.

If the query is recursive, then only the `<conditions>` part of the rule dictates the recursive behavior.

14.3.5 `<conditions>`

The `<conditions>` tag contains a template query described using the extended template syntax. This tag has no special attributes of its own. If it is present, it must be the first child tag of `<rule>`. The recursive nature of a recursive query is fully specified by the content of the `<conditions>` tag.

This tag can contain `<content>`, `<triple>` and `<member>` tags. Its first child must be a `<content>` tag, and there can be only one `<content>` tag per condition. The `<conditions>` tag must also contain at least one `<member>` or `<triple>` tag.

The `<conditions>` tag can also contain a `<treeitem>` tag. If the template is based on a `<tree>` tag, then `<treeitem>` may be used instead of `<content>`. In that case, it is written and acts exactly the same as a `<content>` tag. There is no special reason for this variation; it is just a leftover requirement from the early days of templates. `<treeitem>` is deprecated in favour of `<content>`, but for older versions `<treeitem>` must be used if the template is based on a `<tree>`.

When these tags are used, their order should be the same as the drill-down order used by the template query processor. That order is also the same as the hierarchical arrangement of the facts being examined.

14.3.5.1 <content> The <content> tag must be the first child of the <conditions> tag. It has only one special template attribute:

```
uri
```

This attribute is set to an extended template variable. That variable is then ground to the value supplied to the `ref` attribute in the template's base tag. That value is the starting point for the rule's query. If the query is recursive, the `uri` attribute of the parent query is used instead of `ref`. The <content> tag always has the same form, so by convention it is usually written exactly like this:

```
<content uri="?uri"/>
```

The `uri` attribute is also used on tags that are children of the <action> tag. The variable used in the <content> tag's `uri` attribute must *never* be used as the value of `uri` attributes appearing inside <action> content. If it is used in that way, no solutions to the template query will be found, and no content will be generated. The variable used in the <content> tag's `uri` attribute may appear elsewhere in the <action> tag's content.

If the template is based on a tree, then for versions less than 1.5, the <treeitem> tag is used instead, exactly like this:

```
<treeitem uri="?uri"/>
```

The <treeitem> tag can also be part of the generated content. In that case, it can also appear in the <action> tag, but any `uri` attribute must have a variable different from `?uri` as its value.

14.3.5.2 <triple> The <triple> tag represents one hop (one RDF arc) in the query process. Each <triple> tag used increases the number of hops by one, and increases the number of facts required for a solution by one. The <triple> tag is used to link facts using variables and to select facts.

The triple tag has the following special attributes, which must always be present:

```
subject predicate object
```

- `subject` may be set to an extended template variable or a URI.
- `predicate` must be set to a URI that is a property/predicate name.
- `object` may be set to an extended template variable, a URI, or a literal value.

Variables may not be used in the `predicate` attribute.

It is possible to construct a set of <triple> tags that drills down into the RDF facts and then drills back up somewhere else. It is also possible to construct a set of <triple> tags that create a cycle. Neither of these things are handled correctly in Mozilla. A <triple> tag with zero variables is useless.

14.3.5.3 `<member>` The <member> tag is used to find the contained items of a container tag. It has the special attributes

```
container child
```

The container attribute is the URI of the container tag. The child attribute will be matched to the object of facts that have the container URI as their subject. In all uses of this tag, both attributes are present, and both are set to extended template variables, like so:

```
<member container="?uri" child="?item"/>
```

Because the containment relationship inside an RDF container is just a single fact (with `rdf:_1` and so on as the predicate), an ordinary `<triple>` tag can also be used to find these contained items. The <member> tag is just a specialized version of the `<triple>` tag.

The advantage <member> has over the `<triple>` tag is that no predicate needs to be supplied. The <member> tag is free to apply a container test using the several predicate possibilities described earlier under "`Ref` and `containment:` Container Tests." To do the same job with the `<triple>` tag would require a separate query that hard-coded each URI that can be used as a container test URI.

Although the `container` attribute for a <member> tag often holds the URI starting point of the query, it can be any URI or extended syntax variable used in the query.

14.3.6 `<bindings>`

The `<bindings>` tag is the optional part of an extended syntax query. It has no special attributes of its own and can contain only `<binding>` tags. `<bindings>` and `<binding>` appear elsewhere in Mozilla, particularly in XBL. There is no connection between any other use and the template use. Explained in SQL terms, this part of an extended query provides support for outer joins and null values.

The `<bindings>` tag might better be called the `<extra-groundings>` tag, since there are no bindings in the XBL (or XPConnect or IDL or XPIDL) senses. A *binding variable* is just an additional variable that may be ground by a given query. The same meaning applies to the `<binding>` tag.

The `<bindings>` section of the rule is where extra variables can be set without further restricting the results of the `<conditions>` query. This is done very simply. In the `<conditions>` section, all variables must be ground if a solution to the query is to be found. Such a solution is passed to the bindings section. The query processor also tries to ground all the variables stated in the `<bindings>` section. If only some of the extra variables can be ground, then the processor just gives up and sets the rest to the empty string. This means that the `<conditions>` solution is never rejected by the `<bindings>` section. In effect, the `<bindings>` section is similar to an RDBMS outer join—if something matches, it is reported; otherwise, you get the rest of the query's matched data only.

The variables in the <bindings> section must all be extended template variables. Variables from the <conditions> section may be reused here, but the reverse is not possible. For the <bindings> section to make any sense, at least one variable from the <conditions> section must be used.

14.3.6.1 <binding> The <binding> tag is identical to the <triple> tag in attributes and in purpose. It differs from <triple> only in the rules used to ground its variables, as noted under <bindings>.

14.3.7 <action> and Simple Syntax Content

The <action> tag is used in a <rule> using the extended query syntax. It provides the content that is generated for each query result. The content of simple syntax <rule> tags is generated the same way as <action> content is. That generation system is described here.

The content of an <action> tag consists of ordinary XUL content with embedded extended query variables. The template system substitutes a value for every variable when generating content. Therefore, variables are used in the <action> content, whereas they are defined and ground in the <conditions> content (they are automatically defined and ground for simple syntax queries). The template system also adds an id attribute to one tag each time content is generated.

The content of <action> cannot include a <script> tag.

The content of the <action> tag should be organized as shown in Listing 14.14.

Listing 14.14 Example <action> content hierarchy.

```
<action>                    // simple syntax: <rule>
  <box id="A">
    <box id="B">
      <box id="C" uri="?var"> // simple syntax: uri="rdf:*"
        <box id="D"/>
        <box id="E">
          <box id="F"/>
        </box>
      </box>
    </box>
  </box>
</action>
```

This example is used to explain what works and how it works. In the general case, tags may be nested to arbitrary depth within <action>, and any ordinary XUL tag may be used. The special case of <tree>-based templates is discussed separately.

The content of <action> is divided into the tag containing the uri attribute, that tag's ancestor tags, and that tag's descendant tags. In Listing 14.14, C contains uri; A and B are ancestors; and D, E, and F are children.

Ancestor tags A and B are normally generated as content just once, no matter how many solutions the query finds. If template variables (extended ones for <action> content, simple ones for <rule> content) are used in A or B, then they will have the value of the first solution found by the template. If tags A or B have sibling tags, those siblings may not be generated reliably. It is recommended that such sibling tags be avoided.

Tag C is the start of the repeated content because it contains the uri attribute. Both tag C and all its content will be generated as a unit zero or more times. There are two triggers required before the content will be repeated once. First, a solution must be found to the query. Second, the value of the uri attribute on tag C must be different in that new solution. The easiest way to ensure this is to set that value to a variable quoted in the object of some tuple. One example is the child part of a <member> tag: Use ?item in this case:

```
<member container="?seq" child="?item"/>
```

In the most general case, the uri attribute should therefore be set to a subject or object that is different for every solution found by the query. This unique value is put into the id attribute of each generated copy of tag C during generation. Tag C should not have sibling tags; those sibling tags may not be generated reliably. It is recommended that such sibling tags be avoided.

If lazy building is required, then tag C must be one of these XUL tags:

```
<menu> <menulist> <menubutton> <toolbarbutton> <button> <treeitem>
```

Tags D, E, and F are ordinary content tags that are generated once per query solution. They may have siblings or extensive content of their own. If these tags contain template variables, those variables will be substituted in for each query solution found.

14.3.7.1 Content for <tree>-Based Templates Content for <tree>-based templates can break the rule that ancestor tags of the uri tag are generated only once.

If a template is based on a <tree> tag, then each <treeitem> in the final tree might have a <treechildren> tag as its second child tag. That tag could contain any number of subtree tags for that item. Fortunately, the content held in <action> need only represent a single tree row. The template content builder that processes <tree> templates is intelligent enough to duplicate this content for subtrees. In other words, it is smart enough to detect the need for recursive queries. The <action> content must be constructed carefully if this arrangement is to work. Listing 14.15 shows the correct construction.

Listing 14.15 Example <action> content hierarchy for a <tree> template.

```
<action>                    //simple syntax: use <rule>
  <treechildren>
```

```
    <treeitem uri="?var">   //simple syntax: use uri="rdf:*"
      <treerow>
        ... any normal treerow content ...
      </treerow>
    </treeitem>
  </treechildren>
</action>
```

All the tags in this arrangement can have attributes added. An id should not be added to the <treeitem> tag. The ?var variable usually matches a variable for the object of a <member> or <triple> tag.

It is possible to vary this syntax a little, and even to nest templates inside other templates—for example, so that a <treeitem> comes from one RDF source but its <treechildren> sibling tag comes from another. Such nested syntax needs to be explored carefully because it is not widely used or tested.

Tree-based templates use recursive queries. For each recursion of the query deeper into the tree of facts, the <action> content above the uri tag is duplicated. This means one further copy of the <treechildren> tag stated in Listing 14.15. This new copy is then the starting point for all the solutions found by that new query.

14.3.7.2 <textnode> Simple and extended template variables can appear in XML attributes' values only. Some XUL tags generate content from text between their start and end tags, like <Description>.

The <textnode> tag provides a way to put variables in plain, non-attribute content. Suppose that the variable ?var contains the string "red" at some point. The line

```
<tag><textnode value="big ?var truck"/></tag>
```

is the same as the line

```
<tag>big red truck</tag>
```

<textnode> can be placed anywhere inside the <action> tag. <textnode> cannot be used in templates that have the simple query syntax.

<textnode> concludes the discussion of XUL template tags.

14.4 Common Query Patterns

Here are many of the common queries used in templates.

14.4.1 Containers

The most obvious template queries exploit the standard fact arrangement, and that means using an RDF container. The simple query syntax supports this arrangement.

14.4.2 Single-Fact Queries

Single-fact queries (see the prior discussion) can be specified using the extended query syntax only; they cannot be specified using the simple query syntax. A single-fact query may return zero or more solutions. The only unknown that can be queried for is the object of the single fact. The subject and predicate must be known in advance and hard-coded in the query.

Such a query can be implemented with either a `<member>` or a `<triple>` tag. The `<member>` variation is

```
<rule>
  <conditions>
    <content uri="?uri"/>
    <member container="?uri" child="?data"/>
  </conditions>
  <action>
    <description uri="?data" value="?uri ?data"/>
  </action>
</rule>
```

In this case, if the predicate of the single fact is not a containment predicate (e.g., `rdf:_1`, or a special Mozilla value like `child`), then the containment attribute on the template must specify that predicate. Several predicate alternatives can be listed in that attribute.

The `<triple>` variation is

```
<rule>
  <conditions>
    <content uri="?uri"/>
    <triple subject="?uri"
      predicate="predURI"
      object="?data"/>
  </conditions>
  <action>
    <description uri="?data" value="?uri ?data"/>
  </action>
</rule>
```

"`predURI`" is the predicate to use, expressed as a literal. If predicate alternatives are required, use more than one rule of this kind.

14.4.3 Property Set

A *property set* is a query whose purpose is to retrieve a number of information items attached to a given fact subject. A typical example is treating a fact subject as a JavaScript object and retrieving the property values of that object. A second example is treating a fact subject as the name of a record and retrieving all the data items in that record. These semantic approaches are encouraged by the RDF standard's use of the terms *property* and *value*.

If the subject with associated properties is a member of an RDF container, or a container-like tag, then the simple query syntax is designed with exactly this use in mind:

```
<rule>
  <box uri="rdf:*">
    <label value="rdf:http://www.test.com/Test#Prop1"/>
    <label value="rdf:http://www.test.com/Test#Prop2"/>
    <label value="rdf:http://www.test.com/Test#Prop3"/>
    <label value="rdf:http://www.test.com/Test#Prop4"/>
  </box>
</rule>
```

If the subject with the associated properties is not a member of a container, then the extended query syntax must be used. In that case, the starting point is the same as for the Single Fact Query pattern, using the `<triple>` version. At least one property must be known to exist.

```
<rule>
  <conditions>
    <content uri="?uri"/>
    <triple subject="?uri" predicate="p1" object="?v1"/>
    <triple subject="?uri" predicate="p2" object="?v2"/>
    <triple subject="?uri" predicate="p3" object="?v3"/>
    <triple subject="?uri" predicate="p4" object="?v4"/>
  </conditions>
  <action>
    <description uri="?data" value="?v1 ?v2 ?v3 ?v4"/>
  </action>
</rule>
```

Here, the `p` again stands for full predicate URIs, like `http://www.test.com/Test#Prop1`. There is one `<triple>` for each property in the needed set. If some of the properties may not exist (or could be null), then the matching `<triple>` tags for those properties can be changed to `<binding>` tags and moved to the `<bindings>` section.

14.4.4 Singleton Solution

A single solution is any query that returns just one solution. This usually occurs when the application programmer's knowledge of the facts being queried ensures that only one solution ever exists. That situation requires no special syntax; it is just a consequence of design.

There is, however, another possibility. It relies on the `uri` attribute used inside an `<action>` tag. Because `<action>` is required, this possibility only applies to the extended syntax.

It is possible for a query to find multiple solutions but to generate content for just one. This can happen only when the query is a multifact query. An example illustrates this case. Suppose that the following RDF content exists:

```
<Description about="urn:example:root">
  <link1>
    <Description about="urn:example:child">
      <link2 resource="urn:example:X"/>
      <link2 resource="urn:example:Y"/>
    </Description>
  </link1>
</Description>
```

All the resources of these facts can be recovered with this query:

```
<rule>
  <conditions>
    <content uri="?uri"/>
    <triple subject="?uri" predicate="p1" object="?child"/>
    <triple subject="?child" predicate="p2" object="?res"/>
  </conditions>
  <action>
    <description uri="?res" value="?uri ?child ?res"/>
  </action>
</rule>
```

In this query, `p1` and `p2` should be replaced with suitable URIs for `link1` and `link2`.

Since the variable `?res` changes for each of the two solutions that will be discovered (one with X and one with Y), two copies of the `<action>` content are generated. If, however, the `<description>` tag is changed to the following line, only one copy is generated:

```
<description uri="?child" value="?uri ?child ?res"/>
```

One copy is generated because the `?child` variable can be ground to only one value. The one copy that is generated usually matches the first solution in the RDF document, but that order is not guaranteed.

14.4.5 Tree Queries

All template queries are equivalent to navigating a tree because the query system uses a depth-first solution strategy. Template queries for trees appear complex because (a) they are often recursive, and (b) extensive syntax is required. Disguised by this syntax is the fact that tree-based templates require very simple queries only. Listing 14.16 illustrates this point.

Listing 14.16 Simple extended syntax tree query.

```
<tree flex="1" datasources="test.rdf"
      ref="http://www.example.com/test.rdf">
  <treecols>
    <treecol id="colA" primary="true"/>
  </treecols>
  <template>
    <rule>
```

```
        <conditions>
          <content uri="?uri"/>
          <member container="?uri" child="?item"/>
        </conditions>
        <action>
          <treechildren>
            <treeitem uri="?item">
              <treerow>
                <treecell label="?item"/>
              </treerow>
            </treeitem>
          </treechildren>
        </action>
      </rule>
    </template>
</tree>
```

Listing 14.16 is a straightforward and minimal use of the tree-template combination. Dark text is template markup; light text is tree markup. Although there is a lot of syntax overall, the template specification is very simple. The <rule> section is no more than a single-fact query. The results of that query are used in exactly one place. The code seems complex because the markup overheads of the XUL template and XUL tree syntaxes are interleaved. If the <tree> tag is replaced with a <box> tag and the generated content reduced to a <description> tag, then this template is no more than Listing 14.17.

Listing 14.17 Simple extended syntax tree query.

```
<box datasources="test.rdf"
     ref="http://www.example.com/test.rdf">
  <template>
    <rule>
      <conditions>
        <content uri="?uri"/>
        <member container="?uri" child="?item"/>
      </conditions>
      <action>
        <description uri="?item" value="?item"/>
      </action>
    </rule>
  </template>
</box>
```

Clearly this is a very simple template.

This syntax can be further reduced to the simple syntax if the RDF content follows the standard fact arrangement. If the query is recursive, that change is a little more complex than it first appears. The standard fact arrangement requires two facts if a simple syntax query is to extract a single RDF property value. Those two facts have as subject terms the container identifier and the container member. Both facts must be repeated down the tree of possible solutions that the query searches, since each query step consumes two facts. That means a tree explored using the simple syntax must be twice as big as a tree explored more economically with the extended syntax. In Listing 14.17, only one fact is required per step down the tree.

14.4.6 Unions

There are several ways to generate a set of query solutions that is the union of two or more queries:

- The `datasources` attribute can refer to multiple RDF files or data sources so that the facts examined by a single query are a union of several fact sets.
- The `containment` attribute can add several different container predicates to the one query.
- Multiple `<rule>` tags can be used to ensure that more than one type of solution is found from a given set of facts.
- A set of `<binding>` tags can be used to explore several subtrees of a given query at the same time.

14.4.7 Illegal Queries

This query cannot be handled by the template system:

```
<rule>
  <conditions>
    <content uri="?uri"/>
    <triple subject="?uri" predicate="a" object="?v1"/>
    <triple subject="?v1"  predicate="b" object="?v2"/>
    <triple subject="?v2"  predicate="c" object="?v3"/>
    <triple subject="?v4"  predicate="d" object="?v3"/>
  </conditions>
</rule>
```

In this query, the last `<triple>` works backward from the `?v3` variable, rather than using it as a subject. This effectively decreases the depth that the query penetrates into the fact store by one. That is not implemented; all `<conditions>` content must expand the query in the forward direction only.

14.5 Template Lifecycle

Here is a summary of the processing steps that templates go through.

The first part of the process is the initial generation of XUL content.

1. Mozilla loads the XUL document containing the template. XUL content surrounding the template is layed out as normal, leaving a spot for the template-generated content.

2. All tags, including template tags, are formed into a DOM 1 content tree.
3. When the template part of the content is detected, the browser starts loading facts into memory via the nominated data sources. This is done asynchronously, like images that load inside an HTML Web page.
4. The template tags are examined for rules, and the rules are compiled into an internal, private representation.
5. After the rules are known and the data source is fully loaded, the template query system starts searching for solutions. If the application programmer has added observers, those observers are advised of progress during the search.
6. If lazy building is in effect, the search process might mark parts of the search "don't do this now; maybe look at it later."
7. As each solution is found, content is generated for it from the template rules. This content is added to the XUL document. This is done asynchronously, like images loading inside an HTML Web page.
8. When all nonlazy solutions have been found, initial content generation is complete.

The second part of the process involves interactive response from the template after the initial load is complete.

1. The generated XUL content can react to events and other interactions exactly like ordinary static XUL content. It can exploit event handlers and respond to changes in layout and general-purpose scripting.
2. If the template includes lazy building, then a user clicking on a twisty can cause query processing to explore the RDF graph further. The preceding steps 5-8 are repeated in this case.
3. If the user performs drag-and-drop actions or clicks on sort direction icons, then a `<listbox>`- or `<tree>`-based template must respond to those actions, possibly by updating the fact store. Drag and drop requires extra scripting by the application programmer.
4. If the template is told to rebuild, then the preceding steps 2-8 are repeated, except that the existing generated content is replaced if necessary, rather than created from nothing.

If the template is read-only, so that no fact changes are made, then closing the Mozilla window or removing all the template DOM subtree has no effect on the source of the RDF facts. Such templates cannot damage RDF documents.

If the template includes scripting logic that writes changes to the underlying set of RDF facts, then those changes will be permanent only if (a) the facts come from an RDF file or the Bookmarks file and (b) that file is explicitly written out by a piece of script using the `nsIRDFRemoteDataSource` interface.

14.6 Scripting

Here we will look at how to control and enhance templates from a script and further explore some of the advanced tree concepts discussed in Chapter 13, Listboxes and Trees. Chapter 16, XPCOM Objects, contains extensive discussion of the RDF and data source objects that complement the template system.

14.6.1 Guidelines for Dynamic Templates

Templates expressed in XUL alone are relatively easy because they don't ever change, and they generate content once only. Templates expressed in a combination of XUL, JavaScript, and AOM and XPCOM objects can be very challenging because full functionality is the exception rather than the expected. Here is some collected wisdom:

- ☞ The `dont-build-content` flag, and the other performance flags have no effect when a template as a whole is rebuilt. They affect only the progress of any recursive part of a template query, and the way multiple data sources are merged.
- ☞ The `ref` template attribute or property can be changed any time, and the generated content will be automatically rebuilt.
- ☞ Changes to any part of the template's specification other than `ref` require a manual call to `rebuild()`.
- ☞ The `nsIRDFCompositeDataSource` that holds all the data sources for a given template shouldn't be used to assert new facts (either by `Assert()` or by other means). Always extract and work on one of the data sources that contributes to the composite.
- ☞ For applications, the most reliable data sources for asserting facts are the `in-memory-datasource` (an initially empty data source that usually replaces a value of `rdf:null` for the `datasources` attribute) and the `xml-datasource` (used for externally stored RDF files, and for the URLs stated in the `datasources` attribute). The `xml-datasource` will only assert facts for URLs with a `file:` scheme. It will not assert facts for `chrome:` or `resource:` schemes, or for any other scheme.
- ☞ If you are making extensive fact changes to a data source, remove it from the template first, make the changes, and then add it back. That saves many complex updates to the appearance of generated content. See also the `beginBatchUpdate()` methods for trees in Table 13.3.
- ☞ The `Flush()` method is supported only for data sources based on `file:` URLs.
- ☞ The `Refresh()` method is supported for `http:` and `file:` URLs. When using this method to retrieve a file from a Web server, test equipment must be set up correctly. All HTTP caching effects between the server and Mozilla must be removed or else results may be confusing.

14.6.2 AOM and XPCOM Template Objects

The template system adds JavaScript properties to the objects representing template tags. Properties are added to both the template specification tags and the generated template content tags. These properties are in addition to the properties that exist for the base tag of the template. Table 14.1 lists these properties.

Table 14.1 JavaScript properties added by the template system

Property name	Base tag?	<template> tag?	Rules tags	Generated tags
database	Useful	Null	Null	Null
builder	Sometimes Useful	Null	Null	Null
resource	Useful	Useful—holds tag id	Null	Useful—holds uri value or null
datasources	Useful	Empty string	Empty string	Empty string
ref	Useful	Empty string	Empty string	Empty string

In this table, “Useful” means that the property gains a useful value; “Null” means that the property is set to null; “Empty string” means that the property contains a zero-length string.

- The `database` property is an object that contains references to the data sources used in the template. It implements the `nsICompositeDataSource` XPCOM interface. It exists even if the sole stated data source is `rdf:null`. For chrome-based templates, it always contains the `rdf:local-store` data source.
- The `builder` property is an object used to control the query and content generation process of the template. It can be seen as a highly specialized (and very limited) layout or rendering tool. It implements the `nsIXULTemplateBuilder` interface. It is useful for `<listbox>` and `<tree>`-based templates only.
- The `resource` property is an object that contains a compiled RDF URI. That URI can be a subject, predicate, or object URI. If the tag is `<template>`, it holds the template `id` as a non-URI resource. If the template is a generated tag that has a `uri` attribute, then it holds the value of the specified extended template variable. This object implements the `nsIRDFResource` interface.
- The `datasources` property holds the value of the `datasources` XUL attribute.
- The `ref` property holds the value of the `ref` XUL attribute.

The `database` object contains the `AddDataSource()`, `RemoveDataSource()`, and `GetDataSources()` methods, which are used to manage the data sources that feed facts into the template. The `builder` object contains primarily the `rebuild()` method, which is used to completely re-create and refresh the displayed contents of a template. The `resource` object and `datasources` and `ref` attributes are all available merely for convenience. None of these objects may be replaced by the application programmer.

In addition to these AOM objects are the objects that support builder observers, views, and delegates. They are discussed next.

14.6.3 Builders

Template builders are builders—a piece of code inside the Mozilla Platform that generates the content of a tree. Builders cannot be implemented by an application programmer, but they can be modified.

The simplest use of a builder is to re-create and redisplay a templated `<tree>`. Only one line of code is required:

```
treeElement.builder.rebuild()
```

There are no options. This technique works only on templates whose base tag is a `<tree>` or `<listbox>`. `rebuild()` does not work on other templated tags.

When the tree is rebuilt, the open and closed states of any subtrees will be preserved if lazy building is at work. To stop this from happening, use the `statedatasource` attribute on the `<tree>` tag, and then take that data source away just before rebuilding. To take it away, remove the data source from the databases' property, then remove the tree attribute using a DOM operation, and then call `rebuild()`.

Recall there are two builders used in Mozilla; the XUL content builder and the XUL template builder. The latter deals with templates. This template builder is based on this component and interface:

```
@mozilla.org/xul/xul-template-builder;1 nsIXULTemplateBuilder
```

This interface contains the `rebuild()` method. This builder cannot be modified or replaced by the application programmer.

Inside Mozilla, this template builder has a specialization (a subclass) that is specific to templated trees: the XUL tree builder.

```
@mozilla.org/xul/xul-tree-builder;1 nsIXULTreeBuilder
```

This builder cannot be replaced by the application programmer either. It can, however, be enhanced. It can accept the registration of an object with the `nsITreeBuilderObserver` interface. Although this interface acts somewhat like an observer, it is also very similar to a delegate object. Which of these two design patterns is most accurate is a question of opinion as much as it is of fact.

This nsITreeBuilderObserver interface is a subset of the nsITree-View interface that is used for custom views. It is used to enhance user interactions with the tree, like column clicking and drag-and-drop gestures. In the Mozilla application, two examples of such an observer exist: one in the Bookmark Manager and one in the email folders pane of Classic Mail & News. Both implement drag and drop for their respective trees, and their JavaScript code is a suitable example to study.

This interface is used for drag and drop because of the way that <tree> tags hold their content separate to the rest of the XUL document (see Chapter 13, Listboxes and Trees). The standard drag-and-drop techniques described in Chapter 6, Events, can't be used for a <tree>. In fact, there is no (simple) way to do drag and drop for a <tree> that is not a template.

If an object with the nsITreeBuilderObserver interface is used, it should be lodged as an observer with the tree's DOM object using the addObserver() method of nsITreeView.

All the Mozilla tree builders also support the nsIRDFObserver interface, which means the whole tree can in turn act like an observer. This interface can be added to a data source object (interface nsIRDFDataSource), and it will then be advised each time new facts relevant to the template's queries appear.

14.6.4 Views

If the template is based on a tree, then properties relating to views are also available. Chapter 13, Listboxes and Trees, explains that a view is an automatically created object that is used by a tree builder to perform the actual generation of tree content.

A custom view object completely replaces the content that would be displayed from a template-based RDF file. If the data source for the <tree> template is rdf:null, then a custom view can do the whole job of populating the tree. The simplest way to set this up is to use a <tree> tag with a normal <treecols> section, plus one of these three options for the remaining content:

```
<children/>
<template><treechildren/></template>
<template> ... normal set of template rules ... </template>
```

Such a tree will display its ordinary content first, then when the view is changed and tree rebuilt, the view will take over and determine the content from that point onward. If the attribute flags="dont-build-content" is added, then the ordinary content will not appear at all.

14.6.5 Delegates

A delegate is a very general term in object-oriented design, and many design patterns and software objects have some delegate-like features. In Mozilla, delegates are objects that are used to tie RDF fact URIs to an external system, so that each URI has other baggage associated with it. That other baggage might be vital data of some kind.

In Mozilla, delegates are used to tie RDF facts that are about email information to related information stored on a remote mail server, like an SMTP, IMAP, or LDAP server.

Time and space do not permit a discussion of delegates in this chapter. A starting point is to look closely at the nsIRDFResource and nsIRDFDelegateFactory interfaces, as well as at the XPCOM components whose contract ID's begin with

```
@mozilla.org/rdf/delegate-factory;1?key=
```

14.6.6 Common Scripting Tasks

Here is a brief list of strategies for common template scripting tasks. There is extensive examination of scriptable RDF objects in Chapter 16, XPCOM Objects. In particular, tricks that use the rdf:null data source and other internal data sources are discussed there.

To change a template's data source, use databases.getDataSources(), iterate through the provided list to find the right one, use databases.removeDataSource() with that data source as the argument, and then rebuild. Or remove that data source from the <tree> tag and rebuild.

To change the root URI for a template query, use setAttribute("ref",newURI) on the base tag. The template will rebuild automatically. Setting the ref property has the same effect.

To change rules, use DOM operations or innerHTML to change the template tags directly in the XUL, and then rebuild by calling rebuild(). A better solution is to create all possible rules and disable the one you don't need. Do this by placing a catch-all rule before the rules that should be disabled. The catch-all rule finds solutions for all cases it receives, so the remaining (disabled) rules are never considered.

To change facts in a data source, extract the specific data source using databases.GetDataSources(). Use the Assert() or Change() methods of the nsIRDFDataSource interface. The template will be rebuilt automatically in some cases; to be sure, call rebuild().

To change the results of a query, step back a little. You can't change the solutions that result from the template queries because they are generated by the query. You need to change the query or the original RDF data so that the query solutions become different. To change the facts in the fact store, use the @mozilla.org/rdf/rdf-service;1 component and other RDF components to construct facts and pieces of facts, and then use the data source object's Assert() method to make those facts true. Then rebuild the template.

To change generated content, use normal DOM operations. (The changes will be lost if a rebuild occurs.) To make such changes permanent, change the <content> part of a rule rather than the generated content, and rebuild().

14.7 Style Options

The template system has no related style enhancements, but some new tricks with the existing styles are possible.

Styles can be attached to content in a template, and the style and class attributes can benefit from the use of template variables. This allows some style information to be supplied by the RDF data that drives the template. It also creates an architectural problem because it allows presentation information and raw data to be mixed in one set of RDF facts. If this needs to be done extensively, it is better to use two RDF data sources and keep presentation facts in one and raw data facts in the other.

Styles can also be applied by using `<rule>` tags as data-driven style selectors. Two rules can generate near-identical content, but differ slightly in their queries. The near-identical content can just have different style information.

Finally, styles can be applied to the generated content of a template, using JavaScript DOM operations. If the template is rebuilt, these styles may disappear.

14.8 Hands On: NoteTaker Data Made Live

This "Hands On" session is about using templates to get real data into an application.

In this session, we'll replace some of our NoteTaker XUL code with templates and then test it out with real Web note data.

To begin with, we have the RDF data model of Chapter 12, Overlays and Chrome. Later on we'll put this file in the user's profile, where it belongs. For now, we'll just store it in the chrome with the rest of the NoteTaker tool. It will be in:

```
chrome://notetaker/contents/notetaker.rdf
```

Templates are needed three times in the NoteTaker tool:

1. The form fields on the NoteTaker toolbar should be loaded with data from the current note. We'll see that this takes two templates.
2. The listbox of keywords in the Edit dialog box needs to be loaded with the existing keywords for the current note.
3. The tree of related keywords in the Edit dialog box needs to be loaded with all related keywords that match the keywords in the current note.

The last use requires a special technique; the tree is (very roughly) in a master-detail relationship with the listbox and needs to be coordinated against the contents of the listbox.

Data also appear in the HTML-based note displayed on the current Web page. HTML does not support templates, so we must extract the needed data from RDF using a nontemplate system. That is done in Chapter 16, XPCOM Objects.

14.8.1 Creating Test Data

Before building templates, we need some test data. To that end we create a NoteTaker RDF document containing two notes and their related information. The first note is for a Web page named `test1.html`, which has four keywords. The second note is for a Web page named `test2.html`, which has two keywords. Listing 14.18 shows the full data for these two notes, plus an extra keyword relationship.

Listing 14.18 Test data for NoteTaker XUL templates.

```
<?xml version="1.0"?>
<RDF xmlns="http://www.w3.org/1999/02/22-rdf-syntax-ns#"
    xmnls:NT="http://www.mozilla.org/notetaker-rdf#">
  <Description about="urn:notetaker:root">
    <NT:notes>
      <Seq about="urn:notetaker:notes">
  <li resource="http://saturn/test1.html"/>
  <li resource="http://saturn/test2.html"/>
      </Seq>
    </NT:notes>
    <NT:keywords>
      <Seq about="urn:notetaker:keywords">
        <li resource="urn:notetaker:keyword:checkpointed"/>
        <li resource="urn:notetaker:keyword:reviewed"/>
        <li resource="urn:notetaker:keyword:fun"/>
        <li resource="urn:notetaker:keyword:visual"/>
        <li resource="urn:notetaker:keyword:cool"/>
        <li resource="urn:notetaker:keyword:test"/>
        <li resource="urn:notetaker:keyword:breakdown"/>
        <li resource="urn:notetaker:keyword:first draft"/>
        <li resource="urn:notetaker:keyword:final"/>
        <li resource="urn:notetaker:keyword:guru"/>
        <li resource="urn:notetaker:keyword:rubbish"/>
      </Seq>
    </NT:keywords>
  </Description>

<!-- details for each note -->
  <Description about="http://saturn/test1.html">
    <NT:summary>My Summary</NT:summary>
    <NT:details>My Details</NT:details>
    <NT:top>100</NT:top>
    <NT:left>90</NT:left>
    <NT:width>80</NT:width>
    <NT:height>70</NT:height>
    <NT:keyword resource="urn:notetaker:keyword:test"/>
    <NT:keyword resource="urn:notetaker:keyword:cool"/>
  </Description>
```

```
  <Description about="http://saturn/test2.html">
    <NT:summary>Good place to list</NT:summary>
    <NT:details>Last time I had a website here, my page also appeared on
          Yahoo
    </NT:details>
    <NT:top>100</NT:top>
    <NT:left>300</NT:left>
    <NT:width>100</NT:width>
    <NT:height>200<NT:height>
    <NT:keyword resource="urn:notetaker:keyword:checkpointed"/>
    <NT:keyword resource="urn:notetaker:keyword:reviewed"/>
    <NT:keyword resource="urn:notetaker:keyword:fun"/>
    <NT:keyword resource="urn:notetaker:keyword:visual"/>
  </Description>

<!-- values for each keyword -->
  <Description about="urn:notetaker:keyword:checkpointed"
          NT:label="checkpointed"/>
  <Description about="urn:notetaker:keyword:reviewed" NT:label="reviewed"/
          >
  <Description about="urn:notetaker:keyword:fun" NT:label="fun"/>
  <Description about="urn:notetaker:keyword:visual" NT:label="visual"/>
  <Description about="urn:notetaker:keyword:breakdown"
          NT:label="breakdown"/>
  <Description about="urn:notetaker:keyword:first draft" NT:label="first
          draft"/>
  <Description about="urn:notetaker:keyword:final" NT:label="final"/>
  <Description about="urn:notetaker:keyword:guru" NT:label="guru"/>
  <Description about="urn:notetaker:keyword:rubbish" NT:label="rubbish"/>
  <Description about="urn:notetaker:keyword:test" NT:label="test"/>
  <Description about="urn:notetaker:keyword:cool" NT:label="cool"/>

<!--sufficient related keyword pairings -->
  <Description about="urn:notetaker:keyword:checkpointed">
    <NT:related resource="urn:notetaker:keyword:breakdown"/>
    <NT:related resource="urn:notetaker:keyword:first draft"/>
    <NT:related resource="urn:notetaker:keyword:final"/>
  </Description>
  <Description about="urn:notetaker:keyword:reviewed">
    <NT:related resource="urn:notetaker:keyword:guru"/>
    <NT:related resource="urn:notetaker:keyword:rubbish"/>
  </Description>
  <Description about="urn:notetaker:keyword:fun">
    <NT:related resource="urn:notetaker:keyword:cool"/>
  </Description>

<!-- single example of a cycle -->
  <Description about="urn:notetaker:keyword:cool">
    <NT:related resource="urn:notetaker:keyword:test"/>
  </Description>
  </Description>
</RDF>
```

The combination of RDF documents and XUL templates requires five times as much care as <tree>. If just one little thing is incorrect, the template will produce nothing, and there will be no clues why that happened. We start by carefully testing our data using the advice in "Debug Corner." If you haven't got a text editor with automatic XML syntax checking, then proceed this way: Directly load the RDF document into the Classic Browser to catch all XML syntax errors. Then change the file extension to .xml and load it again, to catch tag-ordering problems. Finally, check it by eye against the format that was decided in Chapter 11, RDF. When all that looks correct, we have a fair, but not perfect, level of confidence that the test data are right.

14.8.2 Simple Templates for Form Elements

The first templates we'll code are the ones in the NoteTaker toolbar. That toolbar requires one value for each of the two textboxes, and a set of values for the dropdown menu. We must use a template that produces one solution for the textboxes and another template that produces a set of zero or more solutions for the dropdown menu.

The dropdown menu is easiest. Looking at the structure of the notetaker.rdf file, we see that we need the label property of the individual keywords. The keywords are collected in the urn:notetaker:keywords RDF container, which is a <Seq> tag. This layout matched the standard fact arrangement required for the simple (template) query syntax, so the template should be easy to create.

We test the template on a simple document first, rather than add it to the toolbar right away. That way we avoid complexities with the menu's popup content. Because templates and RDF give us little feedback, we must proceed step by step. Listing 14.19 is the simple, template-free test document that we'll use.

Listing 14.19 Plain XUL document suitable as a basis for testing templates.

```
<?xml version="1.0"?>
<?xml-stylesheet href="chrome://global/skin/" type="text/css"?>
<!DOCTYPE window>
<window xmlns="http://www.mozilla.org/keymaster/gatekeeper/
          there.is.only.xul">
  <vbox>
    <description value="Static content"/>
    <hbox>
      <description value="Repeated content"/>
    </hbox>
  </vbox>
</window>
```

The details of the needed template follow:

- ☞ Use this RDF file: datasources="notetaker.rdf"
- ☞ Use this query starting point: ref="urn:notetaker:keywords"

- This simple variable is always required on the repeated content for the simple syntax: `uri="rdf:*"`
- This property will be used as a simple syntax query variable: `rdf:http://www.mozilla.org/notetaker-rdf#label`

Merging that information into Listing 14.18 yields Listing 14.20.

Listing 14.20 Plain XUL document templated for the menu query.

```
<?xml version="1.0"?>
<?xml-stylesheet href="chrome://global/skin/" type="text/css"?>
<!DOCTYPE window>
<window xmlns="http://www.mozilla.org/keymaster/gatekeeper/
          there.is.only.xul">
  <vbox
    datasources="notetaker.rdf"
    ref="urn:notetaker:keywords">
    <description value="Static content"/>
    <template>
      <hbox uri="rdf:*">
        <description value="Repeated content"/>
        <description
        value="rdf:http://www.mozilla.org/notetaker-rdf#label"/>
      </hbox>
    </template>
  </vbox>
</window>
```

The `"Static content"` content is outside the `<template>` tag, and so we should always see it. The `"Repeated content"` content will appear once for each solution found by the query. The third description tag displays the values of the sole variable ground by the query. This simple query page results in Figure 14.6.

Now we have the query working. In the preparation of this "Hands On" session, numerous subtle syntax errors had to be ironed out to reach this point; there is nothing wrong with the template system, except possibly a shortage of debugging tools. We can now modify the template for the toolbar. Listing 14.21 shows the dropdown menu both before and after the template is installed.

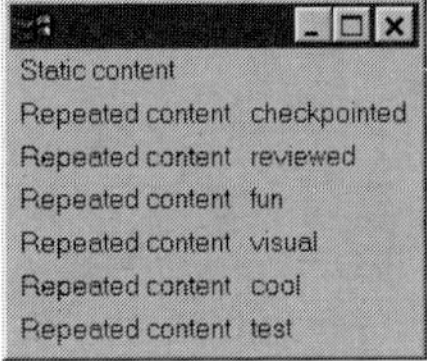

Fig. 14.6 Simple template-generated output using a test page.

Listing 14.21 Templated popup menu for the NoteTaker toolbar.

```
<?xml version="1.0"?>

<menulist editable="true">
  <menupopup>
  <!-- static menu items removed -->
  </menupopup>
</menulist>

<menulist id="notetaker-toolbar.keywords" editable="true">
  <menupopup datasources="notetaker.rdf" ref="urn:notetaker:keywords">
    <template>
      <menuitem uri="rdf:*"
        label="rdf:http://www.mozilla.org/notetaker-rdf#label"/>
    </template>
  </menupopup>
</menulist>
```

The results of these changes are shown in Figure 14.7.

If there are no keywords at all, the menu will contain no items and will lay out poorly in the toolbar. To fix this, we could add a dummy `<menuitem>` tag above the `<template>` tag, or just make sure that this initial `notetaker.rdf` contains at least one keyword. We'll do the latter.

The other template required in the toolbar must retrieve a single solution, since there's only one summary `<textbox>`, ever. To see what that template's query might be, we examine the structure of the `notetaker.rdf` file. The note's URL is a member of a named RDF container (`urn:notetaker:notes`), and it has a property summary. So the standard fact arrangement, required for a simple template query, is present. Perhaps we can use that simple syntax.

In fact, we can't use the simple syntax, because we want to be choosy about which members of the sequence are retrieved. We only want one member, which is the note for the currently displayed URL. Therefore we must resort to the extended syntax. In the extended syntax, we don't have to start

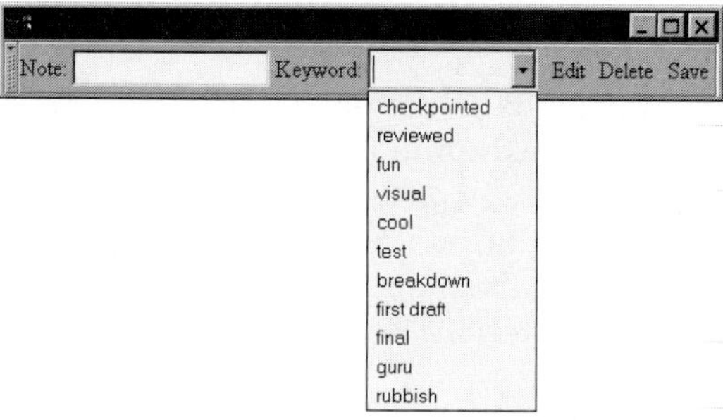

Fig. 14.7 Template-generated menu popup for the NoteTaker toolbar.

at the top of a sequence, so we can be more creative with our query. We can start it directly at the URL of the current note. If we do that, an example of the query fact would be:

```
<- http://saturn/test1.html, http://www.mozilla.org/notetaker-
     rdf#summary, ?summary ->
```

Using the advice in this chapter under "Common Query Patterns," we create the template for the keyword textbox as shown in Listing 14.22:

Listing 14.22 Templated textbox for the NoteTaker toolbar.

```
<box datasources="notetaker.rdf" ref="http://saturn/test1.html">
  <template>
    <rule>
      <conditions>
        <content uri="?uri"/>
        <triple subject="?uri"
          predicate="http://www.mozilla.org/notetaker-rdf#summary"
          object="?summary"/>
      </conditions>
      <action>
        <textbox id="notetaker-toolbar.summary" uri="?summary"
          value="?summary"/>
      </action>
    </rule>
  </template>
</box>
```

This code replaces the single tag `<textbox/>` in the existing toolbar. We've surrounded the textbox with an invisible <box> just to get the template working.

This template code has a fixed URL as the query start point. We'll shortly make this value dynamic using a script and `setAttribute()`. That concludes the XUL changes to the NoteTaker toolbar. We now turn to templates required for the Edit dialog box. The `<listbox>` and `<tree>` tags in that dialog box both need templates.

14.8.3 An Extended Syntax Template for `<listbox>`

The `<listbox>` tag for this dialog box is the easier task, so that's first. To learn what the query should be, we examine the structure of the `notetaker.rdf` file again. We see that a note is part of a sequence and contains a `keyword` property, so it is in the standard data arrangement. The problem is that the URL for the note is a known, fixed quantity rather than being every note in the sequence. This is a similar situation to the `<textbox>` on the toolbar, so we'll need an extended query.

Another reason for an extended query is to dig out the textual strings for the keywords. Those strings are properties of each keyword rather than properties of the note. We can easily retrieve them by extending the query further into the set of facts—one additional <triple> tag will link the keywords found on the note to the labels on the keywords. The template we require looks like Listing 14.23.

Listing 14.23 Templated listbox for the NoteTaker toolbar.
```
<listbox id="dialog.keywords" rows="3" datasources="notetaker.rdf"
          ref="http://saturn/test1.html">
  <template>
    <rule>
      <conditions>
        <content uri="?uri"/>
        <triple subject="?uri"
          predicate="http://www.mozilla.org/notetaker-rdf#keyword"
          object="?keyword"/>
        <triple subject="?keyword"
          predicate="http://www.mozilla.org/notetaker-rdf#label"
          object="?text"/>
      </conditions>
      <action>
        <listitem uri="?keyword" label="?text"/>
      </action>
    </rule>
  </template>
</listbox>
```

Except for the addition of one <triple> tag, this code is effectively the same as the code for the toolbar <textbox>.

We could also use a template for the Edit panel of the Edit dialog box. There are good reasons for not doing that, so we'll leave that panel as it is for now. One of those good reasons is that we don't know which note is the best one to display when the URL loads.

14.8.4 An Extended Syntax Template for <tree>

The last template we consider is for the <tree> of related keywords.

To gain some ideas what the query might be for this tree, we return to the notetaker.rdf file. We will need the label property to display the keyword. We will also need the related property to discover keywords related to a given keyword. Finally, we want the level 0 (zero) of the tree to be the keywords of the current note's URL. We'll use that URL as the top of the query, but we'll display only the children of that URL, not the URL itself.

The facts we seem to need for a full, recursive query go like this:

```
<- current-page-url, keyword, ?keyword -> // level 0
<- ?keyword, label, ?text ->

<- ?keyword, related, ?keyword2 ->        // level 1
<- ?keyword2, label, ?text2 ->
```

```
<- ?keyword2, related, ?keyword3 ->        // level 2
<- ?keyword3, label, ?text3 ->

... and so on ...
```

This set of facts doesn't match the standard fact arrangement, so we can't use the simple query syntax. This set of facts also represents a recursive query, so we really need to use a `<tree>` tag for testing.

What will the recursive query be? We need to concentrate on the narrower question: What is the query needed to probe one level deeper into the tree of solutions? There appear to be two facts per level, so it might seem that each step in the recursive query is a two-fact query. If we examine the `notetaker.rdf` fact structure, it appears that there is only one fact required per level of the query because keywords are separated by a single predicate/property. If we draw the query as an RDF diagram, we can quickly see that one fact is the correct approach. Figure 14.8 shows this diagram.

Clearly, the recursive behavior requires one step along the (vertical) arrows only. So the recursive query must be a one-fact query. The other arrows are side information required at each level but not contributing to the recursive behavior.

We consider first this recursive fact represented by vertical arrows. The problem is that sometimes it is labeled with `keyword` and sometimes it is labeled with `related`. In other words, there are two alternatives for the recursive query:

```
<- current-page-url, keyword, ?keyword ->
<- current-keyword-urn, related, ?keyword ->
```

Somehow the template query must accommodate both cases. One solution is to use a separate `<rule>` for each possibility. In our case, the con-

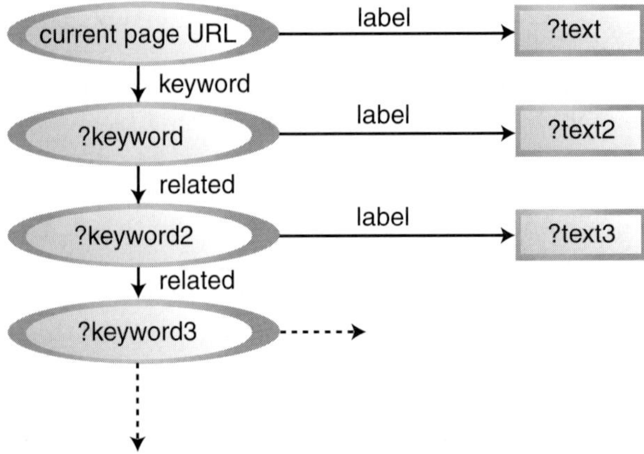

Fig. 14.8 RDF diagram for a recursive template query.

tainment template attribute is a simple solution. We are fortunate that, given any URI, either there will be facts with the related property, or there will be facts with the keyword property, but not both, which means that we can use multiple container predicates at once. We will list both the related and keyword predicates in this attribute's value.

To see why we can use containment, consider the progress of the query. When the query is discovering the top level of the tree, the keyword predicate will find solutions and the related predicate won't, because that's the way the facts are arranged in the RDF file. When the query is discovering solutions deeper in the tree, the related predicate will find solutions and the keyword predicate won't. This is exactly what we want. Listing 14.24 shows the resulting template.

Listing 14.24 Recursive tree template for the NoteTaker Edit dialog box.

```
<tree id="dialog.related" flex="1"
      datasources="notetaker.rdf"
      ref="http://saturn/test2.html"
      containment="http://www.mozilla.org/notetaker-rdf#related http://
          www.mozilla.org/notetaker-rdf#keyword"
      hidecolumnpicker="true"
  >
  <treecols>
    <treecol id="tree.all" hideheader="true" primary="true" flex="1"/>
  </treecols>
  <template>
    <rule>
      <conditions>
        <content uri="?uri"/>
        <member container="?uri" child="?keyword"/>
      </conditions>
      <action>
        <treechildren>
          <treeitem uri="?keyword">
            <treerow>
              <treecell label="?keyword"/>
            </treerow>
          </treeitem>
        </treechildren>
      </action>
    </rule>
  </template>
</tree>
```

The query contains a <member> tag to match the use of the containment attribute. Because this is a recursive query, we can't test it with a plain <description> tag. We must use one of the tags that explicitly supports recursive queries, in this case <tree>.

We have therefore managed to build the recursive query. All that is needed now is to add the ancillary information from Figure 14.8. That is easy to do using a <binding> tag. We add this content just after the </conditions> tag:

```
<bindings>
  <binding subject="?keyword"
    predicate="http://www.mozilla.org/notetaker-rdf#label"
    object="?text"/>
</bindings>
```

Because <binding> tags don't assist with the recursive process, we haven't damaged the query; we've just enhanced the information it retrieves. Finally, we must change the <treecell> to report the label that the binding discovers, rather than the URN of the keyword:

```
<treecell label="?text"/>
```

With these changes, we've completed the tree's template, and all the required templates for the NoteTaker tool. Even though the <listbox> and <tree> tags have template-generated content, our event handlers from Chapter 13, Listboxes and Trees, continue to work; they can browse the DOM structure for template-generated content as easily as they can a DOM structure built from static XUL tags.

We do have one problem with the <tree> template. It does not display related keywords as well as the custom view experiment did in Chapter 13, Listboxes and Trees. It only displays what's in the RDF file. We could improve the output by adding the other keyword-keyword combinations to `notetaker.rdf`, or we could somehow modify the template so that the facts used in the template receive special processing before display, rather than being read straight from the file. We'll consider that latter possibility in Chapter 16, XPCOM Objects.

14.8.5 Coordinating and Refreshing Template Content

The final feature we'd like to implement is keeping the displayed data up to date. That means tying the data in the toolbar, Edit dialog box, and HTML note to the RDF facts about the URL of the Web page currently displayed in the browser. Keeping the HTML note up to date is too hard for the technology we've explored so far, but the other updates are easy. Our plan follows:

1. Update the <textbox> on the toolbar every time the current note changes.
2. Update the dropdown menu on the toolbar every time a note is saved or deleted, in case the total set of keywords changed as a result of that save or delete.
3. Update the Keywords pane of the dialog box every time it is opened.

To do this, we make the following small changes for the toolbar:

1. Update the JavaScript version of the current note to include a URL.
2. Provide a utility function that updates the toolbar display.

3. The timed checks that detect a newly displayed Web page need to update the toolbar <textbox>.
4. A notetaker-delete command is needed on the delete button on the toolbar.
5. A notetaker-save command is needed on the save button on the toolbar.
6. The notetaker-open-dialog command must update the dropdown menu on the toolbar when the dialog box closes.

First, we must implement the existing note object as a full JavaScript object and then give it methods clear() and resolve() and a url property. clear() removes any current note data; resolve() turns a supplied URL into the URL of an existing note and records the results. For this chapter, these changes are trivial, but we'll need to expand on them later. The code for the new note object is shown in Listing 14.25.

Listing 14.25 Basic JavaScript object for a NoteTaker note.

```
function Note() {}  // constructor

Note.prototype = {
  url : null,
  summary : "",
  details : "",
  chop_query : true, home_page : false,
  width : 100, height : 90, top : 80, left : 70,
  clear : function () {
    this.url = null;
  },
  resolve : function (url) {
    this.url = url;
  },
}

var note = new Note();
```

Second, we implement a utility refresh_toolbar() function that updates the toolbar templates. Some of this function we'll have to modify in later chapters. Listing 14.26 shows this function.

Listing 14.26 Template rebuilding code for the NoteTaker toolbar.

```
function refresh_toolbar()
{
  var menu = window.document.getElementById('notetaker-toolbar.keywords');
  menu.firstChild.builder.rebuild();

  var box = window.document.getElementById('notetaker-toolbar.summary');
  box.parentNode.setAttribute('ref', note.url);
  box.parentNode.builder.rebuild();
}
```

The `rebuild()` method causes the template-generated contents to be removed and re-created. In the case of the dropdown menu, the contents will change only if the underlying RDF file changes. In the case of the textbox, the template itself is modified, and so the query is different each time it is rebuilt.

Next, we look at the timed checks. This is all run from the `content_poll()` function, so let's rewrite it slightly so that it updates the toolbar as well as the displayed note. Listing 14.27 shows the new version.

Listing 14.27 Poll the displayed Web page and make all required updates.

```
function content_poll()
{
  var doc;
  try {
    if ( !window.content ) throw('fail');
    doc = window.content.document;
    if ( !doc ) throw('fail');
    if ( doc.getElementsByTagName("body").length == 0 ) throw('fail');
    if ( doc.location.href == "about:blank" ) throw('fail');
  }
  catch (e) {
    note.clear();
    refresh_toolbar();
    return;
  }

  if ( doc.visited ) return;

  note.resolve(doc.location.href);
  display_note();
  refresh_toolbar();
  doc.visited = true;
}
```

If there's no suitable URL present, then clear the current note and the toolbar. Otherwise, find the new current note and update the toolbar, note, and current page.

We can't yet complete the remaining tasks 4 and 6 because we don't know how to modify RDF files yet—we only know how to read them. We can, however, do the template update part of the nominated commands. We update the `action()` function to call `refresh_toolbar()` wherever it's needed. Listing 14.28 shows this trivial code.

Listing 14.28 Full list of NoteTaker toolbar commands with template rebuilding.

```
function action(task)
{
  if ( task == "notetaker-open-dialog" )
  {
    window.openDialog("editDialog.xul","_blank","modal=yes");
    refresh_toolbar();
  }
```

```
  if ( task == "notetaker-display" )
  {
    display_note();
  }

  if ( task == "notetaker-save" )
  {
    refresh_toolbar();
  }
  if ( task == "notetaker-delete" )
  {
    refresh_toolbar();
  }
}
```

That completes management of the toolbar templates. For the dialog box, we need an equivalent effect for the templates in the Keywords pane. We choose to put this in the `notetaker-load` command. In the `action()` function that services that command, we add a call to `refresh_dialog()` and implement `refresh_dialog()` as shown in Listing 14.29.

Listing 14.29 Template rebuilding for NoteTaker Edit dialog box.

```
function refresh_dialog()
{
  var listbox = window.document.getElementById('dialog.keywords');
  listbox.setAttribute('ref', window.opener.note.url);
  listbox.builder.rebuild();

  var tree = window.document.getElementById('dialog.keywords');
  tree.setAttribute('ref', window.opener.note.url);
  tree.builder.rebuild();
}
```

This is identical to the template updates for the toolbar drop-down menu.

14.9 Debug Corner: Template Survival Guide

When templates are phrased and used correctly, everything works. There are almost no syntax-related bugs or unstable features to blame failure on. Most problems come from syntax mistakes in the application code.

On Microsoft Windows, be sure to check that the Mozilla Platform has been fully shut down when the last window is closed. If a badly formed template is used, the Mozilla process can linger on and be reused in later tests, which is very confusing. When this happens, the most common symptom is that recent changes to the XUL code or JavaScript appear to have no effect. It is safest to start each test with a new instance of the platform. If you leave the Mozilla splash screen in place, you can use this as a hint to remind you when a new instance has started.

A second platform flaw involves recursive queries. Only attempt to get these working with a <menu> or <tree> widget; other results are unpredictable and can cause crashes.

The combination of RDF documents and XUL templates requires five times as much care as the <tree> tag discussed in Chapter 13, Listboxes and Trees. If just one little thing is incorrect, the template will produce nothing at all, and there will be no clues why that happened. The right approach is essential.

14.9.1 Building Up a Template

When creating a template, always start with test data stored in an external RDF file. Mozilla has full-featured support for a file-based RDF source. External RDF files are easy to view. You can use the techniques described in "Debug Corner" in Chapter 11, RDF, to run the data through Mozilla once. This lets you confirm that it is loading the way that you expect. Load the file directly into a browser so that Mozilla can report any syntax errors. Load the file as an .xml file so that you can see any indentation problems. Alternately, try out one of the RDF validation tools recommended by the W3C.

After gaining confidence with some test data, the next step is to prove that the query output can be displayed in a XUL window.

If the template query is not recursive, then create a template using a simple <vbox> tag as the base tag. Dump something out into a <description> or <label> tag without any fancy features in the rules. After you have seen something appear, you can be sure that you have at least the query root and part of the query structure right. Even if your goal is to use a deeply nested tree structure, try displaying the top-level items by themselves in a <vbox> first.

If your ultimate source of facts is an internal data source, read the advice in Chapter 16, XPCOM Objects, on these data sources and extract into a test page as much information as possible from that data source. Some data sources can be manipulated directly from a template; others need a script. You need to be familiar with the exact content generated, or your template queries won't work.

Next, build up your queries. The template system is flexible and can handle some changes to the order of content inside <template>, but making those changes is not recommended. For the least headaches, stick closely to the order of tags suggested in this chapter. Even though such order can be varied a little, doing so can confuse the internal rule creation system about what template variables are what. Swapping things around can stop data from appearing.

If the template is to be a recursive one, then you can't easily test the recursion outside of a <menu> or <tree> tag; you can only test the first level of the recursion. To test the recursion through multiple levels, use a <tree> tag, not a <menu> tag. It is not possible to build a recursively generated set of menus out of a single <rule>—at least two rules are required. One rule is for menu items that are <menu>s; the other is for menu items that are <menu-item>s. So for recursive queries, the <tree> tag is the simplest test vehicle.

Only after the queries are yielding results should you think about the real widget you want to use as the base tag. In the case of <tree>, always start with the recommended content described in this chapter, and always make sure that the tree has a primary column. You can alter the other details later. Carefully review the flags and options that can be added to the base tag—some are vital. Automatically add `flags="dont-build-content"` and `flex="1"` attributes to trees, until you can think of a good reason for omitting them.

After your template works properly, you might want to script it so that it has dynamic behavior. "Guidelines for Dynamic Templates" contains very important wisdom. Outside of those guidelines, very little is currently supported.

Finally, note the remarks in "Data Sources" in Chapter 16, XPCOM Objects, about data sources. If your final RDF source is internal, not external, then the data source used needs to be carefully assessed for available functionality. Most internal data sources have unpublished formats for the RDF facts they supply. As a last resort, examine how they are used in the chrome by the already working Mozilla applications.

14.10 SUMMARY

Mozilla's template system extends RDF with a query system and with formatted output of the query results. Those results and output can change dynamically to match dynamic changes to the information underlying the query. Templates work on top of the XUL language and are integrated with the content layout system. They can be used to create dynamic GUI interfaces or just to display changing data in a fixed-sized widget. Templates are not static—they can easily be refreshed or updated if conditions change.

The template system is a technical challenge to learn. It has unfamiliar concepts, it has its share of quirks and stumbling blocks, and it provides very little feedback to the programmer. Awkwardly, the data sources that feed data into the template system are a motley group of individuals whose quirks require further effort to appreciate.

For all those version 1 problems, templates are very powerful tools. An RDF file stored at any URL in the world can be read and displayed using a very brief and concise set of XUL tags. Such simplicity augers well for the future data processing capabilities of the XUL language and the Mozilla Platform. It is likely that templates are only an early step in the data processing capabilities of the platform.

JavaScript and the DOM can be used to generate new content in a XUL document. RDF and templates achieve a similar end, but by a different route. A third way exists to generate content in a XUL document. That method involves XBL, the subject of the next chapter.

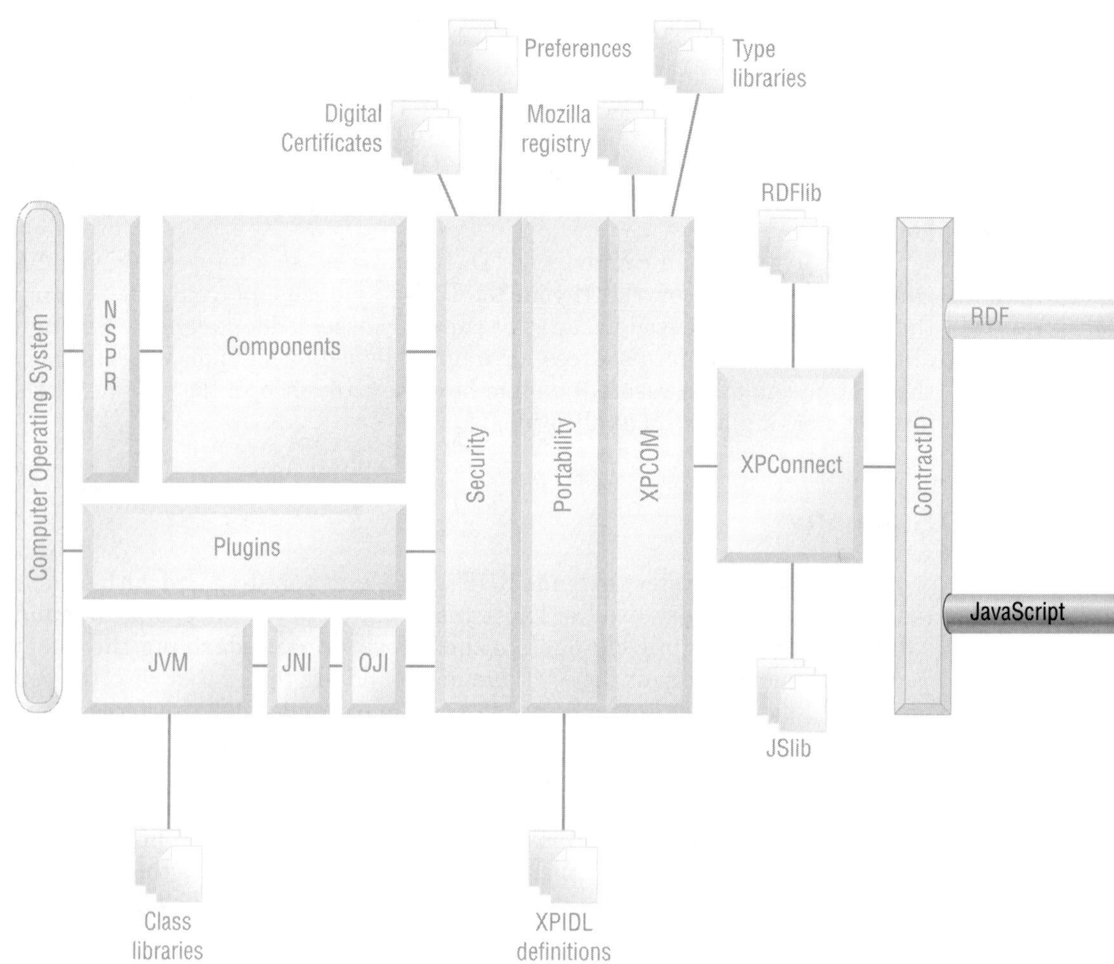

Preferences
Type libraries
Digital Certificates
Mozilla registry
RDFlib
Computer Operating System
NSPR
Components
Security
Portability
XPCOM
XPConnect
ContractID
RDF
Plugins
JavaScript
JVM
JNI
OJI
JSlib
Class libraries
XPIDL definitions

CHAPTER 15

XBL Bindings

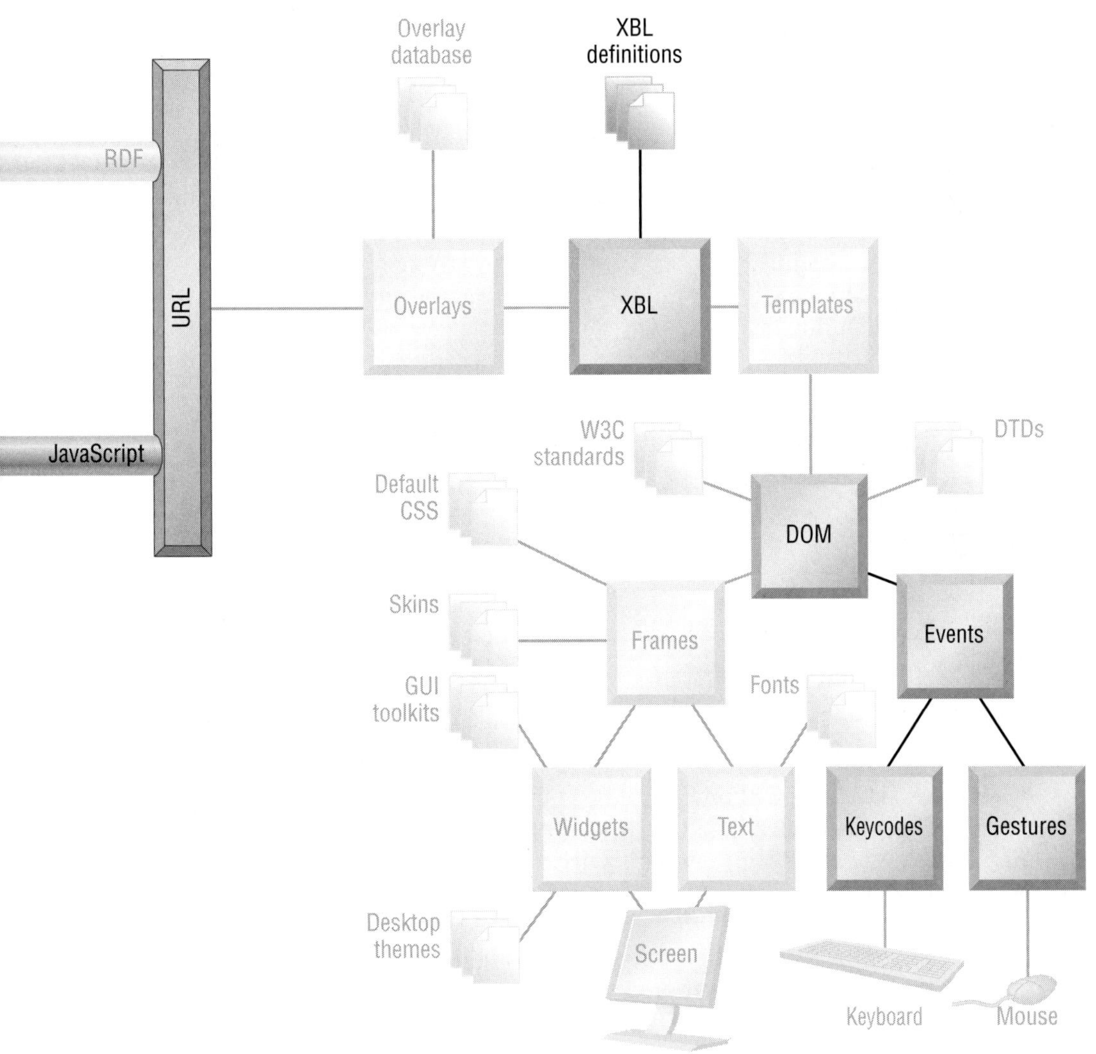

This chapter explains how to enhance the XUL language with new tags and new behavior using XBL (XML Binding Language).

XBL is an XML-based language that allows new, fully featured tags to be added to XUL, HTML, and XML. It is an efficient system for creating new GUI widgets. It is specific to Mozilla.

Plain XUL allows programmers to create user-defined tags like `<mytag>`, but such tags aren't very useful. They can be styled but are merely simple box-like tags. XBL, by comparison, allows for the creation of whole widgets with distinctive appearance and behavior. The content of an XBL widget is made up of tags drawn from XUL and HTML and from other tags based on XBL. An XBL widget is not as flexible as a Java applet or a plugin. It cannot start with a blank, rectangular canvas, and use sophisticated graphics libraries to draw on that plane. XBL can only combine existing tags.

XBL does not create new tags; it creates new bindings. A *binding* is a bundle of tags and scripts that together provide the features of a new widget-like event handler and displayable content. This bundle is a binding, and a binding is like an object. In Mozilla, a binding is matched to a user-defined tag with the Mozilla-specific CSS2 property: `-moz-binding`. After the binding is matched to the tag, they are said to be bound. A trivial binding is shown in Listing 15.1. This is a fragment of an XBL document and implements a widget that is just a smiley face (an emoticon).

Listing 15.1 Trivial example of an XBL binding.

```
<binding id="smiley">
  <content>
    <xul:image src="face.png"/>
  </content>
  <handlers>
    <handler event="click" action="alert('have a day')"/>
  </handlers>
</binding>
```

Such a binding could be attached to a user-defined tag named `<smiley/>` with a line of CSS like so:

```
smiley { -moz-binding: url("smiley.xml#smiley"); }
```

The `<smiley/>` tag will now displays a face whenever it is used in a XUL document. If the face is clicked on, it pops up an alert encouraging you to have a day. This is a very simple widget with its own trivial interactivity. Neither XUL nor HTML supplies a `<smiley>` tag.

The XBL binding system is built into the C/C++ code of the Mozilla Platform, but the bindings themselves are written using only JavaScript and XML. This fully interpreted environment makes bindings as easy to create and manage as XUL or HTML. This ease of use has been well-exploited in Mozilla. Many XBL bindings contribute to Mozilla applications such as the Classic Mail & News and the Classic Browser. Nearly all XUL tags have an XBL binding.

Throughout this book, references are made to `.xml` files in the `toolkit.jar` chrome file. These `.xml` files are XBL bindings, usually several per file. Some XUL tags documented in this book are nothing more than XBL bindings at work. Good examples are highly specialized tags like `<tabbrowser>` and `<colorpicker>`, which are defined purely in XBL. Even simple tags like `<button>` have XBL bindings.

Beyond Mozilla, a technology similar to XBL is the PostScript language. PostScript is used mostly for printing, but PostScript scripts can also be created by hand. Postscript allows chunks of displayable content to be named and reused. This makes it easy to construct large documents. List processing languages like Lisp and Tcl/Tk also provide an interpreted way of constructing GUIs, but they are more program-like than XML-based XBL. Tcl/Tk is probably XBL's biggest competitor in the Linux world. The pre-supplied components that Microsoft's .NET provides and the much simpler behaviors of Internet Explorer are XBL competitors in the world of Microsoft Windows.

An XBL binding has a clearly defined interface and a unique identity, and that makes XBL a tiny component system. Just as XPCOM is designed for 3GL components, XBL is designed for XML components. XBL's component model is much simpler than XPCOM's.

Because XBL bindings are made from XML and JavaScript, bound elements can be freely intermixed with HTML or XUL. HTML intermixing is unusual because the set of tags used in HTML pages is fixed and standard. It is far more common to see XBL used in XUL applications.

The NPA diagram at the start of this chapter shows the extent of XBL in the Mozilla Platform. Despite its status as a component system, XBL is a front-end Mozilla technology. During the loading of a XUL document, XBL bindings are identified and pulled separately into the final document's content. This inclusion process has some similarities with the overlay system. After tags bound to XBL bindings are loaded, they display their content like any XUL tag. The XBL system also has special support for capturing user input events. It uses a capture system almost the same as the XUL `<key>` tag.

This chapter continues with an overview of bindings and then gets down to the specific tags.

15.1 Binding Concepts

XBL extends XML and the traditional Web environment the way C++ extends C. It provides object-like features on top of a system that has no object-like features to start with.

15.1.1 An Example Binding

Every XBL document is just a list of bindings, each stated with a `<binding>` tag. Constructing a binding is similar to constructing an object's class. Listing

15.2 shows a simple XBL binding that is a variant of the XUL <checkbox> tag's binding.

Listing 15.2 Example XBL binding similar to <checkbox>'s binding.

```
<?xml version="1.0"?>
<bindings
  xmlns="http://www.mozilla.org/xbl"
  xmlns:xbl="http://www.mozilla.org/xbl"
     xmlns:xul="http://www.mozilla.org/keymaster/gatekeeper/
          there.is.only.xul"
>
<binding id="checkbox" extends="general.xml#basetext">

  <resources>
    <stylesheet src="chrome://global/skin/checkbox.css"/>
  </resources>

  <content>
    <xul:image class="checkbox-check" xbl:inherits="checked,disabled"/>
    <xul:hbox>
      <xul:image class="checkbox-icon" xbl:inherits="src"/>
      <xul:label xbl:inherits="xbl:text=label,accesskey,crop"/>
    </xul:hbox>
  </content>

  <implementation implements="nsIDOMXULCheckboxElement">
    <method name="check" action="this.checked = true"/>
    <property
      name="checked"
      onset="if (val) this.setAttribute('checked','true');"
      onget="return this.getAttribute('checked') == 'true';"
     />
  </implementation>

  <handlers>
    <handler event="click" button="0"
    action="if (!this.disabled) this.checked = !this.checked;"/>
    <handler event="keypress" key=" ">
      <![CDATA[
        this.checked = !this.checked;
      ]]>
    </handler>
  </handlers>

</binding>
</bindings>
```

Listing 15.2 shows many of the standard features of a binding. The <resource> and <content> sections describe data in the form of styles, images, tags, and plain XML elements. These sections are used to deliver XML content. The <implementation> and <handlers> section describe properties, methods, and event-handling hooks. These sections are installed as JavaScript and DOM content. The content and scripting aspects of a binding are like the data and code forks in a PC or Macintosh program. The pale content is XUL and JavaScript code. It is used *by* the binding, but it is not *part of* the XBL language.

It is common practice to study other people's bindings. "Reading Others' Code: Naming Conventions" in Chapter 16, XPCOM Objects, and Table 16.1 provide some reading hints for bindings created by mozilla.org.

15.1.2 Standards

XBL is an application of XML. Its XML definition can be found at *www.mozilla.org/xbl*. Mozilla does not load this URL; it is just used as an identifier that is recognized when encountered.

The standard suffix for a file containing XBL is `.xml`. The standard MIME type for an XBL document is `application/xml`.

XBL bindings are identified by a URL. There is no separate URL scheme for XBL; instead the two most common access methods are the `http:` and `chrome:` schemes. Like RDF, binding URLs include a `#id` suffix that identifies a given binding within an XBL document. Like RDF, that identified binding is considered a whole resource rather than a resource fragment. An example URL is

```
chrome://global/content/bindings/button.xml#button.
```

XBL has been submitted as a Note to the W3C. This means that a document describing XBL has been submitted to that organization. A W3C Note is a technology description lodged as a proposed solution to an issue that the W3C is considering. It is not a draft standard or "on the standards track"; it is just a proposal. The latest version of the XBL Note can be found at *www.mozilla.org/xbl/xbl.html*.

Mozilla's implementation of XBL is different from the Note submitted to the W3C. It contains additional features and does not implement all the features in the Note. The "Non-Tags and Non-Attributes" topic in this chapter discusses the differences.

Standards competing with XBL include ECMA-290 "ECMAScript Components" which is used by Microsoft in its WSH (Windows Scripting Host) technology. The WSDL standard and its related standards attempt to provide a distributed naming system for components and services, but WSDL is not as closely tied to user interaction as XBL is. Another semicompeting standard is XSL. XSL can process an XML file and replace specified tags with other content. That is the same as XBL, but XSL operates in batch mode, performing a single pass over the supplied document. XBL can be applied after a document is fully loaded. XBL is a helper system, rather than a full processing step like XSL. No other standard really addresses the niche that XBL addresses.

XBL has a broader agenda than most W3C standards. HTML, CSS, and JavaScript can only interoperate to a certain degree. Those three standards all focus on one tag, one style, and one object at a time. Although these standards allow content tags, style rules, and object properties to be grouped together, this grouping is quite narrow. There is no structural support across Web standards for programmers who need high-level object or component concepts to work with. XBL seeks to fill this gap for programmers by integrating XML, scripting, and styles into one structure—a binding.

15.1.3 Relationship with DOM Hierarchies

XBL bindings must be installed into a DOM hierarchy before they can be used.

Before a binding can be used, it must be *bound* to an existing tag in an existing XML document. That existing tag is called the *bound tag*, and the existing document is called the *target document*. If the bound tag has content of its own, that content is called the *explicit content*. If the binding contains a `<content>` tag, then the tags inside that `<content>` tag are called *anonymous content*. There is at most one set of anonymous content per binding, but there can be a different set of explicit content for each bound tag in the target document. Both types of content, plus the other details in the binding, add to the document that uses the binding.

When a binding is bound, the DOM hierarchy in the target document grows. Three changes are made:

1. The bound tag gains the properties, methods, and event handlers of the binding.
2. The bound tag has its content replaced with a mix of explicit and anonymous content.
3. The anonymous content is separately added to the DOM and is available via a special mechanism.

Steps 1 and 2 are repeated for each instance of the bound tag in the target document. This is a content generation process very similar to overlays and templates. Like overlays, content is inserted into the target document at specific points. Like templates, extra content is created by repeatedly copying a standard set of tags. The Mozilla Platform automatically performs these steps.

The full XBL definition of the binding is not available in the bound document. If necessary, it can be loaded and examined just as any XML document can.

These principles are broken down into steps in "How Bindings are Processed" later in this chapter.

15.1.4 Default Actions

The XBL system can be used to implement the default actions that HTML and XUL tags and widgets offer.

An example of a default action is given by the HTML `<input type="submit">` tag. When the button widget associated with this tag is clicked, form data are submitted by a browser to some Web server. No scripting is required to make this submission happen. The default action is part of the DOM Event processing that occurs for all XML tags. But how exactly is a form submission implemented, and how is it connected to the DOM Event processing?

The answer is that a default action can be implemented in an XBL binding. A binding provides a means to specify what DOM event and what JavaScript handler go together. When an event is generated, the XBL binding is automatically detected as the source of the default action, and the right handler is run, causing that action to occur.

A given widget can have a different default action for each kind of user input event. In the case of the `<input type="submit">` tag, pressing the Return or Enter key or clicking the displayed button produces the same effect. This does not have to be the case when a binding is created—every event can cause a different outcome.

Using a traditional even handler, the application programmer can override default actions. This, however, must be attacked correctly. If the application handler is installed as an attribute value (such as an `onclick` handler), then that handler will be used instead of the XBL handler. If the application handler is installed using `addEventListener()`, then this handler must be installed before the XBL handler is bound to the tag. This requirement puts the application handler ahead of the XBL handler on the list of event handlers. To achieve this status, see the remarks in "Scripting."

An XBL binding is not responsible for the event capture and bubbling processes. It is not responsible for maintaining the input focus or the state of the window's focus ring. Those things are done deep in the C/C++ part of the platform and have nothing to do with XBL. Mozilla's accessibility support (for the disabled) is implemented using XBL, but the input system that first captures accessibility commands is part of the core platform.

15.1.5 Object-like Features

A bound XBL binding has object-like features and can be considered an object from a JavaScript or DOM perspective.

An object interface consists of object attributes, methods, and exceptions. Binding interfaces contain object properties, methods, and handlers. Properties are effectively object attributes, and handlers are just special-purpose object methods. Exceptions can also be implemented in a binding, but XBL has no explicit syntax for them. To create an exception, use the `throw` feature of JavaScript instead.

XBL also has support for traditional object-oriented concepts. Table 15.1 is an overview of the OO support that XBL provides.

Table 15.1 XBL object support

Object concept	XBL support
Aggregation	XBL tags collect content (including bound content) and JavaScript code together into a binding, and merge explicit and anonymous content into a final content set.
Containment	The bound tag holds all content and JavaScript logic. An XBL binding can contain other bound tags, and therefore other bindings.
Encapsulation	A bound tag holds all the useful information a binding supplies, although some housekeeping information can be accessed using the JavaScript document object.
Inheritance	XBL supports the inherits attribute, for inheriting XML attributes, and the extends attribute, for inheriting whole bindings.
Information hiding	When a binding is bound, the binding specification is hidden from the bound tag. Only the interface implied by that specification is available.
Interfaces	A binding that implements an interface can be inherited by another binding by use of the extends attribute. A binding can specify what XPCOM interfaces it supports using the XBL implements attribute.
Late-binding	Bindings are loaded independently and asynchronously into a bound document. A binding can be bound or rebound using CSS2 rules at any time. Bindings must always be referred to explicitly. All bound bindings must be concrete. There is no mechanism for finding a base binding for a derived binding.
Object-based	Bound bindings look like objects from a JavaScript perspective.
Object-oriented	The XBL extends attribute supports basing XBL bindings on other XBL bindings. This support includes the concept of an inheritance chain. See following discussion.
Multiple inheritance	XBL only supports single inheritance of bindings.
Run-time type reflection	XBL has no automatic support for type reflection. A binding can implement the nsIClassInfo interface if it wishes.

Each binding can extend (inherit) one other binding. That other binding can in turn inherit a further binding, and so on. Such a set of inherited bindings form an order list called an *inheritance chain*. When a particular binding is bound, that particular binding is at the head of the chain. That binding is also called the *primary binding*. The chain is always at least one binding long. If the chain is exactly one binding long, then there is no inheritance at work.

Figure 15.1 shows an example of an inheritance chain, based on the XUL `<button>` tag.

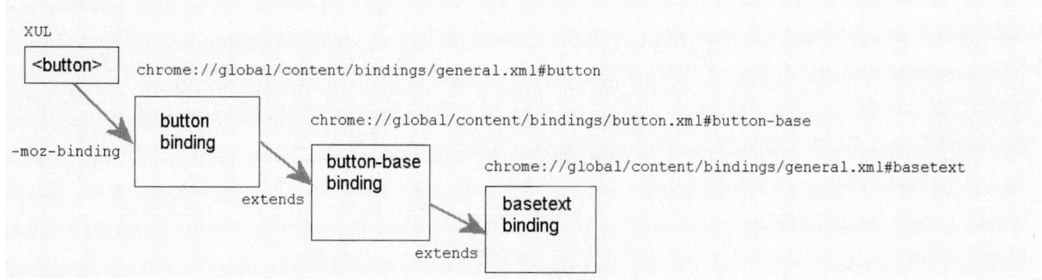

Fig. 15.1 XBL inheritance hierarchy for the XUL `<button>` tag.

This example shows an inheritance chain of three items. The "`button`" binding is bound to the `<button>` tag, and that binding is the head of the chain. The other two bindings are general-purpose bindings that are inherited in many places across XUL. The `button-base` binding is used for all (or most) button-like widgets, and the `basetext` binding is used for all widgets that have a textual component. `button` and `button-base` are defined in the same XBL document (`button.xml`), but `basetext` is defined elsewhere (in `general.xml`). All three of these bindings contribute features to the `<button>` tag's DOM object.

Two bindings can inherit the same base binding, so the full set of inheritance chains can be viewed as a tree (or grove of trees). This treelike structure might be an aid at design time, but there is no way to navigate it or inspect it from a script.

Table 15.2 shows how the various features of XBL bindings are inherited.

Table 15.2 Inheritance of XBL binding features

XBL feature	Inherited?
<resources>	All bindings in the inheritance chain have their resources loaded. All stylesheets have the same default weight, but rules nearest the head of the chain are applied later and override earlier rules.
<content>	No inheritance. The binding at the head of the chain is the sole binding used. If bound tags are contained inside <content>, rather than inherited, then their bindings are applied.
<field>, <property>, and <method>	Properties and methods are inherited. If the derived binding duplicates a name in a base binding, the derived version replaces the base version, and the base version is not available from logic in the derived binding.
<constructor> and <destructor>	Both are inherited. Constructers are run one at a time in order from the ultimate base binding to the final derived binding. Destructors are run one at a time in order from the final derived binding to the ultimate base binding.

Table 15.2 Inheritance of XBL binding features (Continued)

XBL feature	Inherited?
<handlers>	Handlers are inherited. Derived binding handlers override base binding handlers that define the same event.
display attribute	No inheritance. Only the attribute on the most derived binding is used.

15.1.6 XBL Component Framework

The XBL system is a very simple component framework. A component framework allows standardized components to interoperate in a convenient way. A binding is a form of component.

A component system similar to XBL is Perl's module system, which is accessed with the Perl `use` and `require` keywords. Both systems are quite primitive. XBL bindings can be inspected via the DOM just as Perl modules can be inspected via symbol tables. XBL bindings are not directly included the way Perl modules are, but in general terms they are overlaid on other code.

Component names in the XBL system are URLs of the form `Resource#Id`, where `Resource` is a document's Web address and `id` is the value of the `id` attribute for a `<binding>` tag. Like RDF, XBL treats `id`-qualified URLs as whole resources, not as offsets in an existing resource.

XBL has no component registry or name service and no way of querying the specification of a binding. Instead, each XUL or HTML document maintains a simple internal list of the currently active bindings for that document.

The XBL component system is a distributed system because bindings can be retrieved from URLs anywhere. Bindings do not communicate back to the server they are loaded from unless they contain code designed to do just that.

XBL does not have the features of complex component systems like Microsoft's COM, Mozilla's XPCOM, OMG CORBA, or Sun's JavaBeans. Its strengths are simplicity and immediacy, not expressive power or tight integration.

15.1.6.1 Bindings as XPCOM Components

An XBL binding can implement one or more XPCOM interfaces. This allows the DOM object for a bound tag to act like an XPCOM component with those interfaces.

A binding cannot act as an XPCOM component unless it is bound first.

15.2 Constructing One XBL Binding

This topic describes the individual XBL tags and tag attributes.

Some XBL tags have the same names as tags used elsewhere in Mozilla. It is always a good idea to provide full `xmlns` namespace declarations when creating XBL documents. That strategy helps avoid confusion. XBL tag names with meanings in other XML applications supported by Mozilla are

```
<bindings> <body> <children> <content> <image>
```

XBL attribute names with meaning elsewhere are

```
method action command modifiers charcode keycode key name readonly
    text
```

15.2.1 Bound Tags and `-moz-binding`

Most, but not all, XUL and HTML tags can be bound to an XBL binding. For a tag to be bound, it must have a frame—a styleable rectangular area in which it is displayed.

Any tag with this style has no frame and cannot be bound:

```
{ display: none; }
```

A tag that gains this style will lose any binding that it has. For this reason, a bound XUL tag should be collapsed rather than hidden if it needs to be visually suppressed.

Tag instances, not tag names, are bound to a binding. Each style rule that contains `-moz-binding` binds a set of tag instances. Any pattern that represents a CSS2 selector can be used as a set of instances to be bound. Listing 15.3 shows a number of examples.

Listing 15.3 CSS2 selector example for bindings.

```
box            { -moz-binding: url("binding.xml#sample"); }
#id            { -moz-binding: url("binding.xml#sample"); }
.class         { -moz-binding: url("binding.xml#sample"); }
box[X="here"] { -moz-binding: url("binding.xml#sample"); }
box,vbox,hbox { -moz-binding: url("binding.xml#sample"); }
box vbox       { -moz-binding: url("binding.xml#sample"); }
```

The first line binds all <box> tag instances to the same binding. Each tag instance has its own interface and its own set of state. The second line binds just one tag, regardless of its name. The third line binds any and all tags with a given class attribute. The fourth line binds only a subset of <box> tags, those that have the `X="here"` attribute. The fifth line binds all <box>, <vbox>, and <hbox> tags, and so on. Where two style rules bind the same tag instance (a very bad piece of design), the more specific of the two rules takes precedence, or the later of the two, if the two selectors are the same. That is normal CSS2 processing.

This style rule support is used in XUL for tags that have variant types, like `<button>`. Each variant is bound to a different binding. Variant bindings can be seen in `xul.css` in `toolkit.jar` in the chrome.

Bindings can be explicitly avoided as follows:

```
{ -moz-binding : none; }
```

Mozilla (to version 1.4 at least) has some issues adding and removing bindings; the advice in "Scripting" in this chapter should be followed rather than just applying and unapplying style rules.

Finally, a long-standing bug (at least to version 1.4) means that a tag with this style will not display properly if bound:

```
{ display: block; }
```

Because blocks are not part of XUL, this is only a trap for HTML. Avoid combining this style with -moz-binding.

15.2.2 <bindings>

The <bindings> tag is the outermost tag in an XBL document. It has no special meaning of its own and no special attributes. It can contain only <binding> tags.

A <!DOCTYPE> declaration is not needed for XBL documents. If one is added, the minimum required is

```
<!DOCTYPE bindings>
```

15.2.3 <binding>

The <binding> tag holds one binding specification. It can have up to four child tags. Each of the following tags should appear at most once:

```
<resources> <content> <implementation> <handlers>
```

All four are optional. It is recommended that they appear in the order shown, but that is not mandatory. A <binding> tag with no content is useless, except that it will remove all content and default actions from any tag bound to it. That effect is similar to the style "-moz-binding : none".
The <binding> tag has the following special attributes:

```
id display extends inheritstyle
```

The id attribute is unique and identifies the binding. A binding does not have a name, it has a URL identifier. If the #id part of the URL is left off, the first binding in the XBL document will be used.

The extends attribute is XBL's inheritance mechanism. It can be set to the URL of one other binding. A series of bindings specified with extends form an XBL inheritance chain, as discussed in "Object-like Features."

The extends attribute also accepts a shorthand value. That shorthand value is used for the display attribute as well. It consists of a xul: prefix and a XUL tag name. This shorthand says that the binding is based on an existing tag and should use that tag's features. In the case of extends, this attribute provides a base implementation for the binding to enhance. An example is

```
extends="xul:box"
```

The `display` attribute accepts only the shorthand notation used for `extends`. It states what box object to apply for the binding. The box object identified is the one that normally applies to the stated XUL tag. An example is

```
display="xul:button"
```

This causes the binding to adopt the box object that the XUL `<button>` tag has.

The `inherit` style attribute can be set to `false`. It is `true` by default. If it is set to `false`, the bound tag will not benefit from any styles that were associated with the tag before the binding was added.

15.2.4 `<resources>`

The `<resources>` tag states what other documents a given binding requires. It is similar to the `<LINK>` tag of HTML. The `<resources>` tag has no special attributes and can only contain these XBL tags:

```
<image> <stylesheet>
```

Zero or more of either tag can be stated. Order is unimportant, except that later `<stylesheet>` tags will be applied after earlier ones. The XBL system has a little intelligence about the contents of the `<resources>` tag, as described next.

15.2.4.1 `<image>` The `<image>` tag is identical to the XUL `<image>` tag, except that the only useful attribute is `src`. As for XUL, `src` specifies the URL of an image.

```
<image src="icons.gif"/>
```

XBL does nothing with this tag except tell the Mozilla Platform to retrieve the matching image, which is then cached. The `<image>` tag is a hint to the platform that the image is important and may be needed later. Later uses might be in the XUL `<image>` tag, the HTML `<img>` tag, the CSS2 list-style-image property, or in the content part of an XBL definition. Stating an `<image>` tag is just a performance optimization.

15.2.4.2 `<stylesheet>` The `<stylesheet>` tag is identical to the HTML `<style src=>` tag. It cannot contain any inline content of its own.

```
<stylesheet src="chrome://global/skin/button.css"/>
```

Stylesheets are used in XBL to contain all the presentation detail of the XBL widget. This allows the presentation details to be theme-dependent. It also allows style rules to be created that only apply to the anonymous content of the bound tag. In the previous example, all the presentation detail for the XUL `<button>` tag (which is based on an XBL binding with `id="button"`) is stored in a theme-dependent URL.

More than one <stylesheet> tag may be used per binding, but this is rare. If so, the stylesheets are applied in the order they appear.

If a binding has an inheritance chain of other bindings, and those other bindings have <stylesheet> tags, then all stylesheets will be applied. The stylesheets are applied in order from the tail to the head of the chain so that the primary binding has highest precedence.

The standard XUL tag bindings stored in `toolkit.jar` in the chrome have a stylesheet each. Those stylesheets are theme-dependent. A theme designer should implement all these standard stylesheets for a given theme, or else the display of XUL tags will not be consistent under that theme. The same goes for themes that hope to support Mozilla's standard applications such as Messenger. The stylesheets associated with XBL bindings used in the Messenger client should also be implemented by a theme designer if these applications are to benefit from the new theme.

15.2.5 <content>

The <content> tag holds all the anonymous content of the binding. It can hold XML tags from any XML namespace, such as HTML, XUL, or MathML. It can also hold the XBL-specific <children> tag. XUL observers and broadcasters, along with the <script> tag, do not function when used as anonymous content.

The <content> tag used to have two special attributes:

```
includes excludes
```

Both attributes are deprecated and should be avoided. Use the <children> tag in the anonymous content instead. If any other attributes appear on the <content> tag, they will be copied to the bound tag.

Preexisting attributes of the bound tag can be added to the tags inside <content> using the `inherits` attribute. Explicit content of the bound tag can be merged with the tags inside <content> using the <children> tag.

If a binding uses the `extends` attribute, so that it builds on another binding, then any <content> tag in that other binding is ignored.

If the <content> tag of the bound binding is empty, then the bound tag will have no content either.

15.2.5.1 Merging Attributes with `xbl:inherits=` The anonymous content of a <content> tag can be a document fragment of any type and of any size. The XBL <children> tag can appear anywhere inside that document fragment.

Non-XBL tags in the content can use one XBL tag attribute: the `inherits` attribute. This attribute is used to pass parameters and their values from the bound tag to the anonymous content, as though those content tags were observing the bound tag. This parameter passing is done by simply renaming and copying the bound tag attribute values to the anonymous content tags.

This mechanism gives the user of the bound tag some control over the anonymous content. For this to work, the binding creator must anticipate the user's needs and strategically place inherits in the binding's anonymous content.

The inherits attribute holds a comma- or space-separated sequence of attribute mappings. An attribute mapping states what attribute on the anonymous content tag should receive the value of what attribute on the bound tag. Each attribute mapping uses one of the following four syntaxes:

```
att1
att1=att2
xbl:text=att2
att1=xbl:text
```

att1 and att2 are any legal XML attribute names.

- ☞ The first syntax form says that the att1 attribute on the bound tag, and its value, should be copied straight to the anonymous tag.
- ☞ The second syntax form says that the att1 attribute on the anonymous tag should have the value of the att2 attribute on the bound tag.
- ☞ The third form uses the special reserved name xbl:text. It says that the anonymous tag's content (a DOM 1 Text Node) should contain the value of the att2 attribute on the bound tag. This achieves the same effect as <textnode> in XUL templates.
- ☞ The fourth form says that the att1 attribute on the anonymous tag should contain the value of the bound tag's explicit content, which must be a DOM 1 text node.

Because the inherits attribute is an XBL attribute, it can't appear alone inside a non-XBL tag. It must be fully specified with an XML namespace. This is done by prefixing it with xbl: (or similar) and adding another namespace declaration to the top of the XBL document. That is why some XBL documents have two references to the XBL namespace, as shown here:

```
<bindings id="test"
   xmlns="http://www.mozilla.org/xbl"
   xmlns:xbl="http://www.mozilla.org/xbl"
   xmlns:xul="http://www.mozilla.org/keymaster/gatekeeper/
     there.is.only.xul"
>
```

The first XBL namespace is the default; the second is stated specifically for the inherits attribute.

When all these things are put together, a full example of inherits is

```
<xul:label dir="ltr"
     xbl:inherits="xbl:text=value,style,align=justify"/>
```

If the bound tag were defined this way:

```
<mytag value="Test" style="color:red" justify="start"/>
```

then, after substitution, the anonymous <xul:label> tag would be replaced by

```
<xul:label dir="ltr" style="color:red" align="start">
Test
</xul:label>
```

The inherits attribute can be used anywhere in the anonymous content and can map one attribute to many different anonymous content tags if required. Anonymous content tags are always free to specify attributes directly, like dir="ltr". If the special xbl:text attribute is used more than once, all assigned values will appear in the text node of the anonymous tag.

15.2.5.2 Merging Tags with <children> The <children> tag controls the merging of the bound tag's explicit content (if any) with the binding <content> tag's anonymous content (if any). The <children> tag can appear anywhere inside the anonymous content of the binding. It represents any explicit content that the bound tag has. It supports the following special attribute:

```
includes
```

The includes attribute can be set to a comma-separated list of tag names. No namespace qualifiers are required. This attribute modifies the content merge process. What content is merged depends on what content exists. Here is an overview of the possibilities:

1. If there is no explicit content, then any <children> tags in the anonymous content are ignored. This is equivalent to deleting all start, end, and singleton <children> tags from the <content> section but leaving other tags and subtags intact. The final content is a copy of all of the remaining anonymous content.
2. If there is no anonymous content, then the bound tag will contain no content at all after all merging is done.
3. If there is both explicit and anonymous content, then count up the explicit content tags that are immediate children of the bound tag. Each of these tags should match one <children> tag. If this is achieved, then the final content will be a merged copy of all explicit and anonymous content.
4. If none of these three conditions is met, the <children> tag has been used incorrectly in the anonymous content, or unexpected explicit content is present in the bound tag. The final merged results will be unpredictable in this case.

The last two cases require further explanation. How content is merged depends entirely on the <children> tag. This tag creates the illusion that explicit content is added into the anonymous content. In reality, the final merged content is a copy of all the other content. It is convenient and harmless, however, to think of the explicit content as being added to the anonymous content. Here is how such additions can occur:

1. If a `<children>` tag appears without an `includes` attribute, then it stands for all the explicit content, which then replaces the `<children>` tag and its content subtree in the anonymous content. In this case, exactly one `<children>` tag should appear in the anonymous content.
2. If a `<children>` tag appears with the `includes` attribute, then it stands for some of the explicit content only. That explicit content will replace `<children>` and its content subtree in the anonymous content. All immediate children of the bound tag with tag names that match the `includes` list will be inserted. They will be inserted at that `<children>` point in the anonymous content. They will be inserted in the same order they appear in the bound tag.
3. If point 2 is repeated carefully, enough `<children includes=>` tags will exist to cover all the immediate child tags of the bound tag. Such tags provide complete coverage of explicit tags. In that case, all the explicit and anonymous content will be merged neatly.
4. If point 2 is not repeated enough, then some immediate child tags of the bound tag will not find a matching `<children includes=>` tag. That is incomplete coverage of explicit tags. All explicit tags are appended to the final content by Mozilla, and all anonymous content is thrown out.
5. If point 2 is done carelessly, then some child tags of the bound tag will match more than one `<children>` tag. That is a mess and does not work. In this case, content output will be unpredictable.

In summary, the binding designer must either (a) make no assumptions about the explicit content of the bound tag and avoid using includes; (b) fully anticipate what explicit tags may be put into a bound tag and use includes everywhere; or (c) make an educated guess and rely on the XBL system outputting something that is reasonable.

Listing 15.4 shows well-formed examples of this system at work.

Listing 15.4 Source code for XBL content merging examples.

```
<!-- tag to be bound -->
<mytag>
  <image src="face.png"/>
  <description label="Smile"/>
  <image src="face.png"/>
</mytag>

<!-- Example 1: unknown explicit content -->
<content>
  <box>
    <children/>
  </box>
</content>
```

```
<!-- Example 2: known explicit content -->
<content>
  <children includes="description"/>
  <box>
    <children includes="image"/>
  </box>
</content>

<!-- Example 3: known but optional explicit content -->
<content>
  <children includes="image|description">
    <label value="No emoticon supplied"/>
  </children>
</content>
```

In this listing, the `<mytag>` tag is the tag to be bound. The other fragments are from three different bindings. Example 1 adds all the explicit content, regardless of what it is, into a <box>. Example 2 carefully places each type of explicit content in a certain spot. Example 3 repeats back the explicit content, but if none exists, a `<label>` is reported instead. Listing 15.5 shows the final content for each of these cases.

Listing 15.5 Generated content for XBL content merging examples.

```
<!-- Example 1: unknown explicit content -->
<mytag>
  <box>
    <image src="face.png"/>
    <description label="Smile"/>
    <image src="face.png"/>
  </box>
</mytag>

<!-- Example 2: known explicit content -->
<mytag>
  <description label="Smile"/>
  <box>
    <image src="face.png"/>
    <image src="face.png"/>
  </box>
</mytag>

<!-- Example 3: known but optional explicit content -->
<mytag>
  <image src="face.png"/>
  <description label="Smile"/>
  <image src="face.png"/>
</mytag>
```

If the original contents of `<mytag>` are made very different, Example 1 will always work, but Examples 2 and 3 might yield unexpected results.

Listing 15.6 shows an arrangement that will never work reliably because any explicit content <image> tags will match both <children> tags in the anonymous content.

Listing 15.6 Poorly formed anonymous content for an XBL binding.

```
<content>
  <children/>
  <box>
    <children includes="image"/>
  </box>
</content>
```

15.2.5.3 Merging Bound Tags The anonymous content inside the XBL <content> tag can include tags that are in turn bound to some XBL binding. This is just as well because most XUL tags are bound tags.

XBL automatically supports bound tags as anonymous content. Such tags are treated like any other tag. Just use the bound tag as if no binding were involved.

It is possible to create containment and inheritance cycles between one or more bindings. This should be avoided because it doesn't work. The <content> tag should never contain an instance of the tag to be bound.

15.2.6 <implementation>

The <implementation> tag is a simple container tag. It specifies the object-like interface of the binding. This interface is implemented inside the binding using JavaScript. It is then available to JavaScript scripts that run outside the bound tag. The interface created appears as properties and methods on the bound tag.

The <implementation> tag has one special attribute:

`implements`

This attribute can be set to a comma- or space-separated list of XPCOM interface names, like `nsISimpleEnumerator` or `nsIDOMEventListener`. Any interface name can be used. The Mozilla Platform treats the binding as an XPConnected (JavaScript wrapped) XPCOM component and uses these interface names to identify what the binding can do. It is up to the binding creator to make sure that the binding faithfully implements the interfaces it advertises. The XBL system automatically adds functionality equivalent to the `nsISupports` interface.

If any of these interfaces are specified and implemented, they appear as interfaces on the bound tag.

The `type` attribute is not supported by <implementation> or any of its subtags. The language used to define the content is assumed to be JavaScript. Use of `<![CDATA[ ]]>` XML syntax is recommended in all binding code when scripts are nontrivial in size.

The <implementation> tag can hold any number of these tags as children, in any order:

```
<field> <property> <method>
```

The <implementation> tag can also hold up to one of each of these tags:

```
<constructor> <destructor>
```

All five of these tags hold JavaScript scripts as content. Such scripts have access to several well-known JavaScript properties:

```
this window document event
```

The window and document properties are the same as those used in XUL and HTML scripts and refer to the window and document of the bound tag. The this property references the DOM Element object of the bound tag, which contains many useful DOM methods, like getAttribute(). The event property exists only for <handler> code and contains a DOM Event object.

Be aware that within an XBL <implementation> section, the this property has a special feature. All simple values assigned to properties of the this object are automatically turned to String types. Under that rule, the following line of code returns the string "1213":

```
this.dozen = 12; alert(dozen + 13);
```

This conversion shows up only when you use the + operator. For other mathematical operations, Strings will be silently converted to numbers and the behavior is hidden. A simple workaround is to store the values in an Object. This line of code reports 25:

```
this.d = {}; d.dozen = 12; alert(d.dozen + 13);
```

A binding without an <implementation> tag is still useful. It can display content and it can handle events.

Listing 15.7 is a simple example of a partial XBL object. It implements an experimental light bulb. Every time this light bulb's power output is checked, it ages slightly and its power output drops as a consequence. Eventually, trying to turn it on or off won't work at all because it becomes too inefficient.

Listing 15.7 Example object interface using XBL <implementation>.

```
<implementation>
  <field name="rating" readonly="true">60</field>
  <field name="lit">true</field>
  <field name="age">0</field>
  <property name="power"
           onget="age++; return rating-age/1000;"
           onset="age=(rating-val)*1000;"
  >
```

```
  <method name="toggle">
    <body>
      if ( this.power > 30 ) this.lit = !this.lit;
    </body>
  </method>
</implementation>
```

This object has four properties: rating (a constant value, intended here it is Watts), lit (a boolean), age (an integer), and power (a dynamically calculated value). It has one method: toggle(). These property names appear both as attribute values in XBL tags and as JavaScript code within the tag content. For example, the toggle() method uses the power and lit properties, whose names also appear as values of the name attribute in <field> tags.

The interface in Listing 15.7 is equivalent to the JavaScript object in Listing 15.8.

Listing 15.8 Equivalent JavaScript object to Listing 15.6.

```
var bulb = {
  const rating : 60,
        lit : true,
        age : 0,
    get power() { age++; return rating-age/1000; },
    set power(val) { age=(rating-val)*1000; },
        toggle : function () {
          if ( this.power > 30 ) this.lit = !this.lit;
        }
};
```

The two listings are obviously very similar. Why not just use a plain JavaScript object and avoid XBL? Such an object must be hand-attached to every tag that needs it, using a script or scripts. Using XBL, the object appears everywhere the CSS binding rule says it should, automatically.

15.2.6.1 <field> The <field> tag is the simplest part of the binding interface. It is designed to hold a simple variable. It is used to hold programmer-specified state information, for each bound tag. The <property> tag is a more flexible version of <field>.

<field> has two special attributes:

```
name readonly
```

- ☞ The name attribute holds the name of the JavaScript property that the field implements. Therefore, it must be a valid JavaScript variable name.
- ☞ The readonly attribute can be set to true, in which case a field cannot be set from a script.

The syntax for <field> is

```
<field>JavaScript expression</field>
```

Note that the content is an expression, not a statement. Because the expression is evaluated once only, it is usually a constant expression, but it can be a complicated calculation if required. This evaluation occurs when the binding is bound. Examples include

```
<field name="count">3+2</field>
<field name="address" readonly="true">"12 High St"</field>
<field name="phonelist">[]</field>
```

These examples look strange because there is no obvious assignment taking place. Instead, the XBL system evaluates the supplied expression and uses the result. These tags are similar to these JavaScript statements:

```
var   count     = eval('3+2');            // 5
const address   = eval('"12 High St"');   // a string
var   phonelist = eval('[]');             // an empty Array
```

Once created, fields are properties of the bound tag's object, which is the same as this, and can be used normally.

15.2.6.2 `<property>`, `<getter>`, and `<setter>` The `<property>` tag is designed to hold a simple variable, just as the `<field>` tag does. This variable is available as a JavaScript property on the bound tag's DOM object.

The difference between `<property>` and `<field>` is that the `<property>` tag's variable acts like an interface, whereas the `<field>` tag's variable is a simple value.

The `<property>` variable's value can be dynamically calculated when it is either read or written, and either operation can have side effects. This means that scripts using the property can cause other processing to occur just by setting or getting it.

Recall from Chapter 5, Scripting, that a JavaScript property can have its state defined with `__defineGetter__` and `__defineSetter__` functions. A `<property>` tag's property works the same way, except that it is defined with `<getter>` and `<setter>` tags, or with shorthand `onget` and `onset` attributes.

The `<property>` tag has four special attributes:

```
name readonly onget onset
```

- `name` is the name of the JavaScript property that this property defines. It must be a legal JavaScript name.
- `readonly` ensures that the property acts like a const JavaScript variable. It can be read but not written.
- `onget` is a shorthand notation for the `<getter>` tag and takes a script as its value. If both `onget` and `<getter>` are specified, then `onget` is used.
- `onset` is a shorthand notation for the `<setter>` tag and takes a script as its value. If both `onset` and `<setter>` are specified, then `onset` is used. `onset` is useless if `readonly="true"` is also specified.

The <property> tag can hold zero or one <getter> and <setter> tags as content. In turn, the content of these tags is the body of a JavaScript function.

- ☞ The <getter> tag and the onget attribute must contain a sequence of JavaScript statements that result in return being called.
- ☞ The <setter> tag and the onset attribute must also contain JavaScript but should return val. The special variable val contains the value passed in to the setter.

See Listing 15.7 for a simple example of onget and onset. The equivalent syntax using <getter> and <setter> is shown in Listing 15.9. The CDATA sections could be dropped in this example because the code is trivial. The keyword this is used everywhere for clarity—a recommended practice.

Listing 15.9 Example of XBL <getter> and <setter> use.

```
<property name="power">
  <getter><![CDATA[
    this.age++;
    return this.rating - this.age/1000;
  ]]>
  </getter>
  <setter><![CDATA[
    this.age = (this.rating - val) * 1000;
    return val;
  ]]>
  </setter>
</property>
```

If an attempt is made to set such a property when both <setter> and onset are missing, then an error will be reported to the JavaScript console (or an exception will be raised). If an attempt is made to get the value of such a property when both <getter> and onget are missing, then undefined will be returned.

15.2.6.3 <method>, <parameter>, and <body> The <method> tag is used to define an interface method. It contains zero or more <parameter> tags followed by exactly one <body> tag. The <method> tag supports one special attribute:

```
name
```

The name attribute specifies the name of a JavaScript property that will hold a Function object, so it must be a valid JavaScript identifier. The <method> tag does not support the action attribute and Mozilla may crash if that attribute is used.

If inheritance chains are being used, then there is no way for any extended binding <method> to run any base binding <method> that has been overridden by an extended binding <method> with the same name. You cannot work with overridden base-binding methods.

The <parameter> tag has exactly the same syntax as the <method> tag. Its sole name attribute defines one variable name passed in to the methods. The order of <parameter> tags is the same as the order of variables passed to the method.

The <method> and <parameter> tags are not used to create a fully typed function signature. They are just used as names. There is no type checking, or even argument counting. There is no type reflection beyond what JavaScript itself provides. There is no way to specify the type of the return value. These tags are very simplistic.

It is not possible to create two methods with the same names but different numbers of parameters. Because all JavaScript functions support variable argument lists, there is also no need to create such variations.

Finally, the <body> tag contains the JavaScript statements that make up the method. This tag has no special attributes at all. The JavaScript return statement should be used in the code when the method has something to return. The arguments object, which appears in all JavaScript functions, is also available for use in the content of the <body> tag.

Listing 15.10 shows these tags working together:

Listing 15.10 Example of XBL <method>,<parameter>, and <body> tags.

```
<method name="play">
  <parameter name="boy"/>
  <parameter name="dog"/>
  <parameter name="ball"/>
  <body><![CDATA[
    if ( arguments.length != 3)
      throw Components.results.NS_ERROR_INVALID_ARG;

    if ( boy == "Tom" && dog == "Spot" )
    {
      return document.fetch(ball.type);
    }
    return null;
  ]]>
  </body>
</method>
```

This example shows that any checks on the arguments passed in must be done by hand; nothing is done for you automatically. JavaScript's throw statement may be used to terminate the method and return an exception to the calling code. The value returned in this example is one of XPCOM's official error values. By using one of these constants, the method is conforming to XPCOM component standards. The method body is free to interact with any objects that it likes in the current window—in this case, the fetch() method is a method or function stored outside the binding. This piece of XBL is equivalent to the JavaScript function shown in Listing 15.11.

Listing 15.11 JavaScript function equivalent of an XBL <method>.

```
function play(boy, dog, ball)
{
  if ( arguments.length != 3)
    throw Components.results.NS_ERROR_INVALID_ARG;

  if ( boy == "Tom" && dog == "Spot" )
  {
    return document.fetch(ball.type);
  }
  return null;
}
```

The two definitions are hardly different at all, and so it is no surprise that XBL <method> contents are converted to JavaScript soon after an XBL document is loaded and parsed.

15.2.6.4 <constructor> and <destructor> The <constructor> and <destructor> tags are event handlers that fire once only during the bound lifetime of a binding. They are used for initialization and cleanup activities, just as constructors and destructors in most object-oriented languages are. XBL constructors and destructors have standard object-oriented semantics and do not follow the prototype system of JavaScript.

The only special attribute that these two tags support is this attribute:

```
action
```

The action attribute is shorthand for the content of the <constructor> and <destructor> tags. That content is a JavaScript function body, as for the XBL <body> tag. It can be specified between start and end tags or by using the action attribute. If both are specified, the action attribute is used, but it makes no sense to specify both.

The <construction> tag runs its action each time the binding is bound to a target document tag. That could be a large number of times, and if so, it is important that the constructor's action has good performance. There is no way to control the bindings in the inheritance chain using the <constructor> tag. There is no way to control any bound tags in the <content> section from the <constructor> tag. The constructor code is passed no arguments, but the this pointer is always available. The construction code does not need to return a value.

If the current binding inherits another binding, then <constructor> tags will fire in order from the tail to the head of the inheritance chain—in other words, the <constructor> tag of the primary binding will be the last one to fire.

The <destructor> tag runs its action each time the binding is unbound from a target document tag. It is rare that this occurs without the whole target document being destroyed, but if bindings are managed by hand, or if the state shared by multiple windows is maintained, then a <destructor> may be useful. As for the <constructor> tag, there is no special way to affect the status of other bindings that are part of the current binding. The destruction code is not passed any arguments and does not need to return any value.

If the current binding extends (inherits from) another binding, then <destructor> tags will fire in order from the head to the tail of the inheritance chain—in other words, the <destructor> tag of the primary binding will be the first one to fire.

It is common to create XPCOM objects from a constructor. If only one such object is required for a given binding, rather than one per bound tag, then a common idiom for arranging this is shown in Listing 15.12.

Listing 15.12 Creation of global components using an XBL constructor.

```
<constructor><![CDATA[
if (!document.globalPicker)
{
  var Cc = Components.classes;
  var Ci = Components.interfaces;
  var comp = Cc["@mozilla.org/filepicker;1"];
  document.globalPicker = comp.getService(Ci.nsIFilePicker);
}
]]></constructor>
```

In this code, each bound tag checks to see whether the initialization has been done yet, and if it has, the code simply ignores that step. Bindings are all bound at different times, but because Mozilla is single-threaded, it is not possible for two constructors to run at the same time.

15.2.7 <handlers>

The <handlers> tag is a simple container tag that holds all the event handlers associated with the XBL binding. It has no special attributes of its own. It holds one or more <handler> tags. Each handler tag is responsible for executing some JavaScript in response to a single DOM 2 event on the bound tag.

The XBL bindings stored in Mozilla's chrome contain over 500 individual handlers and so are responsible for a great deal of interactivity. Many of the events processed by standard applications like the Classic Browser and Classic Mail & News are the result of XBL bindings rather than specific application code.

The event handlers specified in XBL are one of four sources of handlers in Mozilla. Chapter 6, Events, describes support for on... style event handlers. It also describes the <key> tag. That tag has syntax very similar to the <handler> tag. The last set of handlers is buried deep inside the Mozilla Platform. Those handlers are written in C/C++ and are installed automatically by the platform when a window first opens.

These last handlers are the default handlers that run if nothing else is installed. Just as the Mozilla Platform precreates a special command controller for handling the focus, so too does the platform install a set of special handlers for the most fundamental types of event processing. When `<key>` handlers are added, they sit on top of the fundamental handlers, just as application-defined `onclick` handlers sit on top of the XBL bindings. When `<handler>` tags are added, they sit alongside the fundamental handlers, as if both were registered with `addEventListener()`.

Although this last and most hidden set of handlers is implemented as part of the XBL system, it is not accessible to application programmers. The main thing to note is that some event handling occurs underneath XBL bindings, and that no amount of searching in the chrome will find code that is responsible for it all.

15.2.7.1 `<handler>` The `<handler>` tag is very much like the XUL `<key>` tag. It defines one event target and one action for one highly specific event. An action is either a piece of script or a command to execute.

The `<handler>` tag implements the default action for the given event when it occurs on the bound tag. It can be overridden on the bound tag with a normal DOM 2 Events event handler.

For the handler to run, the matching event must be generated on the bound tag. That means the event must be generated either by a user action, as a consequence of document changes, or via the DOM 2 Events `dispatchEvent()` method. There is discussion of XBL event flow in "Scripting" later in this chapter.

The `<handler>` tag supports the following special attributes:

```
event phase command modifiers clickcount key keycode charcode button
     action
```

- The `event` attribute specifies the event name for the handler, drawing from the events that Mozilla supports. See Table 6.1 for a list of event names. `mousedown` is an example event. `event` has no default value.
- The `phase` attribute says at what stage in the DOM 2 Event cycle the action will fire. It must be set to "`capturing`", "`target`", or "`bubbling`". "`bubbling`" is the default.
- The `command` attribute specifies a command (as described in Chapter 9, Commands) that will be executed when the event occurs. The controller used to find and execute the command, however, will be sought on the currently focused tag, not on the bound tag. This means that the binding must be entirely focusable; otherwise, steps must be taken to ensure that the focusable parts of the binding content have a suitable controller. This attribute is mutually exclusive with `action`. It has no default value.

- The modifiers attribute accepts a space- or comma-separated list of the values shift, control, alt, meta, accel, and access. This attribute is used to specify which modifiers apply to a key event. All stated modifiers must be pressed for the event to occur. accel is the generic, platform-independent accelerator key as described in Chapter 6, Events. access matches the case where a shortcut key (a hot key) for the bound tag has been pressed. Shortcut keys are specified with the XUL key= attribute. The default is no modifiers.
- The clickcount key is only used for mouse events. It contains a single digit that specifies how many user clicks of the mouse are required (down-up is one click). The maximum number of clicks is ultimately an operating system limit. Mozilla supports at least three clicks. The default is any number of clicks.
- The key attribute is used only for key events. It contains a single printable key, such as 'A'. Either key or keycode should be used for key events, but not both. The default is any key press.
- The keycode attribute is used only for key events. It contains a single VK_ key mnemonic from the list in Table 6.3. Either keycode or key should be used for key events, but not both. The default value is any key.
- The charcode attribute is an older, deprecated name for the key attribute. Use key instead.
- The button attribute is used only for mouse events. It contains a single digit that specifies which mouse button is pressed. The number of mouse buttons is ultimately an operating system limit; Mozilla supports at least three buttons. The first button is button 0. The default button is any button. On a two- or three-button mouse, the right button is button 2.
- The action attribute contains the script that should run when the event occurs. This attribute is mutually exclusive with the command attribute. It has no default value.

If neither the command nor the action attribute is specified, then a JavaScript event handler for the event can be put between start and end <handler> tags. An example handler is

```
<handler event="click" phase="target" clickcount="1" button="0">
  this.do_custom_click(); // a <method> of the binding
</handler>
```

This is the default action for a left-button single-click click event. The do_custom_click() method is specified elsewhere in the binding so that it can also be called directly on the bound tag's DOM object.

15.2.8 Non-tags and Non-attributes

The XBL system has its share of tags that don't exist, but appear to exist. The following summary applies to Mozilla versions to 1.4.

The W3C Note for XBL is a proposal and does not exactly match Mozilla's implementation. Mozilla's version of XBL does not support the following aspects of that Note:

- The `type` attribute, used on `<bindings>`, `<method>`, and other tags.
- The `applyauthorsheets` attribute on the `<content>` tag.
- The `applybindingsheets` attribute on the `<children>` tag.
- The `<element>` tag and all references to it.
- The following events are not supported: `contentgenerated`, `content-destroyed`, `bindingattached`, `bindingdetached`.

These two attributes come from the early development of XBL and should be avoided: the `includes` attribute when used on the `<content>` tag and the `charcode` attribute when used on the `<handler>` tag.

The `<script>` tag is not part of XBL and won't work at all inside a pure XBL document.

The following tag attributes do nothing at all:

```
attachto applyauthorstyles styleexplicitcontent
```

15.3 Combining Multiple Bindings

The XBL inheritance system is given an overview in "Object-like Features" earlier in this chapter. This topic is concerned with uses of the inheritance system. Only a binding creator can implement inherited bindings.

15.3.1 Simple Inheritance with `extends=`

Listing 15.13 show two bindings related by inheritance.

Listing 15.13 Trivial example of XBL binding inheritance.

```
<!-- both bindings contained in example.xml -->

<binding id="smileyA">
  <content>
    <xul:image src="faceA.png"/>
  </content>
  <implementation>
    <method name="methodA">
      <body> return true; </body>
    </method>
  </implementation>
</binding>

<binding id="smileyB" extends="example.xml#smileyA">
  <content>
    <xul:image src="faceB.png"/>
```

```
  </content>
  <implementation>
    <method name="methodB">
      <body> return false; </body>
    </method>
  </implementation>
</binding>
```

Table 15.2 describes how different parts of a binding are inherited, so following that table yields these results.

If binding smileyA is bound to a XUL tag, then that tag will have a single `<image src="faceA.png">` tag as content, and one method called methodA(). In this case, the bound tag's XBL inheritance chain is of length one and contains only binding smileyA. This case has no inheritance, and smileyA is the primary binding.

If binding smileyB is bound to a XUL tag, then that tag will have a single `<image src="faceB.png">` tag as content, and two methods named methodA() and methodB(). In this case, the bound tag's XBL inheritance chain is of length two and contains binding smileyB at the head and binding smileyA at the tail. This is the inherited case, and smileyB is the primary binding.

Both of these bindings can be applied to different tags at the same time.

It is impossible to tell whether a binding is extended because its URL might be used anywhere in the world. If a binding resides in the chrome, then an audit of all the chrome files can reveal all uses of a given binding. Even so, secure applications installed outside the chrome might still extend a chrome binding undetectably.

15.3.2 Zero Content Bindings

A very popular XBL technique used in Mozilla is to extract common logic from a set of bindings and build a zero content binding to hold that logic. Such a binding has no `<resources>` or `<content>` section and is rarely (or never) bound directly to a tag. It contains mostly programming logic and state information.

If another binding uses this binding as its base, then the methods and handlers of the zero content binding are added back into the extended binding at run time. The zero content binding can be extended a number of times for different purposes. In object-oriented terms, the zero content binding might be called a "virtual content base class."

An example of such a zero content binding is the button-base binding in button.xml in toolkit.jar in the chrome. It contains:

- properties: accessible type dlgType group open checked checkState autoCheck
- handlers: event="command"

These properties and events are responsible for managing a number of states used by button-like widgets. For example, the checked property has <setter> and <getter> JavaScript logic that allows a bound tag to have <checkbox> or <radio>-like states. This logic does housekeeping tasks on the bound tag, setting and unsetting XML attributes and coordinating the checked state against other attributes that might be present.

The logic in this one binding is inherited by many other bindings. Those bindings in turn are used for many XUL tags: all variants of <button>, all variants of <toolbarbutton>, <thumb>, <dropmarker>, <radio>, <menu>, the buttons in <wizard>, <dialog>-based windows, and so on. Clearly the button-base binding is highly reusable.

A zero content base tag saves unnecessary duplication of code. When such a binding is used, the binding extending it should add a <content> section.

15.3.3 Input Façade Bindings

It is possible to make an XBL binding that concentrates on user input. Such a binding has a large <handlers> section and not much else, although it might also have supporting methods and properties.

Such a binding is called an input façade binding for two reasons. First, it adds a layer of user input and event servicing between the user and the widget, in the form of a set of handlers. That is like the front counter of a shop. Second, it relies on some other binding to supply it with the widget-specific processing power it needs. It is therefore a "thin" binding, and façades are thin. A trivial example of an input façade binding is

```
<binding id="click-facade" extends="bindings.xml#base-widget">
  <handlers>
    <handler event="click"> this.click(); </handler>
  </handlers>
</binding>
```

This simple binding erects an input façade between single-click input and the widget. It does not implement the click() method—that is left up to some other binding. That method might be generic (in which case the base-widget binding would supply it), or it might be highly specialized (in which case a binding that extends click-facade will supply it).

The handler code in this binding could be more complex; it might be required to maintain state that enables and disables certain inputs depending on what the last input was. An input façade is another place to put macro-processing functionality for user input.

Like a zero content binding, an input façade binding is rarely bound to a tag. Its main purpose is to extract from a set of bindings common user input semantics and collect those semantics together into one place. Its lack of <content> means that it should generally be extended before use.

There are no XBL input façades in the Mozilla Platform (to version 1.4), but there is room for them. If you examine the XBL bindings for `<tree>`, `<listbox>`, `<tabbox>`, and HTML's `<select>` (start with `xul.css` in `toolkit.jar` in the chrome), then you will see a common set of keypad navigation keys in all the bindings for those widgets. This subset could be extracted into an input façade binding that would then be reused across widgets, providing a uniform navigation experience.

Mozilla does currently implement one kind of input façade. It consists of the XUL documents that hold sets of `<key>` bindings. These documents are included in most Mozilla application windows via the use of overlays. Where an XBL input façade is specific to an XBL binding, a XUL input façade in the form of a set of `<key>` bindings is specific to a whole XUL document.

15.3.4 Inner Content Bindings

This chapter's title implies that bindings are used to create whole widgets, and that can indeed be done. It is also possible for a binding to supply the insides of a widget only. Such a binding is called an inner content binding.

Inner content bindings are simple to create. Their `<content>` section makes an assumption about the parent tag of the bound tag. The expectation is that the bound tag will deliver content to its parent tag, which is some kind of container tag. That container tag defines the borders of a widget. The inner content binding relies on that parent tag being correctly stated. Obvious containers in XUL are tags like `<box>`, `<button>`, `<menupopup>`, `<scrollbar>`, and `<toolbar>`.

Inner content bindings are dependent on the bound tag's parent and are closely coupled with it. Such a binding might provide methods and properties that the parent expects, or it might reach up into the parent to extract information that it needs. This close coupling means that the bound tag is usually an ugly failure when stated by itself. When stated inside the right container tag, it provides an abstraction that expresses the content of that tag neatly.

Inside Mozilla's XUL, several tags follow the inner content philosophy. The tags used inside `<scrollbar>` are examples: `<thumb>`, `<slider>`, and `<scrollbarbutton>`. These tags do not all have XBL bindings, but they do rely on their parent tags for correct functioning. Examples of tags with XBL bindings are the `<dropmarker>` tag used in some `<button>` tags and the `<tabs>` tag used inside `<tabbox>`.

15.4 How Bindings Are Processed

Here are the steps a binding goes through when it is bound to a tag in a target document:

1. When loading the target document, the Mozilla layout engine detects the need for a binding when it sees a `-moz-binding` style on a given loaded tag.

2. The document's list of things to finish is incremented by one. This list delays the firing of an `onload` event for the target document.
3. If a complete, compiled copy of the binding does not yet exist for the target document, steps 4-7 are done. If it exists, processing continues from step 8.
4. The XBL document for the binding is fetched and put in the Mozilla cache. This is done in parallel with the loading of the target document.
5. The fetched XBL document is parsed and compiled into an internal data structure.
6. If an `extends` attribute exists, steps 2–7 are repeated (in parallel) for each binding in the inheritance chain. So another binding could reach step 7 before the current binding.
7. The compiled binding is added to the document's binding manager. The binding manager is an XPCOM component that holds a list of all bindings used by the document.
8. The full inheritance chain for the binding is now available in loaded and compiled form. The target document's tag is now bound to the binding—ultimately this is just a pointer assignment inside Mozilla. Before this step, a script inspecting the bound tag would see no binding. After this step, a script cannot inspect the bound tag until all the remaining steps are complete. This is because the remaining steps occupy Mozilla's sole processing thread until they are finished.
9. Attributes of the `<content>` tag are copied to the tag to be bound.
10. Explicit and anonymous content are merged, and the result is copied to the bound tag using DOM operations.
11. `<handler>` handlers are installed on the bound tag using the binding manager.
12. `<property>` and `<method>` properties are added to the bound tag's DOM object.
13. Any `<constructor>` code in the inheritance chain is run.
14. If there are any stylesheet changes resulting from all these steps, they are applied as a final step.
15. The list of things to finish before an `onload` event can fire is decremented by one.

15.5 Scripting

A bound tag looks like any other DOM object to JavaScript. Scripts originating from the bound side of the tag can act on the bound tag's object in a number of standard ways:

- ☞ Properties can be invoked as methods, or assigned to, or read.

- Properties can be added or set to `null`.
- Properties that hold methods (`Function` objects) can be changed to user-defined methods.
- Event handlers lodged with on... style attributes, or via the DOM 2 `addEventListener()` method, can override handlers in the binding.
- DOM 1 interfaces can set and unset attributes on the bound tag.
- DOM 1 interfaces can modify the final merged content of the bound tag.

None of these actions affects the XBL binding specification for a bound binding.

The most significant issue for a user of XBL bindings is the issue of load time. There is no general way to tell whether a single bound tag has finished being bound. The only way to be sure is to use an `onload` handler in the bound tag's document and to avoid lazy-loading templates. If the bindings you use are all custom made, then it is good design for those bindings to provide some hint that they are loaded.

Another aspect of scripting bound tags has to do with event handling. There is the matter of ordinary DOM events and the special case of input focus.

Ordinary DOM events travel into the bound tag's final merged content as if it were normal XUL content. From an application programmer's point of view, a bound tag is a single indivisible item and the last step in the capture phase of the event's life. It is only from the binding creator's point of view that the content of a bound tag has any active role. In that case, the `event` continues into the binding where it can be accessed with the event object. The `event.originalTarget` property of that object is of most use in the binding; the `event.target` property is not yet reliable at version 1.4.

If, however, the bound tag is not part of the window's focus ring (such as a XUL <box>) tag, then parts of the merged content can still receive events. In particular, if the merged content contains tags that are focus ring candidates (like `<checkbox>` or `<button>`), then those tags can still be tabbed into and out of by the user. The following principle is at work:

If a tag ought to be able to receive the focus, and its parent tag can't receive the focus, then let it receive the focus.

The XBL binding system does not have a "refresh" or "rebuild" interface that can be used to bring a bound tag up to date. A bound tag can only have a whole binding added or removed. There are two ways to do this.

The first way to change a bound tag's binding is to modify the `-moz-binding` style property with a script. The most straightforward thing to do is to set this property to or away from the special value none. Unfortunately, a Mozilla bug makes this solution unreliable. The recommended alternative is to create two style classes:

```
.binding-installed { -moz-binding : url("test.xml#Test"); }
.binding-removed   { -moz-binding : none; }
```

Rather than set the `-moz-binding` property, set the class attribute of the bound tag to one or the other of these two class names. This works properly.

The second way to change a bound tag's binding is to use the sole XPCOM interface available for the purpose. This interface is

```
nsIDOMDocumentXBL
```

It is automatically available on the document object. Table 15.3 lists the methods of this interface.

Table 15.3 `nsIDOMDocumentXBL` interface

Returns	Method signature
void	addBinding(nsIDOMElement element, String URL)
void	removeBinding(nsIDOMElement element, String URL)
nsIDocument	loadBindingDocument(String URL)
nsIDomElement	getBindingParent(nsIDOMNode node)
nsIDOMNodeList	getAnonymousNodes(nsIDOMElement element)
nsIDOMElement	getAnonymousElementByAttribute(nsIDOMElement element, String attribute, String value)

The `addBinding()` and `removeBinding()` methods add and remove a primary binding to the tag matching the DOM object supplied. If the primary binding implies an inheritance chain, then that is loaded as well. These two methods operate synchronously, so they don't return until the binding change is complete.

The `loadBindingDocument()` method synchronously loads an XBL document with the specified URL into a DOM tree of its own, which is returned. This method can be used to inspect the structure of a binding specification. This method is useful for reflecting the specification of a binding into a data structure, which can then be used to build schema-based tools like designers and inspectors. It also provides a way to change a binding synchronously—that is, to chance a binding so that script execution suspends until the new binding is fully in place.

The `getBindingParent()` method returns the bound tag that has the supplied object as a content tag or text node. It is used to walk up the hierarchy of content from a piece of content is whose origin is uncertain, until a tag that has a binding is found.

The remaining two methods are XBL variations on the `document.getElementById()` method. Instead of returning tag objects from the document DOM tree, they return tag objects from an XBL binding's anonymous content. This is the only part of an XBL binding's specification that can be accessed from a script. In both methods, the DOM Element passed in is the DOM object for a bound tag.

getAnonymousNodes() returns an object containing all the immediate children of the <content> tag in a matching binding. The number of children is specified by a length property on the returned object, and each child is available using the item() method on the returned object, which takes a child index number.

getAnonymousElementByAttribute() returns a single tag from the set of tags inside the <content> tag of a binding. The tag returned has the attribute name and attribute value specified in the method call.

This last method solves a problem created by the XBL merging of anonymous and explicit content in a bound tag. Before the merge, anonymous content tags are in a certain order. After the merge, the relative positions of those tags may be different, owing to the addition of explicit content. This method allows an anonymous content tag to be found, regardless of its position. The tag must have a unique attribute-value pair that can be searched for. The attribute named anonid is a convention used for this purpose. The DOM Element supplied should be that of the bound tag.

A second problem solved by this method has to do with themes. A theme may contain more than style information; specific skins may also include scripts. Those scripts might customize the content of a given widget binding so that it has a look consistent with the theme. getAnonymousElementByAttribute() provides a way for a script-enabled skin to poke around inside an existing binding, or its own replacement binding, and make changes.

The XPCOM system has two components that are related to XBL:

```
@mozilla.org/xbl;1 @mozilla.org/xbl/binding-manager;1
```

Neither of these have any interfaces that are significant for application scripts.

15.6 Style Options

The -moz-binding CSS2 style extension is the only style option specific to XBL. See the topic "Bound Tags and -moz-binding" in this chapter.

Each binding created should have its own stylesheet so that the designed widget can support multiple themes or skins. Such a stylesheet is specified in the <resources> section of the binding specification.

15.7 Hands On: The <noteplacer> Tag

This "Hands On" session is about developing general-purpose code using XBL. In particular, we will create a new XBL binding and matching user-defined XUL tag that might contribute to the content and function of the NoteTaker dialog box.

XUL content should not be converted to XBL bindings just because it is possible. Only code that is used more than once in a given page or that could be reused in another application is a good candidate for XBL. XBL bindings wrap up the content they implement in extra structure. For mostly harmless content, that extra structure is not always desirable from a code maintenance point of view. Only when the binding is used frequently are there complexity savings.

In the NoteTaker tool, there are no repeated parts in the content of the toolbar or dialog box: therefore, there is little need for XBL use. We do, however, need an XBL example to illustrate the technology. The positioning information (top, left, height, width) of the Edit pane in the dialog box is worthy of experiment. Those four numbers are very similar to the positioning styles in the CSS2 standard, and a need for them may crop up in other applications. Furthermore, the existing implementation is a little cumbersome: The user must make an educated guess when entering values, and there is no user feedback on those values until the dialog box is closed, which is too late.

We can improve on that existing positioning system with a new widget. We will create an XBL binding that the user can manipulate graphically to specify the location of a note. This binding will be a special-purpose widget that is a bit like the <colorpicker> tag and a bit like a Print Preview window.

This positioning widget won't be integrated into the final NoteTaker code; we'll just illustrate the possibilities.

15.7.1 Designing Widget Interfaces

We need to find visual, XML, JavaScript, and user input interfaces for the new binding and implement those interfaces in XBL code. The job of the widget is to cue the user to provide positioning information and to make available that information to the rest of the XUL document.

We first look at the visual interface. The visual part of the binding is the inspiration for the widget. That visual must come from creative insight and invention because every widget attempts to provide something unique and different. This is the most challenging part of widget design because each widget must be original. If it's not original, we might as well just copy and enhance an existing widget like <button>.

There is one way to avoid being original. An XBL widget can aggregate other, simpler widgets into a useful group. Such an aggregated system is often called a console, just as an old-fashioned console consisted of a set of switches and knobs. That kind of use of XBL is straightforward.

Because all XUL tags and tag combinations take up a rectangle of screen area, we know that we must start with a rectangle. It's possible to create rather weird widgets that break this rule, but it's rare to go that far. Figure 15.2 shows a simple mockup of our new widget.

This idea came from looking at other software that provides visual configuration options, like print subsystems and image-processing programs, and then reflecting on our own need. The essential thing that is new in this widget

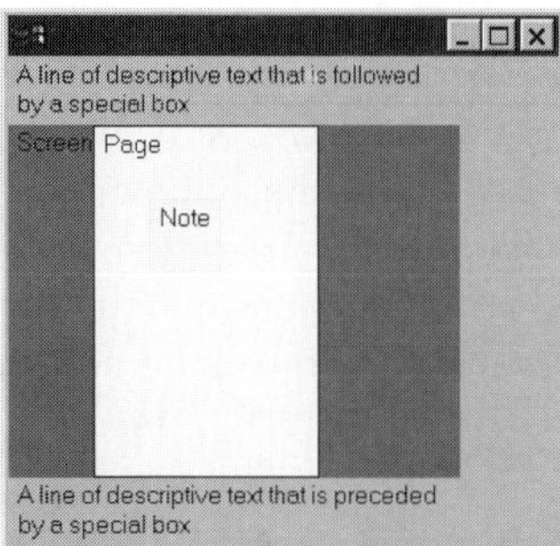

Fig. 15.2 Mockup of an XBL binding that lets the user position a note.

is that it is a fixed-sized model of the whole desktop. In the limited space we have here, we'll just do a simple-minded job of creating this widget. A more extensive solution would use technology similar to the Print Preview feature of the Mozilla Browsers.

In Figure 15.2, the main rectangle will be our new widget. It contains three parts: a backdrop <box> that represents the total screen area of the user's desktop, an optional white <box> that represents a browser window or page, and a yellow <box> that represents the note to be positioned. Each box is labeled in case it's not obvious to the user what they are. The whole rectangle will be sized in a way that reflects the dimensions of the desktop (the display resolution).

This main rectangle accepts user input. If the user clicks with the primary mouse button, the top-left corner of the note is located under the mouse. If the user clicks again, the bottom-right corner is set. This series of clicks can be repeated as long as is necessary. If the user clicks with the alternate mouse button (right-click or apple-click), then the nearest leading diagonal corner of the note is moved to the mouse location.

When the note is positioned, its coordinates are calculated. If the white page is not present, those coordinates are relative to the whole desktop. This case is useful if the user browses with windows maximized. If the white page is present, the coordinates are relative to the edge of the page, which is the edge of a window smaller than the whole screen. The white page is present for psychological purposes: human beings prefer windows that are displayed in the golden ratio, where width and height are in the approximate proportion 1:1.618. It is common for browser windows to end up in that ratio. The white page reminds the user what that ideal size looks like.

The second interface is user input. The widget will support button 0 single click (the primary or left mouse button) and button 2 single click (the secondary, apple-click or right-click button). Both buttons set the position of either the top-left corner or the bottom-right corner of the note. Button 0 clicks alternate between the two corners. Button 2 clicks move the nearest corner. After a quick glance at the visual interface, we should be able to create a widget that is neither a member of the focus ring or of the accessibility system, so there is no user input planning required there. Both possibilities are disqualified because none of the XUL tags in the binding's content is focusable or accessible.

The third interface required for this new widget is an XML interface. In our case, that means a tag name and a set of attributes that are known to the binding and layout behavior. A binding can be bound to any tag, but we'll select `<noteplacer>` as the tag of choice for the binding. The following attributes will have special meaning:

```
scale screenx screeny pageless
```

- `scale` accepts an integer and specifies the size of the noteplacer widget relative to the actual desktop size. For example, set to 4 (the default is 2), the noteplacer widget will be one-quarter the dimensions of the full desktop.
- `screenx` states the width of the desktop in pixels. The default is the value given by the `window.screen.width` property.
- `screeny` states the height of the desktop in pixels. The default is the value given by `window.screen.height` property.
- `pageless` can be set to `true` or `false`. If set to `true`, the white page will not appear in the widget. The default is `false`.

There is also the question of layout. Can the widget flex? What orientation does it have? The list of questions goes on. Because the noteplacer widget mimics the shape of the desktop, it will be a fixed size and won't flex. It will always be oriented horizontally and will have no particular alignment or direction.

The last interface will be the JavaScript XBL interface for the bound tag. We'll support the following properties:

```
top left width height scale screenx screeny pageless
     setFromEvent(e,primary)
```

- `top`, `left`, `width`, and `height` match the fields in the Edit dialog box.
- `scale`, `screenx`, `screeny`, and `pageless` match the XML attributes for the bound tag.
- `setFromEvent()` positions one of the corners of the note based on an event object. If the second argument is `true`, the top-left corner is set; otherwise, the bottom-right corner is set.

Offhand, we can't think of any existing platform interfaces (e.g., `nsI-Accessible`) that we'd like to support. The bound tag will automatically gain the standard DOM interfaces for a DOM 2 Element object; we don't have to do anything to get those.

Together, these four types of interface fully specify our new widget. The final question we should ask is: Can we exploit any existing binding? It doesn't appear likely in this case because the noteplacer widget is so simple.

15.7.2 Adding XBL Content

To create the binding itself, we start with a simple skeleton. In this step, we'll also consider the content parts of the binding. The skeleton is shown in Listing 15.14.

Listing 15.14 Trivial example of XBL binding inheritance.

```
<?xml version="1.0"?>
<bindings id="notetaker"
   xmlns="http://www.mozilla.org/xbl"
   xmlns:xul="http://www.mozilla.org/keymaster/gatekeeper/
          there.is.only.xul"
   xmlns:xbl="http://www.mozilla.org/xbl">

  <binding id="noteplacer">
    <resources></resources>
    <content></content>
    <implementation>
      <constructor></constructor>
      <destructor></destructor>
    </implementation>
    <handlers></handlers>
  </binding>
</bindings>
```

The set of bindings specific to NoteTaker we've called "`notetaker`" and the binding specifically for the `<noteplacer>` tag we've called "`noteplacer`". Because there's no binding inheritance, there's no `extends` attribute on the `<binding>` tag. Because the new widget is based on simple XUL boxes, there's no need for a `display` attribute on that tag either. All we need to do is fill in the four sections of the binding.

We start with the `<content>` and `<resources>` sections. We mock up some content (the basis of Figure 15.3), and then consider how it might best be modified to suit the XBL system. The mocked-up content appears in Listing 15.15.

Listing 15.15 Mocked-up XUL content for the noteplacer XBL binding.

```
<stack minwidth="320" minheight="240">
  <description value="Screen"/>
  <box class="page" top="0" left="86" minwidth="148" minheight="240">
    <description value="Page"/>
  </box>
  <box class="note" top="20" left="106" minwidth="40" minheight="40">
    <description value="Note"/>
  </box>
</stack>
```

This content is of a fixed size and has many attributes hard-coded in place. Most widgets should rely on the platform rather than fixed pixel size to lay out the content neatly. The unique thing about our widget is fixed dimensions, so that's the rule we break to add something new to XUL's widget set.

Before this code will be suitable for the `<content>` section of the binding, it needs some work. We see the following problems:

- The page part of the widget always appears; we want it to be invisible if the user uses full-screen windows.
- The page is very boring and plain white. We might want to put something more suggestive in there, like a browser menu bar and toolbar.
- The attributes quoting pixel sizes for most tags are useless. The real values will be computed based on `<noteplacer>` tag attributes and the current screen size.
- Font sizes are misleading. If the widget is supposed to represent a scaled-down desktop, then the font sizes should be scaled-down as well.

There are simple solutions to all of these problems. Page disappearance is the easiest. We'll let the `<box>` tag holding the page inherit the `pageless` attribute from the `<notepicker>` tag:

```
<box class="page" xbl:inherits="collapsed=pageless" ...>
```

To stop the page from being boring, we let any explicit content of the `<noteplacer>` tag dictate the contents of the `<box class="page">` tag. By carefully reviewing the merging rules for explicit and anonymous content, we conclude that

```
<description value="page"/>
```

should be replaced with

```
<children>
  <description value="page"/>
</children>
```

If there is explicit content, it will all be added in one place; if not, then the `<description>` tag stands as the default.

We next remove the fixed pixel sizes. They were based on a widget that is the size of a 640×480 desktop, scaled down by a factor of two. Instead, values will be calculated at run time in the binding constructor. We can't inherit from the attributes in the `<noteplacer>` tag because the needed values are a mathematical combination of those attribute values, not a direct copy. We'll see shortly how that is done.

Finally, font sizes will be addressed in the constructor as well. We'll add an inline style to any anonymous content that is a `<description>` or `<label>` tag. That style will scale down the fonts to match the size of the widget. In some cases, the text will be unreadable, but it's only intended as a point of reference for the user—the widget is mostly graphical.

For these last two points, we'll add an `anonid` attribute to the anonymous content that we'll want to modify later. Looking ahead a bit, that is the

<stack> tag and two <box> tags. The final <content> part of the binding will be as shown in Listing 15.16. Note the `xul:` namespace prefix on every XUL tag.

Listing 15.16 `<content>` part of the `noteplacer` XBL binding.

```
<content>
  <xul:stack anonid="desktop">
    <xul:description value="Screen"/>
    <xul:box xbl:inherits="collapsed=pageless" class="page" anonid="page">
      <xul:children>
        <xul:description value="Page"/>
      </xul:children>
    </xul:box>
    <xul:box class="note" anonid="note">
      <xul:description value="Note"/>
    </xul:box>
  </xul:stack>
</content>
```

If we test the binding at this stage (a good idea in principle), the results will look odd. They look odd because we have stripped out quite a lot of the final layout information. The binding is working; it's just that we haven't finished it yet.

Next, we can create a simple stylesheet with default values for the anonymous content, as shown in Listing 15.17.

Listing 15.17 CSS2 stylesheet for the `noteplacer` XBL binding.

```
stack {
  background-color : background;
  font-family : -moz-fixed;
}
box.page {
  background-color : white;
  border : solid thin;
  border-color : black;
}
box.note {
  background-color : lightyellow;
  border : solid thin;
  border-color : yellow;
}
```

The background color ensures that the desktop part of the widget will have the same color as the user's desktop. The `-moz-fixed` font (the system font) has the important property that it can be rendered at all sizes. 7px is 14px scaled down by a factor of two. Note that the default namespace for an XBL-included stylesheet is the XUL namespace. This means that tags in the stylesheet do *not* need to be prefixed with a CSS2 namespace. Such namespaces look like this:

```
@namespace url("http://www.mozilla.org/keymaster/gatekeeper/
     there.is.only.xul");
xul|stack { ... styles ... };
```

The stylesheet will go in the `<resources>` section of the XBL specification, using a relative URL. It has a relative URL because the `noteplacer` binding is specific to the `notetaker` package and in the same directory as the binding. It is not a global binding in the `global` package. In general, one CSS file should be used for all bindings for the `notetaker` package, and that file should be called `notetaker.css`. We're using a different name just to emphasize that the file contains only XBL style information and to avoid confusion with the skins created earlier. The finished piece of XBL reads

```
<resources>
  <stylesheet src="noteplacer.css"/>
</resources>
```

Having created the content and stylesheets, we've finished half the binding and have completely specified the visual and XML interface for the widget.

15.7.3 Adding XBL Functionality

The remainder of the `noteplacer` binding is the `<implementation>` and `<handlers>` sections. These two sections provide the JavaScript and user-input interfaces to the new widget. Let's look at the JavaScript side first, based on the bulleted list of wanted features in the earlier part of this "Hands On" session.

It's very common to see XML attributes reflected directly as JavaScript properties on the bound object, and we could do that. Adding such reflected features is trivial, as this example from the button-base binding shows.

```
<property name="type"
  onget="return this.getAttribute('type');"
  onset="this.setAttribute('type', val); return val;"/>
```

We don't use this approach because we don't want to store the state of our widget in XML attributes. That is a design decision that weighs the advantages and disadvantages of XML attributes. The advantages of storing state in attributes follow:

- Very common default cases require no attributes at all, which speeds up widget processing.
- JavaScript properties and XML attributes are automatically coordinated because one always depends on the other.
- The state is accessible from CSS stylesheets.
- The state is more easily accessible from C/C++ platform code.
- Bound tags can inherit values into those attributes if they're used in the `<content>` of another binding.

The disadvantages of storing state in XML attributes follow:

- Access to attributes is slow compared to ordinary JavaScript variables.
- Any attempt at information hiding or simplification is pointless because state is deliberately exposed.
- Scripts inside the binding (and outside) are required to do additional checks for the special null case when a given attribute is missing altogether.

If you are building a general-purpose toolkit of widgets, or building a frequently used widget, then the advantages may outweigh the disadvantages, and using XML attributes should be considered.

In our case, the widget is clearly application-specific, rather than general-purpose. We have no popular default cases. We won't be adding platform code to process our widget or using complex style tricks. The only null case might be the `pageless` attribute, where absence could be equated to `false`. For our widget, we prefer a reliable interface that never yields up a `null` or an empty value. The rest of the application can then use the widget as a true black box. This decision means that we will use JavaScript to store the widget's state.

Overall, we need to create `<field>`, `<property>`, `<method>`, `<constructor>`, and `<destructor>` content for the widget.

For the `<field>` attribute, we'll expose the golden ratio to the user. This is not ideal because the value can't be usefully passed to the XBL object, and so we might question how useful it is. At least it illustrates the syntax:

```
<field name="ratio">(1+Math.sqrt(5))/2</field>
```

This mathematical expression is one of several ways to calculate the golden ratio.

For the `<constructor>`, we observe that our widget tends to be quite large, and that it shouldn't stretch and shrink as a result of surrounding layout changes. This fixed size is unusual, and shouldn't always be a design choice, but it suits our purpose, which is to represent the desktop accurately. It also means that the `<constructor>` can size the widget once, and we won't have to worry about its flexing later. The constructor also must store the state of the widget in JavaScript. The logic for both state and layout is shown in Listing 15.18.

Listing 15.18 `<constructor>` code for the `noteplacer` XBL binding.

```
this.getAEBA = function (x,y,z) {
  return document.getAnonymousElementByAttribute(x,y,z);
}

this.desktop = getAEBA(this,"anonid","desktop");
this.page    = getAEBA(this,"anonid","page");
this.note    = getAEBA(this,"anonid","note");
```

```
this.d = {};        // protect numbers from string-ification

this.d.top      = 40;
this.d.left     = 40;
this.d.width    = 100;
this.d.height   = 100;

this.d.scale     = att2var("scale", 2);
this.d.screenx   = att2var("screenx", window.screen.width);
this.d.screeny   = att2var("screeny", window.screen.height);
this.d.pageless = att2var("pageless", false);

this.d.page_offset = 0;
if ( !d.pageless )
  d.page_offset = (d.screenx - d.screeny/ratio)/d.scale/2;

/* layout the content once */

this.setAttribute("style","font-size:"+14/d.scale+"px;");
placeDesktop();
placeNote();
if ( ! d.pageless ) placePage();
```

The `getAEBA` property is just a shorthand reference to the mouthful that is `document.getAnonymousElementByAttribute()`. We remember the important DOM elements of the widget for our future convenience. The `d` (for data) property saves our numeric state data away from XBL's tendency to force simple values into strings. All the properties of `this.d` are hidden from the user of the widget (the application programmer who places `<noteplacer>` tags). After these properties are calculated, the `<content>` part of the widget has its attributes adjusted, including scaling the displayed text. The `att2var()`, `placeDesktop()`, `placeNote()`, and `placePage()` functions are all methods of the `this` object that are declared at the start of the constructor code. They are shown in Listing 15.19.

Listing 15.19 Private `<constructor>` methods for the `noteplacer` XBL binding.

```
this.att2var = function (name, dvalue) {
  var val = this.getAttribute(name);
  if ( val == "" ) return dvalue;
  if ( isNaN(val) ) return dvalue;
  return val - 0;
}

this.arg2var = function (arg) {
  var err = "Bad argument passed to noteplacer binding";
  if ( arg == "" ) throw err;
  if ( isNaN(arg) ) throw err;
  return arg;
}
```

```
this.placeNote = function () {
  note.setAttribute("top", d.top / d.scale);
  note.setAttribute("left", d.page_offset + d.left / d.scale);
  note.setAttribute("minwidth", d.width / d.scale);
  note.setAttribute("minheight",d.height / d.scale);
}

this.placeDesktop = function () {
  desktop.setAttribute("minwidth", d.screenx/d.scale);
  desktop.setAttribute("minheight",d.screeny/d.scale);
}

this.placePage = function () {
  page.setAttribute("minheight", d.screeny/d.scale);
  page.setAttribute("minwidth",  d.screeny/d.scale/ratio);
  page.setAttribute("top", "0");
  page.setAttribute("left", d.page_offset);
}
```

The `att2var()` method calculates the value for a state variable based on the default value and an optional XML attribute that overrides that default if it is present. The `arg2var()` method checks that a passed-in argument is a legal number. We'll use it shortly. The other methods adjust the positions of the widget content based on the state information and a little mathematics. All these methods, plus the `getAEBA()` method, are private to the widget. They don't appear as properties on the `<noteplacer>` tag's DOM object.

We haven't held any XPCOM components or other big objects during the life of the widget, so there's nothing to let go of when the widget is destroyed. As a consequence, there is no `<destructor>` required for our widget.

We've already made the effort to capture the state information of the widget, and that makes implementing the `<property>` tags very easy. Listing 15.20 shows these tags.

Listing 15.20 `<property>` tags for the `noteplacer` XBL binding.

```
<property name="top"
  onget="return this.d.top;"
  onset="this.d.top = arg2var(val); placeNote();"/>
<property name="left"
  onget="return this.d.left;"
  onset="this.d.left = arg2var(val); placeNote();"/>
<property name="width"
  onget="return this.d.width;"
  onset="this.d.width = arg2var(val); placeNote();"/>
<property name="height"
  onget="return this.d.height;"
  onset="this.d.height = arg2var(val); placeNote();"/>

<property name="scale" readonly="true"
  onget="return this.d.scale;"/>
```

```
<property name="screenx" readonly="true"
  onget="return this.d.screenx;"/>
<property name="screeny" readonly="true"
  onget="return this.d.screeny;"/>
<property name="pageless" readonly="true"
  onget="return this.d.pageless;"/>
```

These properties could hardly be simpler to implement. Note how the setters throw an exception via `arg2var()` if the value passed by the widget user contains rubbish. If our widget were more dynamic, the `placeNote()` function call in each `onget` attribute would be more extensive and might have to do extensive calculations or processing.

Let's now turn to the sole `<method>` tag required.

The widget coordinates used in both XML attributes and JavaScript properties are relative to the pane that the note is placed in. When DOM events occur, however, the DOM Event object generated has coordinates that are relative to the whole window. That is a different coordinate system. The convenience method `setFromEvent()` allows a user of the widget to set a corner of the note using that Event object. The widget handles the required coordinate transformation for the user. This method is shown in Listing 15.21.

Listing 15.21 `<method>` tag for the `noteplacer` XBL binding.

```
this.getCoords = function(x,y) {
  return {
    x: (x - this.boxObject.x - d.page_offset) * d.scale,
    y: (y - this.boxObject.y) * d.scale
  };
}

<method name="setFromEvent">
  <parameter name="evt"/>
  <parameter name="cornerFlag"/>
  <body><![CDATA[
    var coords = getCoords(evt.clientX , evt.clientY);
    if (cornerFlag) {
      d.width  += d.left - coords.x;
      d.height += d.top - coords.y;
      d.top = coords.y;
      d.left = coords.x;
    }
    else {
      d.width  = coords.x - d.left;
      d.height = coords.y - d.top;
    }
    placeNote();
    ]]>
  </body>
</method>
```

The `getCoords()` function converts the supplied coordinates. It is added to the `<constructor>` contents so that it resides with the other utility functions—it is not exposed to users of the widget. The `setFromEvent()` method is exposed to the user. After that method has local coordinates from `getCoords()`, it recalculates the size and top corner of the note based on the location provided and the existing note dimensions. That done, the note is repositioned to match. This method could use some additional sanity checks (e.g., width and height should never be negative), but it does the job for our purposes.

The last part of the binding specification is the `<handlers>` section. We have two handlers, both for the DOM 2 click event, but for different mouse buttons. For the primary button, we introduce another private variable, this time called `this.d.topclick`. If this variable is true, then a primary click will set the location of the top-left corner of the note. If it is false, the bottom-right corner will be set. We initialize this variable to `true` in the constructor. For the secondary button, we rely on the Pythagorean theorem ("the sum of the squares of the sides of a right triangle equals the square of the hypotenuse") to detect the leading diagonal corner of the note nearest the click point. That corner is then updated. The resulting code is shown in Listing 15.22.

Listing 15.22 `<handler>` tags for the `noteplacer` XBL binding.

```
<handlers>
  <handler event="click" button="0"><![CDATA[
    this.setFromEvent(event,d.topclick);
    this.d.topclick = !this.d.topclick;
    ]]>
  </handler>

  <handler event="click" button="2"><![CDATA[
    var coords = this.getCoords(event.clientX, event.clientY);
    var dist1, dist2;
    with (Math) {
      dist1 = sqrt(pow(coords.x-d.left,2) + pow(coords.y-d.top,2));
      dist2 = sqrt(  pow(coords.x - (d.left + d.width), 2)
                   + pow(coords.y - (d.top + d.height), 2)
                   );
    }
    this.setFromEvent(event, (dist1 < dist2));
    ]]>
  </handler>
</handlers>
```

Using CDATA sections avoids a great deal of time otherwise wasted in ebugging. The handler functions reuse both the exposed `setFromEvent()` thod and the private `getCoords()` method, and so their logic is very sim-

ith the `<handlers>` content finished, the `noteplacer` binding is com- about 150 lines of code all told. With no more binding changes ll that remains is to try it out.

15.7.4 Integrating the Binding

Having created the noteplacer binding, we next want to try it out. In fact, the next few steps are a useful way to create a binding test harness. Such a harness is as useful during binding development as it is for final testing.

To connect the binding to a tag, we use a single style rule:

```
noteplacer {
  -moz-binding : url("noteplacer.xml#noteplacer");
}
```

We put this in a file named xulextras.css for now. This file lives in the same directory as the rest of the noteplacer content. This stylesheet enhances the standard set of XUL tags with the new <noteplacer> tag.

In a test of the new widget, we want to see the following things:

- The widget fits properly inside surrounding content.
- The widget reacts properly to user input, including window resizing.
- Attributes set on the widget have the desired effect.
- Explicit content provided to the widget has the desired effect.

To that end, we construct the test XUL document of Listing 15.23.

Listing 15.23 Test page for the noteplacer XBL binding.

```
<?xml version="1.0"?>
<?xml-stylesheet href="chrome://global/skin/" type="text/css"?>
<?xml-stylesheet href="xulextras.css" type="text/css"?>
<!DOCTYPE window>
<window xmlns="http://www.mozilla.org/keymaster/gatekeeper/
          there.is.only.xul"
  onload="install()">
<script>
  var np;

  function install()
  {
    np = document.getElementById("test");
    np.addEventListener("click", report, false);
  }

  function report()
  {
    var str = "";
    str += "Top: "      + np.top + "\n";
    str += "Left: "     + np.left + "\n";
    str += "Width: "    + np.width + "\n";
    str += "Height: "   + np.height + "\n";
    str += "ScreenX: "  + np.screenx + "\n";
    str += "ScreenY: "  + np.screeny + "\n";
    str += "scale: "    + np.scale + "\n";
```

```
      alert(str);
    }
  </script>
  <description>Before Test </description>
    <hbox>
      <description value="Left of Test"/>
      <noteplacer screenx="1024" screeny="768" scale="4">
        <toolbox flex="1">
          <toolbar grippyhidden="true">
            <description value="File"/>
            <description value="Edit"/>
            <description value="View"/>
            <description value="Go"/>
            <spacer flex="1"/>
          </toolbar>
          <spacer style="background-color:white" flex="1"/>
        </toolbox>
      </noteplacer>
      <description value="Right of Test"/>
    </hbox>
    <description>After Test </description>
  </window>
    </handler>
  </handlers>
```

This document surrounds the <noteplacer> tag with other content and provides a fake toolbar as a content hint for the page. It also lodges an event handler on the tag. That event handler will be applied to the `click` handlers specified in the binding. When this document is displayed, it appears as in Figure 15.3.

Obviously, the supplied toolbar is a primitive example of a browser window, but then an indication to the user is all that is required. Perhaps one day the screen capture technology inside the DOM Inspector's XPCOM screenshot components will be complete. Then an actual, scaled-down screenshot can be put where the explicit content currently goes.

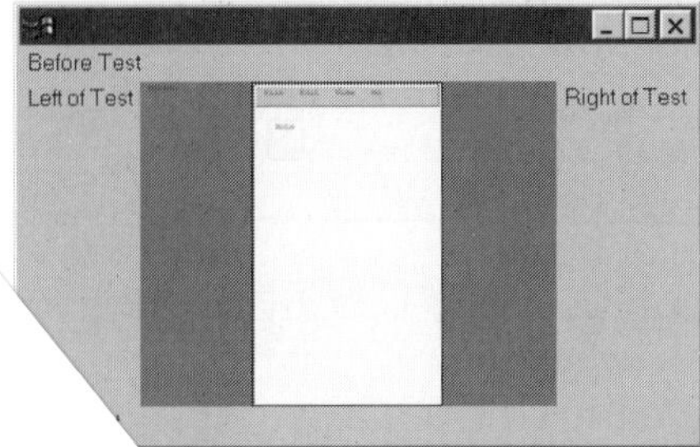

Test XUL document showing customized <noteplacer> tag.

If the click handlers receive input, then an alert box appears that reports the current position of the note. That alert box is shown in Figure 15.4.

A little mathematics and the values displayed can be confirmed as probably accurate.

It is easy to see how the <noteplacer> tag could be integrated into the NoteTaker application using JavaScript. From the Edit dialog box, it could be launched in a separate second dialog box or embedded somewhere in the existing <tabbox>. When the dialog box closes, an onclose event handler reads the state of the widget and copies the values into the matching fields in the Edit pane, or into the matching fields in the toolbar note object.

A single widget by itself gives the user few clues how it should be used. Like many XUL tags, <noteplacer> is functional rather than obvious. This tag should be surrounded by other content when served up to the user. Figure 15.5 shows one possible scenario.

That ends the "Hands On" session for this chapter.

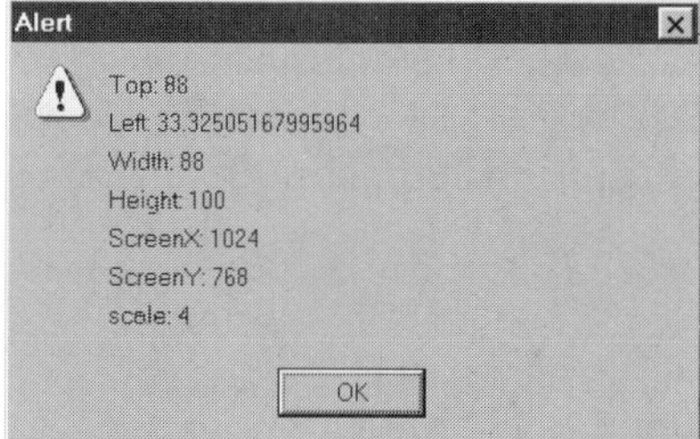

Fig. 15.4 Diagnostic alert box confirming the state of a <noteplacer> widget.

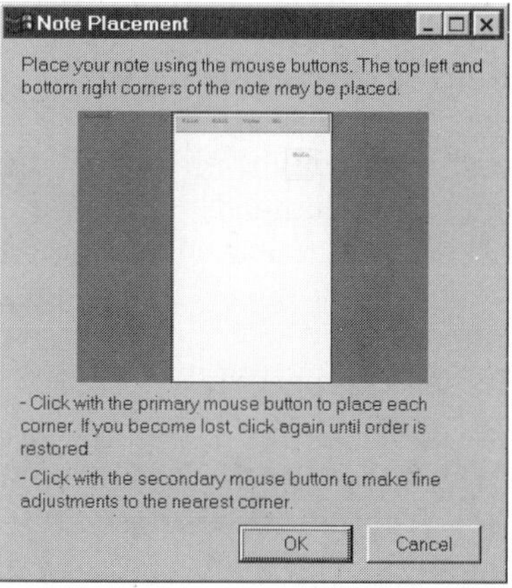

Fig. 15.5 Application use of the <noteplacer> tag.

15.8 Debug Corner: XBL Diagnosis

There is nothing mysterious about XBL bindings; the window and document objects are both available to all property, method, handler, and constructor/destructor code. All the debugging techniques available to normal scripts are also available to scripts used in XBL.

XBL is not as mysterious to work with as RDF either. Syntax errors in an XBL document are reported to the JavaScript console, and the messages supplied are readable.

The two most frequent problems when creating bindings are the result of XML namespaces and internal JavaScript properties. Note the following regarding namespaces:

- ☞ The XBL `inherit` property must be prefixed with a namespace identifier like `xbl:` because the default namespace for the tag that `inherit` resides in will always be either XUL or HTML.
- ☞ XBL must have a separate namespace because it shares some tag names with other XML applications such as XUL, RDF, and HTML.
- ☞ If the standard set of namespaces in which the default namespace is XBL is used, then every XUL or HTML tag in the `<content>` section must have a namespace prefix. If not, nothing will appear.

On internal JavaScript properties of XBL bindings, two simple omissions are:

- ☞ Forgetting to prefix binding variables with `this`.
- ☞ Forgetting that immediate properties of this store simple values as String types.

The most frustrating problem with bindings is the way they load asynchronously. You can't assume when bound methods and properties will be available. There are several trivial solutions to this problem.

The simplest solution is to use a document `onload` handler for any initialization code that is required. This will work only if all the bindings used are bound once directly in stylesheets and never changed.

The next simplest solution is to add this field to every binding created:

```
<field name="loaded" readonly="true">true</field>
```

Before scripting the bound tag, check that this property is set; if it is, then the binding is available.

A more systematic solution might use the `<constructor>` part of a binding's specification. This piece of code is a simple registration system:

```
with (window.document)
  bindTotal = (bindTotal) ? ++bindTotal : 1;
```

If a XUL application window consists of only a few very complex XBL widgets, then it is easy to keep track of how many have finished loading. A timer can be used to consult the in-progress total until all widgets are loaded. If a destructor also decrements this total, then the total can be a running total that keeps track of loaded widgets when their bindings are dynamically changed. For highly specialized XBL widgets, this small amount of coupling between the widget and the containing document can be a practical solution to loading delays. In short, this is the same logic as that used to coordinate frames in a Web document.

A last solution to this asynchronicity is to use the `loadBindingDocument()` method, which prevents the problem entirely.

Finally, XBL widgets have some security restrictions. If the documents represented by two URLs are to have full access to each other, they must pass Mozilla's "Same Origin" test. That test demands that both URLs come from the same server. XBL widgets must also pass this test or be installed where security restrictions are dropped. A XUL application delivered by one server cannot ordinarily use an XBL binding defined at another server. Rather than go through a complex certification and code signing exercise, it is generally simpler just to install the bindings in the chrome.

In all cases, if a binding is to take advantage of XPCOM components, the document that contains the bound tag of interest should be installed in the chrome. Bindings have the same security as the documents to which they are bound.

15.9 Summary

Mozilla's XBL technology adds extensibility and componentization to user interface development. It follows the general philosophy of visual markup languages like HTML: Keep it simple so that it is quick to use. But XBL is also a software engineering tool—it allows common pieces of functionality to be isolated, specified, and reused.

The XBL part of the Mozilla Platform helps glue interactive, visual widgets to the rest of the platform by giving them highly customized object-like features. XBL bindings back nearly every XUL tag, and many HTML tags as well. The default actions supplied by these bindings contribute to the ease of use that those other markup languages enjoy.

In the next chapter, we'll see the objects to which XBL bindings usually connect. These are the many objects supplied by the XPCOM system. Many XPCOM objects have been explored already, but there are always objects complementary to other technologies like XUL and RDF. Many XPCOM components are functional in their own right, and these components dramatically extend a Mozilla-based application.

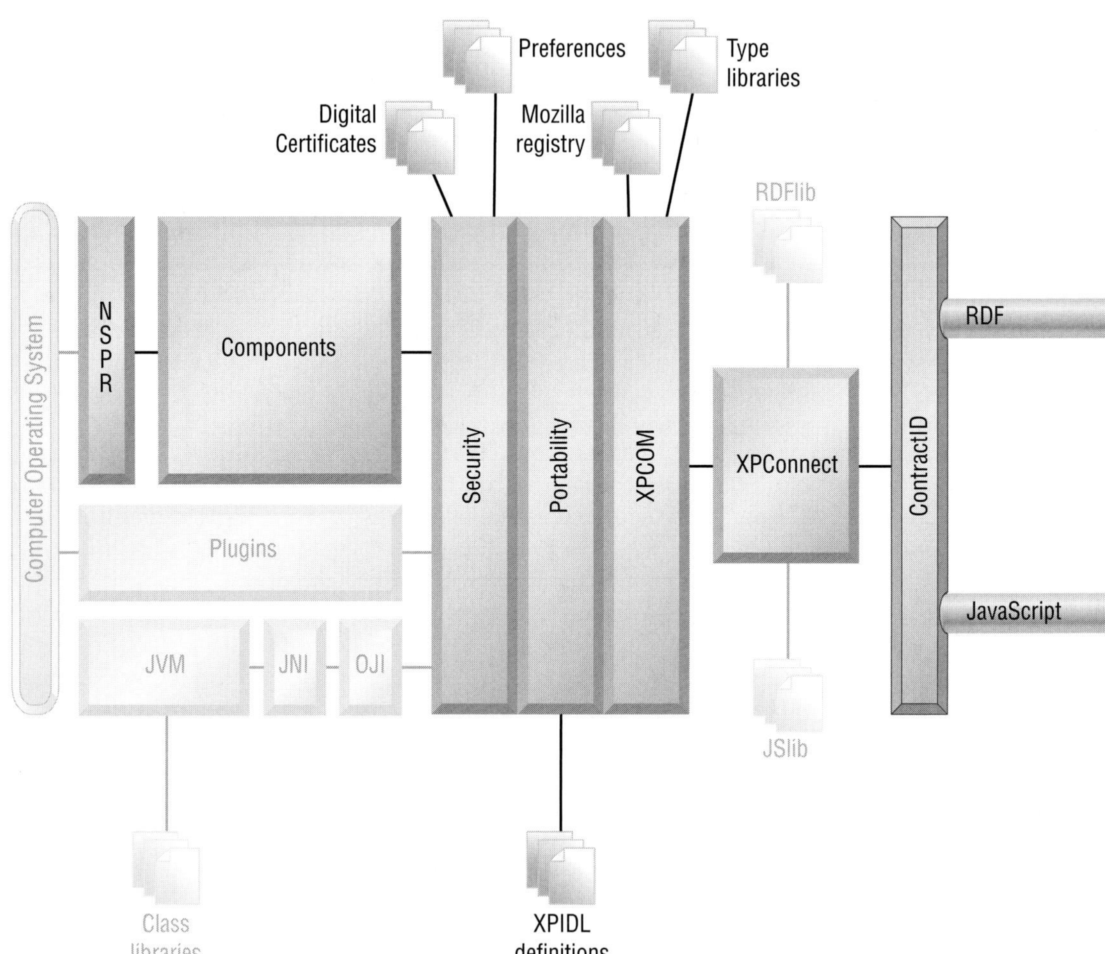

Preferences
Type libraries
Digital Certificates
Mozilla registry
RDFlib
Computer Operating System
NSPR
Components
Security
Portability
XPCOM
XPConnect
ContractID
RDF
JavaScript
Plugins
JVM
JNI
OJI
JSlib
Class libraries
XPIDL definitions

CHAPTER 16

XPCOM Objects

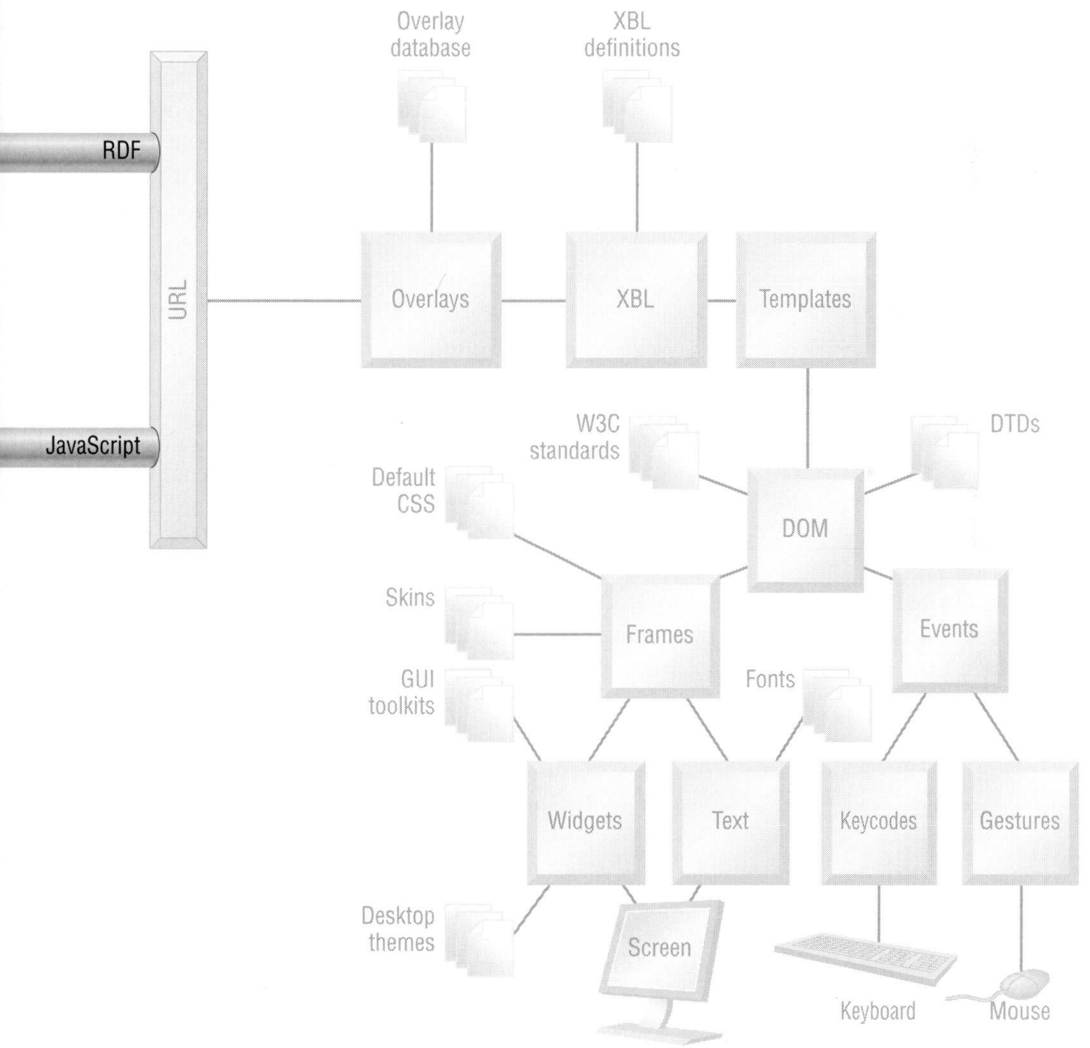

The Mozilla Platform is a base for building software applications. It contains an object library of over a thousand objects. Many of these objects have nothing to do with GUIs. This chapter explains which of those objects solves which common programming problems.

A thousand example scripts is too big a goal for a single chapter—the best that can be done here is to provide some pointers and guidance. In addition to this discussion, you'll need to read the XPIDL interface definitions for the objects discussed. Many script fragments are presented here to complement those interfaces. All solutions presented use JavaScript.

Mozilla's object library consists mostly of XPCOM components. Without XPCOM components, an application programmer is trapped within an XML document, whether it be HTML or XUL. Inside such a document, URLs, HTTP, SOAP, and WSDL are the only mechanisms out. By adding XPCOM components, everything opens up dramatically. Components add support for networking, databases, files, and processes—all the meat and drink of traditional software applications. XPCOM components are available on all platforms where Mozilla runs and are entirely portable with only a very few exceptions.

Mozilla's set of XPCOM components are just like any 3GL or OO library. Just as C++ and Java have a stream concept and stream objects, so too does Mozilla. Just as C, Perl, and numerous other languages have a file concept, so too does Mozilla. Mozilla objects are therefore standard programmer fare—almost.

The reason that these objects are *almost* standard fare is because Mozilla is still version 1. This newness has affected the set of components that are available. Rather than having a very broad range of low-level objects, Mozilla consists of some low-level objects, some mid-level objects, and some very application-specific high-level objects. The platform was first designed to build a Web browser application suite, and so objects exist to support that goal at all levels of abstraction. The platform has not had the extensive, general-purpose design that the Java class libraries have received. On the other hand, a thousand objects is not a trivial total; it approaches the size of Perl's extensive library of modules.

A second nonstandard aspect of Mozilla's objects is that many objects are network-centric. Navigator, Messenger, and Chat applications are all Internet clients that interact with servers, and this is reflected in the object library. Some simple operations, like loading a file, are complex because the file might be anywhere in the world. This complexity affects the interfaces used. Those interfaces are also constrained by Mozilla's security system.

If an application is not a Web browser, email client, or XML display system, then Mozilla's objects still have plenty to offer, but some of the highly specialized objects available will be of little use. On the other hand, if the application contains browser-like functionality, then specialized objects speed the development process greatly.

As shown in the NPA diagram for this chapter, the back half of Mozilla is the home of XPCOM components. The XPCOM and XPConnect technologies rely on various external files; a registry (a simple database like the Microsoft Windows registry) and type libraries (component descriptions) are foremost. Preferences and certificates are two aspects of security also stored external to components. From a programmer's point of view, the most interesting part of the XPCOM system are the externally stored XPIDL files, which contain readable descriptions of all the XPCOM interfaces.

This chapter begins with some of the key concepts of the components' environment. It then moves on to address common programming tasks and Mozilla's solutions. General programming tasks come first: more application-specific tasks come later. Finally, a look is taken at the platform itself and its security systems. The "Hands On" session in this chapter has an extensive series of examples that show how to script objects associated with RDF.

16.1 Concepts and Terms

Mozilla's collection of XPCOM components is large and a world of its own. To write scripts effectively, pick up some of the established jargon used at the scripting level.

16.1.1 Reading Others' Code: Naming Conventions

Mozilla is a huge piece of software, and regular exploration of features is commonplace. Most Mozilla code and documentation have a particular style that is worth becoming accustomed to. That style appears in the following sources:

- The XPIDL definition files that define the existing XPCOM interfaces. These interfaces are help files that you can't do without.
- The numerous at-work examples that can be found in the chrome of a built Mozilla application.
- Less importantly, the C/C++ source code of the platform. This code is more challenging and of less immediate value, but it is also the ultimate authority.

Of these information sources, the XPIDL files are the main item that you need to survive. See the introduction of this book for a URL for those files.

The Mozilla coding style uses naming conventions as usage hints. These hints are especially important in JavaScript code. JavaScript syntax provides only weak signatures for objects and methods compared with compiled languages like Java or C++.

Here follows some examples of naming hints used by Mozilla code.

Mozilla uses prefix characters to hint at the nature of an XPCOM interface. The most common prefix is `nsI`, meaning "netscape Interface." This prefix is used to identify an interface that is available for application programmer use. Other prefixes like `imgI`, `inI`, `jsdI`, and `mozI` (image, inspector, JavaScript debugger, and Mozilla, respectively) serve the same purpose, but they are intended to be application- or technology-specific. They are still available for general use. The plain prefix `ns` (without a trailing `I`) is used for objects that are not intended for application programmer use. Most occurrences of plain-`ns` prefixes are hidden inside the platform.

Second, the ECMAScript standard allows a host object to report its type as a string. In Mozilla, this string is calculated by stripping a prefix from the current XPCOM interface name for that host object. The characters stripped are `nsIDOM`, so an object presenting the `nsIDOMHTMLDocument` interface will report its JavaScript object type as `HTMLDocument`.

Third, capitalization is also used for interface attributes and methods:

- ☞ Constants in DOM-based interfaces are written in `ALL_UPPERCASE_STYLE`.
- ☞ Constants in non-DOM interfaces typically use `initCapStyle`.
- ☞ Variables and methods are written in `initCapStyle`.
- ☞ RDF interfaces are an exception, they use `InitCapStyle` for method names—the first letter is capitalized.

Either way, XPIDL and JavaScript cases always match. Inside the C/C++ of the platform, method names are translated from `initCap` to `InitCap`, and interface names sometimes appear with the XPIDL capitalization and sometimes appear in `ALL_CAPS`.

Mozilla makes frequent use of a single-character prefix for interface attributes and method arguments. This notation is common in XBL bindings, platform C/C++ code, XPIDL interfaces, and ordinary JavaScript. JavaScript's use of these prefixes is somewhat patchy. These single-character prefixes are described in Table 16.1.

Table 16.1 Mozilla single-character name prefixes

Prefix	Frequency of appearance	Meaning
a	Common	aVar is a temporary variable or a function or method argument. It stands for a value or object of ordinary significance, one that is usually subjected to processing. aFile is an example.
e	Occasional	eVar is a value, usually a constant that is one item of an enumeration. eTuesday is an example.
g	Occasional	gVar is a global variable; either global to the current window (the JavaScript global object) or entirely global in the case of C/C++. gMenuControllers is an example.

Table 16.1 Mozilla single-character name prefixes (Continued)

Prefix	Frequency of appearance	Meaning
k	Occasional	kVar is a key value—one of a set of values that some specific variable can take on. It is similar to the e prefix, except that key values are often bitmasks or strings and so don't number sequentially from one. kMimeType is an example.
m	Common	mVar is a member (property or attribute) of an object. It is usually used to store private data. mLength is an example.
n	Occasional	nVar usually holds a total of some kind. It is an ordinary variable.
s,i,b,f,r,p	Rare	These prefixes are used inside the platform's C/C++ to mean a string, integer, Boolean, floating-point number, short integer, and pointer type, respectively. They are not usually seen in JavaScript code, which sometimes uses f to mean file or folder instead.

One further prefix used in the Mozilla Platform is *PR*. PR stands for Portable Runtime, and NSPR stands for Netscape Portable Runtime. NSPR is a library and coding standard designed to overcome the portability problems of C, C++, and operating systems. The Mozilla Platform uses a set of data types that are guaranteed portable, and these types have PR prefixes. This notation is occasionally exposed to XPCOM and to the application programmer.

16.1.2 Modular Programming

The Mozilla Platform breaks technology up into pieces a number of different ways. Almost every technical term for *part* or *piece* that software engineering offers is used by Mozilla. Correct usage of these terms is given here:

- **binding**. A binding is an interface written down in a particular programming language. In Mozilla, a binding is either an ECMAScript interface stated in the W3C DOM standards or an XBL binding.
- **class**. The only classes in Mozilla are the component classes of XPCOM. Each class is used to create zero or more objects. JavaScript 2.0 (ECMAScript 1.4) will have class definitions of a different type, but JavaScript 1.5 does not have these.
- **component**. A component is a thing with unique identity within the XPCOM system. It is a class with a CID (a component identifier) and a matching ContractID (like `@mozilla.org/test;1`), or it is an interface with an IID (an interface identifier). Because interfaces can't be used

without a concrete implementation but classes can, classes are thought of as the only real components.

- **interface**. An interface is a set of access points to an object. XPCOM interfaces are the only interfaces in Mozilla. Any object that supplies those access points is said to implement that interface. Each XPCOM object and XBL binding implements zero or more XPCOM interfaces; JavaScript objects may also implement XPCOM interfaces.
- **library**. The Mozilla Platform has a number of dynamically linked libraries, but those libraries are of no particular interest to the application programmer. General-purpose JavaScript scripts may informally be called libraries. Type libraries are data files that define XPCOM interfaces. These are created when the platform is compiled and automatically used by XPConnect.
- **module**. XPCOM components in the Mozilla Platform are grouped into modules, but this is only obvious to developers of the platform. Modules have no meaning to application programmers, unless a whole new XPCOM module is being created.
- **object**. Mozilla contains XPCOM objects and JavaScript objects. An XPCOM object is of a given class type and implements one or more interfaces. A JavaScript object may be anything from a simple data structure to a complex host object. JavaScript host objects are either XPCOM objects or Java objects.
- **package**. A group of related files installed in Mozilla's chrome is called a package. A package has a name that matches a file system directory name.
- **prototype**. A JavaScript object used as the basis for the construction of a new JavaScript object is called a prototype.

16.1.3 Foreign-Type Systems

The XPCOM system gives JavaScript access to other programming environments. Those other environments have their own basic types. Either those foreign types must be automatically converted to JavaScript types (and back again) or those foreign types must provide some kind of usable interface.

There are five foreign-type systems in Mozilla that are accessible from JavaScript:

- **The fundamental platform types implemented by NSPR**. These are the portable C/C++ types out of which the platform is built out.
- **RDF data types**. These are the types Mozilla can identify in RDF documents.
- **XML schema data types**. Mozilla can intelligently parse files that have this format and can identify the standard primitive types contained inside.

- **XML RPC XDR**. The RPC-over-XML network protocol is supported by Mozilla, which includes underlying XDR network-independent data types.
- **Java**. A Java JVM can be run as a Mozilla platform plugin, which gives access to Java-typed objects.

Of these type systems, automatic conversion to and from JavaScript works only for Java. The other four type systems are available from the following specific XPCOM interfaces:

- The NSPR types are all represented by interfaces that derive from `nsISupportsPrimitive`, like `nsISupportsPRInt32`.
- RDF data types have interfaces `nsIRDFLiteral`, `nsIRDFDate`, and `nsIRDFInt`, all based on `nsIRDFNode`.
- XML schema data types are named as constants in `nsISchemaSimpleType` and `nsISchemaBuiltinType` interfaces.
- The XDR encoding of XML RPC uses the NSPR types. The `nsIXmlRpcClient` interface has a factory method that can create NSPR-typed objects.

In addition to these foreign type systems, the XPCOM architecture and the components specified using that architecture are a type system of their own, one based on object types (classes and interfaces) rather than simple data types. This set of classes and interfaces is the main set of type symbols that application programmers use when building nontrivial scripts.

16.2 General-Purpose Scripting

This topic explains how to solve generic programming tasks using Mozilla.

16.2.1 Command-Line Arguments

When the Mozilla Platform is started up via the command line, it remembers the command-line arguments passed in. On Microsoft Windows, the platform does not remember the command-line arguments used to start up further windows that are managed by the same running instance.

To access the command-line arguments, use this component and interface:

```
@mozilla.org/appShell/commandLineService;1 nsICmdLineService
```

The `nsICmdLineService` exposes `argc`, the count of arguments, but not `argv`, the list of strings making up the arguments. The `argc` count is the number of argument-value pairs, not the number of whitespace-separated strings, which is the traditional UNIX/Windows definition. Because `argv` is not supplied, you must guess what parameters were supplied, using the `getCmdLineValue()` method. A typical call to this method is

```
var url = cls.getCmdLineValue("-chrome");
```

If the argument passed in wasn't supplied at invocation time, then `null` is returned.

This interface also contains a factory method `getHandlerForParam()`, which returns an object with the `nsICmdLineHandler` interface. This returned object is a read-only record that contains configuration information for a handler, such as default values. Each command-line handler that exists adds to the command-line options available to the platform. Such handlers can be created in JavaScript if necessary.

It is not possible to retrieve the original, raw command-line string using JavaScript.

16.2.2 Data Structures and Algorithms

The JavaScript language provides basic arrays and objects, which are enough for most simple needs. Separate from JavaScript, the Mozilla Platform provides a huge data model that is an implementation of the W3C DOM standards. This data model has obvious uses in representing HTML, XUL, MathML, SVG, and XML documents generally. It is covered under the topic "Web Scripting" as well as being described in Chapter 5, Scripting.

Apart from the DOM, Mozilla provides very few data structure interfaces. What exists is used mostly to expose platform-internal data structures to the scripting environment. They are not really intended to be the basis for new data structures, although there is nothing wrong with reusing these interfaces when developing application objects.

XPCOM collection objects that can be used alone are listed in Table 16.2. These collections are not recommended for most uses, but are worth noting.

JavaScript is flexible to start with, and these collections do not add much by themselves. These objects are complemented by a number of cursor or iterator interfaces. There are two varieties of cursor in XPCOM. The simpler variety consists of enumerators:

```
nsIEnumerator nsIBidirectionalEnumerator
```

Enumerators are read-only cursors that step through a given collection. The collection must be static, and only one enumerator at a time is allowed. These interfaces return the `nsISupports` interface for each object they enumerate.

The more complex variety of cursor is called an iterator. Iterators support tasks like: stepping through dynamically updated collections, inserting items into collections, and simultaneous use of iterators on a given collection. These iterators, all with interfaces named

```
nsI{something}Iterator
```

Table 16.2 XPCOM collection objects

Interface	Implemented in	Description
nsIArray	@mozilla.org/array;1	An XPCOM version of a read-only JavaScript array
nsIMutableArray	@mozilla.org/array;1	Adds methods that allow modification of an nsIArray's contents
nsICollection	@mozilla.org/supports-array;1	Adds a simple collection interface to a serializable stream; not generally useful from JavaScript; use any of the other interfaces
nsIDictionary	@mozilla.org/dictionary;1	A simple collection that holds key-to-value pairs (a map), implemented in JavaScript; in Microsoft Windows a dictionary is equivalent to a map; potentially useful
nsIProperties	@mozilla.org/properties;1	A simple collection that holds key-to-value pairs, implemented in C/C++ (a map); in Java a properties collection is equivalent to a map

are rarely needed by themselves but may be useful as a design guide if complex application data structures are required. They are occasionally produced by other XPCOM interfaces.

The DOM 2 Traversal and Ranges standard supplies a powerful iterator. In Mozilla it is named `nsIDOMNodeIterator`. It is occasionally useful when working with DOM data structures.

The Mozilla Platform does not provide much in the area of general-purpose algorithms. JavaScript provides regular expressions and the `Array.sort()` method, but there is little beyond that. The sort functionality used in templated XUL cannot be applied elsewhere.

16.2.3 Databases

The Mozilla Platform has support for databases, but that support is only slowly emerging. Only the most trivial support is available in the default builds of the Mozilla application suite; other support must be sought out and set up before it is available for use. Platform support for databases falls into five groups: flat files, relational databases, application-specific databases, fact stores, and caches.

Table 16.3 describes the flat file databases inside Mozilla.

The last two items deserve some explanation. `dbm` is an old version of the standard Berkeley `db` package. It is used to create several security files stored in the user's profile. This package is not directly exposed to XPCOM and cannot be used from JavaScript.

Table 16.3 General-purpose flat file databases in Mozilla

File format	Application support	Covered under what topic?
Raw files	Read/Write	"Files and Folders," "Data Transfer"
DTD documents	Read Only	Chapter 3, Static Content
Properties files	Read Only	Chapter 5, "Scripting"—see stringbundles example
Preferences	Read / Deferred Write	"Preferences"
XML Documents	Read or Write	"Web Scripting"
RDF Documents	Read / Flushed Write	"Data Sources"
Mozilla Registry	Read / Write	Chapter 17, Deployment
dbm	Unavailable	See text
Mdb	Unavailable	See text

`Mdb`, the "message database," is a custom-designed, single-file database invented for Mozilla's use. It supports the concepts of cursors, tables, rows, cells, and schema information. It supports both relational data and more general attribute value lists, as well as references between rows and tables so that a row can exist in several tables at once. It is not multiuser or multicursor and has no transactions and no recovery process. It is a general-purpose file format for self-referential data and has a low-level format equivalent to the basic structure of RDF. It has an XPCOM interface, but no XPIDL definition, and therefore no matching type library. No type library means it is not available from JavaScript.

On the relational database side, the default version of Mozilla has no direct access to relational databases. Access can be added, though. Table 16.4 lists the options both available and forecast during the release of version 1.4.

Finally, the platform has some application-specific flat file formats. These file formats are all read and written indirectly using high-level interfaces. Their location is fixed inside the current user profile. Table 16.5 lists these databases.

The cookies and bookmarks files are written entirely each time a change is made. The address book file is partially written each time a change is made.

"`Mork`" is a simple flat file database built using the `Mdb` technology, which was described in the discussion of Table 16.3. It provides a set of specifically formatted data structures suitable for storing address book cards and for status information about the user's current email and newsgroup windows. Like `Mdb`, `Mork` is not accessible from JavaScript. You can see `Mork` database content by viewing email and news control files with a text editor. Those files have `.mdb` suffixes.

Table 16.4 RDBMS add-ons for Mozilla

Database	Installation method	Cross platform?	Notes
MySQL	Downloadable XPInstall package	Yes	See *mysqlxpcom.mozdev.org*
MySQL	Recompile Mozilla 1.5+	Linux/ UNIX	See *www.mozilla.org/projects/sql*
PostgresSQL	Recompile Mozilla 1.3+	Linux/ UNIX	See *www.mozilla.org/projects/sql*
Protozilla	Downloadable XPInstall package	Linux/ UNIX	Adds the ability to extend Mozilla's network protocol support to other databases. See *http://protozilla.mozdev.org*
Web-based	Make a Web server available	Yes	Standard Web-based solution for database access; use HTTP GET and POST requests to manage a database client behind the server

Table 16.5 Application-specific flat file databases in Mozilla

File format	Notes
Cookies file	
Bookmarks file	
Address book	Uses Mork
News server control file	Uses Mork
Newsgroup hostinfo	Standard format newgroup control file
Email server control file	Uses Mork
Email folder	Standard UNIX mail(1) format mail folder
Mork	See following discussion in text

The `Mork/Mdb` file format is a disk-based format. The somewhat equivalent memory-based format is an RDF fact store, the best example being the `in-memory-datasource` data source.

The other database-like features in the Mozilla Platform are caches: the Web cache, which caches documents of remote origin, and the fastload (or XUL) cache, which holds chrome files that make up displayed windows.

16.2.4 Environment

The environment of the currently running process can be retrieved one variable at a time using this component and interface:

```
@mozilla.org/process/util;1 interface nsIProcess
```

The `nsIProcess` interface has a method `getEnvironment()` that returns the value for a supplied variable name. Supplied variable names are converted from Unicode to 8-bit extended ASCII, and values returned are Unicode values converted from the 8-bit extended ASCII value retrieved.

The operating system type or version can be detected without use of the environment. Just examine the `window.navigator.userAgent` property.

Versions of Mozilla built with debug support require that the environment variable `MOZILLA_FIVE_HOME` be set to the directory that the Mozilla binaries are installed in.

There is no environment variable that specifies the location of the current user's profile (or any profile). Setting such a variable by hand requires guesswork or foreknowledge since profile names are encrypted. The profile directory can be found using a well-known alias. See "File System Directory."

A number of debug environment variables are available when the Mozilla build is compiled with `--debug-enabled`. To understand their use, the source code for the platform needs to be examined closely. Their output is often too cryptic for general use.

16.2.5 Files and Folders

This topic describes how to locate and specify files and folders on the computer on which the platform is installed. The term *folder* is used for a file system directory because in Mozilla, the term *directory* means directory service.

Handling files in Mozilla is made complex by portability constraints and Web standards. The XPCOM objects used to represent files must be portable across all operating systems (or at least UNIX, Microsoft Windows, and Macintosh), and the idea of a file or folder must somehow interoperate with the idea of a URL.

The need for portability affects the names used for files and folders. The Mozilla Platform does not have a concept of full path name because operating system paths are expressed in different syntaxes and because volume-oriented operating systems like MacOS don't have paths at all. There are a number of volume-oriented operating systems still. Even the pathless file name part of a file identifier can be problematic. Mozilla's response to these constraints is to keep explicit use of paths and file names at arm's length, except in cases where portability is not critical.

This arm's length approach is implemented with the `nsIFile` interface. An object with that interface is frequently used in scripts, but it is rarely specified or inspected directly. Whatever naming information is available inside the `nsIFile` object stays there. Only in nonportable cases is the naming information manipulated directly. That means the `nsIFile` object is only rarely created directly with its standard XPCOM pair:

```
@mozilla.org/file/local;1 nsIFile
```

Instead, objects with this interface are produced indirectly, using methods belonging to other interfaces. Files that are stored locally are represented by objects with a specialized `nsIFile` interface. The XPCOM pair responsible for that specialized interface is

```
@mozilla.org/file/local;1 nsILocalFile
```

Both interfaces apply to folders as well as files. There is also an older interface for files. It is deprecated (unfashionable) and shouldn't be used at all:

```
@mozilla.org/filespec;1 nsIFileSpec
```

The application programmer therefore relies on that object being manufactured, initialized, and returned by a method of some other interface. Overall, there are many ways to bring such an object into existence:

1. A directory service that retains a list of well-known files and folders can be consulted if the nature of the needed file or folder is known in advance.
2. Users can be prompted to identify the file or folder. Whatever they pick is the file or folder required.
3. The file or folder can be deduced from a URL. This does not automatically work; the context of the URL and file are both important.
4. The file or folder can be deduced from another file or folder object, if that other object is somehow related. Finding the parent directory of a given file requires only `nsIFile`'s parent property; finding the contents of a folder requires only `nsIFile`'s `directoryEntries` property.
5. If portability is not an issue, then the file's full or partial UNIX or Windows path name can be specified as a JavaScript string and an object initialized with that string.
6. Finally, if an `nsIFile` object is used to create a stream, channel, or other XPCOM object, then that other object can usually reveal the originating `nsIFile` object at any later point.

Examples of these dot-points are given in "File System Directory."

The `nsIFile` interface addresses portability issues, but the issue of integration with Web URLs remains. URLs are maintained in objects with the `nsIURL` interface. See "Web Scripting" for details on that interface. Files and URLs can be converted to each other using this XPCOM pair:

```
@mozilla.org/network/protocol;1?name=file nsIFileProtocolHandler
```

This interface provides `newFileURI()` and `getFileFromURLSpec()` methods that do the required conversion. `newFileURI()` is also available on the `nsIIOService` interface.

The nsIURL and nsIFile interfaces also allow a URI or file specification to be dissected into its component parts. Those parts can be read or updated. Simple string operations may be sufficient to turn the naming information inside an nsIFile object into an nsIURL object and vice versa. Files and URLs can therefore also be connected by application-specific string manipulation code.

16.2.5.1 Using the File System Directory

The file system directory is described in "Platform Configuration," where some further examples are given. This piece of code gets by the shortest route a folder suitable for holding temporary files. Listing 16.1 illustrates.

Listing 16.1 Directory specification of an nsILocalFile object.

```
var Cc = Components.classes;
var Ci = Components.interfaces;
var dp = Cc["@mozilla.org/file/directory_service;1"];
    dp = dp.createInstance(Ci.nsIDirectoryServiceProvider);

var folder = dp.getFile("TmpD", {});
```

This approach reveals only those files and folders that already have a nominated purpose for the Mozilla Platform. The code revolves around the special folder alias TmpD. It must be looked up in a table. Those tables are compiled in "File System Directory."

16.2.5.2 Using the End User

To create an nsILocalFile object, one solution is to ask the user as Listing 16.2 shows.

Listing 16.2 User-specification of an nsILocalFile object.

```
var file;
var CcFP = Components.classes["@mozilla.org/filepicker;1"];
var CiFP = Components.interfaces.nsIFilePicker;
var fp = CcFP.createInstance(CiFP);

// use whatever nsIFilePicker options are suitable
fp.init(window, "File to Read", Picker.modeOpen);

if ( fp.show() != fp.returnCancel )
  file = fp.file;
```

The nsIFilePicker object manufactures an nsILocalFile object in response to the user's selection.

If the object created holds a folder name, it can be converted to a more specific file or folder using the appendRelativePath() method, which accepts relative path names that do not include "..". The appended path can, with care, be hand-constructed without the loss of portability. Fortunately, all of Microsoft Windows, UNIX, and Macintosh support the forward slash (`/`) character as a path separator for subpaths, even though a Microsoft Windows DOS Box does not. Be aware that some Windows users (and some Linux users in rare cases) may not have Long File Name (LFN) support, which limits file names to "8.3" or 14-character names. The `nsIFile` interface supports a number of attributes and methods that assist with portable path construction.

Finally, if the application does not need to be portable, or if separate implementation code for each supported platform are permitted, then an `nsILocalFile` object can be initialized directly from a string using the `initWithPath()` method. Backslash characters used in Microsoft Windows paths should be escaped (`\\`) or forward slashes used instead. Separate implementation code can be as simple as a series of `if` statements that test the current platform.

16.2.5.3 Using a Literal or a URL If the application does not need to be portable, or if separate implementation code for each supported platform is maintained, then an `nsILocalFile` object can be initialized directly from a string. A suitable piece of code is simply as shown in Listing 16.3.

Listing 16.3 Literal specification of an `nsILocalFile` object.

```
var file;
var CcLF = Components.classes["@mozilla.org/local/file;1"];
var CiLF = Components.interfaces.nsILocalFile;
var file = CcLF.createInstance(CiLF);

file.initWithPath("C:\\WINDOWS\NOTEPAD.EXE");
```

The literal "`C:`" could be replaced with a portable file system root folder using the DrvD alias and the file system directory. Recall that Microsoft Windows supports both forward slashes and backslashes as path separators, so those too could be made more portable.

Alternately, the location of a local file might be contained inside a URL. The portable way to achieve conversion is with this code:

```
var conv = Cc["@mozilla.org/network/protocol;1?name=file"];
conv = conv.createInstance(Ci.nsIFileProtocolHandler);

var url = ... // Some nsIURL that already exists

var file = conv.getFileFromURLSpec(url);
```

That URL will either be prefixed with `file:`, or it will refer to a virtual directory behind a local Web server. In either case, the URI scheme may be chopped off and replaced with a different file system root. For example,

```
file.initWithPath(myURL.filePath.replace(/\|/,":"));
```

Here, myURL is an nsIURL object. The replace() regular expression operation changes a URL fragment like "C|/test" to "C:/test". Beware that under Microsoft Windows, network-mapped paths (UNC paths) like \\saturn\tmp require a prefix of five forward slashes (http://///saturn/tmp) when expressed as URLs, and that convention is not finalized at this time.

16.2.5.4 Working on Files and Folders After a file is located and represented internally by an object, it's usual to read, write, or manipulate that file.

File descriptors, file pointers, and file handles are not available in the Mozilla JavaScript environment. That means that file-descriptor-based pipes cannot be created. The nsIPipe interface creates an application-level pipe, not a traditional UNIX pipe. The platform cannot be used to create named pipes (or symbolic links), but such pipes can be read from and written to if they already exist. In short, direct low-level file access is not the way to go.

Instead of file handles, Mozilla uses objects. Instead of manipulating a single object, a script must manipulate at least two objects. One object identifies the file or folder that is to be used—an nsIFile or nsILocalFile object. This object is a file *name* specifier. The other object is a stream that data are read from and written to. This object is a file *content* specifier. Both objects must be created, and this must be done in such a way that they are connected to each other. "Data Transfer" in this chapter discusses streams and other content specifiers extensively. Streams are similar to Java or C++ streams, but there is no operator overloading at work.

16.2.5.5 Working on ZIP and JAR Archives This XPCOM pair uses nsIFile concepts and provides access to the contents of locally stored .zip and .jar files:

```
@mozilla.org/libjar/zip-reader;1 nsIZipReader
```

Zip files can also be created with this interface.

The stream converters noted in "Stream Content Conversion" can be used to work with a stream of compressed characters in their raw form.

16.2.6 Interrupts and Signals

There is no way to catch or send operating system signals from JavaScript. To catch signals, an XPCOM component must be written in either Java or C/C++.

The nsIThread XPCOM interface is used to manage a piece of code that can be interrupted. This will work only if the code to be interrupted is not JavaScript. The JavaScript interpreter in the Mozilla Platform is single-threaded and can't interrupt itself. This means that thread-based interrupts are not usable for entirely scripted applications.

The event-oriented technologies described in Chapter 6, Events, and the command system of Chapter 9, Commands, are the main alternatives to interrupts.

16.2.7 Network Protocols

Mozilla provides support for well-known network application protocols like FTP. Mozilla assumes the underlying transport layer will be TCP/IP. Other protocols, such as RS232, X.25, or TP4 must be overlayed with TCP/IP before they are usable. Mozilla supports the following low-level protocols:

- ☞ **TCP/IP v4** and **v6**. v6 is not enabled in the default build and must be compiled in with `--enable-ipv6`. The Configuration windows in Classic Mozilla do not yet support IPv6.
- ☞ **DNS**. The platform supports multithreaded (parallel) DNS look-ups.
- ☞ **FTP**. Mozilla supports FTP, but the Download Manager does not support FTP resume as of version 1.4.
- ☞ **RPC**. Mozilla provides support for RPC over XML only, not RPC over NDR/XDR. The latter approach is the traditional method of doing RPC.
- ☞ **SSL (Secure Sockets Layer)** and **SOCKS**. Mozilla supports SSL versions 2 and 3, and SOCKS 4.0 and 5.0. SSL is used for Secure SMTP (SMIME) and Secure HTTP (HTTPS) protocol support.

Protocols are used indirectly in Mozilla. Resources are identified by URL and the access method that prefixes the URL (like *http:*) determines the protocol used. The protocol is then exploited automatically by the platform. In general, a channel object accepts a URL, and everything "just works" from then on. Nevertheless, individual protocols do exist as separate objects and can be created as instances of this XPCOM pair:

```
@mozilla.org/network/protocol;1?name={x} nsIProtocolHandler
```

In this component name, `{x}` should be replaced with a value like `ftp` or `http`. A dump of the `window.Components.classes` array reveals all the protocols (actually URL schemes) for which Mozilla has components.

Mozilla can be configured at the IP port level using preferences. Individual ports can be enabled or disabled. Enabling such ports has no effect unless they are enabled in the operating system as well. Enabled ports can create security holes at the application level and are not recommended unless suitable firewalls are in place. See the preferences displayed by the URL `about:config` that start with `network` for an extensive list of configuration options.

Application programmers also have access to sockets. Operating systems represent a TCP/IP connection with a socket library that maps the TCP/IP connection to a file descriptor. Mozilla wraps the connection and descriptor details up into an object. Such a socket object is the lowest level network data structure available in the default build of the platform.

Finally, the Optimoz project, documented at *www.mozdev.org*, can be used to extend the network support of Mozilla. Using Optimoz, new protocols that are written in JavaScript alone can be added. The requirements for such protocols follow: They must be built on top of a TCP/IP socket; they must be tolerant of small time delays; they must implement the `nsIProtocolHandler` interface; and the JavaScript code must register a full XPCOM component implementation for the created handler.

We now turn to specific low-level network-oriented tasks. For application-level communications, see "Data Transfer" and "Web Scripting."

16.2.7.1 How to Find an IP Address To find the IP address for a given domain name, use this XPCOM pair:

```
@mozilla.org/network/dns-service;1 interface nsIDNSService
```

An object so created returns the IP address for a given domain name, or the current host, as a string like "`192.168.1.10`". Resolving domain names is slow, so if you don't want the application to freeze, use the `lookup()` method, which requires a listener object with the `nsIDNSListener` interface. The request will then proceed asynchronously. Make this listener out of a pure JavaScript object.

16.2.7.2 How to Create a Socket To create a socket connection, several steps are required.

To use a socket you must ultimately create an `nsITransport` object. After you have this object, you can ignore the socket to a degree and, instead, use the techniques described in "Data Transfer." Socket access is quite abstract and high level; there is no `ioctl(2)` API that can be used to configure socket options.

To get this `nsITransport` object, you must first deal with the possibility that there is a network proxy between the platform and the computer at the other end of the socket. Create an object that is an `nsIProxyInfo` object for the desired remote address if you aren't sure whether a proxy exists. An `nsIProxyInfo` object, can be created using the `newProxyInfo()` or `examineForProxy()` methods of this XPCOM pair:

```
@mozilla.org/network/protocol-proxy-service; nsIProtocolProxyService
```

Next, using the resulting `nsIProxyInfo` object, or `null` if it is certain no proxy exists, create the factory object that is responsible for creating `nsITransport` objects for sockets. That factory object is created with this XPCOM pair:

```
@mozilla.org/network/socket-transport-service;1 nsISocketTransportService
```

With that factory object, create an `nsITransport` object by passing the `nsIProxyInfo` object to the `createTransport()` method. The resulting object will also support the `nsISocketTransport` interface, which is the base socket. If a SOCKS socket is wanted, use the `createTransportOfType()` method instead and choose a type of "`socks`" for SOCKS 5.0

or "socks4" for SOCKS 4.0. A UNIX (IPC) socket can be created by specifying a type of "ipc". The final transport object thus created can be used as a socket or as any transport object can.

SOCKS-enabled sockets use digital encryption and can be created only if correct encryption modules and keys are installed and enabled via the preferences. These items are installed and enabled by default in the user profile of the Classic Browser and the Mozilla Browser.

The Mozilla Platform has a number of other socket-related interfaces, but none of them is available from JavaScript. When looking through socket XPIDL files, remember to check for [noscript] before the interface name's declaration. Such interfaces are not available to JavaScript.

Listing 16.4 is a simple Perl program that can be used as a test server for socket connections. It reads from all connecting clients and prints what it gets to stdout. It does not support SOCKS, nor does it write data back to the socket client.

Listing 16.4 Socket server implementation for testing.

```
use IO::Socket;

my ($server, $client, $host);

$server = IO::Socket::INET->new(
    Proto => 'tcp', LocalPort => 80, Listen => SOMAXCONN, Reuse => 1);

while ($server && ($client = $server->accept()))
{
  while ( <$client> ) { print; }
  close $client;
}
```

In order to work, this program also requires correct port setup at the operating system level.

16.2.7.3 How to Create an FTP Session The Mozilla Platform does not directly support a whole FTP session. Each URL request made via an nsIChannel object is a standalone operation. This means that each FTP session consists of at most four FTP commands. In pseudo-code, these are

```
open {hostname and port}
cd   {directory}
dir OR get {file}
close
```

This FTP session is handled inside Mozilla. The FTP session information is not available to the application programmer, and the application programmer can't submit individual FTP commands. This means that the way to conduct an FTP session is to use a URL request that happens to be an ftp: URL. See "Downloading Files" and "Channels" for detailed instructions.

If the application code needs to walk through the FTP hierarchy of an FTP site, then there is still a way to do that. An FTP URL can represent an FTP directory rather than a single file. If that URL is submitted from the platform, the directory listing is returned, but it is converted to an HTML document. This returned document can be walked through to discover files and subdirectories in the original URL directory. Those files can then be retrieved in turn.

To upload (put) a file to an FTP server, the same environment applies. The FTP session is hidden behind a URL. See "Uploading and Posting Files" for how to do this.

If all else fails, two sockets can be set up from JavaScript that implement the FTP protocol directly. If this is done, care needs to be taken to ensure that performance is adequate. This approach is probably as much work as creating a new XPCOM component for FTP in C/C++.

16.2.8 Processes and Threads

Your task may not require a whole thread or process. It may only need to be scheduled as an event on an event queue. If that is the case, see Chapter 6, Events. For larger tasks, read on.

The simplest way to run a separate program is to hand a file to the desktop of the operating system and ask the desktop to activate that file as though it were invoked (usually double-clicked) by the user. Start by using this XPCOM pair to create a file object:

```
@mozilla.org/file/local;1 nsILocalFile
```

Associate the resulting object with a real file (see "File System Directory" for how) and then call the `launch()` method. On UNIX, `launch()` is handled by the GNOME desktop, not by the PATH environment variable. There is no way to shut down that launched application from Mozilla.

More generally, processes can be launched from the platform using this pair of XPCOM objects:

```
@mozilla.org/process/util;1 nsIProcess
```

Be aware that this interface is not yet fully implemented on all platforms. To use it successfully, proceed as follows. As before, create an `nsILocalFile` object associated with the required executable. Because processes are generally operating system–dependent, the non-portable `initWithPath()` method may be used. Pass that object to the `nsIProcess init()` method, and then call `run()` to create the process. That last step requires a method invocation like this:

```
var blocking = true;
var argv =     ["arg1","arg2"];
var result =   {};
nsIProcess_object.run(blocking, argv, argv.length, result);
```

The `result` object is required by the `run()` method; it receives a `value` property that is set to 0 (zero) if the process starts successfully. If blocking is set to `true`, then Mozilla will freeze while the process runs. In that case, windows will not be updated for any reason until the process ends. If set to `false`, Mozilla continues processing. In either case, when the process finishes, the `exitValue` property on the `nsIProcess` object will be set. Some testing is required to match the `exitValue` value to normal exit values returned by the operating system.

Threads are a more difficult matter than processes. To an application programmer, a thread is no more than a piece of code scheduled with `window.setTimeout()`. Although this creates the illusion of a second flow of control, in fact the scheduled code is queued up until the current flow of control (the current piece of script) ends. No script is ever started until the existing running script is complete.

Matters are like this because of the way the JavaScript interpreter (SpiderMonkey) is connected to Mozilla. Deep inside, the platform does support threads. Its XPCOM system has a threading system that is a simplification of Microsoft COM's threading system. This system is used in a number of places; most obviously to manage FTP connections, which require the separate monitoring of two connections. The JavaScript interpreter is embedded in Mozilla using just one of these threads. While the interpreter is built to handle multiple running instances, its use in the Mozilla Platform does not take advantage of that feature.

Even though true threads are not available in JavaScript, interfaces do exist for working with threads. They provide a neater way to organize chunks of code than `setTimeout()` and `setInterval()` provide. Listing 16.5 shows the steps required to create a thread:

Listing 16.5 Simple thread creation code.

```
var Cct = Components.classes["@mozilla.org/thread;1"];
var Cit = Components.interfaces.nsIThread;

var thread = { Run : function ()
                    { alert(this.foo+" thread underway"); }
               foo : "bar"
             };

var mgr = Cct.createInstance(Cit);

mgr.init(code, 0, Cit.PRIORITY_NORMAL, Cit.SCOPE_GLOBAL,
         Cit.STATE_JOINABLE);

mgr.join();
alert("thread created");
```

The code object supports the `nsIRunnable` interface and contains the code to run (the `Run()` method) and any other properties that might be useful to that code. The `thread` object holds the implementation of the thread, which includes the code and some data. The `mgr` (manager) object holds the `thread`'s configuration and state. The `join()` method tells the platform threading system that this thread should be scheduled to run—or to continue running if it was previously interrupted. Such an interruption is not possible if the thread is written in JavaScript. `join()` is not equivalent to `eval()`—the thread is put on a queue that the JavaScript interpreter will get to eventually. Because the interpreter is single-threaded and not interruptible by other threads, the `alert()` in the last line of code will always appear before the `join`ed thread's alert.

There is no race condition in this arrangement—the current script must finish before anything else can run. This single-threaded arrangement means that it is not possible to create blocking or infinite loop threads whose code is written in JavaScript. Such threads may never end, and therefore no other threads will ever run. The only value, then, of using such a system from JavaScript is as a modeling strategy that collects code into handy thread objects or that works with non-JavaScript XPCOM objects that also have the `nsIRunnable` interface.

A JavaScript script can create genuine threads by interacting with Java. Such threads are pure Java threads only.

16.3 Data Transfer

This topic describes the general-purpose structures used to read, write, and process content inside the platform. It picks up where locating files and folders left off. RDF fact processing is also covered, but parsing of XML documents is left to "Web Scripting."

16.3.1 Content Processing Concepts

A major task of the back half of Mozilla is to process content and data. To do this, the platform must have systems that can transfer data and content from place to place. Mozilla has many content and data processing concepts to pick from.

Chapter 6, Events, describes the concepts of listeners, observers, and broadcasters. Those concepts are event oriented and are used only for tiny pieces of information. They are not sufficient for a content-oriented system, although such a system might work better if observers or listeners are added. A content-oriented system must transfer information as large as a document in size.

Mozilla's content-processing concepts are files, folders, streams, sessions, channels, transports, sources (data sources), and sinks.

Files and *folders* are concepts common to all operating systems and are discussed in "General-Purpose Scripting."

A *stream* is Mozilla's lowest level way to transfer data. A stream works on a series of bytes, octets, or characters, just like a C++ or Java stream does, or like redirection (>) in a UNIX or DOS shell. Streams can be read or written, depending on their source and destination. Mozilla also supports Unicode streams, where the fundamental character is a two-byte "wide character" rather than a one-byte "extended ASCII" character.

A *session* is a set of configuration information about a process, task, or activity that is underway. This configuration information is used by the process itself, although it sometimes receives events. It, however, is not the actual process at work; it is an onlooker, a specifier, and a controller.

An example session is an FTP file transfer. The FTP domain name, user name, password, and socket connection are part of the FTP session information. The actual transfer of the file data is done by some other piece of software. The session merely says who, what, where, and when. A session can also be used outside of the networking domain—a Mozilla drag-and-drop mouse gesture has a session object that tracks the progress of the gesture. Sessions are used in a number of places in Mozilla.

A *channel* is the piece of platform architecture that actually performs data transfer. A channel is a sophisticated version of a buffer. In Mozilla, channels are used mostly for retrieving documents that have a URL. Channels sometimes have extensive functionality, but their basic task is fairly simple: They make available a flow of raw data that originates elsewhere, such as behind a Web server. The data transfer might consist of actually copying data, or it might be a conceptual transfer in which the data, once available in form A, is now available in form B. A channel has a management role—actual read and write of data to the channel is usually handed off to a stream.

A *transport* is a piece of networking. While a channel provides a high-level concept for data transfer, a transport does all the leg work by implementing or using a specific network protocol like SMTP or socket-based TCP/IP.

Sources and *sinks* are treated separately next.

16.3.1.1 Sources and Sinks Source and sinks are important concepts in Mozilla. They are used mostly for the wholesale processing of XML documents. They are the highest level information flow concepts in Mozilla and usually do content-specific processing.

Sources and sinks are also a general design concept in both science and engineering. Many programmers are introduced to sources and sinks when dataflow diagrams are taught. In dataflow diagrams (and in an ordinary kitchen sink), it is generally understood that data or content (or water) starts at the source (the tap) and ends at the sink (the drain hole). That, however, is just a matter of perspective. That example can be turned inside out.

If you are responsible for the kitchen sink itself, then matters are arranged in the standard way. You can see water leaving the tap (the source) and entering the drain hole (the sink).

If you are responsible for guiding the water from the tap to the drain hole, then matters are inside out. The first thing you do is collect the water from the tap into some intermediate place, like a jug. The jug is then a sink. The last thing you do is pour the water out from that intermediate place into the drain hole. The jug is then a source. In this example, your data-transfer system starts with a sink and ends with a source, not the other way around.

This second perspective is relevant to Mozilla. Inside the platform, a sink is used to suck up the content of a document into main memory. If any of the content needs to be extracted, then a source is used to get it out.

No matter which way sources and sinks are arranged, in producer-consumer terms, a source is always a producer, and a sink is always a consumer. From the application programmer's perspective, if the document content is not yet available (perhaps because it is stored in an external file), then a sink must be set up first to load that content. A source is set up second, to retrieve the loaded content for application use. The application programmer's job is to set up the water flow. In some cases, the document is automatically loaded. In that case, only a source is required.

This type of arrangement has one complexity. Documents can be modified. Sinks are generally used for the initial loading of data, and so they process data one way. This means that it is up to a source to manage changes. Therefore, sources not only retrieve the document's content but generally can modify it as well.

Mozilla does not provide a general-purpose sink or source interface. There are only specialist interfaces for particular kinds of data. Mozilla's interfaces allow more than one sink or source to operate on an in-memory document at the same time.

16.3.1.2 Specialized Sources and Sinks Sources and sinks operate as content processors and are high-level concepts. Mozilla's sources and sinks are all specialized to a particular purpose.

Data sources are used to process RDF content. Instead of working with tags, parser tokens, or DOM objects, data sources work with RDF facts. The template system of XUL uses RDF data sources extensively, and these templates and sources can be manipulated with scripts. There are no RDF fact sinks, only fact sources. These fact sources (data sources) can also perform insert, update, and delete operations on the fact store that holds the retrieved-to-memory RDF document. Some of Mozilla's data sources, called *internal data sources*, draw their content directly from the platform, rather than from an external RDF document. The origins of the facts in this case are usually data structures inside the platform, or the user's bookmark file.

A *parser* is another kind of sink. It takes a flow of content, usually originating in a document, and transforms it into a data structure. An example is a parser that reads XML and creates a DOM tree. Mozilla includes parsers for all applications of XML that it understands.

A *serializer* is a source that is the inverse of a parser. It turns a data structure into a stream of flat content, typically an XML document.

16.3.1.3 Content Processing Architecture All the data processing concepts discussed here fit together into an informal set of layers, although this layer-

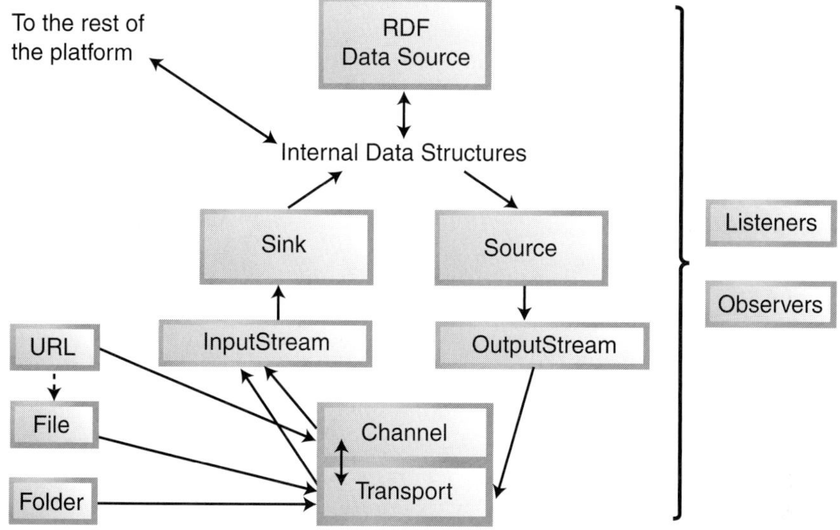

Fig. 16.1 Layered structure of content processing concepts.

ing is not as structured as a network protocol stack. Figure 16.1 illustrates these layered relationships.

Figure 16.1 is a conceptual diagram and does not show strict object relationships. It is, however, close to some specific object relationships inside the platform. We can see that channels and transports are closely connected, but not so closely connected that they can't be used separately. Input and output streams expose the data or content processed to the rest of the platform. Two typically large chunks of processing are the sources and sinks that contain parsers, serializers, and other transformation tools. RDF data sources are somewhat separate from the other concepts because they are very high level and work only on content already broken down into facts. All these concepts support listeners and observers; URLs and files are used to configure the lower levels of processing.

Not shown in Figure 16.1 are the many other interfaces provided by these central concepts, or the many other interactions that occur with the rest of the platform.

16.3.2 Streams

When a file or other information source is available, a stream must be created before that file's contents can be worked on. Streams are central to data processing in Mozilla, and there are a large number of stream-oriented interfaces available. These interfaces include stream creators, loaders, converters, and managers. Several specialized streams also exist such as random-access and string-based streams. There is a stream interface available for all common tasks—just look for any interface with `Stream` in its name.

To illustrate this flexibility, Listing 16.6 shows four methods of creating a stream. This stream is used to read a local file that is a sequence of bytes.

Listing 16.6 Stream creation by several methods.

```
var Cc = Components.classes;
var Ci = Components.interfaces;
var mode_bits = 0x01; // from nsIFileChannel
var perm_bits = 0;    // from Unix/Posix open(2)
var file_bits = 0;    // from nsIFileInputStream

var stream;
var file = ... // same as Listing 16-3 or 16-2

// [1] Created directly

stream = Cc["@mozilla.org/network/file-input-stream;1"];
stream = stream.createInstance(Ci.nsIFileInputStream);
stream.init(file, mode_bits, perm_bits, file_bits);

// [2] Created from a transport

var trans = Cc["@mozilla.org/network/stream-transport-service;1"];
trans = trans.getService(Ci.nsIStreamTransportService);
trans = trans.createInputTransport(stream,0,-1,true);
var stream2 = trans.openInputStream(0,-1,0);

// [3] Created from a channel

var channel = Cc["@mozilla.org/network/local-file-channel;1"]
channel = channel.createInstance(Ci.nsIFileChannel);
channel.init(file, mode_bits, perm_bits);
stream = channel.open();

// In all cases, work on the stream from JavaScript

var s2 = Cc["@mozilla.org/scriptableinputstream;1"];
s2 = s2.createInstance(Ci.nsIScriptableInputStream);
s2.init(stream);

var bytes = 100;
var content = null;
content = s2.read(bytes);
```

In all three cases, the `nsILocalFile` object created earlier is passed in as an initialization argument at some point.

☞ **Example 1**. The file is read and written directly using a stream. The stream interacts with the file synchronously unless special arrangements are made.

- ☞ **Example 2**. This example is a little odd because it both starts and ends with a stream. The transport object must be based on something, and in the absence of a network protocol, a stream is the only other alternative. That underlying protocol is used to retrieve the file's content. The stream handed back by the transport to variable `stream 2` is different from the stream supplied. The handed-back stream will generally have data available on demand because the transport does work to collect the received data ready for the next user request. By comparison, example 1 does work only when the user makes a request. The transport will also close down the "connection" to the file automatically when no more data are available.
- ☞ **Example 3**. A channel allows the file to be retrieved without any assumptions about the retrieval mechanism.

Finally, streams cannot be read or written from JavaScript automatically. This is a piece of design intended to keep streams efficient. Instead, the stream object must be wrapped up in a special object that supplies read/write operations. That is the point of the last few lines, which also read at most the first 100 bytes of the supplied file, less if the file is short.

Examples 1 and 2 can be used to perform file writing instead of reading with only small coding changes. Example 3 cannot be rewritten because channels work only one way. When writing content, the default output is single-byte characters. Any content supplied as UTF16 Unicode strings (like JavaScript strings) is truncated character by character down to the least significant byte. This means that default file output is single-byte extended ASCII. To output Unicode (usually in a UTF8 encoding), content conversion is required. That is discussed next. (see "Stream Content Conversion.")

16.3.2.1 Stream Content Conversion All character strings are represented as Unicode inside the platform. Plain files may be read as raw binary data (use `nsIBinaryInputStream`), as 8-bit character data (the default for plain files), or as correctly encoded Unicode. The last option occurs when XML files are identified and parsed into DOM hierarchies, when a stream of data originates from a source that supplies format information such as HTTP or MIME, or when DTD files are read.

To convert the content produced by a stream, this XPCOM pair will do the job:

```
@mozilla.org/intl/scriptableunicodeconverter;1
    nsIScriptableUnicodeConverter
```

Mozilla also supports many components with Contract IDs of this form:

```
@mozilla.org/streamconv;1?from={mime1}to={mime2}
```

`mime1` and `mime2` are MIME types. These components support the `nsIStreamConverter` interface. Such an object reads a given input stream and

Table 16.6 Stream conversions supported by Mozilla

Original MIME type	Converted MIME type
application/http-index-format	text/html
application/mac-binhex40	*/*
application/x-unknown-content-type	*/*
compress	uncompressed content
deflate	uncompressed content
gzip	uncompressed content
message/rfc822	application/vnd.mozilla.xul+xml
message/rfc822	*/*
message/rfc822	text/html
multipart/byteranges	*/*
multipart/mixed	*/*
text/ftp-dir	application/http-index-format
text/gopher-dir	application/http-index-format
text/plain	text/html
x-compress	uncompressed content
x-gzip	uncompressed content

converts its content. It makes available a new input stream that the converted content can be read from. Table 16.6 lists the conversions that the platform supplies. Such a converter can also be implemented in pure JavaScript.

The XPIDL description for `nsIStreamConverter` explains how such a conversion can be done with two `nsIStreamListener` objects instead of whole stream objects. This approach allows converters to work on any kind of stream, not just input streams.

16.3.3 Transports

Transport layer XPCOM objects are responsible for transferring content from inside the Mozilla Platform to outside it, and vice versa. Transports are therefore more general than streams, which are restricted to the platform and to the local disk. Where streams generally provide data synchronously and directly from a given source, transports can provide data both asynchronously and synchronously, from anywhere. Transports may also handle and buffer up data between user requests.

The currently available transport layers are shown in Table 16.7.

Table 16.7 Supported XPCOM transport layers

Implementation	Interface
@mozilla.org/network/stream-transport-service;1	nsIStreamTransportService
@mozilla.org/network/socket-transport-service;1	nsISocketTransportService
@mozilla.org/network/storage-transport;1	nsITransport
@mozilla.org/xmlextras/soap/transport;1?protocol=http	nsISOAPTransport
@mozilla.org/xmlextras/soap/transport;1?protocol=https	nsISOAPTransport

The five transports in Table 16.7 are responsible for: all streams, including local files; domain sockets; the browser cache; an HTTP transport binding for SOAP requests; and a secure (SSL-based) HTTP transport binding for SOAP requests.

The `stream-transport-service` implementation is fairly new (since 1.3) and replaces the no longer available `file-transport-service`. Be aware that some examples of code may use that older object.

16.3.4 Channels

A channel is a read-only mechanism for getting the content of a URL. Although a channel can work with file objects, it is more natural for a channel to use a URL. Channels are responsible for much of the content-specific work that Mozilla does when retrieving a document. The sole exception to the read-only rule is an upload channel, which is used for submitting forms, uploading files, and publishing Web pages.

In the normal programming case, channels are handled indirectly. Like `nsIFile` objects and streams, it is far more common for a channel to be created for you than to create one explicitly yourself. Just as a file and a stream are a closely associated pair of objects, so too are a URL and a channel. This analogy is not perfect. A difference is that while streams can be created directly, channels rarely are because channels are mostly buried behind a protocol. A second difference is that a channel is an enhanced request (an `nsIRequest` object), which in turn is an enhanced URL. So a channel and its URL are not strictly separate objects.

Use of channels usually starts with this XPCOM pair:

```
@mozilla.org/network/io-service;1 nsIIOService
```

This component provides the `nsIIOService` interface via `getService()`. As for transports, this interface is effectively a name service for URL schemes. Recall that a URL scheme is the characters before the first colon in a fully quoted URL. This component takes scheme names and returns software objects. The `nsIIOService` interface is therefore the fundamental jumping off point for retrieving the content of a URL.

The `nsIIOService` interface can create new URI objects (with `nsIURI` or `nsIURL` interfaces). These objects describe a given URL just as `nsIFile` objects describe a file. These interfaces also expose the protocol handler objects for a given scheme or URL. Those protocol handler objects implement channels. Each protocol handler supports one type of channel; some support more than one type. After a URL object is constructed, either from user input or from a plain JavaScript string, it can be used to find the protocol handler for that URL, and from that found handler a useful channel object can be obtained. The short way to do all this is just to call `newChannelFromURI()`.

When the channel object is available, it can produce a stream object and start the required processing. The stream object is used to deal with the retrieved content. The `nsIIOService` interface has a number of convenience methods so that it is easy to ignore the protocol handler entirely.

Channels do a great deal of processing on behalf of the URL requestor—they locate and retrieve the resource; perform content conversion; and record the MIME type and other configuration details. Table 16.8 lists the channels provided by the platform.

From Table 16.8, most channels are associated with a URL scheme. All channels support the `nsIChannel` core functionality, which consists primarily

Table 16.8 Supported XPCOM channels

Channel interface	URL scheme and/or contract ID implementing
nsIChannel	All the following entries
nsICachingChannel	http:
nsIDataChannel	data:
nsIEncodedChannel	http:
nsIFileChannel	file:
nsIFTPChannel	ftp:
nsIHttpChannel	http:
nsIImapMockChannel	imap:
nsIInputStreamChannel	@mozilla.org/network/input-stream-channel;1
nsIJarChannel	jar:
nsIMultiPartChannel	internal use only
nsIResumableChannel	ftp: (http: not yet supported)
nsIUploadChannel	file:, ftp:, http:
nsIViewSourceChannel	view-source:
nsIWyciwygChannel	wyciwyg: (not spelled 'wysiwyg')

of the `open()` and `asyncOpen()` methods. Those methods yield stream or stream listener objects. The other channel interfaces merely enhance the channel object produced by `nsIIOService` with extra configuration information. They do not represent fundamentally different channels—they are just add-ons.

Table 16.8 presents a few unusual cases. The `nsIUploadChannel` is oriented away from the desktop rather than toward it. It consumes an input stream, rather than providing one, all in order to send the supplied content to some server. The `nsIResumableChannel` is used for FTP downloads that are interrupted. The Download Manager in the Classic Browser does not yet use this functionality.

The second unusual case is that of trivial protocols. A channel need not be associated with a complicated protocol like HTTP or FTP. It can be associated with any simple transfer task. The existing implemented channels support a trivial memory-to-disk transfer (plain file access) and an even more trivial memory-to-memory transfer (which uses a stream object). Neither of these trivial protocols needs to interact with URLs, and so their channel objects can be manipulated directly by hand. That is the origin of the `input-stream-channel` Contract ID that appears in Table 16.8.

Listing 16.6 has an example of the trivial memory-to-disk protocol at work.

16.3.5 Data Sources

Data sources provide the fact-oriented support needed for XUL templates and manipulation of RDF fact stores. The Mozilla Platform contains substantial code that hooks data source objects up to such URIs. For manipulation of fact stores, XPCOM interfaces are coded against directly, and again the platform has substantial preexisting code that does this. The most obvious example is the default builders and content views used to activate templates. Equivalent or different support can be built by an application programmer using these interfaces.

The concept of a data source is expressed by the `nsIRDFDataSource` interface. This interface provides all the semantics of dealing with RDF facts. About 20 XPCOM components implement this interface. The "Hands On" session in this chapter has extensive examples of these interfaces at work. This topic attempts to classify and identify those interfaces.

Individual facts can be constructed from simple XPCOM objects based in the `nsIRDFResource` and `nsIRDFLiteral` interfaces. In general, a data source is always readable and occasionally writable, providing simple query-insert-update-delete functionality, sometimes called get-and-set. Unlike other processing concepts, data sources operate on logical objects (facts) rather than a stream of bytes or characters

Useful XPCOM data source interfaces fall into three categories:

- **Helper tools and utilities**. These are needed just to make something happen.
- **Creative extensions**. Some interfaces extend the functionality provided by the basic `nsIRDFDataSource` interface in novel ways.
- **Content support**. Some aspects of data sources determine content—the type and number of facts that can be accessed. This final category is divided into ordinary and internal data sources. Ordinary data sources draw facts from RDF files. Internal data sources draw facts from the Mozilla Platform itself.

If the wrong data source from this final group is chosen, then hours, days, or weeks can be spent wondering why nothing works. It is therefore important to have good product knowledge on each kind of content support.

The `nsIRDFDataSource` makes poor use of the word *source*. In that interface, *source* and *target* are used to mean fact subject and fact object, respectively—for example, `getSource()`. Source is also used elsewhere in Mozilla to mean source code. Don't automatically assume that source means data source.

16.3.5.1 Factory and Helper Objects If a XUL template is involved, then the DOM objects for that template provide access to `nsIRDFDataSource` objects. If no template exists, then a directly scripted use of data sources requires use of factory objects right from the start. Table 16.9 lists the components used for pure RDF manipulation:

In Table 16.9, the notation `{arg}` indicates that a number of alternatives are possible. The easiest way to see them all is to list the contents of the `window.Components.classes` array. Table 16.9 is divided into four parts as follows.

The first part is the starting point for application use of RDF. The `nsIRDFService` interface is used to create `nsIRDFDataSource` objects from a URI, including a URL based on the `rdf:` scheme. Those URLs are listed in Table 16.11. If an object for a fact subject, predicate, or object is required, it can also be created from JavaScript strings using this interface. The `nsIRDFService` interface's object is accessible via `getService()`, not via `createInstance()`.

The second section of Table 16.9 provides factory interfaces for creating and manipulating RDF containers. The two interfaces supplied provide straightforward ways to create data structures consisting of RDF resource objects. This section also includes the `resource-factory` components. When a `resource-factory` component is used, the fact items created have extra features. Depending on the argument chosen for `name=`, such a created object might contain address book, email, news, or file information, in addition to the basic subject, predicate, or object resource. This information, and its associated methods, follows the resource around as it is manipulated in the fact

Table 16.9 XPCOM components specific to RDF

Component name	Interfaces	Purpose
@mozilla.org/rdf/rdf-service;1	nsIRDFService	Starting point; creates nsIRDFDataSource data sources and nsIRDFNode subjects, predicates, and objects
@mozilla.org/rdf/container;1	nsIRDFContainer	Creates a <Bag>, <Seq>, or <Alt> tag object
@mozilla.org/rdf/container-utils;1	nsIRDFContainerUtils	Manipulates an RDF container tag object
@mozilla.org/rdf/resource-factory;1?name={arg}	various	Creates objects representing parts of a fact
@mozilla.org/rdf/content-sink;1	nsIExpatSink	Turns RDF-based XML objects into a fact store
@mozilla.org/rdf/xml-parser;1	nsIRDFXMLParser	Turns an RDF document into RDF-based XML objects
@mozilla.org/rdf/xml-serializer;1	nsIRDFXMLSerializer nsIRDFXMLSource	Turns a fact store into an RDF document
@mozilla.org/rdf/delegate-factory;1?key={arg}&scheme={arg}	nsIRDFDelegateFactory	Ties a resource (a fact item) to a custom object that synchronizes something else against that resource

store. Only the components that relate to email are fully revealed by XPCOM; the others are entirely unavailable to scripts. The ones that are revealed have `name=` set to the following values:

```
imap mailbox news moz-abdirectory moz-abldapdirectory moz-
    abmdbdirectory moz-aboutlookdirectory
```

The third section of Table 16.9 is only of use for directly parsing RDF documents. That is a deep customization of Mozilla and not particularly required by ordinary applications. The reverse action, which is to generate an RDF document from a fact store, is required for any application that intends to persist the data it manipulates. None of these interfaces is used to manipulate facts.

Finally, the `nsIRDFDelegateFactory` item in Table 16.9 requires a deep understanding of the platform architecture. It provides a way to attach a side effect to the creation or destruction of a resource used in a fact. Using such a delegate ties a fact to whatever system the delegate is designed for.

This is like the tie function in Perl. A delegate is an observer for an individual resource object. Use of that interface is beyond the scope of this book.

16.3.5.2 Structural Options Mozilla provides options that extend the functionality of data sources. These options make data sources more flexible rather than providing further access to their content. These options exist in the form of XPCOM interfaces that add extra functionality to the fact store that holds the data in the data source. Table 16.10 describes these interfaces.

The XUL template system not only uses composite data sources but also supports a list of arguments supplied to the XUL attribute of the data sources. A composite data source is no more than a container that holds other data sources. It in turn implements the `nsIRDFDataSource` interface. Each method of that interface just searches the contained data sources and calls the same method on each one as required.

In-memory data sources are at the core of several of the more complex data sources. Where the content of a fact store needs to be constructed by hand, rather than sourced from some other place, an in-memory data source is the logical starting point. Purging such a data source is just a way of resetting it back to empty. Stopping propagation (preventing broadcast of changed facts) slightly improves performance.

The `nsIRDFRemoteDatasource` interface provides a way to save and load a fact store back to or from the place it originated. That place is typically an RDF file or something equivalent. The file can be local or remote, but there is very limited support in both cases. Save is implemented by the `Flush()` method, and load, by the `Refresh()` method. `Flush()` is only supported on `file:` URLs; `Refresh()` is only supported on `file:` and `http:` URLs.

16.3.5.3 Content Options Data sources are not all created equal. They differ in content and in access to that content. These differences are the main reason why data sources are hard to use. It is not obvious from an application programmer's perspective which data sources can produce what facts or how those facts might be retrieved. All data sources are based on XPCOM components that follow this naming pattern:

```
@mozilla.org/rdf/datasource;1?name={arg}
```

Legal values for `{arg}` are listed in Table 16.12, leftmost column.

The content that a data source provides to the application programmer is obvious only for ordinary RDF files. Those files can be read directly by eye, which lays them completely open. Internal data sources, on the other hand, cannot be viewed at all except by (a) using the data source, (b) studying the platform source code, or (c) finding an example in the user's profile. The bookmark, history, search and local-store internal data sources all drop example files in the user profile; the others do not. Even where there are example files, those files generally aren't RDF documents.

Table 16.10 Interfaces extending the features of `nsIRDFDataSource`

Interface name	Implemented by	Purpose
nsIRDFDataSource	All data sources, but see Table 16.12 for limitations	Fundamental data operations on the data source's fact store
nsIRDFCompositeDataSource	@mozilla.org/rdf/datasource;1?name=composite-datasource	Provides a data source that is a union of the facts in one or more other data sources; inserted facts go into the first of those other data sources
nsIRDFInMemoryDataSource	@mozilla.org./rdf/datasource;1?name=in-memory-datasource	Provides a data source based on a fact store that is independent of all other facts
nsIRDFPurgeableDataSource	@mozilla.org/rdf/datasource;1?name=in-memory-datasource	Allows a data source to be emptied of facts
nsIRDFPropagatableDataSource	@mozilla.org/rdf/datasource;1?name=in-memory-datasource @mozilla.org/browser/bookmarks-service;1 @mozilla.org/rdf/datasource;1?name=bookmarks	Turns on or turns off broadcasting of fact changes to any observers
nsIRDFRemoteDataSource	@mozilla.org/autocompleteSession;1?type=history @mozilla.org/browser/bookmarks-service;1 @mozilla.org/browser/global-history;1 @mozilla.org/rdf/datasource;1?name=bookmarks @mozilla.org/rdf/datasource;1?name=history @mozilla.org/rdf/datasource;1?name=xml-datasource	Provides a way to coordinate the fact store of a data source against the original source of the facts. The XML data source contract ID is for plain RDF files

This anonymity of content is a big problem for XUL templates and scripts that try to navigate an internal data source. In both cases, the structure of the data source needs to be known beforehand. Fortunately, such internal data sources are needed for a narrow class of uses only.

The "Debug Corner" in this chapter has some code that reveals a data source's content. Table 16.11 lists the top-most fact subject and common predicates for most of the internal data sources. The special value `rdf:null` stands for no data source at all. It does not stand for an empty data source.

Beyond content, many of Mozilla's data sources have limited or restricted functionality. This means that even if you know what the content of the data source is, the data source object may not have enough implementation to make that content accessible. This means that even though an XPCOM component may state that it supports the `nsIRDFDataSource` interface, in truth many of the methods in that interface may simply return with an error or exception, without doing anything. Such data source objects are yet to be finished.

Table 16.12 indicates the level of support that is available for each of the implemented data sources. Table 16.12 is based on Mozilla version 1.4 and should be used as an *indication only* of the available functionality. Less-well-known data sources require obscure preparation steps before they are useful. Such steps are not yet covered here.

Data sources that do not have an `rdf:` URI cannot be used in XUL templates using XML attributes. They may still be attached to a template with a script. Data sources that are not registered with XPCOM in the default build of the platform cannot be used from XUL or JavaScript at all. The `composite-datasource` can only be asserted into if one of its collected data sources can be inserted into. It is recommended that you work with the individual data source directly, rather than work indirectly through the composite data source's interface.

16.4 Web Scripting

Web browsers perform tasks that operate in an environment different from traditional 3GL programs. On the Web, there is no such thing as a file or a file name. Instead, there are URLs and the documents that represent those URL resources. Frequently, such documents have complex structure and are XML-based. Such an environment requires a different scripting approach to that described under "Files and Folders" and under "Streams."

Web browsers are also actors in the emerging Web protocols stack, which could be better identified as the XML protocol stack. This stack, a set of standards, uses HTTP (or another protocol) as the first step in a series of application-enabling and application-specific sets of protocols. The XML protocol stack provides a data-oriented transaction system, rather than the simple document request and response-with-retrieval system that Web surfing requires.

Table 16.11 Starting points for internal data sources

rdf: URI	Topmost URN / URI	Predicates used to contain facts
rdf:addressdirectory	moz-abdirectory://	http://home.netscape.com/NC-rdf#child and http://home.netscape.com/NC-rdf#CardChild
rdf:bookmarks	NC:BookmarksRoot NC:PersonalToolbarFolder	Uses RDF containers
rdf:charset-menu	Many (e.g., NC:BrowserCharsetMenuRoot)	Uses RDF containers
rdf:files	NC:FilesRoot	http://home.netscape.com/NC-rdf#child
rdf:history	NC:HistoryRoot NC:HistoryByDate	http://home.netscape.com/NC-rdf#child
rdf:httpindex	URL of index	
rdf:internetsearch	NC:SearchEngineRoot NC:LastSearchRoot NC:SearchResultsSitesRoot NC:FilterSearchUrlRoot NC:FilterSearchSitesRoot SearchCategoryRoot LastSearchMode	http://home.netscape.com/NC-rdf#child
rdf:ispdefaults		
rdf:local-store	None; use any URI	No containers; each URI has a set of properties only
rdf:localsearch	Every find: URI is a root	No containers; each URI has a set of properties only
rdf:mailnewsfolders	No root; use server URLs	http://home.netscape.com/NC-rdf#child
rdf:msgaccountmanager	msgaccounts:/	
rdf:msgfilters	No root; use server URLs	
rdf:smtp	NC:smtpservers	http://home.netscape.com/NC-rdf#child
rdf:subscribe	No root; use server URLs	http://home.netscape.com/NC-rdf#child
rdf:window-mediator	NC:WindowMediatorRoot	Uses RDF containers

Table 16.12 nsIRDFDataSource interface support for each data source

Name used in Contract ID	Has rdf: URI?	Registered with XPCOM in the default build?	Content-specific XPCOM interfaces?	Supports assert()?	Supports ArcLabelsOut()?	Supports GetAllResources() ?	Supports commands?
addressdirectory	✓	✓	✓	✓	✓		✓
bookmarks	✓	✓	✓	✓	✓	✓	
charset-menu	✓	✓	✓	✓	✓	✓	
files	✓	✓			✓		
history	✓	✓	✓		✓	✓	
httpindex	✓	✓	✓	✓	✓	✓	✓
internetsearch	✓	✓		✓	✓	✓	
ispdefaults	✓	✓					
local-store	✓	✓			✓	✓	✓
localsearch	✓	✓			✓		
mailnewsfolder	✓	✓	✓	✓	✓		✓
msgaccountmanager	✓	✓	✓		✓		
msgfilters	✓	✓			✓		
smtp	✓	✓			✓		
subscribe	✓	✓	✓		✓		
window-mediator	✓	✓	✓	✓	✓	✓	✓
chrome				✓	✓	✓	✓
mailsounds					✓		
registry					✓		
relatedlinks					✓	✓	✓
in-memory-datasource		✓		✓	✓	✓	
composite-datasource		✓		maybe	✓		✓
xml-datasource (RDF files)		✓	✓	file: URLs only	✓	✓	✓

This emerging Web protocols stack consists of a set of standards and standards-in-progress. From lowest to highest, the most central standards in the stack follow:

- **XML and XML Schema**. These standards are used to define the underlying syntax of all the other standards. Mozilla implements XML and has some XML Schema utilities.
- **HTTP**. This protocol can act as a "transport binding" that is used to send and receive Web protocol stack messages. Mozilla implements HTTP.
- **SOAP and XML-RPC**. SOAP provides an XML-based format for messages. It adds timing, naming, identifying, data packaging, and message-passing semantics to plain XML. It is to XML what traditional RPC (Remote Procedure Calls) are to C/C++. There are two message formats in the W3C SOAP specification: one that maps efficiently to traditional RPC and one that is a "pure XML" format that uses XML schema types. The former is sometimes called XML-RPC. Mozilla implements both standards.
- **WSDL**. Built on top of SOAP, WSDL is a module packaging and definition language. Client software can exploit it to analyze and use SOAP-based facilities provided by servers. Mozilla support for WSDL is available from version 1.4 onward.
- **UDDI**. UDDI is a protocol that provides a name-mapping service for Web services, just as DNS provides a name-mapping service for TCP/IP addresses. UDDI gives an XML client the capbility to dynamically discover Web services that it doesn't yet know about. Mozilla does not implement UDDI, but UDDI is built on top of SOAP and so can be simulated at the cost of extra programming effort.
- **ebXML (enterprise business XML)**. Defined by the OASIS organization (*www.oasis-open.org*) and the United Nations, ebXML adds business transactions and business identification on top of SOAP. Mozilla does not implement ebXML.
- **Business process modeling standards**. These standards are high-level aggregation and specification standards intended to solve both general and specific business intercommunication problems between software applications. An example of the organizations developing these standards are the Workflow Management Coalition and the Open Application Group. Mozilla does not implement any of these standards.

Mozilla may not ever implement all these standards because some are intended to be used business-to-business, rather than consumer-to-business. The Web protocol stack is somewhat separate from the typical uses of Web browsers—displaying HTML content and email messages. Instead of using a channel, which is the standard way to work with URLs, these Web protocol features have their own separate interfaces, which must be specially scripted.

A Mozilla application might have no GUI at all. For example, it might be based on the `xpcshell` tool. In that case, the application can exploit the advanced XML support in the platform. It can implement servers that provide and use Web protocol stack concepts. A simple example is a content router that sends received XML documents to different destinations, depending on what they contain.

16.4.1 URIs, URLs, and URNs

URIs, and the specialist subformats of URL and URN, are described in the IETF's RFC 2396. It is intended, or at least hoped, that URIs be media-independent and highly portable. They therefore do not have the portability problems that file and path names have. Instead, URIs (especially URLs) have another problem: They are often badly typed, aliased, or carelessly shortened by users.

In Mozilla, a URI can be represented as a plain JavaScript string without loss of portability. If this string is to be usable with other XPIDL interfaces, then it needs to be converted to an object. This XPCOM pair is the most fundamental object available:

```
@mozilla.org/network/simple-uri;1 nsIURI
```

URLs are a specific form of URI and have a specialist object available, one that caters to all the common URL schemes, like `http:` and `ftp:`. This XPCOM pair is a widely used example:

```
@mozilla.org/network/standard-url;1 nsIURL
```

This interface also supports `nsIURI`. In fact, most XPCOM components with `uri` or `url` in their Contract ID support one or both of these interfaces.

If the user enters a URI, some validation may well be required. There are several defenses against bad syntax. This XPCOM pair makes the broadest attempt to fix a user-entered URI:

```
@mozilla.org/docshell/urifixup;1 nsIURIFixup
```

This interface has a method `createFixupURI()`, which can deal with keywords entered as URIs and lazy shortened forms entered as *www.test.com* or even *test.com* instead of *http://www.test.com*. Such a `docshell` component is exposed as an AOM object in a Mozilla Browser window; that structure is discussed in Chapter 10, Windows and Panes, in "`<iframe>`."

A second solution for syntax problems is to rely on this XPCOM pair:

```
@mozilla.org/network/url-parser;1?auth=maybe nsIURLParser
```

This interface will parse a URL according to RFC 2396, but in a lenient way so that many small syntax mistakes are both accepted and corrected. The component subspecifier can also be quoted as `yes` or `no`. In those cases, there are slight variations on the parsing algorithm used.

Finally, the base interface, `nsIURI`, supports a method named `resolve()`. This method compares a supplied relative URI against the current object's URI and returns a fully resolved (unshortened) URI equivalent to the relative one supplied.

There is no XPCOM object specifically for URNs.

The ultimate test of a URL's correctness is, of course, to retrieve the resource that it locates.

16.4.2 Downloading Files

To download a file or document from a remote location, you can use a channel, a URI, and the resulting stream. That is the straightforward approach covered under "Content Processing Concepts." There is also a very high-level alternative, which is to use this XPCOM pair:

```
@mozilla.org/embedding/browser/nsWebBrowserPersist;1
    nsIWebBrowserPersist
```

This interface accepts a URI or a DOM 1 `Document` interface and an `nsILocalFile` object. It performs the whole fetch-and-save operation with a single method call.

To perform a download asynchronously so that other tasks can be attended to during the download, create a content listener or observer object in pure JavaScript. Most interfaces, like `nsIChannel`, describe which content listeners and observers are supported. Each time a chunk of downloaded document content appears in the listener or observer, you process it, save it, or ignore it.

The most common way such a process-by-piece object is built is to implement the `nsIWebProgressListener` interface. Any object that supports the `nsIWebProgress` interface can register such a listener (or more than one), and many other interfaces accept such a listener object as an initialization argument. There are existing XPCOM objects that implement this interface, so for many applications the object you need to get the job done already exists.

To be advised of the progress of an asynchronous download, there are numerous options. Receiving progress advice is in theory a problem separate from that of receiving content. Advice is information about progress, whereas received content is the result of that progress.

The most primitive advice option is to enhance an ordinary content listener so that progress is noted as each chunk of content arrives. This option does not report completion or management events associated with content delivery; it only reports forward progress.

A better tracking option is to create a pure JavaScript object with the `nsIProgressEventSink` interface and to supply it to the object responsible for the download. This sink (an event listener) reports all changes to the status of the in-progress download. An alternative is to create a pure JavaScript object with the `nsIRequestObserver` interface and lodge it with the channel or transport object. Such an observer only notices the beginning and ending of the download, not cancellations or suspensions.

An even more sophisticated tracking approach is to use the XPCOM objects responsible for the Mozilla Download Manager. These objects can be used with or without the Download Manager dialog box, but if that dialog box is employed, lots of scripting is required to tie it to the XPCOM objects properly. With or without a dialog box, this approach is limited to downloading files to be saved to disk. Such a use starts with this XPCOM pair, which implements a service:

```
@mozilla.org/download-manager;1 nsIDownloadManager
```

This single object manages all downloads underway. The `addDownload()` method of the manager is used to create and register a new object with the `nsIDownload` interface for each file to be downloaded.

Through a subtle arrangement, each download object is responsible for informing the Download Manager about progress because it records all the configuration details of a single download operation. These details are specified in the arguments passed to `addDownload()` and include a way of disposing of (saving) the downloaded item—this is the final `nsIWebBrowserPersist` argument. If this argument exists, the download object keeps the Download Manager informed of progress automatically, and the Download Manager uses the download object to clean up if the download is canceled or otherwise interrupted. If this final argument does not exist, then cleanup is up to the application programmer. The need for cleanup can be detected by lodging an observer on the individual download objects.

Mozilla also supports the concept of a load group. This is a variation on the `nsIRequest` interface, which allows a collection of URIs to have group identity. A load group is useful if a summary of the progress of a collection of requests is needed.

16.4.3 File and MIME Types

The MIME type of a file, URI, or file extension can be found with this XPCOM pair, which is a singleton service object:

```
@mozilla.org/mime;1 nsIMIMEService
```

This object consults the MIME information stored in the Mozilla user profile first. If an answer is not available there, then the desktop's operating system is consulted. On UNIX, the type is determined by the GNOME desktop, not by `file(1)`.

The `launch()` method of `nsILocalFile` allows an executable to be run or a data file to be loaded into its application software. This can be done without the application programmer needing to know anything about the file's type.

16.4.4 Uploading and Posting Files

Documents can be posted by means of the AOM `XMLHttpRequest` object. That object is discussed in Chapter 7, Forms and Menus, in "Form Submission." It is based on this XPCOM pair:

```
@mozilla.org/xmlextras/xmlhttprequest;1 nsIJSXMLHttpRequest
```

Uploading of documents is equally easy, if not easier. Follow the approach described in "Channels" in this chapter, specifying the destination of the upload when using the `nsIIOService` interface. That destination will either be a server-side program, in the case of an HTTP POST operation, or an FTP directory, in the case of FTP. After the channel is created, use `QueryInterface()` to obtain the `nsIUploadChannel` interface and supply that interface with an input stream containing the file contents to be sent. To send the content, obtain the `nsIChannel` interface again, and call `open()` or `asyncOpen()` as for any channel object.

16.4.5 Web Protocol Stack Objects

The basis of the Web protocol stack, HTTP, is widely used in Mozilla, and can be scripted in many ways, including direct use of the `XMLHttpRequest` AOM object. The other protocols supported by Mozilla require specific objects separate from the rest of the platform.

A useful set of documentation on support for Web protocols is available at *www.mozilla.org/xmlextras/*.

XML-RPC support is the simplest step up from HTTP. This XPCOM pair:

```
@mozilla.org/xml-rpc/client;1 nsIXmlRpcClient
```

is responsible for creating an XML fragment containing the RPC request, submitting it synchronously or asynchronously to the supplied URL over HTTP, and reporting back results or faults. Faults appear as objects with the `nsIXmlRpcFault` interface.

In traditional RPC, a tool like `rpcgen(1)` is used to create C code that does much of the work. That C code

- Maps native types to RPC portable types.
- Marshals nativeRPC calls into a portable XDR/NDR format "for the wire."
- Handles network communications and timing issues.
- Operates reasonably efficiently.

In Mozilla's XML-RPC, JavaScript is an interpreted language, and the platform is already compiled in most cases. The implementation details and interface are therefore different from traditional RPC. The `nsIXmlRpcClient` is responsible for marshaling JavaScript RPC calls into portable XML, but it delegates the sending and receiving of calls to a Mozilla channel object. This means that timeouts need to be checked for on the channel. The supplied interface delegates to the application programmer the mapping of JavaScript to XML-RPC types. It provides factory methods for creating XML-RPC types, but the application programmer needs to populate and assemble them for use by the RPC request. Finally, the `nsIXmlRpcClient` is implemented in JavaScript and regularly resolves names into objects using the `window.Components` object, so it is not highly optimized for performance.

SOAP is the intended and popular replacement for XML-RPC. SOAP technology is information-dense and requires a book of its own. The SOAP and XML-P standards at the W3C are highly recommended reading. Only the utter basics are presented here. XML-P (P stands for *Protocol*) is the future name for SOAP, assuming the popularity of SOAP as an acronym can be overcome.

A SOAP call is a request message followed by a response message, and so HTTP is a natural transport for SOAP. Both messages are in XML format. Both messages consist of an envelope tag that holds one optional header tag and one mandatory body tag. These tags are defined by the SOAP standard. The body tag contains a document fragment consisting of other tags. Those other tags are defined by the application programmer, who should have gone to the trouble of creating or using a formal XML schema definition for them. Those tags are the data sent and received.

For a programmer to create a SOAP message, objects are needed for the following tasks:

- To manipulate XML schema definitions
- To construct SOAP envelopes and their internal structure
- To set up a connection to a SOAP-enabled server
- To make the SOAP call
- To deal with any exceptions, faults, and failures
- To extract any returned XML document

Mozilla's solution to each of these bullet points is an object based on the matching XPCOM pair in this list:

- @mozilla.org/xmlextras/schemas/schemaloader;1 nsISchemaLoader
- @mozilla.org/xmlextras/soap/call;1 nsISOAPMessage
- @mozilla.org/xmlextras/soap/transport;1?protocol=http; nsISOAPTransport
- @mozilla.org/xmlextras/soap/call;1 nsISOAPCall
- @mozilla.org/xmlextras/soap/fault;1 nsISOAPFault
- @mozilla.org/xmlextras/soap/response;1 nsISOAPMessage

Many minor and ancillary interfaces assist this core set of features. On top of all these things is the need to set up an HTTP and SOAP-enabled server so that something can respond to the outgoing SOAP request.

The interface `nsISOAPMessage` is also exposed as an AOM object named `SOAPCall` and can therefore be created very simply:

```
var soap_call = new SOAPCall();
```

The `nsISOAPParameter` interface is similarly reflected in the `SOAPParameter` AOM object. These two objects allow simple SOAP calls to be made without extensive preparatory use of the `window.Components` array.

The famously available Google SOAP service is a genuine SOAP service that can be used to test Mozilla clients that make SOAP calls. It is described at *www.google.com/apis/index*. It is hard, however, to learn much when you don't control both the client and the server. A better solution is available in the Mozilla source code. This Web-hosted portion of the source contains sample code useful for learning and testing SOAP:

```
http://lxr.mozilla.org/seamonkey/source/extensions/xmlextras/tests/
```

If you have a Web server available with CGI support, then the three small `.cgi` programs in this directory (written in Perl) can be used to receive SOAP requests and respond in kind. The `echo.cgi` version implements a "ping" operation, which by convention should be the first service implemented when a group of related SOAP calls are defined. The other two `.cgis` provide a success response and a failure response. The success response also contains response content.

There is enough XPCOM SOAP support in Mozilla for the platform to act as a SOAP server instead of a client, provided that the clients all use the same transport (ultimately one socket or file descriptor). This means that the platform cannot yet accept SOAP requests sent from anywhere in the world.

The final Web protocol stack protocol that Mozilla supports is the WSDL protocol, or Web Services Description Language. It bundles together a set of individual SOAP calls into a single definition document. Very roughly speaking, it is the XML equivalent of a CORBA IDL file or a Mozilla XPIDL file. WSDL definitions are the responsibility of the application programmer.

WSDL in Mozilla is brand new as this is written. The best place to look for up-to-the-minute information is this URL, which contains the XPIDL definitions for WSDL interfaces:

```
http://lxr.mozilla.org/seamonkey/source/extensions/xmlextras/wsdl/
```

To see the Contract IDs for the components that implement these interfaces, either read the `.h` header files in this directory, or use the Component Viewer tool list component Contract IDs with this prefix:

```
@mozilla.org/xmlextras/wsdl/
```

Such a listing will only work on versions 1.4 and later, which is the minimum version for full WSDL support.

16.4.6 XSLT Batch Processing

The Mozilla XSLT processing system can be exploited by scripts using this XPCOM pair:

```
@mozilla.org/document-transformer;1?type=text/xsl nsIXSLTProcessor
```

An object with this interface accepts two DOM trees or subtrees as arguments: One is a tree of XSLT tags that is a set of processing instructions; the other is the content to be transformed. A third tree or subtree, which contains the processed output, is returned. XSLT parameters can also be supplied as arguments. This system cannot work in-place—the results must be attached to an existing DOM hierarchy if that is required.

16.5 PLATFORM CONFIGURATION

Some scripting tasks inspect, manage, and update the state of the Mozilla Platform itself. To do that, internal aspects of the platform must be revealed via XPCOM interfaces. This topic covers the cache, file system directory, preferences, security, and user profiles.

16.5.1 Cache Control

The Mozilla Browser cache is intended to be transparent to all operations, but it is possible to interact with it if necessary. The cache is at work for all URL requests performed by the platform, unless it is explicitly avoided or turned off. Low-level access to the cache can be had via this XPCOM pair:

```
@mozilla.org/network/cache-service;1 nsICacheService
```

An object built this way also needs access to the constants provided by the `nsICache` interface. The details are surprisingly complex because the cache supports simultaneous access sessions with a single-write, multiple-read locking model. This means that low-level access to the cache can fail as a result of resource contention. It is easier to stay away from the detail and let higher level services like transports and channels manage the interaction for you. One handy use of this interface is the `evictEntries()` method, which can be used to empty the cache.

A very simple use of the cache is prefetching. Prefetching brings an `http:` URL from its original location into the cache without necessarily consuming or displaying it. Prefetching only works for `http:` URLs that are not HTTP GET requests (a request must not have a `?param=` part). Prefetching is accomplished with this pair of XPCOM objects:

```
@mozilla.org/prefetch-service;1 nsIPrefetchService
```

Similar, but finer control is also available on the `nsIRequest` interface, which is the basis for channels and transports. The `loadFlags` property can be used on a per-URI basis to control how a retrieved URI and the cache interact.

16.5.2 File System Directory

The Mozilla Platform has a directory service that allows scripts to locate well-known files and folders.

A Mozilla directory is like a phone book: It is used to look up the detail associated with a given name. Directories are therefore entirely separate from the concept of an operating system's file system and from the concept of a file system directory. Mozilla directories are usually called directory services to emphasize the way in which they serve up details in response to requests. There are many directories in Mozilla.

Of the directories that Mozilla implements, some provide access to remote resources, others provide access to data files on the local file system like the local Mozilla Address book, and still others provide access to internals of the running platform. One of these internally maintained directories holds a set of well-known operating system file and folder names, all of which are used by the platform. That is the only directory service discussed here.

Access to these file and folder names is required by scripts if applications are to use the same file system locations as the platform. The benefits of reusing these locations are that the application is then (a) properly platform-integrated and (b) somewhat protected from portability problems.

This internal directory, called the file system directory service, is implemented by this XPCOM pair:

```
@mozilla.org/file/directory_service;1 nsIDirectoryService
```

Note that `directory_service` contains an underscore, not a dash. This directory holds the locations of all the files and folders about which application programmers and applications need to know. The files and folder locations available in this directory are therefore fundamental to Mozilla applications. After file or folder locations are retrieved from a directory, they can be operated on just like any file or folder.

The `nsIDirectoryService` interface is not that useful by itself. All it can do is manage a set of provider objects. A provider is an object that supplies a subset of the directory contents to the directory service. In the normal case, a directory service object provides none of its own contents. Instead, each directory service has zero or more providers registered. Each provider contributes to the directory and supports the `nsIDirectoryServiceProvider` interface. When a script consults the directory service, that service looks through its providers to see if any of them have the details for the name the script asked about. Providers are entirely hidden from the script when they are arranged in this way.

Apart from providers, the directory service system also uses other interfaces. The `nsIProperties` interface is the standard interface used to retrieve details of a name recorded in the directory. A sought-after name, in the form of a short string (effectively an alias or a nickname), is passed into the directory service via the `nsIProperties` method `get()`. Any item in the directory that matches that alias has its details returned. The file system directory service implements this `nsIProperties` interface. Listing 16.7 shows code that uses this standard interface:

Listing 16.7 Retrieving a file system resource from a directory with an alias.

```
var Cc = Components.classes;
var Ci = Components.interfaces;

var dir = Cc["@mozilla.org/file/directory_service;1"];
dir = dir.getService(Ci.nsIDirectoryService);  // Initialized

// Put calls to dir.registerProvider(provider_object) here

var dir_props = dir.QueryInterface(Ci.nsIProperties);

var file = dir_props.get("myalias", Ci.nsIFile);

if (file == null )
  alert("No Such Location");
```

This code creates the directory service object, adds no providers at all, grabs the `nsIProperties` interface, and retrieves the detail for the `"myalias"` alias. Because the XPCOM file system directory service stores file and folder information, the information returned (an object) is expected to have the `nsIFile` interface.

In this example, the last line of code might produce an alert for two reasons. The string "`myalias`" is not one of the well-known aliases, and so is unknown to the directory. That is trivial to fix—use a known alias. More seriously, there are no providers for this directory service; therefore, we expect that no aliases would be recognized at all. That is a reasonable reading of the code, but in practice it is not true. In practice, this directory has at least two providers at all times.

- ☞ The first of these providers is added by the directory object itself when it is created. This provider adds application-level aliases to the directory. These aliases match the install area files and folders for the Mozilla Platform.
- ☞ The second of these providers is added when the platform starts up. This provider is associated with the current user profile. It adds profile-specific aliases to the directory. These aliases match files and folders that are part of the current user profile.

☞ If the platform is displaying a Web page, and that Web page contains a plugin or a Java applet, then a third provider is added, but only while that page exists. This provider is associated with the plugin manager. It adds plugin-specific aliases to the directory. These aliases are processed differently than the other aliases (as described shortly), but a file object matching the alias is still returned, if it exists.

A rather confusing aspect of the directory implementation is this: The object that implements the directory service also implements a provider. This provider is specified by the XPCOM pair:

```
@mozilla.org/file/directory_service;1 nsIDirectoryServiceProvider
```

This provider is in addition to the three providers just noted. It is never (or rarely) registered with any directory service. Instead, it can be scripted directly. It is not hidden as the other providers are. This last provider adds aliases relevant to the XPCOM system that is at the heart of the platform. These aliases are for the lowest level files and folders required by the platform and include a number of operating-system-specific locations.

This last provider can be scripted as shown in Listing 16.8.

Listing 16.8 Retrieving a file system resource from a provider using an alias.

```
var Cc = Components.classes;
var Ci = Components.interfaces;

var prov = Cc["@mozilla.org/file/directory_service;1"];
prov = prov.getService(Ci.nsIDirectoryServiceProvider);

var result = {};  // an empty object
var file = prov.getFile("alias", result);

if ( file == null ) alert("No such location");

// alert(result.value)
```

Because providers are usually managed by a directory, the `getFile()` method has arguments that suit a directory object. The second argument to `getFile()`, an empty object, allows the provider to return some status information back to the directory. An ordinary script can throw this information away—it is only needed if the script is implementing its own directory service. See the XPIDL file for `nsIDirectoryServiceProvider` for details.

The remainder of this topic lists the aliases supplied by all these producers, starting with this last, special provider.

16.5.2.1 XPCOM File System Aliases These aliases are provided by the special built-in directory service provider that is accessed directly. Tables 16.13 to 16.16 list the alias options available. Table 16.13 applies to all platforms.

Table 16.13 All-platform XPCOM file system aliases

Alias	Description of matching nsIFile
ComRegF	XPCOM component registry file—unused
ComsD	Folder that holds XPCOM components
CurProcD	Folder of the executable for the currently running process; always $MOZILLA_FIVE_HOME on UNIX
CurWorkD	Folder that is the present working directory of the current executable
DrvD	Returns the top of the operating system's file system—Windows: usually C:; UNIX: /; MacOS: the root volume
GreComsD	Folder holding GRE (Gecko Runtime Engine) XPCOM components
GreD	Folder GRE is installed in
Home	Home folder for the current user—Windows: %HOME%; UNIX: $HOME; MacOS: the documents folder
TmpD	Operating system location for temporary files—Windows: %TMP%; UNIX: $TMP; MacOS: the temporary files folder

Table 16.14 lists further aliases and applies only to Microsoft Windows. The stated CSIDL constants are part of the Microsoft Windows User Interface APIs and are used by Windows functions like `SHGetFolderPath()`. Each alias stands for a well-known folder. For a full description of these constants, see *http://msdn.microsoft.com/library/en-us/shellcc/platform/shell/reference/enums/csidl.asp.*

Table 16.14 Microsoft Windows only XPCOM file system aliases

Alias	CSIDL equivalent	Alias	CSIDL equivalent
AppData	CSIDL_APPDATA	netH	CSIDL_NETHOOD
Buckt	CSIDL_BITBUCKET	NetW	CSIDL_NETWORK
CmDeskP	CSIDL_COMMON_DESKTOPDIRECTORY	Pers	CSIDL_PERSONAL
CmPrgs	CSIDL_COMMON_PROGRAMS	PrntHd	CSIDL_PRINTHOOD
CmStrt	CSIDL_COMMON_STARTUP	Prnts	CSIDL_PRINTERS
Cntls	CSIDL_CONTROLS	Progs	CSIDL_PROGRAMS
DeskP	CSIDL_DESKTOPDIRECTORY	Rcnt	CSIDL_RECENT
DeskV	CSIDL_DESKTOP	SndTo	CSIDL_SENDTO
Drivs	CSIDL_DRIVES	Tmpls	CSIDL_TEMPLATES
Favs	CSIDL_FAVORATES	WinD	CSIDL_WINDOWS

Be aware that the aliases prefixed with `Cm` will fail (and throw an exception) on single-user versions of Microsoft Windows, like Microsoft Windows 98.

Table 16.15 lists further aliases; it applies to the Macintosh only.

Finally, Table 16.16 lists the remaining miscellany of aliases. Aliases for OS/2, BeOS, OpenVMS, and others are not shown.

Together, these aliases define all the file system locations known to the XPCOM core of the platform. It is easy to see that application code can become nonportable if these aliases are used more than trivially.

16.5.2.2 Application File System Aliases These aliases originate from the provider that is attached to the directory service when it is created. It is always available. These aliases are standard across all platforms.

The XPCOM system is not the whole of the Mozilla Platform. On top of that core is a large collection of components and infrastructure that makes up the rest of the platform. That platform includes installation areas for browsers and other products, chrome, caches, registries, and so on. Those locations and the location of the user profile system are described by these aliases. They are shown in Table 16.17.

Table 16.15 Macintosh only XPCOM file system aliases

Alias	Folder	Alias	Folder
ApplMenu	The Apple Menu	Exts	The Extensions folder
ClassicPrfs	Mac Classic Profile folder	Isrch	The Internet Search folder
CntlPnl	The Control Panel	Prfs	The Preferences folder
DfltDwnld	The Default Download folder	Shdwn	The Shutdown folder
Docs	The Documents folder	Trsh	The folder holding the Trash
Desk	The folder holding the Desktop		

Table 16.16 Miscellaneous XPCOM file system aliases

Alias	Description of matching nsIFile
Fnts	Macintosh and Microsoft Windows: the folder holding system fonts
LibD	UNIX: /usr/local/lib/netscape
Locl	UNIX: /usr/local/netscape
Strt	Macintosh and Microsoft Windows: the startup folder
SysD	Macintosh OSX only: the system folder
UlibDir	Macintosh OSX only: the /usr/lib folder

Table 16.17 Application install file system aliases

Alias	Description of retrieved object	Path name relative to install area
AppRegF	The global application registry file	Located elsewhere (see Chapter 17, Deployment)
AppRegD	The folder holding the global application registry	Located elsewhere (see Chapter 17, Deployment)
DefRt	The top folder of the defaults area	Defaults
PrfDef	The folder holding the default preferences	Defaults/pref
profDef	The folder holding default profile values for the current locale	Defaults/profile/{locale}
ProfDefNoLoc	The folder holding default profile values for the default locale	Defaults/profile
DefProtRt	The top folder for all user profiles	Located elsewhere (see below)
Ares	The resources folder	Res
Achrom	The chrome folder	Chrome
SrchPlugns	The folder holding plugin search and download configuration files	Searchplugins
AplugінsDL	An nsIEnumerator list of available plugin files	Plugins/*
XPIClnupD	The folder holding uninstall programs	Uninstall
UserPlugins	The folder under the current user profile that holds profile-specific plugins	Located elsewhere
OSXUserPlugins	MacOS X only; the folder holding user plugins	Located elsewhere
OSXLocalPlugins	MacOS X only; the folder holding local plugins	Located elsewhere
MacSysPlugins	Mac Classic only; the folder holding system plugins	Located elsewhere

The `DefProtRt` alias returns the following per-platform values:

- UNIX: ~/.mozilla
- Windows: {CLSID_APPDATA}\Mozilla\Profiles
- Macintosh: :Documents:Mozilla:Profiles

16.5.2.3 Profile File System Aliases These aliases originate from a provider added to the directory service when the platform starts up. In a full distribution of the platform (i.e., one that is not embedded or otherwise cut down), it is always available. These aliases, in Table 16.18, are standard across all platforms.

16.5.2.4 Plugin File System Aliases Plugin file system aliases originate from a provider that is added to the directory service when plugins or Java is required. These aliases are used to retrieve a file implementing a plugin, but they work only on Microsoft Windows.

The other directory service providers merely translate an alias to an operating-system-specific file or folder. This provider does that translation too, but first it analyzes the available resources in more depth. It uses the alias to extract from the platform preference information, which states the minimum version of the plugin that is needed and whether that plugin is enabled. It then compares any minimum enabled version with product versions installed in the operating system. It returns a file for the operating-system-installed version if it is sufficiently new. The version comparison is done using the format described in Chapter 17, Deployment. The known aliases are listed in Table 16.19.

Table 16.18 Profile file system aliases

Alias	Description of retrieved object	Path name relative to user profile
PrefD	The folder holding the preference file; same as ProfD	.
PrefF	The file holding the user preferences	prefs.js
ProfD	The topmost folder of the current profile	.
Uchrm	The folder holding user chrome	chrome
LclSt	The file holding persistent data about the user's Mozilla windows	localstore.rdf
Uhist	Classic Browser URL history file	history.dat
Upanels	Classic Browser user-defined sidebar panels file	panels.rdf
UmimTyp	The platform-wide MIME type information	mimeTypes.rdf
Bmarks	Classic Browser bookmarks file	bookmarks.html
Dloads	Classic Browser download history file	downloads.rdf
SrchF	Classic Browser search engine configuration file	search.rdf
MailD	Folder holding local mail accounts	Mail
ImapMD	Folder holding IMAP mail accounts	ImapMail
NewsD	Folder holding Newserver configuration	News
MFCaD	File holding current visual settings of Classic Mail folders	panacea.dat

Table 16.19 Plugin file system aliases

Alias	Description of matching nsIFile
plugin.scan.SunJRE	The Mozilla OJI Java JRE plugin file
plugin.scan.Acrobat	The Adobe Acrobat plugin file
plugin.scan.Quicktime	The Apple Quicktime plugin file
plugin.scan.WindowsMediaPlayer	The Microsoft Windows Media Player executable
plugin.scan.4xPluginFolder	Netscape 4.x plugin folder

16.5.3 Preferences

The current profile's user preferences, the current global preferences, and a preference file stored anywhere on the local computer can all be manipulated from scripts. This XPCOM pair is responsible:

```
@mozilla.org/preferences-service;1 nsIPrefService
```

Preferences cannot be changed from scripts outside the chrome unless standard Web security restrictions are removed. A user can modify preferences directly in versions 1.3 and higher by right-clicking on the content displayed by the `about:config` URL.

16.5.4 Security

This topic explains how security is implemented. Because security is a big subject, we'll look at only those security constraints that directly bear on scripting.

In Netscape version 4.x browsers, security checks were handled by the Java subsystem of the browser. In Mozilla, that is no longer the case—the Mozilla Platform handles its own security needs with its own security implementation. No Java is required.

A piece of Mozilla code can be in one of four security states: Web Safe, Trusted, Certified, or Domain Policied. In practical terms, code means JavaScript scripts, but these security states also apply to all downloadable documents, including HTML.

New support for WSDL in the platform includes a further wrinkle on security. This wrinkle requires an additional security check when a remotely located Web service is first used. This check is designed to protect the server vending the Web service, not the platform calling that service. It requires that the platform ask the service for permission to use the service. As this goes to print, it is proposed that the `nsIWebScriptsAccessService` interface be the client-side entry point for this check.

Most, but not all, security issues are handled in the XPConnect code that connects JavaScript to the internals of the platform.

In all cases, if a security violation occurs, errors are reported to the JavaScript Console.

16.5.4.1 Web Safe Security Web Safe security is the default security applied to Mozilla applications. It is the security that applies to XUL-based applications installed outside the chrome, and it is the security applied to Web-based applications that run inside a window that displays HTML or XML (a browser). Web Safe security provides a nearly fully secure environment, by putting two obstacles in the way of scripts.

The first obstacle in Web Safe security is a set of restrictions designed to guarantee that the user interface is under end user control. An example restriction is the requirement that all windows be at least 100 pixels wide and high, so they are obvious to the user.

The second obstacle in Web Safe security is the Same Origin test, which is used pervasively throughout the platform. This policy says that a script can only use a resource that originates via the same protocol, and from the same domain name and IP port number, as the script itself. A script downloaded from *www.test.com* cannot affect a Web page downloaded from *www.pages.com* or from *ftp://www.test.com* or even from *www.test.com:99*, where *99* is a different port number.

The Same Origin test prevents scripts from affecting different-origin windows in a running application and from crossing frame boundaries into different-origin documents. Both the contents of the chrome and the entire set of XPCOM components are considered different-origin to all Web sites. Therefore, in the case of scripts with a remote origin, components are entirely unavailable under Web Safe security. They are also unavailable to local scripts stored outside the chrome.

The Same Origin test does not apply to the special URL `about:blank`, which is always accessible.

16.5.4.2 Trusted Security The opposite extreme to Web Safe security is Trusted security. Scripts in the Trusted security state have no security restrictions at all. They can access all XPCOM components automatically and all scripts and documents regardless of origin. Scripts and all other resources installed in the chrome are Trusted. In particular, resources in the chrome never need permissions from the user.

One outstanding issue with the use of chrome is that adding content into the chrome is hard to do securely. The XPInstall system, described in Chapter 17, Deployment, does not yet insist on authentication of chrome installation packages. Such authentication requires digital certificates and signatures. This means that there is no guaranteed check that a package intended for the chrome originates from the source that it claims to originate from. In theory, a malicious chrome package could lie about its origin, and when the user agreed to install it, it would be able to exploit its new, trusted state. In practice, no one has yet bothered to interfere with Mozilla in this way.

16.5.4.3 Certified Security In between the Web Safe and Trusted security states is the Certified state. Scripts and other resources can be decorated with digital certificates that contain public key encrypted digital signatures and that can be authenticated (confirmed accurate) by a respected organization. In this security state, all scripts are treated as Web Safe until their signing information is examined. If the signing proves acceptable, then the script can act as a Trusted script.

Digital certificates are a world of their own; only the consequences for application scripts are noted here. To sign scripts and other resources digitally, the SignTool tool is required. It is not provided by Mozilla, but it is available from Netscape at the *http://devedge.netscape.com* Web site, along with documentation. In addition to signing files digitally, this tool can produce a test certificate that can be used in the absence of a real certificate. Real certificates cost money to acquire.

The use of digital certificates requires two pieces of configuration. First, a database of certificates must be maintained by the platform. In Classic Mozilla, this is held automatically, although some of the more obscure panels in the preferences dialog box allow certificates to be user-managed. The second piece of configuration is that the user must give permission every time a signed script is encountered. That is extremely inconvenient, so browsers can also remember the permissions the user has granted in the past and reapply them silently on future occasions. All this configuration information is held in the user profile.

The difference between Trusted and Certified arrangements is that a Certified arrangement requires at least one interactive confirmation by the user. The only way to avoid this is to build a custom installation of a browser or the platform with the required certificates and permissions already bundled with it.

The Certified security state can be attained without any certificates. This user preference drops the need for certificates or digital signing, but it still requires that the programmer appeal for special privileges and that the user grant permission to use those privileges:

```
user_pref("signed.applets.codebase_principal_support", true);
```

This preference is only useful for developing applications where the ultimate security model will be the Certified model.

If Certified security is the model chosen, then each piece of code that wants to perform a Trusted operation (like using an XPCOM object) must appeal to the user for permission to use that operation. That permission is requested by preceding critical sections of code with a function call:

```
window.netscape.security.PrivilegeManager.enablePrivilege("P1 P2
    P3");
```

This call either asks the user for permission with a dialog box or silently succeeds if permission has been granted and remembered in the past. On success, the security of the following code is raised to the Trusted state for the

Table 16.20 Privilege strings used in code-signing security

Privilege	Affected targets*
UniversalBrowserRead	Reading of sensitive browser data; allows the script to pass the Same Origin check when reading from any document
UniversalBrowserWrite	Modification of sensitive browser data; allows the script to pass the Same Origin check when writing to any document
UniversalXPConnect	Unrestricted JavaScript access to XPCOM components using XPConnect
UniversalPreferencesRead	Read preferences using the navigator.preference() method
UniversalPreferenceWrite	Set preferences using the navigator.preference() method
CapabilityReferencesAccess	Reads or sets the preferences that define security policies, including which privileges have been granted and denied to scripts; also requires UniversalPreferencesRead and/or UniversalPreferencesWrite
UniversalFileRead	Display or submit files that have file: URLs

**The data in Table 16.20 appear courtesy Jesse Ruderman and mozilla.org.

specified privileges only. The Trusted state ends when the current JavaScript scope ends, which is usually at the end of a function or method call.

In this call, P1, P2, and P3 are a space-separated list of privilege keywords—at least one such keyword is required. Table 16.20 lists the available privileges and the targets to which they control access. A target is just any capability or functional feature of the platform.

Inside the platform, each of these privileges might be checked in a number of places so that the overall effect is that the target is fully protected by the security system.

16.5.4.4 Policied Security The final security model available to scripts is a set of user preferences. Policied security grants and denies Trusted access to all documents retrieved from specific origins. An origin is a protocol + domain + port combination, as used in the Same Origin test. This form of security controls use of specific JavaScript properties in those retrieved documents. Those specific properties are therefore the targets for this security model. The set of grants and denials is bundled up into one configuration item, which is called a policy. One policy can apply to several different origins. This security model is the least used of the security options Mozilla provides.

If this security system is not specified, retrieved documents follow the Web Safe security model. If this security system is used, retrieved documents may have more or less restrictions than the Web Safe model. Therefore, if the user's profile can be modified, Domain Policied security can be the most or least restrictive of all the security options.

The Policied security model has no direct user interface in the preferences system of the Mozilla applications. Some of the checkbox preferences in that system are implemented using this security system, but that is not obvious to the user.

This preference system exists for the following reasons:

- To support specific preferences that enable or disable useful functionality.
- To compete with Internet Explorer's zone-based preference system.
- To empower the user so that irritating Web sites can be individually disabled.
- To provide a powerful and flexible system in case it proves useful.

To use this security, new user preferences must be set. Three steps are required: define a policy name; define a set of origins that the policy applies to; and define access rules for the individual object properties that the security model controls. These steps are examined in turn.

There are three kinds of policy names—explicit, wildcard, and default. Every property that might have an access rule can be associated with one of each of these names, and these three names have a pecking order.

At the bottom of the pecking order are the default policies. There is one default policy per JavaScript property, and it is applied if no other policies exist. If no default policies are specified, then the single default policy named `"default"` applies to all properties. This `"default"` default policy may also be modified. It will shortly be clear why more than one default policy is useful.

Next from the bottom is the wildcard policy. It has the name `"*"` (asterisk). It is applied when it is explicitly stated, and in that case it overrides default policies.

At the top are the explicit policies. These policies are named when explicitly stated and are applied first and foremost. These policies override the other two kinds.

To name policies, two preferences are used:

```
user_pref("capability.policy.policynames","p1 test foo");
user_pref("capability.policy.default_policynames","normal,off");
```

The policy names are space- or comma-separated and may not contain a period character. The first line of the preceding code specifies three policies; the second specifies two default policies. The wildcard policy name is automatically recognized and doesn't need to be specified.

Having made up policy names, each policy is then provided with a list of origins. Each policy will be applied only for documents retrieved from those origin names. The names of the policies created are used in the preference string that specifies the sites. For example, the policy called `mypol` has its origins specified thus:

```
user_pref("capability.policy.mypol.sites", "http://test.com http://
    x.org");
```

The argument is a space- or comma-separated list of partial URLs, and the word "`sites`" is synonymous with "`origins`." The partial URLs cannot include specific subparts of the origin's Web site. There should be zero or one of these preferences per site. If the policy name is a default policy name, then the sites listed will have that default policy. This allows different defaults for different sites. If the wildcard policy is required, specify `*` instead of `mypol`.

After the policy names and origins are specified, all that remains is to create the access rules. There are three types of rules. A single preference line is required for each rule that is stated.

The first and most general rule syntax applies to all JavaScript properties, regardless of whether they are simple values or methods. For the policy `mypol`, it has the syntax

```
user_pref("capabilities.policy.mypol.Iface.Prop","Keywords")
```

`Iface`, `Prop`, and `Keywords` must be replaced with specific strings.

- ☞ `Iface` is the name of the JavaScript object holding the property of interest. In fact, it must be the shortened XPCOM interface name that has had the `nsIDOM` prefix removed. Example names are `ChromeWindow`, `HTMLDocument`, and `XULImageElement`. Some DOM objects have shorthand object names like `Image`, but the official `HTMLImageElement` name must be used.
- ☞ `Prop` is the property name to which the access rule applies. It is usually an attribute or method of an XPCOM interface, like the `value` property of many form controls.
- ☞ `Keywords` must be a space- or comma-separated list of privilege names from Table 16.20 *or* one of the sole keywords `AllAccess`, `NoAccess`, or `sameOrigin`. `AllAccess` is the same as specifying all the keywords from Table 16.20. `sameOrigin` means that the Web Safe security rules should apply. `NoAccess` means that the property cannot be read or written at all.

An example rule is

```
user_pref("capabilities.policy.*.History.back","NoAccess");
```

This rule says that the wildcard policy disabled the `back()` method of the `nsIDOMHistory` object. That object is used in the Mozilla Browser only, so this rule serves to prevent the user from navigating backward when surfing the Web.

The second rule syntax, which applies only to nonmethod JavaScript properties, gives control over the ECMAScript `[[Get]]` and `[[Set]]` operations on that property. The syntax is

```
user_pref("capabilities.policy.mypol.Iface.Prop.Access","Keyword");
```

In the XUL template code, we'll still need a data source, or else the content isn't a template. We use Mozilla's empty placeholder data source, named `rdf:null`. After the XUL is loaded, we'll create a new data source from the XPCOM URL object and attach it to each template using JavaScript. In this way, one data source object will be responsible for all the RDF traffic to and from the data source.

This use of a single, coordinated data source is not the only way for a set of XUL templates to share RDF. If two templates have the same data source attribute, then all RDF facts still come from a shared, single set of facts (a single fact store). This must be the case, or else the code written in Chapter 14, Templates, would not have worked. All that we are doing here is detaching the data source from XUL so that we can supply a customized one. We could instead create a custom data source for each template. As long as they were all based on the same URL, they would all still operate on one shared set of facts.

After we have this data source, we can read and write it using our own JavaScript functions and the numerous RDF interfaces available. At the same time, the template system will access the same data source using the built-in XUL template builder.

To make the design neater, we'll complement the `Note` JavaScript object with a `NoteDataSource` object. The `Note` object was last visited in "Hands On" in Chapter 14, Templates. Each time we need to work on the data source, we'll have the option of capturing that work as a method of our new object.

16.6.2 Data Source Setup

To start with, we need to put a copy of the `notetaker.rdf` file (a test version) in the current user profile if testing is to do anything useful.

Our main setup task is to get access to that RDF file. That means starting with a file name and an idea of its location and ending up with an `nsIRDFDataSource` object. We'll hard-code the file name, but not its location. We'll use several of the facilities described in this chapter to ready the data source.

To locate a file portably, we must use a directory service. Inspecting the directory service tables of known aliases in this chapter, we conclude that the `ProfD` alias from Table 16.18 is the most portable way to reach the current user profile's folder. We turn that alias into an `nsIFile` that holds the profile folder, extend the path of that folder to specify our `notetaker.rdf` file, convert the resulting file into a URL, and then finally use that URL to create a data source. Whew. Listing 16.9 shows this code:

Listing 16.9 Finding and initializing a locally stored data source.

```
var Cc = Components.classes;
var Ci = Components.interfaces;

// Note session object
```

```
function NoteSession() {
  this.init();
}

NoteSession.prototype = {
  config_file : "notetaker.rdf",
  datasource : null,
  init : function (otherfile) {
    var fdir, conv, rdf, file, url;

    if (otherfile) this.config_file = otherfile;

    with (window) {
      fdir = Cc["@mozilla.org/file/directory_service;1"];
      fdir = fdir.getService(Ci.nsIProperties);

      conv = Cc["@mozilla.org/network/protocol;1?name=file"];
      conv = conv.createInstance(Ci.nsIFileProtocolHandler);

      rdf  = Cc["@mozilla.org/rdf/rdf-service;1"];
      rdf  = rdf.getService(Ci.nsIRDFService);
    }

    file = fdir.get("ProfD", Ci.nsIFile);
    file.append(this.config_file);

    if (!file.exists())
      throw this.config_file + " is missing";

    if (!file.isFile() || !file.isWritable() || !file.isReadable())
      throw this.config_file + " has type or permission problems";

    url  = conv.newFileURI(file);
    this.datasource = rdf.GetDataSource(url.spec);
  }
};

var noteSession = new NoteSession();
```

The `init()` method of this `NoteSession` object does all the work. In there, we set up three handy XPCOM objects. We extract the current user profile folder as `nsIFile`. The `append()` method makes an in-place modification to that folder so that it fully specifies our configuration file. The `append()` method does not return anything. Next we perform a couple of sanity checks to make sure that the configuration file is in place—in our completed tool we'll supply a skeleton copy at deployment time, so the file should always exist. In real life, some extra logic should be included here to re-create the file in case it has been deleted. Last, we convert from `nsIFile` to `nsIURL` using `newFileURI()`, then from `nsIURL` to `String` with `url.spec`, and finally from `String` to `nsIRDFDataSource` with `getDataSource()`.

This series of steps is a standard approach for readying a data source. If the data source is internal or remote, some steps might vary a bit. For example, if the URL of the data source is known in advance, little more than `GetDataSource()` is required.

16.6.3 Dynamically Allocating Data Sources to Templates

Now that we have a data source available, let's use it. We want to modify the existing templates so that their displayed data come from the data source's URL, not from a hard-coded XUL attribute. To do that, we'll use a placeholder attribute `datasources="rdf:null"` until the real data source is scripted in.

16.6.3.1 Toolbar Changes We will throw away altogether the template used on the NoteTaker toolbar `<textbox>`. We're making this change because it's unnecessarily complex—the textbox need only act as a simple form element. We only included this template in previous chapters to illustrate the simplest of template uses. Templates aren't a final solution for every problem. The plain `<textbox>` returns to

```
<textbox id="notetaker-toolbar.summary"/>
```

This textbox is filled by `refresh_toolbar()`. That function will now do a simple copy from our note object, instead of a template rebuild. That's all for the summary textbox on the toolbar.

The Keyword dropdown menu on the toolbar has a very standard template query. There would be no reason to change it if the profile-specific data source could be hard-coded. Because it can't be hard-coded, we must change code in both XUL and JavaScript.

This menu has been data-driven since Chapter 14, Templates, but it has not been as dynamic as it may seem. In Chapter 14, it was generated at XUL page creation time and remained static thereafter. From now on, it must change anytime a keyword is added. Any XUL content added or removed may cause the document, including the menu, to reflow. Reflow is an automatic process, but it works most reliably on simple tags. For complex tags like `<menulist>`, careful use of XUL is required. Used carelessly, the menu will appear broken.

To see this broken effect, recall that the original `<menulist>` and template has the form of Listing 16.10. This listing has `"rdf:null"` as the placeholder data source.

Listing 16.10 NoteTaker `<menupopup>` before dynamic support.

```
<menulist id="notetaker-toolbar.keywords" editable="true">
  <menupopup datasources="rdf:null" ref="urn:notetaker:keywords">
    <template>
      <menuitem uri="rdf:*"
        label="rdf:http://www.mozilla.org/notetaker-rdf#label"/>
```

```
    </template>
  </menupopup>
</menulist>
```

Note that only the <menuitem> tags are part of the template. With "rdf:null" in place, the complete menu, consisting of static XUL and generated template content, will appear instead as

```
<menulist id="notetaker-toolbar.keywords" editable="true">
  <menupopup datsources="rdf:null" ref="urn:notetaker:keywords">
  </menupopup>
</menulist>
```

Figure 16.2 shows the results of this changed code.

Fig. 16.2 Templated <menulist> with zero items.

This user interface has layout problems and interaction problems; the sources of these problems can be found in Listing 16.10. We might decide to overlook these problems. After all, our code will modify the template from an `onload` handler so that `rdf:null` is replaced right away with our hand-crafted data source. This should generate <menuitem> tags for the menu, and all should be well.

Unfortunately, all is not well. The popup (dropdown) content is sized by the <menupopup> tag, which has a frame. That frame does not dynamically relayout after it is created, or at least not yet. This means the XUL code in Listing 16.10 will not work when its template is modified after display. Listing 16.11 shows a better version of that Listing 16.10:

Listing 16.11 NoteTaker <menupopup> after dynamic support.

```
<menulist id="notetaker-toolbar.keywords"
  editable="true"
  datasources="rdf:null"
  ref="urn:notetaker:keywords"
>
  <template>
    <menupopup>
      <menuitem uri="rdf:*"
        label="rdf:http://www.mozilla.org/notetaker-rdf#label"/>
    </menupopup>
  </template>
</menulist>
```

In this version, the <template> tag and associated attributes have been *moved up one* in the tag hierarchy. Now, the <menupopup> tag pair is regenerated every time the template runs. Only one <menupopup> tag pair will be generated because those tags are outside the spot where the uri attribute is declared. Recall that the uri attribute is the beginning point for per-query solution generation of template content. Because the <menupopup> is generated each time <menuitem>s are generated, there is opportunity for the <menupopup>'s frame, also created each time, to get its layout correct. This is the recommended approach for template-driven dropdown menus whose content must change after the initial display.

Even with this fix, the keywords menu may have one further usability problem, although this problem doesn't appear in our particular application. Figure 16.3 shows a test toolbar before and after a menu dropmarker has been clicked once. The top window is the before case.

Fig. 16.3 Reflow problems with templated menus.

In this test, the <textbox> at the top of the menu has an initial width that is the default for a <textbox> tag. When the menu is clicked, the menu items are exposed, and the textbox is layed out again to match the width of the widest menu item. The net result is that the dropmarker for the menu jumps to one side. This is confusing for the user. A workaround is to set the width attribute on the <menulist> tag. Fortunately, this problem doesn't occur for NoteTaker, provided a real Web page is displayed.

JavaScript changes required for this newly dynamic menu are quite simple. The functions refresh_toolbar() and init_toolbar() must be changed to attach the new data source to the menu template. Listing 16.12 shows these two functions with data source changes.

Listing 16.12 NoteTaker toolbar changes for data-source-based templates.

```
// onload browser listeners work in the capture phase
window.addEventListener("load", init_handler, true);

// load RDF content for the toolbar. Relies on note object.
function init_toolbar(origin)
{
  if ( origin != "timed" ) {
    // avoid running inside any onload handler
    setTimeout("init_toolbar('timed')",1);
  }
  else
  {
```

```
    var menu = window.document.getElementById('notetaker-
          toolbar.keywords');
    menu.database.AddDataSource(noteSession.datasource);
    menu.ref = 'urn:notetaker:keywords';
    setInterval("content_poll()", 1000);
  }
}

// update the toolbar based on the latest content.
function refresh_toolbar()
{
  var box = document.getElementById('notetaker-toolbar.summary');
  box.value = note.summary;

  var menu = document.getElementById('notetaker-toolbar.keywords');
  menu.ref = 'urn:notetaker:keywords';
}
```

In "Hands On" in Chapter 14, Templates, these functions nervously called `rebuild()` every time a template changed in the least. Now, however, it's clear that the template data are based on the `xml-datasource` data source, which supports fully coordinated template updates. A call to `rebuild()` is therefore not required. If in doubt though, always call `rebuild()`.

The `init_toolbar()` function in this listing attaches the new data source to the dropdown menu template, updates the template's `ref` property, and starts `content_poll()`, which watches the content part of the browser for URL changes. Even though the `ref` property doesn't change value, this assignment tells the template to recalculate solutions for the query held.

The `setTimeout()` call is, as before, a workaround for outstanding defects in the onload event handler. Compare `refresh_toolbar()` with the `Refresh()` method of `nsIRDFRemoteDataSource`. The latter method refreshes the fact store on which a given data source is based. The `refresh_toolbar()` function refreshes only XUL content, including XUL content that results from a template query.

That concludes the display-oriented changes to the NoteTaker toolbar. We'll return to the toolbar when we script up support for user data entry.

16.6.3.2 Edit Dialog Changes The NoteTaker Edit dialog box is the other part of the NoteTaker tool that contains templates. Those templates also require script-initialized data sources. The Edit panel of the dialog box doesn't have any templates at all. The Keyword panel has a template on a `<listbox>` and another on a `<tree>`.

The procedure for attaching a data source to these two templates is very similar to the procedure used on the toolbar. We replace `datasources="notetaker.rdf"` with `datasources="rdf:null"` in two places in `editDialog.xul`. We create a function `init_dialog()` in dialog_action.js, and we modify the existing refresh_dialog() function. Those updated functions are shown in Listing 16.13.

Listing 16.13 NoteTaker dialog changes for data-source-based templates.

```
window.addEventListener("load", init_dialog, "true");

function init_dialog()
{
  if ( origin != "timed" ) {
    // avoid running inside any onload handler
    setTimeout("init_dialog('timed')",1);
  }
  else
  {
    var listbox = document.getElementById('notetaker.keywords');
    listbox.database.AddDataSource(window.opener.noteSession.datasource);

    var tree = document.getElementById('notetaker.related');
    tree.database.AddDataSource(window.opener.noteSession.datasource);

    refresh_dialog();
  }
}

function refresh_dialog()
{
  var listbox = document.getElementById('dialog.keywords');
  listbox.ref = window.opener.note.url;
  //listbox.ref = "http://saturn/test1.html";  // test case

  var tree = document.getElementById('dialog.related');
  tree.ref = window.opener.note.url;
  //tree.ref = "http://saturn/test1.html";     // test case
}
```

The init_dialog() function is nearly identical to the init_toolbar() function, adding the same data source to each of the two keyword templates. The refresh_dialog() function is also similar and includes some example URLs from the notetaker.rdf test data that can be used to unit test the template updates. These changes make no difference to the user interface; they merely support the relocated notetaker.rdf file.

In the "Hands On" session in Chapter 13, Listboxes and Trees, we experimented with dynamic listboxes scripted up using the DOM interfaces and no templates. That code required about 30 lines of JavaScript. In the "Hands On" session in this chapter, we have achieved the same effect using a template and only a few lines of scripting.

With these changes in place, all the NoteTaker tool's templates are now driven from the notetaker.rdf file located in the user profile.

16.6.4 Scripted RDF Queries Using XPCOM Interfaces

XUL's template system is just one way to create a query on a set of RDF facts. It is a declarative approach similar to SQL. Another approach is to pick through the RDF facts by hand, using a script. This is equivalent to navigating a data structure, so it is an algorithmic or algebraic approach. This second approach means using the many XPCOM interfaces that are available for manipulating RDF content. Those interfaces provide some navigation assistance, so the scripting effort required is as large as it might seem.

The NoteTaker tool has one query that benefits from a scripted solution. That query is responsible for looking up any existing note for the currently displayed URL. Templates are not an automatic solution for this case for several reasons:

- The destination of the data is JavaScript, not XUL, and templates don't support the `<script>` tag as content.
- This query has no visual output.
- The "Chop Query" feature of the dialog box works two ways. Not only does it optionally remove the parameters from the URL for an HTTP GET request, but it also demands that such a URL be matched to a note with or without the parameter string present. That kind of matching means string operations on the URL.

Templates don't provide string operations, but scripts do, so we'll implement this lookup query with a script.

This lookup query is implemented by the `resolve()` method of the note object, in `notes.js`. This method was created as a stub in past chapters and now gains a full implementation. It loads the RDF details for a note into the properties of the note object. Listing 16.14 shows its implementation.

Listing 16.14 NoteTaker script-based RDF query.

```
resolve : function (url) {
  var ds = window.noteSession.datasource;
  var ns = "http://www.mozilla.org/notetaker-rdf#";

  var rdf = Cc["@mozilla.org/rdf/rdf-service;1"];
      rdf = rdf.getService(Ci.nsIRDFService);

  var container = Cc["@mozilla.org/rdf/container;1"];
      container = container.getService(Ci.nsIRDFContainer);

  var cu = Cc["@mozilla.org/rdf/container-utils;1"];
      cu = cu.getService(Ci.nsIRDFContainerUtils);

  var seq_node = rdf.GetResource("urn:notetaker:notes");
  var url_node      = rdf.GetResource(url);
  var chopped_node = rdf.GetResource(url.replace(/\?.*/,""));
```

```
  var matching_node, prop_node, value_node;

  if (!cu.IsContainer(ds,seq_node)) {
   throw "Missing <Seq> 'urn:notetaker:notes' in " +
          noteSession.config_file;
   return;
  }
  container.Init(ds,seq_node);

  // Try the full URL, then the chopped URL, then give up

  if ( container.IndexOf(url_node) != -1) {
    matching_node = url_node;
    this.url = url;
    this.chop_query = false;
  }
  else if ( container.IndexOf(chopped_node) != -1 ) {
    matching_node = chopped_node;
    this.url = url.replace(/\?.*/,"");
  }
  else {
    this.url = null;
    return;
  }
  else
    return;

  // Something found; grab all the note properties for it.

  var props = ["summary", "details", "width", "height", "top", "left"];

  for (var i=0; i<props.length; i++)
  {
    pred_node  = rdf.GetResource(ns + props[i]);
    value_node = ds.GetTarget(matching_node, pred_node, true);
    value_node = value_node.QueryInterface(Ci.nsIRDFLiteral);
    this[props[i]] = value_node.Value;
  }
}
```

First, this method readies the three main service objects that the RDF system provides. The `nsIRDFService` object is used to turn plain URL strings into `nsIRDFResource` objects, which are a subtype of the generic `nsIRDFNode` type. Most RDF methods do not accept string arguments; `nsIRDFNode` objects are generally required. We create such objects for both the full URL and the chopped URL. The sole use of the `nsIContainerUtils` interface follows. It is used to confirm that the `urn:notetaker:notes` resource is a container in the `notetaker.rdf` file. If this much is not in place, then there is a problem with that file, and the method aborts with an error. The `nsIRDFContainer` interface is then used to link the container (`<Seq>`) URI with the data source, and that link is initialized. Normally, access to the data source is on a fact-by-fact basis. This last interface allows an RDF container and its members to be treated as though they were a data structure. That structure is the RDF equivalent of a table index. With that, the initialization part of the method ends.

The `if .. else` cascade contains the start of the scripted query. In this case, that query is quite trivial. It says: Search for a fully matching resource in the data source, and if that fails, search for a resource that matches the displayed URL without its query parameters. If both fail, give up.

The remainder of the query pulls out all the facts that represent property/value pairs for the found note. `rdf.GetTarget()` always returns an `nsIRDFNode`, so that object must be converted to the type we really expect for the property's value, which is a literal string. We're not storing window measurements as integers. Finally, those retrieved values are copied into the matching properties of the note object. This part of the code assumes that the note is well formed (properly created) in the `notetaker.rdf` file.

Overall, this query is a two-fact query that follows the general pattern of a simple syntax template query, except for the special checks at the start of the different URL strings.

If you test this `resolve()` method, perhaps by adding test code such as this

```
note.resolve("http://saturn/test1.html");
```

then the code will almost certainly fail with unexpected errors. Typically it is the first use of an RDF interface that fails, but failure might occur deeper in the code, or worse, intermittently. The culprit causing these failures is outside the note object—it is in the `noteSession` object. There, the data source for the RDF file is initialized in the `init()` function with this call:

```
this.datasource = GetDataSource(url.spec);
```

This initialization is wrong for our purposes. It causes the data source to be loaded asynchronously so that the fact store for that data source will only fill over time. Meanwhile, our scripts have raced forward and the note object is trying to probe the data source before it is ready. No wonder that RDF methods complain that expected containers or resources aren't present in the data source. The solution is to load the data source differently:

```
this.datasource = GetDataSourceBlocking(url.spec);
```

This causes a tiny delay when the browser window is first displayed, but it's livable for our simple case.

We could work around this tiny delay with a more sophisticated strategy that perhaps uses the `nsIRequestObserver` or `nsIStreamListener` interfaces of the `xml-datasource`'s XPCOM component. Those interfaces can be used to detect the ending of an asynchronous load. Some XPCOM objects created in this method are also created in other methods. Overhead could be reduced by adding created XPCOM objects to the `noteSession` object, where they would be available for reuse. That's a job for another day.

In past chapters, we wrote scripts to push the note object's data out into the form fields and into the HTML document of the browser's GUI. Now we've connected the note object to the RDF fact store and configuration file that persistently holds the notes. As a result, the display of existing notes works. We only need to change a small omission in the `toolbar_action.js` file. In function `content_poll()`, this

```
display_note()
```

should read this

```
if (note.url != null ) display_note()
```

That leaves Web pages without notes free of any decoration. Much better!

16.6.5 When to Move User-Entered Data into RDF

In addition to displaying RDF content, the NoteTaker tool is designed to capture it. The last time this was properly organized was in Chapter 7, Forms and Menus, when we sent the captured data to a Web server. This session puts that data into an RDF fact store, and ultimately into a local file. The main alternate solution is to use a relational database.

For our purposes, entering data means adding it to a data source. It will sit in memory until either the user chooses an action that makes it permanent or the platform is shut down. That is a design choice.

Data can be entered either via the NoteTaker toolbar or via either panel in the dialog box. Let's look at each of these, starting with the toolbar.

The summary and keyword fields of the toolbar provide a quick way to create or update a note. Such a note can have its summary modified and a single keyword added. If the user fills these fields, but doesn't press any of the toolbar buttons (Edit, Save, or Delete), then nothing happens. Therefore, user changes to these fields can be handled in the commands available from the toolbar. There is no need for onchange event handlers or anything like that.

The Edit panel of the dialog box is the same as the toolbar. Changes made by the user only need to be recorded if the user presses the Ok button; they can be discarded if the dialog box is canceled. The Keywords panel, however, is more complex.

The Keywords panel allows any number of new keywords to be collected using the Add and Delete buttons on that panel. The question is: Where should these values be kept while the dialog box is displayed? If the user ultimately cancels the dialog box, these new keywords should be thrown away. If the user ultimately accepts the changes, these new keywords should be preserved. The problem is that we want the `<listbox>` and `<tree>` parts of the panel to update when keywords are added. This means that those keywords must be stored in RDF where the templated tags can find them, even when we're not sure if they are ultimately to be kept or not.

In a nutshell, we have an undo or transaction rollback problem to solve. We want to be able to insert keywords into a data source where they're shared, but possibly remove them later if they're not ultimately wanted. The solution we choose is to implement a new command controller. That controller will record the keyword changes in an undo buffer. If it receives a rollback command, it will reverse all the commands made to date, and consequently any RDF changes. This solution is a design choice, but it is easily applied to most applications.

The result of this design is that all data entry processing is processed behind the command infrastructure. That is a very neat arrangement. In summary, data sits passively in form elements until the user causes a command to run. The command may push that data into a fact store where it is then more generally available across the application. This is particularly useful for templates. If the command is responsible for persisting the information, then the fact store will also be flushed to disk or sent over a network.

16.6.6 Enhancing Commands to Process RDF Content

Finally, we turn to the code that pushes data from the user to disk, rather than the other way around. We will update the `action()` function for the toolbar and the dialog box and implement a new controller for the special keyword support in the dialog box.

The toolbar `action()` function supports the `notetaker-open-dialog`, `notetaker-save`, `notetaker-display`, and `notetaker-delete` commands. Only `-save` and `-delete` require RDF processing. These two commands are quite lengthy, so Listing 16.15 only shows the simpler `notetaker-save` command.

Listing 16.15 NoteTaker script-based RDF update and save.

```
function action(task)
{
  var ns = "http://www.mozilla.org/notetaker-rdf#";

  var rdf = Cc["@mozilla.org/rdf/rdf-service;1"];
      rdf = rdf.getService(Ci.nsIRDFService);

  var container = Cc["@mozilla.org/rdf/container;1"];
      container = container.getService(Ci.nsIRDFContainer);

  var url_node;

// ... other commands removed ...

  if ( task == "notetaker-save" )
  {
```

```
var summary = document.getElementById("notetaker-toolbar.summary");
var keyword = document.getElementById("notetaker-toolbar.keywords");

var update_type = null;

if ( note.url != null )
{
  if ( keyword.value != "" || summary.value != note.summary )
  {
    update_type = "partial"; // existing note: update summary,
      keywords
    url_node = rdf.GetResource(note.url);
  }
}
else if ( window.content && window.content.document
     && window.content.document.visited )
{
  update_type = "complete"; // a new note
  url_node = window.content.document.location.href;
  url_node = url_node.replace(/\?.*/,""); // toolbar chops any query
  url_node = rdf.GetResource(url_node);
}

if ( update_type == "complete" )
{

  // add the note's url to the note container
  var note_cont = rdf.GetResource("urn:notetaker:notes");
  container.Init(noteSession.datasource,note_cont);
  container.AppendElement(url_node);

  // add the note's fields, except for keywords
  var names = ["details", "top", "left", "width", "height"];
  var prop_node, value_node;

  for (var i=0; i < names.length; i++)
  {
    prop_node  = rdf.GetResource(ns + names[i]);
    value_node = rdf.GetLiteral(note[names[i]]);
    noteSession.datasource.Assert(url_node, prop_node, value_node,
      true);
  }
}

if ( update_type != null)
{
  // update/add the summary
  var summary_pred = rdf.GetResource(ns + "summary");
  var summary_node = rdf.GetLiteral(summary.value);
      noteSession.datasource.Assert(url_node, summary_pred,
      summary_node, true);

  // begin work on a single new keyword
```

```
      var keyword_node = rdf.GetResource("urn:notetaker:keyword:" +
          keyword.value);
      var keyword_value = rdf.GetLiteral(keyword.value);

      // make this keyword related to one other keyword for this note
      var keyword_pred = rdf.GetResource(ns + "keyword");
      var related_pred = rdf.GetResource(ns + "related");
      var keyword2 = noteSession.datasource.GetTarget(url_node,
          keyword_pred, true);
      if (keyword2)
        noteSession.datasource.Assert(keyword_node, related_pred,
          keyword2, true);

      // add the keyword to this note
      noteSession.datasource.Assert(url_node, keyword_pred, keyword_node,
          true);

      // state the keyword itself
      var label_pred   = rdf.GetResource(ns + "label");
      noteSession.datasource.Assert(keyword_node, label_pred,
          keyword_value, true);

      // add the keyword to the container holding all keywords
      var keyword_cont = rdf.GetResource("urn:notetaker:keywords");
      container.Init(noteSession.datasource,keyword_cont);
      container.AppendElement(keyword_node);
    }

    // write it out

        noteSession.datasource.QueryInterface(Ci.nsIRDFRemoteDataSource)
        .Flush();

    note.resolve();
    display_note();
  }
```

This code contains the RDF equivalent of one database transaction. It starts with some standard preparation—access to the XPCOM RDF interfaces—and then examines the GUI to see what kind of save is required. By collecting the summary field, the keyword field, the `note` and `noteSession` objects, and the state of the currently displayed URL, the code determines whether a note already exists. We cheat a little and reuse some information from the `content_poll()` function, such as the visited property.

If the note already exists, the only changes must be toolbar changes, so the saving of the note is a partial update of the existing note facts. If the note doesn't exist, then the note needs to be added (inserted), which requires a complete update of those facts. When a note is added from the toolbar, we also chop off any HTTP GET query string from the URL. At the end of all that examination, the `update_type` variable says what to do.

Because a partial update is a subset of a complete update, the partial case is shared by all updates. This branch in the code

```
if ( update_type == "complete" )
```

contains the complete update logic, except for the shared part; this branch

```
if (update_type != null )
```

holds the shared part used by both the complete and partial updates. Let's look at each one in turn.

The complete update code grabs the `urn:notetaker:notes` container and adds the URL for the note to it. That's one fact. It then steps through all the properties that a note has, except for the summary and a keyword. It adds those as well. That's five more facts for a total of six. All strings must be converted to `nsIRDFNote` objects or equivalent subtypes before they can be submitted to RDF.

The partial update code is then called in all cases where it's possible to create a note. You can't create a note for an `about:blank` URL or for an FTP site, so it's possible that the `notetaker-save` action will do nothing. The summary is straightforward—we just add one more fact. If the fact already exists, then the `Assert()` statement that adds it again will have no effect. By default, and in all normal circumstances, duplicate facts aren't allowed in a data source, so it's safe to assert a fact that might already be there.

The partial code then addresses the trickier matter of an entered keyword. If the note already has a keyword, then we want this keyword to be "connected" (related) to the other keywords in the note. That means a fact stating that (any) one keyword in the note is related to this new keyword. So we fish out an existing keyword value; if one's found, we add a fact stating the relatedness of the new and existing keyword. We do this first to avoid relating our new keyword to itself. That might happen if we added the new keyword first. The remaining code is straightforward: We add the keyword to the note; we add the keyword to the list of all keywords in the `urn:notetaker:keywords` container; and we add the keyword itself. That is four more facts.

At the end of this code, we've added 1 + 4 (+ optional 5) facts to the data source. Because the data source is based on the fully featured `xml-datasource`, these changes are automatically pushed to all templates using the data source. We then call the `Flush()` method to push the data source out to disk. Be aware that this command will write out the `notetaker.rdf` file with the facts in a near-random order, so any pretty formatting of that file will be lost. To finish up, we update and display the note, bringing our non-RDF data structures and the GUI into agreement with RDF.

That concludes the processing required for the `notetaker-save` command. The `notetaker-delete` command is equally detailed; the challenge in that command is to identify keywords no longer needed and to identify keywords still needed by other notes. That requires some analysis of the many different cases that are possible, which we won't do here. The Delete button on the Keywords panel has very similar logic; we'll discuss it shortly.

The Edit dialog box's `action()` function supports commands `notetaker-nav-edit`, `notetaker-nav-keywords`, `notetaker-save`, `notetaker-load`, and `notetaker-close-dialog`. Of these, the `notetaker-save` command is the only one requiring RDF work. In fact, we can reuse the `notetaker-save` command on the toolbar if we're organized enough: Listing 16.16 illustrates.

Listing 16.16 Improvements to the dialog box `notetaker-save` command.

```
if (task == "notetaker-save")
{
  var field, widget, note = window.opener.note;

  for (field in note)
  {
  widget = document.getElementById("dialog." + field.replace(/_/,"-"));

  if (!widget) continue;

  if (widget.tagName == "checkbox")
      note[field] = widget.checked;
  else
     note[field] = widget.value;
  }
  window.opener.setTimeout('execute("notetaker-save")',1);
}
```

This single extra line runs the toolbar's `notetaker-save` command. We can't call `window.opener.execute()` directly because the function would run in the dialog window's context. We want it to run in the browser window's context. Calling the browser window's `setTimeout()` method ensures that the right window context starts up when the timed command is run.

Finally, extra commands are required for the Keywords pane of the Edit dialog box. These commands will be collected into a controller that supports `commit` and `undo` operations. It will support these commands: `notetaker-keyword-add`, `notetaker-keyword-delete`, `notetaker-keyword-commit`, and `notetaker-keyword-undo-all`. Because these commands are closely tied together and will share data, it's not convenient to implement them separately in the `action()` function. Instead, they'll be implemented directly in the controller. We'll make a new file named `keywordController.js` for this controller. Listing 16.17 shows the structure of this controller.

Listing 16.17 Command controller for dialog box's RDF keywords.

```
var keywordController = {
  _cmds : { },
  _undo_stack : [],
```

```
  _rdf : null,
  _ds : null,
  _ns : "http://www.mozilla.org/notetaker-rdf#",
  _related : null,
  _label : null,
  _keyword : null,

  init              : function (ds) { ... initialize ... },
  _LoggedAssert     : function (sub, pred, obj) { ... },
  _LoggedUnassert   : function (sub, pred, obj) { ... },

  supportsCommand   : function (cmd) { return (cmd in this._cmds); },
  isCommandEnabled : function (cmd) { return true; },
  onEvent           : function (cmd) { return true; },
  doCommand         : function (cmd) {
     ... preparation code ...
    switch (cmd) {
    case "notetaker-keyword-add":
    case "notetaker-keyword-delete":
    case "notetaker-keyword-commit":
    case "notetaker-keyword-undo-all":
    }
  }
};

keywordController.init(window.opener.noteSession.datasource);
```

Like all command controllers, this controller has the standard four commands, starting with `supportsCommand()`. The `doCommand()` method implements a different case statement for each command attempted. The controller also has many custom features. The controller holds a number of variables, and an array called `_undo_stack` will hold the steps that need to be reversed. The `_LoggedAssert()` and `_LoggedUnassert()` methods perform RDF manipulation as for `Assert()` and `Unassert()`, but they also make a record of their actions in the undo stack. Let's first make the `init()` method, which is trivially shown in Listing 16.18:

Listing 16.18 Initialization of keyword command controller.

```
init              : function (ds) {
    this._rdf = Cc["@mozilla.org/rdf/rdf-service;1"];
    this._rdf = this._rdf.getService(Ci.nsIRDFService);
    this._ds = ds;
    this._related = this._rdf.GetResource(this._ns + "related");
    this._label   = this._rdf.GetResource(this._ns + "label");
    this._keyword = this._rdf.GetResource(this._ns + "keyword");
    window.controllers.insertControllerAt(0,this);
  },
```

This method assigns some handy objects to the controller—the RDF service, the supplied data source, and three commonly used predicate terms. The controller then registers itself with the dialog window. By putting it first in the controller chain, we ensure that it is the first controller to be examined for any commands that might occur.

The next two functions `_LoggedAssert()` and `_LoggedUnassert()` show how a controller can retain and share information about the commands it executes. In this case, that information is `undo` history about the RDF facts asserted and removed by commands. Listing 16.19 shows these two functions.

Listing 16.19 Implementation of fact assertion undo log.

```
_LoggedAssert      : function (sub, pred, obj)
  {
    if ( !this._ds.HasAssertion(sub, pred, obj, true))
    {
      this._undo_stack.push( { assert:true, sterm:sub, pterm:pred,
          oterm:obj } );
      this._ds.Assert(sub, pred, obj, true);
    }
  },

  _LoggedUnassert    : function (sub, pred, obj)
  {
    if ( this._ds.HasAssertion(sub, pred, obj, true))
    {
      this._undo_stack.push( { assert:false, sterm:sub, pterm:pred,
          oterm:obj } );
      this._ds.Unassert(sub, pred, obj, true);
    }
  },
```

Each function is a simple replacement for `nsIRDFDataSource.Assert()` and `nsIRDFDataSource.Unassert()`. In both cases, the fact store is first tested to see if the RDF change would have any effect. If it would, then a record of the change to be made is created (as a four-property object) and that record is put on the undo stack. The property `assert` states whether the fact is asserted or unasserted. The genuine RDF change is then made as normal.

These two functions are directly complemented by the `notetaker-keyword-commit` and `notetaker-keyword-undo-all` commands. The fragment of the `doCommand()` method responsible for these two commands appears in Listing 16.20.

Listing 16.20 Committing and undoing fact changes using an undo log.

```
case "notetaker-keyword-commit":
 this._undo_stack = [];
 break;

case "notetaker-keyword-undo-all":
  while (this._undo_stack.length > 0 )
```

```
{
  var cmd = this._undo_stack.pop();
  if ( cmd.assert )
    this._ds.Unassert(cmd.sterm, cmd.pterm, cmd.oterm, true);
  else
    this._ds.Assert(cmd.sterm, cmd.pterm, cmd.oterm, true);
}
break;
```

The `notetaker-keyword-commit` command is trivial; it forgets the existing undo commands so that they can't be accidentally undone. The `notetaker-keyword-undo-all` command is marginally more complex. It steps through the stack `Unassert()`'ing every previously `Assert()`'ed fact, and `Assert()`'ing every previously `Unassert()`'ed fact. At the end of this processing, no items remain on the stack, so in this implementation, it's not possible to "undo an undo."

Even though this undo system works on fact assertions, not commands, it is easy to see how the stack could hold records of whole commands as trivially as it holds records of whole facts. That possibility is also suggested in Chapter 9, Commands.

The remainder of the `doCommand()` method appears in Listing 16.21.

Listing 16.21 `doCommand()` initialization with save and delete operations.

```
doCommand         : function (cmd) {

  var url     = window.opener.content.document.location.href;
  var keyword = window.document.getElementById("dialog.keyword").value;

  if (keyword.match(/^[ \t]*$/))
    return;

  var keyword_node = this._rdf.GetResource("urn:notetaker:keyword:" +
          keyword);
  var keyword_value = this._rdf.GetLiteral(keyword);
  var url_node     = this._rdf.GetResource(url);

  var test_node, keyword2, enum1, enum2;

  switch (cmd) {

  case "notetaker-keyword-add":
    // This keyword should be related to an existing keyword, if any
    keyword2 = this._ds.GetTarget(url_node, this._keyword, true);
    if (keyword2)
      this._LoggedAssert(keyword_node, this._related, keyword2);

    // add this keyword
    this._LoggedAssert(keyword_node, this._label, keyword_value);

    // add this keyword to the current note.
```

```
      this._LoggedAssert(url_node, this._keyword, keyword_node);
      break;


    case "notetaker-keyword-delete":
      // remove this keyword from the current note.
      this._LoggedUnassert(url_node, this._keyword, keyword_node);

      // remove this keyword and related facts if it's not used elsewhere
      enum1 = this._ds.GetSources( this._keyword, keyword_node, true);
      if (!enum1.hasMoreElements())
      {
        // this keyword
        this._LoggedUnassert(keyword_node, this._label, keyword_value);

        // this keyword is related to that keyword
        enum2 = this._ds.GetTargets(keyword_node, this._related, true);
        while (enum2.hasMoreElements())
          this._LoggedUnassert(keyword_node, this._related,
            enum2.getNext().QueryInterface(Ci.nsIRDFNode));

        // that keyword is related to this keyword
        enum2 = this._ds.GetSources(this._related, keyword_node, true);
        while (enum2.hasMoreElements())

            this._LoggedUnassert(enum2.getNext().QueryInterface(Ci.nsIRDFNod
            e), this._related, keyword_node);
      }
      else // this keyword is used elsewhere.
      {
        // delete related facts where keywords that this keyword
        // relates to are only found in the current note.
        enum1 = this._ds.GetTargets(keyword_node, this._related, true);
        while (enum1.hasMoreElements())
        {
          keyword2 = enum1.getNext().QueryInterface(Ci.nsIRDFNode);
          enum2 = this._ds.GetSources(this._keyword, keyword2, true);

          test_node = enum2.getNext().QueryInterface(Ci.nsIRDFNode);
          if (!enum2.hasMoreElements() && test_node.EqualsNode(url_node))
            this._LoggedUnassert(keyword_node, this._related, keyword2);

          // delete related facts where keyword that relates to this
          // keyword are only found in the current note.
          enum1 = this._ds.GetSources(this._related, keyword_node, true);
          while (enum1.hasMoreElements())
          {
            keyword2 = enum1.getNext().QueryInterface(Ci.nsIRDFNode);
            enum2 = this._ds.GetSources(this._keyword, keyword2, true);

            test_node = enum2.getNext().QueryInterface(Ci.nsIRDFNode);
            if (!enum2.hasMoreElements() && test_node.EqualsNode(url_node))
              this._LoggedUnassert(keyword2, this._related, keyword_node);
          }
```

```
    }
  }
  break;
```

The ten or so lines of code prior to the `switch()` statement initializes some local variables and aborts the command if there's no current note. The switch statement shows the `notetaker-keyword-add` and `notetaker-keyword-delete` cases. Adding and removing keywords would be easy if we didn't try to maintain a sense of which keywords are related to which other keywords. That information makes the adding and removing tasks longer.

Both commands assume that a note either already exists or is currently being created for that URL. So the keywords added and removed are done so in the context of a particular URL. The comments in the code describe the steps involved, but here is a more explanatory discussion.

All this code is constrained by the fact that duplicate facts don't exist in a normal fact store. There are no variables in a fact store, so we can't set both A and B equal to 5. Every fact stored is unique. We need to manage the fact store globally; we must consider the impact of adding or removing a fact on all other facts in the fact store.

The keyword addition case is the easier case. It adds these facts to the data source:

```
<- keyword-urn, related, keyword2-urn -> (optional)
<- note-url, keyword, keyword-urn ->
<- keyword-urn, label, keyword-literal ->
```

We want to ensure that all related keywords can be found for a given note. That means any keyword belonging to a note with existing keywords must be related to all the other keywords in the note. In our RDF model, we capture this information by relating that one keyword to at least one of the other keywords for that note. So we first check for other keywords and, if there are any, relate the new keyword to one of them. After this is done, we're free to add this keyword in as well, first to the note as a fact object term and then in its own right as a fact that states that the keyword exists and what its value is. Each of the required facts asserted is done so through the `_LoggedAssert()` interface.

The keyword deletion case is quite complex. It is easy to remove information specific to one note, but keywords may be used by several notes, which means that keyword-to-keyword relationships can also be used by several notes. The first and last of the three facts stated in the addition case therefore can't be deleted without some careful checks of their use elsewhere in the fact store. How we proceed depends on whether the keyword to be deleted is used in other notes. The required tortured logic follows.

If the keyword in question is used only in a single note, then all information about that keyword is confined to a single note. We can delete all record of the keyword in a straightforward manner.

If the keyword in question is used in several notes, we proceed more carefully. We can remove the keyword reference from the current note, but we can't delete the keyword's own fact. Removing facts where this keyword is related to some other keyword is the hard part. If a keyword-related-to-our-keyword fact is used by another note, we can't remove it. We'll know if that fact is so used by checking the other keyword in the keyword. If that other keyword appears in any other note in the fact store, the fact applies to that other note as well as the current note, so leave it. Otherwise, remove it. We do this twice because the keyword to be deleted could be fact subject or fact object in such a related fact.

Astute readers will note that the `urn:notetaker:keywords <Seq>` should also be updated by these `-add` and `-delete` commands. We haven't done that because these commands are complicated enough as it is, and some trickery is required to fit those further updates in with the undo system. In fact, a more general solution is to couple data source observer objects with the undo stack—a project for another day. That concludes RDF enhancement of the NoteTaker commands.

To get all this working, we need to hook the new controller and command calls into the dialog box. Several pieces of code are required. The `editDialog.xul` file requires an additional `<script>` tag:

```
<script src="keywordController.js"/>
```

That file also needs extra handlers on the `<dialog>` tag. These handlers are for the keyword changes made in the dialog box.

```
<dialog xmlns="http://www.mozilla.org/keymaster/gatekeeper/
     there.is.only.xul"
  id="notetaker.dialog"
  title="Edit NoteTaker Note"
  onload="execute('notetaker-load');"
  ondialogaccept="execute('notetaker-keyword-commit');
                  execute('notetaker-save');
                  execute('notetaker-close-dialog');"
  ondialogcancel="execute('notetaker-keyword-undo-all');
                  execute('notetaker-close-dialog');"
  >
```

These handlers are getting large, and any further changes should probably be aggregated into single functions or some kind of transaction. The dialog box has some other handlers in the file `dialog_handlers.js`. Two of these other handlers reduce to trivial code now that the keyword controller has been written:

```
function add_click(ev)
  {
  execute("notetaker-keyword-add");
}

function delete_click(ev)
{
  execute("notetaker-keyword-delete");
}
```

With these last changes, the NoteTaker tool is complete—or at least as complete as space allows in this book.

16.6.7 Custom RDF Tree Views and Data Sources

In "Hands On" in Chapter 13, Listboxes and Trees, we briefly experimented with custom views. That experiment can be extended to RDF if desired. If that is done, then the `<tree>` tag with the custom view can be powered from an RDF data source without using any template. Space here does not permit a long examination of that implementation option, but a few remarks are worth making:

That Chapter 13, Listboxes and Trees, experiment implemented a method named `calcRelatedMatrix()`, which built information out of a constant JavaScript array named `treedata`. If that method is reimplemented to extract the pairs of related keywords from a data source instead of an array, then that experiment will work immediately, but using RDF data instead of JavaScript data.

Such a simple replacement strategy is, however, a primitive use of the facilities of data sources. A better solution is to use the `nsIRDFObserver` interface. If the JavaScript object implementing a custom view also implements this interface, then that object can be registered as an observer on a data source (it must be an `nsIRDFCompositeDataSource`). The view will them receive notification every time a fact in the data source changes and can incrementally update the tree's view rather than recalculate the whole view in one batch. That is a more sophisticated strategy that supports event management consoles and other "server push" data systems.

Finally, we point out that an object with the `nsIRDFDataSource` interface can be created entirely in JavaScript. Such an object can be used to pretend that the data it supplies is RDF-based. Alternately, such an object might wrap itself around one or more other data sources, in which case it is a variation on the composite data source implementation supplied by the platform. Either way, such an object can be lodged (via JavaScript only) with a template and can drive the appearance of the GUI just as the presupplied data source does.

16.7 Debug Corner: Working with Data Sources

Some of the most common problems that hit when working with data sources include the following:

- **Capitalization**. Unlike the rest of XPCOM, data source interface methods are stated in `InitCaps`, not in `initCaps`. Thus it is `GetResource()` not `getResource()`.
- **Asynchronous loading**. If the `nsIRDFDataSource` interface's `GetDataSource()` methods is used to create a data source instead of `Get-`

`DataSourceBlocking()`, the data source loads “in the background.” In that case, any statements manipulating that data source immediately after its object is created are at risk. The risk is that the data source has not finished loading yet, and so not all anticipated facts may yet be present.

- **Syntax problems in test data**. If RDF files containing test data have syntax errors, then facts in that RDF file will be loaded into a data source only up to the point where the syntax error occurs. No error messages will be given.
- **Attempting to push content back over the Web**. Data sources originating from over a network cannot yet be “saved” back to their origin directly. Only local files can be saved (updated). To push a changed data source back over the Web (or over FTP), turn the data source into an RDF document using a content source interface and then use the file upload system. For a lower level solution, use a socket.
- **Using `false` as an argument to `Assert()` or `Unassert()`**. The fourth argument to these methods should always be true. Using `false` expands the logic system used in the RDF facts stores in an unhelpful way. This fourth argument says nothing about the existence of facts. Always use `true`.
- **Passing strings to `Assert()` or `Unassert()`**. These methods only accept objects of type `nsIRDFNode` and subtypes of that type.
- **Problems with multiple return values.** Methods such as `GetTargets()` return an `nsISimpleEnumerator` object that provides a list of possible URIs that fit the fact requested. Each object returned by this enumerator has interface `nsISupports`, and `QueryInterface()` should be used to extract a more useful `nsIRDFNode` interface, or a subtype of that interface.
- **The `nsIRDFContainerUtil` interface and objects implementing it generally have no life of their own**. They work on other objects passed in as arguments.

16.7.1 Revealing Data Source Content

RDF internal data sources are one of the trickiest aspects of the Mozilla Platform. Listing 16.22 is a piece of code that can be used to probe their contents.

Listing 16.22 Stream creation by many methods.

```
function _dumpFactSubtree(ds, sub, level)
{
  var iter, iter2, pred, obj, objstr, result="";

  // bail if passed an nsIRDFLiteral or other non-URI
  try { iter = ds.ArcLabelsOut(sub); }
  catch (ex) { return; }
```

```
  while (iter.hasMoreElements())
  {
    pred = iter.getNext().QueryInterface(Ci.nsIRDFResource);
    iter2 = ds.GetTargets(sub, pred, true);

    while (iter2.hasMoreElements())
    {
      obj = iter2.getNext();
      try {
        obj = obj.QueryInterface(Ci.nsIRDFResource);
        objstr = obj.Value;
      }
      catch (ex)
      {
        obj = obj.QueryInterface(Ci.nsIRDFLiteral);
        objstr = '"' + obj.Value + '"';
      }

      result += level + " " + sub.Value + " , " +
                pred.Value + " , " + objstr + "\n";

      result += dumpFactSubtree(ds, obj, level+1);
    }
  }
  return result;
}

function dumpFromRoot(ds, rootURI)
{
  return _dumpFactSubtree(ds, rootURI, 0);
}
```

The function `dumpFromRoot()` is the API to use. It relies on very few aspects of the `nsIRDFDataSource` interface and should work for most internal data sources and for all plain RDF files. It performs a recursive breadth-first search of a fact store using a given starting point and assumes that the RDF graph in the fact store is structured as a tree.

This function should be passed an `nsIRDFDataSource` object and an `nsIRDFResource` object. The data source the first object represents should be fully loaded, or else the report generated in the result string will be incomplete. The `rootURI argument` should be a URI that is suspected of being a container or container-owner in the RDF graph for the data source's fact store. The URIs listed in Table 16.11 are typical candidates. If the RDF graph contains cycles, then the code will recurse forever, probably crashing the browser eventually. It's only a simple testing tool, so treat it that way.

16.8 Summary

The Mozilla Platform contains more object facilities than can possibly be covered here. Because of its portability requirements, and because of its application focus, those objects tend to be high-level ones. Perhaps one day there will be a full POSIX interface, but the high-level application focus of the platform reduces the urgency of any such need.

Mozilla's XML processing facilities are particularly strong, which is no surprise. Heavyweight XML-based networks tend to be business-to-business rather than consumer-to-business, but Microsoft's .NET initiative suggests that there is plenty of need for sophisticated XML-based client-oriented software.

Having explored first the front half and now the back half of Mozilla-based applications, we have only to deploy those applications. Mozilla's build system, which is used to create compiled applications, is complemented by a remote install system. That system, XPInstall, is the topic of our last chapter, which follows.

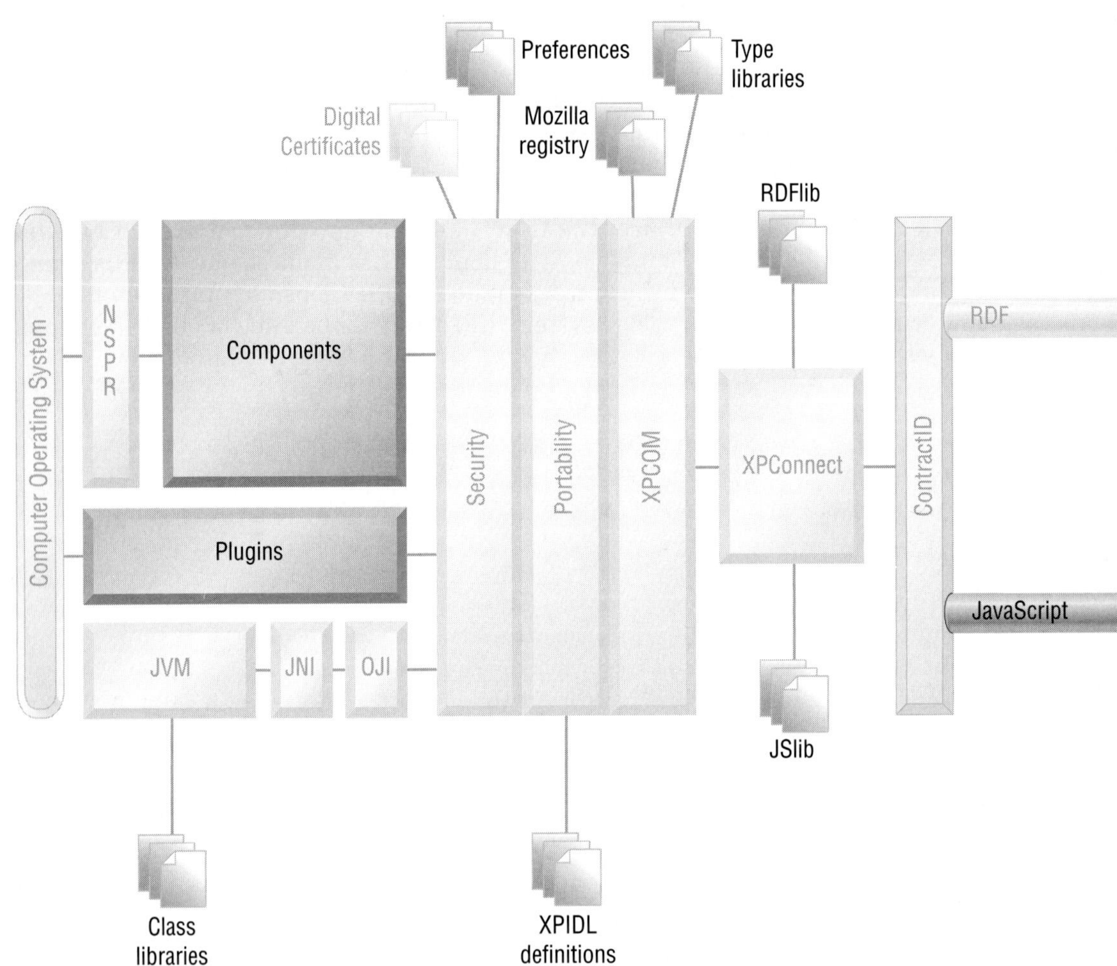

Preferences
Type libraries
Digital Certificates
Mozilla registry
RDFlib
Computer Operating System
NSPR
Components
Security
Portability
XPCOM
XPConnect
ContractID
RDF
Plugins
JavaScript
JVM
JNI
OJI
JSlib
Class libraries
XPIDL definitions

CHAPTER 17

Deployment

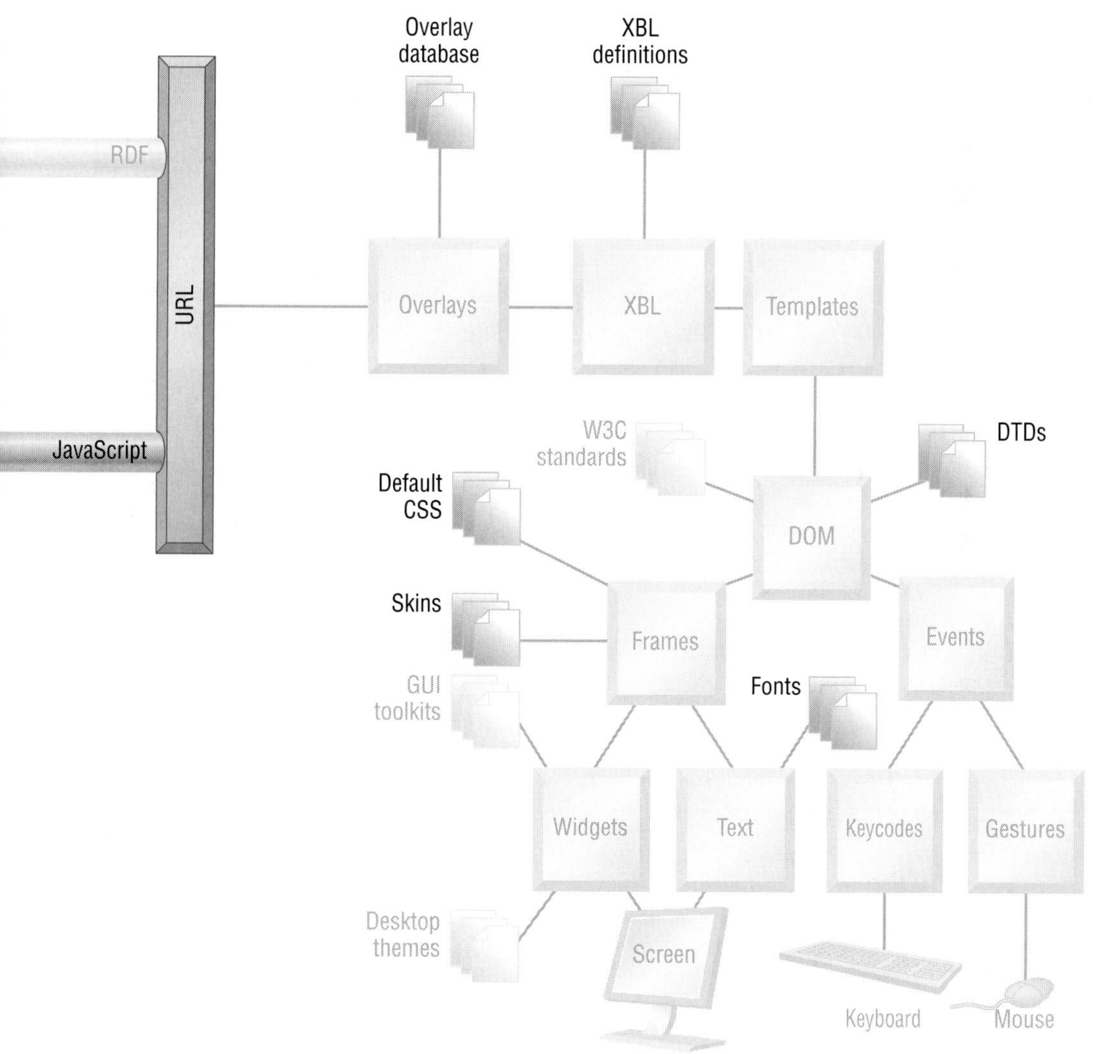

This chapter describes how to distribute your application to the world from a Web site. Doing so is one use of Mozilla's XPInstall (Cross Platform Install) system.

Most Mozilla applications are built to be used. Before one can be used, it must be installed on some computer. Installation is part of the general problem of deployment. Mozilla supports a variety of deployment strategies. This chapter notes all those strategies but focuses on automatic deployment of applications from a URL served up by an ordinary Web server.

Deploying software from a remote server has been a glamorous idea ever since Java applets first appeared, and now is part of Microsoft's .NET strategy. Such an approach makes reaching the user or customer easy, reduces the cost of distribution to nearly nothing, and naturally fits with traditional client-server architectures. As the speed of the Internet increases, the arguments for locally managed applications weaken in favor of service providers, especially in business. Even when the application is a standalone one, a flow of patches, revisions, and news items can preserve a vital communication channel with the users.

Mozilla contains a portable installation system called XPInstall. There is no need for tools outside Mozilla like InstallShield or `rpm(1)`; XPInstall is all you need. XPInstall can be user activated from any running Mozilla application, like a browser, or it can accompany a batch-oriented standalone executable.

Deployment doesn't have the same glamour as throwing together a bunch of windows for a demo—deployment is supposed to just work. That supposedly simple goal, however, is a major test of your ability to be organized. If your deployment system is well organized, the world will give you silence, but may use your application. If your deployment system has any flaws at all, your application will probably sink without a trace.

Central to deployment is the idea of a bundle. A *bundle* is just a collection of files and scripts that make up an application. RPMs, tarballs, and executable archives are all examples of bundles. By talking about bundles, this chapter avoids clashing with other terms like *package*, *application*, and *installer*, which all have their own meanings within Mozilla. In Mozilla, bundles are XPI (`.xpi` suffix) files or executables. XPI is an acronym for Cross(X) Platform Install. XPI files are just ZIP files, with a few extra conventions imposed.

The other side of deployment is installation. In this chapter, installation means copying pieces of the bundle to the local computer. It is possible to bundle an application so that it can be installed on any operating system that Mozilla supports. Because operating systems have their differences, installation sometimes has to dip down into platform-specific details. Nevertheless, at least 90% of bundle preparation can be done in a portable way.

In the case of remote deployment, XPInstall retrieves XPI files like Java's JVM retrieves applet JAR files. Unlike JAR files, XPI files are not held within a "sandbox." They can install to any part of the platform or to any part of the underlying operating system. Both the platform and the operating system can be damaged if a bundle is poorly organized. The safest and most common strategy is to install only into the chrome area.

Mozilla's Platform source code is not required to make a deployable application, but if a complex install strategy is chosen, then access to a working Mozilla compilation environment becomes more important.

The NPA diagram at the start of this chapter shows the impact that XPInstall has on the Mozilla Platform. From the diagram, XPInstall can be used to install all the various files that a running platform instance relies on. In fact, the whole NPA diagram could be highlighted because XPInstall can be used to replace even dynamic link libraries and executables—everything. Such broad-brush changes are a rare event, however. Two things are entirely missing from the diagram: application files and XPInstall itself. Application files, like XUL, CSS, RDF, and JavaScript files, are separate from the platform proper but are the most commonly installed files. XPInstall is a small world unto itself, which is why it doesn't appear. It is best seen as a specialized download tool like an FTP client or WinAMP.

XPInstall both uses and provides familiar technologies. The deployment process is scripted with JavaScript, and there are specialist objects available that assist. XPInstall presents a series of interactive windows to the user. A few XUL tags aim to do the same thing.

This chapter begins with a quick review of all the install options. It follows that with a description of remote install and finishes with a run-down of the technologies involved.

17.1 Overview of Install Strategies

Every option you can imagine is available for installing Mozilla-based applications. The options considered here are *no install*, *manual install*, *piggy-back install*, *native install*, and *custom install*. *Remote installs*, the main subject of this chapter, have a separate and extensive discussion of their own.

The simplest way to access a Mozilla-based application is with *no install* at all. In this case, the users already have the Mozilla Platform on their computers. Your application is served over the Web as a series of XUL files and their various inclusions, such as overlays, stylesheets, and scripts. To serve XUL documents from a Web site, just make sure that the Web server sets the MIME type for `.xul` files to be

```
application/vnd.mozilla.xul+xml
```

If suitable digital security is in place, such an application can have as much access to the local computer as any chrome-based application.

The Web is still slow, so some attention to performance helps. XUL documents, scripts, and stylesheets are cached in the browser cache just as all Web documents are, so if cache space is available, that is a start. Correct cache settings in the client browser and on the server can reduce to near-zero the overhead of downloading. On the client, the XUL cache should be enabled, and Quick Launch functionality should be turned on for the Windows platform. FastLoad raises the platform into memory at operating system boot time, just like Internet Explorer. FastLoad is enabled when Mozilla or Netscape is first installed; it is a simple preference. XUL applications can also be deployed as JAR files, which further assists with performance. The URL of a file stored in a JAR file has the form

```
jar:{url}!{path}
```

where `{url}` is the location of the JAR archive, and `{path}` is the location of a given file within it. If the JAR file `example.jar` is stored at the top of the chrome and contains the file `test/sample.xul`, then the full path name for `sample.xul` would be

```
jar:resource:/chrome/example.jar!test/sample.xul
```

As discussed in Chapter 12, Overlays and Chrome, the `resource:` URL scheme is a scheme that points to the top of the platform install area, and `chrome:` URLs are typically mapped to `resource:` URLs.

If the `-chrome` command-line option or an application-specific command-line option is used (like `-jsconsole`), a XUL application may be started so that no hint of browser-like functionality appears. Such an application looks the same as any native executable.

If an install system seems like a good idea, then the options are as follows.

If a local install is required, then the most primitive solution is to do it manually. *Manual installation* requires access to the file system and operating system shell of the target platform.

There are good reasons for doing a manual application installation. For developers, it is a quick way to test work that is in progress. For system administrators, manual installation steps can be rolled up into existing deployment tools and processes. For systems integrators, the resources used by manual installations are the COTS (common-off-the-shelf) interfaces needed to combine applications into larger, integrated systems.

The different kinds of manual installations are *platform install*, *component install*, *application install*, and *security install*. Platform install means installing the Mozilla Platform itself. This always requires an operating-system–specific executable and is called a *native install* here. After that is done, other types of manual installations are possible.

Manual component install adds new XPCOM components and interfaces to the installed platform. These components are then available to all applications installed. To install new components and interfaces:

1. **Create a Mozilla module**. A module is an implementation of one or more components and one or more interfaces, so this is a programming task. The module will be either a JavaScript `.js` file or a compiled language like C or C++.

2. **Create components**. To do this, turn the module into executable code. Nothing needs to be done for a `.js` file. C/C++ implementations need to be compiled into a dynamic link library using the Mozilla build environment.
3. **Create interfaces**. An interface is specified in an `.idl` file, which the component creator must write. Run the XPIDL `.idl` file through the `xpidlgen` tool to produce an `.xpt` type library file. `xpidlgen` is part of the build environment of Mozilla, so interface creation requires that you build the Mozilla source, or find a build with debug turned on.
4. **Copy the `.js` and `.xpt` file to the `components` directory under the platform install directory**. Alternately, copy the dynamic link library there. Ensure that copied files are readable (and executable if libraries).
5. **Run the tool `regxpcom` from the Mozilla install directory**. This tool is supplied with the platform. It generates manifests in files called `compreg.dat` and `xpti.dat`.
6. **Restart the platform**, which then benefits from the new `.dat` files. The component and its interfaces can now be used from scripts.

The Mozilla source code contains an example component called `nsSample` with an example interface called `nsISample`. See the source code directory `xpcom/sample`.

Manual application install adds new XUL-related files to the chrome. Such files are divided into packages. To add packages to the chrome, follow these steps:

1. **Create a package**. A package is a set of files layed out using the standard chrome directory structure of content, skins, and locales. Such files may be bundled into a JAR archive or left as a simple hierarchy of folders and files.
2. **Create and add `contents.rdf` files to the package**. A package is not really a package without these files. There should be one for the content directory, one for each skin, and one for each locale.
3. **Copy the package or folder hierarchy to the chrome directory**.
4. **Update the file `installed-chrome.txt`**, located in the chrome directory. At most one line should appear for each of the content, locale, and skin subparts of the package.
5. **Delete the `chrome/overlayinfo` directory**, if this package has been installed before (you are updating it). This will cause the overlay system to be recalculated.
6. **Restart the platform**.

All of these steps are illustrated with the NoteTaker examples in the first five chapters of this book. Chapter 12, Overlays and Chrome, discusses the mechanics of the chrome registry, which is the user of these files.

Lines added to installed-chrome.txt should be of the form

```
skin,install,url,{url}/
locale,install,url,{url}/
content,install,url,{url}/
```

where {url} must refer to a local directory and should generally be a jar: or a resource: URL. The resource: scheme points to the very top of the Mozilla installation area—the parent directory of the chrome directory. Locale URLs must include a locale name, like en-US; skin URLs must include a theme name, like modern.

A security install may be required for applications installed outside the chrome. Such applications can be installed on a local disk, or served from a Web site, and still run in a secure environment. If this secure environment is to be available without user effort, custom configuration files must be added to the platform. Such files must be created manually but can be installed either by hand or in an automated way.

To create these files, start by creating a new user profile using the Mozilla Profile Manager. Copy all files in that profile to one side so that the originals are preserved. Next, install the application in its final location. Run the application using that profile, with no special preferences or other changes. Every time the platform asks you to grant security access (perhaps to a digitally signed file or to a form submission), agree. Every time the platform offers to remember such a decision, confirm that it should. When all security aspects have been run through, shut down the application and copy any files in the profile that have changed from the originals. These are the files that need to be manually installed into the user profile on all computers to which they are deployed. Alternately, these can be installed into the default user profile.

Both piggy-back and native installs require use and modification of the Mozilla build environment. The build environment is not addressed in this book, but a few remarks are worth making.

A piggy-back install is a normal distribution of Mozilla modified to include extra application files. Such a distribution has two strengths: It contains an absolutely standard version of the platform (and Mozilla application suite), and it collects all required install tasks together into one familiar bundle. When the platform is installed, the additional applications are automatically available.

To make this work, the Mozilla build system must be altered. Fortunately, some of that system is data-driven. A small start is to look at example files under the directory xpinstall/packager. At least three changes are required:

1. The manifest that lists all the files to put into the final bundle must be updated. Files like packages-unix should be changed to do this.
2. The configuration of the interactive wizard that installs the platform must be updated. This configuration exists in files with .it suffixes.

3. The additional application files must be made available so that they can be included. Somehow they must appear in the `dist` (distribution) directory created by the build process at the top of the source tree. That directory is where the results of the make process are collected together. Hand-copying the required files is at best a temporary hack, but it can work.

If these first steps are done correctly, then a full compile of the product will produce a modified installation, but with one caveat. That caveat is that the build system has many subtlies and so no quick changes are immune from problems. Extensive study is likely before all this will work in a polished manner.

A native install involves a core part of the XPInstall subsystem. This core part is a small piece of platform-specific code. That code does not use XPCOM or any of the facilities of the Mozilla Platform; it is an independent program with its own support for TCP/IP, FTP, and HTTP. To do anything with this code requires familiarity with the Mozilla source code. It can be used three ways:

- In a full install, this XPInstall code is part of a large archive holding all the platform and application, which on Microsoft Windows is also an auto-install binary.
- In a so-called stub install, the distribution file is small (a stub) and contains this XPInstall code and a little configuration information. When the installation is started, the code connects to the Internet and downloads the platform components selected by the user.
- In an application install, this XPInstall code is used as a specialist installer for a particular application, separate from the core platform. This use is as close as XPInstall gets to acting like InstallShield or the `rpm` system. This use is not yet common and is really a variation on a full install.

The Netscape Client Customization Kit can slightly customize a native install, provided it is based on a Netscape 7.0 release. This tool is available at *http://devedge.netscape.com*. It has a very restrictive license, which makes it nearly useless for Open Source purposes, or even for commercial purposes.

XPInstall's native code also has some portable features. It contains a JavaScript interpreter, some XUL-like GUI code, some objects, and some operating system access. Together these are enough to extract the contents from one or more XPI bundles and to place them in the operating system's file system. This portion of XPInstall deploys both the platform and applications in the style of InstallShield.

The remote install case that is examined in this chapter uses this same native infrastructure. Not only is that infrastructure available in an installation binary, but it is also available inside the running Mozilla Platform. A hook in the browser object model allows an XPI file to be passed to this special native code, causing installation to commence.

Finally, a Mozilla application can ignore the XPInstall system altogether. That is a custom install. XUL and XPCOM technology is sufficiently powerful that all steps required to install an application can be done from the chrome. If you really need your own installation system, then there is nothing stopping you from creating one. The XUL tags described under the topic "Install Technologies" allow a dialog window that acts like an installation wizard to be easily created.

Netscape's Smart Update feature is an application built on top of XPInstall.

17.2 Steps Toward Remote Deployment

Overall, remote installation is an information distribution method that follows the publishing model of the traditional media. To build an application bundle for remote deployment via the Web is to be a publisher.

To deploy an application remotely, several things must happen. The application programmer, in the role of a release engineer, must prepare a little and write two scripts. The end user must agree to install the application. The platform itself must act on the instructions provided.

Remote deployment relies on the use of a URL. Mozilla's remote deployment system can use a `file:` URL just as easily as an `http:` URL. Therefore, all the remarks made here can also be applied to a deployment that starts and ends on the local file system.

17.2.1 What the Programmer Does

Here are the tasks that the programmer needs to complete so that an application can be deployed remotely by the user. The deployment system can be developed in parallel with other application development tasks.

17.2.1.1 Assigning Names and Versions The first step of deployment is to give the application names. Several names are needed for XPInstall to work. These names include a *text name*, a *package name*, a *registry application name*, and a *version*. Platform-specific names are also required. On Microsoft Windows, a Windows registry key is useful. Macintosh Aliases and Microsoft Windows Shortcuts might also be required. It is sensible for all these names, except for versions, to have the same root. A root is just a word that other words grow from. Other marks, like mastheads, brands, and command-line names aren't an explicit part of XPInstall. XPInstall does not support a graphical representation of the application, such as an icon.

The text name is a Unicode string that appears in the dialog boxes that XPInstall presents to the user. Because it is Unicode, it can contain © or ® or ™ symbols, among others. XPInstall presents this string in Latin left-to-right order, which is restrictive for some languages. An example text name is

```
Frederick's Amazing Shopping Spree System, Gold Version
```

The package name is the name of the chrome package that the application will be installed under (assuming that it is to go into the chrome). It is an 8-bit extended ASCII name and, for absolute portability, should be 8 characters or less and alphabetic (UNIX: 14 characters or less). Because it is used as a folder (file system directory) name, it shouldn't contain any punctuation, except perhaps the underscore. There isn't any need to include a version number (e.g., `netscape7`) in the package name, unless two different versions are to be installed at the same time. If the application is not installed under the chrome, then an install directory name has much the same rules as a package name. An example package name is

```
fredshop
```

The registry application name is a name that the Mozilla Platform uses to manage the application on the local host. It is used for version management, installation, and uninstallation. Mozilla's registries are described later in "Install Technologies." A registry name looks like a UNIX path, except that it can include Unicode characters. It is encoded in UTF8 inside the registry. Most registry application names follow a syntax convention like this:

```
/Application Publisher/short-name/subproduct
```

The `Application Publisher` part might be corporate or technical. A corporate version might just state `Alpha Trading Company`. A technical version might be a domain name in a similar convention to Java packages, like "`mozilla.org`". The short-name part is the application's name and usually is similar to the package name (e.g., `Navigator`). The subproduct part is optional and is used where the application is a suite of tools—one such tool might be a subpart of the larger application. An example from Mozilla is

```
/mozilla.org/Mozilla/JavaScript Debugger/Venkman Chrome
```

This example shows subproducts nested two levels deep. `Venkman Chrome` is a subproduct of the `JavaScript Debugger`, which is a subpart of Mozilla-the-application.

If the leading `/` is left off, then the path is considered to be a subpath and will be prefixed by `/mozilla.org/Mozilla/` (or by `/Netscape/` for Netscape versions of the platform).

In fact, the registry application name can be any path delimited by forward slash characters; there isn't any implicit meaning to the first or subsequent parts. The name does not need to match a directory name; it is just a hierarchical key in the style of Windows Registry keys. It has a length limit of about 2,000 characters. An example is

```
/Fred's Pyramid Company/Amazing Shopping Spree System/Gold Version
```

Mozilla application versions have a fixed format, which is a four-part number. A version can be expressed as four 32-bit integers or as a string of period-separated integers. The string should be easily convertible to four integers—it should not have a "beta" suffix or other junk. The string version has the format:

```
"{major}.{minor}.{revision}.{build}"
```

- The major number starts from 0 and should change only when the application's designer significantly changes the application's design.
- The minor number starts from 0 and indicates feature additions to the base application. Applications based on earlier minor numbers should be able to interoperate with this version.
- The revision number starts from 0 and indicates bug fixes and trivial changes at most. Except for these fixes, earlier versions should operate identically.
- The build number is used to track a specific attempt at generating the application from its source. It comes from the build process and is a unique key of some sort.

An example version string is

```
"1.0.2.20021018"
```

Many unenforced conventions apply to these numbers. Some of these conventions follow:

- The build number uniquely identifies a single compilation or packaging pass. It might be a sequence number or a date. A 32-bit integer is big enough to hold a decimal number consisting of digits from the sequence full year-month-day-hour, until at least year 2200. An example for 9 A.M., 28 February 2003 is 2003022809. This is the system that Mozilla uses.
- The Linux kernel and some other products use even minor numbers to indicate a stable release, and odd minor numbers to indicate an in-progress work. Mozilla does not use this system. Minor numbers always indicate user releases.
- If the major number is zero, the product is considered to be under fundamental construction. No user should expect such an application to work with any previous version, no matter how minor. Any such compatibility is just a lucky convenience.

17.2.1.2 Organizing the World Naming an application is easy. Organizing one is harder.

It is in the application developer's best interest to ensure that when the user deploys the application, that user has a good experience. This is because when users choose to deploy, they also choose to trust the Web site that offers the application. That trust must be maintained, or a bad reputation will be the only result.

Therefore, the second step for deployment is a release review. For the deployment strategy to work cleanly, the release engineer must have a clear understanding of what is being deployed and where. That means capturing some configuration information. The README document supplied with the Mozilla browser suite is an example of this information, but such thinking should go further. Three sets of information need to be captured: a *baseline*, a *footprint*, and a *target*.

A *baseline* is a reference point for the origin of an application bundle. It can be as simple as a CD burn of all the source files in the application or as organized as a CVS tag that includes a fully automated build and bundling system. If you can't re-create an application's bundle reliably, you can't test the deployment system properly or offer patches later. If your application is based on an Open Source license, then you are required by that license to produce a baseline ("the source") and to make it available to everyone.

For simple applications, just copy the source to a backup before each release.

A *footprint* represents the impact an installed application has on the end user's computer. It is a list of all the files on the destination computer that are affected by the application installed. The purpose of a footprint is to nail down every place on the user's computer that might be modified by the installing or running application. When user number 52,345 rings up for help with a messed-up PC, the footprint describes the boundaries of the problem space.

Examples of common footprint items are the Windows Registry, desktop shortcuts, `.ini` or `.rc` files, environment variables, global MIME types, and boot scripts. Inside Mozilla, running applications might also affect preferences files, security settings, and local MIME types. Applications might add components to the Mozilla components directory, add special-purpose binary utilities, or modify shell scripts used to start the platform.

If a bundle deploys files outside the platform install area, then those files should not automatically be put under `C:\Program Files` (Windows) or under `/usr` (UNIX). That is a very irritating practice for IT people who must configuration-manage their systems. Instead, ensure that the application can be entirely installed under a single folder of the user's choosing. Never put files in `/etc` or `C:\Windows` or `C:\Winnt` unless it is impossible to avoid doing so.

For simple applications, the footprint should go no further than the chrome directory and Mozilla registries. If users elect to save application-generated files elsewhere, that is their business.

Finally, a *target* is a description of the computing environment for which the application is designed. Such a description includes hardware, operating system, existing applications, specific files or configurations, required disk space—everything. A target description is the basis of a README file that the user might see. It is also used to identify checks that installation scripts need to do.

For simple, portable applications, a target consists of no more than a minimum version of the Mozilla Platform.

These three documents keep the application deployment process orderly and sane. You don't want the wrong software on the wrong computer complicating the wrong operating system files.

17.2.1.3 Scripts To automate application deployment, you must write up to two scripts.

The first script runs in an ordinary HTML Web page or in a XUL document. No special security arrangements are necessary. This script works only when the page is viewed with Mozilla technology. The rest of the page holds an invitation to the user to grab the application. The second script, called `install.js`, runs inside the XPInstall part of the platform, where it is isolated from the Web and from XPCOM.

Both scripts benefit from JavaScript host objects. The objects noted in the following overview are covered in full in "Install Technologies."

The first script is a so-called trigger script; it starts the application deployment. Two objects are available, and a third must be created from pure JavaScript. The two objects available are the `window.InstallTrigger` object and the `InstallVersion` object, which is also available as `window.InstallVersion`.

The `InstallTrigger` object contains diagnostic methods, plus the `install()` method, which starts the download of XPI files and eventually calls one or more copies of the second script, `install.js`. The diagnostic methods can be used to do some basic version checks and to tell whether `XPInstall` is enabled.

The `InstallVersion` object is a convenience object that can compare two application versions and report which is greater and which of the four version numbers are different.

The third object, which the application programmer must make, has this form:

```
var xpi_container = {
    "Test app part 1"  :  "URL1",
    "Test app part 2"  :  "URL2",
    ...
}
```

This object represents all the XPI files that together make up an application and is passed to the `InstallTrigger.install()` method. The preceding example object contains two properties, and so represents two XPI files. Any number of properties greater than zero is allowed. Because both properties have names that are literal strings, they can only be read using array notation like this:

```
var url = xpi_container["Test app part 1"];
```

Each property name is a text name for that application component, and the user will see it. Each property value is a URL (relative or absolute), which must be an XPI file. The URL may have a parameter string appended. That parameter string starts with ?, which is the same as parameters in an HTTP GET request. The remainder of the parameter string can follow HTTP GET syntax, or it can be any string (although that is a poor design choice). An example URL is

```
/downloads/apps/mozilla/shopcart/main.xpi?java=yes;flash=no
```

This URL is a relative URL, so Mozilla will add `http:` and a domain. In this example, the trigger code has detected the presence of Java and the absence of the Flash plugin and has passed that information to the second script `install.js` via parameters `java` and `flash`. The parameter portion of an XPI URL is passed directly to the `install.js` script without further processing.

All these objects are combined into a function that is usually called from an `onclick` handler on a link or a button. Listing 17.1 is a skeleton of such a function that shows most of the functionality it might contain.

Listing 17.1 Skeleton for a full-featured XPInstall trigger script.

```
function deploy()
{
  if ( !is_moz_browser() ) { return false; }
  if ( !window.InstallTrigger.enabled() { return false; }
  if ( !is_target() ) { return false; }
  if ( !is_app_version_ok() } { return false; }

  var       error_flag = false;
  function error_handler(url, err) { error_flag = true; };

  calculate_params();
  var       xpi_container = { ... };

  with (window.InstallTrigger)
    install(xpi_container, error_handler);

  return !error_flag;
}
```

Most of the functions used in this script need to be filled out for each application. The initial series of tests aborts the deployment if anything is wrong, including problems with the user's computer and problems with applications already installed. The `error_handler()` function is simplistic and can be made more complex if necessary. The `calculate_params()` function prepares whatever information needs to be passed to the second script. That information is used in the creation of the `xpi_container` object. Finally, `install()` is called to make the whole thing go. Of course, nothing happens if JavaScript is disabled, or if the preference `xpinstall.enabled` is set to `false`.

Testing the user's computer to see if it matches the target is a challenging task. The browser environment is limited to Web Safe scripts, and the XPInstall environment cannot access XPCOM components. Tests may need to be split over both places. If complex testing is needed, then write a separate application devoted to platform testing and ask the user to install that first. That application can then be used in trigger scripts from then on.

The second script to be written is always called `install.js`. Each XPI archive must contain one of these scripts. This second script is responsible for putting each file in the XPI archive in the correct spot in the local file system. The file-copying work is not done directly in the script. Instead, the script provides the XPInstall system with a series of file placement instructions. When all the instructions are scheduled, XPInstall is told to go ahead and do them all. When that happens, XPInstall automatically executes, records, and logs its actions; handles errors; and saves information for a future uninstall. At any point before the go-ahead is given, the `install.js` script can abort the installation. `install.js` can hack on the operating system a little as well.

The environment that `install.js` runs in is very restrictive. It runs in a separate JavaScript interpreter context and has its own global object, which is not an HTML or XUL window object. Only a few objects exist with which the script can work. Their names are

```
Install InstallVersion File FileSpecObject WinProfile WinReg
```

The `Install` object is the global object for the JavaScript context, so its methods can be called directly as though they were functions. It is the central object and has factory methods that can be used to create objects of the other types.

The `Install` object has useful properties. The `platform` property states the operating system. The `arguments` property contains any parameters, and the `url` property contains the full XPI URL.

The `Install` object also has useful methods: `initInstall()`, which primes XPInstall so that it is ready to accept instructions; `cancelInstall()`, which aborts everything; `performInstall()`, which runs the install according to instructions; and `uninstall()`, which removes applications. There are also useful diagnostic features.

The `File` and `FileSpecObject` objects are separate from any XPCOM file concepts—they are separate and different implementations with similar features. They can be used to manipulate files and directories anywhere on the local computer. Some special names that allow this to be done portably are available. The `File` object can also perform a few tests on the operating system and other miscellany.

The `WinProfile` and `WinReg` objects are Microsoft Windows specific. `WinProfile` provides read/write access to an `.INI` configuration file, and `WinReg` provides read/write access to the Windows Registry.

Depending on its contents, the `install.js` script might require that the platform be restarted; it also might require that the platform reassess the chrome or plugins when that restart happens. None of these side effects affects the processing of the script itself. As for the trigger script, `install.js` has a standard pattern of use. Listing 17.2 shows this pattern.

Listing 17.2 Skeleton for a full-featured XPInstall `install.js` script.

```
var TEXT_NAME = "Test Application Release 3.2";
var REG_NAME  = "/Test Company/Test Application";
var VERSION   = "3.2.0.1999";
var params;
var rv = SUCCESS;

function prepare()
{
  if ( !(params = parse_args())) return INVALID_ARGUMENTS;
  if ( is_target() != SUCCESS )   return getLastError();

  initInstall(TEXT_NAME, REG_NAME, VERSION);

  /* -- as many functions like this as required -- */
  if ( schedule_folders()!= SUCCESS) return getLastError();
  if ( schedule_files() != SUCCESS ) return getLastError();
  if ( modify_os() != SUCCESS )      return getLastError();
  if ( run_any_programs() != SUCCESS)return getLastError();
  if ( register_chrome() != SUCCESS) return getLastError();

  return SUCCESS;
}

rv = prepare();
(rv == SUCCESS) ? performInstall() : cancelInstall(rv);
```

The script relies on error codes that the `Install` object maintains and returns when something goes wrong. The first step is to ensure that any arguments passed from the trigger script are in good order, and that the user's computer is suitable for install. If that is all okay, then `initInstall()` primes XPInstall to receive install instructions. Each function that follows does part of the work required to set up the installation. When these functions are called, few errors result because each installation instruction is only recorded, not performed. Finally, if all goes well, everything is run at once with `performInstall()`. Not shown are logging messages that can be recorded to a file with the `logComment()` method, or progress reports that can be sent to the user with `alert()` or `confirm()`. `prompt()` is not available as a method.

The simplest version of this skeleton, useful for testing, is shown in Listing 17.3.

Listing 17.3 Complete `install.js` script for a simple chrome application.

```
var TEXT_NAME = "Test Application Release 3.2";
var REG_NAME  = "/Test Company/Test Application";
var VERSION   = "3.2.0.1999";
```

```
var rv = SUCCESS;

function schedule_folders()
{
  var tree = getFolder("Chrome"); // Special keyword
  setPackageFolder(tree);
  addDirectory("chrome");         // topmost directory
}

function prepare()
{
  initInstall(TEXT_NAME, REG_NAME, VERSION);
  if ( schedule_folders()!= SUCCESS) return getLastError();
  return SUCCESS;
}

rv = prepare();
(rv == SUCCESS) ? performInstall() : cancelInstall(rv);
```

This example cuts down the `prepare()` function so that it is nearly trivial and adds an implementation of the `schedule_folders()` function. That implementation contains the critical step of matching a directory hierarchy in the XPI file against a directory hierarchy on the local file system. The hierarchy in the file will be copied to that file system.

The mechanics of this process are as follows. The special keyword `Chrome`, one of only a few such keywords, is used to pick out the chrome folder in the platform's install area. This keyword is independent of operating system, but other keywords exist that are operating system specific. That folder is made of the target directory (effectively the current directory). Finally, the folder named "`chrome`" in the XPI file is singled out to be copied. In fact, only the children of that XPI folder (and all their descendants) will be copied.

In Listing 17.3, all files in the XPI bundle (except `install.js`) have as their topmost directory the name `chrome`. That part of the path could be replaced with `X` or `Part1` or any other text string because it is just a placeholder. Everything will still work, provided that the `addDirectory()` call is changed to match.

If the XPI file is layed out using "`chrome`" as the placeholder, then good choices of file names within it are

```
chrome/content/TestApp/TestApp.xul
chrome/locale/en-US/TestApp/master.dtd
chrome/skin/classic/TestApp/global.css
```

Folders in the file system are matched against folders in the XPI bundle, and this can be repeated several times in the one bundle. An XPI bundle can contain several trees with different topmost directories. For example, if an XPI contained three installable subtrees, each subtree can be matched to a different location on the local disk. Such an XPI file might contain

```
install.js
subtree1/file1
subtree1/file2
subtree2/file3
subtree2/file4
subtree3/file5
subtree3/file6
```

Each subtree of two files can be placed in a different location by the one install script.

Finally, if an application is to be uninstalled, then the `uninstall()` method can also be used between `initInstall()` and `performInstall()`. It schedules an instruction that will uninstall an application based on historical information in the Mozilla registry. That uninstall will also occur when the other scheduled instructions are executed.

17.2.1.4 XPI Files An XPI file has the format of an ordinary ZIP file. Use WinZip, `pkzip`, or similar programs on Microsoft Windows; use `zip(1)`, not `gzip(1)`, on UNIX. Path names in ZIP files are always relative paths.

Such a file has one content requirement: It must contain at the top level an `install.js` file. It is common practice that the rest of the content directory structure matches the directory structure of the platform's installation area. If the XPI file directory structure doesn't match that area, then the `install.js` script will be more complicated.

It is possible to sign an XPI file digitally. Digital signing is done with the Netscape SignTool tool, as for all digitally signed files in Mozilla, but there is one restriction. The digital signature must be the first item in the XPI ZIP file. The digital signature is a file with path `META-INF/{signature}`, where `{signature}` is a file name indicating an encrypted signature of a type that Mozilla supports. Be aware that tools like WinZip use sorted views that can confuse the apparent order—display the ZIP file in "original order" to be sure or use `unzip(1)` or `pkunzip`. For more about SignTool and digital signing, consult *http://devedge.netscape.com*.

Figure 17.1 shows the contents of the XPI bundle for the Chatzilla instant messaging client. It is a ZIP file. This bundle is typically installed when the Classic Mozilla application suite is installed. That installation is done locally by Mozilla's native install system. The file could equally be installed from a remote location using the remote install part of the platform.

The topmost directory, named `bin` in this case, collects together all the files into one subtree. There are versions of this XPI for each operating system platform; for example, the UNIX version replaces `.ICO` files with `.XBM` files. On all platforms the `chatzilla.jar` file inside the bundle contains all the chrome files for the Chatzilla application. This JAR file can be seen in the `chrome` area of any installed copy of the Mozilla application suite. The `chatzilla-service.js` file is a new XPCOM component that is delivered with the application. That component registers command-line options

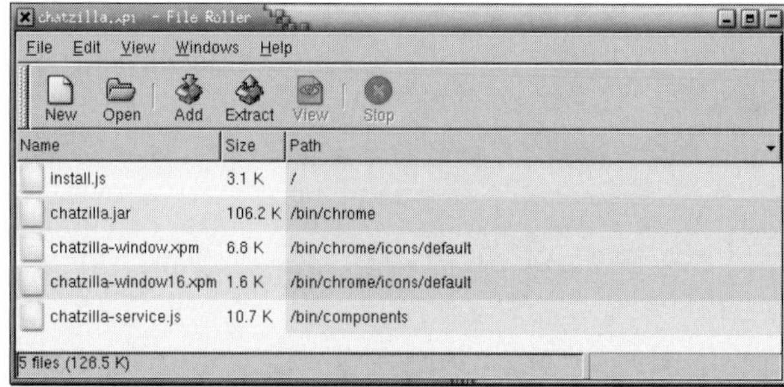

Fig. 17.1 Chatzilla XPI file for Microsoft Windows.

(`-chat`) and a URL scheme (`irc://`) with the platform that integrates Chatzilla with the rest of the platform.

17.2.1.5 Shorthand for No-Content XPI If the XPI file only implements a skin or a locale, then the scripting process can be shortened. No `install.js` script is needed in that case. In the trigger script, call `installChrome()` instead of `install()`. Because installing skins or locales cannot fail (unless disk space is very low), the trigger script is reduced to a single line.

In this case, files inside the XPI file are copied directly into the chrome directory. Those inside files should be JAR files.

17.2.1.6 Shorthand for MIME Types If the XPI file is served up by a Web server so that it has MIME type

```
application/x-xpinstall
```

then the XPInstall system will handle that file automatically. In that case, there is no need for a script placed on an event handler in the application code. Any `install.js` script provided inside the XPI file will still be run.

The application programmer also has the option of avoiding the XPInstall system entirely. The XUL tags described in "Install Technologies" allow a dialog box that acts like an installation wizard to be created easily.

17.2.2 What the User Does

The user chooses whether to deploy the application. The experience he has with the install process is shown in the following sequence of figures. The first thing he sees is a document separate from the to-be-installed application, as shown in Figure 17.2.

This is an HTML page, but it could be a XUL document, in which case the trigger script might be less obvious than a button. In this example, one application consisting of three XPI bundles is specified by the trigger script. Next, the user sees a dialog box as in Figure 17.3.

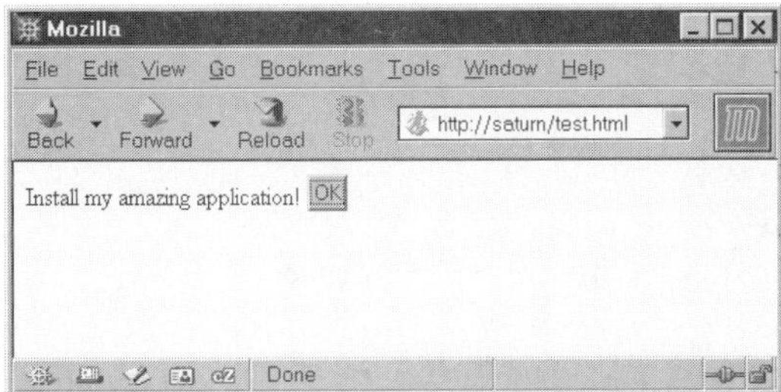

Fig. 17.2 Step 1 of remote deployment: an HTML page.

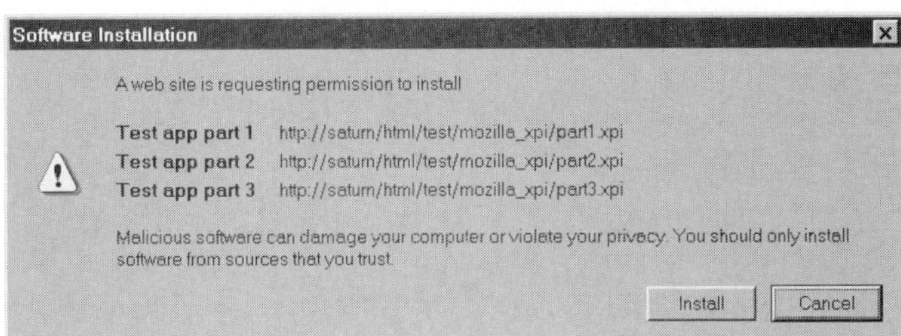

Fig. 17.3 Step 2 of remote deployment: picking list display.

This dialog box reports the goods to be received. If the user chooses Cancel, everything is aborted. If the user agrees, the installation starts immediately and may complete with no further opportunities to back out. After this picking list, a progress dialog box is displayed, as shown in Figure 17.4.

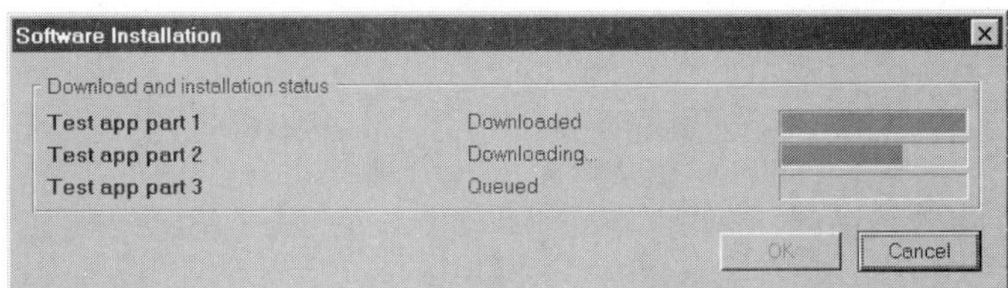

Fig. 17.4 Step 3 of remote deployment: application bundle download.

The listed bundles are downloaded in order. The contained `install.js` files are run as soon as their XPI bundle is available. Unless they contain specific code, these scripts finish without user interaction. If prompts are displayed by the code in the script, they look just like ordinary JavaScript prompts, as Figure 17.5 shows.

After the `install.js` scripts have run, the outcome is either a canceled, a failed, or a completed installation. The user next sees a summary of the processing, as in Figure 17.6.

If the installation process requires that the application be restarted, then a final dialog box will advise the user of this.

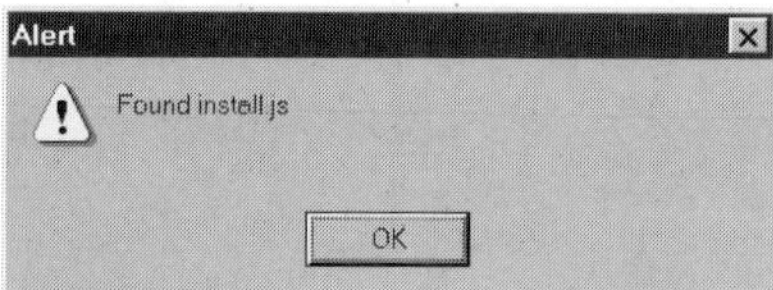

Fig. 17.5 Step 4 of remote deployment: optional user interaction.

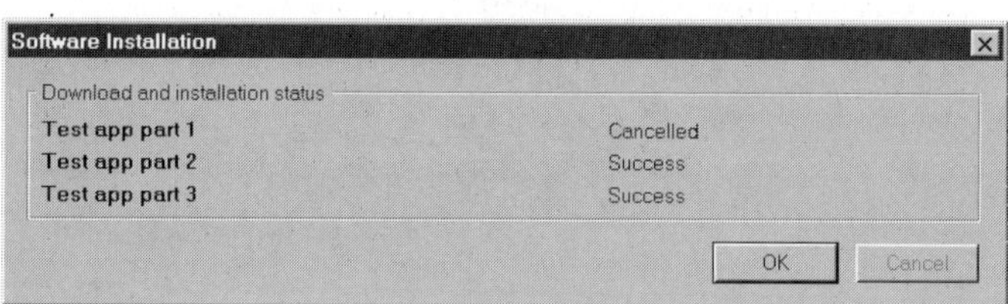

Fig. 17.6 Step 5 of remote deployment: results.

17.2.3 What the Platform Does

During remote deployment, the platform manages the process, receives instructions from the `install.js` script, does all the actions specified, and keeps a record of everything done. The following steps are performed:

1. Start the XPInstall system when `InstallTrigger.install()` or `InstallTrigger.installChrome()` is called. Present and manage the windows that the user sees.
2. Maintain a list of XPI archives to download. Download them to the operating system's temporary files directory. Don't use the Mozilla cache.
3. If the first item in a downloaded archive is a digital signature (detected by path name), then verify the signature. Fail only if verification against the right certificate is possible and fails; in that case, cease the download. Otherwise, continue.
4. Run each `install.js` file one at a time. There is no coordination between different `install.js` files other than their initial order. If one XPI file needs to know if an earlier one finished successfully, then application code must be written that separately tracks progress. That code might create a "touch file" or use Microsoft Windows registry keys as counters to track progress.
5. During the execution of an `install.js` file, record the information in steps 6 to 11.
6. Record any logged messages, plus some automatically produced text, in the file `chrome/install.log`.
7. Record in a Mozilla registry all the things that would need to be undone if the application were uninstalled.

8. Record in a Mozilla registry that this application and its version now exist.
9. Record in `chrome/installed-chrome.txt` the results of all calls to `registerChrome()`.
10. Record if the chrome or components need to be reassessed by the platform.
11. Record if a reboot is required.
12. Next, proceed to the scheduled instructions for the install.
13. Unpack whatever files are required. If file names or path names in the XPI bundle don't match those supplied in the script, do nothing and move to the next instruction.
14. Perform other operating system manipulations as instructed. If the instructions aren't possible or aren't sensible, report an error and do nothing, and then move on to the next instruction.
15. When the user restarts the platform, go through normal post-installation initialization: recalculate chrome overlays, XPCOM components, and available locales and skins.

That is the whole of the remote installation process. Version checking is entirely up to the application programmer and the `install.js` file.

The XPInstall system occasionally must reach out to the rest of the platform to get its job done. An example is the use of alert dialog boxes. If this is necessary, then scripts running elsewhere in the platform will be blocked until XPInstall has finished with the resources it needed. Usually any such blockage is brief and of little consequence.

17.3 Install Technologies

The remainder of this chapter describes the pieces of technology used or usable for remote installation.

17.3.1 File Uses and Formats

The platform's installation uses several different kinds of data files. There are three main uses for these files, and they are written in several different file formats. The three uses are registries, manifests, and logs.

- *Registries* are read/write files that the platform uses as simple databases that can be updated. Configuration, application, and version information is stored in registries.
- *Manifests* are read-only files. They act as bills-of-lading or picking lists; in other words, they describe what's provided. Mozilla uses manifests to list available XPCOM components, plugins, chrome files, overlays, and

some aspects of the build process. Manifests can sometimes be generated from other information.

- *Logs* are write-only files that can be independently examined. Mozilla creates logs for the initial platform install and for subsequent remote application installs. Extensive extra logging is possible if the platform used was compiled with `--enable-debug`.

Formats used for these files include the Mozilla registry format (described next), Microsoft Windows `.ini` format, and RDF and plain text. Table 17.1 lists all these formats and their uses.

17.3.2 Mozilla Registries

A Mozilla registry is a file that is similar in format to the Microsoft Windows registry. There is very little direct access to the registry, but a peek inside clears up some mysteries about the platform.

A Mozilla registry consists of a hierarchy of keys, each of which can have a set of attribute-value pairs. The keys can be named using a hierarchical description, which is effectively a path. At the top of the hierarchy is a root key named `/`, and several special names point to important parts of the hierarchy. These are equivalent to Microsoft's `HKEY_` names. Mozilla uses UTF8-encoded Unicode strings for the names in a registry path.

Unlike the Windows registry, the Mozilla registry uses forward slashes (`/`) to delimit steps in a key's fully qualified path. There are other differences as well.

Table 17.1 Installation documents used by the platform

File type	File names using this type	Use
Mozilla registry	mozver.dat, mozregistry.dat, registry, registry.dat, appreg, global.regs, versions.regs, "Mozilla Registry," "Mozilla Versions"	Registry of platform and application names and versions, uninstall information, plugins, and created user profiles
Microsoft Windows .ini	pluginreg.dat, pluginreg, xpti.dat, compreg.dat	Manifest of current plugins, current components, and XPConnect type libraries
	manifest.ini, master.ini, talkback.ini	Configuration files for Talkback-enabled releases
XML RDF	overlays.rdf, contents.rdf, various other per-profile files	Manifests of overlays and of JAR archive content
Line-formatted plain text	installed-chrome.txt, chromelist.txt	Manifests of chrome files that need to be considered for overlays, themes, and locales
Free format text	install.log, install_status.log	Log files for native and remote installation

- ☞ Mozilla does not, as yet, have a tool equivalent to `regedit` or `regedit32`.
- ☞ Interfaces to registries are not yet fully exposed to application programmers.
- ☞ Registries are cross-platform and appear on UNIX, MacOS, and other platforms.
- ☞ The platform maintains more than one registry per platform installation.

All Mozilla registries have the same top-level structure. Each registry consists of exactly one root (named `/`) with four immediate children:

```
"/Users/"
"/Common/"
"/Version Registry/"
"/Private Arenas/"
```

If special compilation options are turned on, then a fifth child exists: "`/Current User/`". This fifth child is not present in the default builds. A key held under one of the four names might have a full path like so:

```
"/Version Registry/mozilla.org/Mozilla/XPCom/bin"
```

This key does not look like an application registry name by accident—that is exactly what the string after "`/Version Registry`" is.

A Mozilla registry is effectively the boot information for the platform. A running platform instance seeks information from the registry after the operating system launches that instance. The most confusing aspect of registries is that there are several, and each one holds a different subset of the information. Table 17.2 attempts to clarify this.

The "chrome registry" is not a file in Mozilla registry format. It is a term that covers the RDF-driven configuration of the chrome, including the overlays database and supporting text files like `installed-chrome.txt`. See Chapter 12, Overlays and Chrome, for more on it.

The Mozilla registry cannot be accessed from an `install.js` script, unless a separate executable is run. It can be accessed from an ordinary application script using this XPCOM pair:

```
@mozilla.org/registry;1 nsIRegistry
```

This interface provides read/write methods and methods that can be used to traverse the tree of registry keys. The interface provides no obvious way to dump out the whole hierarchy from the root. A dirty trick, which has worked in the past, is to use the magic number `32` (hex 0x20) as an `nsRegistryKey` argument. That is the number of the root key. Be aware that neither the root nor its immediate children (the four well-known children) have any attribute-value pairs stored against them. Do not look for such pairs; only look for pairs further down the tree.

Table 17.2 Mozilla registries maintained by the platform

Everyday name	Single user O/S has	Multiuser O/S has	File names used	Keys populated	Use
Versions registry	One	One per O/S user	mozver.dat, "Mozilla Versions", Versions.regs	Versions Private arenas	Global registry of version information for all platform installations, including Netscape Global registry of uninstall information for all platform installations, including Netscape
Global registry	One	One per O/S user	mozregis-try.dat, "Mozilla Registry", registry, Global.regs	None	No current use
Application registry	One	One per O/S user	appreg, registry.dat	Common	Registry of all user profiles and of all available plugins and Java support
Component registry	One per platform installation	One per platform installation	compon-ent.reg , "Component Registry"	Common	Registry of all XPCOM components available

17.3.3 XUL Wizards

Occasionally an application needs to guide the user through a complicated procedure. Deploying software is one such procedure. A traditional way to manage the complexity is to provide a window or dialog box that assists the user step by step. Such a dialog box is sometimes called a *wizard*.

XUL supplies a `<wizard>` tag to assist with complex processes like installation. `<wizard>` is like a fancy combination of a `<deck>` and a `<dialog>` tag. Each `<wizard>` tag holds one or more `<wizardpage>` tags. Each of the `<wizardpage>` tags holds any XUL content.

Like the `<dialog>` tag, the `<wizard>` tag represents a whole window and is used in place of a `<window>` tag. Like cards in a deck, the set of `<wizardpage>` tags are laid on top of each other. The `<wizard>` tag supplies Next, Back, Cancel, and Finish buttons that let the user navigate between the pages, just as the tab labels in a `<tabbox>` provide navigation between tabs. Both `<wizard>` and `<wizardpage>` tags are based on XBL bindings stored in the file `wizard.xml` in `toolkit.jar` in the chrome.

In `toolkit.jar` in the chrome, there are also a number of files prefixed with "`wizard.`" These files add value to the basic `<wizard>` tag, particularly in the form of the WizardManager JavaScript object. If your application needs several wizards, it is worth examining this code for its value as a time-saver. It allows you to create a central object that holds all the scripting logic that ties the wizard GUI to your application. It is therefore an orderly way to proceed.

Figure 17.7 shows a window based on the `<wizard>` tag. This window is used in the Mozilla Email client to create a new News or Email account.

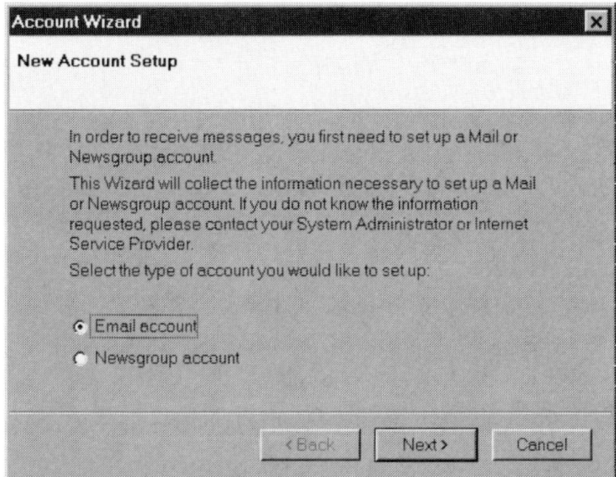

Fig. 17.7 Email account creation system based on the `<wizard>` tag.

None of this markup is used or usable from the normal remote install system discussed in this chapter. It can be used only for custom installs, in the chrome, or in remotely hosted applications.

17.3.3.1 <wizard>

The `<wizard>` tag provides some content, navigation logic, and event processing for the window it manages. The minimum the application programmer needs to do is supply the remaining content as a set of `<wizardpage>` tags (which usually consists of form elements and explanatory text) and scripts to validate and act on the choices the user makes. The `<wizard>` tag supports the following special attributes:

```
title pagestep firstpage lastpage onwizardnext onwizardback
     onwizardcancel onwizardfinish
```

- `title` specifies the string that will appear in the top part of the window, after the words "Welcome to the."
- `pagestep` specifies how many pages to jump when the Back or Next buttons are pressed. The default is 1 (one).
- `firstpage` is set to `true` by the wizard when the first page is being displayed.
- `lastpage` is set to `true` by the wizard when the last page is being displayed.

The remaining attributes are event handlers and fire when the Next, Back, Cancel, and Finish buttons are clicked. These event handlers all have sensible default actions. Like `<dialog>` and `<window>`, the `width`, `height`, `screenX`, and `screenY` attributes do nothing for the `<wizard>` tag. `<wizard>` automatically sets `width="500px"`, `height="380px"`.

In addition to attributes, the XBL definition for `<wizard>` has methods and properties that allow scripts to mimic the user's actions. Figure 17.8 shows the content that the `<wizard>` tag provides for free.

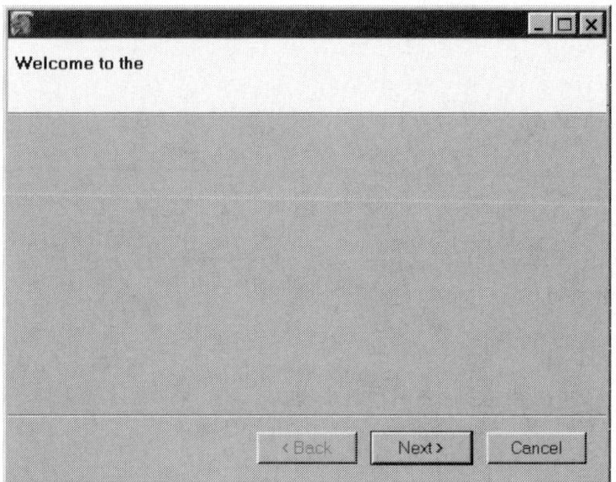

Fig. 17.8 Bare-bones wizard based on the `<wizard>` tag.

17.3.3.2 `<wizardpage>` The `<wizardpage>` tag is a simple boxlike tag. It is operated on extensively by its parent `<wizard>` tag and is of little use by itself. Put any XUL content inside it, but beware of messing up the simple navigation strategy of the wizard—it is better to add more pages than complicate an existing page. `<wizardpage>` supports the following special attributes:

```
pageid next onpagehide onpageshow onpagerewound onpageadvanced
```

- ☞ `pageid` is an identifier for the page separate from `id`. It is used by the logic internal to the `<wizard>` tag and should always be supplied.
- ☞ `next` provides a way of disrupting the normal page order of the wizard. It holds a `pageid` identifier. If it is set, the wizard will abandon its simple strategy of stepping forward and backward through the pages. Instead, it will rely on the `next` attribute for all navigation. If this is to work, the attribute must be set by assigning to the next property of the DOM object for the `<wizardpage>` tag, not by directly adding it to the `<wizardpage>` tag. After this is done, all wizard navigation relies on all `<wizardpage>` tags having a next attribute.

The remaining four attributes are event handlers. They fire when the page appears and disappears, and when the user goes forward a page and backward a page. They have no default implementations. `<wizardpage>` is trivial at best.

17.3.4 Web-Side Objects

The XPInstall remote install system provides the application programmer with two objects usable in ordinary HTML and XUL documents: `InstallTrigger` and `InstallVersion`. `InstallTrigger` and `InstallVersion` are properties of the global (`window`) object; `InstallVersion` objects can also be made from the `InstallTrigger.getVersion()` method.

17.3.4.1 `InstallTrigger` Table 17.3 describes the `InstallTrigger` object.

17.3.4.2 `InstallVersion` Table 17.4 describes the `InstallVersion` object. Note that extra constants are available but that the meaning is the same.

Table 17.3 The XPInstall `InstallTrigger` Object

Constant, property or method signature	Use
SKIN (1), LOCALE (2), CONTENT (4), PACKAGE (7)	bitmask flags for installChrome()
MAJOR_DIFF(4), MINOR_DIFF(3), REL_DIFF(2), BLD_DIFF(1), EQUAL(0), NOT_FOUND(-5)	Constants returned by compareVersion() indicating where two versions differ; values of opposite sign are also possible, except for 5
Boolean enabled()	True if XPInstall is enabled in preferences
Boolean install(Object xpi_list, function(url, err))	True if a list of XPI bundles installs correctly; the function argument will be called for each XPI URL that fails to install; see "Scripts"
Boolean installChrome(Number flags, String url, String name)	Same as install(), except flags is a bitwise OR that says what the content is, and install.js is not run; name is the application's text name
Number compareVersion(String name, String version) Number compareVersion(String name, InstallVersion version) Number compareVersion(String name, Number major, Number minor, Number release, Number build)	Compare the version of the application with registry name "name" against the supplied version; returns positive constants if the supplied version is greater
InstallVersion getVersion(String name)	Return the version of the supplied application registry name, or null

Table 17.4 The XPInstall installversion object

Constant, property, or method signature	Use
MAJOR_DIFF(4), MINOR_DIFF(3), REL_DIFF(2), BLD_DIFF(1), EQUAL(0), BLD_DIFF_MINUS(-1), REL_DIFF_MINUS(-2), MINOR_DIFF_MINUS(-3), MAJOR_DIFF_MINUS(-4), NOT_FOUND(-5)	Constants returned by compareTo() indicating where two versions differ
major	Holds the major version
minor	Holds the minor version
release	Holds the release version
build	Holds the build version
void init()	Initializes this object to version "0.0.0.0"
void init(String version)	Initializes this object to the version number supplied
String toString()	Returns a string representation of the version held, or null
Number compareTo(String version) Number compareTo(InstallVersion version) Number compareTo(Number major, Number minor, Number release, Number build)	Compares the held version against the supplied version; returns positive constants if the supplied version is greater

The `InstallVersion` object is also available to the `install.js` scripting environment.

17.3.5 XPInstall-Side Objects

The following objects are available to `install.js` scripts:

```
Install InstallVersion FileSpecObject File WinProfile WinReg
```

The `InstallVersion` object is described in "Web-Side Objects"; the others are described here.

17.3.5.1 `Install` The `Install` object is the global object within the `install.js` scripting environment. That object's methods may be called directly or prefixed with `Install`. `Install` is equivalent to the window property in a Web page.

The `Install` object is a factory object and can produce all the other objects that exist. It holds all the arguments passed in from the install trigger script. It provides access to a global error number similar to `errno` in C/C++

and has a concept of the current directory during the installation. It can do very basic logging, user interaction, and execution of native programs.

Tables 17.5,17.6, and 17.7 describe this object. All the properties of the `Install` object are read-only.

Table 17.5 The `XPInstall` Install object

Constant, property, or method signature	Action deferred until install?	Use
SKIN (1), LOCALE (2), CONTENT (4), PACKAGE (7), DELAYED_CHROME(16)		Bitmask values for flags property and for registerChrome(); use of DELAYED_CHROME delays registration until the platform next starts up
Number buildID		The build version of this installation of the platform (e.g., 2002060411)
Error constants (see Table 17.6)		
String platform		Holds the operating system type and version, which closely follow the style of window.navigator.userAgent
String jarfile		Full path name of the copy of the XPI file on the local computer
String archive		Same as jarfile
String arguments		Holds any string after ? in the XPI file's URL, or null
String url		The full XPI URL passed to install() or installChrome()
Number flags		Flags passed to InstallTrigger's installChrome(), or zero
Number _finalStatus		Value returned back to the remote install progress dialog box
Boolean _installedFiles		False after cancelInstall() is called
File File		Reference to a File object
Object Install		Self-reference to the global Install object

Table 17.5 The `XPInstall` Install object (Continued)

Constant, property, or method signature	Action deferred until install?	Use
Number addDirectory(String XPItree) Number addDirectory(String name, String XPItree, FileSpecObject OSpath, String localPath) Number addDirectory(String name, String version, String XPItree, FileSpecObject OSpath, String localPath) Number addDirectory(String name, InstallVersion version, String XPItree, FileSpecObject OSpath, String localPath)	✓	Copy the supplied XPItree path to the local file system; install under the current application or the one with registry name name, if supplied; always install under the latest version, or, if a version is supplied, use it to check if any existing application is newer; don't install if this check says it is newer; if no destination is supplied, install the contents of XPItree under the current directory; if OSpath and localPath are supplied, concatenate them and store XPItree under the result; return any errors
Number addFile(String XPIfile) Number addFile(String name, String version, String XPIfile, FileSpecObject Ospath, String localPath, [Boolean force]) Number addFile(String name, InstallVersion version, String XPIfile, FileSpecObject OSpath, String localPath, [Boolean force])	✓	Copy the XPIfile in the XPI archive to the local file system; install under the current directory, current application, and current version if no other details are supplied; if an application registry name is supplied in name, use that instead of the current application; if a version is supplied, don't install if an existing application is more recent than the version; if OSpath and localPath are supplied, concatenate them and install the file under the resulting folder; if force is supplied and set to true, don't do version tests—always install in that case; return any errors
Null alert(String value)		Display a modal dialog window showing value until the user acknowledges it
void cancelInstall() void cancelInstall(Number reason)		Don't perform any of the scheduled instructions; if a reason is suppled, set it as the error code, otherwise, set to INSTALL_CANCELLED
Boolean confirm(String value)		Display a modal dialog window showing value until the user accepts or rejects it; Return false if it is rejected

Table 17.5 The `XPInstall` Install object (Continued)

Constant, property, or method signature	Action deferred until install?	Use
Number execute(String XPIpath, String args, Boolean blocking) Number execute(String XPIpath, String args); Number execute(String XPIpath);	✓	Execute the program at path XPIpath in the XPI archive; Optionally supply it with operating system–specific arguments; Optionally supply it with blocking set to true, which pauses the install until the executed program is finished; The default for blocking is false
Number gestalt(String selector)		On the Macintosh only, reports the value of selector according to the Gestalt Manager; Otherwise, return null; Also see text accompanying below this table
FileSpecObject getComponentFolder(String name) FileSpecObject getComponentFolder(String name, String subpath)		Return the folder for the application with registry name name; return the folder of the subpart of that application if subpath is present; otherwise, return null
FileSpecObject getFolder(String keyword) FileSpecObject getFolder(String keyword, String subpath) FileSpecObject getFolder(FileSpecObject folder, String subpath)		Return the folder matching the supplied keyword or a subfolder of that folder if subpart is supplied: if subpart is a JAR file name rather than a folder, then step into the root virtual folder of the JAR file; alternately, specialize an existing folder to one of its subfolders; return null on failure
Number getLastError()		Return the last error status code encountered, which could also be SUCCESS
WinProfile getWinProfile(FileSpecObject folder, String filename)		Return a WinProfile object for the supplied .INI file; returns null if the operating system is not Microsoft Windows
WinReg getWinRegistry()		Return a WinReg object
Number initInstall(String text_name, String reg_name, String version) Number initInstall(String text_name, String reg_name, InstallVersion version);		Begin the scheduling process for this install; set the current application to text name text_name, registry name reg_name, and current version to version; return any errors

Table 17.5 The `XPInstall` Install object (Continued)

Constant, property, or method signature	Action deferred until install?	Use
Object loadResources(String XPIpath)		Return a JavaScript object modeled on a properties (stringbundle) file in the XPI archive; that properties file has XPI relative path name XPI-path; each property in the file appears as a property on the Java-Script object; returns null on failure
Null logComment(String text)	✓	Write the text, plus some formatting, to the install.log file
patch()	✓	This method allows a single file to be updated based on a byte-by-byte delta (a series or diff of changes); not recommended for applications; use addFile() instead
Number performInstall()		Execute all the scheduled install tasks and return an error status
Number registerChrome(Number flags, FileSpecObject folder) Number registerChrome(Number flags, FileSpecObject folder, String rdfpath)	✓	Tell the platform that these chrome files should be reexamined for overlays, locales, and skins; flags says what kind of thing is being registered (see below), folder is the location of the files to consider, rdfpath is an optional subpath (including file name) from folder that says where to find the contents.rdf file for overlays
Number refreshPlugins() Number refreshPlugins(Boolean reloadPages)	✓	Make the platform recalculate the available plugins and then reload all windows depending on them; if reloadPages is false, reload is skipped
void resetError() void resetError(Number error)		Set the last error encountered to zero or to error if it is supplied
Number setPackageFolder(FileSpecObject folder)	✓	Change the current directory to the supplied folder
Number uninstall(String name)	✓	Schedule the given application registry name for uninstall; returns an error code

The following notes expand on aspects of Table 17.5.

It is important to realize that error values returned from scheduling methods only report problems with the scheduling process. They do not report problems with the execution of the scheduled instruction. Even if no error is received during scheduling, the instruction can still fail when it is executed during installation.

Error values are usually negative integers. Values between `-200` and `-299` are reserved for the platform; values smaller than `-5550` are Macintosh specific; `0` is `SUCCESS`, and `999` is `REBOOT_NEEDED`. All values produced by the platform have matching property names that hold constants. Table 17.6 lists these names.

A list of valid selectors for the `gestalt()` method and their meanings and values can be viewed at *www.rgaros.nl/gestalt/index.html.*

The special folder keywords submitted as arguments to `getFolder()` are listed in Table 17.7.

The "`Program`" keyword matches the top of the platform installation area. The "`file:///`" keyword matches the top of the local file system. To see the value of a specific keyword on a specific computer, use this line of code:

```
alert(getFolder(keyword).toString());
```

17.3.5.2 `FileSpecObject` The `FileSpecObject` is a value-like object that is passed between the methods of other objects in the XPInstall system. It is rare that this object type is manipulated directly. It is never created with `new` from JavaScript. The `FileSpecObject` has only one useful property:

```
String toString()
```

This method returns a nonportable path for the folder that the `FileSpecObject` represents.

17.3.5.3 `File` The `Install` object is in part responsible for the overall matching and installing of files, folders, and subtrees of files. By comparison, the `File` object is responsible for inspecting and manipulating one file or folder closely. Some of the `Install` object's methods schedule tasks to be done when the install gets going. All of the `File` object's methods schedule tasks for later execution.

Only one `File` object is ever needed, and that object is available as a property named `File` on the global object. All methods on this object are therefore accessible just by calling:

```
File.method_name(args);
```

Table 17.8 describes the `File` object.

Table 17.6 Mozilla platform property names

Name	Name	Name
ACCESS_DENIED	INSUFFICIENT_DISK_SPACE	READ_ONLY
ALREADY_EXISTS	INVALID_ARGUMENTS	REBOOT_NEEDED
APPLE_SINGLE_ERR	IS_DIRECTORY	SCRIPT_ERROR
BAD_PACKAGE_NAME	IS_FILE	SOURCE_DOES_NOT_EXIST
CANT_READ_ARCHIVE	KEY_ACCESS_DENIED	SOURCE_IS_DIRECTORY
CHROME_REGISTRY_ERROR	KEY_DOES_NOT_EXIST	SOURCE_IS_FILE
DOES_NOT_EXIST	MALFORMED_INSTALL	SUCCESS
DOWNLOAD_ERROR	NETWORK_FILE_IS_IN_USE	UNABLE_TO_LOAD_LIBRARY
EXTRACTION_FAILED	NO_INSTALL_SCRIPT	UNABLE_TO_LOCATE_LIB_FUNCTION
FILENAME_ALREADY_USED	NO_SUCH_COMPONENT	UNEXPECTED_ERROR
GESTALT_INVALID_ARGUMENT	PACKAGE_FOLDER_NOT_SET	UNINSTALL_FAILED
GESTALT_UNKNOWN_ERR	PATCH_BAD_CHECKSUM_RESULT	USER_CANCELLED
INSTALL_CANCELLED	PATCH_BAD_CHECKSUM_TARGET	VALUE_DOES_NOT_EXIST
INSTALL_NOT_STARTED	PATCH_BAD_DIFF	

Table 17.7 Keyword identifiers for Install.`getFolder()`

Cross-platform	Microsoft Windows	Macintosh	UNIX
"Plugins"	"Win System"	"Mac System"	"Unix Local"
"Program"	"Windows"	"Mac Desktop"	"Unix Lib"
"Temporary"		"Mac Trash"	
"Profile"		"Mac Startup"	
"Preferences"		"Mac Shutdown"	
"OS Drive"		"Mac Apple Menu"	
"file:///"		"Mac Control Panel"	
"Components"		"Mac Extension"	
"Chrome"		"Mac Fonts"	
		"Mac Preferences"	
		"Mac Documents"	

Table 17.8 The XPInstall File object

Constant, property, or method signature	Action deferred until install starts?	Use
Number copy(FileSpecObject src, FileSpecObject target)	✓	Copies a file or folder to a new destination.
Number dirCreate(FileSpecObject local)	✓	Creates the local directory given by local.
FileSpecObject dirGetParent(FileSpecObject dir)		Returns the parent directory of dir, or null.
Number dirRemove(FileSpecObject local)	✓	Removes the local directory given by local.
Number dirRename(FileSpecObject local)	✓	Removes the local directory given by local.
Number diskSpaceAvailable(FileSpecObject local)		Returns the disk space available on the volume/drive holding the file or folder local. Returns bytes.
Number execute(FileSpecObject file [, String args [, Boolean blocking]])	✓	Runs the executable given by file, with optional arguments args. If blocking is also supplied and set to true, the install will halt until the program finishes. blocking is false by default.

Table 17.8 The XPInstall File object (Continued)

Constant, property, or method signature	Action deferred until install starts?	Use
Boolean exists(FileSpecObject local)		Returns true if the local file or folder named local exists.
Boolean isDirectory(FileSpecObject local)		Returns true if the thing named local is a local folder (file system directory).
Boolean isFile(FileSpecObject local)		Returns true if the thing named local is a local file, and not a folder.
Boolean isWritable(FileSpecObject local)		Returns true if the local folder or file named local is writable.
Number macAlias(FileSpecObject src, String filename, FileSpecObject target) Number macAlias(FileSpecObject src, String filename, FileSpecObject target, String alias)	✓	Creates a Macintosh Alias in the folder target, based on the file file name that resides in the folder src. If alias is supplied as an argument, make that the text of the new alias.
Number modDate(FileSpecObject local)		Returns when local was last changed in milliseconds. This time is calculated differently for each platform.
Boolean modDateChanged(FileSpecObject local, number modDate)		Returns true if the file local has changed since the date modDate (from modDate()).
Number move(FileSpecObject src, FileSpecObject target)	✓	Moves the file src to the folder target. Cannot move Microsoft Windows directories.
String nativeVersion(FileSpecObject local)		Gets Microsoft Windows version information about the file local (e.g., DLL version), or return null.
Number remove(FileSpecObject local)	✓	Removes the file or folder local.
Number rename(FileSpecObject local, String name)	✓	Renames the file or folder local to name.
Number size(FileSpecObject local)		Returns the size in bytes of the file local.
String windowsGetShortName(FileSpecObject local)		For Microsoft Windows only, gets the 8.3 (non-LFN) file name for the supplied file; otherwise, returns null.

Table 17.8 The XPInstall File object (Continued)

Constant, property, or method signature	Action deferred until install starts?	Use
Number windowsRegisterServer(FileSpecObject local)	✓	For Microsoft Windows only, registers the file local as a server.
Number windowsShortcut(FileSpecObject local, FileSpecObject target, String linkname, FileSpecObject dir, String params, FileSpecObject icondb, Number index)	✓	For Microsoft Windows only, creates a shortcut for file local. Puts the shortcut in directory target. Gives the shortcut the name linkname, plus an .lnk extension. Makes the working directory of the shortcut dir. Gives the shortcut parameters params. Uses the indexth icon in the file at path icondb for the shortcut's desktop icon.
String windowsVersion(FileSpecObject local)		Gets Microsoft Windows version information about the file local, or return null.

17.3.5.4 `WinProfile` The `WinProfile` object, manufactured by the `Install.getWinProfile()` method, can perform operations on a Microsoft Windows specific `.INI` file, such as `C:\WINDOWS\WIN.INI`. It contains two methods only:

```
String getString(String section, String key)
String writeString(String section, String key, String value)
```

Since an `.INI` file is in extended ASCII format, Unicode information cannot be put in such a file.

17.3.5.5 `WinReg` The `WinReg` object, manufactured by the `Install.GetWinRegistry()` method, provides access to the Windows registry. Operations on the registry happen immediately; they are not deferred.

The `WinReg` object holds the current registry root key. By default the current root key is `HKEY_CLASSES_ROOT`.

Path names for Windows registry keys are delimited by backslashes (\). Backslashes in JavaScript strings must be stated doubly (\\) if they are to be treated as normal characters.

Table 17.9 describes the `WinReg` object. Some of the methods listed return data, but many of the methods merely return a status code. When a status code is returned, `null` means that the Mozilla Platform couldn't assemble the registry change correctly. This usually means problems were encountered with the arguments supplied. If a non-null-value is returned, that value comes from the actual registry operation. Even when the return value is ordinary data, a `null` value means failure of the method, again most likely the result of argument problems. In summary, always check return values for `null`.

Table 17.9 The XPInstall WinReg object

Constant, property, or method signature	Use
HKEY_CLASSES_ROOT, HKEY_CURRENT_USER, HKEY_LOCAL_MACHINE, HKEY_USERS	Predefined constants for well-known root keys.
Number createKey(String subkey, String name)	Creates the subkey subkey with the class name name. name may be a zero-length string.
Number deleteKey(String subkey)	Deletes the subkey named subkey.
Number deleteValue(String subkey, String name)	Deletes the attribute-value pair of subkey whose name is name.
String enumKeys(String subkey, Number index)	Returns the indexth subkey for the key named subkey. Returns a zero-length string for non-existent subkeys.
String enumValueNames(String subkey, Number index)	Returns the indexth attribute name for the key named subkey.
Number getValueNumber(String subkey, String attr)	Returns the DWORD value of the attr attribute of the subkey key.
String getValueString(String subkey, String attr)	Returns the String value of the attr attribute of the subkey key.
Number getValue(String subkey, String attr)	Returns the DWORD value of the attr attribute of the subkey key.
Boolean isKeyWritable(String subkey)	Returns true if the subkey key is writable.
Boolean keyExists(String subkey)	Returns true if the subkey key exists.
void setRootKey(String key)	Sets the root key to one of the predefined roots listed in the first row of this table. Returns null on failure.
Number setValueNumber(String subkey, String attr, Number val)	Sets the attr attribute of the subkey key to the val value. Returns null on failure.
Number setValueString(String subkey, String attr, String str)	Sets the attr attribute of the subkey key to the str value. Returns null on failure.
Boolean valueExists(String subkey, String attr)	Returns true if the subkey key has an attr attribute.

17.3.6 XPCOM Objects

The XPInstall system does not make XPCOM interfaces available to `install.js` scripts.

There are, however, a number of components and interfaces available outside of the XPInstall environment that duplicate the XPInstall functionality. If a custom deployment system is required, or deployment-like design is needed, then these components and objects are perhaps worth exploring.

This XPCOM pair provides access to the Mozilla registry, although it is not complete or completely flexible:

```
@mozilla.org/registry;1 nsIRegistry
```

This interface treats the different registry files as though they were all one file. The registry is also expressed as an RDF data source. At the time of this writing, that RDF data source is not available for use. Its XPCOM pair is forecast to be

```
@mozilla.org/registry-viewer;1 nsIRDFDataSource
```

A different registry interface is provided by the so-called chrome registry. This interface allows the platform to recalculate its view of the chrome. That includes refreshing overlay, skin, and locale information. It can also install chrome packages, skins, and locales. The XPCOM pair providing this functionality is

```
@mozilla.org/chrome/chrome-registry;1 nsIXULChromeRegistry;1
```

Of particular interest to Microsoft Windows developers are two pairs of XPCOM items:

```
@mozilla.org/winhooks;1 nsIWindowsRegistry
@mozilla.org/winhooks;1 nsIWindowsHooks
```

These interfaces provide much of the low-level access to Microsoft Windows that the platform-specific operations need.

Separate from these registration-like interfaces are the many file and network manipulation interfaces that are covered in Chapter 16, XPCOM Objects, including interfaces that can unpack a ZIP archive.

All that remains is some observations about XPInstall's own objects. The Web-side objects `InstallTrigger` and `InstallVersion` have no useful XPIDL interface definitions. They do happen to have Contract IDs registered with XPCOM, along with the XPInstall infrastructure itself:

```
@mozilla.org/xpinstall/installtrigger;1
@mozilla.org/xpinstall/installversion;1
@mozilla.rg/xpinstall;1
```

There is no point in using these Contract IDs from a script since no useful interfaces are available. The objects available in the `install.js` scripting environment are not exposed to XPCOM either. In fact, in that second case, not even Contract IDs exist for those objects.

17.4 Hands On: Bundling Up NoteTaker

This "Hands On" session bundles up the already working NoteTaker tool into an XPI file that can be installed using XPInstall. In theory, the tool could run directly from a remote Web server, but merging local content with server-based overlays is a messy approach that defies common sense. In practical terms, it may not even work. We'll stick with a downloadable installation.

Although the running code for the tool is complete, several small bits and pieces must be added. Our strategy for bringing them all together is the sum of the issues brought to light in this chapter. That means

- Determine any names for the tool.
- Determine the content of release documents.
- Determine the content of the final tool.
- Create download pages, installation scripts, and support files.
- Create a final XPI file.

Let's run through these tasks.

17.4.1 Release Preparation

First we pick suitable names for our tool:

- **Text name**. We choose "`NoteTaker Web Notes`". We save the advertising and promotional hype for the Web page that will offer the tool.
- **Package name**. Throughout this book we've been using "`notetaker`", which we'll stick to. That's more than the eight characters that very old Microsoft Windows computers support, but perhaps that's a small loss only.
- **Registry application name**. That's "`/Nigel McFarlane/NoteTaker`". If this tool were absorbed into the main Mozilla Browser development stream, then the name might be merely "`NoteTaker`", which would be appended to something like "`/mozilla.org/Browser/`". In that case, the full name would be "`/mozilla.org/Browser/NoteTaker`". There's no such affiliation at this time.
- **Version number**. There's a shortage of real-world testing for the tool so far, but it appears to work. Call it version 0.9. That version is 0.9.0.0 when stated in full. Many enhancements and modifications are possible, but they would bump the version over 1.0, probably.

We also review the software to be delivered.

- **Baseline**. Whatever is discussed in this book is the basis of this release of the tool. I keep a copy of all code relevant to each chapter in a directory under that chapter and do incremental backups daily and full backups weekly and monthly. Since I'm finished on the 30th, tonight's monthly backup will freeze everything. My baseline will be source files for this book (edition 1, author's final draft), plus the final installable XPI file plus a backup date. That backup will also contain any test files and test data, which is handy.

- **Footprint**. The footprint for the NoteTaker tool is very small. It has only three items: the chrome directory hierarchy; the Mozilla registries; and the `notetaker.rdf` file in the current user profile.
- **Target**. The target for the software has several parts. Because of recent changes to XPCOM objects (file-based streams), this release requires platform version 1.4 final, minimum. It is tested on the Classic Browser only, not on the Mozilla Browser. The application is portable, so the operating system doesn't matter that much; however, there are bound to be a few constraints we haven't identified yet. The platform version and Classic Mozilla application suite will be the whole target, and we note that future versions are not automatically supported.

That's all the logistics required.

17.4.2 Creating Support Files and Scripts

The NoteTaker 0.9 release requires files above and beyond the application code.

We'll include a `README.txt` file for developers exploring the source code. We'll make one up based on the information in the last topic.

We'll need a `contents.rdf` file for the `notetaker/contents` directory and to register the NoteTaker package. We'll use the one specified in Chapter 2, XUL Layout, and include the enhancements made in Chapter 12, Overlays and Chrome.

We want to show a trivial example of locale support. For that we'll need a `contents.rdf` file and a DTD file for a sample locale. We'll use the `contents.rdf` file from Chapter 3, Static Content, and make up a trivial DTD file—one that has no effect.

We also want to show a trivial example of skin installation. For that we'll need a `contents.rdf` file and a CSS file for a sample skin (theme). We'll use the `contents.rdf` file from Chapter 4, First Widgets and Themes, and make up a trivial style sheet—one that has no effect.

Finally we'll need the installation support. That amounts to an HTML file and two scripts. The NoteTaker tool is small and almost entirely reliant on the platform and the Classic Browser application. We expect the install scripts to be lightweight rather then complex.

Because the HTML file might be displayed in any Web browser, it had better be highly portable as shown in Listing 17.4.

Listing 17.4 Download Web page for the NoteTaker tool.

```
<html>
  <head>
    <script src="deploy.js"/>
  <body>
    <h1>NoteTaker Download</h1>
    <p>The NoteTaker tool adds Web Notes to your Mozilla-based Web
          browser. Web Notes are placed on top of displayed Web pages.
          They hold information that you record for your own purposes.
    </p>
    <p>Only the Classic Browser, version 1.4, is supported. It is part of
          the established Mozilla Web application suite. The standalone
          Mozilla Browser is not yet supported.
    </p>
    <p>Download here:
      <a href="notetaker.xpi" onclick="download(event)">NoteTaker tool
          0.9</a>
    </p>
  </body>
</html>
```

The `deploy()` function follows the outline of Listing 17.1. In this case, the full script is shown in Listing 17.5. Bullet-proof browser detection is a lengthy matter; this code covers most common alternatives only.

Listing 17.5 XPInstall trigger script for the NoteTaker bundle.

```
function download(e) {
  if ( ! deploy() )
    alert("NoteTaker 0.9 requires Classic Mozilla 1.4");
  e.preventDefault();
}

function is_moz_browser() {
  return (
    window.navigator &&
    window.navigator.userAgent &&
    window.navigator.userAgent.search(/^Mozilla\/5\.0/) != -1
  );
}

function is_target() {
  var agent = window.navigator.userAgent;
  return (
    agent.search(/rv:1\.4/) != -1 &&   // matches
    agent.search(/Phoenix/) == -1 &&   // no match
    agent.search(/Firebird/) == -1     // no match
  );
}

function is_app_version_ok() {
  var it = window.InstallTrigger;
```

```
    var result = it.compareVersion(
      "Nigel McFarlane/NoteTaker", "0.9.0.0");

    return ( result == it.NOT_FOUND ||
             Math.abs(result) <= it.REL_DIFF );
  }

  function deploy()
  {
    if ( !is_moz_browser() ) { return false; }
    if ( !window.InstallTrigger.enabled() { return false; }
    if ( !is_target() ) { return false; }
    if ( !is_app_version_ok() } { return false; }

    var xpi_container =
      { "NoteTaker Web Notes" : "notetaker.xpi" };

    with (window.InstallTrigger)
      install(xpi_container, null);
    return true;
  }
```

There are no parameters required, so that part of the skeleton in Listing 17.1 is gone. If the user attempts to install to the wrong platform or the wrong application, we complain. There is no error handler for the `install()` function because there is nothing we could do to rectify a failure. In a large organization, we might display an HTML page that allows a problem report to be filed. We'll rely instead on the `install.js` file issuing a useful user-oriented complaint.

The three detection functions are simple. Any browser whose `userAgent` starts with "`Mozilla/5.0`" is likely to be a mozilla.org browser. If the `userAgent` contains "`Firebird`" or "`Phoenix`", then it's the Mozilla Browser, not the Classic Browser, which we don't support. The `is_app_version_ok()` test is lenient; it allows, for example, the installation of version `0.9.1.0` on top of `0.9.0.0`. This is a guarantee from the developer that going backward in a release version is minor enough to be safe. That might be required if a new release proves more defective than anticipated.

The final piece of the install system is the script `install.js`. Listing 17.6 is most of that script, based on Listing 17.2.

Listing 17.6 `install.js` script for the NoteTaker tool.

```
var TEXT_NAME = "NoteTaker Web Notes";
var REG_NAME  = "/Nigel McFarlane/NoteTaker";
var VERSION   = "0.9.0.0";
var rv = SUCCESS;

function prepare()
{
  initInstall(TEXT_NAME, REG_NAME, VERSION);
```

```
  if ( schedule_files() != SUCCESS ) return getLastError();
  if ( register_chrome() != SUCCESS) return getLastError();

  return SUCCESS;
}

rv = prepare();
if (rv == SUCCESS) {
  performInstall();
}
else {
  alert("Installation failed. (Error = " + rv + ")" );
  cancelInstall(rv);
}
```

As for the install trigger script, the `install.js` script is simplified from the skeleton of Listing 17.2. There are no parameters to check. We assume that the install trigger script proceeds with the download only if platform conditions are right. Because the NoteTaker tool is a browser enhancement, we don't have desktop menu items or icons or shortcuts to add. NoteTaker is such a small tool that checking available disk space is pointless. Because the tool is written entirely in JavaScript, we don't have any executables or binary libraries to manage either. All we need to do is place the contents of the `.XPI` file correctly and to advise the platform that new chrome content exists.

To do those few steps, we need to know the contents of the XPI. Looking ahead to "Final Bundling," we see that the XPI content is

```
install.js
notetaker.jar
extras/README.txt
extras/notetaker.rdf
```

The whole application resides in the `notetaker.jar` archive. Files in the extras virtual directory won't ever be used at run time. The `README.txt` file is there for curious programmers to find and read; the `notetaker.rdf` file is the initial copy of the user's note database. It needs to be copied into the current user profile.

Listing 17.7 shows the two missing functions from Listing 17.6. They perform the required manipulation of the XPI file and of the chrome registry.

Listing 17.7 Deploying files and registering chrome from `install.js`.

```
function schedule_files()
{
  addFile(TEXT_NAME, VERSION, "notetaker.jar",
          getFolder("Chrome"), "notetaker.jar", true);

  addFile(TEXT_NAME, VERSION, "extras/notetaker.rdf",
          getFolder("Profile"), "notetaker.rdf", true);
```

```
  return SUCCESS;
}

function register_chrome()
{
  var jar_root = getFolder("Chrome", "notetaker.jar");

  registerChrome(PACKAGE | DELAYED_CHROME,
                 jar_root, "content/notetaker/");
  registerChrome(SKIN | DELAYED_CHROME,
                 jar_root, "skin/modern/notetaker/");
  registerChrome(LOCALE | DELAYED_CHROME,
                 jar_root, "locale/en-US/notetaker/");
  return SUCCESS;
}
```

The second `addFile()` function call shows how any file path in an XPI file can be matched to any path on the local file system. The `getFolder()` call in the function `register_chrome()` shows how the top of the folder hierarchy inside the JAR file can be returned as an object. Both `schedule_files()` and `register_chrome()` complete without touching the `notetaker.xpi` file. Their `addFile()` and `registerChrome()` calls are scheduled for later execution when `performInstall()` is called.

That is the whole of the `install.js` script.

17.4.3 Final Bundling

Having located or created all the required files, the `notetaker` XPI file can finally be assembled. It must contain at least the `install.js` file (because it is more than a skin or a locale), so a start is to create a ZIP archive containing that one file.

The NoteTaker tool should be the main contents of the XPI file. It is a neat and efficient arrangement to have the NoteTaker package in a single JAR archive in the chrome. Such a file is faster to read from disk because it is small. It is also easy to manage if the number of installed packages is high. We'll do that, and we'll put that JAR archive inside the XPI install archive for delivery. Unfortunately, JAR archives are very fiddly to set up for two reasons.

In all chapters to date, the NoteTaker tool has resided under the folder `resource:/chrome/notetaker` as a set of discrete files and subfolders. If we delivered the package arranged this way, we could create the required XPI file simply by zipping up a working NoteTaker folder, with an `install.js` file added. A JAR archive, however, has its directory structure arranged differently to support fast access. Our installed NoteTaker packages look nothing like the hierarchy that a JAR file requires:

```
Chrome test package          JAR archive
notetaker/content      <---> content/notetaker
```

```
notetaker/locale/en-US <---> locale/en-US/notetaker
notetaker/skin/modern  <---> skin/moder/notetaker
```

The only solution to this set of differences is to make a copy of the test files from the chrome and rearrange them in a temporary folder hierarchy that reflects the JAR convention. A systematic solution is to write a Perl, WSH, or shell script that automates the rearrangement process. That second hierarchy can then be zipped up; the JAR file results.

A second wrinkle with JAR files is that the order of the files in the archive matters if the archive is large. The most time-critical files should be near the start of the archive, where less effort is required to find them. To achieve this, put the package files in a hierarchy matching the JAR convention as before. Create a text file that lists the files in the order required, and pass that list to a suitable command-line zip tool like `pkzip` (Microsoft Windows) or `zip(1)` (UNIX). It's possible to create the JAR file correctly by adding files and folders to it a piece at a time from the desktop, but that is quite a tedious process.

Figure 17.9 shows a JAR file for the NoteTaker package that has some trivial ordering. The content part of the package is put first because it is used the most. In fact, the skin and locale files in this package are just placeholder files that illustrate where such things might be put. For such a small application, this ordering is probably of no benefit.

We now have two files for the final XPI: `install.js` and `notetaker.jar`. To these we can add a README file and the beginning `notetaker.rdf` file. The final XPI file (in which ordering is not important unless digital signatures are present) appears in Figure 17.10.

Nothing more is required except to upload the HTML page with the download link and the XPI file to a Web site. That concludes the NoteTaker running example in this book.

Name	Size	Ratio	Path
contents.rdf	929	57%	content\notetaker\
toolbar_action.js	11,422	73%	content\notetaker\
controllers.js	1,461	68%	content\notetaker\
dialog_action.js	2,302	67%	content\notetaker\
dialog_handlers.js	2,154	65%	content\notetaker\
editDialog.xul	4,920	75%	content\notetaker\
keywordController.js	5,960	75%	content\notetaker\
notes.js	3,602	62%	content\notetaker\
browserOverlay.xul	1,599	66%	content\notetaker\
contents.rdf	605	53%	locale\en-US\notetaker\
example.dtd	44	14%	locale\en-US\notetaker\
contents.rdf	611	56%	skin\modern\notetaker\
example.css	109	12%	skin\modern\notetaker\

Fig. 17.9 JAR archive holding the NoteTaker package.

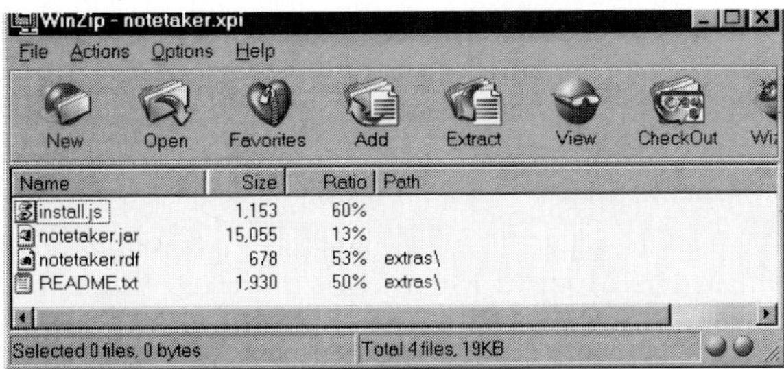

Fig. 17.10 XPI archive holding the full NoteTaker distribution.

17.5 Debug Corner: Logging and Testing

The `logComment()` method of the `Install` object is the only way to produce diagnostic messages from the `install.js` file, unless `alert()` is considered. Messages are logged to the `install.log` file, which is stored in the top directory of the platform install area.

A common source of problems in the install process is poor matching between hierarchical path names in the XPI file and hierarchical path names on the local file system. If the two are not stated correctly, or do not match correctly, then zero files might be copied by that step of the installation process. This can easily be detected by examining the `install.log` installation log and by checking the file system.

If nothing (or the wrong thing) is happening, a good debugging strategy is to simplify the installation process. Remove any digital signatures, and then remove any code that performs version checks and balances. Start with an XPI file whose contents need only to be copied into the chrome. Concentrate on ensuring that the archive's subtrees of files are installing to their correct locations. If there is no fancy version checking done, then the same XPI file can be installed over and over again harmlessly—there is no need to uninstall between installs. In simple cases, it is also safe to delete custom portions of the chrome by hand. Don't ever delete any of the standard JAR files that come with the platform.

If overlays are included in the application, beware of corrupting the overlay database. If any of the overlays have syntax error or incompatibility problems, the platform or an initial window may fail to start, and the installation will be useless. To fix this, delete the `overlayinfo` database, the installed files, the `chrome.rdf` file, and the line items added to `installed-chrome.txt`. Then restart.

In general, it is recommended that any install testing be done on a separate installation of the platform to that used for everyday purposes. That separate installation can be a "crash and burn" area where experiments can be freely undertaken. On Microsoft Windows, a separate computer is even better because there is only one central Mozilla and Window registry per host. It is also possible to corrupt the Windows registry from an XPInstall script if you try hard enough.

17.6 Summary

The XPInstall subsystem of the Mozilla Platform has many faces and can be exploited in many ways. Application programmers who don't want to learn how to build and package the platform itself use only a few of these faces.

The most attractive of the XPInstall technologies is remote install. Remote install holds the promise of delivering to users and customers service-provision software that has a low cost of distribution and the possibility of ongoing updates.

The mostly portable XPInstall system highly complements the other portable aspects of Mozilla applications. Rather than dividing the world into Visual Basic, AppleScript, and Perl, Mozilla-based applications can be uniformly deployed and used across most popular operating system platforms.

Application programmers can veer toward custom installs or native installs once their applications gain some maturity and a user base. The XPCOM system provides enough features that a separate installation system can be written on top of the platform if required. The only part of the platform that is difficult to reproduce without C/C++ code is the native installer stubs that first boot the platform into being.

With XPInstall covered, this book's overview of Mozilla technologies is complete. Today the Mozilla Platform is a feature-rich and practical development environment. It is a highly visible and substantial Open Source project, and its future is certainly bright. Good luck with your Mozilla work.

INDEX

D

M

N

Q

R

S

T

Z

About the Author

Nigel McFarlane is a science and technology writer, analyst, and programmer. He is the author of many articles on Web, XML, JavaScript, and other technologies, and his work has appeared in periodicals such as *DevX* and *The Sydney Morning Herald*, and on *www.builder.com*. Nigel is also the author of *Instant JavaScript* and *Professional JavaScript*. He lives in Melbourne, Australia.

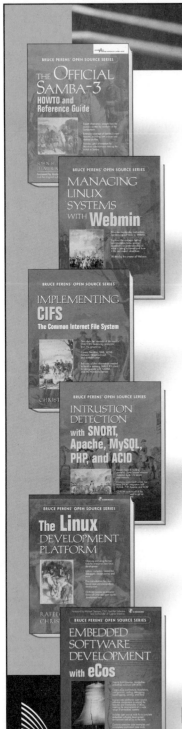